The Calculus of Violence

THE CALCULUS

of

VIOLENCE

How Americans Fought the Civil War

AARON SHEEHAN-DEAN

Harvard University Press

CAMBRIDGE, MASSACHUSETTS

LONDON, ENGLAND

2018

First printing

Library of Congress Cataloging-in-Publication Data
Names: Sheehan-Dean, Aaron Charles, author.
Title: The calculus of violence : how Americans fought the
Civil War / Aaron Sheehan-Dean.
Description: Cambridge, Massachusetts : Harvard University Press, 2018. |
Includes bibliographical references and index.
Identifiers: LCCN 2018001864 | ISBN 9780674984226 (alk. paper)
Subjects: LCSH: United States—History—Civil War, 1861–1865. |
United States—History—Civil War, 1861–1865—Historiography. |
Violence—United States—History—19th century.
Classification: LCC E468 .S35 2018 | DDC 973.7—dc23
LC record available at https://lccn.loc.gov/2018001864

Book design by Dean Bornstein

For Megan

CONTENTS

The Calculus of Violence

INTRODUCTION
The Puzzle of the Civil War

The US Civil War was, by a wide measure, the bloodiest conflict in American history. It consumed 750,000 lives, including nearly one-quarter of the white men of military age living in the South. The Civil War featured traditional battles that pitted uniformed soldiers against one another and gruesome acts of irregular warfare committed by guerrillas against regular soldiers and civilians. It incorporated hostage-taking, imprisonment, banishment, and mass killings. Nonetheless, at many points, Northerners and Southerners chose restraint. Soldiers on both sides took prisoners, respected flags of truce, and directed their weapons at each other rather than at noncombatants. Politicians and citizens demanded their nations observe the laws of war. And enslaved people sought freedom rather than revenge in the chaos of the conflict. If not for these actions, the already high death toll could have escalated dramatically. In order to understand this puzzle—a catastrophic war that could have been much worse—this book examines how people on both sides justified the lethal violence of the conflict and when, how, and why they balanced cruelty and destruction with restraint and mercy.

Who could be killed in the Civil War? Who could do that killing? How did they justify their actions? In short, why was the Civil War so bloody? And, conversely, how did participants avoid what Lincoln most feared, a "remorseless revolutionary struggle?" The answers lie in the thoughts and actions of the Civil War's participants. Sometimes they drew upon deeply held beliefs, and at other times they acted spontaneously in unanticipated situations. The answers changed over time; and in the uncertainty of war participants contradicted themselves from moment to moment. As a result, the patterns of violence in the conflict did not follow a path of steady growth. The "limited to total" war paradigm, which argues that the war inexorably grew more violent each year, dominates both academic and popular histories of the war, but it mischaracterizes the conflict. The reassurance offered by this narrative—common to descriptions of nearly all wars—conceals the more complicated reality of a conflict in which local patterns of violence and peace varied across time and space. In some places, the war was more unrestrained in 1861 than 1865, and in other places, the opposite held true. The Civil War was not either restrained or violent; it was both.[1] Malice and charity occurred simultaneously, sometimes in the same places. Moving beyond a binary formulation helps us see the ways in which people understood some acts of violence as immoral and wasteful and others as necessary and just.[2]

This book brings together the regular and irregular aspects of the war. It examines the behavior of politicians, officers, soldiers, guerrillas, prisoners, and citizens. It analyzes what they did and how they justified what they did. It explores the gaps and discrepancies between action and rhetoric, between reality and theory. The result is an analysis of the war that operates on two levels. Within the conflict, I track how Federals and Confederates engaged with each other over those issues that could most easily enable lethal violence to spiral out of control: guerrillas, emancipation, prisoners, and occupation. If we look only at the ground level and focus on these issues, as previous historians have done, we see a war that is often bloody and only occasionally restrained. If we pull back, employ hindsight, and broaden the frame of reference to include other civil and national conflicts in the mid-nineteenth century, the American experience appears unusual for the degree of restraint exercised by participants. These conflicting conclusions—that the Civil War was defined by unnecessary violence and death and also by restraint—are produced by shifting our own perspective on the event, as we must do with the passage of time. Recognizing that the US Civil War, compared to contemporaneous conflicts, included more moments of restraint and charity does not minimize the degree of suffering, even unjust suffering, borne during the conflict. Like F. Scott Fitzgerald's definition of "first-rate intelligence," a full understanding of the Civil War requires that we hold two contrary ideas in our heads simultaneously.

In three important spheres of the war, participants engaged each other in ways that discouraged restraint and escalated the war's violence. The Confederacy's willingness to tolerate guerrillas proved a fateful choice.

Their presence in the war subjected noncombatants to lethal violence and compelled the Union to devise a counterinsurgency strategy that exacted a devastating toll on Southern civilians. In response to the Union's mid-war endorsement of emancipation and its enlistment of black men into US armies, the Confederacy subjected black soldiers to unjust violence throughout the conflict. The last factor stimulating violence was the strong sense of nationalism that bound participants to their cause and encouraged a vision of the enemy as corrupt and unworthy. This message came from newspaper editors, politicians' speeches, and ministers' sermons, and it increased over the course of the war, compelling people to fight longer and tolerate greater bloodshed, both their own and their enemy's.

The most important restraining influence countering these forces was the state. In the Union and the Confederacy central governments set limits on violence. Because both states curried the favor of international observers, they professed adherence to the laws of war, which sanctioned lethal violence only against combatants. Neither side observed this principle perfectly, but the experience of the Civil War reveals that states matter. The most destructive nineteenth-century wars, like the Caste War of the Yucatán or the Taiping Civil War, involved actors who did not aspire to statehood or who rejected the Western laws of war.[3] The state's role in regulating behavior can be seen in several ways. First, both places practiced regular war, with the important exception of the Confederacy's use of guerrillas. Even potentially catastrophic moments like sieges and artillery bombardments of towns and cities occurred in legal and deliberate ways. Second, both sides took prisoners of war rather than treating enemy combatants as criminals and executing them, as happened in the wake of the Paris Commune in 1871, although many Civil War prisoners suffered and died needlessly while incarcerated.[4] Third, despite the outcry by Confederate civilians, Union occupation of Southern cities rarely entailed much lethal violence. One last factor that manifested itself through official channels also encouraged moderation in the Union's pursuit of military victory. Abraham Lincoln, most US military officers, and a majority of the Republican Party regarded Confederates as wayward citizens who could be restored to loyalty and then to full civic life. Black Northerners and white abolitionists opposed this view and sanctioned a more destructive and sometimes more violent conflict with the Confederacy, but they rarely held the levers of power. This political dynamic ensured that the Northerners who created and implemented war policy restrained themselves in ways that did not occur in similar conflicts in other places.

Any useful study of violence in the war must take stock of victims' attitudes as well as perpetrators. The story begins with how each side justified their resort to war. I also consider how they explained the violence they committed. During the war, we can see cycles of conflict, escalation, and resolution in different places at different times, so we move chronologically through each crucial event of the war in many theaters. These cycles varied over time. Sometimes the war's participants produced more violence under the guise of retribution and sometimes participants deterred additional violence. The experiences of the Civil War do not reflect some natural or inevitable escalation of violence that rules all wars. For instance, in 1863, the Union endorsed emancipation as a war strategy, which the Confederacy regarded as a violation of the rules of war. Confederate president Jefferson Davis then announced a policy of killing rather than capturing black soldiers. In response, Lincoln issued his own threat to retaliate against Confederate prisoners. Confederates never treated black soldiers fairly but neither did they execute all those they defeated in battle. Similarly, Lincoln did not execute captured Confederates. The narrative that follows examines these cycles, the moments that ignited them, and how actors on both sides took responsibility for suppressing them. The pattern of violence in the war was uneven, contingent, and often contradictory.

I spend ample time considering Lincoln and Davis, but this story, of necessity, ranges across the full spectrum of politicians, legal scholars, military officers, enlisted men, and regular citizens whose actions together shaped the war. I chronicle the attitudes and behavior of different constituencies over time. Americans divided by region, ideology, race, and religion in their perspectives toward military violence. Even if we could isolate each of these variables, the task would be a hard one; these forces interacted with each other in unpredictable ways. For instance, some evangelical Protestants (mostly abolitionists) began the war as committed pacifists, but the prospect of emancipation inspired many of them to support the war and, surprisingly, to advocate vigorous conduct against the South. Northern and Southern blacks differed too, with the former espousing aggressive policies while the latter, hemmed in by armed whites on all sides, pursued more cautious strategies.

Northern policymakers, such as Abraham Lincoln and moderate Republican congressmen, sought a full and equitable reconciliation of both regions. They recognized early on that unnecessary violence would only exacerbate difference and alienate Southerners from the national government. A vocal body of white elites in the North promoted moderation in war. Some of these were recent converts to the Republican Party while others remained within the ranks of the Democratic Party. They were counterbalanced by black elites, such as Frederick Douglass, and some white abolitionists who promoted a more aggressive war. This shift also came from the bottom up, because Northern soldiers experienced a profound disillusionment during their first year in the South. They expected to be greeted by the nonslaveholding majority of the region as liberators but were more often regarded as invaders and repulsed with whatever tools could be mustered.[5] Soldiers reacted by encouraging a harsher treatment of white civilians, whom they assumed to be disloyal and potential supporters of guerrilla units (which they often were). Those same soldiers grew more generous toward enslaved people as they came to support the plans of radicals in the North who saw the war as an opportunity to destroy the power of slaveholders and remake the region.

Confederate society possessed at least as many divisions as did the North. During the war, Southern policymakers sanctioned harsh treatment of the enemy, most importantly with regard to black Union troops. But even here, there were moderates who advocated adherence to the laws of war, if only in the strategic hopes of earning European support. Like their Northern peers, Southern soldiers sometimes diverged from official policy, often mistreating Southern civilians if they suspected them of Unionism. Confederate soldiers also exceeded their ambiguous orders and inflicted cruel and lethal violence on black soldiers.[6] Even more than in the North, social cleavages divided Confederate society. Dissenters and enslaved people represented a serious internal threat. Their actions, often geared around personal or family survival, complicated Confederate

THE CALCULUS OF VIOLENCE

efforts to govern. Last, the South produced a wide range of irregular combatants, some of whom supported the Confederacy, some of whom opposed it, and still others who engaged in murder and plunder for personal gain.

Most historians limit their analysis to North America when studying the war, but this method distorts the nature of the conflict and its place in history. Approaching the question of violence and morality in the Civil War from a global context allows us to recognize that the conflict was not the bloodiest civil war, either in terms of absolute numbers of casualties or when weighted by population. These distinctions belong, respectively, to China's Taiping Rebellion, which claimed the lives of over twenty million people between 1850–1864, and Mexico's Caste War of the Yucatán, 1847–1872, which killed 35 percent of the region's population.[7] A global framework restores the perspective of the war's participants, who saw their conflict through the lens of past conflicts, and partly explains how and why they acted the way they did. The laws of war, to which participants made continuous reference, both limited and exacerbated the violence of the conflict.[8]

Respect for the laws of war created standards that also operated internally—each nation's populace policed itself. Because these were both modern democracies, dissenting and supporting constituencies demanded that their armies behave in ways that reflected people's fundamentally benevolent vision of themselves. But for all the restraint that both sides manifested (and they talked more about restraint than they practiced it), they also authorized and accepted atrocities. Genuine noncombatants suffered hardship, banishment, property seizure, detention, and death. The North banished citizens that supported guerrillas from its occupied cities and, in the most extreme case, 20,000 inhabitants of western Missouri.[9] Global influences could also encourage violence when it concerned the effort to maintain a civilized nation against that of the savage. Both North and South identified themselves with a crusading, European virtue and their enemy with a barbaric, immoral nature.

The US Civil War was not a world war in the modern sense of total engagement and impact, but it drew the attention of observers around the world. Participants framed their arguments in global terms and broadcast their positions to every person who would listen and possibly lend them aid.[10] The world of the nineteenth century differed from our own in important ways, most importantly for this story because of the rising prominence of nation-states. The war's participants made nationalism a central force in the Civil War, inspiring solidarity with one another and hatred for their enemy. At the same time, claiming nationhood, for both North and South, required citizens to behave as modern civilized people should. Sometimes this meant committing the violence necessary to ensure the success of their way of life and at other times it meant abstaining from violence to claim the moral high ground in the eyes of the world. The result was a war that left us a seeming paradox—a catastrophically bloody conflict that could have been much worse. This Civil War does not yield the heroes that so often populate our stories, but it does reveal the ordinary people—acting intentionally but without perfect foresight, hoping to win a virtuous war and sometimes committing atrocities—who stumbled through the conflict.

This story is full of surprises. Enslaved people, who had the greatest claim to righteous fury, abjured violence and sought their freedom instead. Soldiers on both sides observed the customary laws of war by generally respecting the lives of noncombatants. But at times they also cynically manipulated the law to sanction greater violence. For instance, Northern soldiers referred to their own rules of conduct to defend the summary execution of guerrillas and unnecessary violence against civilians. Confederate soldiers referred to the law to defend wanton cruelty and murder against black Union troops. Commanders North and South justified their hard war against soldiers and civilians by resort to necessity, but over time they also developed an apparatus of military law and oversight that tempered those measures. The democratic structure of both nations produced a similar split vision. The public of both regions lived a vicarious war that encouraged a descent into vengeance and bloodshed, but the presence of minority parties and dissenting politicians in both sections ensured the persistence of contrary voices. And despite all the violence and bloodshed, the laws of war helped produce meaningful boundaries. Civilians never became direct targets of lethal violence as they had in Indian wars of the previous decades and as they did in twentieth-century conflicts. From these sometimes contradictory trends, Northerners and Southerners created a calculus of violence that helped them respond to the contingencies of the conflict. In mathematics, calculus empowers its users to determine points along a curve or the area encompassed by it. It operates according to natural law and generates accurate predictions. No such certainty, however, could be found in the Civil War. Participants fashioned a wartime calculus through which they balanced the moral, strategic, and political dimensions of their actions, but that calculus itself changed as the war evolved.

Neither the US nor the CS governments maintained a monopoly on violence. As in other civil conflicts, both institutional and individual actors seized opportunities to perpetrate violence to advance their own ends. Usually, these irregular combatants were classified as guerrillas or bushwhackers. Sometimes, third parties acted in synchrony with the goals of the nation to which they pledged loyalty, and in other cases they used national affiliation to mask personal or communal vengeance or simple financial opportunity. In recent years, scholars have grouped such actions under the heading of guerrilla warfare. While earlier generations of historians saw guerrilla conflict as marginal, current scholars view it as central to understanding the experience of the Civil War.[11]

The guerrilla war is usually mapped onto an East-West framework that cleanly divides the regular war from the irregular war. We now have a good sense of where guerrillas operated and of the Union's counterinsurgency strategies. As a result, we can map these zones and identify the dangerous ground where these spaces overlapped and guerrillas and soldiers found each other in their sights. The linear connotation of "zones," in fact, misrepresents these areas, which were porous and unevenly shaped. We might more profitably imagine periodically colliding waves. Sometimes when waves intersect, a larger one absorbs the smaller one and the water returns to calm. This occurred when uniformed soldiers met guerrillas and captured them instead of killing them. Other waves crash together and create a higher peak that unleashes more turbulence. Sometimes in the Civil War, regular soldiers responded to guerrilla attacks with executions and town burnings; the intersection of these contrary modes of fighting created a more dangerous world for everyone. Whether we think of them as zones or waves, we need to integrate the experiences of the war's irregular dimension into the standard accounts of regular military action.

One of the challenges of any history is finding a language that accurately represents the historical reality of the past while making sense to current readers. Anachronistic terms create a false continuity between past and present; antiquated terms alienate readers and encourage us to regard ourselves as uniquely virtuous. In this case, we are confronted by the same words but ones whose underlying meaning has changed. A nineteenth-century just war is not a twenty-first-century just war. The shifting definitions of "justice" over the last century and a half, to say nothing of the differences between Saint Augustine's time and ours, complicate any analysis of the nature of violence in the Civil War. This temporal difference is part of why behavior that may appear cruel or vindictive to us appeared natural and proper to Civil War Americans. We also need precise language. Although historians of the Civil War have offered increasingly thoughtful and capacious histories of the conflict, when they turn to the war's violence the terms become more allusive and obscure. Cities are "devastated," "destroyed," or "obliterated." But burning the public buildings of a town or even its private homes is not the same as killing its inhabitants. The latter rarely occurred in the Civil War, though it was commonplace in twentieth-century warfare. This was a difference that mattered to the war's participants, and it should be clear to readers.

In what follows, I take pains to distinguish between Union and Confederate definitions of fair and responsible behavior in war. They began the war with similar perspectives but diverged quickly over guerrillas, occupation, emancipation, and prisoners. Confederates denounced the US Army's treatment of Southern citizens from the war's opening moments. The fatal break came with the Union's enlistment of black soldiers, which Confederates regarded as a breach of civilized behavior in war. In turn, Northerners regarded the Confederates' willingness to mistreat and often murder black soldiers as evidence of Southern depravity. Because wars are dialectical processes, the narrative that follows offers a holistic account of the nature of Civil War violence. Northern and Southern contestants defined their own virtue and their failings based partly on their opponent's position. When military officers negotiated with the enemy, usually through letters, they often changed their behavior, even while denying any wrongdoing. Participants on both sides adjusted their moral reckoning with the war in relation to each other.

Instead of posing the question "Was the Civil War a just war?" which has led some historians to impute a single meaning to the conflict, my goal is to investigate how participants defined justice in the midst of war.[12] Declaring a conflict just after its conclusion is the purview of ethicists and does little to help us understand why or how it happened. As a historian, my hope is to enable readers to see the contrary conceptions of violence and mercy that animated Northerners and Southerners in the Civil War. As in most wars, people on each side believed they had the stronger claims to justice, but events forced them to re-evaluate the wartime calculus and their right to this moral high ground. My concern is not with adjudicating the past but with explaining how people believed they were right. With such a background, readers may draw their own conclusions.

Evaluating the violence of the US Civil War from the perspective of the participants' moral frameworks forces us to confront the war not as a tragic misunderstanding between brothers but as a violent conflict like so many others. It forces us to admit wrongdoing on both sides. This latter admission topples America from its perch—a city on a hill, a beacon of virtue, and a model of democratic civility for the world to emulate. Instead, a full recognition of both the horror and the civility of the Civil War positions the United States within the mainstream of history.

A study of the war's violence is also important in moral terms. For many Americans, our current sense of the Civil War's meaning in American life hinges on two truisms: first, that it destroyed slavery, and second, that the human cost was enormous. For Lincoln, these two facts expressed a mathematical relationship: "every drop of blood drawn with the lash shall be paid by another drawn with the sword." Revisionist historians of the 1920s and 1930s, some of whom regarded slavery as a benevolent institution, rejected Lincoln's logic—they did not believe the liberation of 4 million people was worth the war's cost. Today, most Americans take the opposite view, retaining something of Lincoln's sense of cosmic justice, that the deaths of Union and Confederate soldiers redeemed in some way the gross injustice of American slavery.[13] Using a war's outcome to justify its course may make good politics, but it makes poor history. Instead, we need to investigate the violence of the Civil War during the war years rather than reading backward from Northern victory and emancipation. It is also true that historians too often write about war as an autonomous force, all the more so in an age of unlimited and timeless war on terror.[14] But in a democracy, the choices that voters and citizens make about who they support and the military policies they condone structure what our armies do on the ground. Lincoln knew this as well, which is why at the end of the war he tried to steer a Northern public, buoyed by a victory that confirmed their sense of righteousness, back toward a more conciliatory posture. In March 1865, when Lincoln promised "malice toward none and charity toward all," he was looking forward to a postwar era in which he would be responsible for integrating ex-Confederates into the national fabric. Charity, as Lincoln and his contemporaries understood it, required that they judge and treat others, especially opponents, with a generous spirit.[15] Lincoln announced his intention because it marked a change from how the war had been fought. For Northerners and Southerners, malice and charity defined the boundaries of the wartime calculus.

For those who have seen the horrors of war firsthand, perhaps the simultaneous presence of malice and charity seems routine, but historians have been slow to appreciate what it means for the Civil War. Kurt Vonnegut, who witnessed some of the worst moments of World War II, opened his novel *Slaughterhouse Five, or The Children's Crusade* by asserting that "there is nothing intelligent to say about a massacre."[16] Nineteenth-century Americans held a more optimistic view of the possibility of learning from history, even the most painful kind. George Caleb Bingham, painter, politician, and Union soldier, argued after the Civil War that "'the burnt child dreads the fire,' only because the hurtful properties of that element are impressed upon its memory by the injury they have inflicted. If it suffers itself to forget them, it profits nothing from its costly experience, and is liable to be burnt again." "In like manner," Bingham believed, "the history which fails to record the public and individual crimes which convulse society and sap the foundations of civil liberty, leaves future generations exposed to like evils from like fatal causes."[17] Perhaps I have more of the nineteenth century than the twentieth in me. I retain enough optimism to believe that trying to say something intelligent about a massacre is a worthy cause. With all due respect to Mr. Vonnegut, this study examines the fire in the hope that we will not burn ourselves again.

[I]

Who Can Make War?

Even the most casual student of American history knows the terrible death toll of the Civil War. The foundational role of this information in histories of the conflict may lead us to think that Americans anticipated or easily accepted the war's increasingly high casualties. In fact, the war's participants had to reconcile themselves to the conflict's scale at each new threshold, never knowing where its pinnacle lay. It would be easy to assume, as some do, that the war's violence flowed naturally from an irreconcilable animosity between the regions. In this telling, the American *Iliad* derives its tragedy from the same source as its Greek ancestor: "Rage, Goddess, sing the rage of Peleus' son Achilles."[1] Disagreement over the fate of slavery drove Northerners and Southerners to envision each other as enemies; deceit, betrayal, and wounded honor compelled Yankee and Rebel as it did Achilles and Agamemnon. The bitter invective spewed by wartime commentators lends credence to this interpretation, but the full historical record offers a more mixed portrait of attitudes toward both the enemy and wartime violence. To be sure, prewar political conflicts, mostly over slavery, alienated Northerners and Southerners. By 1860, many believed their differences made continued coexistence impossible. At the same time, the connections built over decades of national life continued to exist. Federals and Confederates were not inevitable enemies. The way they fought and the ways they explained and justified how they fought generated much of the antagonism in the war. Only a few lines after so clearly identifying the motive of the Trojan War, Homer poses a similar question: "what God drove them to fight with such a fury?" Not having recourse to the meddlesome Greek pantheon, we must identify the sources of fury among Northerners and Southerners themselves.

Unexceptional America

Americans entered the Civil War with strongly held ideas about nation-hood, war, and violence. The dynamism and unpredictability of the conflict compelled some to abandon old ways of thinking while others found their beliefs confirmed. Regardless, all Americans tested the new conceptions, habits, and attitudes they formed during the bewildering changes of the 1840s and 1850s. Three categories of thought shaped the war most profoundly. First, how did people think about their communities and their nation—what held people together and legitimized their voice? Second, what were their attitudes about morality and the law generally? Third, what was the nature and experience of violence in antebellum America?

Nineteenth-Century Americans

Americans in both North and South lived local lives before the Civil War.[2] National and even state government touched most people lightly, and the economic, social, and cultural communities that shaped their lives existed within a day's horse ride. Throughout the 1840s and 1850s, Americans built networks to connect these places. Some networks, like railroads, canals, and turnpikes, were physical pathways while others, like newspapers and the postal system, created virtual communities, as subscribers and readers exchanged ideas with strangers linked by common religions, political ideologies, or charitable motives. But the presence of these connections, which tied Americans to new national and even global markets for goods, ideas, and practices, did little to disrupt the essentially small-scale communities of antebellum America. This meant that when the war came, Americans experienced it at different scales. Missourians and Arkansans knew the guerrilla conflict; Virginians and Tennesseans knew the habits and effects of regular armies. Coastal communities, along the Mississippi River and the Atlantic Ocean, knew occupation. Northerners experienced the war through the letters of soldier-relatives and newspaper reporting.

The war narrative assembled by participants was fragmented. With hindsight, we possess a panoptic view that encompasses all these various aspects, but this was not how the war looked to those who experienced it, even for those men at the center of their respective nations who had the media at their command. Some events broke through the local frameworks in which most people were immersed. Presidential speeches and newspaper reporting offered a common language of people, events, and practices. In what follows, we need to consider both the broad historical perspective that explains outcomes and the contemporary, blinkered view that explains why people made the decisions they did from one moment to the next.

The changing structure of the midcentury economy facilitated a more destructive war in the South. In the antebellum decades, the United States developed an increasingly commercial economy and one with active markets in corporate stocks and government bonds.[3] For Northerners, this meant a dynamic commercial economy that could shift with surprising speed into war production. In contrast, the vast majority of Southerners' wealth existed in the form of property and slaves. During the Civil War, these proved much more vulnerable to seizure and destruction than the North's commercial resources.

Politics was in transition too. By the 1850s, nearly all Northern and Southern states had liberalized their voting and office-holding requirements. The rise of the second two-party system, which pitted Whigs against Democrats, energized voters and enabled a vibrant culture of partisan politics. The elites who controlled politics pursued public policies that favored native-born white men, creating a sense of entitlement about the purpose of American politics. The responsiveness of that system meant that people in both sections felt empowered to monitor, debate, and help shape military policy during the conflict.

Daily newspapers flourished in both parts of the United States, contributing to the new political infrastructure.[4] By 1860, readers around the country devoured hundreds of daily newspapers, many with national reach. Most editors affiliated themselves with a political party and published material that advocated their beliefs. Despite these partisan roots, the collective system of the American media gave access to diverse voices. These papers circulated information faster and more broadly than any previous medium in wartime. Although the immediate after-battle reports, coming over telegraph wires from the first generation of war reporters, were notoriously inaccurate, the volume and flow of information shaped how the war happened. The competition among newspapers ensured that most reports had outlets and the expanding audience encouraged editors to find provocative stories. The political disputes generated by the Civil War as well as the daily narrative of bloodshed and drama provided more opportunities to attract new readers than editors could handle. Papers played an outsized role in shaping public attitudes throughout the war. The economic and political institutions of American life did not create the bloodshed of the Civil War, but they did create a more interconnected, polarized public familiar with and even eager to consume information amid the mayhem of modern life.

Because Southern leaders organized the new nation around the protection of racial slavery, it may seem odd to designate Confederate society a democratic one. Abolitionists and antislavery Republicans certainly objected to the designation. They regarded the antebellum and Confederate South as aristocratic societies.[5] No consensus about the essential features of a democratic society existed in the 1850s, even among Northerners, and most of the markers that we use today—universal adult suffrage, full civil rights, and an independent press—did not exist. The salient democratic features of the Confederacy were a representative political system, competitive elections, a free press, and the presence of a strong dissenting political tradition. Because of these institutions and practices, the Confederacy operated much like the United States in terms of the participation of the general public in setting the nature and course of the war.

Values and the Law

What values defined Americans midcentury? Many citizens, though certainly not all, developed moral frameworks grounded in the evangelical Protestantism that emerged from the Second Great Awakening of the 1830s. This movement called them to renew or initiate a faith that would purge sin from the world. The effort to build a more Christian world took slightly different shape in different parts of the country. In the North, adherents campaigned for the reform of prisons and other places of suffering, for temperance, for respect for the dignity of all people, and among the more radical believers, for women's rights and the abolition of slavery. Northerners and Southerners clashed over the particular content of the social reforms that various groups advocated, but they came together around a belief in the justice, goodness, and naturalness of the United States as a historical entity. Regardless of the regional particulars, adherents of the Second Great Awakening celebrated the New Testament messages of hope and salvation. The wrathful God of the Old Testament never disappeared from view—he often starred in wartime tracts—but the benevolent message of Jesus attained more prominence. For strict adherents to this new evangelical faith, the war presented a serious challenge. Some devout Northern abolitionists refused to abandon their pacifism to support the Union war effort. Many others accommodated themselves to the conflict, reasoning that the good that would come from emancipation outweighed the bad inherent in military conflict. But even those who found a way to reconcile their religious beliefs and the violence of war experienced a persistent tension.

Alongside religion existed a body of philosophical and legal thought articulating modern ethics. The law offered a rational and transparent system to regulate behavior. One of the most important works—*International Law; or, Rules Regulating the Intercourse of States*—was written by Henry W. Halleck, a US Army officer (and soon to be Lincoln's general-in-chief). During the Mexican-American War, Halleck served as a legal adviser on the staff of the commander of the Pacific Squadron. Halleck's treatise rested on the substantial body of writing on nations, laws, and war developed by Europeans over the preceding centuries. It was an ample tome. The book opened with a historical survey of writing on international law and war beginning with the ancient Jews and continuing for 907 pages through hundreds of years of European history, ending with the contemporary United States.[6] Halleck's book substituted for the absence of specific rules in the *Military Regulations of the US* and *Articles of War*, the two official volumes published by the army. Halleck offered the closest thing to a manual of conduct then available, albeit one burdened by detailed citations. Halleck's footnotes sometimes consumed more space than the text itself. His average citation ran several lines and referenced many works:

Vattel, *Droit des Gens*, liv. 2, ch. 18, §§326, et. seq.; Wheaton, *Elem. Int. Law*, pt. 4, ch. 1, §1; Phillimore, *On Int. Law*, vol. 3, §2; Wildman, *Int. Law*, vol. 1, ch. 5; Polson, *Law of Nations*, sec 6; Wolfius, *Jus Gentium*, cap. 5; Heffter, *Droit International*, §106; Bello, *Derecho Internacional*, pt. 1, cap. 11, §1.

This was not a case of academic pedantry run amok. Halleck established a foundation for his rules that readers would respect. He grounded the work in European history and thought, intending the sheer volume of his citation system to guide but also overwhelm readers. They could check each of his notes but were more likely to marvel at the weight of western tradition they represented, which clearly lay on the side of the nations and the lawyers. The most important wartime commentator on the laws of war, the German-born Francis Lieber, was likewise steeped in the classic literature. Lieber's fame rests on his facility at translating the historical rules surrounding just war theory into nineteenth-century practice. These rules came to be called the Lieber Code, issued as General Orders No. 100 in April 1863 to the US Army. In 1861 Lieber gained renown when he published a set of public lectures on the laws of war in the *New York Times*, which was reprinted in other national papers.[7]

These legal scholars and philosophers hoped to build a recognizable and enforceable collection of the laws of war, but before the Civil War commenced they were mostly writing and speaking to one another. It is safe to assume that few outside the War Department read Halleck's volume, but they still held opinions about the laws of war. In the decades before the Civil War, common people regarded the law as a public, social, and fluid institution.[8] This attitude continued during the Civil War, when most people treated the laws of war as a set of practices and beliefs undergirded by experience and history, something more akin to the common law of the antebellum era than to the intellectual apparatus articulated by Lieber.[9] For lawyers, especially military officers, Lieber, Halleck, and the European Emer de Vattel served as the foundation when they implemented the laws of war in the war itself.

Just as common people understood and used the law, so they framed their ethical understanding of the world through the patterns they absorbed

Francis Lieber, a German-American legal scholar, made himself one of the leading rule-makers of the Civil War. In 1863, he drew on the global laws of war to draft the Union army's code of conduct for its soldiers.

from history.[10] Few people received the thorough grounding that luminaries like Jefferson and Madison drew upon to frame the Declaration and Constitution two generations earlier but, nonetheless, popular and private conversations during the war reveal the deep imprint of historical examples and analogies that helped Americans make sense of their conflict. They drew upon ancient, European, and more recent global conflicts to interpret their own actions. Most Americans (North and South) assumed the United States occupied a special place in world history— Lincoln called the nation "the last best of hope of earth"—but they also saw how easily the country could follow the dispiriting examples of other peoples.[11] Mexico served as a cautionary tale—a republic that could not maintain itself. The political turmoil of Mexico in the 1840s and 1850s conjured the nightmare that would come with Confederate victory. "If the United States submits to a division now it will not stop, but will go on until we reap the fate of Mexico, which is eternal war," William T. Sherman prophesied.[12] To avoid these dangers required confidence, will, and force. Watching the success of the British as they built a global empire, many Americans learned that sometimes violence was necessary to expand civilization.

The debate about the legitimate ways to maintain national unity was an old problem. Educated Americans rooted it in Greek history, in particular Pericles's famous funeral oration memorializing Athenian soldiers killed in their campaign against the Spartans during the Peloponnesian War. This speech became a touchstone in the nineteenth century and served as a reference for Lincoln at the dedication of the Gettysburg cemetery. Our record of Pericles's words comes from the historian Thucydides, and most Americans would have read his words as a celebration of the virtues of Athenian democracy. In Thucydides's view, Athenian freedom made them powerful, and they used that power to advance the cause of liberty, even through war. "Make up your minds that happiness depends on being free, and freedom depends on being courageous. Let there be no relaxation in the face of the perils of the war." Far from it. Thucydides conveys both the benefits and dangers of making war upon a free power like Athens. "Our adventurous spirit has forced an entry into every sea and into every land; and everywhere we have left behind us everlasting memorials of good done to our friends or suffering inflicted on our enemies."[13]

Regardless of the particular lessons Americans drew from the past, they believed that they could draw clear moral conclusions about the causes and meaning of military conflict. This perspective is so different from our modern, often cynical, posture that it bears mention. Consider

THE CALCULUS OF VIOLENCE

the attitude of one of the North's leading ministers in late 1861: "it is a matter of thanksgiving that this war promises to solve those difficult problems which have baffled the wisdom of our wisest counsellors." Henry Ward Beecher's cultural opposite, the proslavery theorist George Fitzhugh, came to a similar conclusion, writing that wars came because "God, who is wiser than we, has instituted them for salutary purposes, and promoted mankind to prepare for them." This faith in war to solve social and political problems was widely shared by Americans both north and south.[14]

Antebellum Violence

For at least the last several decades, Americans have regarded themselves as an unusually violent people. Studies, polls, and anecdotal reporting all indicate that residents of the United States recognize that they live in a more violent society than any comparable western industrialized democracy.[15] Further, many people read this evidence backward in time. They assume that because more Americans die of gun violence than the residents of any other nation, this must always have been the case. It is a curious case of inverted American exceptionalism, in which the thing that marks the United States as distinct is our least desirable characteristic. But only a few decades ago, a host of researchers reached the opposite conclusion. Their studies demonstrated that Americans before the twentieth century lived violent lives, but no more violent than residents of comparable places around the globe.[16] What, then, was the nature of American violence before the Civil War? What were Americans' attitudes toward warfare and killing? What sources did they draw upon to form these attitudes? These questions are essential to answer clearly before we can attempt any assessment of why people behaved in the ways that they did during the war itself.

Violence played a central role in the creation of European colonies in the New World in the seventeenth and eighteenth centuries. After decades of ignoring its role, or of subsuming it under the rubric of "encounters," historians now recognize the terrible violence committed against and among native peoples all across the Americas.[17] The territory Europeans explored and occupied was already filled with interpersonal and communal violence. As the British came to dominate North America, they harnessed war and killing to support land acquisition and control of labor. Almost from the point of first contact, Anglo Americans regarded violence as a legitimate tool in their efforts to subdue native populations. According to one student of this process, bloodshed lies at the heart of the American experience. "From the onset of the Seven Years' War in 1754," she writes, "until the United States' victory forty-one years later at the Battle of Fallen Timbers, atrocity and retaliation turned the West into a 'dark and bloody ground,' from the Mohawk Valley to the Carolinas, from the Great Lakes to Kentucky."[18] This pattern of violent interaction continued in the nineteenth century in a national rather than imperial context. Americans experienced a series of terrible clashes between native communities and the US government in the decades after the War of 1812. These involved the forcible dispossession and exile of thousands of people from their homes in the southeastern United States. The violence culminated in three wars with the Seminoles, which ended only in 1842.

The long nineteenth century opened in the fratricidal conflicts of the American, French, and Haitian Revolutions. National and civil wars around the globe consumed millions of lives before the century culminated in the apocalypse of World War I. In the new, crowded cities, fueled by industrial growth and conflict that came to typify the modern world, interpersonal violence took the lives of many. Lethal violence, defined by murder rates, escalated in the United States in the 1840s and 1850s. It did so for a variety of reasons: the influx of immigrants who intensified job competition and cultural anxiety among the native born; regional conflicts over slavery's expansion; political disputes over the country's future; racial violence inside and outside of slavery; and class conflict as the market economy upset old standards. All of these factors transpired against a background of historical dismay and lack of confidence in the government and the nation itself.[19] The arbitrary nature of the era's violence increased people's sense of their own vulnerability.

In addition to the personal violence that characterized the era, the political struggle over slavery had overflowed the churches in which it started, coursed through Congress, and spilled into the open in the mid-1850s. From the plains of Kansas, where pro- and antislavery forces fought each other, to the abolitionist and antiabolitionist riots of north-eastern cities, the elemental brutality of slavery engulfed many people be-yond plantation boundaries. Yet, even while some Americans accepted the use of mass violence to further their political or social agendas, others drew away. Abolitionists and evangelicals rejected the casual killing prac-ticed in Jacksonian America. Pacifists criticized American militarism in the Seminole Wars and the Mexican-American War of the 1840s. These competing currents ensured that the Americans who lived through the Civil War entered it seasoned by public debate and personal introspec-tion over the proper way to wage war.

In both North and South, violence was pervasive but also contained within certain parameters. In the South, personal violence suffused and defined slavery. A whole world of violent acts that free people never faced could be committed against enslaved persons. White Southerners used violence against enslaved people continually. From routine beatings or "discipline" that occurred in all manner of public and private settings to the vivid signs on enslaved peoples' bodies as punishment for attempted escapes and other high crimes, the evidence of slavery's violence was omnipresent. Southern historians rarely consider the impact of this daily exposure on popular attitudes toward violence itself, but abolitionists and even many conservative Northerners assumed it reduced white Southerners' sympathy for suffering more generally.[20] Northerners saw evidence of this as soon as the war started. Charles Wills, an Illinois sol-dier, described the whip marks on the back of a white Alabamian who joined his regiment: "his back looks harder than any one I ever saw." The man had received thirty lashes because of his support for the Union in the war's opening days. Still, he was luckier than the nine men hanged for the same offense the day before he lit out for the North.[21]

Slavery made violence in the South different from that in the North. Violent punishment of enslaved people happened everywhere and in every context in the antebellum South. The public nature of these acts, which ran the gamut from simple chastisement to outright killings, made violence pervasive in Southern life. Another important regional dif-ference was the greater role Southern white women assumed in the punishment of enslaved people. Although men occupied the primary po-sitions as protectors of the slave system, mistresses also used violence in their supervision and direction of slaves within and outside their homes.[22] With rare exceptions, neither masters nor mistresses were punished for the harm they inflicted on their slaves.[23] In cases where owners beat or killed their slaves and such actions reverberated in the community (as they often did given the degree of cross-plantation marriage and family networks), other masters might informally censure such behavior, but masters rarely faced legal prosecution for actions taken against enslaved people. The result was a culture that sanctioned elite-sponsored violence against social inferiors and expected that such practices could exist within an otherwise orderly and lawful society. These would prove to be perfect preconditions for the irregular violence that wracked much of the South during the war.

The system of slavery structured the role of violence in Southern life, both between blacks and whites and among whites themselves.[24] Slaves used violence to rebel and, increasingly in the nineteenth century, antislavery activists used violence to try and destroy the system. Accounts of chilling cruelty by masters toward slaves circulated widely throughout the antebellum period. Although denounced by slavery's sympathizers as aberrations or exaggerations, photographs and records of the physical evidence on slaves' bodies and the metal implements of torture and confinement that rest today in museums reveal the constitutive role that violence played in managing American slavery. Some slaves lashed out at owners, and enslaved people organized at least fifty-four slave revolts or conspiracies between the Revolution and the Civil War.[25] But the counterresponse by whites to these events, whether they were isolated acts of personal violence or broader political movements, generated higher death tolls than the liberation efforts themselves.

A different constellation of potential violence encircled white men in the cult of honor. Although duels occupy much of the historical imagination, violence enacted to preserve or redeem honor often involved other types of personal attacks. In 1825, the mayor of Pensacola, Florida, Peter Alba, Jr., described as "a man of gigantic size and athletic strength," jumped Joseph White, a fellow politician and opponent of Alba's friend Richard Call, and began hitting him with a club. Alba's intent was to cut off White's ears (he had a brought a stiletto along for the procedure), but White wrestled free and escaped.[26] For the next decade, White and Call, and their allies and stand-ins, continued to battle for physical and political supremacy in frontier Florida. Most Southern men understood that the two elements—bodily integrity and political leadership—reinforced one another. If Alba had succeeded, White would have carried a public mark of his inferiority and probably lost the support of his followers. As scholars have shown, the cult of masculine honor structured much of the Southern social and political world before the Civil War.[27] According to one historian, Southern men "considered politics and rhetoric personal matters" and their inability to ignore insults "infused the whole system with violence."[28] The necessity of maintaining a good image in public required immediate and often violent responses to threats or slights to one's honor. The particular nature of American politics in the antebellum period amplified the potential for harm resulting from Southern interpretations of honor. According to another historian, "politics raised the stakes of honor: nowhere was the possible esteem higher, nowhere the danger of assault on one's honor greater."[29] Honor was not the only factor; demography, regional insecurity, and Southern culture all encouraged "the overwhelming acceptance of violence by almost everyone in the society."[30]

Like Southerners, Northerners also accepted high rates of violence in certain spheres of their lives. The North's increasingly dense urban spaces, especially Lower Manhattan, produced legendary stories of thieves, bare-knuckle fighters, and outright gang warfare. Though few places were as rough as Five Points, the notorious Bowery neighborhood ruled by immigrant gangs, Boston, Philadelphia, and a host of second-tier Northern cities incubated dangerous neighborhoods defined by routine violence. In these same places, working-class men also resorted to unruly and sometimes violent street protests in response to bad working conditions and anger over competition with immigrants. These street actions, which happened in Southern cities as well, sustained the Revolutionary-era practice of joining public destruction and personal violence to political protest.[31]

Yet another group of Northerners marshaled public violence against slavery. From 1835 to 1861, Americans participated in at least 1,200 riots, many of them designed to protest or protect slavery.[32] In the Christiana Riot, for instance, a mixed group of free blacks and their white neigh-

bors helped protect a group of runaway slaves who had reached the security of Pennsylvania. In this riot, the defenders killed one of the slave
catchers sent to return the newly freed people to bondage.[33] Episodes of
this sort happened all along slavery's border, and they generated conflict
between blacks and whites and among whites from either side of the
struggle.[34] One scholar notes that "by the mid-1830s vigilance committees had been established by African Americans in the major cities of the
East Coast."[35] These groups armed themselves, trained, and actively defended their own people and runaways escaping slavery. Blacks had been
resisting slavery in the South since its inception, and by the 1830s, some
whites joined in the effort. But this change produced deep divisions within
the antislavery community. Many reformers had come to abolition
through the evangelical revivals of the 1820s and 1830s, and these people
often advocated a rigid pacifism. So even as a strategy of violence helped
bridge racial gaps in the movement, it produced new rifts among whites.
The violence directed against slavery was a precursor and partly a cause
of the violence of war.[36] Herman Melville famously referred to John
Brown and his 1859 raid on Harpers Ferry as the "meteor of the war,"
foreshadowing the coming conflict.

The most famous instance of political violence over slavery in antebellum America—the caning of Massachusetts senator Charles Sumner
in 1856—spurred the growth of the Republican Party and accelerated the
sense of sectional alienation, but what stands out from the episode is its
singularity. In the days after the event, Virginia newspapers gleefully listed
other abolitionist senators who deserved a beating. In Boston, abolitionists demonstrated and organized. According to one observer, "if a leader
daring & reckless enough had presented himself, he might have raised
any number of men to march on Washington."[37] But no more senators
were caned and no army marched on the capital. The most important
effect of the violence was its impact on public attitudes in each section.
In the North, one man reported that "I have never before seen anything
at all like the present state of deep, determined, & desperat feelings of
hatred, & hostility to the further extension of slavery, & its political
power."[38] The physical violence enacted as a part of the sectional conflict was tightly circumscribed, but its political and rhetorical impact rip-
pled far beyond the individuals affected.

If Sumner personified sectional violence, Kansas gave it a spatial focus. The best recent chronicle of events in the territory (Kansas became a state in 1861) describes the escalation of violence that so alarmed easterners after 1854. The most famous event in the period was the "Sack of Lawrence" by proslavery forces in which the free-state capital was targeted. The leading hotel was burned to the ground, newspaper presses destroyed, and several houses looted, though the only death was of a proslavery settler killed by falling masonry. John Brown's massacre of five proslavery settlers along Pottawatomie Creek and the later murder of five free-state partisans in the Marais des Cygnes massacre stand out as the deadliest events of the period. The years 1856–57 witnessed frequent attacks by one camp or the other, but as with the caning of Sumner, the more important change came as Kansans and easterners (both North and South), who eagerly consumed reports of the conflict, inured themselves to the presence of violence in a political conflict that politics could not solve.[39]

The white abolitionist John Brown played a key role in escalating the Kansas conflict. He also led the most dramatic Northern attack on slavery in American history. In 1859, he directed a small group of men in an assault on the US Armory and Arsenal at Harpers Ferry, Virginia, intending to distribute the weapons he seized to enslaved people in the state, whom he would then guide to freedom. The raid failed when the US government dispatched soldiers to suppress it, as they had in previous slave rebellions going back to the nation's founding. Like the Sumner caning, the public reaction to the Brown raid on Harpers Ferry belied its small scale. Southerners regarded it as proof that abolitionists desired not only the end of slavery but the end of white Southerners as well. Most actual abolitionists venerated Brown but repudiated his actions. The raid's violence and ironies—its first victim was a free black watchman for the Baltimore & Ohio Railroad—made them reluctant to commit to such extreme methods.[40]

Justifying War

Americans' reactions to the ubiquity and varieties of violence in the antebellum world offer only part of the context for understanding how the Civil War was fought. We must also investigate American attitudes toward war. Steeped as they were in European history, most educated Americans regarded military conflict as inevitable, and many viewed it as an affirming signal of national maturity. A general sense of war's creative and productive possibilities was widely shared. The first true pacifists in the American experience emerged out of the religious awakening of the 1830s and 1840s. In the midst of the Mexican-American War, for instance, William Lloyd Garrison declared a "moral abhorrence which war excites in my soul," so strong that it "causes me instinctively to recoil whenever I see a soldier, as I should to see a rattlesnake running at large."[41] This categorical opposition to war was regarded by many as not only naive but absurd. Nonetheless, Americans, like their Europeans counterparts of the time, recognized boundaries around warfare.

Who could create wars, and how could they be fought? The answers to these important questions determined what was a just conflict. These questions were not simply academic. As Henry Halleck explained in his treatise on international law, "all modern ethical writers regard an *unjust* war as not only immoral, but as one of the greatest of crimes—murder on a large scale."[42] The first question could be answered easily: states could wage wars. In an era before modern nongovernmental organizations, the only legitimate international actors were nation-states. The question of who comprised a nation contains much of the core problem of the American Civil War, but regardless of whether participants recognized the Confederacy as an independent state, they all regarded nation-states as the sole actors in war. The issue of *how* wars should be fought—of what qualified as just conduct—elicited a much wider range of responses. Although both Northerners and Southerners claimed adherence to a supposedly timeless conception of just war, they, like their European peers, also recognized the situational nature of just behavior in military conflicts. Contrary to popular conceptions of the United States as maintaining an isolationist stance until well into World War I, nineteenth-century Americans regarded domestic and foreign policy as reciprocal and dynamic. The most important public policies of the early republic and antebellum eras concerned expansion, development, and trade, all of which encouraged American growth by protecting and fostering markets overseas.[43] The Civil War era was no different. The ways people on each side chose to fight reflected both immediate military and political concerns and the wider global resonance and judgment of such practices. Participants in the war also defined justice in relation to each other. The historical experience of the Civil War reveals that, in practice, just war is more dynamic than the transhistorical theory it claims to be.

Nationhood and Sovereignty

If only nations could fight wars, what made a nation? This was the question of the century, as ethnic and linguistic communities built nation-states across Europe and the Americas. In the process, nineteenth-century Westerners labored to establish the nation as the natural and universal form of political community. Elite Americans and their peers in Europe regarded the nation as the final stage in political development. This was most visible in the legal treatises on international law, an old body of thought that touched on trade, diplomacy, migration, and conflict. Henry Wheaton's definitive *Elements of International Law* (in its sixth edition by the start of the Civil War) declared that "the peculiar subjects of international law are Nations."[44]

The centrality of nations to global trade, diplomacy, and war only increased the importance of clarifying their foundations. An honest accounting would have seen a global conversation about the mechanisms by which people could dissolve and rebuild new political entities, something along the lines of what flourished briefly in the wake of World War I. In the event, national leaders forestalled this effort. The creation of nations reflected local and situational power struggles as much as it did any broader effort to capitalize on a natural affinity among people of a defined area.[45] The differing demands of these contests ensured that elites in any given country sought to project their nations as natural and perpetual entities, which required obscuring the actual historical origins of such places. This was more complicated in the United States, where the American Revolution clearly marked an origin moment. To help naturalize America, national histories of the early nineteenth century identified the gradual coalescence of Americans as a people in the eighteenth-century British colonial world.

The success of this effort—to create a permanent and inviolable American nation—was tested in the secession crisis of 1861. If the Southern people comprised an autonomous nation, they could claim a right to govern themselves. If the United States comprised the only legitimate American nation, then Southerners could assert their rights as a minority section but could not dissolve the whole. The initial federal response to this elemental threat was temporizing. The secession of seven Deep South states in late 1860 and early 1861 paralyzed President James Buchanan. He denounced the constitutionality of Southern withdrawal from the Union but believed he was unable to act against it. Buchanan proclaimed that "the Executive has no authority to decide what shall be the relations between the Federal Government and [the States]" and believed that their duty to solve the problem devolved upon Congress. Bravely, he counseled, "the course of events is so rapidly hastening forward that the emergency may soon arise when you may be called upon to decide the momentous question whether you possess the power by force of arms to compel a State to remain in the Union." Although he believed in federal supremacy, Buchanan offered no plan to maintain it in the event of secession. "It may be safely asserted that the power to make war against a State is at variance with the whole spirit and intent of the Constitution," he announced.[46] Buchanan personified the problem of sovereignty at the heart of the Civil War—he seemed not to understand who had the authority to make or unmake a nation.

Southerner fire-eaters filled the vacuum left by Buchanan's inaction. They strived to establish both the coherence of a unique Southern nation and the legitimacy of asserting such a project from within the existing United States. To do so, they emphasized the natural right of a people (defined with great selectivity) to determine their own political future. The fluid nature of nation-building in the nineteenth century offered them hope. Henry Halleck's definition of statehood seemed to hold promise for would-be Confederates. "*A sovereign state,*" he wrote, "may therefore, be defined to be *any nation or people organized into a body politic and exercising the rights of self-government.*"[47] After Deep South delegates created the Confederacy on February 4, 1861, in Montgomery, Alabama, they claimed themselves to be a "body politic" deserving of sovereignty and recognition. Southerners also drew support from Wheaton's *Elements of International Law.* Confederate ambassadors carried copies of Wheaton's work with them when they traveled abroad. Perhaps they wanted to avail themselves of his particularly modern framework for thinking about sovereignty and statehood. Wheaton recognized that states did not require external support to establish legitimacy. Offering a framework that passed no judgment on the ideological purpose or composition of a state, he affirmed that "it is a State because it exists."[48]

From Lincoln's election in November through the early 1861 creation of the Confederacy, Southern elites advanced an interpretation of American constitutional history that legitimized the new nation. Jefferson Davis led this effort in his inaugural address. According to Davis, the creation of the Confederacy "illustrates the American idea that governments rest upon the consent of the governed, and that it is the right of the people to alter or abolish governments whenever they become destructive of the ends for which they were established." Because this slaveholding conservative rejected the label of revolutionary, Davis needed to show continuity rather than change: "we have changed the constituent parts, but not the system of our Government . . . we have a light which reveals its true meaning."[49] In many of his public addresses, Davis articulated the state compact theory of the Constitution, asserting the states as the proper actors in the case of secession.[50] The trend of the early nineteenth century was toward liberal nationalism, producing states that broadened access to property, curtailed the power of hierarchical institutions (like the Catholic Church in Latin America), and expanded the franchise. But there was nothing inevitable about this alignment. It was (as the second half of the century showed) possible to create a new popular nation on behalf of a conservative politics, as happened in Germany.[51]

Rather than rehash the debate about whether white Southerners had a legitimate right to secede, we need to understand *how* they went about asserting that right. Confederates emphasized this effort because it was central to their bid for independence and their hopes of legitimizing the Confederacy as a sovereign nation, and especially because only a sovereign nation could legitimately make war. The fire-eaters who led Southern states from the Union pursued secession in a manner that anticipated this challenge. Most importantly, they claimed to instigate and pursue the process through regular democratic means. In the Deep South, popularly elected representatives attended special conventions that decided the issue. In the Upper South, the decisions of similar conventions were also subject to popular referendums. The question of whether secession received popular support is a hard one to answer. In Southern states outside South Carolina, popular support for secession, as measured by votes for convention candidates committed for or against remaining in the Union, exceeded 50 percent of eligible voters, but often just barely. The limits of universal white male suffrage as the marker for a true democracy are obvious today but received little attention in the South at the time. White Southerners trumpeted the fact that a majority of those empowered with the right to vote in a majority of the Southern states supported secession. Would-be Confederates believed that they possessed popular support, a historical claim, and a compelling economic case for secession. In their eyes, secession and war were just acts.

Northerners disagreed. They regarded the United States in 1860 as a sovereign state, unable to dissolve as white Southerners proposed. Lincoln dismissed secession as the "essence of anarchy," as did many Southern conservatives. White Southerners' decision to destroy the American government because they were unhappy with the outcome of a presidential election seemed sheer madness. "The dissent of a minority," explained the conservative *North American Review*, "may be entitled to respectful attention, but it cannot furnish the rule of government." To do so would threaten self-government itself. According to Lincoln, if secession succeeded, the lesson of political instability would doom democracy as a global experiment. Northerners marshaled historical, legal, and economic arguments of their own, all of which emphasized the perpetuity of the Union. Travers Twiss, the other key interpreter of international law alongside Wheaton and Halleck, emphasized "the Cardinal Right, upon which all others hinge . . . that of Self-Preservation." For these writers, and for the many Northerners who absorbed their view on international law, the American nation was an inviolable unity, justified in defending its integrity against enemies both foreign and domestic.[52]

Lincoln and Northerners took refuge with Wheaton as well, who asserted that "sovereignty is the supreme power by which any State is governed. This power may be exercised either internally or externally." He categorized the American Union in unequivocal terms as permanent. "It is not merely a league of sovereign States," Wheaton wrote, "but a supreme federal government, or compositive State, acting not only upon the sovereign members of the Union, but directly upon all its citizens in their individual and corporate capacities." Northerners emphasized the permanence of the federal Union. The Confederate assault on Fort Sumter, US property in the harbor at Charleston, South Carolina, constituted a rebellion against the legitimate authority of the national government. Henry Halleck's definition of "civil wars" fit the bill perfectly: "those which result from hostile operations, carried on between different parts of the same state," like the War of the Roses in England or recent factions in Mexico.[53]

Some scholars believe that a state's standing depends on whether foreign powers recognize it, in which case the Confederacy must be regarded as a failure. Foreign powers played a pivotal role in establishing the sovereignty of the US government during the Revolution and in sustaining it during the Civil War. Britain, France, and Russia all refused to recognize the Confederacy as an independent nation. In doing so, they explicitly sanctioned Lincoln's claim that the Washington government exercised legitimate authority over Southern citizens. The British and French, both dominant global actors with grand colonial pretensions, understood that casting Confederates in the position of rebels against established power weakened the ability of white Southerners to mount their campaign for autonomy. More importantly (from the European perspective), it helped create a precedent for central power over that of subnational or ethnic communities that might one day push against London or Paris. As much as theories of justice and natural rights might have informed debates about just war, we should not underestimate the influence of geopolitics and strategy.

Defensive War

Southern fire-eaters dismissed the likelihood of a war in public, but few believed that the United States would let the South leave in peace. War could only be fought by nations and just wars only by just people. Most new Confederates felt they had established the moral and legal legitimacy of the Confederacy in February. Having created their state, Confederates prepared for war. The Confederate Secretary of State emphasized as much in his instructions to the foreign deputies sent to Europe in March: "You will not fail to explain that in withdrawing from the United States the Confederate States have not violated any obligations of sovereignty. They have merely exercised the sovereignty, which they have possessed since their separation from Great Britain and jealously guarded."[54]

Both Northerners and Southerners labored to prove to themselves and the world that they had the right to make war. Ancient and modern scholars of just war agree that states can resort to war only when they are attacked or face an imminent threat of such an attack. Offensive war violates the cardinal principle of just war doctrine—that states have a natural right to self-defense but not to committing violence against others. Defining "imminent threat" can be a tricky proposition. Strictly speaking, Confederates fired the first shot when they turned their cannons on a US military installation, Fort Sumter. As Lincoln had hoped, this empowered the United States to adopt a defensive posture.

People at the time disagreed about when, where, and why the Civil War started, and historians have faithfully maintained this tradition. As in recent conflicts, both sides advocated a particular chronology that demonstrated to the world the justness of their respective causes. Southerners had a harder pitch to make, as they knew at the time. The Confederates attacked Fort Sumter before a supply ship arrived in April 1861. Although some Southern papers argued that Lincoln's decision to resupply the fort represented a hostile act, they seemed to sense the weakness of their position. The stronger Southern argument, one that fire-eaters had been making in different forms since at least the mid-1850s, was that the North's refusal to observe their obligations under the Constitution, especially the return of runaway slaves, effectively relieved Southerners of their duty to respect federal authority. That is, they were not rebels against a legitimate government but conservatives seeking to uphold the original American faith against its appropriation by Northern radicals. In the words of one Confederate congressional resolution: "the war in which we are now engaged with the Government and people of the United States was not provoked or inaugurated by the Confederate

States, and is now prosecuted and maintained by them only in vindi-
cation of the highest and most sacred rights of a people resolved to be
free and independent." This position had the merit of being grounded
in a consideration of how polities organized themselves. As Southerners also knew, the constitutional pose reflected an essentially unan-
swerable question about when and how people can reorganize their
national connections and institutions. But the lack of a clear answer
did not dissuade Confederate thinkers from asserting the justice of
their cause. Even more, as one historian notes, "secessionists . . . tried
to reassure everyone that their crusade was a holy one." In the language of just war theory, they claimed *jus ad bellum*, a legitimate right
to make war.[55]

Like Davis, Lincoln understood he must win world opinion on the
question of who had *jus ad bellum*. Accordingly, he explained the war's origins in a way that cast the North as a victim. As he described the difference between the Confederacy and the United States: "one of them would
make war rather than let the nation survive; and the other would *accept*
war rather than let it perish."[56] More significantly, he crafted a response
to the Southern contention that a popular minority could constitution-
ally dissolve their relationship as a part of the American nation. Lincoln
conceived of the Union as perpetual and secession as impossible. "Perpetuity is implied, if not expressed, in the fundamental law of all national
governments," Lincoln wrote. "It is safe to assert that no government
proper, ever had a provision in its organic law for its own termination."[57]
From his earliest experiences with government Lincoln cherished, even
worshipped, the rule of law. Secession, predicated on Southerners' fears
over the consequences of electing a Republican president, rejected that
rule. As a Whig, Lincoln had grown used to seeing his party lose national
elections. The remedy for an election that did not produce the desired
result was to wait and try again. As Lincoln saw it, secession destroyed
self-government because everyone who disliked the outcome of an election, at whatever level, could simply proclaim independence. In democracies, he wrote, there could be "no appeal from the ballot to the bullet." So
in response to Southerners' contention that secession was a preemptive
strike against an imminent threat from the federal government, Lincoln

averred that not only was secession undemocratic; secession made democracy impossible.

Davis and Lincoln directed their arguments for their respective national sovereignties at both external and internal audiences. To function as a nation, they needed the respect and support of other nations. More importantly, they needed to inspire their own people. Neither man anticipated the full scope of the war that came, but both knew that they faced skeptical, divided publics and that war of any sort would require a firm moral foundation. The challenge for each administration was to explain their own posture in a way that convinced their public of their righteousness. Once justice had been proven, they could expect not just an eager public but a committed one, ready to bear sacrifice and weather setbacks, secure in the authority of their cause.

The sovereignty struggle was never an even fight. The United States began the war with an eighty-year history as an independent nation. The Confederacy could claim only two months. Lincoln exploited that difference and sought every opportunity to deny the independence of the Confederacy. In his writing, he used "rebellion" far more often than "civil war." Despite its assumption of a dispute among common people, "civil war" granted too much autonomy to the Confederacy.[58] He often referred to it as the "Confederate States" (with quotation marks) or the "so-called Confederate States." This was both a logical consequence of his belief in a perpetual Union and one of his rhetorical weapons against the Confederacy. The Confederates, for their part, recognized the United States as a legitimate member of the community of nations. They denied its sovereignty over the Southern states—a logical consequence of their belief in secession—but they could claim magnanimity in tolerating the presence of a bona fide national neighbor to their north.

The Laws of War

Even as both Northerners and Southerners labored to build a secure moral edifice from which to claim national sovereignty and the right to defend it, they also anticipated fighting a just war in practice, what theorists of this tradition call *jus in bello*. During the war, this pride in observing limits (or claiming to) represented a way to make a virtue of what was often a necessity imposed by physical, logistical, or tactical limits. "If this is a civil war . . . then it should be carried on *as a war* and according to the usages of *civilized* nations, and by such means only as are deemed legitimate modes of warfare," proclaimed one Northerner. Victimhood and the incapacity, rather than the unwillingness, to respond to violence or destruction could fuel its own kind of moral righteousness. But the desire to respect global laws of war also stemmed from how participants on both sides visualized themselves as a people. One military historian characterizes the 1850s as "the crucial decade in the accelerating development of more formal efforts to define appropriate conduct in war." Early in the war, the *New York Times* bragged, "it is for the rebels to persecute, lynch and hang the innocent and feeble that fall into their hands. But let the Stars and Stripes float only over a peaceful and law-abiding Union, where all the rights and franchises of freemen are preserved." With the nouns reversed, this sentiment could easily have been expressed by the Richmond papers.[59]

Certain of its own just conduct, each side assumed that the other intended to commit outrages upon its citizens, and each exploited every opportunity to report, embellish, exaggerate, or falsify stories about the mistreatment of its noncombatants. Both North and South claimed continuity with American military practice and global standards, and made comparisons to justify their own policies and condemn their enemy's. The Napoleonic Wars set a benchmark for much nineteenth-century fighting, and the Crimean War later in the century provided a contemporary example. The interstate dimensions of these conflicts diminished their applicability, however. The Indian Rebellion of 1857 offered a more useful example and was frequently mentioned in American discussions of the Civil War. It featured a quasi-national movement claiming territorial and political sovereignty from a larger, well-established polity, the British Empire. It entailed a history of complicated claims and counterclaims of atrocities. And it drew substantial international attention focused on questions of national autonomy, violence, and legitimate warfare.

When discussing just conduct in war, Federals and Confederates claimed continuity with a line of thinkers dating back to Saint Augustine and Thomas Aquinas, but most focused on sixteenth-, seventeenth-, and eighteenth-century European writers such as Francisco de Vittoria, Hugo Grotius, and Emer de Vattel.[60] Francis Lieber, writing to the US attorney general, referred to Grotius as "one of your and my greatest masters."[61] Both sides sought historical and contemporary legitimacy as sovereign nations by connecting their methods of waging war to established traditions.[62] Mississippi congressman Henry Foote hoped to accomplish this by postponing "the adoption of harsh measures until all other proper resources in vogue among civilized nations were exhausted."[63] He understood the diplomatic importance of positioning the Confederacy as an equal among civilized nations. Even as nations build themselves in a geographic context, they must also do so in a historical context. Theorists of nationalism emphasize the historical roots of a given nation—that to claim nationhood, a people must link themselves to discrete ancestors.[64] In addition to this vertical support, nations require tangential branches on their family tree. These connect the nation to established traditions parallel to its own. This practice adds strength to claims for sovereignty because foreign nations see something of themselves in others.[65]

American policymakers regarded Vattel as the leading contemporary interpreter of the laws of war. He was raised in Neuchâtel (today's Switzerland), then controlled by Prussia, but he received a polyglot education, studying in Basel, Geneva, and Dresden. His main purpose in the *Law of Nations* (published in 1758 and translated into English by the end of the eighteenth century) was to apply natural law theory to the interactions and integrity of nations. Vattel was primarily concerned with political economy and establishing a system for trade that would enable Europe to advance. His advice on these matters resonated with a wide array of readers, including a young William T. Sherman, who took the book with him on a months-long voyage from New York around Cape Horn to Monterey, California, in 1846–47. Vattel offered both specific arguments about what was permissible in war and what constituted sovereign authority (especially important for Northerners). Getting right with Vattel enabled each side to affiliate themselves with a respected intellectual and cultural tradition.[66]

By the time of the Civil War (and still today), there were two basic divisions of just war conduct: *jus ad bellum* or questions relating to the justice of the war's cause, and *jus in bello* or questions relating to how the war was fought. Some people start wars with just cause but behave illegitimately during them. Others might initiate a war on insufficient grounds but behave according to established practice while fighting it. In theory, these categories of analysis remain fundamentally distinct. In practice, these categories are in constant tension because nations have an obligation to end wars as soon as possible (indeed, a swift and decisive war satisfies an important measure of justice), but doing so might compel actions that would violate rules of *jus in bello*. As a result, nations must balance these competing goals. The Union, in particular, struggled to find the point of equilibrium. The difficulty was fighting a hard war that did not alienate the white Southerners Lincoln hoped to bring back to the Union. According to a recent study, Francis Lieber, for one, understood that "warfare was not unrestricted violence, but violence limited by an end."[67] The end for which both Lieber and Lincoln fought was reunion, and the political imperatives of reunion—the importance of ensuring that Southerners *wanted* to be part of the American union—encouraged restraint in how they fought.

The questions of *jus in bello* are easier to pose (if not easier to answer) because they surround specific kinds of action. The most important issue pertaining to justice in war is directing war violence only at legitimate targets. Noncombatants can be injured or even killed under specific circumstances (a separate body of just war theory called the *doctrine of double effect* governs these conditions), but adhering to just war requires that combatants selectively identify their targets. There can be no indiscriminate killing; enemy soldiers are the only legitimate targets of lethal violence.[68] This means that the laws of war direct, or focus, a war's violence rather than simply reducing it. Conversely, soldiers who commit violence against enemy combatants as a part of regular uniformed armies cannot be charged with assault or murder. They possess immunity for actions that in peacetime would ensure criminal prosecution. But soldiers do not possess unlimited immunity. When they perpetrate violence against noncombatants, including civilians or enemies taken as prisoners, soldiers may be tried for violations of various international conventions. Today, we have an elaborate system at both the national and international level that investigates and punishes wrongdoing by members of the military. That system only began after the Civil War (the first Geneva Convention was written in 1864, in part because of the violence that Europeans saw in the US conflict). The same court of global public opinion that functions today was in session then, however, and its judges (the newspaper-reading public of European countries) evaluated Northern and Southern behavior carefully.

It is a truism that complicates the study of war to note that every nation believes that it fights a just cause. And in retrospect, most readers seek to adjudicate which side in a conflict had a stronger claim to justice. The challenge for historians is to establish the context within which people made this claim. Despite the theoretical continuity of just war doctrine over centuries of western philosophy and war, the question of which actions are permissible changes subtly in each age. We need to be cautious about assuming a universal, transhistorical standard of justice and instead work to restore the debate over just war to its historical framework. Part of that context for the US Civil War involves acknowledging that enslaved people and their allies made a different claim on justice. In their view, justice demanded abolishing slavery, even if war was necessary to accomplish it. At some points, Lincoln's rhetoric shifted from the legalistic framework of traditional just war doctrine to incorporate this broader social claim to justice. The competing ideas about what constituted a just war and just practice within it demand that rather than asking if the Civil War a just war, we can more profitably frame different questions: Why did each side think they behaved justly? How did they defend those claims? How did their claims compare to the prevailing sentiment at the time? Such philosophical distinctions may seem arcane or the exclusive province of military planners and legal thinkers, but the language of just war and the laws of war (which often stood in for the former) circulated among a surprisingly wide range of people, soldier and civilian alike.

The conspicuous labors of American leaders to cite European authorities suggest an effort to create a kind of moral genealogy of acceptable and prohibited behavior. More than intellectual lineage, these efforts—mostly in the congresses and the newspapers of both sections—sought to build international recognition behind claims to legitimacy. According to one historian, "Civil War Americans felt bound to explain their positions in legal terms. Law and the Constitution provided the common vernacular for people on all sides of this civil conflict."[69] An important marker for inclusion in the world of nations was waging warfare like other modern European nations. Leaders of both sides understood the strategic value of articulating and enacting a civilized war. They were also no doubt relieved when humanitarian sentiment dovetailed with military interests. As other conflicts have revealed, the weaker (insurgent) side in a military conflict often trumpets the laws of war with greater enthusiasm. They have more to gain from enforcement than the dominant power does. The Civil War was no exception. Confederates celebrated their restraint and denounced Yankee violations more often in public conversation, but both sides were engulfed in the same tensions and contradictions between rhetoric and practice.

It may surprise modern readers to learn that a key part of the laws of war that governed the violence of the conflict was retaliation. Although today we may use the words *retaliation* and *revenge* interchangeably, in the nineteenth century they had distinct definitions. Retaliation and reprisal (the latter term sometimes substitutes for the former) come from distinct root words but both emphasize the compensatory nature of the practice. According to the *Oxford English Dictionary* (*OED*), the Latin root of *retāliāre* means "to make amends for (a wrong done) by an equivalent punishment." Reprisal, from Anglo-Norman and Middle French, indicates the "seizure of property or persons of foreigners as compensation for loss sustained, retaking, repossessing." Revenge, in contrast, emphasizes the pleasure of payback. As the *OED* defines it, the "satisfaction obtained by repaying an injury or wrong." Just war scholars elaborated the concept of retaliation thoroughly before the Civil War. Grotius insisted that retaliation was only lawful when practiced against the original perpetrators of an unjust act, never as mere punishment. Building on Grotius, Emer de Vattel used the mistreatment of ambassadors to condemn revenge. "What right have you to cut off the nose and ears of the embassador of a barbarian who had treated your embassador in that manner?," he asked. Vattel expressed reservations about the role of retaliation, but believed that when practiced, "the punishment ought to bear some proportion to the evil for which we mean to inflict it."[70]

Francis Lieber applied these conceptions to the Union's rules of war. "The law of war," wrote Lieber, "can no more wholly dispense with retaliation than can the law of nations, of which it is a branch. Yet civilized nations acknowledge retaliation as the sternest feature of war. A reckless enemy often leaves to his opponent no other means of securing himself against the repetition of barbarous outrage." According to Lieber, "retaliation will therefore never be resorted to as a measure of mere revenge, but only as a means of protective retribution, and moreover cautiously and unavoidably."[71] Although Confederates spurned Lieber's definition as an invitation to barbarism, they expressed the same attitude in their discussions of retaliation. When Confederate congressman Theodore Burnett introduced a resolution demanding that for every Confederate soldier "incarcerated in the dungeons and felon cells of Northern prisons . . . [we] shall . . . administer the same treatment received by our men in the hands of the enemy," he did not anticipate a limitless cycle of vengeance. Instead, the purpose of his resolution was to "bring the enemy back to a sense of humanity."[72] Similarly, US senator Benjamin Brown explained that "it was for the purpose of putting an end to these barbarities, and not for the purpose of enhancing them, that they recommended the joint resolution now before the Senate."[73] Brown's Senate colleague James Harlan went even further, asserting that "war . . . is in itself in its very nature retaliatory. No just war can commence by an organized community except for the punishment of injuries received or insults offered by another organized community or civil power."[74]

In practice, both sides used retaliation as a method of ensuring compliance with global standards of conduct. Some of the officers and officials who used retaliation seem to have arrived at it independently after recognizing it as a method of forcing one's opponent to respect the rules of war. But many more came to retaliation because of their awareness of its place in international law. Even ordinary civilians demonstrated an implicit awareness of the parameters of retaliation established by just war scholars. In some cases, commanders rejected retaliation because they believed that unjust suffering would redound to their benefit. Midway through the war, Robert E. Lee explained to Jefferson Davis, "I am not in favor of retaliation except in very extreme cases, and I think it would be better for us to suffer, and be right in our own eyes and in the eyes of the world. We will gain more by it in the end."[75]

Both Northerners and Southerners deployed retaliation not as an excuse for revenge but as a method of ensuring that their opponent operated in accordance with global standards of war. Retaliation enmeshes soldiers in a contradiction. They violate the rules of war in order to enforce the rules of war, but the threat and occasional use of retaliation deterred unrestrained war. The foremost modern authority on just war recognizes that the use of retaliation can quickly become a slippery slope. He notes that "it is the express purpose of reprisals . . . to break off the chain, to stop the wrongdoing *here*, with this final act."[76] From the perspective of just war theory, the objection to reprisals comes because they punish innocent people for the crimes of others, but the war's participants and later observers recognized that the "responsive, restrained, and proportional" nature of reprisals and their intent to end a breach of the war convention make them valuable. During the Civil War, they played this role. Ironically, retaliation became the last best hope of man.

The dangers of retaliation emerged most fully around the problems of slavery and emancipation. Both sides found themselves threatening and practicing retaliation over conflicts related to the status of enslaved people and black soldiers more than any other issue. The problem of slavery was woven into the moral fabric of the conflict from the beginning, but especially once the North, in 1863, made emancipation its official policy. In order to understand the decisions that Confederates made throughout the war regarding how to fight, we need to remember their bedrock belief in the legality and morality of slavery. Vice President Alexander Stephens's characterization of slavery as the "cornerstone" of the new Confederacy was no exaggeration. Once the North committed itself to ending slavery in the United States, the moral dynamics of the war changed as well. Even previously proslavery Northerners grasped the advantages such a posture promised. Confederates regarded the shift in Union policy as illegal, immoral, and a gross violation of the military traditions of civilized nations. The result of this impasse was that the remainder of the war constituted an extended conflict over how to reconfigure the laws of war and military practice to adapt to the new environment. This elemental division over slavery emerged before the Emancipation Proclamation, as did clashes over other questions of just conduct in war.

[2]

The Rising of the People

The secession of seven Deep South states in late 1860 and early 1861 exposed the problem of sovereignty at the heart of the Civil War—who had the authority to make a nation? Who could unmake it? What steps could be taken to ensure the perseverance of an existing nation or the creation of a new one? Initially surprised by white Southerners' willingness to assert their independence, Northerners responded with a robust defense of American democracy and the federal union. Beyond their claims to a defensive and hence just position, the language each side used to frame its recourse to war in 1861 shaped how they behaved in the years to come. Southerners asserted the natural right of a people to determine their own political future. Northerners emphasized the inviolability of the Union, the only bulwark, they believed, for the future of representative government in a hostile world. The war that came surprised both sides. It started in street riots before the Battle of Bull Run that brought soldiers and citizens into lethal confrontations and it generated irregular conflict almost immediately. In the war's first year, both sides struggled to define their rules of conduct. The Union faced two challenges, both of which involved the status of people under the laws of war. Committing to those laws meant taking prisoners, but this action created the danger of recognizing their opponent as a legitimate and sovereign entity. Second, US commanders had to respond to the exodus of enslaved people from the Confederacy who hoped the Union promised freedom. For the Confederacy, the problem was organizing and controlling the military resistance they had kindled. The rise of guerrilla units challenged traditional norms of regular warfare, complicating the question of who deserved protection if captured.

No solace for these questions could be found in the Constitution, which nineteenth-century Americans regarded as the final arbiter of law in the United States. It had frustratingly little to say about the rights of citizens or noncitizens in times of war. According to Lincoln's solicitor general, William Whiting, this was why they took recourse to the "law of nations" (and within it, the laws of war), which existed before and above the Constitution. Only in these international frameworks could the war's participants find rules for how to behave. Whiting, an influential voice in the administration, argued that "none of [the] rights, guaranteed to peaceful citizens, by the constitution belong to them after they have become belligerents against their own government." In 1861, when Whiting penned his thoughts, he was concerned primarily with clarifying the president's power to seize property, but the legal logic carried him to a starker conclusion about military power. "This right of seizure and condemnation is harsh," he observed, "as all the proceedings of war are harsh, in the extreme, but it is nevertheless lawful. It would be harsh to kill in battle a loyal citizen who, having been impressed into the ranks of the rebels, is made to fight against his country; yet it is lawful to do so." According to Whiting, the right to destroy and to kill was implicit in the right of national self-defense.[1] The Confederate administration operated according to the same principles. Jefferson Davis and his cabinet believed that their national sovereignty justified creating an army and using lethal force when necessary to defend the new country.

The process of organizing armies, launching campaigns, and encountering the enemy in person blurred the clear boundaries around lethal violence marked out by just war theory. Northerners initiated military campaigns that destroyed Southern property and killed those whom they hoped to draw back to the Union. Lincoln hesitated to declare captured Confederates prisoners of war because he feared that doing so would confer legitimacy on their state. Refusing them prisoner-of-war status, however, would have initiated a terrible sequence of tit-for-tat executions of captured men. And despite being a slave republic, the US Army tentatively endorsed a form of military emancipation. Confederates struggled with their own paradoxes. They articulated a national rhetoric of individual liberty on behalf of a new nation dedicated to expanding slavery. And even while organizing a regular army, some Southern citizens engaged in irregular warfare that violated the laws of war to which they claimed adherence. The war's participants resolved some of these contradictions, but during this first year of the conflict both sides struggled to implement methods of waging war that accomplished their military goals without subverting their values or compromising their standing in the international arena.

Commencing War

The contradictions manifested themselves immediately. The Civil War began as a regular war and an irregular one. It started at Fort Sumter in Charleston Harbor and in the streets of Baltimore. It involved soldiers and civilians. It imposed a steep learning curve. In 1861, Civil War soldiers began fumbling toward a set of common practices on the battlefield, as volunteers learned how to fight according to the laws of war. Off those regular battlefields, irregular fighters subjected both regular combatants and noncombatants to hardship and death.

The War in the Streets

On April 20, 1861, the *Philadelphia Press* declared "Civil war has commenced." The article anchored its claim not to Fort Sumter, the moment typically given prominence in accounts of the Civil War. Instead, the basis for this assertion—echoed in newspapers across the North—was bloody fighting in Baltimore. For many participants, the Civil War started not with an artillery attack on a US fort but in the streets, with civilians and soldiers mixed together. In the days after April 15, when Lincoln called up the state militias to help enforce the laws of the United States, tens of thousands of men began making their way toward Washington. Volunteers from northeastern cities moved by railroad down the seaboard, which brought them through the secessionist stronghold of Baltimore. Northern soldiers traveling to Baltimore eyed it warily; violent riots on election days had become a ritual in the city, and the tradition of mob violence in a pro-secession town presaged rough passage. Maryland's governor was nominally pro-Union, but Baltimore, from its mayor to its chief of police, was governed by prosecessionists and this divided leadership inhibited a coherent response to the first bloody conflict of the Civil War.[2]

"The Sixth Regiment of the Massachusetts Volunteers Firing into the People in Pratt Street, While Attempting to Pass through Baltimore *en route* to Washington, April 10, 1861." The violent clashes between soldiers and civilians in the streets of Baltimore alerted Americans that the Civil War would not be fought exclusively on battlefields.

The First Pennsylvania Volunteers passed through the city on April 18 and had to run a gauntlet of angry Baltimoreans as they switched trains. Despite protection from a regular army unit stationed in the city, the novice Pennsylvanians suffered injuries from the bricks, rocks, and bottles thrown at them by crowds. The Sixth Massachusetts Volunteer Regiment, heading south behind the Pennsylvanians, listened to reports about the assault. Colonel Edward Jones, the regiment's commander, told his men to resist provocations from the mob but also instructed them to "select any man whom you may see aiming at you, and be sure to drop him."[3] The Massachusetts men arrived in Baltimore midday on April 19. Fire-bells rang to announce their arrival and pro-Southern men, "Plug Ugly roughs" in the local parlance, poured into the streets to jeer and bombard the troops.[4] The violence quickly exceeded the previous day's events

as thousands of Baltimoreans attacked a small group of the soldiers separated from the main body. After the crowd pitched into the troops with
missiles and bullets, the volunteers responded in kind. Before they could
reach the safety of the station, four soldiers were killed and several dozen
seriously wounded. Following their commander's advice, they took careful
aim and killed dozens of rioters.[5] The mayor's understated report to Lincoln explained, a "collision between the citizens and the Northern troops
had taken place."[6] Northerners read reports of the events with growing
indignation and horror. Their word of choice to describe this behavior
was "mob." In all its various forms—"rebellious mobs," "mobocratic,"
"mob violence," "mob rule"—this description distanced these disloyal
Americans from the rational and orderly Northerners who defended the
flag.[7] It situated the Baltimore actions as criminal conduct rather than
the political action Confederates considered it to be.

The events in Baltimore and the secession of Virginia on April 17 inspired panic in residents and officials in Washington, DC. Lincoln received reports of Maryland civilians organizing themselves to force the
state out of the Union and perhaps turn on the capital. The fighting in
Baltimore stirred the first threats of revenge as an act of war. A prominent Pennsylvanian encouraged the Secretary of War to use a firm hand
against traitors. "The administration will be sustained in everything except halfway measures," he wrote, "If Baltimore was laid in ashes, the
North would rejoice over it." Lincoln weighed the competing reports and
contrary advice coming into his office. Some Northerners had already
called "for Baltimore's immediate bombardment as retribution for the
deadly riot against the Sixth Massachusetts on April 19." This would have
represented an overreaction under the traditional guidelines of
retaliation—which mandated proportional action—but perhaps the
threats of such action, which appeared in regional papers, helped curtail
more violence.[8]

A similar street fight, this one more deadly still, exploded in St. Louis
two weeks later. Fearing violence from prosecessionists, army officers
organized an ad hoc federal force, composed partly of native-born men
and partly of German immigrants who had settled in the city over the
preceding dozen years. On May 10, these men forced the surrender of a
group of several hundred state militia recently enrolled by the proseces-

sion governor. As in Baltimore, a large group of anti-Republican specta-tors heckled and abused the soldiers, singling out the "Damned Dutch" for special harassment. As the soldiers marched their captives through the city, violence broke out, and several dozen soldiers and civilians were killed. The Union general, Nathaniel Lyon, overlooked the civilian ca-sualties in his official report, but the state militia commander asserted that after surrendering, "a number of my men [were] put to death, together with several innocent lookers-on,—men, women, and children." Violence erupted the next day, again between German-American soldiers and ci-vilians, claiming another dozen lives. In both encounters, US soldiers treated the men firing at them as irregular combatants who could be legitimately killed. In the phrase of one Northern paper, "the Secession-ists, in a word, are to be taught that they are no longer a privileged class—that when they shoot they must expect to be shot—when they stab that they will be disemboweled on the spot." Unionists celebrated this as "the first blow struck at the Great Rebellion. Heretofore it had always been aggressive."[9]

Northerners applauded the firm hand used to keep Union control of the city even as they denounced the noncombatant deaths. Like their critique of the Baltimore riot as a crime rather than war, Northern reac-tion to the St. Louis affair foreshadowed an approach that would span the war—to condemn, often publicly, those occasions when their sol-diers directed lethal violence against civilians but to endorse the result itself. According to the *Philadelphia Press*, "when communities permit ruffians and murderers to assault the soldiers sent among them by the constituted authorities of the land, these communities must suffer. The innocent may fall with the guilty, but while we may wish to mourn the sad fate which sends them to the grave, inexorable duty can permit few con-siderations of sympathy."[10]

Most historians mark the war's opening with the firing on Fort Sumter. Starting the narrative in Charleston Harbor—at a military installation by uniformed soldiers of two hostile nations—presents the Civil War as a regular military conflict. But the Civil War also began on the streets of Baltimore and St. Louis. And from the beginning, it was a conflict de-fined as much by its irregular as by its regular features. These cities both lay along the border between North and South, the region where the war's irregular violence was worst. Observers pondered: Would Fort Sumter or Baltimore define the coming conflict? The irregular fighting in Baltimore inspired one Northern paper to declare it a "reign of terror," intentionally summoning the specter of the French Revolution.[11] The Civil War never generated a terror of the sort led by Robespierre, but that does not mean its participants exercised the gentlemanly restraint we might imagine characterized warfare in the age of honor.

Becoming Soldiers

After the capture of Fort Sumter by Confederate forces and the bloody clashes in Baltimore and St. Louis, Americans knew they were at war. In the coming weeks, the call to arms in both regions drew hundreds of thousands of volunteers. The Union enlisted 2.1 million men during the conflict and the Confederacy roughly 900,000. The prewar US Army contained 17,000 men. This meant that only one-half of 1 percent of Civil War soldiers entered the conflict with professional military training. This figure excludes those men who attended military academies such as Norwich, in Vermont, or the Virginia Military Institute, and did not take into account Mexican War veterans, but the basic fact remains: the overwhelming majority of Civil War soldiers entered military service with little training in the rudiments of war. The antebellum militia system, in the words of one historian, was "a dismal failure" in terms of training men.[12] As a result, both sides subjected their eager volunteers to intensive boot camps where men received instruction in formations, drill, maneuver, and the basics of military camp life. They received less instruction in the equally important issues of how to identify a target and which actions were acceptable and which ones outlawed.

Officers at recruitment centers received copies of the standard guides—*Hardee's Tactics*, which choreographed the movement of soldiers on battlefields, and the US Army's *Regulations* and *Articles of War*. These latter manuals included the forms needed for quartermasters to requisition supplies but offered only vague guidelines in terms of who could be subjected to the lethal violence exercised by the armies. Neither the *Regulations* nor the *Articles of War* (which were adopted in the same form by the Confederate army) offered instruction on how to differentiate friend from foe or who among enemies was a legitimate target of an army's power. What little guidance they gave was intended to build a strong and efficient army, not necessarily a just one. During sieges, for instance, the *Regulations* included exactly one line of advice for curtailing violence against noncombatants once a place had been captured: "The officers exert themselves to restrain the men." In fact, a conquered city existed mostly at the whim of the commanding officer: "whether the place be taken by assault or by capitulation, the provisions and military stores, and the public funds, are reserved for the use of the army."[13]

The lack of clarity about acceptable behavior by soldiers in the *Regulations* and *Articles* generated conflicts between and within each side as the war progressed. That said, Regular Army soldiers (and they played key roles in both Union and Confederate armies) had a clear and tightly bounded sense of the legitimate targets of military violence. Robert E. Lee explained to his soldiers: "it must be remembered that we make war only upon armed men."[14] Lee was not unique in this regard. According to a historian of the antebellum army, "almost all old army men, Union and Confederate, remained committed to the conventions of organized nation-state war waged by soldiers in uniform, subject to military discipline."[15]

Even if the volunteers received little counsel on the boundaries of their behavior, the training methods of 1861 succeeded. Despite their novice status, federal and Confederate armies proved themselves disciplined and dedicated enough to sustain four years of vigorous war. The results of that work are well known: 750,000 soldiers died in the US Civil War, and hundreds of thousands more were injured, maimed, or disabled. These casualties, for the most part, occurred through legitimate combat or disease (twice as many from the latter as the former). This is the Civil War that we encounter most often in battle and campaign studies, the biographies of generals, and sweeping military histories of the conflict. Officers and enlisted men on both sides generally observed the customary rules of engagement when they met on battlefields. The defining feature of these battles, as described by a legal scholar, was the way they segregated military violence. A "classic pitched battle, is by no means an unambiguous descent into horror. It is a ritualized means of focusing, and therefore containing, the violence of war." This expert identifies the US

Civil War, along with the Franco-Prussian War, as the conflict that marked a turn away from decisive, "pitched" battles. Although there is no question that even the largest battles of the Civil War—Shiloh, Gettysburg, Atlanta—failed to end the conflict, the battles themselves contained the war's violence. They did so because soldiers signaled their participation by donning uniforms, fighting under distinct national flags, and targeting each other for violence. Flags of truce were respected, wounded men (in most cases) were taken from the field, and, most importantly, soldiers could surrender or be captured outright. Once their status shifted from soldier to prisoner, they became, in effect, noncombatants. The general adherence to these practices created a mostly just Civil War on the battlefield.[16]

The First Dangers

Both volunteers and their respective publics, counter to their expectations, encountered the difficulties of fighting a regular war from the start. These derived not from innate bloodlust or sectional animosities, but from tensions between the laws of war and the political and military objectives of both sides. Two foundational problems manifested in the war's early days, one related to slavery and the other to the issue of nationhood. Officers devised solutions to these challenges, but the policies they adopted were ad hoc and situational. Their policies solved immediate crises, but both issues—the future of slavery and the question of whether Lincoln should treat Confederates as citizens of another nation—complicated the war until its conclusion.

Contraband of War

Soldiers and civilians became entangled in the violence and paradoxes of slavery as soon as the war began. One of the most surprising and consequential moments took place before any major battles had occurred. In spring 1861, Confederates labored to build fortifications along the peninsula bordered by York River and James River below Richmond. Lacking sufficient manpower, they impressed slaves from nearby plantations to build their defenses. The US Army's position in Fort Monroe, at the tip of the peninsula, proved alluring to enslaved people who already sensed the possibilities inherent in a war between North and South. On the night of May 24, three enslaved men—Frank Baker, Shepard Mallory, and James Townsend—escaped the Confederate lines and fled to the Union fort, where they surrendered themselves. The following day, Major John B. Cary, a Virginia native serving in Confederate forces, appealed to the fort's commander, Major-General Benjamin Butler, for the return of the men under the auspices of the Fugitive Slave Act of 1850. Butler's response held far-reaching consequences. He told Cary: "the Fugitive Slave Act did not affect a foreign country, which Virginia claimed to be, and that she must reckon it one of the infelicities of her position that in so far at least, she was taken at her word."[17]

Butler's clever sarcasm resonates with our modern rejection of slavery, making it hard to see anything noble or consistent in Cary's request, which exposed him as a Confederate still desiring the protection American law offered for slavery. Notwithstanding Cary's hypocrisy, his assumption that the war would not interfere with slaveholding represented a common belief across the South and the North in 1861. Even if the Fugitive Slave Act no longer applied, Cary no doubt expected that Butler would honor the sanctity of private property. Many conservative Union generals did, ordering their soldiers to return runaway slaves to Confederate masters. Butler recognized the manpower advantage such a policy would give the Union. Shortly after Cary's visit, he issued an order declaring Baker, Mallory, and Townsend "contraband of war," making them subject to seizure by US troops and thus potentially free of slavery.

Historians have spent considerable time analyzing the contradictions inherent in this position and the revolutionary potential contained within the "contraband" designation.[18] What has remained less noticed is the significance of Butler's reliance on the laws of war to achieve his goal of depriving the Confederacy of manpower.[19] Though Lincoln would always deny it, Butler's frank admission to Cary revealed that secession had worked—Virginia was now out of the Union and without the protection of its laws. The Fugitive Slave Act had no more power in Virginia, Butler effectively declared, than it did in Canada, where many fugitives found refuge. But the success of secession did not create an environment of lawlessness. To the contrary, the condition of war between hostile powers activated the global laws of war. Among their many purposes was regulating the conduct of soldiers. Under these rules, it was illegal for soldiers to plunder wounded or dead enemies after a battle. The only items that could be seized from the enemy—whether combatant or noncombatant—were those that could be used for military purposes—guns, ammunition, animals, food, and in the case of the Confederate South, enslaved people. Confederates objected to the seizure of enslaved people by the US Army because such an action seemed tantamount to emancipation (not to be confused with the "impressment" of slaves practiced by the Confederate government, a distinction that many slaveholders came to view as strictly semantic). They also objected because such people, once employed by the US Army, became themselves, if only to a limited degree, agents of war against them.

The tangled issues of emancipation and the role that African Americans would play in the war pressed themselves with even greater force on the US Army in the Lower Mississippi River Valley. Two preconditions helped ensure this region played a key role in the Union's turn toward emancipation. One was strategic: Admiral David Farragut captured New Orleans and extended Union control up the Mississippi River in early 1862. Second, the region contained an educated, propertied, and politically aware black community. These two elements enabled Louisiana's free blacks and enslaved people to claim a defining role in the struggle. Once again, Benjamin Butler placed himself at the center of the action, having been transferred to the Department of New Orleans, where he commanded the occupation of the city. Despite the seeming liberality of his initial contraband order, Butler held many of the same prejudiced views of black Americans as other white Northerners. He described those enslaved people he met whose masters had fled the region as comparable to shipwreck victims, with "all [their] social ties and means of living gone." Butler mistakenly believed that slaves identified themselves with their masters, something freedpeople proved false as they defended their interests throughout the war.[20]

Butler hoped his contraband order would destabilize the Confederacy, but he resisted any broader role for freedpeople in the war. John W. Phelps, one of Butler's subordinates and a dedicated abolitionist, felt no such reluctance and began working to enlist black men into US armies in mid-1862. Butler deferred to Lincoln's opposition to the practice, prompting Phelps to resign. But manpower demands and the desire of black New Orleanians to participate in the war overwhelmed Butler's hesitancy. He hit upon a novel solution that incorporated black soldiers into the army without giving license to servile insurrection. He accepted the enlistment of Louisiana's Native Guard, a regiment of black and mixed-race men that had fought for Louisiana since the mid-eighteenth century. By Butler's reasoning, because these men had been first incorporated into the Confederate army, a short-lived experiment that failed, the Confederates could have no legal objection to his enlisting them as well. A Treasury Department agent reported that he "admired the characteristic shrewdness with which Gen. Butler has managed the affair."[21]

But white Southerners saw a difference. It was one thing for them to accept loyal black men who seemed to support Confederate interests and quite another to accept an invading force composed of those men, or perhaps of slaves recruited from the countryside. White Southerners regarded any effort by enslaved people to free themselves as an unlawful and unjust assault on their society. William Porcher Miles, a Confederate congressman from South Carolina, wrote to Jefferson Davis in June 1862 about reports that the United States was organizing a regiment of formerly enslaved men in his state. (Another abolitionist Union general was duplicating Phelps's efforts, this time along the Sea Island coast.) "As these negroes are slaves in open insurrection," Miles advised, "they are liable by the laws of the State to be hung whenever taken." Some Confederates worried that these men would be treated like regular prisoners of war, but Miles assured them this fear was unfounded. "I do not contemplate for a moment any such proceeding on the part of this Government."[22]

Rumors of slave insurrection circulated among Unionists and Confederates in Texas, Louisiana, Georgia, South Carolina, Mississippi, and Arkansas in 1861 and 1862. In Louisiana, most escaping slaves made their way, directly or indirectly, to Butler's headquarters. Brigadier General Daniel Ruggles of the Confederacy condemned Butler's style of warfare by disparaging the efforts of the United States, "in violation of its constitutional obligations, inaugurating deliberately servile war by stimulating the half-civilized African to raise his hand against his master and benefactor, and thus make war upon the Anglo-Saxon race—war on human nature." Although he paid little heed to Ruggles, Butler seems to have held similar fears, writing to his wife in July 1862 that "we shall have a negro insurrection here I fancy. . . . If something is not done soon, God help us all. The negroes are getting saucy and troublesome, and who blames them?" Some Northerners, reluctant to see enslaved people as agents of their own fates, accounted for unsettled conditions in Louisiana by reference to the environment. Having listened to an incredible story of escape, in which runaways braved bloodhounds and alligators, one man observed that "the swamps [of Louisiana] were never free of negroes. They constituted a species of asylum and that fact had its effect upon the character of the negro and upon the workings of the system."[23]

A conservative in many respects, Butler paid as much heed to stories of rebelliousness as did the most anxious slaveholder. When Union Brigadier General Godfrey Weitzel took several regiments of Union soldiers, including some the Native Guard, to the western reaches of the state, Butler hoped to minimize the social impact of the presence of such men clad in Union blue. "We must leave force enough to take care of any rising of the negroes," Butler instructed. To ensure this, he advised Weitzel to meet with leading black men in the area and explain that the army would ensure order regardless of where they lived, so they should remain with their owners for the time being. "Caution them that there must be no violence to unarmed and quiet persons." Butler's recommendations failed to mollify Weitzel, who appeared paralyzed with fear over the slave rebellion he believed he was engendering. "[The Native Guard's] moral effect in this community, which is stripped of nearly all its able-bodied men, and will be stripped of a great many of its arms, is terrible," he reported to army headquarters. "Women and children, and even men, are in terror. It is heart-rending, and I cannot make myself responsible for it." Weitzel represented the attitudes of many white Northerners who opposed emancipation and the enlistment of black men because they believed that once released from white control, enslaved people would revolt in a paroxysm of violence.[24]

Personal misgivings aside, Butler would have none of it. "Does not this state of things arise from the very fact of war itself?," he lectured Weitzel. "You are in a country where now the negroes outnumber the whites ten to one, and these whites are in rebellion against the Government or in terror seeking its protection." Reversing the polarity of blame that white Southerners asserted (and that Weitzel seems to have adopted), Butler reassured him that "you are in no degree responsible for it. The responsibility rests upon those who have begun and carried on this war, who have stopped at no barbarity, no act of outrage, upon the citizens and troops of the United States."[25] Butler echoed William Whiting's justification for the fate of people killed in the war. Disloyalty put Southern people in a position where they exposed themselves to violence, property destruction, and the confiscation of their slaves. Butler instructed Weitzel to meet with local whites and tell them to stop resisting the Union. That mission accomplished, he would then explain that the army would put down insurrection. This assurance would have been cold comfort to most white Southerners, as Butler well knew, but it also appears to have been unnecessary. None of the statewide newspapers document anything like the mass uprising that Weitzel imagined. Thousands of black Louisianans escaped their bondage by fleeing to Union lines, but few of those instigated the violence that Weitzel and Butler feared.

Privateers and Prisoners

Notwithstanding Butler's blithe assertion that Virginia's secession actually removed it from the United States, the Lincoln administration remained adamant that such an action was impossible. Lincoln and his subordinates consistently referred to the "so-called Confederate States" to avoid accidentally lending it the prestige of sovereign nationhood. Because the purpose of the war, from Lincoln's perspective, was preserving the Union, any recognition of the Confederacy as independent was tantamount to defeat. Despite their assertion, Lincoln and Republicans treated the Confederacy as a nation even if they refused to recognize it.[26] They took a page from international law, which defined what could be done by central states in the context of insurrections. Global practice recognized that at certain points rebellions could become full-fledged civil wars that required treating each side equally. According to a recent history, respecting this precedent "enabled federal authorities to treat the Confederates as public enemies who fell under the rules of war, while not forgiving them for treason."[27] The first and most pressing problem that forced this awareness was prisoner exchange. Taking prisoners embodied a central proposition of just war but created the danger of recognizing the opponent as a legitimate and sovereign entity. Prisoners merited protection from harm because they fought as legitimate belligerents in a conflict. Despite the resolution that the Lincoln administration reached in 1861, the problem of belligerent rights haunted the Civil War until its end.

Foreign observers expected from the war's start that both sides would take prisoners of war rather than execute captured enemies. Americans likewise adopted the language of "prisoners of war," assuming that any men captured would be treated fairly. At the same time, Northerners worried that treating captured men as prisoners would give legitimacy to the Confederacy. As the *New York Times* framed the issue, "a prisoner of war, to be provided with rations and comfortable subsistence until the peace . . . is a very different thing from a captured traitor to be tried by the courts and judged by the laws against treason. The one enjoys an honorable restraint, while the other may have to swing for it." One of the premier Northern newspapermen of the day identified this tension early in the conflict, arguing that "the government should not treat its captured rebels as prisoners of war. . . . To do [so] . . . is a virtual admission that the rebels are a lawful enemy."[28]

Although both sides took prisoners after skirmishes in early 1861, it was clashes on the seas that provoked a reckoning. Just after Lincoln's militia call in April, Jefferson Davis issued letters of marque to ship captains willing to interdict Northern vessels for the Confederacy. These authorized the ships to operate as privateers, which meant that privately owned vessels could conduct maritime war against the enemy. In this case, it allowed Southern captains to seize US flagships and their contents. The practice of privateering was well established—the Confederate Constitution copied the language on the practice verbatim from the US Constitution. The Declaration of Paris ending the Crimean War in 1856 had outlawed privateering, but the United States had refused to sign it. So the Confederacy could claim an old American right to engage in privateering. Southern ship owners responded to Davis's call by organizing and outfitting ships, and they soon began to ply the Atlantic and Gulf Coast waters. In midsummer 1861, the Union navy captured three Confederate privateers, the *Savannah*, the *Petrel*, and the *Jeff Davis*. The *Savannah* went to New York, where the sailors were put into the notorious city jail, the Tombs. The other ships went to Philadelphia, where the sailors were also imprisoned and accused of piracy. The court refused to recognize their letters of marque or their claim to represent, as privateers, a sovereign state. Instead, they would be tried as criminals and, if convicted, sentenced to death.

Jefferson Davis was appalled by the decision to prosecute these men and concerned about the war presaged by such a decision. As he explained, the crew of the *Savannah* "has been indicted by the grand jury of New York for treason and piracy, which . . . indicat[ed] an intention of not considering them as prisoners of war."[29] In response to the Northern actions, Robert E. Lee advised moving three US officers held by the Confederacy into close confinement. In early July, Davis wrote Lincoln directly: "It is the desire of this government to so conduct the war now existing, as to mitigate its horrors as far as may be possible: and with this intent its treatment of the prisoners captured by its forces has been marked by the greatest humanity and leniency consistent with public obligation. . . . It is only since the news has been received of the treatment of the prisoners taken on the *Savannah*, that I have been compelled to withdraw these indulgences, and to hold the prisoners taken by us in strict confinement." That is, the treatment of his sailors in the North justified Davis's harsher treatment of Union prisoners. "A just regard to humanity and to the honor of this government now requires me to state explicitly, that painful as will be the necessity, this government will deal out to the prisoners held by it, the same treatment and the same fate as shall be experienced by those captured on the *Savannah*."[30] Davis discussed the fate of the imprisoned men in many different venues, using it as an example of the cruelty and illegal conduct of the North.[31] He justified his actions by recourse to the practice of retaliation—using the threat of equivalent treatment of Union prisoners to correct Lincoln's conduct, which he regarded as unjust.

In Philadelphia, the judge's strict instructions to the jury assured a guilty verdict. "'Judge the tree by its fruits,' [the presiding judge] said, 'and we see the results of this miserable political heresy in the present situation of our country.'" In New York, the court allowed more evidence and the defense attorney worked to prove the existence of the Confederacy. For the *Savannah's* crew, "the [defense counsel] pointed out that in every way the men complied with the code of war as recognized by all civilized nations." The New York jurors were clearly confused about how to proceed. One of them "sent word to the judge that a verdict depended on whether a civil war existed." The judge refused to answer, leaving the men to do it on their own. Perhaps as a result of the confusion, the jury deadlocked on the charge of piracy.[32]

In the meantime, the Confederacy escalated its response to the Philadelphia decision. Judah Benjamin, then secretary of war for the Confederacy, wrote to John Winder, commander at Richmond, where several Union prisoners were held: "You are hereby instructed to choose by lot from among your prisoners of war of highest rank, one who is to be confined in a cell appropriate to convicted felons, and who is to be treated in all respects as if such a convict, and to be held for execution in the same manner as may be adopted by the enemy for the execution of a prisoner of war, Smith, recently condemned to death in Philadelphia. You will also select thirteen other prisoners of war, the highest in rank of those captured by our forces, to be confined in the cells reserved for prisoners accused of infamous crimes, and will treat them as such so long as the enemy shall continue so to treat the like number of prisoners of war captured by them at sea, and now held for trial in New York as pirates." Winder obeyed, selecting one colonel for execution, and twelve more—a mix of lieutenants, colonels, and captains—as hostages to balance the remaining Confederates still held. Then Lincoln blinked. He moved the Confederates to a regular military prison and allowed them to be exchanged and returned South, in spite of the strong Northern sentiment that regarded the privateers as little better than robbers and murderers.[33]

Both Confederates and Federals claimed victory. Confederates used this episode to further their cause around the world. Henry Hotze, a Confederate propagandist in Europe, raised the issue in his British campaign, explaining in the London *Morning Post* that the United States initially acted "in strict accordance with its theory that the war was only the suppression of an insurrection, in which the belligerent rights belonged exclusively to itself."[34] Hotze asserted that global opinion—which recognized the captured sailors as legitimate participants in a real war—forced Lincoln to commute the initial death threat. This not only furthered the cause of Confederate recognition but positioned the Confederacy as conforming to international law and the United States as violating it.

Francis Lieber, in the *New York Times* in August 1861, offered a legal argument "to reassure Union leaders that they could have it both ways: they could abide by humanitarian restraints of the laws of war without extending de facto recognition to the Confederacy as a nation." The US Supreme Court considered the issue as well, ruling in the *Prize Cases* that, given the legality of the blockade, privateering (when properly sanctioned by government-issued letters of marque) was legal. The court's opinion gave Lincoln the authority to treat the Confederacy and its soldiers as regular enemies in a war without recognizing the nation behind them. "A state of actual war may exist without any formal declaration of it by either party," the court declared, eliminating the need for Lincoln to acknowledge or even name the conflict. Echoing Lincoln's view, the justices asserted that "the present civil war between the United States and the so-called Confederate States has such character and magnitude as to give the United States the same rights and powers which they might exercise in the case of a national or foreign war." Lincoln had already claimed this right, but conservative Democrats had long objected. Securing the backing of the court, still presided over by the old Jacksonian Roger Taney, strengthened Lincoln's political hand.[35]

Former Massachusetts governor Edward Everett, who later shared the stage with Lincoln at Gettysburg, explained the pressure requiring this concession. "We are compelled," he observed, "by the magnitude of the forces engaged, and by the course of the great maritime powers in recognizing them as belligerents, to regard them ourselves in that light. Instead of punishing them as traitors and rebels when they fall into our hands, as the municipal law of our own and all other countries, and their practice too, would warrant us in doing, we treat them of necessity as alien enemies." Everett positioned US policy as consistent with international law. "Prisoners are exchanged and paroled, flags of truce sent and received; and they enjoy in all respects the privileges and are subject to all the obligation, which by the Law of Nations pertain to public war."[36] Treatment as a public enemy ensured that soldiers would be captured rather than killed as criminals. But it did not ensure easy treatment; the Confederacy was now effectively a foreign power at war with the United States. This meant, according to a recent study, that "Confederate rebels were public enemies, subject to the *international* rules of war-making, which gave the president the 'sovereign power' to do most anything against enemies, within the dictates of morality."[37]

Francis Lieber made this same argument in advice to the administration. "We do not acknowledge the Carolinians as an independent nation," Lieber counseled, "by blockading Charleston any more than we declare the 'Confederacy' a sovereign government by treating their captured soldiers as prisoners of war." As Lieber expected, the *Prize Cases* decision established that a state of war existed between two belligerents. The Confederacy never organized more than a very small regular navy, but Davis's letters of marque covered many privateers who effectively constituted an arm of the Confederate war power. By treating those sailors captured from privateers as prisoners of war, Lincoln forestalled the retaliatory spiral that Davis's July decision would surely have touched off if applied more broadly during the war. It also publicly brought US military policy on this issue into line with international law, something that both Confederates and conservative Unionists had been calling for since the conflict's opening. In this instance, though not in every one to come, strict adherence to the laws of war limited the conflict's bloodshed on both sides, especially for those Southern sailors held in New York and Philadelphia jails.[38]

Righteousness in War

In the dilemmas over emancipation and prisoners, legal and political elites decided the outcome, but of nearly equal weight in shaping the moral boundaries of the war were the attitudes and perspectives of the general public. Northerners and Southerners drew on what they knew and what they experienced, whether firsthand or through print, to create a language of metaphor and comparison with which they justified their behavior and condemned that of their enemy. Once developed, this language revealed and perpetuated each side's sense of righteousness. Confederates and Federals emphasized different aspects of their history and purpose at different times but they shared a surprising amount as well. These languages were turned inward—to explain war to themselves, in effect—and outward to the world. Like other practices, intellectual trends often worked at cross purposes. The attention to just war and civilized conduct, broadcast to the world with pride, was balanced by fiery rhetoric about the savageness of the enemy.

The Rhetoric of Just War

Most importantly, leaders on both sides presented themselves as acting defensively. As the insurgents, Confederates integrated a rhetoric of victimhood into nearly every public comment. The 1861 debate over the legitimacy of the Confederate nation and their right to initiate defensive war began this process. The bedrock of this argument was laid in the same claims made by American revolutionaries eighty years earlier. "The tyranny of an unbridled majority, the most odious and least responsible form of despotism, has denied us both the right and remedy," proclaimed Jefferson Davis. "Therefore we are in arms to renew such sacrifices as our fathers made to the holy cause of constitutional liberty." This assertion of the Confederacy's right to self-defense remained a staple of Southern rhetoric, though it failed to sway its primary audience—Europeans.[39]

Without ever abandoning their belief in the justice of their cause, after 1861, Confederates sought to generate sympathy among observers by emphasizing the practice of war. Already by mid-1862, Confederates felt alienated from their former countrymen because of how they fought. When one of Union Major-General George B. McClellan's staff members met with Confederate Brigadier General Howell Cobb, he reported that "the invasion of the seceding states, with its consequent slaughter and waste, had created in the Southern mind such feelings of animosity and spirit of resistance that the war could only end in separation or extermination." According to Cobb, "the blood which has been shed has washed out all feelings of brotherhood." In official correspondence and public pronouncements, the Confederate secretary of war and the army's inspector general condemned Northern practices. Jefferson Davis, in the war's first year, began his habit of denouncing US Army behavior in the strongest possible terms. In his message to Congress of July 1861, before the Battle of Bull Run had even been fought, Davis declared that Federals "are waging an indiscriminate war upon them all, with a savage ferocity unknown to modern civilization. In this war, rapine is the rule; private residences, in peaceful rural retreats, are bombarded and burnt; grain crops in the field are consumed by the torch; and when the torch is not convenient, careful labor is bestowed to render complete the destruction of every article of use or ornament remaining in private dwellings, after their inhabitants have fled from the outrages of a brutal soldiery." This characterization wildly exaggerated Union soldiers' behavior, as Davis surely knew.[40]

Davis seems to have decided that using such inflammatory rhetoric was essential to consolidating public support early in the war. Confederate newspapers and ministers took their cue from the president and mischaracterized Union behavior throughout the war. Southern pulpits rang with condemnations of vile Yankees. Within a week of Bull Run, a South Carolina pastor denounced Lincoln as a "blind and infatuated power that in madness rends the pillars of democratic liberty, invades the South, confiscates her property, blockades her ports, burns her cities, insults her daughters by a mercenary and brutal soldiery, and threatens to subjugate, enslave, and annihilate her sons." Confederate congressmen used similarly unrestrained rhetoric. Charles Russell of Virginia declared that by August 1862, "the Federal government had repudiated all restraints upon violence, and waged upon the South a war of extermination, to which history presents no parallel." How could ordinary Confederates, subjected to a persistent characterization of the war as nothing short of apocalypse, not have envisioned the Union as a sinful and unjust combatant? In public and private discussions, political leaders and many common people used the language of hyperbole and analogy. Yankees were fiends, felons, and blood-maddened barbarians, more vile and treacherous than Indians, Huns, or wild savages.[41] Confederates needed analogies that resonated with the public and that generated outrage. The elusive nature of allegorical language also concealed those differences that Confederates wanted hidden, especially the central role of slavery in their nation.[42]

Union partisans asserted their blamelessness surrounding the war's origins as well. "This rebellion must be crushed," proclaimed Archibald Dixon, senator from Kentucky. "Let it require a longer or a shorter time, let it cost more or less money; a greater or less sacrifice of human life, still it can be, it must and it will be, crushed. If the ordinary means of warfare can do this, let them, as I hope they may, suffice; but if more shall be required, more must be resorted to." In the cogent and dangerous conflation of one midwesterner, it was "a necessary, just, and glorious war." Edward Everett proclaimed that "the government and loyal people of the country are the party assailed, and that they are clad in the triple armor of a just cause." The North's shift toward emancipation in 1862 brought them more fully in line with the prevailing moral sentiment in the western world, which allowed them to trumpet their cause with greater openness and enthusiasm. "Our government is standing on the defensive. It is defending its life. . . . It is not a war which the government has made, but a war forced upon the government—a war which the government could not refuse to accept," proclaimed Indiana governor Oliver Morton.[43]

Always, Northerners presented themselves as acting in response to secession, usually with regret but fortitude. "My whole nature abhors the bloodshed and misery that mark war's path, and the blackened and desolate track it leaves behind," one speaker intoned. "But there are some things I love more than those which war destroys, and those are the very institutions and blessings that would be destroyed if the rebellion should triumph. I love the principles that elevate humanity more than I hate war—and I accept war, with its horrors, as the least of the evils presented to us."[44] For his part, Lincoln extolled the Union as "the last best hope of earth." Framing the stakes of the conflict in terms of its global effects strengthened the necessity of a strong response. "A rebellion against the principle of democracy—a rebellion against the law of representative government—is a rebellion against mankind itself," proclaimed the North's "Loyal League." "In the success of destruction of the rebellion are involved not the happiness of America only—not the liberties of Americans only—but the peace and welfare of a world."[45] Francis Lieber went even further, asserting a divine sanction for the nation. "Every one agrees," he told Edward Bates at the war's start, "that the <u>Integrity of the country</u>

must be maintained at any price, under any circumstances. God has given us this great country for great purposes; He has given it to us, as much as he gave Palestine to the Jews."[46]

By 1862, the Northern press and Northern publishers working in many media (fiction, nonfiction, poetry, and drama) explained to their readers the role of virtuous citizens. In the midst of a crisis that threatened their interests, their nation, and the future of democracy itself, "true patriots should 'trust the government'" to manage the war. At home, supporters were enjoined to "speak out boldly for the right."[47] One of the most popular arguments for the justice of the Northern side came in Charles Stillé's pamphlet, *How a Free People Conduct a Long War.* Over half a million copies circulated among Northern readers. Stillé used the example of the campaign against Napoleon on the Iberian Peninsula as his reference point. Fought jointly by Spain, Portugal, and England, the effort was long and costly, but the benefit of reversing Napoleon's plan for continental domination merited the effort. Similarly, Stillé urged Northerners to commit themselves to military victory: "in military success alone . . . is to be found the true solution of our whole difficulty, the only force which can give vitality or permanence to any theory of settlement."[48] Northern ministers echoed these arguments from the pulpit. As one historian has shown, they "insisted that there was no conflict between being a good Christian and supporting a just war."[49] Indeed, Christians had a special obligation to endorse the war. As a New York minister admonished, it was not sufficient simply to love one's country; "that love, like all others, is essentially active, and demands a cheerful and ready loyalty when the cause of public righteousness and order is involved."[50] Another minister, echoing his peers, proclaimed it "a holy war . . . a war in defence of the fundamental principles of this government—a war in defence of American Nationality, the Constitution, the Union, the rights of legal majorities, the ballot-box, the law." More ominously, he urged that, once justified, the war must be fought with "unflinching earnestness, energy, and self-sacrifice."[51] A later scholar worried that this shift in thinking about the war facilitated a more total and destructive conflict. "The defensive war," he wrote, "born out of sheer necessity, was transformed into a crusade for the moral regeneration of America, if not indeed for the salvation of the world."[52]

History on Our Side

Along with the philosophical consistency that came from aligning one's side with the just war tradition, both sides relied on historical examples to build rhetorical support. For many Northerners, the Peloponnesian War was a logical place to start because they believed they were lineal descendants of Greece. In this example, the South was always warlike Sparta and the North democratic Athens. "In this respect [Sparta] differed from Athens as much as the South at this day differs from the North, and from precisely the same causes, the principal of which, in each case, was barbarism—barbarism deliberately organized, and maintained in conscious preference to intellectual refinement." Drawing on more recent history, Southerners claimed allegiance to the American Revolution, a contention with which Northerners disagreed. "This rebellion bears no resemblance to the popular uprisings in Europe against oppression, or to the Revolution of our fathers," argued one Northerner.[53]

One of the most ubiquitous parallels may be unfamiliar to many twenty-first-century readers. In 1857, people in India asserted their separate nationality against the British empire then occupying their country. Current scholars of the Indian conflict continue to debate the proper terminology—an "insurrection," an "uprising," or a nationalist "rebellion"—but most interpret the event in the long context of resistance to British imperialism.[54] What the English-language newspapers of the day termed the "Sepoy Mutiny" bore enough similarity to the American Civil War that participants on both sides used it as a shorthand to characterize unjust or uncivilized conduct in war. The conflict, touched off by fears over British attempts to forcibly convert India's Hindu and Muslim population, revolved around the native "Sepoy" units employed by the British administration. These units—the overwhelming majority of the imperial forces in India—revolted at a moment of transition within the empire as control shifted from the East India Company to the British government, which reached deeper into Indian life. Because the anti-British coalition included Hindus and Muslims, modern scholars characterize the movement as nationalist or at least protonationalist. Civil War Americans knew that the conflict was characterized from the beginning by atrocities committed by Indian forces against British soldiers, administrators, and their families, and by British forces against Sepoy units and their supporters.

Because it was the most recent large-scale international conflict and because it offered the most salacious examples of atrocities committed against both regular troops and noncombatants, the Indian Rebellion served as shorthand for savage treatment at the hands of an enemy. This acknowledgment began at the very beginning of the Civil War. A Northern war correspondent in Charleston during the initial firing on Fort Sumter reported being taken captive and told that "the Government meant to make an example of me and shoot me, a la. Sepoy from the mouth of a sixty-four pounder."[55] Another early war example appeared in a report from Kentucky, where "a Union man, named THOMPSON . . . was visited by the 'Regulators' [Confederate guerrillas]—himself abused, and his two daughters, one about sixteen and the other fourteen, taken out into his yard and outraged in the most shameful manner possible—after the manner of the Sepoys of Hindostan."[56] This account was given by a Northern officer charged with assessing conditions along the western frontier: "the outrages which have been committed against the towns and people of Kansas by our common foes exceed any atrocities committed by Sepoy or savage warfare."[57]

Northerners hoped that Confederates would earn the same infamy through their behavior. "Foreign nations must . . . consign to lasting odium the authors of crimes which, in all their details, exceed the worst excesses of the Sepoys of India," the *New York Times* argued.[58] Even more important than a shameful legacy was the international repudiation the paper advocated. The process of characterizing and explaining how the war was being fought—done primarily in the language of global examples—helped shape whether and how strongly foreign nations intervened in the conflict. The use of "Sepoy" to mark unforgiveable behavior continued throughout the war. "Indeed, so far as their conduct of the war is concerned, it is not easy to draw a very marked distinction between the Southern rebels and the Sepoys in the late East Indian rebellion," a Northern paper noted, "but we are confident that the memory of these atrocities will be carried into battle, and that sooner or later they will be most terribly and amply avenged. Curses are like chickens, and still come home to roost."[59]

Southerners made the same references as their Northern foes. They used "Sepoy" as shorthand for northern atrocities to arouse European ire over US behavior, just as Northerners did. At the same time, Southerners heralded British executions of rebels as a wise policy. Predictably, the *Charleston Mercury* took the most extreme position. Reacting to the capture of black troops during a battle later in the war, the paper approvingly noted that "the general impression is that Col. Logan should have dealt with them summarily—hanging them to the first tree, or shooting them sans ceremonie—that their fate might be a warning and example to others." The *Mercury* defended this policy with reference to the 1857 uprising. "England carried out this extreme penalty—this paramount right—in her dealings with the insurrectionary *Sepoys* in India, with excellent effect and France and Spain have repeatedly and successfully tested its efficacy among their colonial insurrectionary blacks."[60] Northern editorialists must have thrilled to this report, which proved that the Confederacy endorsed the very practices the North had so magnanimously repudiated in the fight against Southern rebels. It was ironic, though not entirely inconsistent, that Southerners endorsed the justice of suppressing rebellion, especially one waged through atrocity. Because many Southern conservatives rejected the idea that secession was revolution and looked past their own record of atrocities, the only thing they could see when confronted with the idea of violent insurrection was the history of slave uprisings in the American past and those yet to come under Lincoln's malign hand. And in the face of such a revolution, most white Southerners strongly endorsed the *Mercury*'s proposed remedy.

If the Indian example helped Northerners (and Southerners, to a lesser extent) define just practice in war, it could also help them define *jus ad bellum*, or the justice of the war's cause. What Northerners wanted, indeed expected, was that the global sanction offered to England for its suppression of the rebellion of 1857 would sanction their own suppression of Southern secession. In this accounting, the US decision to oppose secession and make war against the Confederacy reflected the natural right of sovereign and self-governing polities to preserve their territorial integrity.[61] Even US radicals asserted a similarity of purpose and reminded the British of how the United States had supported them in 1857. William Lloyd Garrison's *Liberator* explained that during the Indian Rebellion "the universal feeling [in the United States] was in favor of the most severe punishment of the murderous traitors. . . . The government affirmed no belligerent rights in favor of the Sepoys, showed no signs of sympathy with the insurgents, and congratulated the English in every success of their arms."[62] Some Englishmen agreed, blurring the line between imperial control and territorial integrity in a way useful to both England and the United States. For these men, British nonintervention in the US conflict helped preserve the continuity of consolidated power. "All wars are deplorable, especially civil wars" wrote one English observer. "But almost every country has been compelled to engage in them at some period of their history, and they have worked out the solution of their difficulties by sacrifices and bloodshed, as the Americans are now doing, purchasing by these means peace and security for the future." This correspondent noted that "during our Indian mutiny the French Press assured us that our efforts to recover our supremacy were quite vain, and that our Sepoy executions and heroic battles were but so many needless cruelties and bootless sacrifices. I do not think we listened with much patience to these opinions, or that we should have been willing to accept the mediation of any one in our quarrel."[63] But if this call to be left alone seemed to come mostly from a desire to avoid public scrutiny, the Indian parallel more generally served to constrain and limit violence. Each side reacted with indignation when their goals were likened to those of the Sepoy rebels, but each accusation forced a public explanation of policy (fodder for both foreign and domestic critics) and potentially a change in behavior. Neither combatant wanted to be fairly compared to a Sepoy.

Nor did they want to be compared to an American Indian. When Federals or Confederates wanted to stigmatize their enemy with a domestic reference, they accused each other of fighting like Native Americans. Doing so drew on the long and bloody practices of war in North America. White Americans interpreted that history as evidence of native peoples' fundamental unsuitability for inclusion in modern America, demonstrated most vividly in how they made war. Beginning in the colonial era, Americans of all regions compiled evidence of Indian atrocities in warfare that they believed divided their civilized European practice from savage indigenous habits. As historians have shown, both sides in these conflicts usually shared the same behavior, but in the mid-nineteenth century, few white Americans approached the subject with objectivity or dispassion.[64] Instead, they relied on old stereotypes as they deployed a language of metaphor and innuendo to condemn their opponents. US and Confederate newspapers deployed references to "savage" warfare throughout their coverage.[65] Even African American newspapers traded in the same malevolent imagery. The *Christian Recorder*, reprinting another paper's editorial, lamented that "we shall be brought to adopt the conclusion that the presence of Indian *savages* cannot greatly intensify the horrors of the internecine strife into which" the Confederates had plunged the country.[66]

Defending themselves and condemning their opponents preoccupied Northerners and Southerners throughout the war. On both sides, people espoused a greater sense of moral virtue as the war progressed. The repetition of atrocity stories confirmed the stereotypes that each side brought into the conflict and yielded a bloodier war. They each relied upon perceptions of their enemy as uniquely debased and themselves as uniquely victimized. The use of global and historical examples, like the Sepoy, proved important because they obscured origins and context. This analytical slipperiness makes them particularly tricky to use for rigorous historical thinking. But the sometimes intentionally muddled language of participants should not blind us to the strategic postures they adopted—using language to rally their publics, generate sympathy abroad, and justify to themselves policies that contradicted the laws of war they claimed to be upholding.

Both sides also drew on religious notions of righteousness to buttress their claims to moral superiority. Ministers in both North and South explained the justice of their cause to their parishioners and the world (in printed sermons) in order to encourage global sanction for the violence they committed. Henry Ward Beecher's assertion that "God hates lukewarm patriotism as much as lukewarm religion" would have been approved by Christians on both sides. Continuously throughout the war, ministers reaffirmed the wisdom and authority that would carry their side to victory with God's favor. Defeats were harder to reconcile, but ministers regarded every success as a sign of divine sanction.[67]

In the Civil War, righteousness developed as a consequence of the ways that people on each side portrayed their own actions and those of their enemy. One historian explained the escalation of violence in the Civil War as a product of what he called the "vicarious war." In this interpretation, the "experience of war was partly a flight into unreason: into visions of purgation and redemption, into anticipation and intuition and spiritual apotheosis, into bloodshed that was not only intentional pursuit of interests of state but was also sacramental, erotic, mystical, and strangely gratifying."[68] This concept captures an important aspect of the Civil War—indeed, any war—as the propulsive demands of military conflict draw participants toward positions they never imagined taking. But vicarious experience did not displace reason. The war's evidence reveals that Northerners and Southerners came to loathe one another, but this was itself a historical, and often reluctant, process. Hate developed from what they did to each other, not because of who they were. The language of justice and righteousness had to be built. Arguing that reason operated alongside unreason hardly mitigates the deadliness of the war. Because participants believed they were justified by experience, they regarded their hatred as more legitimate. The intentionality of these languages did not produce consistency. The rhetoric of righteousness contradicted the language of just war. The latter emphasized restraint and reached out to a global audience to celebrate the virtues embodied in lawful warmaking; righteousness turned inward and inflamed passion, which often generated conduct that violated the laws of war. Together, they formed the edges of a lethal blade wielded by citizens against each other.

The Guerrilla War Begins

The nonviolent solution reached in the case of privateers and prisoners did not prevail in the irregular war. Citizens, both North and South, demonstrated terrific martial enthusiasm in April 1861, but neither side was prepared to equip, train, and organize large national armies. Many of the men who failed to find a home in regular Confederate units resorted to irregular war. In some parts of the South, guerrillas and other irregular combatants mobilized faster than regular forces. In 1861, Jefferson Davis arrived at a policy of selective defense, guarding those parts of the Confederacy deemed most valuable and most easily defended. This decision left the less populated or more remote parts of the new nation without the presence of regular armies. In these places, guerrillas took the lead in defending their communities, often from what they regarded as internal enemies as much as Northern invaders.[69] In early 1862, Confederate leaders responded to public pressure for local defense units by passing the Partisan Ranger Act, which allowed communities to organize local defense forces that operated independently, with Richmond's sanction but little oversight. Historians of war distinguish between partisan forces, which are organized and legally obligated to a nation, from guerrillas, who are locally constituted and often pursue personal gain. Few people in either the North or South could make the distinction as clearly.[70] Northern newspapers blurred the differences between raiding expeditions by regular Confederate cavalry and true guerrilla actions, with a predictable outcome: Northerners believed their enemy waged an unprincipled war. As a result, Northern antiguerrilla policies escalated in 1862, leading Confederate civilians to the conclusion that the Union was bent on a war of extermination.[71] The Confederacy's decision to sanction guerrilla warfare produced the first pronounced increase in the war's destructiveness, especially as it concerned noncombatants. This first phase of the guerrilla war generated policy responses from both sides that shaped the war for years to come.

The Realities of Irregular War

Already by June 1861, one man could report from Missouri that "we have civil war in our midst. We have union men & secessionists and there is a deadly hostility existing between them. . . . Men seem to have lost their reason and gone mad."[72] Civil War historians agree with this grim assessment; Missouri experienced the most sustained and most destructive guerrilla conflict. By the summer of 1861, Missouri "fell into chaos," in the words of a leading scholar.[73] The state's population divided their loyalties, and when the pro-Confederate state guard retreated into the southwestern corner of the state, guerrillas organized themselves to attack the railroad lines that enabled Union troops to move across the state. From these legitimate targets, guerrillas turned on Unionist neighbors and used hit-and-run attacks against the few, poorly led Northern soldiers in the state. Union Major General John Pope responded by holding civilians responsible for damages done to property by guerrillas, but his subordinates and successors escalated the destruction and violence meted out to pro-Confederates, and the state descended into bloody internecine conflict earlier than much of the country.[74]

Missouri was unusual for the intensity and duration of its irregular conflict, but every Confederate and several Union states experienced periodic guerrilla war that replicated many of the problems identified in the Missouri clashes. Eastern Tennessee, eastern Texas, northern Alabama, upcountry South Carolina, northeastern Florida, Appalachian Virginia, and North Carolina all contained divided communities. In these places, citizens split, with some remaining obedient to the federal government while their neighbors endorsed secession. Political loyalties formed the first line of definition. In western North Carolina, according to one history of the region, Unionists "were 'robbing, stealing, and plundering almost all the time and shooting at southern men when ever they can get a sly chance.'" In eastern North Carolina in mid-1862, Union soldiers "took particular delight in roughing up suspected guerrillas." One Union soldier "admitted to his brother, 'I would go twenty miles enny day to get a squint across my old musket at one of the cowardly devils.'" North Georgia witnessed a guerrilla conflict that spiraled out of control as pro-Union and pro-Confederate supporters attacked each other's homesteads. In one episode, Confederates captured a deserter from their army, whom they "mutilated in the most horrible manner, and then, bleeding as he was, they hung him to a tree in sight of his own house." Pro-Union men interpreted actions like these to signal that "it was a war of extermination between them."[75]

East Tennessee was Union territory that suffered under Confederate control for the war's first two years. Confederates treated East Tennessee civilians the same way the Union treated suspect populations in Missouri, Kentucky, and western Virginia. From mid-1861 until the seizure of the region by Union troops in 1863, pro-Union guerrillas harassed Confederate troops and pro-Confederate civilians throughout the area.[76] According to a regional historian, "unionist and secessionist guerrilla bands beat civilians holding the wrong political views, ambushed them on the road, shot them in their homes, and plundered their houses, barns, and possessions."[77] The intermittent presence of regular armies encouraged civilians to publicly identify with one side or the other, which made them vulnerable if that side left the area. The result was a high incidence of guerrilla war in this region. "As the war dragged on . . . East Tennessee faced economic disaster. Guerrillas and brigands continued to destroy homes and barns, steal food and livestock, and murder the farmers." In all these places, noncombatants and regular combatants alike were confronted with the threat of irregular war.[78]

Sanctioning Guerrillas

Despite Richmond's ambivalence, Confederate civilians expressed strong support, both rhetorically and often in material terms, for irregular fighters. The idea of local defense resonated with white Southerners. Although the image of a lawless South, where every slight drew swift revenge, exaggerates the reality, antebellum Southerners often stepped outside the formal legal and political system to settle problems. Slaveholders exercised their will on plantations with little regard for formal systems of justice. Traditions of local autonomy had deep roots in the region and this impulse continued to be felt as volunteers transitioned into regular soldiers. For those who did not want to be subject to an officer's command or who distrusted the new national framework established in Richmond, irregular service in one's own community held great appeal. Even if Richmond had opposed their organization, stopping it may have proved impossible. In the Shenandoah Valley, M. G. Harman called on locals to "drive back these Northern Vandals and Traitors from the soil of the Old Dominion." "FLY TO ARMS! and let us RAISE A LARGE FORCE AND REDEEM THE NORTHWEST FROM A Ruthless Abolition and Fanatical Foe."[79]

Guerrilla units, especially pro-Confederate bands, targeted soldiers but also turned against civilians. The most common tactics of guerrillas and other irregular actors in the war were beatings and assaults. In many cases, they punished civilians for supporting the enemy, hoping to dissuade future support. In other cases, assaults accompanied robbery or other property-based crimes that bore no relation to the national or ideological goals of the war. While generally focused on the adult men whose position in a community could shape local patterns of loyalty,

"Southern Chivalry: Dedicated to Jeff Davis." Northern newspapers printed lurid accounts of the attacks waged by Southern guerrillas, leading readers to regard the Confederate war effort as unjust and immoral.

ample evidence exists of assaults directed at women and children. Knowledge of these events comes almost entirely from incidental notices in personal and public papers. Beatings and whippings were so ubiquitous in regions characterized by irregular war that they did not receive official notice.

The Confederate state did little to inhibit the operation of these units, except in isolated instances when they preyed on Confederate civilians. In some places, like Missouri and Arkansas, Confederate officers encouraged men to organize and operate irregularly. Richmond's implicit, and sometimes explicit, support raises the questions of why Confederates tolerated pro-Confederate guerrillas and how they expected such men to be treated. The rise of guerrilla units challenged traditional norms of regular warfare, complicating the question of who deserved protection if captured. In order to safeguard noncombatants from the violence of war, soldiers must be able to identify enemy combatants. Guerrillas, who are defined in part by their failure to wear uniforms, make this impossible.

According to this theory, by blending into civilian life by dress, habit, or residence, guerrillas put true noncombatants at risk because their enemies would be unable to distinguish among them. Confederates, especially those who had served in the prewar Regular Army, knew these arguments, but they looked the other way during the Civil War.[80]

Some scholars, particularly those writing outside a traditional national framework of war, regard guerrillas as a legitimate manifestation of a people's army. How else could an insurgent community fight except by organizing locally and in an ad hoc fashion? One modern theorist concludes: "any significant degree of popular support entitles the guerrillas to the benevolent quarantine customarily offered to prisoners of war."[81] The historical role of guerrillas likewise encouraged some measure of respect. Guerrillas originated in popular resistance to invading armies. The term—meaning "little war"—derived from the Spanish resistance to Napoleon when he invaded the Iberian Peninsula in 1808. The global opposition to Napoleon's plan of conquest lent legitimacy to Spanish efforts, particularly after his bloody efforts to subdue guerrilla resistance. The thousands of men he executed, immortalized in Francisco Goya's painting *The Third of May, 1808*, sanctified the practice of local, ad hoc military resistance. Confederates also drew on domestic historical experience. During the American Revolution, rebels often organized irregularly to fight the British, particularly in the southern colonies.

The Confederate communities that supported guerrillas did not respect the legal distinction that the Union drew between regular and irregular soldiers and demanded that their guerrillas be treated as public enemies. Although very few civilians articulated a clear perspective on the legal status of guerrillas alongside Confederate armies, they generally attributed their presence and actions to what we would call a "People's War." This concept had only recently developed and is usually connected in the historical literature to the French Revolution, which is regarded as the first truly popular conflict.[82] In democratic societies, it referred to the reality that a truly national event, like a war, could only happen with the support of most of the citizens. White Southerners claimed this was the case with the Confederacy and further claimed that in places where a national army failed to appear, citizens were empowered to act on their own. The elastic definition of a people's war—whether it referred to cause and origin, popular support, or mode of fighting—made it useful to Confederate partisans who took advantage of the successes guerrillas scored against Union soldiers without taking responsibility for an unlawful form of warfare.

Confederates divided on the legality and wisdom of sanctioning guerrilla forces. In April 1862, Senator Henry Burnett of Kentucky introduced "a resolution to facilitate the raising of guerrilla companies for the war." Because he represented a Union state in the Confederate Congress, perhaps Burnett recognized the impossibility of raising regular forces on a widespread basis. William Preston, from Virginia, emerged as his sharpest critic. Initially, Preston couched his opposition in terms of efficiency. Allowing rival recruiters to solicit men for guerrilla duty might undermine the regular army, he argued. Then he turned to the ethical and diplomatic aspects of his argument. Preston objected to the message that official sanction of guerrillas would send to the world. "War was a unit," he argued, "and no country could succeed without perfect organization of its army. All the forces must be subject to the same military laws."[83]

Later iterations of this debate avoided direct reference to "guerrillas," presumably because that was sure to attract negative attention. Instead, they emphasized the natural right of "local defense." Despite Preston's arguments, in October 1862, the Confederate Congress authorized bands of twenty or more men to self-organize and "be considered as belonging to the Provisional army of the Confederate States." The statutory language asserted that men in these units were *entitled, when captured by the enemy, to all the privileges of prisoners of war.*"[84] Confederate congressmen knew that the decision to accord rights as a public enemy was for the Union to make, but the language provided justification for retaliation if they were mistreated. Only one senator, Edward Sparrow of Louisiana, anticipated the problems such a policy would engender for their own people. "It would permit the organization of bodies of men who would not be responsible to the Government," he prophesied, "and for whose acts it would not be proper for the Government to be responsible, for they might be entirely in contravention to all the rules of civilized warfare. A number of bad men might league themselves together and, under the protection the bill gave, commit all kinds of outrages on all parties."[85] The "Provisional Army" envisioned in the October legislation never materialized, and Confederate congressmen continued to wrestle with the issue throughout the war. Perhaps the clearest evidence that Confederate congressmen recognized the fundamental unjustness of guerrilla warfare was that they never authorized retaliation for the Union's execution of Southern guerrillas.[86] Their ambivalence reveals the frustrations of an organized state facing a larger foe against whom an insurgency might be useful.

Speaking for the Davis administration in early 1862, the Confederate secretary of war explicitly repudiated the idea of guerrilla fighting. "Guerrilla companies are not recognized as part of the military organization of the Confederate States," Judah Benjamin wrote, "and cannot be authorized by this department."[87] Because the attacks of guerrilla units came outside the conventions of regular warfare, members of those units did not merit the protections enjoyed by regular troops. In short, they could and often were executed on the spot if captured in the process of waging an irregular action. Some Confederates protested this policy and others complicated it. The inspector general for the Confederacy, James Cooper, came close to defending "bushwhackers," defining them as "citizens of this Confederacy who have taken up arms to defend their homes and their families."[88] Unlike Robert E. Lee, who, after a thirty-two year career in the US Army, took pains to denounce and oppose the use of guerrillas, Jefferson Davis spent little time discouraging this behavior. According to one recent biographer, "he showed relatively little interest in guerrilla warfare."[89]

Outlawing Guerrillas

How did the Federals treat guerrillas, and how did the North explain this decision? Before he wrote his full treatise on the laws of war, Francis Lieber tackled the problem of guerrillas in a pamphlet he wrote for the Union's high command. Lieber identified different sorts of guerrillas, at least one of which merited something like ambivalent support from him. Lieber deferred to current opinion among theorists of war about what he termed "the rising of the people." If a people, lacking a central government, organized themselves "to repel invasion," this "entitles them to the full benefits of the law of war." What Lieber had in mind were undoubtedly the original guerrillas—Spanish civilian resistance to Napoleon. Lieber himself was baptized in military conflict in German resistance to Napoleon in 1812, so it should not surprise us that he made an allowance for some forms of irregular war. But Lieber included two caveats to his approval of guerrilla warfare that were met in the European but not American cases. Men who organized themselves to resist invasion had to do so in substantial numbers and had to do so publicly. In Spain and in parts of the territory that later became Germany, Napoleon's swift conquest incapacitated whatever central governments existed. In their absence, communities sent their men to fight the French troops. These defenders met Napoleon's soldiers on regular fields of battle, often with little success, but for Lieber what remained important was their public and transparent character. They stood in lieu of the regular soldiers, who should have been protecting their communities.[90]

Lieber's report came in late 1862, long after the irregular war had claimed lives and spurred a strong response from Union officers on the ground. In March of that year, the Union commander in Missouri issued clear instructions to his subordinates: "death to bushwhackers is the order. Have a commission always ready to try, determine, and execute immediately, if they are unfortunately taken alive." Lieber recognized that soldiers on the ground would issue summary punishment regardless of what theorists like him wrote. Men caught "prowling near the opposing army," would be killed, he observed, regardless of whether they were in or out of uniform. Most Union officers agreed. Like many in the army, Major General Nathaniel Banks believed that severe punishment for unlawful conduct was the most effective deterrent to its widespread use. "I respect the rights of men engaged in War, because they are responsible for their acts; and whenever any man falls in battle, or is captured, I am desirous of extending to him to the utmost of my power," Banks pledged. He recognized, as we still do, that whatever a soldier did "it is because as a soldier he is bound to perform the duties of a soldier, and ought to suffer only the legitimate consequences of his acts." Guerrillas, acting outside the control of the state, merited no such respect. "Men who abandon the ranks of their army, lagging behind upon plantations, in villages and towns, throwing off the equipment and costume of a soldier, have no right to the immunities of soldiers, if they assume to exercise his power of wounding or killing those who they assume to be enemies. Such acts are not legitimate acts of war, and can only be considered and punished if attended with fatal consequences, as assassinations."[91]

Guerrillas and their treatment also created another, more sinister problem, one that threatened to spread beyond the irregular war and shape how the regular war was fought. As Lieber explained: "guerrilla bands cannot encumber themselves with prisoners of war; they have, therefore, frequently, perhaps generally, killed their prisoners, and of course have been killed in turn when made prisoners, thus introducing a system of barbarity which becomes intenser in its demoralization as it spreads and is prolonged." Although Lieber respected the "rising of the people," he denounced their tendency to "interfere with the mitigation of the severity of war, which it is one of the noblest objects of the modern law of war to obtain." He thus defended the North's sometimes draconian guerrilla policies as an effort to create a more just war overall. Doing so, from Lieber's perspective, required ensuring that Union soldiers were not compelled to behavior that paralleled that of the guerrillas. As one historian explains, the danger came from guerrillas' willingness to repudiate "the basic requirements and assumptions of the citizen-soldier concept. Their identity as civilians-turned-combatants relied on murder and secrecy, evident in their disregard for moral law and military custom." The danger was that "Union occupiers had to adapt to this model themselves or be killed." As Lieber defined the problem, soldiers were belligerents and deserved protection as prisoners if captured. Guerrillas were not legitimate belligerents, and so their role in the war could only produce confusion and death. The Union's legal response drew from both strategic and moral motives.[92]

[3]

Soldiers and Citizens

By the middle of 1862, participants and observers could see certain broad patterns of violence in the Civil War. Though the death toll rose far beyond what either side had anticipated, on the battlefields, soldiers treated each other under the conventions of the Western laws of war. Beyond the reach of the regular armies, guerrilla and partisan forces operated with greater impunity, often targeting citizens alongside soldiers. In response, Union officers arrested Southern citizens (both men and women), seized hostages to negotiate with guerrilla units, destroyed whole towns, and banished communities. They also, on rare occasions, killed Southern civilians. The areas of regular and irregular war changed over time and across space as the armies moved and conditions on the ground shifted. Throughout 1862, US forces pressed deeper into Confederate territory, bringing them into contact with a hostile white population. Union occupation created numerous administrative and legal challenges, including how to control a disloyal citizenry while fighting a regular war and an insurgency. Although conditions in occupied places could oscillate between peace and violence with surprising speed, Union forces supervised a mostly peaceful occupation.

Few people at the time recognized that it was Union military success—mostly along southern rivers—that generated the new problems of occupation. Despite the relative lack of lethal violence as US troops acquired control over Southern cities, the terror that accompanied occupation—and that regular soldiers encountered in the protracted fighting around Richmond, through central Virginia, and in central Tennessee and Kentucky—generated new attitudes about who could be subjected to military violence. White Southerners, some of whom may have reluctantly supported secession, recoiled from the Union's hard war and committed themselves to Confederate victory. In the North, as abolitionists evolved from the age's leading humanitarians into the war's most eager militants, they enabled a more vigorous and more sustained Union war effort, especially one that targeted slavery.

Union Occupation

Like most wars, the Civil War drew civilians into its storm from the opening moments. Whether they were Baltimore secessionists, St. Louis German-Americans, or East Tennessee Unionists, civilians found themselves caught in the war's violence. Some transformed themselves into irregular combatants, effectively abandoning the status of true civilian, but many more—especially women, children, and elderly men—remained noncombatants who were nonetheless subjected to military violence.

Even as Civil War soldiers collectively found their way toward a set of common practices on the battlefield, soldiers' interactions with civilians in places off the battlefield created new opportunities for unnecessary and counterproductive violence. The US Army's instructions for how to interact with noncombatants, formalized in 1863 but present in army norms before that, established a high standard: "private citizens are no longer murdered, enslaved, or carried off to distant parts, and the inoffensive individual is as little disturbed in his private relations as the commander of the hostile troops can afford to grant in the overruling demands of a vigorous war."[1] The easiest place for these rules to bend or break was when soldiers moved the battlefield into cities and towns. Here, the density of noncombatants, the complicated physical space, and the ability of defenders to exploit these features left attacking armies facing difficult choices. Once the army had successfully captured a city, the problems multiplied. Distinguishing loyal from disloyal citizens and determining which privileges of civil society would be extended to people from each group preoccupied commanders across the South. Doing so while defending a city from Confederate counterattack, identifying and organizing local resources that the Union could use for military purposes, and managing the process of emancipation taxed the talents of even the most talented Union generals.

The Moment of Conquest

New Orleans—the first major Southern city occupied by Northern forces in the Civil War—presented a heady brew of these challenges. Thanks to a well-planned attack by Flag Officer David Farragut and a disorganized and poorly managed defense by Confederate Major General Mansfield Lovell, Union forces conquered the city itself with almost no violence. But the issue of how to manage relations between soldiers and civilians in occupied places pressed itself upon the Union in the hours after conquest. Some Americans, then and now, rejected the idea that the US Army could, in military terms, occupy parts of Southern states. But Union military planners saw the issue differently. As one historian explains, "drawing from French theories of a state of siege and from British notions of martial law, many Republicans claimed that rebellious territories could be occupied almost as if they were foreign as long as the victorious nation maintained the state of war."[2]

The narrative of the city's surrender is worth considering in detail because the actions of both sides at New Orleans (and the disputes about those actions) helped set the terms for how the United States handled the surrender of other Confederate places. New Orleans presented an attractive target for conquest. It was the largest, most economically important city in the South, and it was strategically accessible, located close to the Gulf of Mexico. From those waters US ships could bring their heavy guns to bear on any attack. But the city also presented serious obstacles in terms of administration. It held one of the most diverse populations (in terms of religion, ethnicity, and race) of any place in the country. Travel accounts from both Americans and Europeans "pronounced it the dirtiest city in the country," meaning it posed a health threat to potential occupiers. With 168,000 residents, New Orleans was the sixth largest city in the United States. It suffered serious problems of poverty and working class strife. Like many urban areas of the South, it also contained a substantial body of conditional and even many outright Unionists. Despite the importance of the city to the Confederacy, it remained an afterthought in preparations for defense through spring 1862.[3]

Farragut's flotilla subdued Fort Jackson and Fort St. Philip about seventy miles below the city and then sailed upriver. The Union's easy victory caught most New Orleanians by surprise. They anticipated a vigorous resistance from Confederate soldiers in and around the city, but these forces melted away as Farragut moved past the forts. Lovell, commanding only several thousand underequipped militiamen, evacuated his troops and supplies. Residents improvised efforts to ship out money, cotton, tobacco, and other valuables, and they greeted Butler in a foul mood. Civilian panic reached a peak on April 25, when Farragut's men entered the city. "By noon, civil order collapsed," and mobs took over parts of the city. One historian describes the city population as divided among actual Unionists, who came out of hiding, Confederate supporters, who believed surrender would ensure protection for their property, and "an irresponsible majority [who] insisted upon expressing its defiance of the Yankees. This last group soon brought matters to a crisis." Despite the Union's dominant position—its gunboats floated high on the river with unobstructed access over the levees to the city's interior—the mayor and city council delayed surrendering, probably to buy time to evacuate more goods.[4]

Leading up to his attack, Farragut wanted to avoid a catastrophic encounter, such as cutting the levee to swamp the city or turning his guns on it, but he also had limited patience with stalling tactics designed to hold off the inevitable Union capture. One of the captains in the advance flotilla went ashore and raised a US flag above the mint, one of the most prominent federal buildings in the city. "Leaving it unguarded, he warned the crowd which had gathered that he had left orders with his men on the ships to fire howitzers loaded with grapeshot if the flag were molested." The flag held both strategic and ideological purpose. To Union sailors it signaled a pacified city from which they should expect no resistance. To New Orleans residents, it signaled their defeat. Almost immediately, John Mumford, a local man, lowered the flag. In response, the USS Pensacola fired one shot, which struck a building near the mint, but otherwise the fleet resisted the provocative act. Farragut then demanded the surrender of the entire town, which the mayor reluctantly gave. Benjamin Butler, commanding the army force on Farragut's flotilla, entered the city to a vicious round of taunting and threats from citizens along the streets.[5]

Through a series of quick actions Butler established Union control in this fluid and unpredictable atmosphere. Most infamously, he arrested

John Mumford and sentenced him to death. According to a historian of the city, Mumford was "forty-two . . . a rather 'fine-looking man, tall, black-bearded . . . bold, reckless, and defiant,' [who] acted as overlord to the city's gamblers but was well educated, owned property, and exerted considerable influence among the lower class."[6] Mumford was tried by a military commission and convicted "of treason and an overt act thereof."[7] Very few Civil War combatants, irregular or otherwise, were executed for treason, though at this early stage in the war Union commanders experimented with a variety of methods of establishing control. By pulling down the US flag, Mumford broadcast to the Union flotilla the continued resistance of the city. If the naval commanders had taken the provocation seriously, they would have been justified in firing on the city. If actually unleashed, the grapeshot with which the mint captain had threatened the onlookers would have killed many people. Butler made this point in his defense of Mumford's execution to Secretary of War Edwin Stanton: "the lowering of the flag might, nay ought, by every military rule to have brought a bombardment upon the city resulting in no one can know what destruction of property and life."[8] But if the laws of war justified Butler's decision, what motivated him? In a letter to Stanton before he issued Mumford's arrest warrant, Butler explained his purpose: "I find the city under the dominion of the mob. They have insulted our flag, torn it down with indignity. This outrage will be punished in such manner as in my judgment will caution both the perpetrators and the abettors of the act, so that they fear the *stripes* if they do not reverence the stars of our banner."[9]

Butler did not budge on Mumford. Up until the moment of the execution, many residents and even many Union soldiers anticipated a reprieve. Butler listened to the counterarguments and even met with Mumford's wife and children but refused clemency. Thousands of New Orleanians walked to the town square, most perhaps expecting a last-minute reprieve. None came. After witnessing the event, the crowd "turned away and quietly dispersed—confused, dumbfounded, and silently angry."[10]

The rest of the Confederacy was anything but silent. Mumford's execution set off a chain of accusations, complaints, and threats that preoccupied Confederate officials, up to and including President Davis, for the rest of the war. Confederates drew upon the execution as a cause for outrage without end. They compared Butler to the worst of military tyrants from the past—a barbaric Hun was their preferred slight, but Confederate propagandists imaginatively plumbed history for the worst examples they could find. The *New Orleans Delta* reported that "the miserable hireling Butler is playing the tyrant with a high hand. His savage instincts are far ahead of the most ferocious native of Dahomey or Patagonia," an editorial judgment quoted or echoed in papers across the South.[11]

Confederate outrage ignited a political firestorm. Secretary of War Judah Benjamin instructed Robert E. Lee to demand a response. Lee recapitulated the secretary's arguments verbatim in a letter to Union Major-General George McClellan: "we are informed that Mr. Mumford pulled the flag down when the enemy were not yet in possession of the city, but had merely anchored their vessels before it and had made a demand for a surrender which had not been complied with. A party landed, hoisted the flag and retired. The city was not in their possession nor subject to their jurisdiction." This was a curious complaint to make, as Lee must have known, because it seemed to prefer a Union naval attack to peaceful means in subduing the city. Farragut knew the strategic hopelessness of the Confederates' position in New Orleans and demanded surrender to limit bloodshed. But because the city had not yet officially capitulated, Lee regarded "the execution of Mr. Mumford [as] the murder of one of our citizens." McClellan forwarded the correspondence to the War Department along with a lecture for Secretary of War Stanton on General Orders No. 71, which forbade the execution of "prisoners taken in arms." In a break with his usual practice, Jefferson Davis followed up, writing to Lee on August 1 to see what response he had received and threatening the use of retaliation. Henry Halleck, responding for the War Department, promised Lee that once he received all the materials regarding the case he would assess the legality of the execution. Lincoln may have wished that Butler exercised more leniency or tact in his actions or correspondence, but he never reprimanded the general or criticized his actions.[12]

Although generations of historians have obscured our vision of Butler with a thick layer of scorn, even when he acted from instinct Butler's decisions were both legally defensible and strategically effective. Confederates (and many subsequent chroniclers) assumed that he acted solely with a spirit of malice, but like all occupiers he was trying to create order in a chaotic environment. In retrospect, the occupation of New Orleans seems distinguished more by the limited number of casualties than by any particular atrocity.[13] Butler arrested many pro-Confederate civilians, but over the next three years only a handful died. He also arrested Union soldiers when they violated orders protecting citizens and executed criminals who masqueraded as soldiers, actions that locals supported.[14] His public and private correspondence all reveal his urgent desire to pacify the city. Writing to Secretary of War Stanton on May 8, just a week after his troops occupied the city, Butler explained that he "thought it necessary to make so large a display of force in the city. I found it very turbulent and unruly, completely under the control of the mob, no man on either side daring to act independently for fear of open violence and assassination." Butler did not conceal the methods he planned to use: "There is however here a violent, strong, and unruly mob that can only be kept under by fear." The need to impose fear did not diminish with Mumford's arrest. "It will become necessary for me to use the utmost severity in breaking up the various rebel recruiting associations here, which overawe the Union men and give expression to the feelings of the mob, by assassination and murder . . . and usurp the functions of government when a government was here pretended to. I propose to make some brilliant examples."[15] Mumford served as one of those examples whose rough treatment might cow the overt acts of disloyal citizens in the city.

Butler's treatment of Mumford shaped the experiences of soldiers in both armies for years to come. The consequences transcended the propaganda battle waged between Union and Confederate officers. It interfered in the establishment of the prisoner exchange cartel between the two sides in 1862. Whenever Union and Confederate officers sought to negotiate ground rules for exchange, the case of Mumford arose. Davis and Lee's protests failed to elicit any meaningful response from the Lincoln administration. Rather than follow through on their threats of retaliation, they contented themselves with rhetorical revenge. In fact, Butler served Confederate national interests more effectively as a living symbol of Yankee misrule. Denunciations of Butler became a staple part of the rhetoric of Confederate leaders, Jefferson Davis especially, who singled out Butler and his mismanagement of New Orleans. Davis issued a proclamation listing Butler's crimes and offered a $10,000 bounty for his capture. Despite being treated as an outlaw by the Confederacy, Butler remained an active part of the Union command until the war's end. In fact, the Lincoln administration appointed him as their representative for negotiations over prisoner exchange, a position that nearly upset the whole arrangement in 1864.[16]

New Orleans was the first and largest city that the Union occupied in the course of the Civil War, but not the only one. The leading historian of this process explains that "no fewer than a hundred Southern towns were occupied and garrisoned as Federal army posts at one time or another during the war."[17] At each of these places, Union commanders, local civil authorities, and whatever military officers may have been present had to negotiate either the peaceful surrender or the military resistance of the town. For shorter or longer moments, they all teetered on that same precipice where Farragut had contemplated a bombardment of civilian space. Many would have considered themselves lucky to escape with a single death.

US Secretary of the Navy Gideon Welles instructed his naval officers to "exercise great forbearance with great firmness."[18] These instructions applied regardless of whether vessels approached hostile places from the sea or from rivers. When US Captain Samuel Phillips Lee approached Vicksburg, he wrote to the mayor that he hoped "the same spirit which [induced] the military authorities to require from the city of New Orleans, rather than wantonly sacrifice the lives and property of its inhabitants, would have been followed here." In mid-1862, Union Lieutenant-Commanding Edward T. Nichols drew on the precedents established at places like New Orleans and Baton Rouge to persuade the residents of Rodney, Mississippi, to capitulate quietly. Only a few days after a deadly incident at Baton Rouge and an even more serious one at Grand Gulf, Mississippi, where a Union ship was fired upon by a shore battery, Nichols advised Rodney's town leaders that "I deem it my duty to inform you that should any battery or artillery fire upon any of our vessels while passing up or down from or near the town of Rodney the punishment for the offense will be visited on the town." Nichols expected that residents would understand that the Union's overwhelming strength along the river made any opposition both unlawful and ill-advised. Mansfield Lovell accepted

"Bluebeard of New Orleans." Union General Benjamin Butler earned lasting infamy because of how he managed the occupation of New Orleans. Southern newspapers vilified Butler as heartless and cruel, particularly because of his treatment of female civilians.

the basic position articulated by Nichols, admitting that if a shore battery fired on a ship, the "assaulting party does not claim, any immunity by reason of the presence of women and children."[19]

The situation Nichols hoped to avoid transpired at Natchez later in the year, when a large group of guerrillas fired on the USS *Anglo American* from shore. According to one of the sailors, "we immediately opened our Batteries and commenced Shelling the City. We kept the fire up for 2 ½ hours. The inhabitants kept up a fire of Musketry all the time. Our shells set fire to several houses Under the Hill and did a great deal of damage to the City." By mid-1862, Union sailors had learned to fear the dark spots on shore that could conceal guerrillas. The nature of these interactions degraded the relationship between Northerners and Southerners. According to a naval historian, the sailors "did not understand why men who were trying to kill them would flee from a pitched fight . . . gunboatmen came to view guerrillas and their methods as cowardly, unmanly, and uncivilized." These interactions "bred an instinctive distrust of all Southern civilians save contrabands." Another historian has categorized the Union's response to guerrilla attacks along the river as "punitive," intended to chastise Southern civilians for the irregulars who attacked Union ships. Farragut, Butler, and Sherman argued that their actions were strategic, not punitive. Without any effective way to reach the guerrillas, who scattered before Union soldiers could disembark and engage, they hoped to deter communities from supporting such behavior. At the same time, there is little doubt that these commanders hoped the terror they sowed among civilians would weaken their support for the Confederacy.[20]

In the discussions around Rodney, Lovell admitted that the Confederacy sited its artillery batteries where they could best allow defense "without reference to or connection with the people of the town." This surprising admission drew an immediate response from Farragut: "You say you locate your batteries at such points on the river as are deemed best suited, &c., without reference to the people of the town, and claim no immunity for your troops. Now, therefore, the violation is with you. You . . . should therefore see that the innocent and defenseless of your own people are out of the way before you make the attack; for rest assured that the fire will be returned, and we will not hold ourselves answerable for the death of the innocent."[21] Farragut, like other Union officers, knew that defenders who surrounded themselves with civilians held responsibility for whatever fate befell those civilians. Some Confederate commanders agreed. These lessons in surrender, taught at places like New Orleans, Rodney, Grand Gulf, Natchez, and others found attentive students around the Confederacy. X. B. Debray, the Confederate general defending Houston, explained to the commander at Galveston: "the enemy having possession of Galveston Bay with an overwhelming force of artillery, you will avoid making within the city a resistance, which would bring about the destruction of the property of our citizens without resulting in any good to the country."[22] Debray, unlike some others, had learned that if the Union military encountered Confederate resistance, they countered with overwhelming force.

The Fruits of Occupation

The Civil War abounded in ironies. Historians are fond of noting that the harder Confederates fought the more they doomed slavery and that the harder Federals fought the less likely Confederates would willingly return to the Union. If our awareness of irony is to yield genuine explanation, we must also accept that the historical actors we chronicle recognized these ironies as well. Lincoln hoped to revive white Southerners' sense of loyalty to the United States, but the permanent presence of Union troops in Southern cities created new opportunities for violence and persecution that alienated those people Lincoln hoped to attract. The scale of the war and the tenacity of Confederate resistance meant that the war would not be won in a single, quick sweep. Instead, the North would have to subdue the South one region at a time, which meant that Union soldiers would have to occupy and control Southern cities and towns while other parts of the army advanced upon strategic points.

Occupation was legal and within the laws of war, but it confounded Lincoln's hope of quickly reaffirming white Southern loyalty. By bringing soldiers and civilians together in crowded urban spaces, occupation created new opportunities for violence that reverberated far beyond the streets where it played out. The initially gentle occupation policies of

1861 yielded to more punishing practices as Confederate civilians expressed scorn for their occupiers. Union officers fined disloyal citizens to support impoverished residents of garrison towns, confiscated property when necessary, arrested Southern citizens (men and women) when they refused to acquiesce to Union control, and destroyed property or seized hostages to counter the guerrilla units that proliferated in the countryside around garrison towns. On a handful of occasions, occupation commanders killed Southern civilians. This spectrum of behavior, which encompassed lawful and orderly occupation according to established practice as well as unjust violations of noncombatant immunity, bedeviled Lincoln's efforts to paint the Union as a benevolent force.

Once Union soldiers pacified a Southern city, they established an administrative apparatus to ensure order. Each department hosted a provost marshal general, who appointed deputy provost marshals that administered towns and cities. Part judge, part administrator, and part military officer, provost marshals adjudicated a great deal of the Civil War.[23] They administered loyalty oaths, creating lists of reliable and suspect citizens. They were the first line of response when civilians felt they had been wronged by Union soldiers. Provost marshals also helped reestablish and regulate economic markets in garrison towns. They settled complaints between workers and managers and resolved charges of theft or ill treatment in lieu of often idle local courts. Provost marshals also disciplined Union soldiers. Above all, provost marshals energetically produced files—the National Archives contains thousands of records for each occupied place. Many of these concerned the routine crimes committed by stationary soldiers: drunkenness, gambling, fighting, theft, and more serious charges.

Civilians could also be arrested by provost marshals when they committed mundane crimes well as political ones. The Departments of North Carolina and Virginia operated unevenly with a rotating cast of provost marshals appearing at different places and times. In other departments, continuity in office helped produce stability. The Little Rock provost marshal made his district of Arkansas one of the calmer parts of an often chaotic state. The provost marshal general of Tennessee demanded that Union soldiers adhere to a high standard in their conduct with local civilians, both loyal and disloyal. Captain William M. Wiley, serving in the

Department of the Cumberland, was fastidious about the law.[24] In contrast, the New Orleans provost marshal, James Bowen, dealt more harshly with enemy civilians.[25] In all these places, provost marshals mediated between civilians and soldiers. A good one could ensure that the inevitable friction generated between civilians and soldiers produced only smoke, but a negligent or lax provost marshal might allow a spark to ignite these dangerous compounds. The potential for missteps was legion. The occupation experience in Baton Rouge, upriver from New Orleans, illuminates the precariousness of Union control and the ways that violence could flare, even in the midst of an otherwise orderly occupation.

The first clue was the missing flag. Just as in New Orleans, when US forces occupied Baton Rouge in early May, they required that a US flag fly from the roof of the city arsenal night and day. And just as in New Orleans, when the flag came down, trouble followed. On May 28, it was absent, and Flag Officer David Farragut issued a curt note to the mayor asking for it to be raised. Shortly afterward, Farragut's chief engineer went ashore with four boys in a dinghy. As they landed, several dozen men on horses galloped toward the boat firing buckshot, which injured the engineer and two of the boys. Farragut surmised that these horsemen were guerrillas, bold enough to ride within eyesight of the Union ships. His response came swiftly. Within fifteen minutes, two ships in his flotilla had maneuvered into position and fired on the town. The response was a legitimate one under the laws of war, though federal sailors seized the opportunity to exceed the needs of the moment. A Union officer observed from his ship that "most of the sailors blazed away right into the houses without regard to the position of the foe." Remarkably, the incident ended without any civilian deaths. A citizens' group came forward to explain that the horsemen were from the country and not local residents. Whether the townspeople knew the guerrillas or not (and the sailors assumed they did), it was locals who suffered. Their homes and their churches bore the pockmarks of Union artillery, and they lived in fear of another round of still more vigorous cannonading.[26]

The conflict over how to view the bombardment can be seen by juxtaposing a Confederate and Union view of the event. Sarah Morgan, a young woman in Baton Rouge, experienced the day firsthand, fleeing with her family east of town. Morgan condemned Farragut's decision as one that needlessly subjected innocents to deadly attack. "Hurrah for the illustrious Farragut, the 'Woman Killer!!!'"[27] Farragut never denied the action but rejected Morgan's moral reckoning. He admonished Lovell to protect noncombatants before launching an attack. Farragut admitted that innocents suffered at Baton Rouge "when an attempt was made to kill one of our officers landing in a small boat manned with four boys. They were, when in the act of landing, mostly wounded by the fire of some 30 or 40 horseman, who chivalrously galloped out of the town, leaving the women and children to bear the brunt of vengeance."[28] Under the laws of war, then and now, Farragut was within his rights to return fire (as Lovell earlier admitted), though whether he needed to do so remains open to debate.[29] Guerrilla attacks continued, though none as brazen as what occurred on May 28. Morgan's professions of innocence also rang hollow. Her recollection of May 28 (written two days later) contains a telling admission. Her sister, Lily, ran into her room explaining "Mr. Castle has killed a Federal officer on a ship, and they are going to shell—Bang! went a cannon at the word, and that was all our warning."[30] Rather than the outside agitators that locals claimed the guerrillas to be, Morgan and undoubtedly others in Baton Rouge knew who they were.

As the clash of May 28 revealed, one of the most serious problems arising from Union occupation was the likelihood that their presence would attract Confederate guerrillas. Unlike the irregulars of 1861, who organized in regions abandoned by the Confederacy, these fighters mobilized in response to Union occupation. Union commanders had to decide to what extent they could hold local civilians responsible for the actions of guerrillas that circulated through their territory. The threat in Louisiana was quite real. Louisiana's governor, Thomas Moore, demanded that "every able bodied citizen must hold himself in readiness for immediate service." In a public address on June 18, Moore authorized local leaders to raise bands of Partisan Rangers. "Let every possible assistance be rendered them in forming, arming, equipping, or mounting their companies, and in giving them support and information when possible. Let all our river banks swarm with armed patriots to teach the hated invader that the rifle will be his only welcome on his errand of plunder and destruction."[31] Swarm they did. Union soldiers commented in dark terms about contending with guerrillas along the state's waterways.[32] This sounded to Union ears like an invitation to boundless war, as it did to some Confederates. Robert E. Lee, never enthusiastic about irregular war, urged the state's military commander to solicit "bold and judicious partisans who can raise proper corps," the latter phrase indicating regular soldiers under the command of commissioned officers.[33]

The Union experimented with different techniques, many pioneered in Missouri, to curtail guerrillas active in occupied regions. First came monetary punishments. Major General John Pope inaugurated this practice in 1861 in Missouri in the form of "taxes to be levied on those citizens deemed guilty of supporting or tolerating guerilla attacks on the railroad." Commanders in other theaters copied this approach. Victims filed reports with provost marshals, who assessed fines on disloyal people in the region and then used this money to compensate local Unionists for their losses from guerrilla raids. If money could not be posted as bond or extracted as punishment, creative Union officers found other ways of exacting resources. In central Tennessee, Union officer Thomas Worthington reported that Confederate guerrillas had raided a town, robbing civilians and behaving "in a most shameful and cowardly manner more resembling savages than persons professing to be civilized." Worst of all, the guerrillas "were particularly severe upon the negroes who were left in the place and took particular pains to burn every negro cabin house rude shanty in town." Worthington's solution was to impress the labor of leading Confederate (and guerrilla) sympathizers in the community to "build up every house owned or occupied by Negroes that were destroyed and place in as good if not better condition than they were before." The thirty-two town leaders summoned to do the work no doubt wished they only had to pay fines for the guerrillas' damage.[34]

When assessments failed to produce loyalty and peace, the Union moved to confiscation. If confiscation failed, the next step was outright destruction. Butler's response to the rise in guerrilla activity in Louisiana after reading Moore's proclamation was predictable: "punish with the last severity every guerrilla attack and burn the property of every guerrilla found murdering your soldiers." Officers at Baton Rouge implemented the strategy. In early June, Colonel Nathan M. Dudley reported on his efforts to track down three reputed guerrillas: Keller, Penny, and Castle. His men arrived unannounced at the plantation residences of each man but could not locate them. Instead, the soldiers destroyed machinery and supplies at each place and seized slaves as punishment. At Keller's residence, they took animals and destroyed the cotton gin and 30 bales of cotton, fences, and ornamental trees. "This," Dudley reported, is "the most painful duty of my military life, I executed it in the most delicate manner I possibly could, first tendering the ladies an escort and transportation to the next plantation before I commenced the destruction of anything belonging to the estate." Even Keller's father-in-law admitted his son-in-law's guilt, adding that he had warned him of precisely these consequences. At Penny's plantation, Dudley "burnt every building on the estate except such as were required to cover the negroes left behind, including an extensive and valuable sugar-mill, and also destroyed the fences—in fact, left nothing but the blackened chimneys as monuments to the folly and villainy of its guerrilla owner."[35]

In 1862, Union officers adopted one last method, nonlethal but still quite severe, to deter guerrillas in occupied areas: they destroyed whole towns. Donaldsonville, northwest of New Orleans on the west bank of the Mississippi River, suffered this fate. Farragut ordered its destruction after it fired on Union ships. Butler concurred in the decision, as he explained in a letter to the Mother Superior of the Sisters of Charity in Donaldsonville. "The destruction of that town became a necessity," Butler wrote. "The inhabitants harbored a gang of cowardly guerrillas, who committed every atrocity, amongst others that of firing upon an unarmed boat, crowded with women and children." Butler opened the letter by apologizing for the damage done to the Sisters, then justified the policy. "It is impossible to allow such acts," Butler noted, "and I am only sorry that the righteous punishment meted out to them in this instance, as indeed in all others, fell quite as heavily upon the innocent and unoffending as upon the guilty."[36]

Confederate citizens in Donaldsonville responded with an unusual letter of complaint to the Davis administration. Noting that "the most valuable portion of the town" had been destroyed, they criticized the irregular war being waged upon the Union as the source of their suffering. "Firing upon and destroying a few unarmed [Union] boats (for hitherto no armed vessels have been assailed) can be productive of no results which would justify jeopardizing the lives and the total destruction of the property

"Ruins at Donaldsonville." Riverfront towns from which guerrillas attacked Union shipping on the Mississippi drew increasingly strong military responses. After one such attack, Northern soldiers destroyed the public buildings and most private homes in Donaldsonville, Louisiana, to deter future guerrilla actions.

of our people and the demoralizing of our servile population." Preston Pond, Jr., a prominent area Confederate, echoed the citizens of Donaldsonville when he denounced the actions of Confederate partisans. Writing to Union Major General William Franklin, Pond guessed that the Union troops in the area have "been provoked by the action of some parties, some of whom are regular Confederate troops, while others are of irregular formation; both of which, however, are pursuing a very irregular system of warfare. I wish to say to you that this system of warfare is not approved here but that we are powerless to prevent it. These guerrillas ... are regarded universally with as much disapprobation by us as by you and our people suffer much from their lawlessness." These sharp rebukes of Confederate strategy reflected a local view of the war—if the Confederacy could not match Union force, they should not fire at transports.[37]

Benjamin Butler happily reported on similar evidence of Confederate dissension. He wrote to the secretary of war that during a late June meeting "I had a visit from a dozen or more Gentlemen of Baton Rouge and

Vicinity representing some five or six millions of property and had conversation with them upon the new system of Partisan Rangers just now inaugurated, i.e.: Guerrilla Warfare. They deprecate it, will do every thing possible to discountenance it."[38] Butler's confidence in the Union's ability to stifle guerrilla warfare was misplaced. Despite the escalated punishments, the guerrilla threat expanded in the years ahead, both in Louisiana and elsewhere. It may have been harder for Butler to recognize his own culpability in this process, the ways that occupation generated new dangers, not just for Union soldiers but for noncombatants in the region. As Butler's and Farragut's experiences reveal, a lawful and just war could also be a destructive and deadly one. Subjugating Southern towns, sometimes by force, enabled military control over parts of the region, but it also stimulated irregular resistance that impeded that goal.

Escalating War

Most Americans had been shocked by the scale of the Battle of Bull Run in July 1861. It generated more than 4,000 total casualties, making it one of the bloodiest battles in North America up to that time. This was not the war that Northerners and Southerners anticipated when they mobilized armies amid parades and celebratory dinners; 1862 proved even worse. The casualty lists printed in newspapers after battles extended from paragraphs to columns to pages. The Battle of Shiloh, which took place April 6–7, 1862, in southern Tennessee, marked a terrifying threshold recognized by participants and later observers alike. Union forces moved down the Tennessee River toward Mississippi. Confederate forces surprised these men and pushed them back nearly to the river in the first day's fighting, but on the second day Union reinforcements reclaimed the lost ground. Observers and participants were shocked to read reports of the casualties—nearly 24,000 over the two days, or six times the number of fatalities at Bull Run.[39] Witnesses at the scene were incredulous. Ulysses S. Grant, commanding the Northern forces, remembered the field "so covered with dead that it would have been possible to walk across the clearing, in any direction, stepping on dead bodies, without a foot touching the ground."[40] Equally deadly battles followed throughout the year.

"A Harvest of Death, Gettysburg, Pennsylvania." The Battle of Gettysburg, like the Battle of Shiloh, generated a nearly unimaginable number of casualties— almost 50,000 over three days of fighting. Although photographs could not yet be reproduced in newspapers, their presence in albums and exhibitions alerted viewers to the true scale of loss in the war.

Historians typically present the story of Shiloh as an example of the escalation inevitable in all wars. In this view, people at the time accepted the increase in battlefield deaths as a natural but unavoidable part of the Civil War. This interpretation treats violence as an autonomous force, something with its own inertia. There is some degree of truth in this characterization. Like many complex systems built by people, wars often slip the leash to wreak havoc on the plans and intentions of their creators. But historians' business is to explain how people make change in the world, intentional or unintentional. With the benefit of hindsight, historians are compelled to pay particular attention to the decisions that wars' participants made to accelerate or decelerate the conflicts in which they participated. Violence does not, on its own, escalate. Politicians or senior officers order or sanction policy changes, soldiers implement them, and enemy combatants and civilians of all stripes react.

Northerners and Southerners absorbed these losses because they came in a familiar form—regular battlefield clashes between uniformed soldiers. Historically, this was how wars happened. And history, especially that of the American Revolution, demonstrated the importance of perseverance and sacrifice. Whether in the service of victory or defeat, death demanded respect and compelled citizens to greater commitment to their cause. Death encouraged people to find meaning in it. What proved harder to understand or assimilate was the escalation of irregular war. Despite the contribution of irregular violence to the enormity of the scale of regular loss, noncombatants both North and South accepted these new approaches. Some people dissented for political, strategic, or moral reasons, but in most events the people who fought the Civil War sanctioned increasing violence in 1862. Portions of this choice came from combatants, who reacted to their experiences in contested places. Other portions came from policymakers, who rethought their approaches to what looked like a longer war. Both ideas and actions merged to make the Civil War of 1862 a more dangerous time for everyone involved. For Confederates, this manifested in impromptu, ground-level resistance to occupation and, more formally, increasing guerrilla attacks on Union soldiers. Federals, for their part, adopted a harsher approach to noncombatants, exerting more pressure on civilians who supported guerrillas and escalating the lethal treatment of guerrillas themselves.

Off the Battlefield

Irregular war came unevenly to America. In Missouri, it exploded at the war's opening moments. In Arkansas, it sparked to life in 1862, as Union soldiers invaded the state and Confederate soldiers exited it. After the Union victory at Pea Ridge in March 1862, Confederate regulars evacuated Arkansas. In response, Thomas C. Hindman, the general in command of most of the trans-Mississippi Confederacy, issued what became known as the "band of 10" order. On June 17, 1862, he "instructed the *people* of Arkansas: 'for the more effective annoyance of the enemy upon our rivers and in our mountains and woods, *all citizens* from this district . . .

are called upon to organize themselves into independent companies' of ten men, led by an elected 'captain,' to conduct guerrilla warfare 'without waiting for special instructions.'"[41] Hindman's call turned out perhaps as many as 5,000 men who slowed down the federal advance just as he intended. Snipers killed Union soldiers on transports as they moved down the state's rivers. Others ambushed small detachments of Federals as they marched.

In places like New Orleans or Memphis (captured by Union troops in June 1862), the Union garrison's overwhelming strength deterred irregular violence. But outside the zone of Union power in places subject to thinner occupation or only periodically visited by Union troops, guerrillas organized and attacked.[42] In the broad middle of the country along the Ohio and Missouri Rivers, one historian states that after 1862, "divided allegiances paralyzed social relations. Driven by war tensions, the breakdown of community institutions ensued. Societal organizations locked their doors for months and even years."[43] In the absence of the traditional social glue that held this region together, guerrilla violence annealed it through fire. Despite the popular assumption that irregular war was solely a feature of the western and trans-Mississippi theaters, the East was not spared. Irregular fighters attacked Union troops and Unionist civilians in western Virginia, Maryland, western North Carolina, Kentucky, and eastern Tennessee. According to best estimates, 7,000–9,550 pro-Confederate guerrillas were active in the South throughout the whole war with another 10,000–15,000 "quasi-guerrillas" who operated in deserter bands in the region.[44] Though small in numbers compared to the regular armies, guerrillas exercised an outsized influence.

As the US Army mobilized more and more men in 1862, it forced Confederates to shift their smaller forces within or even between regions to discourage federal attacks or to probe for weaknesses. This arrangement left sizeable areas of the Confederacy without the presence of either army for long stretches of time. After March 1862, Northern troops spent little time in Missouri, Arkansas, or the Indian Territories. Coastal attacks on Texas and Florida yielded little in the way of concrete gains and, as a result, citizens of these states saw few soldiers in blue. Because these states were relatively sparsely populated and located far from the national capitals, the Union did not identify them as a strategic necessity. As a result, irregular warfare predominated. In light of the Union decision and the contemporary focus on the eastern theater, some historians have relegated these areas, and consequently the guerrilla conflict, to the status of "sideshow."[45] But the trans-Mississippi states of Missouri, Arkansas, Louisiana, and Texas held nearly three million residents. For at least one-third of the Southern population, irregular war was more the rule than the exception.

The most important factor disrupting previously stable communities or pacifying unruly ones was the armies' mobility. Vacuums of power developed as armies came and went, leaving civilians at the mercy of irregular forces. The Confederate frontier was loosely governed from Union garrison towns but subject to periodic Confederate raids. Neither national army controlled the no-man's-land, and people in these regions experienced a violent and haphazard conflict. Confederate Major General Richard Ewell, well aware of this feature of warfare, advised his wife to "remember that the Country is not safe, in case of occupation by the enemy. Any town is so, comparatively, but in the Country you are subjected to insults from small marauding bands of the enemy and even our own lowest class would take advantage of such times. In a city the enemy always are in organized bodies, commanded by Officers of rank who wish to conciliate." Ewell accurately summarized the relationship between violence and the presence of regular troops: "the more out of the way a place, the more exposed to outrage as there is less restraint over the parties who spread around."[46]

Ewell, like uniformed officers of both sections, recognized that parties who practiced such "outrage" contributed little to the national war effort. In some regions, guerrillas focused their violence on Union troops while in others they targeted Unionist civilians they regarded as collaborators. This latter violence quickly spread to encompass other noncombatants. The fruits of this shift could be seen in one of the single worst episodes of irregular violence in the US Civil War. In 1862, pro-Confederate irregulars hanged forty-two men in north Texas. A mixed group of state militia and Partisan Ranger units had arrested more than 150 men. Impromptu "trials" were convened that assessed the men's involvement with a local Peace Party. Unlike many of the victims of irregular violence in other places, the executed men in Gainesville displayed little sympathy for the Union. The victims constituted a varied group of nonslaveholders, immigrants, and genuine Peace Party members. State officials sanctioned the killings, and the Davis administration did nothing to punish those responsible. Though extreme, this event illustrates the degree of chaos that could prevail in contested regions within the South where regular troops yielded to irregulars.[47]

Blood Grows Hot

Lincoln knew that his armies had to deter irregular violence without alienating the whole white South, and especially the lukewarm secessionists that he believed composed a majority of the population. In practice, this meant that federal authorities tried first to ferret out guerrillas and target them alone. Identifying guerrillas—distinguishing them from the noncombatants among whom they lived—required locating sympathetic Southern civilians who would inform on their neighbors. This created grave dangers, as collaboration in war always does. When control of a town or region flipped, residents found themselves scrambling to conceal or explain away the loyalties they had expressed when the previous army was in control. Army records are full of documents such as a "List of Enrolled Disloyal and Sympathizers with the Rebellion at Russelville Cole County, MO" which included the names of ninety-four men from age 18 to 54. The longer list containing 329 names of Missouri men, their personal and real estate, and residence, along with remarks like "noted rebel," "bushwhacker," "sympathizer," living at home," and so on. The provost marshal in Arkansas kept careful lists of suspected guerrillas in the area with simplistic designations—"bad," "very bad," "very bad indeed." One entry among these included the vital note: "will give information." For the provost marshal, such a source was invaluable, even if the man was listed as a "bad character." For the informant such a list posed grave risks. If the Union publicly exposed people's loyalties, it created the grounds for future violence.[48]

Union provost marshals combined a variety of information-gathering tools, each with a different level of reliability and coercion. In most occupied cities, provost marshals could compel men to take the loyalty oath and post a bond in order to remain at large in the local community. Most nineteenth-century Americans regarded the taking of an oath as a serious commitment, but some Union officials suspected that white Southerners cynically signed in order to insulate themselves from harassment and gain access to markets, courts, and other public institutions. Provost marshals often went further and required men to write out affidavits asserting their loyalty to the Union. The more detailed and personal nature of these documents may have discouraged casual oath-breakers from signing them. Other provost marshals went further still, setting up investigative committees that called men to testify against one another, to report on associations to which they were invited or to which they belonged, and above all to ferret out disloyalty.[49]

Some white Southerners came willingly to provost marshals to report disloyal neighbors, especially when they had been the victim of theft or violence at the hands of Confederate irregulars. A. P. Appleby, resident of Carroll County, Missouri, for instance, volunteered that in "the month of July 1862, I was taken prisoner by Capt. Merrick—a notorious bushwhacker," and that "while in his camp I saw John D. Fowler in a line with a company of bushwhackers."[50] Depending on Appleby's reliability, Fowler's name might have been added to the Union's list of potential bushwhackers. Although his motives remain obscure, George Pottiser, residing in Carrollton, Missouri, requested the local provost marshal take action against a notorious group of irregulars. One had participated in the murder of two members of the Missouri Militia. He detailed more: "Norman Halsey, another vile rebel, said to be a recruiting officer under Bill Anderson. This wretch is a Southern Methodist preacher. A low cunning, intriguing scoundrel—and no doubt a bare spy."[51] Best of all was when a former guerrilla could be turned. The information gained from them was regarded by Union officers as particularly valuable. Men and women alike were subject to scrutiny, particularly if they crossed the lines and gave evasive answers. Provost marshals combined all this data into lists that tracked reliable Union men, confirmed guerrillas, and all those points along the wide spectrum between these two extremes. Once they identified troublemakers, Union military commanders organized raids to capture or kill them. The increasing sophistication of the Union's military intelligence apparatus enabled this more aggressive antiguerrilla strategy.

One of the places where guerrillas proved most effective was along the Mississippi River.[52] Moore's and Hindman's calls in 1862 for men to resist the advance of Union troops along the waters drew thousands of men into irregular service opposing the Union advance. Though small in numbers, these men exploited their secure position on land to shoot into the slow and vulnerable troop transports and supply ships that traveled southern waters. William T. Sherman held the residents of coastal towns responsible for the actions of guerrillas who operated out of them. Randolph, Tennessee, experienced repercussions for harboring guerrillas similar to those of Donaldsonville, Louisiana. From the shore near Randolph, Confederate irregulars fired on Union ships moving along the river. Sherman's explanation for his response used the same logic that Butler deployed in his conversations with the Sisters of Charity: "the Regular packet 'Eugene' from St. Louis, with passengers & Stores (not public) landed on Tuesday, at the town of Randolph, and came near falling into the possession of a Band of Guerrillas, and was fired into by some 25 to 40 of the Band. I immediately sent a Regiment up with orders to destroy the place. . . . The Regiment has returned and Randolph is gone." The punishment, he reasoned, must fall on the place that sanctioned the guerrillas, even if not all the people there supported the irregulars. "That boat was laden with stores for the very benefit of families, some of whose members are in arms against us; and it was an outrage of the greatest magnitude, that people there or in connivance with them, should fire on an unarmed boat . . . the Example should be followed up on all similar occasions."[53] It was.[54] According to Sherman, the remedy worked, at least for a few months: "Since ordering the destruction of Randolph there have been no more problems."[55]

Butler and Sherman adopted broad remedies because small-scale actions against guerrillas rarely produced much success, as one Union officer admitted. "The expeditions sent out to break up guerrilla dens & seize & bring in there effects are always attended with a good deal of fatigue, & sometimes, but rarely, with skirmishing," reported General Thomas Williams, because irregulars "skulked" through the woods. This created a cultural distance between regular soldiers and guerrillas that allowed much more cavalier treatment of the latter than of fighters they encountered on battlefields. The guerrilla's "appearance & his qualities

[are] those of a white Indian," explained Williams dismissively. The result of this can be felt in the thinly veiled anger of Union commanders when they issued orders related to guerrillas. Ulysses Grant instructed a subordinate, "where you can suppress Guerrillas with the force at your command do it." "Suppress," in this instance, offered wide latitude for lethal violence. "Where Citizens give aid and comfort to these fellows who amuse themselves by firing into them, arrest them." Conservatives in the North condemned the policy of logistical devastation that escalated in 1862. After Secretary of the Navy Gideon Welles heard about the use of churches as hospitals and the seizure of private homes (including that of a Southern friend), he remarked, "there is malice in this."[56]

The Union's more aggressive approach toward guerrillas appeared simultaneously in different theaters. Destruction was the order of the day on Union raids of the countryside around New Bern, North Carolina. "'If you can see the ruin, devastation and utter abandonment of villages, Plantations and farms, which but a short time ago was peopled, fenced and stocked,' one soldier wrote his wife, 'no cows, horses, mules, sheep, or poultry to be seen where ever the Union army advances.' The soldier concluded, 'This whole country for all purposes of maintenance for man or beast for the next twelve months is a desert as hopeless as Sahara itself.'" In Arkansas, Union officers dismantled public and private buildings used for attacks on Union shipping, burned foliage and cover along the riverbanks, and destroyed whole towns, creating great hardship for Arkansas residents, both Unionist and Confederate. Hindman defended his "Band of 10" order and threatened to retaliate against Union prisoners if guerrillas were not treated as soldiers. William T. Sherman, commanding in the region, advised against an unrestrained war. "Remember," he wrote Hindman, "that we have hundreds of thousands of men bitter and yearning for revenge. Let us but loose these from the restraints of discipline and no life or property would be safe. . . . You initiate the game, and my word for it your people will regret it long after you pass from earth." Neither side enacted the draconian policies they threatened, but the violence and destruction created by the guerrilla conflict and its suppression generated enormous suffering among true noncombatants.[57]

Ignoring the role of guerrillas, Confederates condemned any property destruction that affected civilians. One of their strongest protests came in response to antiguerrilla actions in Missouri. The event happened in Palmyra, Missouri, in September 1862, when Union Brigadier General John McNeil executed ten Confederate guerrillas.[58] McNeil killed them because local guerrillas had captured and presumably executed a pro-Union man from the area. That pro-Union man was himself a viable target because he had "performed valuable services as a guide, leading Union forces to guerrilla hideouts, and as an informer, identifying disloyal people in the area." His presumed execution highlights the dangers of collaboration.[59] Complaints over the incident escalated from the departmental commander to Robert E. Lee and eventually to Davis himself. Lee, acting for Davis, initiated a correspondence with Henry Halleck, acting for Lincoln.[60] Pro-Southern newspaper reports identified the victims as "Confederate citizens of Missouri," and Davis felt political pressure to defend even this distant star in the Confederate galaxy.

Despite the high-level exchange, neither side took action. The Confederates did not retaliate, and the Union executed no more prisoners. McNeil's actions did not qualify as just retaliation—only one execution would have been justified if evidence of the Union man's death had been confirmed. Nonetheless, as Davis undoubtedly knew, he could not make a compelling legal case against the execution of guerrillas anywhere. As Samuel Curtis, the Union commander of the Department of Missouri, explained to his Confederate peer, "the idea of 'Confederate citizens of Missouri,' in Missouri, is inconsistent with a state of war between opposing sections, and utterly repugnant to the attitude heretofore allowed you as a belligerent. . . . You have no military power in Missouri . . . much less a civil organization which would induce any man to call himself a 'Confederate citizen.'" Curtis strongly connected himself with Lieber and Halleck's position on guerrillas: "persons in the State, who congregate without commissions of any kind, to steal and rob, under the color of warfare, have deserved death." We do not know if Davis was swayed by this argument, but the lack of formal complaints about the execution of guerrillas offers a tacit admission that they knew these irregular fighters operated outside of the protective sphere of the laws of war. The best Davis could do was keep McNeil alive in Confederate propaganda. He soon occupied a spot alongside Ben Butler in the pantheon of Yankee villains.[61]

Lincoln never issued a public statement on the Palmyra Massacre, as Confederates called it, but he retained McNeil in command, which shows at least a willingness to tolerate his actions in Missouri. Unionists in the state praised McNeil precisely because of his firmness with guerrillas and their supporters. Lincoln once again had to accept that Union policies would evolve as the war continued and be inconsistent in different areas of the country. His vision of the least punishing war rarely aligned with the needs of Union troops on the ground. Lincoln's famous fatalism shaped his view of Missouri: "actual war coming, blood grows hot, and blood is spilled. Thought is forced from old channels into confusion. Deception breeds and thrives. Confidence dies, and universal suspicion reigns. Each man feels an impulse to kill his neighbor, lest he be first killed by him. Revenge and retaliation follow." The inevitability of this sequence might have led him to despair, but Lincoln seemed preoccupied with how he could craft policy that could mitigate the next, even worse, phase. "Every foul bird comes abroad, and every dirty reptile rises up. These add crime to confusion. Strong measures, deemed indispensable but harsh at best, such men make worse by mal-administration." Here Lincoln offered an accurate description of how army policies—"strong measures"— could, by poor officering, create unfortunate consequences.[62]

The irregular war shaped the thinking of the Union officers who managed the regular war. Most important among these was Henry W. Halleck. As the author of a treatise on international law, Halleck began the conflict committed to established principles. His expertise, widely known and respected, helped ensure that he eventually found his way to Washington, where he served as Lincoln's general-in-chief and later chief of staff. In both roles, he helped coordinate military strategy across the various Union departments. Before he became general-in-chief, Halleck commanded the Department of the Missouri. His experience battling guerrillas and other irregulars in that state pushed him away from the restrained warfare he articulated in print in 1861. Halleck's attitudes can be read as roughly emblematic of the shift made by many Northerners. Halleck slowly abandoned his belief that a limited war could succeed. "We have tried three years of conciliation and kindness without any reciprocation," he wrote in 1864; "on the contrary, those thus treated have acted as spies and guerrillas in our rear and within our lines . . . I would destroy every mill and factory within reach which I did not want for my own use."[63] Halleck took Missouri with him, and he was not alone.

Grant and Sherman both spent time there, and they too adapted to a harder, longer war before most other Union officers. But doing so did not necessarily mean advocating for a more lethal conflict. Despite his satisfaction after the burning of Randolph, Sherman continued to struggle with the problem of guerrilla attacks on Union boats on the river. Instead of burning every town that harbored guerrillas, he proposed "to expel ten secession families for every boat fired on." Sherman recognized that his policy shifted exposure to violence from his soldiers to citizens. "It may sometimes fall on the wrong head," he admitted, "but it would be folly to send parties of infantry to chase these wanton guerrillas." In truth, he did not entirely exempt the noncombatants from a role in the guerrilla war. To a Memphis woman who wrote to request a postponement of his order until the Confederate government could disavow the actions to which he objected, Sherman asserted a democratic power to such women that may not have existed to change Confederate behavior. "I know you will say these poor women and children abhor such acts as much as I do. . . . Then let the Confederate authorities say so, and not employ their tools in such deeds of blood and darkness." As a Regular Army officer, Sherman dealt in blood and light, but his exposure to guerrillas convinced him that the South fought outside the laws of war. Not until late 1862 and 1863, when Confederates faced black soldiers, did the white Southerners undergo a similar radicalization.[64]

War at Home

Although women were almost never subjected to the lethal violence experienced by the Texans at Gainesville or the guerrillas at Palmyra, they nonetheless suffered from the escalating war. Occupation, in particular, produced new opportunities for exposing women to unjust violence or mistreatment. Women staffed the home front, so when Union soldiers moved into Southern places, they interacted with Southern women. As such, women came under the rule of all the policies that Union commanders created to administer Southern places. When they violated these rules, women were arrested and imprisoned by Union commanders. Thousands of women served time in the jails of Union provost marshals across the South.[65] In the most extreme cases, provost marshals banished families from cities or regions in the South. Women had to manage these expulsions. Union commanders viewed banishments as mild punishment, but becoming a refugee exposed people to unknown dangers and the violence of the roving bands that populated the edges of the Confederacy.[66] More explicitly partisan women (both Unionist and Confederate) living in contested areas were also subjected to beatings and assaults by irregulars as punishment for their national loyalties and behavior. Last, some women made themselves vulnerable to direct military action when they supported guerrillas.

By the middle of 1862, the attitudes of Northern soldiers toward the Southern civilians with whom they interacted had shifted from a skeptical sympathy to something closer to outright hostility. The destruction and confiscation that accompanied occupying forces stopped worrying Union soldiers. "Men in the ranks agreed that destruction was strategically justified, but many also came to rationalize it as an act of righteous vengeance," as one scholar of this process has noted. Despite this change, Yankees never abandoned their humanity. "Even at their fiercest," this historian argues, "Northern invaders maintained a clear distinction between humane and inhumane war making . . . they drew the line at bodily assaults on unarmed civilians; even at the height of the hard policy, violence of that sort remained rare and was never officially sanctioned."[67]

As always, Benjamin Butler established himself at the center of the problem. His execution of John Mumford earned him scorn, but his treatment of women in New Orleans earned him infamy. After the city's quick capture, some women in the city began showing disrespect for US soldiers and symbols. "Insult rather than injury became many of these women's weapons of choice. . . . Butler's men were treated . . . to all manner of verbal and symbolic insults," writes a Louisiana historian. Butler's response was to issue General Orders No. 28, which threatened that "when any female shall, by word, gesture, or movement, insult or show contempt for any officer or soldier of the United States, she shall be regarded and held liable to be treated as a woman of the town plying her avocation." Confederates, and some sympathetic Britons, regarded this as a license for Union soldiers to sexually assault the town's women at will, though no evidence supports this assertion. Nonetheless, Confederates featured their interpretation of the order in most catalogs of Yankee atrocities for the remainder of the war. Butler celebrated his own cleverness, citing the order as a key part of his effort to pacify the city. Although some women may have been deterred because of the order, evidence suggests that they continued to oppose the occupation, often publicly. Or, as another recent historian concludes: "Confederate women of New Orleans did not resist General Orders No. 28—they distanced themselves from it—thus reasserting what power they could claim by virtue of their class, if not their gender." In New Orleans and every occupied city, women made their political presence known, which is why Union commanders treated them like men in so many cases.[68]

Regardless of where they lived, the first challenge for Southern women, white and black, was finding safe ways to interact with Union troops while protecting and feeding their families. After the Union navy captured New Bern and Beaufort, North Carolina, in March 1862, for instance, white residents there tried to maintain what one historian has called a kind of "dual citizenship . . . [in which] the strength of their convictions rested on a sliding scale—liable to be more pro-Union or pro-Confederate at any given time, depending on their individual circumstances." This response reflected both a genuine prewar skepticism about secession and the reality of trying to live in novel and uncertain times. Although perhaps an effective way for citizens to exploit whatever advantage they could in the ambiguous context of war, this dualism also led soldiers to mistrust what civilians told them and thus created more opportunities for violence. Most white residents found amicable ways to work with Union forces, but those that did not caused real problems. In June 1862, one New Bern woman fired a revolver from her porch into a crowded street, killing one person. The Union guard arrested everyone in the house. Other women took up the habit of firing on Union sentries and guards who traveled through the city. When a Massachusetts soldier was wounded during such an incident, the commanding general arrested the occupants of the house and leveled it.[69]

Many women chronicled the abuses and hardships they suffered under Union occupation, and Union records themselves offer additional testimony. In 1863, the region around Little Rock, Arkansas, was subject to loose Union oversight and surveillance, but as the Union provost marshal J. L. Chandler discovered, one regiment of troops abused their position. The First Iowa Cavalry found itself the target of repeated stories and rumors about their behavior. Chandler did not believe all the stories, but nonetheless warned the unit's commander that "your men are allowed to straggle into the country, as I am informed by evidence unimpeachable, in squads of from three to ten or more and they often plunder the citizens of almost every article that can be carried off." Chandler demanded access to the camp in order to search for stolen goods; he had earlier given access for a local woman to search the camp for "bed clothing and cooking utensils" that she claimed had been stolen by the soldiers. The problems in Arkansas continued into the fall with Chandler persisting in his efforts against the Iowa regiment and others. He returned property when civilians could prove it was theirs, and he kept Union commanders informed about the quality and quantity of complaints filed against various Union regiments. But not all places received oversight as scrupulous as that enacted by Chandler, and other zealous officers might have found less support from the commanding generals in their department.[70]

The presence of Union soldiers and the absence of Confederate men from the Southern home front created still more dangers for enslaved women. Historians have chronicled the abusive relationships that plantation mistresses maintained with their slaves, removing the last vestiges of the veil of civility draped over slavery by nineteenth-century apologists. For some of these mistresses, the threats to themselves and their households that appeared during the war could only be addressed with more violence. Harriet Robinson suffered under a "mean" woman before the war, but "during the war she beat us so terrible . . . Miss Julie would take me by the ears and butt my head against the wall."[71] Like the uncertain violence that so many Missourians faced, some of these interactions may have been rooted in prewar habits, but the changed context of the wartime South made enslaved women still more vulnerable.

The treatment of women in the war's first years vividly illustrated the contradictory nature of Union military policy. Women factored as military actors in the irregular war's domestic supply line and as political actors in most occupied cities.[72] They played key political roles in secession and the whole life of the Confederacy.[73] Union soldiers knew they formed an essential part of the enemy and for this reason subjected them to increasingly harsh military policies. But the prejudices of antebellum men, most of whom believed that women required and merited protection, tempered Union policy, at least in 1861 and 1862. Whatever the quarrel between the Confederacy and the Union, men agreed that it should not be fought out in the lives of the country's women. Further, the gendered nature of the laws of war meant that women were specifically exempted from war's lethal violence.[74] But women's active role in the war, especially in the South, shattered their proscribed role and exposed them to the war's damage.

A War of Beliefs

The changing nature of the war—especially the twin problems of occupation and guerrilla conflict—compelled citizens on both sides to endorse harsher methods, but other shifts in attitudes about what was just in war came from outside the war itself. In the North, ideological or political beliefs shaped this transformation. Sometimes people endorsed the trends, sanctioning the earnest vindictiveness with which Northern soldiers pursued guerrillas. Sometimes people pushed against the current, condemning the war's new course and the actions of their own soldiers. Republicans usually supported the army's increasingly aggressive posture, whereas Democrats, hostile to emancipation and wary of Lincoln, criticized the violence. Most surprising, abolitionists and radical Republicans who had long condemned violence came to see the war as an opportunity to end slavery, and they accepted the bloodshed that was necessary to accomplish that long-sought goal. How did civilians exercise ethical judgments about what was appropriate in war? In the words of one of the protagonists, how did the war's participants "explain ourselves to ourselves?"

Violence and Emancipation

The ideological-military alignments of the Civil War surprised many people during the conflict, and they retain their ability to shock. Northern radicals had embraced the era's humanitarian sensibility most fully. They led campaigns to reform prisons and mental institutions, to protect women and children from abusive (usually alcoholic) men, and to end slavery. Motivated by a vision of Christian perfectionism spurred by the Second Great Awakening, these reformers sought to protect the innocent and reduce suffering in the world. Yet they became champions of hard war. Conservatives, on the other hand, ridiculed and rejected the social policies advocated by the radicals and had long championed American military action. Yet they levied the most serious critique of the Union's armies. Radicals and conservatives in the North possessed very different visions of what the Civil War could and should do. Their divergent, in some respects incompatible, perspectives about the purpose of the war brought them into conflict over how the North should fight.

Because radicals believed only emancipation could justify the violence of war, the Union's turn against slavery in 1862 transformed how they viewed the war's increasing cost. Ohio congressman James Ashley, later the author of the Thirteenth Amendment, believed that by going to war against the United States, rebels had committed treason and their property (including human property) should be seized. Ashley suggested polling soldiers, who knew firsthand how slavery empowered Southern armies. "If this question of the confiscation of property and the liberation of slaves of rebels could be submitted to a vote of our Army," he told the House of Representatives, "there would be no doubt about its passage."[75] By 1862, radicals like Ashley wanted to empower enslaved people to fight lawfully, and they held less concern for the punitive nature of an armed and violent emancipation process.

William Lloyd Garrison led radical opinion in the North for most of the war. Garrison established himself as the leading white abolitionist beginning in the 1830s, when he called for immediate emancipation. He began publishing his newspaper, *The Liberator*, in 1831, the same year as Nat Turner's bloody slave rebellion in Southampton County, Virginia.

Conspiracy-minded slaveholders linked these two events, but the violence of the Nat Turner revolt horrified Garrison. "I deny the right of any people to *fight* for their liberty, and so far am a Quaker in principle." He sympathized with Turner's goal but not his means. This disapproval extended even to white antislavery activists. When Garrison learned that abolitionist publisher Owen Lovejoy had armed himself and his assistants, he was "shocked" and refused to grant Lovejoy (who was murdered by an antiabolitionist mob) status as a "Christian martyr."[76]

The Mexican War stimulated Garrison's pacifist leaning still more. Writing to a friend in 1846, he asserted that "no matter what may be the success of American arms, it cannot alter the criminality of the war. The more success, the more crime, and the more guilt. The more Mexicans slain, the more murders committed." From this perspective, consistent with his broader aim of more humane political and social relations, an unjust war could not be redeemed by victory or even good practice (though he did not believe the United States manifested much of that in Mexico). Garrison shared his pacifistic posture with the black abolitionist Frederick Douglass: "Such is my deep, firm conviction," Douglass wrote in 1846, "that nothing can be attained for liberty universally by war, that were I to be asked the question as to whether I would have my emancipation by the shedding of one single drop of blood, my answer would be in the negative." As late as 1858 Garrison was pleading with audiences to resist being seduced by violence. "I pray you, abolitionists," he lectured one Sunday morning, "still to adhere to the truth. Do not get impatient; do not become exasperated ... do not make yourselves familiar with the idea that blood must flow. Perhaps blood will flow—God knows, I do not: but it shall not flow through any counsel of mine."[77]

Other abolitionists were not so sanguine about the power of moral persuasion. African Americans, both enslaved and free, took direct action against slavery and counseled their white allies to do the same. H. Ford Douglas, a fugitive slave and activist, explained the necessity: "You must either free the slaves, or the slaves will free themselves. All history confirms this fact."[78] Garrison's opposition to direct action split the abolitionist movement in 1840. Under his leadership, the American Anti-Slavery Society continued to oppose any violent or forcible measures to achieve emancipation. The American and Foreign Anti-Slavery Society reflected the greater influence of black abolitionists and espoused a more vigorous opposition to slavery and the slave power.[79] Two decades of fruitless activism pushed many pacifists closer to those who counseled active resistance. Lydia Maria Child, a prominent writer and abolitionist, despaired after the violence in Kansas. She had "always dreaded civil war," but now concluded, "If there is no *other* alternative . . . I am resigned to its approach. In fact, I have become accustomed to the thought that it is inevitable."[80] This frustration culminated in the sympathetic response to John Brown's 1859 raid on Harpers Ferry. Abolitionists of all stripes lavished praise on Brown, especially after his execution, including Garrison, who urged "success to every slave insurrection at the South, and in every slave country."[81]

Nonetheless, when the war came, it confounded Garrison and his supporters. The goal for which they had fought for decades suddenly seemed accessible only by abandoning the moral posture they had cultivated over those years. The change was wrenching. War would bring death not just to the guilty slaveholders but to the innocent as well. As a historian of abolitionists explained, in order to abandon pacifism, they had to "conceive of the war as a national judgment, an act of God, for which the guilt of the nation rather than the decision of any man was responsible."[82] The pages of Garrison's paper, *The Liberator*, analyzed the process of emancipation from every possible angle throughout the war. In 1861 and 1862, the paper republished reports from around the South regarding the slow deterioration of slavery and the rise of contraband camps. The editors paid particular attention to the legal dimensions of emancipation. They regularly reprinted John Quincy Adams's prophetic comments about the possibility of wartime emancipation: "when a country is invaded, and two hostile armies are set in martial array, the commanders of both armies have power to emancipate all the slaves in the invaded territory."[83] Made in a congressional speech in 1842, antislavery Northerners regarded Adams's opinion as a sacred text that proved the constitutionality of emancipation. Identifying wartime emancipation as legal as well as moral helped abolitionists support military action.[84]

Those abolitionists who had promoted more aggressive policies during the 1850s as slaveholders and the federal government reinforced the system of slavery in the United States were ready for a hard war, even one that punished Northerners until they too recanted for the sin of slavery. One Pennsylvania minister proclaimed that "'the North is not yet worthy of victory—not morally ready for it.' 'I pray that God may withhold his hand, that disaster on disaster may come upon us, until we are ready, nay anxious, to do the right.'" For Garrison himself, endorsing state-controlled violence on a mass scale required a moral compromise that he had long refused. But the possibility of ending slavery won him over. Garrison shifted from a position of "non-resistance" to support for the Union's new policy of emancipation. A scholar of abolition explains, "non-resistants like Garrison . . . always held that, if violence were ever justified, it was in the case of a slave rebellion, and in the decade before the war, many Garrisonians had already warmed to the idea that force directed at slavery or used in defense of democratic principles was sometimes legitimate." As Garrison's most recent biographer concludes, "Garrison would not sacrifice his voice for abolition at the culminating moment of struggle, even if that meant acceptance of the violent measures he had always deplored. . . . He held an antislavery war to be a stronger good than a proslavery peace."[85]

In making this shift, Garrison followed the lead of other abolitionists who had given up faith that slavery could be ended without violence. Thomas Wentworth Higginson, a fellow Massachusetts man, believed slavery would not go peacefully. "It is destined, as it began in blood, so to end." Radicalized during his confrontation with slavery in the 1850s, Higginson celebrated the opportunity to martial manly violence against the slave power. As one historian has recently observed, "the outbreak of war, which meant government-sanctioned violence against the South, cheered him." These radicals built a public case for the constitutionality and necessity of army-driven emancipation. David Child, an antislavery theorist, penned a series of articles published in the *Liberator* in the war's opening months. Child drew on both history and the laws of war to justify military emancipation. Although he did not draw on a deep well of legal knowledge, Child's articles pioneered an abolitionist confidence in military action. This confidence in war as an engine of social change culminated in the Thirteenth Amendment, which George Julian, an abolitionist congressman, celebrated as the "glorious fruit of war."[86]

"Much as they had done before the war," one historian notes, "in advocating a higher law than the Constitution—and advocating for the spirit rather than the letter of the biblical statements concerning slavery—they favored an expansive interpretation of the fundamental law and the powers of Congress."[87] During that prewar debate over slavery, radicals had been criticized for ignoring the law altogether. William Seward, for one, failed to receive the Republican nomination for president in 1860 in part because of the radicalism of his "higher law" speech, which encouraged supporters to respect a "law higher than the constitution," meaning the Bible. Those same conservatives who had condemned Seward denounced abolitionists' wartime plans as "liberty run mad."[88] But during the conflict, abolitionists happily found that the international law of war buttressed their advocacy for emancipation.[89] Domestic law, to that point in the war, gave them no support. The willingness of Garrison and other radicals to lean on legal standards at all represented a shift away from their profound antiestablishment tradition. "Our Northern people, who had got to be so tender-hearted that could not hang a villain for the worst of crimes now talk familiarly of hanging and bloodshed," one skeptic noted.[90]

Debating War

Abolitionists' new attitudes emerged from the robust wartime debate among radicals, moderates, and conservatives in the North. The opinions and behavior of Northern governors offer one way to track this national conversation.[91] Although usually considered among the elite, governors operated closer to regular people than national politicians. They commanded militia forces and so invested themselves in enlistment and military affairs. And because they were prominent political leaders, they helped steer public opinion. The divisions among them reveal the wider rifts in the Northern public. Massachusetts governor John Albion Andrew embodied the willingness of radicals to sanction violence.[92] Andrew began the war as the most radical governor in the North. He seems to have moved easily from a posture of nonviolent abolitionism to hard war, making the switch from the New Testament to the Old, from honoring Christ to Joshua.[93] Long an abolitionist, Andrew recognized early in the war that his control over Massachusetts forces gave him a way to finally act against slavery. In December 1861, angry after learning that Massachusetts soldiers participated in the "dirty and despotic work" of returning runaway slaves in Maryland, he prohibited the practice for units under his command.[94] Predictably, Andrew's interference with military operations riled General George McClellan, commanding the Maryland men, who asserted that once the troops were inducted into national service the governor had no authority over them.[95] Andrew no doubt knew this, but his opposition to slavery overrode his concern with the nuances of federal-state authority.

Within a month of Fort Sumter, in fact, Andrew had already pushed far ahead of the Lincoln administration on what became one of the most controversial Union policies of the war. In May 1861, Andrew had publicly advocated arming southern blacks—in one proposal a force of forty thousand to be recruited from eastern Virginia.[96] Lincoln was still organizing Northern troops at this point, and there were no provisions for enlisting free black men from the North let alone enslaved men in the Old Dominion. Undeterred, Andrew looked for other ways to achieve the same end. When a Massachusetts general sent to Maryland to help suppress secessionist mob violence proposed offering troops to the Old Line State to suppress slave insurrections, Andrew rebuked him: "I think that the matter of servile insurrection among a community in arms against the Federal Union is no longer to be regarded by our troops in a political, but solely from a military point of view, and is to be contemplated as one of the inherent weaknesses of the enemy." "We are under no obligation," Andrew wrote, "to guard them in order that they may be enabled to . . . prosecute with more energy their traitorous attacks upon the Federal Government and Capital."[97] Andrew asserted that in a state of war, the North had no responsibility to protect enemy civilians from the harm caused by war.

The general chastised by Andrew was Benjamin Butler. His response to Andrew revealed the tension among white Northerners over the way the war should be fought. He asked what Andrew would advise "in a *moral* and *Christian* as in both a *political* and *military* point of view." "I appreciate fully the force of your Excellency's suggestion as to the inherent weakness of the rebels arising from the preponderant servile population.

This question then is, in what manner shall we take advantage of that weakness? By allowing, and of course arming, that population to rise upon the defenseless women and children of the country, carrying rapine, arson, and murder, all the horrors of San Domingo a million times more magnified, among those whom we hope to reunite with us as brethren[?]" Even at this early date in the war, Butler offered a perceptive observation about the nature of the conflict. "Would your Excellency advise the troops under my command to make war in person upon the defenseless women and children of any part of the Union," he asked Andrew, "accompanied by brutalities too horrible to be named? You will say, God forbid. If we may not do so in person, shall we allow others to do so over whom we can have no restraint and exercise no control?" Butler effectively juxtaposed the obvious military gain with the moral duty. "Could we justify ourselves to ourselves, although with arms amid the savage wildness of camp and field we may have blunted many of the finer moral sensibilities, in letting loose four millions of worse than savages upon the homes and hearths of the South?"[98] Andrew's exchange with Butler marked out rival Northern positions about acceptable modes of warfare.

As the war proceeded, Andrew remained a vigorous proponent of emancipation and also of hard war. In 1862, he wrote to Secretary of State Edwin Stanton advocating harsh measures, again well before the Lincoln administration or most Northerners adopted such tactics. "If our people feel that they are going into the South to help fight rebels who will kill and destroy *them* by all the means known to savages as well as civilized man; will deceive them by fraudulent flags of truce and lying pretenses (as they did the Massachusetts boys at Williamsburg); will use their negro slaves against them as laborers and as fighting men, while they themselves must never fire at the enemy's magazine, I think they will feel that the draft is heavy on their patriotism."[99] This phrase—to "fire at the enemy's magazines"—metaphorically called for hard war before such a change was commonplace in the North. It signaled what conservatives regarded as a reckless if not desperate will to wage unrestrained warfare against an enemy that deserved (according to conservatives) mercy not vengeance.

Other radicals, like Senator Zachariah Chandler of Michigan, believed that "without a little bloodletting, this Union would not be worth a rush." Chandler tracked the same course as Andrew. The radical leaders in

Congress, including Chandler, exercised unusual influence because of their position on the Joint Committee on the Conduct of the War, a bicameral investigative body that they used to critique what they viewed as the slow and incompetent policies of the Lincoln administration. Because the committee possessed subpoena power, it could and did recall generals from the field to interrogate them. The victims of these proceedings were almost always Democrats who, among their military problems, failed to pursue emancipation with vigor. The Joint Committee took these men to task. The closest student of the Joint Committee concludes that radicals like Benjamin Wade, George Julian, and Chandler "felt instinctively that only harsh measures such as confiscation, the arming of black troops, and emancipation would crush southern society." Julian himself conjured apocalyptic visions: "if I had the command of armies," he told an audience in 1863, "I would chastise these rebels as they deserve. I would batter down their cities; I would lay waste their plantations. I would free and arm the negroes; I would write desolation and death on the very soil; and if I had the power, I would paint hell on the very sky that bends over the rebel states, so that all the world might see what it costs to conspire against such a government as this."[100]

Arrayed against Julian, Andrew, Garrison, and other radicals were a host of moderate and conservative Northerners who envisioned a different purpose to the war and, consequently, a different method of how the North should fight it. Conservatives wanted only reunion, not emancipation, which required a restrained conflict. They articulated their position by celebrating their own ideological consistency: they wanted to restrain the power of the state, whether in peace or war. This was the zealotry of the recent convert. In previous wars, (the Seminole Indian Wars of the 1830s and Mexico in 1846) and subsequent ones (the Plains Indian Wars of the 1870s and 1880s), conservatives expressed little concern about atrocities committed by American troops. Where they had been consistent was in opposing federal action against slavery. By 1860, the Republican Party won a majority of Northern votes by opposing the expansion of slavery, but most moderates and conservatives in the region believed the federal government could not regulate or abolish slavery where it existed. This attitude manifested most clearly in the passage of the first version of the Thirteenth Amendment in 1861, which prohibited the passage of any constitutional amendment "which will authorize or give to Congress the power to abolish or interfere" with slavery in those states where it existed.[101] The willingness of Northern congressmen and senators, including Abraham Lincoln, to support this measure—the polar opposite of the Thirteenth Amendment actually incorporated into the Constitution in 1865, which abolished slavery—reveals the divisions in the Northern public at the war's start.

Samuel J. Kirkwood, the Republican governor of Iowa, represented a midwestern strain of the moderate position. From the beginning of the conflict, Kirkwood sought to bring Republicans and Democrats together around loyalty to the Union, preferring to sideline the issue of slavery in order to promote political harmony. In his inaugural address of January 14, 1862, Kirkwood made plain the hierarchy of Northern goals. Anticipating Lincoln's famous response to Horace Greeley later the same year, Kirkwood proclaimed, "This war is waged by our government for the preservation of the Union, and not for the extinction of slavery, unless the preservation of the one shall require the extinction of the other." Kirkwood eventually came to support emancipation, though he explained this in more limited and functional terms than Andrew of Massachusetts. To midwestern critics of Lincoln's policy, Kirkwood explained, "The President gets the power under the Constitution to take their negroes, just where he got the power to take Vicksburg." Morality was not involved. Like other moderates, Kirkwood evolved into a supporter of using black soldiers but only well into the war and after the policy of conciliation he initially supported had failed.[102]

Pennsylvania's Andrew Curtin, another moderate Republican, regarded the possibility of arming black men for the Union as tantamount to violating the laws of war. The son of an iron furnace operator and himself a successful industrialist, Curtin came to the Republican Party by way of free labor and economic uplift. Although hostile to slavery, Curtin approached the problem, like Abraham Lincoln, within the narrow confines of American constitutional law. An aide recalled an interview the governor had a few days after the war began with an agent supposedly sent by Governor Andrew, who hoped to obtain safe passage for one of John Brown's sons to move through Pennsylvania into Virginia "for the purpose of causing an uprising of slaves against their masters." According to the aide, "as the horrors of a servile insurrection, in which innocent women and children would be the chief victims, loomed up before him, Curtin seemed paralyzed for a moment at the cold-blooded proposition. Then, recovering himself, his frame quivering with majestic anger, his tones surcharged with indignation, he dismissed the agent, saying, 'No! I will not permit John Brown's sons to pass through Pennsylvania for such a purpose, but I will use the whole power of this commonwealth to prevent his doing so. Go! Tell those who sent you here that so far as I am concerned this war will be conducted by civilized methods.'"[103] Although this account is almost certainly exaggerated to make Andrew look worse and Curtin better, it reflects the wide divergence in Northern attitudes about the purpose and practice of war. Pennsylvania later enlisted a sizeable share of US Colored Troops, but Curtin's initial attitude—that "the war will be conducted by civilized methods"—reflected the belief among white Northerners that in order to adhere to the laws of war, it must be fought by white men. Whereas Andrew began the war galloping past such restraints, Kirkwood, Curtin, and probably a majority of white Northerners cautiously approached these limits.

By the end of the Civil War, Governors Kirkwood and Curtin had moved much closer to the position occupied by Governor Andrew at its start. The North never endorsed all the measures advocated by the Massachusetts radical—few fired on the enemy's magazines and enslaved people were not indiscriminately armed and urged to revolt. But the war's duration and intensity propelled Northerners to sanction an increasingly violent and deadly war. The story of how moderates and conservatives found themselves adopting radical positions under the pressures of war and came to endorse both uncompensated emancipation and a hard war against Southern civilians has been told well by others. One of the less noticed aspects of this transition was that no clear line from prewar ideological orientations to military practice existed. The prewar radicals most infused with the humanitarian sensibilities of the age advocated the most vigorous measures while conservatives who had sanctioned such measures in Mexico and elsewhere urged policies of restraint.

Even more than Curtin and the moderates, Democrats and Northern conservatives opposed the evolving nature of the Northern war effort in 1862. Moderate white Northerners resisted the shift of opinion on the topic of military confiscation and, especially, emancipation because of a deep-rooted belief in the inviolability of private property. If Southerners remained Americans, as Lincoln claimed, what right had the Union to take or destroy their property?[104] More worrisome than even the policy changes was the rhetoric that radicals used to inspire the cause. One antiabolitionist complained about the rhetoric issuing from churches across the North. The results of such recklessness were plain to be seen: "desolated homesteads and impoverished communities attest our capacities for destruction, awhile the cry of the widow and the fatherless call of God for that vengeance which sooner or later is visited on all iniquity. Whole States are converted into charnel houses." For conservatives, the outcomes were bad enough, but the process reflected something even more sinister. The conservative critique of abolitionist war-making assailed Northern reformers for adopting God's authority to change the world. The true sin, according to one traditionalist, was "their zeal to do what God has reserved for Himself, and vainly think to inaugurate a millennium of bliss, by their imaginary reign of liberty and equality."[105]

Edward Bates, Lincoln's conservative attorney general, observed the secular analog to this process: "surely Cicero was right when he said that 'in every Civil war, Success is dangerous, because it is sure to beget arrogance and a disregard of the *laws of Government.*'" "These men, flattered with a little success, have opened up to themselves a boundless source of power. When the constitution fails them, they have only to say 'this is a time of war—and war gives all needed powers!' I am afraid that this Congress is becoming perfectly Radical and revolutionary." As the social conservative Henry Ward Beecher intoned from the pulpit, "revolution is not the remedy for rebellion."[106]

For much of the twentieth century Americans have used the parlance of hawks and doves to identify those eager to use military force to resolve problems and those reluctant to do so. The ideological and partisan alignment that developed after World War II cemented popular impressions that conservatives are hawks and liberals are doves. Even more, the impression has taken root in popular politics that conservatives are quick to defend our own military from excesses and accusations of atrocity while liberals are quick to judge and blame. In terms of the global laws of war, the common assumption today is that conservatives deny that the laws of war apply to the United States while liberals regard them as an essential framework for bolstering the American image abroad. If these generalizations are true now (and this quick sketch may conceal more than it reveals), it certainly was not the case in the nineteenth century. We cannot draw a clear connection between peacetime political ideologies or partisan affiliations and what kind of respect people will pay to the rules of just war in armed conflicts. What the US Civil War teaches us is that beliefs about what a war should accomplish determine peoples' attitudes about how their army can behave. Those who wanted a revolutionary experience (with emancipation) advocated a harder and less restrained war. Those with narrow political goals (reunion) wanted a softer affair. Much as we might like to believe that the American political tradition, broadly conceived, has always worked in synchrony with the traditions of just war, the political gyrations of the war's participants suggest that a commitment to restrained and just war follows rather than precedes the ultimate purpose of a conflict.

The Millennium Had Come

The fight among Northerners about how to fight a just war assumed new salience in December 1862 when urban warfare returned to the Civil War. The Battle of Fredericksburg, Virginia involved five aspects that prompted observers and participants on both sides to rethink how they understood what was morally permissible in war: an artillery bombardment of a city; soldiers battling through streets and private houses; widespread looting; civilian exile and suffering; and an unbalanced and horrific death toll. In most Civil War narratives, Fredericksburg plays a clear role. It was an overwhelming victory for the Confederates, which demoralized the Union's Army of the Potomac and undermined the Lincoln administration. For military historians, Fredericksburg offers a grim example of the futility of massed charges in the mid-nineteenth century. Waves of Union soldiers threw themselves against the Confederate line on Marye's Heights to no avail. These interpretations of the battle offer important insight into the political and military consequences of December 12, but the experience shaped the war in other ways as well.

Union Major General Ambrose Burnside's men reached the northern bank of the Rappahannock River in late November but found themselves unable to cross the river because of the presence of Confederate snipers in public and private buildings along the river. Union Major General Edwin Sumner, commanding the army's "Right Grand Division," responded under the laws of war. He informed Fredericksburg's mayor that if the city was not surrendered, he would begin shelling it. Sumner justified his actions under the following conditions: "that under the cover of your city, shots have been fired upon the troops of my command. Your mills and manufactories are furnishing provisions and the material for clothing for armed bodies in rebellion against the Government of the United States. Your railroads and other means of transportation are removing supplies to the depots of such troops."[107] The mayor delayed as long as he could while conferring with Robert E. Lee, whose men entrenched along Marye's Heights on the southern part of the town. Sumner let his deadline slip, but Lee started evacuating the women and children even as he fortified his position.[108] Sumner and Thomas Slaughter (the aptly named mayor of Fredericksburg) negotiated away the prospect of an artillery bombardment of a town occupied by civilians, but Confederates would later regard Sumner's threat as a reliable description of the event.

In reality, neither Union troops nor artillery shells crossed the river for weeks. Late on the night of December 10, Union engineers began assembling pontoon bridges over the Rappahannock, but once the morning fog lifted, Confederate sharpshooters opened fire. They killed and wounded several Union engineers working on the bridges. The battle's best chronicler explains the logic: "although an eventual Federal bridgehead could not be prevented, [Confederate Major General] McLaws intended to make it as costly as possible."[109] Frustrated by what he regarded as a violation of the earlier agreement with Mayor Slaughter that the town's buildings would not harbor snipers, "Burnside finally ordered his artillery chief, Brig. Gen. Henry J. Hunt, to 'bring all your guns to bear upon the city and batter it down.'"[110] Although this failed to dislodge the sharpshooters, the effect on the town was considerable: "After two hours of intense artillery fire, entire blocks lay in ruins with only walls standing as stark reminders of what had once been homes or businesses . . .

the town had been knocked to pieces."[111] Hunt commanded 150 cannons, a firepower that compelled more than one soldier to adopt apocalyptic rhetoric to characterize what he saw. Sergeant Summerhayes of the Twentieth Massachusetts observed that "[O]ur batteries on the banks opened fire throwing into the devoted city perfect showers of shell and solid shot, and the din of the exploding shell, and the reports of one hundred and thirty pieces of artillery, together with the crashing of the shot through the empty houses, and the falling of the walls of houses partially burnt, caused one to imagine the millennium had come."[112] Some Union men felt conflicted. As one man cautiously explained, "there are many things connected with this war that seem hard for an enlightened and Christianized nation such as we claim to be."[113]

The failure of the bombardment compelled a new tactic. The Seventh Michigan Infantry rowed themselves across the river and provided a breach for subsequent Union units to tackle the Confederate snipers in person. Many of the Confederates (mostly Mississippians from William Barksdale's brigade) occupied private homes and warehouses along the river. In the ensuing clash, they fought not as a unit but as individuals, and this irregular position spurred a violent and excessive Union response. Other Confederate units fought in a more organized fashion, and although no one on either side had been trained in urban warfare, Confederates used the tight streets and obscured lines of sight in the city's downtown grid to exact maximum casualties from the Union before retreating back to Lee's lines. Lee had never expected Barksdale to hold the abandoned town. The additional time did not affect how he organized his troops or how they entrenched. From the view of many Union soldiers, the fighting in the streets was pointless and unjust.[114]

As darkness settled, Union soldiers released their anger and frustration on the empty buildings around them. According to the definitive history of the battle, Northern "soldiers looted with an awesome, frightening alacrity and thoroughness." They attacked public facilities, businesses, and private homes indiscriminately, piling furniture and other belongings in the street for easier access or simple destruction. Another historian categorized the various motives: "greed, hunger, demoralization, and the refusal of most officers to impose discipline," but also "revenge." Herbert Mason, another officer in the Twentieth Massachusetts, which had experienced the street fighting, wrote his father that "as we had been fired upon by the enemy's sharpshooters enclosed in the houses . . . no guards were placed over the latter." Even avowedly upper-class Northern officers relished the opportunity to seize goods from homes. All this unfolded in a weirdly festive atmosphere as Union soldiers cooked food stolen from Fredericksburg kitchens among the dead bodies of their enemies and comrades.[115]

Few Fredericksburg residents witnessed the violence and destruction war wrought on their homes. Most civilians evacuated the town in early December, but news of the looting traveled quickly through the mass of refugees who wandered south across Spotsylvania and Caroline counties. These noncombatants, mostly women and children, faced serious hardship in the bitter cold of December.[116] When reports reached them that the goods they carried might be all they now owned, their despair only deepened. The wealthiest had moved by train or carriage south to Richmond and competed for housing in the overcrowded market. It was their pianos and libraries that went to the torch or axe.

After this depressing and unexpected sequence of violence, destruction, and exile, the Battle of Fredericksburg itself appears in retrospect almost anticlimactic. On December 12, 1862, Union General Ambrose Burnside ordered a simultaneous advance along the whole Confederate front. He concentrated too much manpower in a broad plain leading uphill toward a low stone wall behind which Confederate infantry lay, supported by ranks of artillery. Wave after wave of Union blue approached but never reached the wall. The Union lost 12,000 men at Fredericksburg and gained nothing. The futility of the Union assault and the brutal efficiency with which it was suppressed by Lee led many people on both sides to regard the battle as little more than murder. But who was responsible for the act? Henry Livermore Abbott, a Massachusetts officer whose unit experienced the worst of the fighting and lost nearly half their regiment, blamed his own command. "I firmly believe," Abbott told his sister, "that as the rebel Gen. Lee told us, the men who ordered the crossing of the river are responsible to God for murder. I believe that Alley was just as much murdered as if he had been deliberately thrown into the river with a stone tied around his neck." Few Federals blamed Lee, perhaps because they would have responded the same way if Union troops occupied the high ground (as they would at Gettysburg a few months later). But Lee himself offered, perhaps apocryphally, a strange benediction on the battle. An aide recalled him telling James Longstreet as they witnessed the stunning repulse of Union soldiers, "It is well this is so terrible! We should grow too fond of it!" This ambiguous comment suggests that the brutal violence of conflict, and Fredericksburg's unequal killing in particular, could dampen the romantic enthusiasm for war that manifests in nations and their people.[117]

Fredericksburg was one of those events that broke through the local framework within which most people interpreted the conflict. Stories of the violence there—against engineers, against civilians, against private homes, and against soldiers—circulated widely in Northern and Southern newspapers. Their Civil War became *the* Civil War. But these stories retained a strongly sectional cast. For white Southerners, Fredericksburg functioned as a kind of talisman, demonstrating the depravity of the Yankees, the victimhood of Confederate civilians, and the bravery and competence of Confederate soldiers. Despite a civilian mortality toll of four people, rumors of more civilian deaths "reaffirmed deeply held convictions about Yankee barbarism," writes one historian. Confederates read the evacuation of civilians from Fredericksburg as the result of Yankee savagery and condemned the looting in historical (sometime hysterical) terms: "'a monument to the barbarity of the abolitionists,' fumed a young staff officer," in what emerged as a typical reading of Yankee behavior. Comparisons to Goths, Huns, "Bedouin Arabs," and other savage people followed in close succession, reflecting the Southern belief that Northern soldiers fought without regard for the rules entertained by civilized people. In later discussions of this event, Confederates blended property destruction and civilian suffering and confused the issue of responsibility.[118]

Federals, in contrast, knew who to blame: Lee, who chose to fight at Fredericksburg. Just as in a siege, his decision to fight in a town imposed unnecessary hardships on the civilians there. Lee could have set up a defensive line along the North Anna River (as he would in spring 1864) and allow the town to be occupied. This would have entailed a strategic concession, a worse defensive position from which to fight, and would have exposed Confederate civilians to Union occupation, but that experience would have been much less disruptive to Confederate noncombatants. Lee lamented the fate of Fredericksburg's civilians, but he never blamed their condition on the US Army because he knew their plight resulted from his military decision. In his correspondence with Confederate officials during the week and in his after-battle report, Lee commented on the destruction of private homes but never condemned the artillery bombardment or subsequent attack that spurred the exodus. Many Northerners, both soldiers and civilians, regretted and criticized the looting of the town, but they also found ways to explain it. As one historian notes, "for those soldiers from godly homes whose families worried about the effects of army life on their moral character, a spirit of righteous vengeance might cover the proverbial multitude of sins."[119]

More menacing still, perhaps, was how much death the North would accept in order to rebuild the nation. After the terrible Union loss at Fredericksburg, Abraham Lincoln observed that "if the same battle were to be fought over again, every day, through a week of days, with the same relative results, the army under Lee would be wiped out to its last man, the Army of the Potomac would still be a mighty host, the war would be over, the war would be won at a smaller cost of life than it will if the week of lost battles must be dragged out through yet another of camps and marches, and of deaths in hospitals rather than upon the field." According to one of his secretaries, Lincoln recognized the truth of this "awful arithmetic" but could not find a general willing to fight hard enough to make it happen.[120] As Lincoln feared, a prolonged war with a seasonal fighting schedule had exposed soldiers to the dangers of disease. But even this, Northern civilians sanctioned. Two years later, the armies returned to the Rappahannock and inflicted even worse casualties on each other. The people of both sections accepted the losses at Fredericksburg—whether combatants or noncombatants—and it was this popular support that produced such a bloody conflict.

[4]

Kindling the Fires of Liberty

Despite all the ill will generated by battles like Fredericksburg, emancipation generated the widest ethical gulf between the Union and the Confederacy during the war. The action that embodied a great moral virtue for the North was viewed by white Southerners as the greatest immoral act of the war. As a result, black civilians (both enslaved and free) and black soldiers were subject to unjust violence by Confederates. Lincoln threatened retaliation and forced Confederates to treat black soldiers more (though not entirely) like white ones. The disagreement about the legitimacy of black soldiers destroyed the prisoner exchange agreement that prevailed in the war's first years. As a result, prisoner-of-war populations skyrocketed, ending the lives of thousands of prisoners on both sides. In sum, white Southerners' defense of slavery and white Northerners' gradual turn against it escalated the stakes and the nature of the conflict.[1]

Because emancipation made the war more violent, historians have overlooked the degree to which it could have stimulated an even worse turn. The end of slavery held the potential to multiply the war's death toll many times over. But this was a path not taken. The half a million enslaved people who fled their bondage rarely stopped to harm their former masters or other whites. Unlike the nightmare scenarios envisioned by Southern whites, few plantations were burned and few families murdered in their beds. Instead, the violence accompanying emancipation most often turned against black Americans. The measured response of enslaved people to emancipation and war diminished the conflict's potential violence, but by pursuing freedom and supporting the Union, black Southerners drove white Southerners into a vengeful frenzy. The latter perceived every action of the former as betrayal and responded with a vindictiveness rarely seen in American wars.

Historians who explain the Civil War's bloodshed usually focus on the animus that white Americans felt for each other.[2] In this telling, arguments over slavery generated sectional antagonisms and secession generated outrage, but it was the war itself and its escalating death toll that drove soldiers to regard each other as mortal enemies. There is considerable truth in such a framing. But by excluding slavery from this story, we misunderstand and oversimplify the war's violence. Because of its centrality to the war's origins and because slavery was so deeply intertwined with all aspects of Southern life, challenges to it shaped nearly every aspect of the war.

The story of wartime emancipation is much better understood today than thirty years ago.[3] Historians now write about the *process* of emancipation, which improves on the older interpretation that saw emancipation as an *act*—instantaneous, irrevocable, and definitive. *Process*, however, conveys a uniformity and coherence that freedpeople in the wartime South never experienced. Like other wartime policies—toward guerrillas, occupation, and prisoners—the US Army's movement against slavery developed unevenly in different places and at different times. Emancipation proceeded in fits and starts, sometimes accelerating, sometimes braking, and sometimes reversing course or swerving unpredictably. There were few linear routes to full freedom. For at least three men, freedom came in May 1861, when they surrendered themselves to Benjamin Butler on the peninsula below Richmond. Thousands of enslaved people transformed themselves into "contraband" over the coming year, claiming a quasi-freedom under the protection of sometimes friendly and sometimes hostile Union commanders. Even as conservative Union officers returned runaway slaves to Southern masters, generals in Louisiana, Kansas, and South Carolina recruited black soldiers in late 1862, sometimes within contraband camps and other times through raids into the Confederate interior. The Union's support for emancipation accelerated with the Second Confiscation Act, passed by Congress in August 1862, which made the slaves of all Rebels subject to seizure and emancipation by Union troops. The Emancipation Proclamation, signed by Lincoln on January 1, 1863, formalized the Union's commitment to ending slavery and provided for the recruitment of black soldiers into Northern armies. The use of black troops on battlefields after mid-1863 and their presence as prisoners of war in late 1863 and 1864 marked a new phase in the conflict. The sequence sketched here suggests a consistency that the war's participants could rarely see. Instead, the contingency and uncertainty of emancipation created more insecurity for all.

Emancipation and Its Consequences

Emancipation confounds the very language that historians must use to describe it. I can write that enslaved people *freed* themselves, or I can write that they *were freed* by the US Army. Both descriptions are grammatically and historically correct, but they do not carry the same moral weight. The historiography and public memory of slavery in the United States makes any analysis of it fraught. Generations of slaveholders and historians regarded African Americans as subjects of history, not actors. This line of thinking can be seen whenever enslaved people resisted their bondage— whether in 1739 at Stono, South Carolina, in 1831 in Southampton County, Virginia, or during the Civil War. In every case, white observers and historians attributed whatever initiative they perceived among enslaved people to outside agitators—the Spanish, abolitionists, and US Army officers in the examples above. White people understood that slaves could and did run away, but many Northerners and Southerners believed that organized rebellion required some external guiding hand. White Southerners regarded the process of emancipation as a strategy by which Northerners incited blacks to violence and encouraged them to do the dirty work of defeating the South. Enslaved African Americans regarded emancipation as a social and political act of liberation that also held military significance. White Northerners' perspective varied and changed as the war progressed.[4] Some reluctantly endorsed emancipation because they feared the idea of arming black men while others, especially abolitionists, supported both emancipation and black enlistment because it promised to anchor postwar claims to black citizenship.

Waging Insurrection

In his book on war and violence in the post-9/11 world, John Sifton writes that "it seemed like the world was straining under the assaults of linguistic perfidy. It was an era of loose language. Words acted as subtle buckshot fired in formulaic blasts."[5] In the early twenty-first century, words like democracy, freedom, and terror became slippery and difficult to define. Civil War Americans must have felt something similar. The contradictions in the ideas that served as central anchors in their self- and national definitions were suddenly visible. Did freedom guarantee the right to be free or the right to enslave others? Did self-government enable participants to end that government? Insurrection, not a word that we use much today, was one of the loose concepts that drew Civil War Americans into the densest problems of their era.

What was an insurrection? Americans of all stripes used the word to characterize the behavior of people during the Civil War, but their varying definitions did more to confuse the conflict than to clarify it. Most people distinguished mob violence, which could concern domestic politics, diplomacy, or cultural anxieties, from insurrections.[6] The latter term usually designated violent resistance to slavery, and it produced most of the deaths from public violence—nearly 400 people in the decades before the war (about 80 percent of whom were enslaved people).[7] Abraham Lincoln used the word continuously, most often in the phrase "the present insurrection." He conceptualized the refusal of white Southerners to recognize national authority as an insurrection.[8] This legal framing leaned on Article I, Section 8 of the US Constitution, where Congress is granted the authority to raise the militia in order to "suppress insurrections." It moves practitioners of insurrection into a dangerous position where they may be legitimately subjected to military force in order to compel their obedience to the laws.

White Southerners defined insurrection differently. They used the word to describe the refusal of enslaved people to follow their commands. In their hands the word indicated not a violation of the law but of the will of a master. "The negroes were in a state of insurrection, some of them refusing to work," complained a Louisiana planter in 1862. On other occasions, white Southerners used the word to describe violent resistance by enslaved people to their state of bondage. Historians of antebellum slave rebellions describe these as the most serious threat to the Southern social order that its white residents could imagine. Death was the only possible response. In either case, white Southerners believed that insurrectionaries merited swift and brutal treatment to restore them to obedience. Insurrectionaries abounded in the Civil War. Like the fight to claim justice in war, this debate over a word drew participants' attention to the widely varying intentions of people in the conflict and to its stakes. Who were the real insurrectionaries of the Civil War?[9]

The Momentum of Emancipation

The actual movement of enslaved people to freedom during the war proceeded largely independent of the sometimes arcane debate among white Americans over how to describe and understand the process (as it had in the antebellum decades). Freedpeople themselves left few written records that capture their perspective on the historic change they wrought. Instead, what we retain is evidence of their behavior, much of it gleaned from military records, governmental reports, or the passing observations of soldiers and civilians. Historians have mined these sources to creatively reconstruct the process of emancipation at the grass-roots level. Above all, escaping slaves sought to "kindle the fires of liberty," in the words of a black abolitionist. We know that freedom required the US Army, which meant that the process developed unevenly across the South and over time. Enslaved people saw freedom in its shadow, even though reaching Union lines sometimes meant being returned to their masters or being exploited by white Northerners instead of Southerners. The process started along the coasts—Atlantic and Gulf—as the Union navy captured islands and ports in late 1861 and early 1862 and followed the path blazed by Union forces as they followed rivers into the Southern heartland.[10]

Running to the Union lines presented grave risks. All the physical dangers and hurdles that obstructed escape before the war remained in place. The high enlistment rate in Confederate forces reduced the manpower available for local defense of slavery, but Confederate armies functioned as giant slave patrols. Regardless, runaways kept coming because they saw promise in the Union's antagonism toward their owners. And they knew that if the US Army enabled freedom, the Confederate army enabled only more slavery. When Lee's army marched north into Maryland in 1862, it seized runaways escaped from Virginia and Pennsylvania's free people of color without distinction.[11] In other southern places, the rebel army ruthlessly enforced the laws of slavery, seizing, punishing, and returning enslaved people who sought their freedom.[12]

When the war began, Union commanders (largely Regular Army Democrats) protected slavery and returned runaways because they were defending the state of the Union as it existed in 1861. As Irvin McDowell's army marched toward Manassas in July 1861, Northern soldiers violated his orders to protect civilian property at their own risk. McDowell arrested several volunteers. Charles Stone, another Democratic general, rebuked his soldiers for encouraging "insubordination" among Maryland slaves by explicitly comparing secession with slaves' disobedience. "The immediate object of raising and supporting this army was the suppression of rebellion," Stone lectured, "and the putting down by military power of those ambitious and misguided people, who (unwilling to subject themselves to the constitution and laws of the country) preferred the carrying out of their own ideas of right and wrong." George McClellan, who assumed command in the fall of 1861, policed his army's interactions with civilians with even greater vigilance. He feared that accepting slaves within Union lines would alienate white Southerners and demanded that his subordinates return them to masters who tracked them to Northern camps.[13]

The pressures of war made this position increasingly untenable in 1862. Even McClellan's corps commanders sometimes failed to mimic his zealotry on this issue. The clearest example of how emancipation overwhelmed the US Army despite the policies intended to fortify it against freedpeople's claims occurred on the peninsula below Richmond in mid-1862. McClellan used the navy to ferry Union troops to Fort Monroe, at the peninsula's tip. They arrived in April and marched toward the Confederate capital. As the Confederate army retreated, Major General John Magruder impressed 1,300 slaves to build fortifications intended to obstruct the Union advance. This first self-inflicted blow initiated the collapse of slavery in the region. Masters objected to impressment, particularly as enslaved people seized chances to escape to Northern lines. As Union soldiers moved through the area, slavery deteriorated still more. Prince de Joinville, a Frenchman traveling with McClellan's army, observed that as the Union advanced up the peninsula, enslaved people "decamped in the direction of Fortress Monroe . . . that is to say, of freedom, carrying their wives and children with them in small carts." The sheer volume of freedom seekers combined with the disruptive effect of 100,000 Union soldiers (two and a half times the population of Richmond itself) to generate chaos. This was not planned or even managed emancipation. Instead, it was the ad hoc process of war eroding slavery. By 1864, 31,654 freedpeople lived in contraband camps in the region south of the peninsula.[14]

The Peninsula Campaign presents the story of the concentrated collapse of slavery under the pressure of a giant US Army amid an active military campaign. In other regions, the process unfolded more slowly or unevenly, but everywhere the army went, it threatened slavery. Along the Sea Islands of South Carolina and Georgia, Confederates fled in late 1861, when the Union navy occupied Port Royal. With no real military struggle and few Confederates left to manage when Sea Island planters moved inland, the US Army imposed order on the autonomy of the new freedpeople. The Treasury Department sent agents who organized the freedpeople into teams of laborers on Union-controlled cotton plantations. Though no longer slaves, their lives were tightly circumscribed by the North's hunger for cotton and the Treasury's hope for a demonstration of the ennobling power of free labor. Farther north along the Atlantic coast, on Roanoke Island, another experiment in freedom yielded a similarly ambiguous conclusion. As in South Carolina, the Freedmen's Colony in North Carolina drew Northern missionaries, both black and white, who came to teach and uplift the freedpeople. The missionaries' naive blend of paternalism and sympathy yielded improved literacy, but the army's casual cruelty and relentless focus on exploiting freedpeoples' manpower left mixed results. In places where the US Army did not establish a permanent presence, the results were even worse. In southwest Georgia, which the US Army never really reached, slaveholders ignored the Emancipation Proclamation and escalated the customary violence of slavery to retain control. Even here, however, enslaved people took inspiration from the news reports and rumors to push against the system of slavery. The Northern congress tried to assert control over the process through the First and Second Confiscation Acts, but these acts failed to achieve any coherence over the US Army's practice on the ground.[15]

Regardless of where it happened, emancipation endangered enslaved people, freedom seekers, and Union and Confederate soldiers. Union officers tried to control the process, but they succeeded only to the extent that Lincoln claimed to have directed the course of the war—like a pole boat captain whose job is ensuring the raft avoids the banks and dangerous shoals but whose direction is determined by the river's current. Emancipation developed its own momentum, fueled by the desire among enslaved people for their freedom and the varied responses of Union and Confederate soldiers encountered on that torturous path. The outcomes were never certain or necessarily permanent, and they generated insecurity for the war's participants. A careful student of Missouri and Kentucky explains how emancipation in the contested borderland unleashed a still more fraught contest: "Beginning in the fall of 1863 . . . a brutal federal counterinsurgency raged in both states including the use of black troops and increased executions of guerrillas. Squads of militia, home guard, and federal cavalry, white and black, blanketed the countryside, burning the homes of known guerrillas and hunting down and executing all those found in arms."[16] Freedpeople experienced the worst of the physical violence generated by this process. Nonetheless, white Southerners perceived themselves the most imperiled, and they escalated the war's violence in response.

Because enslaved people knew well the capriciousness of their white neighbors, they anticipated this behavior. Some black Southerners achieved not absolute freedom or the destruction of the slave system (a goal that, however much desired, had seemed very remote during the antebellum period) but more autonomy. The length of work days contracted just a little, enslaved people seized opportunities for greater mobility to see spouses or children on nearby plantations, and masters exercised less oversight in the daily lives of their slaves. A historian of the region notes that small if significant changes were visible in 1863, once Union soldiers occupied New Bern and Beaufort, North Carolina. Black people "repudiat[ed] their slave heritage, blacks sought control over their own bodies, minds, and material conditions. They asserted their independence, validated their manhood/womanhood and self-sufficiency, and improved the educational and material conditions for themselves and their children." Some fled slavery altogether (tens of thousands in this region), but the majority remained in place. Despite the modest nature of these measures, white Southerners interpreted any change in slaves' status as a threat to the established order. As another historian comments, "lurking in the shadows of every white Southerner's mind was the figure of a murderous black insurrectionist, a specter as old as the South but now grown more palpable and frightening than ever as white power withered and blacks grew more obstreperous." Whatever white Southerners thought of the war's direction, Northerners knew that emancipation brought a harder war to the South, though they disavowed any punitive intent. Abolitionists could claim that the process of making freedom truly national was more a matter of restoring the natural order than enacting any real change. But outside of that small band of true believers, most white Northerners viewed slavery as the standing order in the South and the US Army's emancipatory offensive as a radical act.[17]

Lincoln and Emancipation

Abolitionists toiled for generations to end slavery, but slaveholders marshaled the power of the federal and state governments to protect the institution. The Civil War marked a turning point in the use of state power against slavery. How did Abraham Lincoln, one of those moderate Northerners who respected slavery as legal under American law (despite what legions of Confederate publicists warned), justify the shift to an emancipatory war? Lincoln was perhaps the most powerful rulemaker in the Civil War and one of the most adept at explaining his decisions. In 1864, Lincoln spoke in Baltimore, where he identified the lack of consensus about the meaning of "liberty" as one of the problems of the war. "With some the word liberty may mean for each man to do as he pleases with himself, and the product of his labor; while with others the same word may mean for some men to do as they please with other men, and the product of other men's labor." According to Lincoln, the conflict between these views caused the war. The previous year Lincoln adopted emancipation as Union policy, and this act spurred a new round of recriminations between North and South. Jefferson Davis and the Confederates accused Lincoln of trying to incite a servile insurrection, a clear violation of just war. Lincoln reversed the moral polarity, establishing the Union decision as both necessary and just. "The shepherd drives the wolf from the sheep's throat," he wrote, "for which the sheep thanks the shepherd as a *liberator*, while the wolf denounces him for the same act as the destroyer of liberty, especially as the sheep was a black one." Lincoln's language reflected the paternalistic position of most white Northerners—that he, as shepherd, could give freedom to enslaved people—but its obvious moral conclusion empowered his armies. Lincoln understood that the rhetorical high ground was as important to hold as the hills themselves.[18]

Lincoln's summary of the war—dividing the contestants into shepherds and wolves—reflected the competing claims that each side made for the justice of their cause. Northerners and Southerners believed that each had an exclusive claim to a just cause. In the case of the US Civil War, those claims revolved around competing visions of the meaning of freedom. Lincoln had long defined liberty as the right to earn a fair wage from one's own labor. He declared it strange "that any men should dare to ask a just God's assistance in wringing their bread from the sweat of other men's faces." The shepherd's job required ensuring that people were free to support themselves. Confederates countered with a vision of freedom that required slavery. Despite how contradictory this may seem to us today, freedom and slavery had been closely wed since the earliest days of English settlement in North America. Jefferson Davis drew on a long intellectual lineage when he argued that freedom for white people depended upon the enslavement of black people and that threatening slavery "endangered the liberty of white southerners." His vice president, Alexander Stephens, offered the most cogent defense of this position, asserting that black slavery formed the "cornerstone" of white liberty and the Confederacy. "This, our new government, is the first, in the history of the world, based upon this great physical, philosophical, and moral truth," Stephens declared.[19]

Lincoln's metaphorical language also obscured the agency of enslaved people during the war. By labeling them "sheep," Lincoln consigned them to a passive role in the conflict—needing to be protected by a benevolent shepherd. In fact, as Lincoln knew, black Southerners acted on their own initiative to escape slavery and, in the process, created the humanitarian and policy crisis that propelled him toward the Emancipation Proclamation. Enslaved men and women certainly did not act like sheep during the Civil War, but neither did they resort to wolflike behavior. Their single-minded focus on freedom rather than revenge proved one of the key factors that limited the violence of the conflict. White Southerners considered themselves shepherds for their wayward flock of black dependents, but they preyed on them like the wolves Lincoln described. Many black soldiers died unjust deaths at the hands of Confederate soldiers. More self-reliant than even Northern whites understood, blacks shepherded themselves out of slavery, into uniforms, and through battle with Confederates.

Explaining emancipation as just was critical to winning the rhetorical battles of the Civil War. Alongside occasional public addresses like the one in Baltimore, Lincoln offered more formal defenses of his policy of emancipation. In these explanations he obscured the raw necessity created by the hundreds of thousands of runaway slaves and focused instead on the policy's legal soundness. Anticipating the Confederate (and conservative Northern) counterargument that because slavery was controlled by state law the president had no power over it, Lincoln drew upon the global laws of war. Those same rules that curtailed the war's most egregious violence now sanctioned the most dramatic escalation of the conflict. According to Lincoln the war changed the context within which his actions should be interpreted. "You say [the Emancipation Proclamation] is unconstitutional," he stated. "I think differently. I think the constitution invests its commander-in-chief, with the law of war in time of war."[20] The particular element of the laws of war relevant to emancipation was that regarding property. Sounding like Benjamin Butler on the issue of "contraband," Lincoln offered a clear reading of the role of property in war: given that "slaves are property. Is there—has there ever been—any question that by the law of war, property, both of enemies and friends, may be taken when needed?"[21]

Various public figures had been formulating arguments on behalf of emancipation since the war's opening days. Frederick Douglass, the most gifted wordsmith of the group, inaugurated this effort in 1861, arguing "war for the destruction of liberty must be met with war for the destruction of slavery." By connecting a proposition with which most white

Northerners would have agreed—that secession threatened liberty—to emancipation, Douglass hoped to demonstrate the inevitability of emancipation. Other black abolitionists hoped to inspire in whites a sense of the justice of emancipation. As H. Ford Douglas, one of the few commissioned black officers in the Northern army, asserted "strong in resources . . . we are [illegible word] stronger in the righteousness of a just cause." In case readers were not persuaded, Douglas referred them to "those words of Shakespeare: That he is doubly armed who has his quarrel just."[22]

Opposed to the abolitionists were a substantial body of white Northerners who hesitated to endorse emancipation because they feared that violence would ensue. Conservatives denounced what they believed was an irresponsible act on its own terms and the bloody insurrection it would inevitably yield. One Northern minister wondered "if [slaves] take their liberty violently, can they afterward live there peaceably? Suppose we aid them in a servile insurrection and succeed, vast numbers of both masters and slaves must be slaughtered. Can we afterward make the bloody remnants of the two parties settle down happily and profitably together? Such a scheme is the wildest dream." Even Salmon Chase, Lincoln's Treasury secretary and the most radical member of the cabinet, feared that the proclamation would lead to "depredation and massacre." Lincoln faced opposition within his administration, from lawyers who believed that whatever the justice of the Union cause, emancipation itself constituted an unjust act.[23]

The same was true abroad. Just after Lincoln issued the proclamation, a leading Scottish paper proclaimed that "the Federals in desperation have invoked to their aid the unutterable horrors of a servile war." They "seek to paralyse the victorious armies of the South by letting loose upon their hearts and homes the lust and savagery of four million negroes. The die is cast. Henceforth it is a war of extermination. The North seeks to make of the South a desert—a wilderness of bloodshed and misery."[24] Secretary Chase and most Britons opposed slavery and supported its abolition but feared that emancipation as a war policy would precipitate a more violent conflict. White Northerners responded as they did partly because they had been active consumers of the noxious racial science of the 1850s. One of its young acolytes, the Alabamian

Henry Hotze, explained the dilemma that emancipation would produce: "it is obvious that, were it possible thus to rekindle in the negro the savage instincts of his African descent, the white man, being numerically, as well as in every other respect, the stronger, must in very self-defense turn against and exterminate him as he would a dangerous beast."[25]

Because of the disagreement in the North over this most important war policy, Lincoln marshaled his best talent to defend the justness of the order. Before he was called upon to write on the nature of guerrillas, Francis Lieber commented on emancipation. In a long letter he wrote to Attorney General Edward Bates, and which was subsequently published in the newspapers, Lieber explained, "slavery exists by municipal law, not by the law of nature. Even the ancient Roman law, originating in pagan times lays it down among its first principles that men by nature are free. . . . It does not belong to the law of nature and nations," which was the context Lincoln (and even Jefferson Davis) agreed they inhabited. "Where men are arrayed against each other as belligerents municipal law falls from them like scales," Lieber explained. "Men stand opposed to one another in war simply as men under the laws and usages of war, which is a branch of international law." From this, Lieber concluded that not only was emancipation consistent with the global laws of war, but any effort by armies to return fugitive slaves amounted to re-enslaving them, a power the US government never possessed.[26] Lieber codified this line of argument in General Orders No. 100, published in April 1863. Articles 42 and 43 elaborated the argument he made to Bates: "slavery, complicating and confounding the ideas of property, (that is of a thing,) and of personality, (that is of humanity,) exists according to municipal or local law only. The law of nature and nations has never acknowledged it." He concluded: "in a war between the United States and a belligerent which admits of slavery, if a person held in bondage by that belligerent be captured by or come as a fugitive under the protection of the military forces of the United States, such person is immediately entitled to the rights and privileges of a freeman. To return such person into slavery would amount to enslaving a free person, and neither the United States nor any officer under their authority can enslave any human being."[27]

The practice of enticing an enemy's slaves to desert was hardly novel, as Lieber and most Americans knew. An infamous example from the

American Revolution—when Lord Dunmore promised freedom to Chesapeake slaves who fought for the British—was well known throughout the South. Despite the inconsistencies of British policy and practice, according to a recent history, "tens of thousands of slaves served as soldiers and sailors throughout North America and the Caribbean." American revolutionaries resisted the idea because of their personal stake in slavery, but the paucity of their manpower compelled them to adopt some of the same strategies as their British enemies. As a result, one study concludes, "the American Revolution occasioned major innovations in the arming of slaves, in the functions they performed, and in the scale of their operations."[28]

Lincoln also drew on the arguments advanced by his solicitor general, William Whiting, who published several long pamphlets on the legal dimensions of the war during the conflict. Always skeptical of anything that came from Seward or Stanton, Secretary of the Navy Gideon Welles found little to appreciate in Whiting, but observed in July 1863 that he had "for several months been an important personage here. I have been assured from high authority he is a remarkable man." That high authority included several cabinet secretaries and the president himself. Whiting argued that in a state of war, even one against a civil rather than an alien enemy, the rules of common belligerents applied. Insurgents like the Confederates placed themselves beyond the protections offered by the constitution and risked not just property confiscation but death. "This right of seizure and condemnation is harsh," he wrote, "as all the proceedings of war are harsh, in the extreme, but it is nevertheless lawful." Like any good lawyer, Whiting's argument separated the legal dimensions of emancipation and war from their moral and strategic aspects. He showed that Lincoln *could* emancipate if he believed it necessary and wise. Even Southern Unionists came to this conclusion. "I never would have lifted my arm against slavery," proclaimed a Texan, "if it had not lifted its arm against me and against the Government I love."[29]

Consistent with his advisors and his own belief in emancipation as militarily necessary and lawful, when he came to explain the order, Lincoln did not rely on morality. It was, in Lincoln's words, "a fit and necessary war measure for suppressing said rebellion." Defeating the Confederacy required shifting the manpower embodied in slaves from the South to the

North. Although this dissatisfied abolitionists at the time, it reassured moderate Northerners that the war would not corrupt the system of law and order that underlay their opposition to secession in the first place. Lincoln argued from this position not because of political expediency; he advocated a strenuous war because the future of self-government demanded it. And he could authorize a strenuous war because, as a legal scholar recently concluded, "the president had learned that the law of war permitted him to do anything to defeat an enemy, except for a few acts that were inhumane." This framing inverts our modern sense of the relationship between slavery and war. Lincoln did not emancipate slaves in order to make his cause just. Instead, the justice of his cause enabled emancipation.[30]

The Confederates' Just War

For their part, Confederates could not imagine a more unjust practice in war than emancipation. Southern officers objected to many features of the Union's war, but they did so within the context of the laws of war. Even when they rejected Northern interpretations of those laws, they nonetheless believed they could compel changes in Union behavior by reminding Northerners of their common commitment to civilized behavior. But, according to Confederates, emancipation abandoned the war convention altogether. Rather than a military policy, they regarded the Emancipation Proclamation as inciting insurrection, a policy outside regular war that struck not just the Confederate army but the cornerstone of their society. War, they argued, makes claims on soldiers' lives, but emancipation, as an Alabamian asserted, "incites and employs servile insurrection, with the attendant horrors of rapine and murder, which are crimes like against the laws of God and man." Although we tend to regard emancipation as something more than simply a war policy today, participants viewed it in the context of the time, and for Confederates, that context was the justness of the Union's behavior in the war. As Jefferson Davis's best and most recent biographer observes, "for Davis, the Emancipation Proclamation represented the culmination of the savage war waged upon his country."[31]

As soon as it was issued, denunciations sprang from Confederate pens. In the Confederate Congress, Senator Raphael Semmes of Louisiana called it "a gross violation of the usages of civilized warfare, an outrage upon private property and an invitation to servile war." Confederate Secretary of War James Seddon concurred, arguing that "the employment of a servile insurrection as an instrument of war is contrary to the usages of civilized nations." Seddon's real concern was that "the enlistment of negro slaves as a part of the Army of the United States . . . is a part of the system . . . to subvert by violence the social system and domestic relations of the negro slaves in the Confederacy and to add to the calamities of war a servile insurrection. The savage passions and brutal appetites of a barbarous race are to be stimulated into fierce activity." An editorial writer in Arkansas resorted to biblical language: "the crime of Lincoln in seducing our slaves into the ranks of his army should be ranked, 'amongst those stupendous wrongs against humanity, shocking to the moral sense of the world, like Herod's massacre of the Innocents.'" Jefferson Davis proved himself a master of the genre, characterizing emancipation as "the most execrable measure recorded in the history of guilty man." The specific source of this outrage was not just emancipation but what Davis assumed would follow: "they are encouraged to a general assassination of their masters." He foresaw a stark set of outcomes: "the extermination of the slaves, the exile of the whole white population from the Confederacy, or the absolute and total separation of these States from the United States."[32]

Despite the vigor of Confederate rhetoric, their policy actions displayed reticence and even confusion over the best way to respond. None among them doubted the unjustness of emancipation, but they argued among themselves over how to respond without spurring a counterresponse from the Union. Shortly after the Emancipation Proclamation was announced, Mississippi senator James Phelan asserted that the North's emancipation policy, "so atrocious and infernal[,] is unparalleled in the blackest and bloodiest pages of savage strife, surpasses in atrocious cruelty the most signal despotism that every disgraced the earth." Phelan followed the logic of this characterization to its consistent end; because the Union had abandoned the rules of war, so should Confederates. Phelan proposed that "all rules of civilized warfare should be disregarded in the future defense of our country . . . and that a war of extermination should be waged against every invader whose hostile foot shall cross the borders of these Confederate States." Phelan's was not the only such proposal, but none of the black flag responses to emancipation were passed into law or made standard practice by Confederate armies. Instead, the Confederate Congress passed a statute in October 1862 that escaped slaves captured in battle be turned over to state authorities, who would then prosecute them under anti-insurrection laws, which almost always mandated death penalties. This statute made no provision for what to do with free men of color captured as Union soldiers, a problem that increasingly bedeviled Confederate and state authorities. Whatever the particularity of their responses, Confederates believed in the "justice of our cause," as Robert E. Lee said, even more strongly after the Union endorsed emancipation.[33]

Confederate policy continued to evolve as the war changed. Confronted with the capture of six black soldiers by Confederate troops in coastal Georgia in November 1862, Secretary of War James Seddon denied them protection as soldiers. "Summary execution must therefore be inflicted on those taken," he wrote the field commander.[34] This draconian threat never became policy. On December 23, 1862, Jefferson Davis approved a Confederate congressional resolution advising commanders that "all negro slaves captured in arms be at once delivered over to the executive authorities of the respective States to which they belong to be dealt with according to the laws of said States."[35] Southern states regarded any slave caught with arms as fomenting insurrection, punishable by death. Despite Davis's statement, Confederate senators and congressmen continued to offer resolutions intended to halt the Union's emancipation policy.[36] This resulted in a harsher law, passed in May 1863 with Davis's support, that promised captured black soldiers would be tried by state authorities and required the execution of white officers commanding black units.[37] Even more ominously, the resolution specified that black people who "shall give aid or comfort to the enemies of the Confederate States" should also suffer death, which authorized more killing because so many black Southerners helped Union armies.

In response, Lincoln issued an order threatening retaliation if Confederates executed black soldiers captured in battle. Confederate policymakers (military and civil) once again found themselves unsure how to proceed. South Carolina's governor engaged in a lengthy correspondence with the secretary of war trying to ascertain the proper way to handle both ex-slave and free black soldiers captured in the assault on Fort Wagner in mid-1863. The confusion he manifested in this discussion revealed significant disagreement within the Southern high command about how to respond in a way that remained consistent with customary norms and how to avoid a Northern counterresponse that would expose Confederate soldiers to execution. In contrast to the hard line articulated in the late 1862 discussion, by late 1863, the Confederate Congress entertained a proposal to distinguish between free men of color and former slaves who fought for the US Army. It may be a "barbarous thing for the North to enlist negroes in its armies," Congressman Henry Foote argued, "but . . . we were bound to recognize them as prisoners of war." Foote worried that if the Confederacy did not exchange at least free black soldiers, the Union would never return another Confederate prisoner. In the event, the Union required the Confederacy to treat all its black soldiers the same before commencing exchanges, and that only happened in early 1865. The result was that black men still suffered an unjust war, even when Confederate policy should have protected them. The free black soldiers captured outside Charleston in July 1863, for instance, continued to linger as "nonpersons" held in terrible conditions in Charleston separate from regular prisoners.[38]

The Confederate response came from the bottom as well as the top. Davis set policy (with Congress often intervening), but the dozens of Southern generals sometimes diverged in their interpretations of that policy. Junior officers and soldiers on the ground had their own response to the presence of black Union soldiers. Lee's "Old War Horse," Lieutenant General James Longstreet, inspired his men before an 1862 battle by asserting that "Northerners 'care not for the blood of babes nor the carnage of innocent women which servile insurrection thus stirred up may bring upon their heads.'" Confederate soldiers (at all levels) subjected black soldiers to greater and more unjust violence than they did white ones. As black soldiers discovered to their dismay, their encounters with Confederate soldiers did not possess the chronological, regional, or situational variety that their white peers experienced.[39]

Although Lincoln bore the brunt of Confederate chastisement, white Southerners focused their anger on enslaved and free black people in the South. The violence generated by emancipation turned against slaves rather than masters. This process began well before formal emancipation. As one historian notes, "lethal violence against blacks became common on the frontier, as whites grew nervous about the fate of slavery." They did not distinguish by potential combatants (that is, by age and gender). In Virginia, the sight of black people escaping slavery drew white citizens to the riverbank "with shotguns and rifles [who] ambushed the fugitives from the river bank, shooting down men and women alike." Black Southerners owned relatively little property, so the hard war tactics that Union soldiers waged against white Southerners would not avail; instead, physical violence was the tool of choice. The first targets were those people, like the black Virginians, caught in the act of escape, but any enslaved person asserting his or her autonomy risked a beating or worse. Rather than conceal the violence, as many masters had done in the prewar era when whippings occurred on plantations, Confederates used the public nature of antiemancipation violence to deter freedom seekers. In Baton Rouge, one Union sailor reported that over two days, dozens of enslaved people had come to the wharf seeking security. He was shocked when "a band of Guerallis came down and shot one of them tied another one both hands and feet then threw him into the River. That is what they call making an example to prevent the Niggers from running away." The next day Northern sailors shifted their boats closer to the wharf "to prevent such scenes in the future."[40]

Everywhere freedpeople congregated, they were subject to targeted violence from Confederates. Individual kidnappings were a constant threat, and in July 1863 a Confederate regiment consoled itself for losing the Battle of Helena by burning nearby Camp Ethiopia's cabins and beating and killing many of the inhabitants.[41] In South Carolina, a planter hanged three runaways that he recaptured, "noting that neighboring 'blacks were encouraged to be present' when he hanged them. He expected that 'the effect' would 'not soon be forgotten.'"[42] From the

Kansas-Missouri border, Union Brigadier General Clinton Fisk reported that "Slavery dies hard. I hear its expiring agonies & witness its contortions in death in every quarter of my Dist." "I blush for my race," he confessed, "when I discover the wicked barbarity of the late Masters & Mistresses of the recently freed persons of the counties heretofore named. I have no doubt but that the monster Jim Jackson is instigated by the late slave owners to hang or shoot every negro he can find absent away from the old plantation."[43] The Confederate government stood squarely behind masters in their physical violence toward blacks. In Louisiana, Major General Daniel Ruggles issued an order (ironically on July Fourth) that neither slaves nor free people of color could pass through Confederate lines. "Every negro, slave or free, who shall violate this order," he commanded, "will be shot, in the attempt, unless he or she shall immediately submit to arrest."[44]

Deliberate overreaction was an old pattern in white Southern life. Whenever black people had taken up arms to pursue individual freedom or to attack the slave system, white Southerners responded with ferocious violence. In fear over Nat Turner's rebellion, which claimed the lives of fifty-six white residents of Southampton County, Virginians killed perhaps two hundred black people, many residing hundreds of miles from Turner but accused of collaborating. Whites connected to slave rebellions received the same treatment. In 1836, white Mississippians, spurred by a fantastical story of an impending slave rebellion masterminded by a poor white man named John Murrell, killed a dozen people, including several slaveholders who were inexplicably accused of supporting insurrection. Only months before the war broke out, Mississippians again succumbed to their fears, lynching a host of men, white and black, supposedly planning a slave rebellion at Second Creek. The predictability of white paranoia and overreaction does nothing to explain or mitigate the violence enacted against black Southerners, but it does highlight the gulf between the white and black responses to emancipation.[45]

Even the usually restrained Robert E. Lee greeted formal emancipation with the same shock and horror expressed by Davis and other Confederates. He regarded the Emancipation Proclamation as a "savage and brutal policy," one that left Confederates "no alternative but success or degradation worse than death." He pleaded for more soldiers in order to "save the honor of our families from pollution, our social system from destruction."[46] As Lee's apocalyptic language reveals, he regarded emancipation as an existential threat. The Union's practice of executing guerrillas elicited nary a word from him. Its policies on prisoners drew periodic complaints, and specific episodes (Mumford's execution and the Palmyra execution, for instance) inspired strongly worded letters, but emancipation existed in a different category. For Lee, as for most Confederates, Lincoln's promise of freedom for the slaves was an unjust measure, a signal of the Yankees' willingness to wage unrestrained war. Just as the Union responded to what they regarded as the Confederacy's unjust guerrilla war, the Confederacy escalated the war's violence in response to emancipation, convinced of both the righteousness and the legality of their action.

Emancipation on the Ground

Taking their cue from W. E. B. Du Bois, who referred to the Civil War as a "General Strike," over the last decade historians have started calling the Civil War a "slave rebellion."[47] By this, they generally mean that the movement of half a million enslaved people to freedom during the war dealt a fatal blow to the institution in the United States. Although three and a half million people remained in bondage to the end of the war, the number of fugitives was many orders of magnitude larger than any previous collective blow against slavery in American history. Historians have persuasively shown that the actions of enslaved people eroded the power of masters and destabilized the institution across the country. From the perspective of telling an accurate history of slavery in the United States, one that accounts for the active role that African Americans took against slavery, this historiographical turn is long overdue and essential. But not all rebellions are equal. The Emancipation Proclamation never spurred the Haitian-style slave rebellion that white Southerners feared. No matter how often white Southerners invoked the "horrors of servile insurrection," actual experience contradicted their rhetoric. The revolution on Saint Domingue entailed over a decade of ferocious warfare and violence in a kaleidoscopically shifting sequence of alignments among the participants. Many French slaveholders died at the hands of their slaves in the war's opening phase. Nothing similar, in nature or scale, occurred in the United States. The absence of such emancipation-related violence is the single most important factor that limited bloodshed in the US Civil War. White Southerners knew the history of Haiti well. Since 1791, when the first reports emerged of the uprising of enslaved people on the French-owned island of Saint Domingue, Southern slaveholders had lived in fear of a similar event at home. They consumed newspaper reports and later books and pamphlets about the event. They encountered white and black refugees from the war, many of whom made their way to New Orleans.[48] And they suppressed with great diligence any public traffic in memories or histories of the event. Despite this, Haiti functioned as shorthand among white Southerners for the horrors of what happened when a war became an emancipatory struggle waged off the battlefield and on plantations.

Despite their often hysterical rhetoric, Confederates responded ambivalently to the threats of rebellion that they encountered. In the antebellum era, slaveholders assumed that their slaves loved and obeyed their masters by choice. If this was true, they did not need to fear rebellion. The persistence of this attitude into the war years can be seen in responses to rumors that reached the high command. Even before black soldiers had taken the field, Governor Zebulon Vance of North Carolina forwarded an order supposedly drafted by a Union officer that detailed a plan "to induce the blacks to make a concerted and simultaneous rising, on the night of the 1st of August next, over the entire States in rebellion; to arm themselves with any and every kind of weapon that may come to hand and commence operations by burning all railroad and country bridges and tearing up railroad tracks and destroying telegraph lines, &c., and then take to the woods, the swamps, or the mountains." Although the order's author hastened to add that "no blood is to be shed except in self-defense," it seems designed to reinforce Confederate fears, especially coming on the date (August 1) typically celebrated as West Indian Emancipation Day by free blacks before the Civil War. The scheme is so ignorant of Union military protocol that even Vance must have recognized it was probably a forgery. Nonetheless, Davis responded to Vance and promised to notify his generals, but his secretary of war's laconic comment when he forwarded the material to governors revealed perhaps more than he intended: "while attaching no great importance to the matter, I deem it prudent to place Your Excellency in possession of the information." If Davis had actually taken the matter seriously, he would have contacted Lincoln, as he did on numerous occasions throughout the war for much less dramatic matters.[49]

Nonetheless, in every circumstance of public conversation, when Confederates condemned the Emancipation Proclamation, it was the horrors of Haiti they invoked. Senator Semmes, the Louisianan quoted earlier, connected his routine condemnation of Yankee soldiers to the way that emancipation changed the character of the war. As he understood it, the Union planned "to emancipate their slaves with the atrocious design of adding servile insurrection and the massacre of families to the calamities of war." The specter of a Haitian-style irregular conflict, in which Lincoln encouraged enslaved people to carry the conflict off the battlefield and into Southern homes, haunted Confederate discourse in 1863 and proved a turning point. Northerners were aware of Southern concerns. Some even sought to use Southern fears as a weapon of war. Although a New York state representative did "not believe [the Emancipation Proclamation] will cause a single insurrection," he nevertheless relished that "it weakens our enemies by awakening the chronic fear in the southern mind of negro insurrection. . . . This has been the great night-mare of the southern states."[50]

Because of the specter of Haiti, the process of emancipation and black enlistment became a momentous test of Lincoln's contention that these measures were both militarily necessary and legally justifiable. If the war continued without the chaotic personal violence that white Southerners predicted, then Lincoln would be vindicated. He knew this and articulated two policies in the Emancipation Proclamation itself that he hoped would minimize and direct the violence associated with emancipation. Lincoln had no authority or control over enslaved people, but he nonetheless counseled patience and nonviolence. "I hereby enjoin," he wrote, "upon the people so declared to be free to abstain from all violence, unless in necessary self-defence." But he neither anticipated nor wanted passivity. Instead, he hoped to take advantage of black Southerners' determination to free themselves and end slavery by marshaling that power for the US Army. "I further declare and make known, that such persons of suitable condition, will be received into the armed service of the United States to garrison forts, positions, stations, and other places, and to man vessels of all sorts in said service."[51]

United States Colored Troops

After Lincoln's call, the army established the US Colored Troops (USCT), a separate organization of black men enlisted into federal armies. Lincoln understood both the psychological and physical advantage such a program would possess. He famously wrote to Andrew Johnson that "the bare sight of 50,000 armed and drilled black soldiers along the banks of the Mississippi would end the rebellion at once." Less hyperbolically, he told Johnson that "the colored population is the great available and yet unavailed of, force for restoring the Union."[52] As this statement made clear, Lincoln continued to think of emancipation as a war strategy that enhanced the ability of the Union to achieve reunion rather than a shift in the broader purpose or effect of the conflict. Regardless of what Lincoln said or believed, the USCT became a way to channel the efforts of black Americans in a legal and strategic way.

Those black men who enlisted proved Lincoln right. They volunteered in high numbers and fought tenaciously within the laws of war. The testimony of enslaved men who responded to Lincoln's call expresses a common theme of being dedicated to a corporate sense of self-defense. One man resigned his $20-a-month post as a carpenter to take up a rifle for half his former pay. Queried about why he would make this sacrifice, he responded, "money was worthless to him without freedom and if freedom were worth having it was worth fighting for and that, in his opinion, the colored people should learn to fight and be able to take care of themselves when the white soldiers had gone away." The self- and communal empowerment that came with organizing a black regiment drew many men into the service. "In secesh times," said one man, "I used to pray the Lord for this opportunity to be released from bondage and to fight for my liberty, and I could not feel right so long as I was not in the regiment." These men envisioned their military service as an act of

Some USCT regiments, like the 1st US Colored Infantry pictured here, organized in Union territory and included mostly free men of color. Those organized
in the occupied Confederacy included most former slaves. In both cases, these
men met Confederate opponents within the auspices of a sanctioned part of the
Regular Army.

justice. Not a just war narrowly defined in terms of conduct, though
black soldiers adhered to the laws of war like white soldiers, but the historical reckoning that came from ending the injustice of slavery.[53]

The recruitment of black men into Union armies started unevenly,
throughout 1862, with individual commanders exercising their authority to
recruit locally. Generals in Louisiana, South Carolina, and Kansas all
initiated experiments. Enlistment in these places was haphazard, and
training and equipping often worse; all of the efforts occurred without
official sanction. Once the US Congress formalized the process in early
1863, it proceeded smoothly. By May of that year, the adjutant general's
office centralized the recruitment and organization of black soldiers.
USCT regiments included both former enslaved men who escaped their
masters or the South altogether and free men of color from the North.
The most famous regiments, like the 54th and 55th Massachusetts, contained the sons of prominent abolitionists or well-established Northern
black families, but most of the recruits came from the slave South. By

war's end, they numbered 180,000 soldiers organized into 165 units, nearly 10 percent of the Union's total fighting force (equivalent to 20 percent of the whole Confederate military force). The Union took pains to assert that black men, whether slave or free, would obey the rules of the army like any other soldiers. Brigadier General Lorenzo Thomas, who organized black troops in the Mississippi River Valley, claimed that "they carry [their] habit of obedience with them." Even abolitionists espoused confidence in this idea. When the American Freedmen's Inquiry Commission reported on their survey of freedpeople, they assured readers that "the law in the shape of military rule takes for [former slaves] the place of his master, with this difference, that he submits to it heartily and cheerfully without any sense of degradation."[54]

Some of these new soldiers were liberated during Northern army raids into the Confederate interior. The first and fullest such experiment came in the Department of the South. From the Union naval base at Beaufort, South Carolina, the First and Second South Carolina regiments (organized in early 1863 and staffed with escaped slaves from nearby plantations) raided along the coast and into the interior following the St. Mary's River. They destroyed Confederate salt works, confiscated lumber, and liberated nearly a thousand people. Led by a corps of committed abolitionists in the department, the raids, as a historian notes, were "intended first and foremost to ignite the destruction of slavery." Although no other Union commander replicated the effort, it drew wide attention around the country. Northern conservatives condemned the raids, fearing that they were the servile insurrection prophesied for so long. Republican newspapers celebrated the accomplishments, particularly the capture of Jacksonville, Florida. The *New York Times* proudly noted that "the people were in great fear of an indiscriminate massacre [when the troops first appeared]; but the negroes behaved with propriety, and no one was harmed." Many of the enslaved people liberated during the raids seized the opportunity to bring the fight back to the Confederates and enlisted in the army. Lorenzo Thomas recruited and organized almost 3,000 officers and 78,000 enlisted men between March 1863 and April 1865, nearly half of the total USCT troops used by the North. Thomas worked against racist resistance among white officers in the region and the regular incapacity and disinterest among commanders in the field to manage enlistment. He did so, in part, by appealing directly to men of color. In Memphis in mid-1863, he spoke to a large crowd of black men: "President Lincoln had set you free," he announced, "will you fight? Suppose I would give you guns, and you should see a party of guerrillas in the woods, what would you do?" Thomas and the black men of Memphis knew the answer: "we'd kill them, the crowd roared." Killing under the auspices of the US Army was deemed legitimate.[55]

Black soldiers demonstrated their value to Northern skeptics in 1863. That skepticism, resulting from white fears of insurrection and a belief that black men would make poor soldiers, changed slowly under the pressures of war. The raids and capture of Jacksonville (which held against several Confederate counterattacks) generated good press. Several small but dramatic battles along the Mississippi River drew national attention, most importantly Port Hudson and Milliken's Bend. Throughout 1864, Northern reporters chronicled the experiences of black soldiers in most of the states of the Confederacy. Just as with white soldiers, these experiences ran the gamut from cowardice to Medal of Honor winners. What Lincoln knew from the beginning and what white Northerners came to appreciate was that black soldiers fully devoted themselves to the cause they advanced. Coming late in the war, they were the most valuable volunteers the Union could hope to attract. White people in the North and South had long regarded military service as a unique measure of their virtue, so many were surprised to find black men performed just as well. At Milliken's Bend, where black troops slowed down a Confederate attack at great cost, they earned the praise of white soldiers on both sides. An Illinois soldier reported that "the negroes on that day demonstrated their character as fighting men," and even Confederates conceded that they encountered "some hard fighting."[56]

When black soldiers fought in more irregular circumstances, their experiences rarely generated sympathy. This occurred in theaters (North Carolina and coastal Georgia and Florida, most famously) where abolitionist commanders used the USCT to attack slavery directly. In North Carolina, Union Brigadier General Edward Augustus Wild organized four regiments into what came to be called Wild's African Brigade in 1863. Late in the year, he ordered these units into southeastern Virginia and northeastern North Carolina to catch guerrillas, confiscate supplies, and emancipate slaves. For guerrillas, Wild allowed no laxity. If any fired on the troops, "'you will *at once*, hang the man who fired' and label the body according to the crime. 'Guerrillas are not to be taken alive.'" Most field executions of commanders occurred under the authority of the commander on the scene, rather than under the auspices of a blanket rule from a departmental commander. In the event, Wild's men hanged Daniel Blight as a guerrilla and left his body hanging at a prominent crossroads to deter guerrilla actions. They also arrested other guerrillas, burned homes, liberated slaves, and took civilian hostages. According to a sympathetic *New York Times* journalist who accompanied the campaign, Wild's raid left secessionists "completely panic-stricken. Scores of families fled into the swamps on [Wild's] approach."[57]

Although Blight's execution (if not the hanging of his dead body) remained consistent with Union treatment of guerrillas more generally, it put black soldiers in a tight position because of how viscerally whites responded to field executions, even when they knew they were lawful. Many of the white Union troops in the area were local men not eager to support emancipation or confiscation. Confederate troops responded even more violently, executing Samuel Jordan, a USCT soldier in Wild's brigade captured by irregulars some weeks earlier. Six months later, part of the African Brigade conducted another raid into southwest Virginia, freeing about 600 slaves and seizing 275 cattle and 160 horses and mules. Confederates regarded the raid (and others like it in other regions) as unjust violence directed at civilians. As the North Carolina example illustrates, black soldiers could only establish themselves as legitimate soldiers if observers regarded them as behaving within the bounds of the regular war. Wild, David Hunter, and James Montgomery (commander of the Second South Carolina) did not do black men any favors by assigning them to places rife with irregular war and giving them ambiguous instructions.[58]

Despite the respect earned by the USCT at Milliken's Bend, the battle was also noteworthy for the unjust treatment of black prisoners, another persistent feature of black men's experiences in battle. The closest student of the episode suggests the possibility that black troops were killed while surrendering, but the evidence of Texas troops fighting under a black flag (as some Yankees later claimed) is hard to sustain. "Although the excited nerve and adrenaline of men in their first combat—especially men who recoiled at the very idea of black soldiers—may well have led some individual Confederates to shoot wounded black soldiers or other who had thrown down their arms," he concludes, "the Texans apparently had no prearranged plan or order to massacre the African American soldiers." As Fort Pillow and other sites of racial atrocities would reveal, Confederate soldiers did not need a concerted plan to do great harm to black soldiers. Nonetheless, the experience at Milliken's Bend showed that Confederates could also treat black men as regular opponents. Confederate Brigadier General Henry E. McCulloch captured black soldiers and held them as regular prisoners of war. At least sixty appeared as prisoners of war in Monroe, Louisiana a week later, and others were released in Texas at war's end. McCulloch's postbattle confusion about the disposition of these men also became typical of engagements with black soldiers. The confusion generated by the proposals, resolutions, and policies spun out of Richmond left officers with little guidance.[59]

In the absence of explicit instructions, many field commanders acted on their own initiative. That initiative drew upon their antebellum and wartime experience, and for the slaveholders who enlisted in great numbers in the Confederate army (well above their proportion of the Confederate population at large) and filled the officer corps, the threat of facing uniformed black men in battle seemed especially dire.[60] As a result, many Confederate officers targeted black soldiers for special violence. Confederate Major General Edmund Kirby Smith, for instance, identified an ominous strategy that he hoped would avoid Union retaliation. He instructed his subordinate Richard Taylor to recognize "the propriety of giving no quarter to armed negroes and their officers. In this way we may be relieved from a disagreeable dilemma."[61] Kirby Smith's instructions to kill all black soldiers on the battlefield revealed the lethal animosity that characterized many white Confederates throughout the Civil War.

This behavior began as soon as the first black soldiers took the field. In Louisiana, Confederates captured twenty-one black enlisted men and their black captain (all members of the First Native Guard). As the commanding officer of the 17th Arkansas Mounted Infantry later reported, his unit escorted the men toward Jackson, Louisiana, but several black soldiers purportedly attempted to escape. The Arkansas cavalry shot them as they fled, though such a report could well have been used as an excuse after the fact. The unit's commander reported the full event with surprising honesty: "in the confusion, the other negroes attempted to escape likewise. I then ordered every one shot, and with my six shooter assisted in the execution of the order." Just as quickly, Union commanders protested the mistreatment of their men. Perhaps in response to this very event, Union Brigadier General George L. Andrews wrote his Confederate peer J. A. Logan that he had "been informed by several eyewitnesses that two of the Colored Soldiers of this command have been recently hanged at or near Jackson La by the men of your command." Andrews began the exchange as all officers did in these contexts, by professing that he did not believe Logan was responsible for the actions but that he must take account and punish the perpetrators. "The severest measures of retaliation will certainly be adopted on my part if such outrages should be again committed" or if the perpetrators were not properly dealt with, Andrews threatened. Although Logan responded with his own counter-threat, promising retaliation if Andrews harmed any Confederate prisoners, he also denied mistreating black soldiers. "I will state that if any negroes in arms have been hung by the troops of this command it was without my knowledge or was done by some one if at all without authority from me." On the one hand, this response could be read as the typical dodge of a guilty conscience. On the other hand, Logan implicitly acknowledged that he did not have any legal or moral authority to treat black soldiers differently from white ones.[62]

Jefferson Davis expressed no such ambivalence. Although Davis recognized that gross mistreatment of black soldiers risked a debilitating Union response, even in the postwar period he insisted that because the Confederacy regarded slaves as property, the army had the legal right to re-enslave any former slave they found in the Union ranks.[63] The problem Davis confronted was not just the offense he and other white Southerners took at facing black soldiers. It was one of the most fundamental of the war and one at the heart of much of the war's unnecessary and unjust violence—who could fight? The Confederacy regarded the Union's use of black soldiers as the Union regarded the Confederacy's use of guerrillas— as an illegal and immoral tactic that destroyed the covenant of civilized warfare, subjected civilians to potential harm, and sanctioned the victimized side to perpetrate more harm. The Confederacy and the Union maintained their decisions about who could fight—guerrillas and black men, respectively—though they both also recognized that these decisions made the war more violent.

No Distinction as to Color

Confederate politicians and officers exploited fears of a slave rebellion among their constituency, just as Southern elites had done in the antebellum South, but they also genuinely anticipated that emancipation would unleash a race war. This never transpired, largely due to the restraint exercised by enslaved people. The white South was also held in check by fears of how the North would respond if they used unjust violence against black soldiers or black Southerners more generally. The Andrews-Logan exchange quoted earlier was typical for how field commanders in the Civil War adjudicated disputes about conduct. A tit-for-tat execution struggle never developed in the Civil War partly because the possibility of one restrained such violence. Black soldiers were killed in the act of or after surrendering—probably hundreds, perhaps more. The treatment of black soldiers by Confederates stood as the largest violation of the rules of war customarily observed by uniformed soldiers throughout the conflict. But the move to sell black soldiers into slavery or to kill everyone captured (plus their officers) risked too great a threat to the deteriorating Confederate manpower base.

The potential for a Union counterresponse to Confederate mistreatment of black soldiers (rather than the episodic exchanges that prevailed) emerged in mid-1863. News stories of Confederate atrocities against freedpeople had already circulated for years, but the murder of black prisoners generated a stronger demand for action. Protests from abolitionists and especially from the families of black soldiers reached Lincoln's desk. Hannah Johnson, a black resident of Buffalo, New York, whose father had escaped as a slave from Louisiana, implored Lincoln to stand up for black Union soldiers. Johnson's son served in the 54th Massachusetts, and she expressed concern over the Confederate policy of selling captured soldiers into slavery. She demanded equal treatment. "Why should not our enemies be compelled to treat him the same, Made to do it." Making them, she knew, would involve having Lincoln "rettallyate" for any discrepancies in treatment suffered by Union men.[64] Johnson did not ask for special treatment—she knew her son risked his life as a soldier—but she expected Lincoln to impose equivalent terms on captured Confederates in order to ensure fair treatment.

On the same day Johnson wrote her letter—July 31, 1863—the War Department issued General Orders No. 252, Lincoln's retaliatory threat to the Confederacy. Its basis was a recognition that civilized customs "permit no distinction as to color in the treatment of prisoners of war as public enemies," and accordingly the US government pledged that it would execute an equal number of Confederate soldiers for every black soldier unjustly killed and would hold indefinitely an equal number of Confederate prisoners for every volunteer sold into slavery. Lincoln's decision reflected international law, noting that "the law of nations, and the usages and customs of war, as carried on by civilized powers, permit no distinction as to color in the treatment of prisoners of war as public enemies."[65] Lincoln's order is rarely discussed within the framework of retaliation and just war, but this was the context from which it sprang. Jefferson Davis's threat to treat black soldiers under Southern state law as enslaved men in the act of rebellion promised to initiate a cataclysmic cycle of violence. Lincoln relied upon the enlistment of black soldiers, and he could not afford to deny them the protections of the government. Black Americans and some white abolitionists criticized Lincoln for failing to follow through, but his threat functioned as a preemptive retaliation policy and helped curtail the mass murder of black soldiers.[66] The legislation, orders, questions, and counterorders among Confederate policymakers that followed in the wake of Lincoln's retaliation threat revealed confusion among the Southern high command about how to treat black soldiers in a way that would not initiate a cycle of executions.[67] Confederate soldiers still murdered black Union troops even after Lincoln's warning, but they did so without official sanction and in smaller numbers. In short, Lincoln's threat of retaliation created a more just and symmetrical conflict.[68]

Frederick Douglass and other abolitionists believed that Lincoln came too slowly to his defense of black soldiers. "'The slaughter of blacks taken as captives,' Douglass complained, 'seems to affect him as little as the slaughter of beeves for the use of his army.'" When Douglass met with Lincoln at the White House in August 1863, he criticized the president for being "somewhat slow" in issuing the retaliation order. Lincoln's response reflected the ambivalence that almost all Civil War commanders who considered retaliation experienced. According to Douglass, Lincoln felt it was a "terrible remedy." If the actual perpetrators of racial atrocities could have been arrested, their conviction and punishment would have been an easy matter, but "hanging men for a crime perpetrated by others was revolting to his feelings." With his lawyerly perspective and precision, Lincoln identified the moral quandary at the heart of retaliation. Lincoln also worried that acting too vigorously on behalf of black soldiers might generate antagonism among Northern whites. Critics accused Lincoln of favoring black men over white because of the retaliation order. But among abolitionists, the order found strong support. Charles Drake, a radical Missouri Republican, asserted in a public address that "he who fights the battles of his country is a man and no chattel, whatever his color; and were he as black as a moonless and starless night, he is as much entitled to the protection of his Government as any other man." Drake argued strongly for sustaining the Retaliation Order, even to the point of threatening Lincoln if he quailed. "If the President should abandon our colored soldiers to the fiendish malice of slave-driving rebels, after having called them into the ranks of his country's defenders, his name would deserve to be execrated in every part of the globe where civilization has redeemed man from barbarism, or Christianity has raised him above the level of a brute."[69]

The US Army never actually retaliated for the mistreatment of black soldiers by Confederates. Lincoln believed, as army commanders on both sides usually did, that the threat of retaliation would ensure good behavior in the future. He may have been correct, though establishing cause and effect for things that did not occur remains a historian's most difficult task. Even members of the Confederate Congress, who rarely exercised a responsible attitude toward military action, recognized that black soldier policy required a deft touch. Henry Foote concurred with Jefferson Davis that the Confederacy must respond to the North's emancipation policy, "yet he could not be unmindful of the fact that while this course was unavoidable, it would have a tendency to greatly embitter the existing war-fare, greatly to increase the scenes of bloodshed."[70] If Lincoln had hewed strictly to his retaliation order, much more blood would have been shed.

The process of emancipation generated even more complications in slaveholding Union states, especially Missouri and Kentucky. The Unionist leaders of these states opposed emancipation even as the US Army recruited soldiers from among the states' black populations. A com-promise allowed enlistments only with a master's approval, but this proved hard to enforce. US provost marshals in Kentucky and Missouri received petitions from angry masters, indignant black soldiers, and the panicked families of enlistees. Masters sometimes moved families out of state or tried to re-enslave men who had enlisted. Martha Glover begged her soldier husband, Richard, to alleviate the conditions produced by his enlistment: "they abuse me because you went & say they will not take care of the children & do nothing but quarrel with me all the time and beat me scandalously the day before yesterday." The Union officers charged with recruiting protested the mistreatment of black soldiers and their families. Colonel H. W. Barry, who commanded a black regiment in western Kentucky, flatly disobeyed his superior's order to return fami-lies of men in his charge. "I cannot return to Slavery, the wives and Children of men, whom you acknowledge, fought so gallantly, and saved yourself and Command, from *massacre*, and further, I was sent here . . . for the purpose of protecting union people, whether *Black* or *white*." De-spite this protest, Union policy required the return of black men who fled slavery from Union states to enlist, and many commanders complied.[71]

In some cases, where clear evidence of the inequitable treatment of black soldiers could be established, the Union did respond. But Union officers also seem to have accepted unjust black soldier deaths in a way that they did not for white soldiers. When Ulysses Grant received intel-ligence from a white Southern man that a white captain and several black soldiers were hanged after the fight at Milliken's Bend, Grant wrote the Confederate commander, Richard Taylor. He advised Taylor that he had captured several men who had been fighting under the flag of "no surrender" but had so far treated them as regular prisoners. "I feel no inclination to retaliate for the offenses of irresponsible persons," Grant wrote, "but if it is the policy of any General, entrusted with the command of troops, to show 'no quarter' or to punish with death prisoners taken in battle, I will accept the issue."[72] Taylor may have been following the order Kirby Smith issued, but in this instance, as in others concerning the treatment of black soldiers, Grant assumed the rumor was erroneous and was prepared to wait until positive evidence arrived before acting. Grant's behavior in this case does not demonstrate any special racist outlook. He acted consistently with how commanders often responded to all manner of asserted atrocities, but the frequency with which Union commanders deferred action on accusations of the unjust treatment of black soldiers effectively gave Confederate troops a freer hand against them.

Striking a Blow for Freedom

Through the institution of the US Colored Troops, black men seized the opportunity to legitimately contest slaveholders and the power of the slave system. The regularity and justness of the US Army anchored them in a process larger than themselves. This collective action, conducted under military norms recognized around the world, inoculated them against Confederate charges that black men could only behave like savages. As Lincoln proudly noted in his 1863 address to Congress, "No servile insurrection, or tendency to violence or cruelty, has marked the measures of emancipation and arming the blacks."[73] For nineteenth-century Americans, the way that people fought wars reflected their state of civilization and their fitness for self-rule. White Americans perceived their victory over Mexico in the 1840s as evidence of their superiority. Confederates, by the act of secession and especially by their use of guerrilla warfare, ruled themselves out of the family of civilized men. By joining the Northern army and fighting alongside white soldiers rather than resorting to the insurrectionary pose prophesied by Southern elites, black men elevated themselves in the eyes of skeptical white Northerners.

Similarly, the willingness of black civilians to abjure unnecessary violence reflected their commitment to a future defined in traditional terms. Enslaved people did not rise up en masse to murder their owners.[74] This decision relieved white Northerners of their anxiety about emancipation as a war measure and ensured they would continue to support the fight against slavery. If enslaved people had waged an internecine race war, white Northerners might well have abandoned their support. No less a personage than Ulysses S. Grant had speculated about such a possibility in 1861. He feared that the political turmoil of secession might encourage slaves to revolt. If that happened, "a Northern army may be required . . . to go south to suppress a negro insurrection," he told his father. "As much as the South have vilified the North they would go on such a mission and with the purest motives."[75] Although the attitudes of most white Northerners (including Grant's) changed significantly by 1863, Grant's assumption that Northern men would eagerly crush a slave rebellion reflected the deep concern about such an event. The refusal of black Southerners to play the part scripted for them by whites brought great dividends. The ironies were palpable, as many recognized at the time. White Southerners feared a black irregular war as much as they celebrated their own against the Union. The more black people resisted the temptation of revenge, the more support they generated among white Northerners.

Northern observers took pains to navigate between the competing and contradictory stereotypes that devalued black men's military service. They needed to account for the lack of violence while still respecting the courage that volunteers demonstrated. The American Freedmen's Inquiry Commission, sent south to investigate conditions in contraband camps, tried to walk the narrow space left by respecting black soldiers as men. "That the indiscriminate massacres of a servile insurrection have been spared us, as addition to the horrors of a civil war, is due, it would seem, rather to that absence of revenge and blood-thirstiness which characterizes this race than to the lack either of courage or of any other quality that marked the hardy combatant." To the contrary, the report's authors argued, it was white Southerners, raised with the "boisterous passions" that Thomas Jefferson had long ago denounced, who might resort to unjust conduct. Those, like slaveholders, who possess "arbitrary and irresponsible power," almost always abuse that power. "A beneficent despotism is the rarest of exceptions."[76]

Even as white Southerners reluctantly recognized that the many enslaved men who had joined the USCT behaved like other Union soldiers, they maintained the apocalyptic tone, reserving their strongest rhetoric for what they assumed would be the unmediated violence enacted by enslaved people acting on their own. But nearly all of the actions that enslaved people took demonstrated a desire to avoid physical conflict with whites. Runaway slaves moved toward US Army outposts and garrison towns because the army's presence there promised freedom and some degree of protection from the capriciousness of white anger. The wartime populations of garrison towns—Memphis, Nashville, Little Rock, and Mobile—mushroomed as enslaved people fled to their safe recesses. Once the US Army captured Mobile Bay, the city beckoned as a refuge. During the war the city's black population increased 47 percent, much of that in the months after Union occupation. Looking at a map of the wartime South, two separate refugee flows can be seen—white and black—almost always moving in opposite directions. White Southerners sought escape from the US Army and black Southerners sought escape to the US Army. Rather than remaining in place in order to seek vengeance, enslaved people who had the chance fled.[77]

Perhaps the most notable absence in the wartime record is reports of black men attacking white women. This absence has been observed by historians, usually in the context of an attempt to understand the sudden emergence of a rhetoric of black-on-white rape in the 1880s and 1890s South. The assumption that black men lusted after white women undergirded the lynching rhetoric of the New South and historians have shown that it was invented whole cloth in the postwar era. Confederate chroniclers for many decades, in fact, celebrated the loyalty of black Southerners living on home fronts with almost no masculine supervision. A 1920s history of Jefferson County, Georgia, for instance, praised "the slaves [who] gave love and service to their white folks." Although many of those narratives were written to create black loyalty more than remember it, it is hard to imagine white Southerners ignoring widespread wartime sexual violence against white women. In the Mississippi Delta, where blacks outnumbered whites by a wide margin, there were no reports of rape by black men during the war. A scholar of the region explains that "only three rumors of black violence upon white women were reported to the governor."[78]

Black restraint did not mean passivity. The dangers to which enslaved people exposed themselves when they escaped slavery in the wartime

South reveal a well of courage and determination with few precedents. And the eagerness with which enslaved men volunteered and fought for the USCT reveal a similarly deep spring of martial spirit. In the words of the father of an enlisted man, "he is a truly loyal Boy and says, he will serve his Country faithfully." Part of that confidence came from the historic mission against slavery. Enslaved people had two hundred and fifty years of experience arguing against slavery on the grounds of natural rights. The refusal of black noncombatants to engage in a bloody uprising drew on longstanding patterns of active but not needlessly bloody resistance to slavery.[79]

The experience of slave rebellions in the antebellum era and the brutality with which they were repressed provides the strategic explanation for why enslaved people sought freedom rather than revenge. Black people knew their history and so avoided needless violence because it was counterproductive. The Civil War produced a dramatic escalation of the number of firearms in the United States, with the vast majority of these going into the hands of white people. Additionally, most freedpeople were in no condition to launch sustained campaigns of violence against white Southerners. In the face of food and medicine shortages, just surviving the war as an enslaved person required considerable effort. For those who risked escape, the costs increased. A field report from an agent of the Western Sanitary Commission recorded a typical scene in the wake of Sherman's army: "just at dusk the train of contrabands came in. Slowly and sadly they dragged along through the streets. Wagons were loaded with children, whose weary, despairing look will haunt me, I believe, as long as I live . . . all clothed in the dirt-colored homespun they always wear, worn to rags and tatters, leaving them, in many cases, almost naked. Hundreds of them had not the rags to be decent."[80] These people had neither the tools nor the energy to seek revenge.

In their focus on freedom, black Southerners followed the model of previous slave rebellions, which used organized violence to break the power of slaveholders. Despite white efforts to characterize slave uprisings as murder writ large, enslaved people used violence strategically to effect social change that they could not achieve through moral suasion or political change. The imprint of this model could be seen in colonial rebellions as well as more recent events. The Stono Rebellion of 1739 in

South Carolina, when a group of 200 enslaved people marched south toward what they hoped would be freedom in Spanish Florida, left a legacy that resonated into the twentieth century. When interviewed in the 1930s, George Cato identified himself as the great-great-grandson of the man who led the rebellion. In his recollection of family lore, Cato did not shy away from the killing that accompanied the event, but the historical memory centered around the slaves' march south toward Florida. His father and grandfather kept the story alive by literally walking the "route of de rebel slave march."[81] For Cato, the meaning of his ancestor's resistance lay in the movement toward freedom, not the violence that was necessary to enable it.

The most important and most misrepresented of these liberation events was the Haitian Revolution. Two generations of white Americans matured believing that the enslaved people on the island engaged in an orgy of brutal violence. Rather than just military violence as a part of legitimate rebellion, French reports portrayed black insurgents as glorying in murder for its own sake. Ideologically, this reporting functioned as an antecedent if not ancestor of Confederate propaganda about the coming "servile insurrection." French planters (still alive) in Haiti or refugees who moved to Philadelphia, Baltimore, or New York created the bloody mythology in written histories of the event.[82] The Haitian Revolution was unquestionably violent, but many of the atrocities that French writers trumpeted in order to generate sympathy for the planters came from later, secondhand sources.[83] Violence sustained the practice of slavery on this Caribbean island as on other sugar holdings. Once the insurgency began, French planters and the French state vigorously resisted the effort of the island's inhabitants to free themselves and to liberate Saint Domingue from colonial rule.

As in the Civil War, the issue of violence on Saint Domingue was not whether but what kind. In the war's first phase, from 1791 to 1793, both French and insurgent forces committed atrocities as slaves fought to free themselves. In the war's second phase, previously enslaved fighters joined with the French to battle British and Spanish soldiers intent on capturing the island. After their repulse, the island's black and mixed-race populations forged a new alliance aimed at breaking French rule. The final phase witnessed gross atrocities committed by both sides, usually in retaliation for the enemy's actions. Even then, however, the violence grew out of the dynamics of the war rather than expressing some natural bloodlust inherent in black men. As a British naval officer observed, the black soldiers in Haiti "have certainly not exceeded in either atrocity or in folly" the French. Confusing the issue at the time, the United States, under President John Adams, supported Toussaint Louverture's drive to independence. From 1798 to 1801, the US government, seeking to upset French authority in the hemisphere and to secure advantageous trade relations with a key neighbor, extended diplomatic and even military assistance to the rebellion. This cooperative stance turned out to be brief, but it revealed the potential for a harmony of interests between revolutionary regimes.[84]

Free and enslaved people in the United States identified their military participation in the Civil War with the black revolutionary tradition that found its apotheosis in Haiti. They were what one scholar calls "American Toussaints, committed, disciplined, and talented slave soldiers who were eager to both die and kill for freedom."[85] Black memory carried a different story and a different moral than the island's white inhabitants promulgated, one that celebrated the destruction of the gins, fields, barns, and plantation homes that enabled and depended upon their bondage.[86] As a recent scholar remarked, "slaves and free colored people in Saint-Domingue pushed republican principles to the radical conclusion that all men, regardless of race, are free, equal, and entitled to the rights of citizens."[87] A handful of white American abolitionists had drawn this conclusion at the time. New England minister Abraham Bishop asserted the similarity of the American and Haitian revolutions. "We believe that Freedom is the natural right of all rational beings, and we know that the Blacks have never voluntarily resigned that freedom," Bishop wrote. "Is not their cause as just as ours?"[88] Black Southerners agreed; they supported Northern victory in the Civil War because it promised to restore the freedom that was the natural state of man. Two Ohioans who wrote the secretary of war promised that if given the "poor priverlige of fighting—and (if need be dieing)" they promised "a regiment of colard men can be raised in this State, who we are sure, would make as patriotic and good Soldiers as any other."[89] White abolitionists joined black Southerners in the fight against slavery, and they too marshaled the memory of Haiti in the current war. Wendell Phillips, one of the most famous New England abolitionists, lionized Toussaint Louverture in an address to a packed house at the Smithsonian Institution in 1862.[90]

Sailors and travelers who circulated through the islands brought news of Haiti and later of West Indian emancipation.[91] Because Southern state laws made it illegal to teach enslaved people to read, this knowledge circulated via word of mouth. Story, song, and myth carried the truth of the Haitian Revolution to residents of the black Atlantic.[92] Black Americans celebrated the success of Louverture and other Haitians at building the only independent republic controlled by people of African descent in the hemisphere. After British and French emancipation in the West Indies, both accomplished peacefully through legislative change, black Americans celebrated West Indian Emancipation Day.[93] Even still, the image and model of Haiti remained important in abolitionist literature and speech-making throughout the antebellum era. William Wells Brown, a former slave and a leading abolitionist in the 1850s, found the United States wanting compared to Haiti. While "Washington's government incorporated slavery and the slave-trade," "Toussaint's government made liberty its watchword . . . and made freedom universal among the people."[94] Black-owned Northern newspapers such as *Freedom's Journal* provided a steady stream of coverage, both historical and contemporaneous, about Haiti, lauding it as a model for liberation.[95]

Before the war, few black Americans publicly celebrated the Haitian Revolution (Southern whites would surely have regarded such behavior as cause for punishment), but this changed during the Civil War.[96] In 1862, the Lincoln administration granted formal diplomatic recognition to Haiti, offering it a measure of legitimacy as a sovereign republic that previous American administrations had denied. In 1863, a huge crowd of black Northerners gathered from across the Midwest in Chicago to celebrate British emancipation, the Emancipation Proclamation, and the inauguration of diplomatic ties with Haiti.[97] Prospective soldiers heard it in the call to arms: in the midst of the debate over whether black men should enlist, the *Weekly Anglo-African* asked its readers: "Did Toussaint L'Overture stop to ask that question? Did his followers stop to ask that question? No, no, not at all. They rose up with all their strength and struck blow after blow for freedom."[98] This use of the historical image of

Haiti to mobilize a justly waged war for liberation could not have been more different than white Southern propagandists' use of Haiti to conjure anticipations of unchecked bloodshed.[99] As a white abolitionist noted at the time, in the histories of slave rebellions, "each time has one man's name become a spell of dismay and a symbol of deliverance."[100] Black Americans regarded their own liberation and black Haitian liberation as of a piece: they both required war, but war directed at the goal of freedom, rather than at revenge.

Alongside this historical argument for just behavior, the religious foundations of antebellum black life reinforced the restraint that characterized how black Southerners related to white Southerners in the conflict. By 1860, hundreds of thousands of black Southerners counted themselves as members in the Methodist and Baptist churches, the main religious communities in the antebellum South. The white Americans who shared the tenets of Christianity in the late-eighteenth and early-nineteenth century hoped to save souls and teach docility and obedience. White Southerners, in particular, believed the two were complementary goals; because black people were fitted to be servants, being respectful ones would demonstrate their faith. According to one minister, white evangelicals taught only "the prominent portions of Scripture which shew the duties of servants and the rights of masters." The effort to use religion as social control failed, as black Southerners fashioned spiritual lives that met their own needs. Instead, Afro-Christianity enabled black Southerners to weather the vagaries and suffering meted out in the Civil War.[101]

More specifically, enslaved people built a theology that responded to the stories of redemption and suffering in the Old Testament. A historian of slavery explains that "slaves' identification with the children of Israel took on an immediacy and intensity which would be difficult to exaggerate. The slaves' religious community reached out through space and time to include Jacob, Moses, Joshua, Noah, Daniel, the heroes whose faith had been tested of old."[102] Enslaved people identified with the suffering of Jesus, but a prophetic faith modeled on the Jewish experience of deliverance attuned enslaved people to millennial time frames.[103] This framework enabled black Southerners to maintain a faith that a more narrow expectation of divine intervention could not sustain. The gulf between white and black visions of how God acted and for what purpose could be seen in the exchange between an enslaved woman named Maria and her mistress, who asked her slaves to pray for the South. The more they prayed the more it appeared the Union won, which dismayed the mistress, who suspected her slaves were praying for the North.

> "One day my mistress came out to me. 'Maria, M'ria . . . what *does* you pray for?'
> 'I prays, missus, that de Lord's will may be done.'
> 'But you musn't pray that way. You must pray that our enemies may be driven back.'
> 'But, missus, if it's de Lord's will to drive 'em back, den they will go back.'"[104]

By the time of the Civil War, southern Afro-Christians had the confidence to believe that God would answer their prayers. This did not mean passivity. To the contrary, it required rigorous belief and right action. In an analysis of antebellum black Christianity, one historian emphasizes the importance of Gospel discipline—the willingness of Afro-Christians to submit to a moral order because "acknowledgement of one's moral status in society is acknowledgment of his claim to be honored as an independent, adult person." This self-discipline introduced a spiritual practice that had real world consequences, especially when the war upset the social order and opened possibilities for active resistance or outright violence that did not exist previously. Black Southerners seized the moment to find freedom but not to wreak revenge. The moral discipline of Afro-Christianity protected white Southerners too. As a scholar of southern religion observes, decades of worship had produced a people for whom "forgiveness and forbearance were clearly the attitudes which enabled the weak and powerless to make the oppressor and his instruments psychologically irrelevant." Given the centrality of parables of revenge in modern American life, it may be hard for contemporary readers to empathize with the strength of forgiveness, but by the time of the war, it had come to embody "the essential expression of the black Christian faith." Black Southerners did not absolve their former bondholders, but their focus on freedom rather than vengeance embodied an ethic of forgiveness.[105]

That said, not all enslaved people hewed to the narrow path of nonviolence. Some threatened or used violence against owners and overseers in order to secure greater autonomy or protect themselves from the arbitrary brutality of slavery. Such behavior produced a plantation with "the negroes getting so free and idle" in Tennessee, one woman reported to her husband, because "most every one is afraid to correct them." In other cases, enslaved people killed masters or other figures of authority. Sometimes, these actions displaced white people from plantations, while in others they served as a prelude to black people fleeing and reorganizing themselves in a place where they could make war against slavery. Conspiracies and revolts against slavery occurred in nearly every slave state during the war. Most of these revolts, whether real or imagined, were violently suppressed by whites, often at the cost of dozens of black lives. In other cases, violence was a more intimate tool, wielded within a household against a master or mistress. John Ogee, who joined the US Army in 1863 after escaping slavery, recalled a woman who bludgeoned her overseer with a piece of iron and buried his body. One of the most famous of such events, but hardly the only one, occurred when Betsey Witherspoon, a prominent South Carolina mistress, was murdered "by her own people. Her negroes." Witherspoon's cousin, Mary Chesnut (the war's most famous diarist) worried that she faced the same fate. Despite the benevolence Chesnut believed characterized her relations with slaves, Witherspoon's death revealed the tenuous protection that paternalism promised her.[106]

Breaking Slavery

Although black people rarely sought lethal revenge for its own sake, they used the uncertainty of the war and especially the newfound power of their representatives, black Union soldiers, to attack the institution of slavery. As the black lawyer John Rock noted, "they have not gone to the battlefield for the sake of killing and being killed; but they are fighting for liberty and equality."[107] As a result, the Southern home front became a place of instability. "The conditions of war," one historian writes, "presented bondpeople with opportunities to move in new ways."[108] This was true especially in areas under Union control, where the Northern army attracted runaways, and news of freedom encouraged resistance. Even after the Union had controlled southern Louisiana for two years, the Union provost marshal for St. Marys, on the west side of New Orleans, reported an attack on the plantation of Mrs. Oxley that cost her sugar and molasses, later found in the cabins of her slaves.[109] The citizens of Baton Rouge requested help from the Union. According to them, "negroes . . . are permitted to roam at large without molestation, several murders having already been committed and mules, horses, &c. carried off." This state of affairs, if true, was also "subversive of the first principles of good order and military discipline." Perhaps recognizing the broader shift against slavery, the provost marshal took no action, despite the fact that this region fell within the exemptions Lincoln had written into the Emancipation Proclamation. White Southerners were left to face the deterioration of slavery on their own.[110]

Sometimes, the chaos that slaveholders feared manifested in unusual ways. In North Carolina, a mixed-race group of men ransacked the property of two Confederates. The leader of the gang was a white loyalist named Griffin, who had taken the Union's oath of allegiance early in the war and was then driven from his county by secessionist neighbors. The two Confederates, William and James White, had "availed themselves of the products of his labor feeding their hogs on the corn of his fields & reaping large benefits from his farm." Griffin, supported by a group of armed black and white men, returned for his revenge. The men moved between the two White homesteads, taking household articles, clothing, farm tools, and meat from the smokehouses. At James White's they left with 400 pounds of smoked meats after assaulting the residents "with threats and abusive language." Although the Whites filed a complaint, Griffin's vengeance mission appeared successful. As in Louisiana, the Union's efforts to stem the disruptions of war found a limit. "The place at which these difficulties occurred," the recording officer noted, "was some ten miles beyond our pickets out of New Berne . . . thus virtually leaves the locality devoid of protection & perhaps as suggested by council, beyond the power of law." When enslaved people asserted their autonomy without actually escaping (as happened all over the South throughout the war), they sometimes required the threat of violence to enforce it. William Moore remembered the pivotal moment on the plantation where he was raised. "Billie and Sam told Marse Tom they is taking charge of the niggers themselves and they ain't goin' to stand for any more beatings." The enslaved men gathered the shotguns on the property. "Then one day a group of men approach and the slaves warn Tom that if any approach the house, they will be shot." Tom relayed the message and the men—sent by neighbors to discipline Tom's slaves—beat a retreat.[111]

Enslaved women exploited the uncertainty of war whenever they could, even if they never left the plantations on which they were bound. As the most perceptive historian of this process has noted, "slaves did not rise up en masse, as in the common usage of the phrase, but they did rise up." They broke tools, burned plantation homes, refused to work, or fled altogether. "They spoke openly of freedom, calling for an end to the brutalities associated with slavery, especially the violence against women." These women no doubt took succor from seeing black soldiers in blue attacking slavery, even if their vision was limited to rumor or news reports rather than firsthand liberation.[112]

In August 1863, four soldiers from Louisiana's First Native Guard traveled to St. Bernard Parish and wreaked havoc. Ostensibly a recruiting trip, like those launched by USCT regiments on the Georgia-Florida coast, the men of the Native Guard sought not just additional soldiers but anyone desiring to leave slavery. According to the Union provost marshal for the area, "they visited plantations of loyal & peaceable men, putting guards over their houses, threatening to shoot any white person attempting to leave the houses and there seizing horses carts & mules for the purpose of transporting men women & children from the plantations to the city of New Orleans." In 1863, Louisiana remained in an awkward condition: in those parts of the state occupied by the Union, loyal slaveholders counted on the army to protect their slave property. Yet when in Confederate controlled areas, a small group of Northern soldiers liberated plantations at will. St. Bernard had been under Union control since early 1862, with slavery ostensibly preserved. Four soldiers apparently could undo that. Their presence inspired "a band of negroes thus assembled to the number of seventy five [which] went signing shouting & marauding through the parish disturbing the peace." The soldiers used their guns to intimidate planters and other white authorities, and the Union provost marshal clearly had little recourse except to complain to his superior. Meanwhile, some of those who had been freed returned, seeking to liberate their wives from loyal owners.[113]

A Ride for Liberty—The Fugitive Slaves. During the Civil War, enslaved people sought freedom rather than revenge. As this wartime painting by Eastman Johnson reveals, escaping often entailed a perilous and uncertain journey.

On the same day of their raid into St. Bernard, the Native Guard later ran afoul of a more responsive officer, S. W. Sawyer, the Union commander at Camp Chalmette. He witnessed the same actions—"stopping all work on plantations where they have been, placing guards over the owners and threatening to shoot any dammed white man who interfered in any manner"—and detained some of the men and those they had freed. A superior officer, no doubt pleased with Sawyer's actions, condemned the soldiers as "subversive of the first principles of good order and military discipline."[114] This may well have been true. It remains difficult to know exactly what happened in St. Bernard and similar environments. The soldiers may have been freeing relatives from bondage, may have been impressing men against their will into the army, or may simply have been reveling in their ability to cause chaos. Despite his Massachusetts origin and antislavery leanings, Major General Nathaniel Banks (who replaced Benjamin Butler) did not advance an abolitionist agenda in the Department of the Gulf. When a headquarters officer recommended trying the four Native Guard soldiers before a provost judge, Banks concurred. Regardless, the episode no doubt left the planters of St. Bernard worried about the fate of their slave property and demonstrated to black men that they could use their authority to break slavery.

In other places, the route out of slavery was more solitary. Thomas Cole's experience reveals the capricious path that many enslaved people followed to freedom. Cole's parents had been sold away from the plantation on which he was born while he was still a child. When the Civil War began, Cole was sixteen and already familiar with the vulnerability he faced as a bondsperson. By 1862, Cole feared his overseer was out to get him. Rather than risk an attack on the man, he decided "I's gwine to run off de first chance I gits." Cole's goal reflected the pursuit of liberty that motivated freedpeople during the war: "I's gwine north," he remembered, "where dere ain't no slaveowners." Cole bided his time until supplies ran low on the plantation where he lived and a new, less attentive overseer took charge. Joining a group of enslaved men sent out to hunt, Cole separated himself from the party and hid out for several days until discovered by Union soldiers. Accused of being a Confederate spy, Cole survived his initial encounter by persuading the soldiers he sought only freedom. They sent him to work for the US Army outside Chattanooga, where he participated with the artillery in the Battles of Chattanooga, Lookout Mountain, and Orchard Knob.[115]

Like Thomas Cole, the overwhelming majority of black Southerners who broke out of bondage during the Civil War did so peacefully.[116] To be sure, the raw fact of escape allowed slaves to strike a blow against the slave system, but the method of attack shaped both the experience of enslaved people and the course of the war. By choosing freedom rather than revenge, enslaved people de-escalated the Civil War. Their decision forestalled the immediate violence they might have committed and denied white Southerners the excuse, eagerly anticipated by many, to commit yet more violence against the enslaved and freedpeople still within their grasp.

[5]

Unnecessary Violence

Some historians regard 1863 as a turning point in the Civil War. The Union's twin victories at Gettysburg and Vicksburg altered the momentum of the conflict, though few people at the time believed these battles made Union victory in the war inevitable. The year 1863 should have been a turning point in other respects. In April, the Union issued General Orders No. 100 (the Lieber Code), committing itself publicly to the laws of war. Lieber codified the prevailing wisdom regarding permissible conduct and spelled out in practical terms what Northern soldiers could legally do in the process of suppressing rebellion. Although some historians doubt the reach and efficacy of the code, most regard its effect as salutary.[1] In many instances, this proved to be the case. But the laws of war, as defined by Francis Lieber, created an ambiguous standard for violence in the context of pursuing victory. Lieber licensed lethal violence against irregular combatants. Thousands of guerrillas were captured and pacified, but executed nonetheless, and the US Army banished tens of thousands of civilians from their homes. Both summary executions and banishment flourished in 1863 in Missouri and extended roots across the country, where other commanders reproduced them. The contrary forces visible in the Lieber Code—one toward greater respect for a lawfully conducted war and one toward a more violent and destructive conflict—were hard to distinguish in the popular attitudes on each side. Instead, the popular media of both sides condemned the worst actions of their enemy and ignored those committed by their own armies. Ministers played a key role in creating popular impressions of justice in war and of the enemy. For both Northerners and Southerners, a religious sanction exacerbated the distance between combatants and encouraged a more violent conflict.

The Lieber Code contained the same sharp double edge that defined the Civil War experience prior to 1863. It incorporated both malice and charity, especially in one of its central provisions: the definition of military necessity. "Military necessity," Lieber wrote, "as understood by modern civilized nations, consists in the necessity of those measures which are indispensable for securing the ends of the war, and which are lawful according to the modern law and usages of war."[2] Confederates howled that the first clause authorized anything that was necessary to win the war. Federals emphasized the second clause, which used global precedents to check American power. They argued that by anchoring necessity to "indispensable" measures—acts without which it was *not possible* to win—the code restricted Union military action. As a legal scholar recently showed, this was, in fact, a humanitarian improvement on existing precedent. In previous conflicts, European armies took what they wanted from civilians in their path without regard to the military purpose of such confiscation or destruction. Under Lieber's rules, "military necessity," he argues, "was not a legal prerequisite to visiting indiscriminate destruction on the unarmed subjects of an enemy state."[3] The code limited the war's violence by connecting destruction to military, not political or social, requirements. This rule loosened over time, and Union commanders inflicted violence on Confederates that could be sanctioned under the laws of war but that was not strictly indispensable. When the Union Navy destroyed a Mississippi River town in 1863 for harboring guerrillas who fired on a convoy, one of the soldiers on board condemned it as "one of those unnecessary acts" that he believed would extend rather than shorten the war.[4] This phrase aptly describes much of the war's violence against noncombatants, though it is important to note that both sides rarely used lethal violence against civilians; that bright line remained intact. Although the Confederacy never issued an equivalent military code, its soldiers followed similar protocols, and they too committed lawful but unnecessary violence.

Silent No More: The Laws of War in the Field

The commanders and regular soldiers of both armies, though overwhelmingly volunteers, behaved according to standards of conduct then common among the professional armies of Western Europe. These were unwritten but deeply felt rules, what Ulysses Grant referred to as "what I conceive to be my duty."[5] That said, combatants in a given battle or campaign rarely agreed about the right way to interpret those standards and expended considerable energy in denouncing each other for violations of them. Confederates regarded the Union's use of black soldiers as an abandonment of the laws of war, while Federals regarded the Confederacy's use of guerrillas in a similar way. Neither could agree among themselves about an appropriate response. The year 1863 was a crucial one for both sides. The Union committed itself to emancipation and the enlistment of black soldiers. Within the Confederacy, guerrilla gangs expanded their numbers and created even more mayhem. Driven by these twin challenges—and their common foundation in disagreement over who could legitimately fight the war—Francis Lieber chaired a committee that drafted the first comprehensive rules of conduct for the US Army. These rules proved that the laws of war in the nineteenth century were a labile thing. They could restrain or they could license brutal behavior. They could protect the innocent or condemn the guilty.

The Lieber Code

Despite the frequent references by people on both sides to the "laws of war," these rules existed mostly as philosophical disputes, a form that inhibited easy reference, comparison, or judgment. The European thinkers who interpreted the laws of nations and national conflict did so in long, complex treatises, heavily footnoted and replete with evidence from previous writers. Henry Halleck's 1861 effort in this vein, *International Law; or, Rules Regulating the Intercourse of States,* followed the script with care. As a result, it provided little practical guidance for how soldiers could actually behave. This was where Francis Lieber entered the picture. Fully versed in the historical literature on the topic, Lieber produced something original—a manual of conduct with short paragraphs explaining what was lawful for Union soldiers to do.

The problem of how to handle irregular fighters presented the most serious ethical dilemma Union commanders faced in the war. Only a month before the army issued General Orders No. 100, Ulysses S. Grant, then commanding US forces in Tennessee, pled for a public system of rules that would reduce friction between enemies and improve the conditions of the war for noncombatants. "There has been much done by the citizens of the Southern States that is not in accordance with any known rules of civilized warfare," Grant complained. The "citizens" he referred to here were guerrillas: "these are persons who are always in the guise of citizens, and on the approach of an armed force remain at their homes professing to be in no way connected with the army, but entitled to all the indulgences allowed non-combattants in a country visited by an opposing army. These same persons, many of them, are ready to fire upon unarmed vessels, and to capture, and sometimes murder, small parties of Federal soldiers who may be passing." This practice troubled him, as it did other Union commanders, from a strategic but also legal perspective. "In the absence of any standard authority on this subject, I believe all persons engaged in war must have about them some insignia by which they may be known, at all times, as an enemy to entitle them to the treatment of prisoner of war. Then their hostilities must be carried on in accordance with the rules of civilized warfare."[6] What Grant was proposing, Lieber would articulate, and General Orders No. 100 would formalize. If these conditions were adopted, Grant believed that the army's lethal power could then be directed with precision against only legitimate targets.

Military necessity was only one inspiration for the code. Lieber possessed enormous ambition, and he cultivated relationships with a variety of Union officials as a way to both influence the course of the war and establish himself as a thinker on par with Grotius and Vattel. Commanders on both sides also demonstrated a genuine desire to set parameters on war. Last, the code signaled to a global audience that the United States followed established rules. Although neither Lincoln nor Seward nor Stanton gave the code much attention in their correspondence, it served an important diplomatic purpose by positioning the Northern army within the western military tradition.

What kind of war did Lieber recommend? Following the central tenet of just war—the necessity of discriminating between soldiers and civilians—the Lieber Code established strict rules regarding the treatment of noncombatants. Article 44 specified that "all wanton violence committed against persons in the invaded country, all destruction of property not commanded by the authorized officer, all robbery, all pillage or sacking, even after taking a place by main force, all rape, wounding, maiming, or killing of such inhabitants, are prohibited under the penalty of death, or such other severe punishment as may seem adequate for the gravity of the offense." Against this scrupulous regard for the rights of true noncombatants, Lieber offered no leeway for irregular combatants. Guerrillas could be executed on the spot. Although Confederate authorities only rarely contested any particular execution of guerrillas, they rejected, on principle, Lieber's classification of irregular fighters as outside the pale of law and the protections offered to regular soldiers.[7]

Northerners supported Lieber's code for a variety of reasons. Some saw the strategic value of occupying the moral high ground in the war. Others hoped that the publication of the code would show Southern civilians that the US Army intended to spare them and only punish the soldiers opposing them. Still others maintained an abstract commitment to the rule of law, seemingly without concern about how this position would benefit or harm the Union cause. The provost marshal for southern Tennessee fit this latter description. Captain R. M. Godwin's jail periodically filled up with men accused of being bushwhackers in the area. When superiors reprimanded him for releasing men, he issued the following explanation: "the prisoners were retained three days; no evidence was forwarded all we had was the above mentioned. I talked to each one separately & they claimed to be good, honest men, guilty of no offence; which might be doubted, but no testimony could be procured to prove the contrary." Godwin was not a Confederate sympathizer. He assumed the guilt of the accused but could find no legal way to hold them. "Under the circumstances, nothing could be done; the provisions of the 'Magna Charta' are still in force."[8] Although other provost marshal generals confined suspected insurgents indefinitely, Godwin's actions reflect Lieber's relatively high standard for what harm could be done to noncombatants.

On the other hand, guerrillas found no reprieve from General Orders No. 100. Just as Godwin was releasing his civilian prisoners, Union Brigadier General William Dwight, commanding a brigade near Cheneyville,

Louisiana, announced the fate of R. H. Glaze. Glaze had been a regularly enlisted sergeant in the 8th Regiment Louisiana Volunteers but now "by his own admission being entirely discontinued with any regular military organization in the service of the so called Confederate States of America" and having been captured alone "with his overcoat strapped upon his saddle, arms in his possession to wit a Kentucky rifle, evidently for the purpose of shooting down our soldiers," he was tried as a guerrilla. Dwight followed protocol by trying Glaze and publishing a Special Order explaining his fate. He was shot, Dwight wrote, "as a warning to all men not soldiers to remain peaceably at their homes, if they desire the protection of the Government of the 'United States.'" More ominously, Dwight threatened that "the fate of this man shall be the fate of every man found with arms in his hands not belonging to the so-called Army of the Confederate States of America."[9]

It remains difficult to assess the exact influence of the Lieber Code. Union soldiers were convicted of violations of General Orders No. 100, though many had been tried by court martial or military commission in the war's first two years as well.[10] Like all General Orders, the code was printed in bulk and distributed to Union commanders and to troops, a point Henry Halleck emphasized when John Schofield assumed command in Missouri. Halleck knew from experience how vexing the state could be and warned Schofield that "administrative matters . . . will constitute the most [illeg], arduous, perplexing, and responsible duties of your command. On this subject I commend to your attention the 'Field Instructions' published in General Orders, no. 100."[11] Some historians find little to suggest it constrained Northern actions.[12] According to this view, on the question of treatment of civilians the code was "ambiguous"—it established protections for civilians but included few sanctions for soldiers who violated the rules.[13]

The Confederacy never created a set of rules of conduct comparable to the Lieber Code, though they behaved according to the same prevailing customs of war. In 1861, the Confederate army adopted the *Military Regulations of the United States* and the *Articles of War*. As discussed earlier, these two prewar Regular Army manuals featured guidelines intended to facilitate military efficiency rather than regulate conduct between the army and civilians. Unlike the North, where the Joint

Committee on the Conduct of the War and different permanent congressional committees monitored how the administration fought the war, the Confederate States Congress responded mostly with shrill hysterics. Despite containing many distinguished prewar politicians, the CS Congress displayed little initiative in terms of fighting the war. The Confederacy's decision to abolish political parties generated a more personal and less productive form of oppositional politics. As a result, Confederate legislators exercised little real influence over the Southern army. Jefferson Davis's various secretaries of war (he had five in four years) exerted more rational policymaking. James Seddon, who served longest as head of the War Department, frequently referred to the laws of war in his correspondence with officers in the field. The Lieber Code he condemned as "a confused, unassorted, and undiscriminating compilation from the opinion of the publicists of the last two centuries, some of which are obsolete, others repudiated."[14]

Guerrillas and the Code

On paper, the Lieber Code established a hard line against irregular fighters. Captured guerrillas, Article 82 declared, "are not entitled to the privileges of prisoners of war, but shall be treated summarily as highway robbers or pirates." In practice, Union officers often stopped well short of the irrevocable punishment it demanded. This reflected Lincoln's attitude. When Union Major General John C. Frémont issued an order authorizing his soldiers to kill anyone captured in arms against the US government, Lincoln revoked the order. "Should you shoot a man," Lincoln wrote Frémont, "the Confederates would very certainly shoot our best man in their hands in retaliation; and so, man for man, indefinitely." Lincoln gently indicated that Frémont's proclamation was both strategically unwise and morally suspect. "It is therefore my order that you allow no man to be shot, under the proclamation, without first having my approbation or consent," Lincoln explained.[15]

All over the Confederacy, even in Missouri (where Frémont commanded), Northern commanders pursued less violent strategies of suppressing guerrillas than what Francis Lieber called for in his code.

Although Union commanders could and did resort to executions, especially when units that lost soldiers to guerrilla attacks captured those
suspects, not all guerrillas were killed outright.[16] For instance, when
Union soldiers in Perry County, Arkansas, captured suspected guerrilla
Thomas B. Atterberry, he received a regular hearing rather than a drum-
head court-martial. Accused of "consort[ing] with Roberts [sic] Guerrillas and Bushwhackers opposed to the Government of the U.S. who do
not belong to or compose a part of the regular organized forces of the so
called Confederate States," he was eventually found not guilty and released.[17] Other records from the Little Rock provost marshal demonstrate
that imprisonment was a widely used option for guerrillas.[18] Some were
tried quickly while others languished. Some were imprisoned locally
while being tried and others, once convicted, were sent to Northern
prisons. Several men who were suspected of active disloyalty suffered
long stretches in prison on thin evidence, so these suspects hardly escaped
punishment. In November 1864, a group of men in the district were
charged with theft, parole violations, and operating as guerrillas. They
were released in February 1865.[19] A similar case transpired in northern
Louisiana, where a provost judge found a group of nine men guilty of
being guerrillas and sentenced them to hard labor during the war. The
local Union commander approved the verdict and within a few weeks
the men were sent to Ship Island, where they labored until war's end.[20]
Not every provost marshal or field commander was as thorough as the
Arkansas officers seem to have been, but evidence demonstrates that the
United States did not treat guerrillas in a uniform fashion. The deposi-
tions that remain are not detailed enough to see the cases with perfect
clarity, but they reveal that judges evaluated evidence, character, charges,
and context and that commanders could adjust sentences. Some men
were dealt with severely and others released immediately while still
others were held without any real charges.

The Union housed captured guerrillas at different locations. Many
of the men suspected of functioning as guerrillas were detained, tried, and
jailed locally throughout the South. Others, especially those whose who
seemed inveterate in their opposition to the Union, were sent north.
Among the prisoner-of-war camps created by the federal government, the

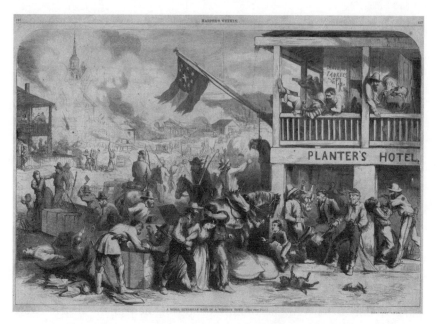

"A Rebel Guerrilla Raid in a Western Town." This illustration, published in late 1862, captures the intimate violence and social chaos caused by guerrillas in the western and trans-Mississippi theaters.

facility at Alton, Illinois, housed many irregular combatants.[21] Between 1863 and 1865, records indicate at least 455 prisoners held there.[22] The irregular combatants at Alton were primarily men captured during the campaigns of the western armies through Missouri, Kentucky, Tennessee, Mississippi, and Georgia. In Arkansas, Union Major General Frederick Steele filled the military prison at Little Rock with guerrillas.[23] Ulysses Grant, who led these campaigns, seems to have been particularly careful to avoid mixing captured soldiers with guerrillas, bushwhackers, and sympathizers. Reporting to Henry Halleck in late 1862, Grant reported that a cavalry detachment had captured forty prisoners from "Haywoods partizan Rangers Seven." Considering these men guerrillas, Grant sent them to Alton.[24] But three months later, Grant had a change of heart and wrote the Alton commandant asking for the return of "Captain Haywood's Cavalry," whom he now respected as "regularly in the confederate service, and entitled to the same treatment as other prisoners of war."[25] Grant instructed his subordinates to pursue the same approach, distinguishing between regular and irregular Confederate soldiers and segregating the prisoners accordingly.[26] Grant's treatment reflected his understanding of the laws of war—regular soldiers were entitled to parole and exchange while guerrillas were not. With their tales of bushwhacking horror, he may also have anticipated the deleterious effect that mixing irregulars into the general prison population could produce.

Grant had good reason to suspect that the stories swapped in Alton might engender more bitter hostility toward the Union. In addition to the bona fide guerrillas held there, Northern commanders also sent to its confines civilians whom they suspected of supporting irregulars or whose loyalty could not be determined. Among them was a Missourian "accused of being a Southern Sympathyzer," held six months, and then released on parole. Another was a Louisianan, seized, according to his wife, with thirteen other men from the small town of St. Joseph as Union forces moved through the region. How long he remained confined is unclear. Women too could be sent to Alton. One woman nearly ended up there after being banished from federal lines at Helena, Arkansas, for being "a camp follower and Common Woman." If she returned again, the provost marshal threatened to have her listed as a spy and sent to Illinois. These civilian prisoners gave weight to the Confederate accusation that Lincoln's regime made war on noncombatants as well. They were the stuff that turned regular soldiers, especially those humiliated by capture and imprisonment, into guerrillas.[27]

Noncombatants they may have been, but hardly innocents. Union commanders regarded the decision to send men (and women) to Alton Prison as a nonlethal method of achieving their larger goal of establishing order and loyalty within the South. Occupied places were unstable places because provost marshals and local commanders never trusted that the complacent face presented to them by Southern whites was genuine. Exiling community leaders, especially if they had proven ties to irregular fighters, could help ensure a peaceful occupation. "The longer Union officials supervised an area," one scholar argues, "the more they became motivated to rid themselves of suspicious noncombatants."[28] By sending men to Alton, officers hoped to preempt the ground-level resistance that plagued so much of the Union's occupation of the South. When Southern places resumed their allegiance to the Union and when those men sent north manifested true loyalty, they could be reunited with their families.

But if commanders regarded this approach as an effective strategy against the irregular war, why did Union commanders not confine more guerrillas? Surely, a policy of imprisoning rather than executing guerrillas would have alienated fewer white Southerners. Very few field commanders explained their decisions either to detain or kill the guerrillas they captured, so we are left with frustratingly few records from which to recreate the process. What is clear is that when irregulars were captured in the process of what resembled regular combat, as happened in the case of Haywood's Partisan Rangers described above by Grant, officers were more likely to consider nonlethal punishments. When guerrillas were captured in the midst of clearly irregular actions—attacking pickets or guard houses, sniping at wagon trains, or attacking civilians—they received no mercy. The law, as Lieber wrote it, did not protect them, and commanders angry over the unjust deaths of their men or civilians they had sworn to defend rarely granted clemency. When Confederate Major General John Pemberton confronted William T. Sherman with evidence that a Mississippi citizen had been killed by a Union officer, Sherman regretted the outcome but regarded it as an inevitable result of the Confederacy's half-guerrilla war. "I assert that his killing was unfortunate, but was the legitimate and logical sequence of the mode of warfare chosen by the Confederate Government by means of guerrillas and partisan rangers." Another report, typical in its brevity and its curt anger, came from a Union soldier: "the Bushwhackers who we Captured 5 miles from Ft. Smith was hung at the Guard house, to-day, it was proved on him as a bushwhacker." This soldier, like Sherman, felt justified, perhaps even obligated, to execute the bushwhacker because doing so might deter would-be guerrillas. In addition, fewer irregular enemies enabled easier Union control. Executions also satisfied soldiers' desire for revenge within the confines of the law. But executing guerrillas could also generate sympathy for irregulars among some locals. Nonlethal strategies may not have offered the same emotional satisfaction, but Union commanders' frequent use of imprisonment suggests they recognized the long-term utility of a softer approach.[29]

Sieges and Civilians

Guerrilla violence was not the only war process that generated paradoxes for the Union. Sieges and artillery bombardments of towns and cities were a crucial feature of nineteenth-century warfare, but entailed using a blunt instrument against a vulnerable population.[30] The Lieber Code, like the *Military Regulations* before it, assumed the legitimacy of sieges as an act of war and set only a few narrow limits—for instance, that hospitals, libraries, and art repositories should be protected. In the course of the Union Navy's efforts to establish control of the Mississippi River in 1861 and 1862, the Union bombarded Southern places, but these sieges rarely lasted long enough to do serious damage. They produced few civilian casualties. As the Confederacy retrenched in the western and trans-Mississippi theaters, it narrowed the range of places it held. This, in turn, allowed the Union to focus its resources on a handful of spots along the river as it sought full control of the Mississippi and its major tributaries, especially Vicksburg, which was subject to a full siege. The armies of both sides also used bombardments to dislodge enemies from inland towns. Like waterborne attacks, these were brief and directed at hostile forces but inevitably produced hardship for civilians as well. The experience of bombardments in the Civil War did not anticipate the massive civilian death and destruction meted out through air campaigns of the twentieth century. Neither did it return participants to the devastating and prolonged sieges of the medieval period. Although the use of artillery against civilian space injured and occasionally killed noncombatants, it could have produced much worse outcomes.

Even if Civil War bombardment campaigns were lawful and produced comparatively few civilian casualties, they killed people unnecessarily. Although the besieged usually cited sound military reasons for defending a given place—strategic location, industrial or governmental resources, or simply a large population they were sworn to protect—defenders who sequestered themselves among civilians put innocent lives at risk. This dilemma was historical. From the earliest records of organized warfare, combatants struggled with the question of how best to balance the sometimes conflicting demands of protecting people and places. The laws of war evolved to accommodate these demands. Grotius clarified that strangers to a country should be given the opportunity to leave before a siege when they would be subjected to lethal violence along with the regular residents. Those people who were "really Subjects of the Enemy, that is, from a permanent Cause, if we respect only their Persons, may in all Places be assaulted, because when War is proclaimed against a Nation, it is at the same Time proclaimed against all of that Nation." Union soldiers understood this idea because of how white Southerners received them and because of the state organization of the Confederacy. Henry Halleck's 1861 treatise on international law defined the process: "a *siege* is a military investment of a place . . . instituted by the rights of war, and for the purpose of injuring the enemy." The "capitulation" that besiegers sought could be obtained by artillery bombardment or more slowly by denying the entry of food, water, medicine, and other necessities into a place until its defenders were forced to surrender. Under the latter conditions, when formal sieges were initiated and lasted for prolonged time, everyone—soldier and civilian—suffered in tandem. Halleck followed the conclusions of earlier generations of writers on the topic in assigning responsibility for the civilian inhabitants of a city to the army that located itself there. Attackers were not required to limit their military campaign in order to protect civilians. Because "every besieged place is, for the time, a military post," Halleck concluded, "its inhabitants are converted into soldiers by the necessities of self-defense."[31]

Building on this foundation, US and CS military regulations instructed officers in the method of organizing their forces and conducting sieges. Both specified that commanders maintain a record of the experience, with the Confederates singling out artillery officers who should note "the effect of the fire," an agnostic comment that reverberates with special irony considering what Confederates came to say about Union artillerists. Experience confirmed the legitimacy and the efficacy of sieges. The most recent American war—against Mexico—had involved their use. During the Battle of Vera Cruz, one historian notes that Winfield Scott directed "a four-day bombardment that threw 463,000 pounds of hot iron into the city, and [caused] the deaths of several hundred Mexican civilians and troops." The outcome justified the toll: "the garrison surrendered both the city and the covering fortress of San Juan de Ulúa." The officer directing the artillery fire at Vera Cruz was Robert E. Lee.

Scott moved from this victory westward to the capitulation of Mexico City, and his men—including Lee, Jefferson Davis, and many other future Union and Confederate generals, learned the utility of this old form of warfare, even when it extracted high costs in terms of civilian casualties.[32]

When Lieber drafted the code, he built upon what Halleck wrote. General Orders No. 100 includes six references to sieges, most of them restrictions on the behavior of besiegers. For instance, attackers could not intentionally target "classical works of art, libraries, scientific collections, or precious instruments, such as astronomical telescopes, as well as hospitals," and messengers coming from besieged cities must be accorded protection as legitimate combatants. The CSA *Army Regulations* likewise specified that once captured, besieging armies were required to protect "churches, asylums, hospitals, colleges, schools, and magazines."[33] But these were minor points that offered limited protection. What marked the Lieber Code as both traditionally restrained and potentially devastating is the clear sanction for bombardment of civilian spaces. Article 19 encouraged but did not require commanders to notify an enemy of a bombardment in order to remove women and children from the place. Under the scope of military necessity, surprise might compel an unannounced attack.

Lieber's consistency with historical practice in war extended to his latent assumption that by retreating into a city, a belligerent exposed civilians to potential harm and this fact could be exploited by an attacker. He declared it within lawful precedents for a besieging force to "drive back" noncombatants expelled by a besieged commander in order to reduce the ration life of his soldiers "so as to hasten on the surrender."[34] Grant used this strategy at Vicksburg, but Northern commanders made clear that Confederates bore the responsibility for civilians injured in a siege. The Northern officer commanding the Charleston siege wrote to his Confederate counterpart that "women and children have been since retained by you in part of the city which has been for many months exposed to fire is a matter decided by your own sense of humanity."[35] The same silence in the Lieber Code regarding civilian casualties manifested within the Union high command. In the full-scale sieges conducted by Northern forces (at Vicksburg, Charleston, Atlanta, and Petersburg), officers never openly discussed the issue of moral responsibility for noncombatants. This silence was not the product of conspiracy or oversight.

Nor was it exclusive to the North. During those occasions when the Confederacy bombarded towns or cities, commanders focused exclusively on military objectives. Robert E. Lee's report on the battle at Harpers Ferry during the 1862 Antietam campaign reflected the same single-mindedness that characterized Grant. "The attack on the garrison began at dawn," Lee reported. "A rapid and vigorous fire was opened from the batteries of General Jackson and those on Maryland and Loudoun Heights." Jackson bombarded gun emplacements in the upper section of the town as well. He was clear about who bore responsibility for the safety of noncombatants. "Should we have to attack let the work be done thoroughly; fire on the houses when necessary," Jackson instructed a subordinate. "The citizens can keep out of harm's way from your artillery. Demolish the place if it is occupied by the enemy, and does not surrender." Lee celebrated the victory over "the garrison" without acknowledging the civilians who were exposed to Confederate fire.[36]

The same rules applied when Confederates bombarded Cumberland, Maryland, the following year. The town sat along the line of the Baltimore & Ohio Railroad and also the Chesapeake & Ohio canal, which the Union held, and which Confederates attacked throughout the war, often with guerrillas. In June 1863, Confederate General Brigadier John Imboden led a raid on the canal. Lee issued clear instructions to Imboden: "do them all the injury in your power by striking them a damaging blow at any point where opportunity offers, and where you deem most practicable." Lee wanted to confine Union troops as he marched into Pennsylvania. Imboden took Lee's instructions as authorization and when Imboden's party arrived at Cumberland they "drove away Federal patrols, and then shelled the town." No Cumberland civilians were injured, but like the encounters along the Mississippi River where Union forces bombarded towns without fatalities, this seems to have been more a result of luck than intention. Besiegers knew that their conduct could be justified under the rules of war, so they focused on the mechanics of the operations. As with execution of guerrillas, because the rules of engagement sanctioned the violence, attackers felt little compunction about unnecessary violence that might result from their actions.[37]

Despite Union commanders' seeming callousness about civilian casualties, during sieges they focused on capturing, not destroying, Southern places. They only targeted sites of strategic or political importance: the high bluffs of Vicksburg, Mississippi, offered control of the Lower Mississippi River, essential for the Union's goal of securing dominance over the corridor; Charleston, South Carolina, birthed the secession movement and housed a key deepwater port on the Atlantic coast; Atlanta, Georgia, controlled a key junction of railroad lines and contained a wealth of war materiel; and Petersburg, Virginia, guarded access to the Confederate capital at Richmond. These military targets also happened to hold tens of thousands of civilians. Second, the Civil War's siege cites held large armies, because Confederate commanders (John Pemberton, Joseph Johnston, and Robert E. Lee) retreated into them. When Vicksburg fell, Ulysses Grant captured 30,000 Confederate soldiers, almost 5 percent of the Confederacy's total enlistment for the war. Last, these places contained industrial infrastructure that both sides regarded as legitimate targets: arsenals, foundries, shipyards, and ordinance and uniform factories. "To destroy these means of continuing the war is therefore our object and duty," a Union officer noted.[38]

Grant's campaign to capture Vicksburg took nearly a year and culminated in the first large-scale siege of the war. It created a model that other Union commanders followed when they resorted to bombardments of civilian towns. Once his army successfully crossed the Mississippi River (south of Vicksburg), Union forces pushed across the Mississippi countryside, defeating their opponents in a wide arc toward Jackson and then back toward the coast. Grant failed to defeat Pemberton's army before it reached the safety of Vicksburg. Against his better judgment, Grant ordered an attack on the city, which failed and cost his army thousands of casualties. After this, he realized that "the place is so strongly fortified . . . that it cannot be taken without either a great sacrifice of life or by a regular siege. I have determined to adopt the latter course and save my men." At nearly the same time that Grant initiated his bombardment of Vicksburg, Nathaniel Banks coordinated a similar attack on Port Hudson, Louisiana, a smaller but still important Confederate outpost farther south on the river. Port Hudson served as shipping depot for cotton grown along the Mississippi River. It consisted of little more than a few blocks on a single street, but contained several hundred residents. Banks's instructions to the region's naval commander reflected no concern about civilian casualties: "we mean to harass the enemy night and day . . . I shall want you to shell the town at night uncesasingly. I think if you can get past the range of the centre of the town and then drop the shells on the right and left, front and rear, for the space of half a mile from the town that it will harass the enemy without injury to us."[39]

Like Banks, Grant's priority in protecting his soldiers remained not just legal under the laws of war but standard practice (as it is today), even when the Confederacy occupied a place where it put civilians in harm's way. Instead of planning another attack or simply waiting them out, Grant ordered a round-the-clock bombardment of Vicksburg beginning May 21, 1863. But even this did not have the effect that many expected. Union soldiers who had anticipated an immediate surrender once their artillery barrage began were surprised to find themselves still outside the city weeks later. The continued Confederate defiance offered evidence that the bombardment was not as damaging as the sound portended. Only a handful of civilians died in the siege and even these fatalities were not definitively the result of the bombardment itself. "I don't imagine this tremendous cannonading has much effect," one observed, "they are so well protected." Like Grant, his soldiers regarded the siege as a legitimate form of warfare even if it produced medieval results. "It seems impossible to take this place, except by close investment, and starvation of the garrison." Grant explained the situation to his wife, Julia: "Everything looks highly favorable here now. I have the town closely invested and our Rifle Pitts up so close to the enemy that they cannot show their heads without being shot at. . . . They dare not show a single gun on the whole line of their works. By throwing shells every few minutes the people are kept continuously in their caves. They must give out soon even if their provisions do not give out. . . . Troops are on less than half rations and many poor people without anything. I decline allowing any of them to come out." This was a harsh but routine and lawful practice under the laws of war. Northern opinion stood firmly behind Grant. One advocate declared that the Union would sail the Mississippi "through to the sea, if we have to raze to the ground every dwelling and every market in Vicksburg. This is our right and our duty."[40]

Whatever Grant's moral reasoning and no matter how scrupulous he may have been about confining the bombardment to Confederate gun emplacements and rifle pits, civilians felt the effects. Although compared to the sieges of Charleston and Petersburg, the Vicksburg campaign concluded quickly, the degree of control Grant exercised ensured that hunger and malnutrition became serious problems before its end. One historian argues that hunger was relatively unknown among white men before the war so the siege, in effect, pushed them back in time and equalized, to a limited extent, conditions between whites and blacks in the city. He interprets Grant as being very deliberate about the punishment that a siege entailed. "It could end only in abject, humiliating, gut-gnawing, surrender and was designed to achieve that particular end. He made no apology. He was a merchant of war." Grant's portrayal in Southern newspapers at the time was even worse—a merchant of death, not war. The *Richmond Daily Dispatch*, after weeks of boasting that the bombardment had no effect on the Gibraltar of the South, reprinted the account of an officer in Pemberton's army who claimed that "the shells, indeed spared no house in the devoted city. Men on their knees at public workshop were killed by them, the sick were killed on their beds, and many who lay down at night to sleep, undisturbed by the report of the bursting missiles to which they had been accustomed, slept the sleep that knows no waking." The report, and Confederate newspapers more generally, obscured the fact that despite its vigor, fewer than ten people died from Grant's siege, a small number in a city of 5,000. After the surrender, some Northern partisan found a functioning press and printed a "Confederate Bill of Fare" for July 4, 1863. The entrees included "Mule head, stuffed, a la Reb; mule hoof, jerked, a la Yankee; mule ears, fricasseed, a la getch; mule side, stewed new style, hair on; and mule liver, hashed, a l'explosion." The casual mockery conveyed by this artifact suggests little sympathy for the victims of the siege.[41]

War on Citizens

It was not sieges alone that increased noncombatant vulnerability and suffering. In the eastern theater, two great armies battled each other across a confined territory while in the western theater, smaller armies and detached units advanced and retreated, bringing them into greater contact with noncombatants and civilian space. In the trans-Mississippi theater, even smaller units of combatants moved in unpredictable and often unsustainable feints and maneuvers. Combined with the region's pattern of irregular violence, this produced a dangerous environment for civilians and soldiers alike. When Lincoln made emancipation a Union war aim in 1863, it exacerbated the region's disorder.[42] The uncertainty generated by this process compelled Union commanders sent to pacify the region to adopt harder tactics against its residents. The fighting in this region, especially Missouri, Kentucky, and west Tennessee, involved much smaller numbers of soldiers and drew less press attention, but the treatment of noncombatants (many of them strongly opposed to the Union) established precedents for policies later implemented in the East.

Nonlethal policies had their own complications. Even Lincoln's attorney general had a hard time parsing the administration's war powers. In a revealing letter to the secretary of war, Edward Bates admitted that "it is hard to draw the exact line of separation between the different kinds of arrests . . . that is, judicial arrest, whose only object is to secure the presence of the accused, so that he may be tried for an alleged crime before a civil court, and <u>political</u> arrests (which is usually executed by the military arm) whose object is to secure the prisoner, and hold him subject to the somewhat broad, and as yet undefined discretion of the President." Arrest and imprisonment, whether it was military, judicial, or political, generated intense opposition. Both conservative Northerners and Confederates condemned Lincoln as a tyrant for the people he jailed during the war. From Lincoln's perspective, detention was a nonviolent practice that deescalated what could have been a runaway death toll. Many people in the North regarded Confederates as traitors, against whom capital punishment was not just possible but required. Later in the war, Ulysses S. Grant encapsulated the military logic of indefinite imprisonment: "every man we hold, when released on parole or otherwise, becomes an active soldier against us at once, either directly or indirectly. If we commence a system of exchange which liberates all prisoners taken we will have to fight on until the whole South is exterminated." Like Lincoln, Grant understood that the political goal of the war—reunion—mandated as much restraint as Northern soldiers could muster.[43]

Civilian Pawns

The US War Department instructed commanders in contested regions to pacify secessionist civilians and establish order. Union officers faced external and internal challenges to this goal. The former challenge manifested in the form of guerrilla bands, composed of men who refused to enlist in the regular Confederate army or who deserted and returned home to fight an irregular war near their homes. Unable to defeat the irregulars in traditional combat, Union officers resorted to irregular methods to counteract guerrillas' worst features. In some cases, this meant more lethal force; soldiers could refuse to give guerrillas quarter when they fought. After several frustrating months, one Illinois soldier reported home "thare has been some tall slautering done here with the rebels. Bush whackers lately." In April he had promised to give every guerrilla he encountered one of "Uncle Sams pills," and in August he announced, "every one we cach without killing some how dont get into camp. You can juge for yourselfe what becomes of them."[44] In other cases, Union officers adopted nonlethal strategies, including a method they learned from guerrillas themselves—holding people hostage in order to negotiate conclusions to specific incidents.[45] Already by fall 1861, Ulysses Grant could explain that he had arrested and confined "three citizens of Blandville by the names of Bak, Corbett, and Vaughan. The two latter are held as hostages for the safety and return of a Mr. Mercer, a Union man and citizen of Ky. who was arrested by the rebels and carried into Columbus a few days since."[46] The War Department never sanctioned the practice, but it emerged ad hoc in different theaters regardless.

Rather than proscribing conduct as most of General Orders No. 100 does, Lieber offered an uncharacteristically elusive definition of a hostage. A hostage, he wrote, "is a person accepted as a pledge for the fulfillment of an agreement concluded between belligerents during the war" and must be treated "like a prisoner of war." Lieber was quoting Halleck's *International Law* almost verbatim, though Halleck's discussion of hostages came in the context of the historical practice of ransoming prisoners, a subset of the ways that belligerents relate to each other during war. Anticipating the objection to a practice based on piracy that treated soldiers as personally liable for their participation in war, Halleck shielded himself by relying on the famous jurist James Kent who noted that the United States had never outlawed the practice of ransoming captives.[47] Lieber signaled an equal ambivalence about the practice, writing that "hostages are rare in the present age."[48] Although military commanders shared Halleck and Lieber's reluctance, hostage taking was unusual but not exceptional in the Civil War and more common on the Union than Confederate side.[49] Despite its manifest mistreatment of noncombatants, hostage taking enabled nonviolent resolutions of a number of tense confrontations.

The practice came into wider use in 1862 and 1863, but earlier examples from divided regions demonstrate the spontaneous nature of how commanders resorted to hostage taking. The guerrilla war in Missouri frustrated Union commanders, who could rarely catch guerrillas in action or even find them after clashes occurred. In one case, Union Colonel C. C. Marsh received advance information about a planned attack on the town of Commerce. He seized two pro-Confederate sympathizers, including one whose uncle led a local gang of "marauders." Under Marsh's instruction, they wrote a short but effective note: "the colonel says that if you attack Commerce to-night he will hang us." Confederates protested that the young men were simply citizens and threatened to retaliate for what they regarded as violations of the laws of war. Marsh happily confessed "to the charge of having written the note mentioned, and would have done as I promised had Captain Price committed the threatened outrages on the peaceable citizens of Commerce." Marsh explained to his superior that he acted as he did because the guerrillas did not communicate as regular soldiers did and the men he arrested "had been notoriously active in aiding the enemy," so could not truly claim noncombatant status in any event.[50]

Similar problems developed in the Union's campaign in western Virginia, which had achieved great success in the northern reaches of the state but stalled in the more mountainous and more Confederate southern region. By late fall 1861, Union Major General William Rosecrans was stymied in his attempts to push east through the mountains. The terrain, weather, and irregular resistance all retarded what could have been a key Union campaign in this strategically important region. Rosecrans, still a bit player, though one with a bright future in the Union command, took twelve civilian men hostage because he was "desirous to put a stop to the marauding of the Rebles and believes this to be the most effective way to accomplish it." Rosecrans's open-ended proclamation—he ordered the men held "until he shall order their release"—was unusual, but as a tactic to address irregular warfare it became occasional practice. In western Tennessee, where guerrillas preyed upon both Union soldiers and Unionist civilians, one commander pleaded for the authority to respond in kind. After the murder of four Unionist men in his department, he requested "authority to arrest the fathers, brothers, and sons of these murderers, and hold them in prison as hostages for the safety of and good treatment of our citizens friends."[51]

Confederates expressed reluctance to engage in hostage exchanges because they feared that it would sanction the Union's control over what it regarded as its citizens. In the summer of 1862, Confederate Secretary of War George W. Randolph advised Jefferson Davis about a proposed swap of Unionist citizens seized as hostages for the release of several residents of Fredericksburg, Virginia, that the Union held. Randolph warned that "we cannot offer an exchange without recognizing the right of the enemy to seize our citizens." Union officers sometimes tried to justify the practice by explaining it as "retaliation," but because the exchanges so often involved civilians for soldiers or regular prisoners for guerrillas, they lacked the equivalency essential to lawful retaliation. Confederate Major General Braxton Bragg, a close follower of military rules, identified this inconsistency in his correspondence with the high command in Richmond. By late 1862, both sides had seized so many civilians that the United States formally proposed exchanging them, as they did prisoners. Bragg criticized the US practice of arresting Confederate sympathizers and sending them to jail in Ohio "for acts which the Confederate forces commit and for which they alone should be held responsible." Bragg was on firm ground in arguing that the laws of war demanded a strict protection of noncombatants, though he ignored the fact that the "acts" the United States was seeking to counteract were usually committed by irregular, not regular, forces.[52]

Because it usually targeted civilians, hostage taking held the potential to be one of the most egregious violations of the laws of war. In one of his more frustrated moments, Ulysses Grant pondered a dramatic escalation in the hostage policy. At the start of Philip Sheridan's 1864 Shenandoah Valley campaign, Grant gave this advice: "the families of most of Mosebys men are known and can be collected. I think they should be taken and kept at Ft. McHenry or some secure place as hostages for good conduct of Mosby and his men."[53] Sheridan never took this exceptional step, perhaps because he recognized how far outside the bounds of regular war it would take him. Hostage taking was nonlethal but hardly nonviolent. It often allowed commanders to negotiate solutions to crises that resisted other solutions, but it imposed serious costs on the people jailed. Some were released quickly, but others spent months in poorly supplied jails. It also imposed psychological costs on the victims, who did not know their fate. The two Missouri men threatened with execution by Colonel Marsh knew that Union officers routinely killed guerrillas. Their uncle's quick compliance ensured they did not have to test Marsh's sincerity, but many other hostages suffered through prolonged periods of uncertainty.

The personal anxiety experienced by hostages multiplied many times over as the stories of hostage taking and exchanges circulated within Confederate communities. Despite the irregularity of the practice, commanders needed to publicize hostage taking in order to achieve their goals. When Confederate Lieutenant General Simon Bolivar Buckner discovered that the Union commander at Pensacola, Florida, had jailed three prominent citizens who refused to take oath of allegiance, he put three Union officers already taken as prisoners into close confinement. These men, according to Buckner's letter, were held "as hostages for Judge Wright, Mr. George Wright, and Mr. Merritt." The method worked. In less than a week, the Union commander responded to Buckner, indicating that Judge Wright was in Pensacola, George Wright has "passed out of our lines," and Merritt left for New Orleans. Like retaliation, hostage taking only worked when all parties to the situation knew what each was doing. In 1864, Congressman Edwin Webster wrote Secretary of War Stanton asking that he order the arrest of three residents of Winchester, Virginia, to be used as hostages in exchange for the return of his cousin, a Maryland state's attorney who was seized by Lee's army as it marched toward Gettysburg in June 1863. Webster identified the men he thought should serve as hostages: Robert Conrad, Daniel H. McGuire, and one other.

McGuire he described as an "active, bitter, uncompromising rebel—original secessionist before war." Robert Conrad was a different story; though a Confederate supporter himself, his father had been one of the county's holdouts against secession and tried to sit out the war neutrally. They were among the most prominent members of the community, and Conrad's arrest would have drawn widespread notice, as Webster no doubt hoped.[54]

Banished Beyond the Lines

When hostage taking failed to deter guerrillas, Union officers adopted another punishment that targeted noncombatants: banishment. In these cases, Union soldiers notified civilians to abandon their homes and then physically escorted them beyond the limits of army lines with orders not to return. In some cases, the homes of banished people were destroyed, and in others the US Army seized them. Civilians arrested as hostages suffered both physically, from the poor conditions in which they were often housed, and psychologically, from the uncertainty about their ultimate fate, but most were returned. The armies who took them, because they were administered by men trained in the laws of war, generally protected the lives of hostages. The same cannot be said for banished civilians. Once released outside of their lines, army officers maintained no responsibility to protect or safeguard the lives of enemy civilians. Like hostage taking, banishment was another policy perfected in places where irregular war predominated and that Union commanders adopted for use in other theaters of war. Also like hostage taking, banishment existed in something of a legal gray zone. The Lieber Code prohibited "all wanton violence . . . against persons in the invaded country" but did not explicitly speak to the prospect of banishment. The code gave Union commanders the right to administer an area once conquered under the terms of martial law, and officers regarded banishment as a viable tool with which to accomplish that goal. Solicitor General William Whiting drew on Revolutionary War precedents, when the American government banished Tories and confiscated their property, to defend the policy as a just response to treason.[55]

Before late summer 1863, when banishment was used on a huge scale in western Missouri, it was primarily a targeted punishment directed at

Confederate women living in Union-occupied cities. In order to create an atmosphere of calm and order, provost marshals and other Union officers needed to identify those people who undermined the project. One way to flush out inveterate Confederates was to require adults to take a loyalty oath before allowing them to participate in civic life. Initially, Northern commanders assumed only men possessed the political identity necessary for a loyalty oath, but they soon learned that white women often manifested as much antipathy to the Union as their husbands, brothers, and fathers. Both men and women objected to taking the oath, which required them to pledge before God to "support, protect and defend the Constitution and Government of the United States against all enemies, whether domestic or foreign, and that I will bear true faith, allegiance and loyalty to the same." William S. Rosecrans, the Union general who managed the occupation of Nashville in 1863, struggled with suppressing Confederate sentiment. Eventually, he resorted to requiring the oath of citizens under the threat of banishment, as Butler had done in New Orleans. Thousands took the oath; he banished perhaps one hundred unrepentant Confederates. It is probably true that some people took the oath cynically, as a ploy to obtain its advantages and protections, but because it was sworn on the bible and sometimes accompanied by a monetary bond, the loyalty oath became a public record that compelled respect.[56]

Dedicated Confederates sometimes refused to take the oath. In a large city, provost marshals could never expect to administer it to everyone, though they could require that prospective consumers produce a bond in order to conduct regular business transactions. In this case, if a woman refused to take the oath, she needed to have a proxy who could purchase goods at a market. Those women who refused the oath (and some who took it cynically) often led the opposition to Union occupation, a practice that could extend from mere discourtesy to Union officers to active spying and express support for Confederate irregulars. These latter were the women most often banished by Union officers. Union soldiers, faced with female hostility firsthand, advocated the policy before it was enacted. Writing from Tuscumbia, Mississippi, one Union soldier noted the change that was coming over men in his regiment. Initially appreciative that local women condemned guerrilla warfare, he observed that "the murders of

Bob McCook, a dozen other men in this command, and hundreds in the army, all tend to dissipate such soft sentiments for we are satisfied that citizens do ten-elevenths of such work; and nothing less than the removal of every citizen beyond our lines, or to north of the Ohio river, will satisfy us."[57]

Usually, banishments came after repeated warnings. When Mrs. C. E. Murray was banished beyond Union lines in central Mississippi, the official charge was for refusing to take the loyalty oath. If she returned, the provost marshal threatened to arrest her as a spy.[58] This step could only be taken if she had had previous encounters with Union officers, probably coming back and forth through Union lines. Memphis, Tennessee, captured by Union naval forces in May 1862, proved difficult to pacify. A succession of commanders there resorted to banishment as a method of control. Grant, in departmental command of the region, complained to Halleck, "there are a great many families of Officers in the rebel army here who are very violent." His solution, which Halleck approved, was to send them south of Union lines. He issued Special Order No. 14, which authorized "the expulsion from Memphis of families of soldiers, CSA and state officers" except for those who took the oath of allegiance. Protests about the form of expulsion (how far they had to walk to reach safety rather than an outright objection to the banishment) from Confederate Brigadier General Jeff Thompson failed to dissuade Grant. The local commander responded in his stead, assuring Thompson that because more Memphis citizens preferred the Union to the Confederacy, relatively few would be affected. His closing admonition reflected the attitude of Union officers: "you are too well versed in the science of War, to be ignorant of the fact that these orders are far more mild than could have been expected after the treatment that helpless Union families have received at the hands of rebels in this city."[59]

The piecemeal strategy of banishment adopted in 1862 failed to solve problems in Memphis. Grant was particularly concerned about guerrilla attacks on the Memphis and Charleston Railroad, a crucial east-west link in the Southern transportation infrastructure. Grant regarded control of the line as essential to his task of pacifying the Deep South. Accordingly, he instructed Union Major General Stephen Hurlburt to inform Memphis citizens in January 1863 that "I will also move south every family in

Memphis of doubtful loyalty, whether they have taken the oath of allegiance or not, if it is necessary for our security, and you can so notify them. For every raid or attempted raid by Guerrillas upon the road, I want ten families of the most noted secessionists sent south."[60] Grant clarified that he would not act against civilians when the line was attacked by regular Confederate units, but because guerrillas operated with the sanction of local residents and outside the laws of war, he held noncombatants liable for their actions. The continuing unrest in eastern Arkansas likewise compelled Union Major General Benjamin Prentiss to issue a threat of banishment against a whole class of the population. Prentiss restricted participation in market life only to those who had taken the loyalty oath. "All male citizens, above the age of 18 years, within the lines of the army stationed at and near Helena, refusing to comply with the provisions of this order," his order specified, "will be immediately arrested and conveyed under escort beyond the lines and released with instructions not to return."[61]

Even after the negative press generated by the banishment of 20,000 Missouri residents, Union officers continued to use the practice to rid themselves of problematic individuals.[62] John F. Philips, colonel of the 7th Missouri Cavalry, requested permission to send two families, mothers and their six and four children respectively, outside Union lines. "They are the families of notorious bushwhackers operating in the vicinity of their homes," Phillips explained.[63] Women whose husbands served as Confederate soldiers continued to present the most trouble.[64] In mid-1864, Union officials in St. Louis struggled with how to respond to a group of women, several married to Confederate officers, who moved between Union and Confederate lines in Missouri and Arkansas. Despite having been banished once, at least one of the women (in this group of four) returned to St. Louis. When captured by the provost marshal, the woman objected indignantly to being questioned. A search revealed that one carried a piece of human skull on which had been carved, "Dec. 31st 1861—Wilson's Creek," the date and location of a Missouri battle. Nina E. Hough, whose husband served as a captain and assistant inspector general in the Confederate army, admitted that she kept it as a memento. Although impressed by her honesty, the questioner concluded that "the true character of this woman, and the object of her coming here cannot be mistaken. She came here in disregard of all military rules and regulations."[65] In a similar situation, Union officials would probably have shot a man who attempted to pass through the lines carrying a piece of a desecrated body of a Union soldier. Banishment actually seems lenient treatment, given the context.

Confederates regarded banishment as a symbol of the viciousness of the Union's war against civilians, and references to it became a staple of Confederates' anti-Union rhetoric.[66] For their part, Union officers seem to have regarded banishment as an unpleasant but nonviolent solution to the problem of women who collaborated with regular or irregular Confederate forces. Lincoln was certainly aware of the practice, just as he must have known about hostage taking. He reversed some orders banishing people beyond Union lines, but he never commented directly on the practice. In one of the most famous cases in the war, the president himself banished the Peace Democrat Clement Vallandigham south of Union lines.

General Orders No. 11

The use of banishment escalated dramatically in Missouri in mid-1863. In response to the guerrilla war along the western side of the state, Union Brigadier General Thomas Ewing "removed" 20,000 citizens of four counties. Ewing sought to end the long-running guerrilla conflict in that part of Missouri and to avenge the worst civilian massacre of the war, William Quantrill's raid on the town of Lawrence, Kansas. The consequences of General Orders No. 11 (as the Union policy was called), in addition to the immediate suffering it caused to noncombatants, were far-reaching. Union officers created an unusually comprehensive intellectual justification for the practice, establishing a precedent for civilian relocation on a massive scale. Like many of the Union's hard war policies, the banishment addressed regional military objectives while contradicting Lincoln's national political goals. The ironies of the decision revealed again the unpredictable nature of the Civil War: a policy that banished thousands of civilians may have avoided an even deadlier solution.

The guerrilla violence in Missouri drew from a variety of sources, some stretching back to antebellum grievances. Lincoln's decision to support emancipation in 1863 complicated the military situation in Missouri still more, as it did in Kentucky, Louisiana, and other parts of the Union-occupied South.[67] The political divisions generated by emancipation created a deeply fractured politics in Missouri, which inhibited the establishment of military order.[68] The wartime Republican governor, Hamilton Gamble, resisted Lincoln's efforts to encourage Missouri to lead the way against slavery. Instead, he was challenged in the state and the region by military officers who championed emancipation.[69] James Lane, the Kansas politician and military leader who led the antislavery and anti-Missouri forces in his state, directed punitive raids into Missouri, which spurred reprisal raids by pro-Confederate Missourians. The long-running border war over slavery meant that residents of the Kansas-Missouri border had battled each other for years, accumulating grievances and learning the landscape.[70] When the Civil War started, the veterans of this border war outfitted themselves with better weapons, learned new tactics, and escalated the conflict.[71] This western region experienced the Civil War's most destructive guerrilla conflict, something qualitatively different from the piecemeal guerrilla attacks against Union outposts or Unionist households in 1861–1862. By 1863, a scholar of the region notes, the "Trans-Mississippi frontier had turned into a lawless and unpredictable environment rife with unmitigated violence."[72]

The fault lines widened by the Union's emancipation policy fractured the Union command in a place where coherence was essential. Some places in eastern Missouri, especially St. Louis itself, were securely defended by large contingents of Union soldiers. Several well-trained and well-equipped regiments remained in the city throughout the war. In contrast, Kansas City, the second largest community in the state and located on the western border, contained only a small detachment of Union soldiers. Rather than imposing order on the region, this vulnerable outpost attracted guerrillas. A recent analysis of attacks in Missouri reveals a pattern to guerrilla violence that helps us understand, in retrospect, the importance of stable, permanent occupation forces. Where Union forces established durable and sizeable occupations, they could deter guerrilla activity. If the Union created temporary or undermanned garrisons (smaller than a regiment), these encouraged irregular violence, against both soldiers and civilians.[73]

Union efforts to stem the guerrilla conflict in Missouri failed to accomplish their goal. Pro-Confederate guerrillas continued to target Union soldiers, especially those in undermanned and temporary outposts in the Missouri countryside, while some groups degenerated into simple banditry, assaulting civilians indiscriminately. Regardless, the security problem created by Missouri's irregular war complicated Union occupation and demanded a solution. The rotating cast of general officers brought into the state to establish peace and security for its Unionist citizens created inconsistencies in Northern policy. Some directed punishments toward guerrillas and their supporters while others imposed policies that affected true noncombatants as well, unintentionally creating more Confederates in the process. As McNeil's executions at Palmyra in 1862 demonstrated, retributive violence, even if it satisfied some emotional need, accomplished little in terms of securing the protection of peaceful citizens. By 1863, Union officials continued to direct missions designed to break up guerrilla bands while also devising a commission system to evaluate the loyalty of residents and to assess fines on those people who supported guerrillas. The bitterness of the guerrilla conflict also inflamed tensions between regular soldiers. Confederate General Thomas Hindman's instruction to his army in the region reminded his soldiers that the opponent they faced was uniquely depraved, by nature and practice. "Remember that the enemy you engage has no feeling of mercy or kindness toward you," Hindman instructed. "His ranks are made up of Pin Indians, free negroes, Southern tories, Kansas jayhawkers, and hired Dutch cut-throats. These bloody ruffians have invaded your country, stolen and destroyed your property; murdered your neighbors; outraged your women; driven your children from their homes and defiled the graves of your kindred." This rhetoric did not encourage a civil conflict.[74]

A four-sided struggle developed along Missouri's western border in 1863. Union forces sought to empower local Unionists, Kansas Jayhawkers aligned with the Union hunted down Missouri guerrillas who, in turn sought to disrupt Union control, while Gamble's state forces failed to support emancipation or adequately confront the guerrilla threat. Union General John Schofield was driven to more and more vigorous policies to create order in the region. His primary concern was eliminating the guerrilla threat, and to do this he targeted the domestic supply line that sustained irregulars. In June, he appointed Thomas Ewing as commander of the recently created District of the Border but failed to furnish him with enough soldiers to administer the region. By August, Ewing had 4,400 men ready for duty, but these troops had to guard Kansas City, establish secure outposts to protect vulnerable citizens, and track down mobile guerrilla bands.[75] There may have been only several hundred guerrillas in the area—accurate numbers are difficult to ascertain— but they drew support from thousands of civilians spread across the region.[76] The pro-Union *Kansas City Daily Journal of Commerce* explained the manpower problem: "It is an utter impossibility to rid the country of these pestilent outlaws, so long as their families remain. . . . With the aid of these spies, dotted all over the country and living in perfect security, a hundred bushwhackers may defy the utmost efforts of five hundred soldiers to exterminate them."[77] A local Union cavalry commander offered even more pessimistic math: "It will be impossible for the United States soldiers to drive them out of this country unless the Government can afford to send ten soldiers for one guerrilla." It was not special prescience that led this officer to identify a solution. "The only way to get them out is to destroy all subsistence in rocky and brushy parts of the country," advised Colonel Penick, "and send off their wives and the children; also the wives and children of sympathizers who are aiding and abetting them."[78] Penick offered this counsel in March 1863. What he envisioned was a broader application of the policy of banishment that Union officers had used elsewhere.

Although neither Schofield nor Ewing responded to Penick's suggestion, by midsummer they inched closer to his position. Ewing understood how the domestic supply line operated, and he targeted it, writing to Schofield in early August to ask if he could deport several hundred families of the worst guerrillas to Arkansas. Perhaps remembering Sherman's and Grant's use of the tactic in Memphis, Schofield approved the order, and banishments commenced. Schofield and Ewing also understood the role of slavery in sustaining military opposition. Accordingly, General Orders No. 10 included an emancipatory component for this Union state. The Emancipation Proclamation included only places in active rebellion, which left Missouri unaffected by the order. Nonetheless, the war was eroding slavery for both loyal and disloyal Missourians. According to Schofield, part of the guerrillas' effort "was to protect their disloyal friends in the possession of their slaves." Ewing wanted to make this impossible. He also cracked down on civilian supporters of the guerrillas. In Kansas City, Ewing arrested a handful of women, several related to the state's most prominent irregulars. These civilian prisoners, like most of those arrested by Union officials around the South, were housed locally rather than being sent to Northern prison camps. Though Ewing had no way of knowing it, the building housing the jail space for these women had been made structurally unsound because of changes to adjacent buildings over the previous decades. On August 14, the jail collapsed. Of the ten women housed there, four were killed and several seriously hurt. Among the casualties were the sisters of "Bloody Bill" Anderson, one of the most active members of Quantrill's band of guerrillas. Anderson and other guerrillas sought revenge.[79]

The response organized by Quantrill stands as the largest premeditated massacre of noncombatants in the Civil War. Quantrill's band rode to Lawrence, Kansas, a refuge for the antislavery free state wing of the western border wars since the 1850s. They arrived in a whirlwind of violence and destruction on the morning of August 21. After sacking the town, Quantrill's men lined up between 150 and 200 of the town's males aged fifteen and over and shot them dead in the street. Both the number of fatalities and the nature of the massacre at Lawrence mark it as the purest large-scale atrocity in the Civil War by a military force (albeit an irregular one). General Ewing's official report summarized the material and human damage cogently. "They robbed most of the stores and banks," he explained, "and burned one hundred and eighty-five buildings, including one-fourth of the private residences and nearly all of the business houses of the town." More alarmingly, Quantrill's raiders "with circumstances of the most fiendish atrocity, murdered 140 unarmed men, among them 14 recruits of the Fourteenth Regiment and 20 of the Second Kansas Colored Volunteers. About 24 persons were wounded."[80] By referring to the massacre's victims as "men," Ewing deemphasized one aspect of the event that could have generated even more Northern anger. Even though some fifteen-year-olds served in Civil War armies (and some regiments listed volunteers even younger than that), most people, if asked, would have classified these "men" as children. The Lawrence Massacre violated not just the usually secure boundary between civilian and soldier but between adult and child as well.

It took several weeks for accurate reporting on the event to reach the rest of the country. Even when news did circulate, Confederates refused to admit the true nature of what had occurred or even to censor Quantrill's actions, an act that commanders on both sides regularly took against subordinates who violated the laws of war. Only a handful of Southern papers classified Quantrill's actions for what they were—mass murder. Instead, most contextualized the event as a part of the violent and ongoing war between Kansas Jayhawkers and Confederate guerrillas in Missouri. The *Richmond Daily Dispatch*, one of the Confederacy's leading papers, expressed the ambivalence that typified many Southern reactions. The editors admitted that they believed "it possible that Quantrell may have departed from the general Confederate custom of fighting wolves and hyenas according to the rules of the knightly tournament." On the other hand, they celebrated his actions by proclaiming him "the Avenging Angel of the wild Western border," one who was "destined, we trust, to scourge to the death the outlaws and murderers who have made Missouri and Kansas shudder with their crimes." The *Augusta Chronicle* offered only excuse and thanks: "The border ruffians of Lawrence have met with a deserved fate. . . . The Lawrenceites set the ball in motion. If they have been crushed by it, they are the only ones to blame. . . . Besides Quantrell has only done to the Lawrenceites what the Federalists have long been doing to our people everywhere." Confederates' willingness to take refuge in the imagined sanctity of revenge marked the dark boundary in responses to unjust violence in the war.[81]

The neutral or supportive tone of the Southern press inspired more anger in the North. Headlines such as "The Rebels applaud and indorse the Lawrence Massacre" suggested to Northern readers that Confederate depravity could be found among soldier and civilian alike. Northern newspapers positioned the story at the top of their pages for weeks. Western papers led the way, printing survivors' accounts and commentary from reporters who quickly assigned blame among the Union military commanders. As with other atrocities, writers put the event in historical or global comparison to help readers understand its scale.

"Our Kansas dispatches partially lift the veil and disclose to us a scene of horror and carnage which can only find its parallel in the butcheries of the Sioux or the massacres of the French revolution." By this point in the war, both sides understood the advantage of explaining to their readers, domestic and foreign, the degree to which such behavior signaled a departure from the laws of war. "The deed of Quantrell embraces the infamy of all these gradations and an infamy more fearful, for it was the desolation of peaceful homes, the murder of peaceful men, and the robbery of peaceful banks and places of business. There is no military law, no military necessity, that will excuse such a crime."[82]

The Union response came in the form of General Orders No. 11, issued by General Ewing four days later on August 25, 1863. It required all inhabitants of Jackson, Cass, Bates, and some of Vernon counties to vacate their homes by September 9. Residents who pledged loyalty to the Union were allowed to relocate to military stations within the District of the Border or to Kansas. But those who could not—the pro-Confederate civilians who presumably supported the guerrillas—had to leave the district entirely or face punishment.[83] Regardless of loyalty, the homes and other buildings in the region were burned to prevent resettlement. Estimates suggest that the order compelled the removal of 20,000 people from their homes (of a prewar population of 40,000 for the area). Ewing's order destroyed the domestic supply line in western Missouri.

General Orders No. 11 emerged from an established tradition in American warfare, especially when soldiers faced an uncivilized enemy. In the event that a combatant engaged in irregular modes of fighting, the army could target the enemy's homes and food supply. This practice began simultaneously with the first permanent English settlement in North America. Less than a year after arriving at Jamestown, John Smith led his soldiers in a "feedfight," itself derived from tactics the English used to suppress Irish uprisings in the sixteenth century.[84] Europeans adopted the technique many times in the long, unpleasant history of warfare with Native Americans in North America. During the American Revolution, Major General John Sullivan, under orders from George Washington, led a prolonged and devastating campaign against the villages and families of the Iroquois in western New York state who fought alongside the British. The Second Seminole War, fought between 1835–1842, involved similar efforts by the 5,000 US Army troops sent to Florida because Seminoles refused to abandon their land. The use of this method against Confederates suggested that army commanders viewed them more like Indian enemies of old rather than fellow citizens.

The banishment of pro-Confederate civilians was predicated on the support they gave to irregulars. Ewing ordered their expulsion because these civilians too often acted like irregular combatants themselves. Even if they did not raid Union camps, they supplied, protected, and gave intelligence to those people who did. In Kentucky, such behavior earned members of the domestic supply line time in jail. In Missouri, it earned them banishment. Schofield later claimed that "the execution of this order was carried out . . . without the loss of a single life or any great discomfort to the participants," but this was patently false. The exile occurred in early September, before the cold weather of the midwestern winter had set in, but the weakened condition of the citizens, already punished by years of warfare and conflict, ensured a high casualty rate. The banished people were generally poor and without the resources to move. The exile created enormous suffering for the civilians, who complied with the order out of necessity and fear of still worse retribution. Within a day, a Union officer observed, "the border was largely 'a desolated country of women and children, some of them allmost naked.'" Much of the order was enforced by Kansas troops, who did so with a vengeance. One such soldier observed: "chimneys mark the spot where once stood costly farm houses, cattle and hogs are fast destroying large piles of corn, prairie fires are burning up miles of good fencing every day or two, and turn which way you will, everything denotes a state of utter desolation and ruin."[85]

Perhaps because of the scale of the order and its singular targeting of noncombatants, the commanders responsible for General Orders No. 11 offered careful public explanations of its necessity and its legality. General John Schofield, the commander of the Department of Missouri, stood fully behind it: "the measure which has been adopted seems a very harsh one, but after the fullest examination and consideration of which I am capable, I am satisfied it is wise and humane." Rather than allow Southerners to claim the order was simply knee-jerk vengeance, Schofield contextualized it around the ongoing guerrilla problem. "It was not adopted hastily as a consequence of the Lawrence massacre. The subject had long been discussed between Genl Ewing and myself, and its necessity recognized as at least probable." This was a true claim—Penick's advice regarding banishment circulated among the regional commanders in March 1863. Schofield knew he would be criticized for subjecting noncombatants to harm but for that, too, he had an explanation. "I had determined to adopt the milder policy of removing all families known to be connected; with, or in sympathy with the guerrillas and had commenced its execution before the raid upon Lawrence." Northern newspapers expressed enthusiasm for General Orders No. 11 as soon as the order was issued.[86]

The Lincoln administration likewise supported the policy. "With the matters of removing the inhabitants of certain counties *en masse;* and of removing certain individuals from time to time, who are supposed to be mischievous, I am not now interfering, but am leaving to your own discretion," Lincoln wrote to Schofield. Henry Halleck, himself an early veteran of Missouri's guerrilla conflict, propounded the legality of the order. "It has been proposed to depopulate the frontier counties of Missouri, and to lay waste the country on the border so as to prevent its furnishing any shelter or subsistence to these bands of murderers." "Such measures are within the recognized laws of war; they were adopted by Wellington in Portugal, and the Russian armies in the campaign of 1812," Halleck observed. Halleck knew his references. Still, he recommended that such orders "should be adopted only in cases of overruling necessity." As Halleck knew, his November report came well after the damage had already been done, which was why he led his report with a defense of the order's legality. Last, but perhaps most importantly, from the perspective of military officers justifying the order, it worked. As a recent scholar has persuasively shown, "nothing more successfully ended irregular violence in Civil War Missouri than Ewing's assault on the guerrillas' domestic supply line."[87]

General Orders No. 11 caused a great deal of harm to civilians, but Ewing and Schofield also sought to prevent worse retaliation by Kansans against the residents of western Missouri. Their concern to prevent such an attack appears throughout all the higher-level discussion of the order. "The great danger of retaliation by the guerrillas upon those who should remain were the chief reasons for adopting the present policy," explained

Schofield.[88] From Ewing all the way to Lincoln, Union commanders worried as much about the counterresponse from enraged Kansans as they did about controlling pro-Confederate guerrillas.[89] The threat was a real one. According to one historian of the region, "from two to three thousand Kansans were then in arms preparing to carry out raids into Missouri."[90] Just days after the event, James Lane organized Kansas men, some active Redlegs and others new to irregular war, for an attack on western Missouri. "Not for mere butchery, not for the gratification of mere prejudice, but for self-preservation, we believe in a war of extermination," Lane told his recruits. "Extermination! I repeat here that for self preservation there shall be extermination of the first tier of counties in Missouri, and, if that won't secure us, then the second and third tier, and tier on tier till we are secure."[91]

Despite the manifest illegality of his plans, Lane shared them with General Schofield: "Mr Lane explained to me his views of the necessity, as he believed, of making a large portion of Western Missouri a <u>desert waste,</u> in order that Kansas might be secure against future invasion." The Union command prevented such a potentially deadly turn of events. Schofield posted guards along the border to keep Lane's Kansans bound within it. But that could not quell the spirit of unrest. A conservative Unionist reported from Platte City that he was organizing "Independent Companies citizens for the defense of this county against the marauders and thieves which now infest it, and for the purpose of defense against the raids which are threatened from Kansas." Northern papers encouraged the sort of action they had condemned among Confederates only days earlier: "Hands off! Let no Copperhead or pro-Slavery General interfere with him. There will be fire and death along that Border, until the great revenge of Kansas is attained. We may not be Christian in these utterances, we are human."[92]

Thomas Carney, governor of Kansas, confirmed the state of affairs in a short note to Schofield just after the massacre: "I must hold Missouri responsible for this fearful fiendish raid." He demanded that people of western Missouri feel the power of military law or else "the people themselves, acting upon the common principle of self-defense, will take the matter in their own hands and avenge their own wrongs." Schofield pledged Carney that the perpetrators of the murders would be punished.

"Be assured that nothing in my power shall be omitted to visit just vengeance upon all who are in any way guilty of the horrible crime." But his language betrayed the boundaries of his conduct—he promised only "just" vengeance—and he opposed any irregular raids by Kansans. "The action of such an irresponsible organization of enraged citizens would be indiscriminate retaliation upon innocent and guilty alike. You cannot expect me to permit anything of this sort." Lincoln agreed with Schofield about this as well, cautioning Halleck, "it is not improbable that retaliation for the recent great outrage at Lawrence, in Kansas, may extend to indiscriminate slaughter on the Missouri border, unless averted by very judicious action." Beyond avenging Lawrence or even curtailing the guerrillas, Lincoln's chief concern appeared to be avoiding a duplication (or worse) of Lawrence. In this context, the banishment imposed by General Orders No. 11 created hardship but avoided massive and deliberate lethal violence. "While no punishment could be too sudden, or too severe for those murderers," Lincoln wrote to a group of Missouri Unionists, "I am well satisfied that the preventing of the threatened remedial raid into Missouri, was the only safe way to avoid an indiscriminate massacre there, including probably more innocent than guilty." General Orders No. 11 thus possessed the same paradoxical nature as so many other violent practices in the Civil War. Despite the severity of its impact on noncombatants, it likely forestalled a much worse response.[93]

The most famous contemporary critique of General Orders No. 11 was created by the artist and sometime politician George Caleb Bingham. Bingham was a Unionist from western Missouri who objected strenuously to what he perceived as a malicious and unjust imposition of military violence against civilians.[94] Bingham served in the US Volunteer Reserve Corps and the Missouri state government during the war but denounced the order nonetheless. "Whatever may have been the motive of 'Order No. 11,'" he maintained, "it is very certain that it had no basis in law, justice or humanity."[95] Bingham painted a famous image that has come to define the terrors of wartime, though few observers today probably understand the context or the liberties he took in representing Ewing and Union soldiers in the painting. Perhaps unintentionally, what Bingham conjured in the painting was a parallel to the Trail of Tears, the expulsion of thousands of Indians from the Southeast in the 1830s.[96] That order too

Order No. 11. George Caleb Bingham's painting offers one of the most famous critiques of the Union's antiguerrilla policy. Although the painting misrepresents the reality of the Union's policy, especially in its portrayal of lethal violence against citizens, it captures the perceived victimization of western Missourians in the wake of General Thomas Ewing Jr.'s order.

was enforced at gunpoint by the US Army and resulted in the deaths of thousands of Cherokees and others who walked through the winter to Indian Territory. Most white Americans supported the Indian Removal Act, signed by President Andrew Jackson, but as Bingham vividly portrayed in his painting, General Orders No. 11 turned that federal power against white civilians. Lincoln, for his part, probably did not see the order in racial terms or as anything equivalent to Jackson's infamous expulsion of the Cherokee. Writing to a group of Missouri radicals, who blamed the Lawrence Massacre and the chaotic violence of the region more generally on the Union commanders who oversaw the area, Lincoln proposed what he called a "more charitable, and, I think, a more rational hypothesis. We are in civil war."[97]

The reciprocal nature of Civil War violence, clearly illustrated in the experience of General Orders No. 11, reveals an additional irony. Union occupation begat guerrilla attacks, which spurred the use of banishment, which, in western Kansas, escalated to the level of wholesale depopulation. The war's participants, their vision clouded by their national and political allegiances and their lived experiences, rarely perceived the holistic nature of the conflict. Unionists, for instance, supported federal authority in the state and regarded the guerrillas as unjust irregular combatants who preyed on soldiers and civilians. They treated the Lawrence Massacre as abominable but not surprising given what they had experienced during the preceding years. For them, there was no justice to the Confederate side and no injustice to civilians punished for aiding it. Pro-Confederate Missourians maintained a similar tunnel vision. They believed themselves subject to illegal occupation and merciless violence since the state's unraveling in 1861. As a result, participants on each side supported policies that worsened rather than lessened the tensions and conflict in the region, increasing their own vulnerability in the process. The rootedness of participants' viewpoints creates friction with our own position, which benefits from both hindsight and ideological distance.

Missouri civilians, Confederate and Unionist, were not the only ones whose actions rebounded against their own professed goals. Carl von Clausewitz, the most famous European theorist of war, published *On War* in 1832, though it was read by few Americans before the Civil War. In that book, Clausewitz offered what amounted to the most famous modern aphorism on war, that it was "politics by other means." This definition helpfully directed subsequent thinkers to focus on the origins and purposes of war, but means and ends in war do not always align perfectly. When Civil War officers took actions that undermined the political goals of their side, some force—institutional rules, political control, or public pressure—was required to restore order. But because of the decentralized communications infrastructure and the comparatively limited electorate, these pressures, even if present, might not bring about change. Abraham Lincoln understood the political purpose of the war—to preserve the Union—and he knew that excessive force against Southern civilians would impede that goal or befoul postwar America. But not all of his commanders possessed Lincoln's political skills, and they had to weigh the safety of their soldiers against the security of hostile noncombatants. Sometimes, Union commanders took military actions that protected their soldiers or

Unionist civilians but that contradicted the political goals of the war. Something like this occurred in western Missouri in August 1863, when the political goal of the war and operational level of military action worked at cross purposes. As the twentieth-century philosopher Simone Weil wrote, "war effaces all conceptions of purpose or goal, including even its own 'war aims.' It effaces the very notion of war's being brought to an end."[98]

General Orders No. 11 may not have directed lethal violence at pro-Confederate civilians but, aside from the important exception of the Emancipation Proclamation, it was the broadest action taken against noncombatants during the Civil War. It also set a precedent for the use of banishment as a tool against large populations by the US Army. William T. Sherman famously repeated the practice in Georgia in 1864, when he exiled civilians in his campaign to capture and secure Atlanta. Sherman has received more notoriety for his expulsion orders, but Ewing's order affected twenty times as many people as Sherman's, and he offered less aid for the refugees themselves. Why does an imagined past—like Sherman's supposed destruction of Georgia—stand out more sharply in our history than a real one—like Ewing's expulsion of pro-Confederate Missourians? Perhaps part of the problem lies with recognizing that our military history is typical rather than exceptional. Ewing's order reflects the process that we fear in all wars—escalation. What we fear about escalation and what seems un-American about it is the degree to which it renders violence inevitable and automatic. Rather than recognize and investigate why this happens in wars, we too often imagine what appears in hindsight to be a sharp break with traditional military practice (and thus something we can deny) when in fact the action we decry developed out of existing habits. Ewing's decision, which required the expulsion of 20,000 people in a loyal state from their communities and the destruction of their homes, evolved logically and consistently from the US Army's use of banishment as a punishment for disloyal citizens. It was neither un-American nor historically exceptional.[99]

The Rhetorical War

The Civil War's violence came from the passions of irregular fighters, the orders of officers, the whims of soldiers, and the pens of politicians. The violence also came from ordinary people. Civilians outside the path of the armies watched, debated, and helped shape the war. As democratic states, both the Union and the Confederacy responded to the demands and whims of their publics. Historians often frame this subject around the question of "morale," which reduces a dynamic and multi-faceted relationship to one assessment: whether civilians were confident in their armed forces and whether that confidence encouraged soldiers to continue fighting. Public support, or its absence, for a military conflict is clearly important to the outcomes of the wars of democratic nations, but popular attitudes shaped the war in other ways as well.[100] For instance, the hard war endorsed by Northern abolitionists propelled the violence inflicted on Southern civilians (and the reverse would have been true if Confederate armies had the opportunity to follow their public's desire to wreak vengeance on Northern communities). In some cases, civilians, angry over the mistreatment of soldier relatives, encouraged an escalation of the war's violence. In other cases, civilians expressed outrage over the behavior of their own troops, and that criticism could restrain military behavior. Peoples' attitudes about the justness of the war's cause and about the justness of the world they expected it to generate also shaped what kind of fighting they sanctioned.

It was, indisputably, a popular war. "*Our army is the people in its military phase and capacity*, the fighting development of the nation," asserted one observer. "Our civil war," proclaimed another Northern author, "is the first in history which is emphatically one which the people imposed upon the rulers, and not one which the rulers imposed upon the people." In their letters, newspapers, sermons, and speeches, people shaped the rhetorical dimensions of the conflict—the exchanges, both direct and indirect, between the two sides, and the broader culture through which observers, both domestic and foreign, interpreted the conflict. One of the most important books on Civil War violence argued that civilians, reading negative accounts of their enemies in newspapers and in soldiers' letters, sanctioned an increasingly violent and bloody conflict. The author argues, "this process of taking the war to heart worked as strongly as any other influence toward making it more inclusive and more destructive." Civilians did experience the conflict vicariously, though it did not inevitably produce only a bloodier conflict. Sometimes this rhetoric produced more intelligible exchanges, and sometimes it disrupted and complicated communication. Sometimes it tempered anger, and sometimes it spurred calls for revenge.[101]

The Popular Press

For civilians who did not experience the war firsthand, and this included almost all Northerners and many Southerners, newspapers provided the most comprehensive view of the conflict. Newspapers allowed people to talk among themselves and to project an image to the world. The primary aim of newspaper publishers was to report on the status of military engagements, but the difficulty of assembling accurate information in a timely manner left many editors free to print what they wanted. Initial reports of battles often included wildly inaccurate casualty estimates and wrong-headed conclusions about who could claim victory in a given encounter. Even though seasoned readers knew to discount for poor reporting and editorial biases, newspapers shaped public opinion nonetheless. Beyond chronicling battles, newspapers alerted readers to reports of misbehavior by the enemy, whether these concerned soldiers in battle or violence directed at civilians. In both the North and South, largely unrestricted popular presses responded with enthusiasm for the national cause of their side. It was rare when a paper celebrated or propagandized unjust violence directly, but editors on both sides included frequent references to the misdeeds of the enemy.

By reprinting administration and congressional speeches, newspapers propagated the rhetoric of war crafted by national leaders. According to Jefferson Davis, white Southerners suffered "outrages of the most despotic character." This was because, as Davis said, the US Army "convert[ed] their soldiers into incendiaries and robbers and involved us in a species of war which claims non-combatants, women, and children as its victims." The *Richmond Dispatch* followed the president's lead. Their August 8, 1862, editorial could stand in for many Southern papers on almost any day during the war: "the day of retribution must come, and we trust it will not long be delayed. That day will be when we are enabled to cross the line and return the desolation to those who first spread it broadcast amongst us. Then let the poisoned chalice be commended to appropriate lips—let the angel of desolation hover over the people who have prayed and fought that we should be plunged in misery and woe—and let no forbearing hand check the tide of retribution until the cry for mercy comes from the persecutor." The use of ornate, sometimes biblical language was typical as well. Editors seemed to believe that ordinary prose would fail to inspire their readers or convey the full measure of their outrage. As the *Dispatch*'s language indicates, its editors neither anticipated nor desired reunion. Scorning reunion, Southern editors did not worry about offending enemy readers, as Lincoln did.[102]

In addition to their reporting about the battlefield practices of each side, newspapers trafficked heavily in reports that the enemy had desecrated the dead, a practice that was especially feared in nineteenth-century America.[103] Both sides assumed and presented evidence that their opponents did this. Reports began after the first major engagement at Manassas. Northern soldiers and newspapers circulated stories of a Confederate blackguard that had mutilated Union soldiers left on the field after the battle. A Unionist minister from Winchester, Virginia, reported that a fellow clergyman described how "'Yankee skulls' were hawked about his town, after the Bull Run battle, at ten dollars a piece. Spurs, also, were made of jaw bones, to his personal knowledge. A member of his own Church, who was at Bull Run, told him that hundreds of bodies were left headless for such purpose."[104] Though hardly common practice, evidence supports charges of grave robbing and desecration by soldiers of both armies.[105] Unionists were incensed by reports of scalping—several of the men still alive—committed by the Indian Regiments under the command of Confederate Brigadier General Albert Pike at the Battle of Pea Ridge. Complicating the situation, both sides only hastily buried bodies after battles, and they resurfaced throughout the war, subject to violation by animals and the weather. The abolitionist *Liberator* regularly reported and reprinted any act of desecration that reached Northern ears.

Another element fueling bad blood between the war's adversaries was the way that newspapers created popular legends that helped the people of each side assimilate themselves to the violence of war. Three figures stand out as emblematic of the unplanned but vigorous use of stories and rumors from the war to glamorize violence in war. Turner Ashby, a Virginia cavalry colonel, led a brief, bloody career cut short by his death in 1862. He became a legend early on—the "knight of the Valley." Ashby's celebrity developed out of his daring exploits in the Shenandoah Valley and his willingness to engage in hand-to-hand combat against Yankee troopers. As his most astute modern biographer argues, Ashby's story assured Confederates that "vengeance *would* be part of this war. Bloodlust *would* become an essential element of Ashby's enthralling presence."[106] Another historian sees Thomas J. "Stonewall" Jackson and William T. Sherman as embodying each side's desire for and endorsement of a violent war. Both commanders fought hard, but the public perceptions of them exaggerated the degree to which they actually waged unrestrained war. Jackson died in 1863 and quickly became the leading star in the Confederate firmament. The image of him as a bold and fearless Christian warrior was meant to inspire further sacrifice. Sherman is a more complicated subject because he wrote so much more about his intent and methods than Jackson. His use of apocalyptic rhetoric—of the Confederates being "wiped out of national existence"—concealed the more deliberate use of force and the substantial restraint he exercised against noncombatants. Sherman contributed to the Northern endorsement of a destructive war by crafting a language that justified unlimited resistance to the crime of disunion.[107] Sherman's quotability and Jackson's noble silence offered Northern and Southern papers ample material from which to spin stories of them and the necessity of hard war.

On rarer occasions, newspapers criticized the conduct of soldiers on their own side, though blame, if assigned, always fell on officers rather than volunteers. After the massacre at Fort Pillow, in Tennessee, the Macon *Daily Telegraph* offered both a summary of the battle and an indictment of Forrest's soldiers under the heading "Rebel Atrocities." The correspondent described the conditions after Confederates captured the fort in much the same language that Northerners did, with bloodthirsty Confederates killing black and white soldiers rather than allowing them to surrender. He concluded that "several such cases have been related to me, and I think, to a great extent, the whites and negroes were indiscriminately murdered." Although the writer closed by noting that Forrest reportedly shot one of his men who was shooting prisoners, nonetheless, "he is responsible for the conduct of his men."[108] The paper stopped shy of calling for his dismissal, but any criticism on this sensitive topic stands out as honest reporting.

In the North, the clear partisan division produced a more unusual situation. Republican papers justified the administration's policies, even when those entailed violence directed at civilians. Democratic newspapers mantled themselves in the laws of war in order to criticize Lincoln. They condemned both the war's origins and its ongoing nature. Not accidentally, their critiques called for a softer war against the South, particularly the protection of private (that is, slave) property. Even late in the war Democrats could be heard denouncing the injustice of Union conduct. In 1864, one midwestern partisan condemned the abolitionists who struck the war's first, unjust blow. "These men intended to plunge this country into civil war. Their criminal intent existed from the outset."[109] Democrats' newfound commitment to restrained military action would have surprised Native Americans, who had been on the receiving end of brutal military campaigns strongly endorsed by Democrats.

The proliferation of newspapers in the 1830s and 1840s ensured that every city and many towns in the United States contained a printing press. As a result, pamphleteers, whether secular or religious, easily reproduced their work. The robust postal system allowed for cheap and fast distribution. The result was a huge and varied pamphlet literature, deeper on the Northern side but nonetheless prevalent in both places. Soldiers, politicians, ministers, and writers of all kinds churned out pamphlets during the war. In New York City, boosters organized the most famous and influential pamphlet society, called the Loyal Publication League (LPL). Composed, like most of the "Loyal Leagues" organized in Northern cities during the war, of elite Republicans, they published more than eighty pamphlets, ranging from three to thirty pages. In 1863, they distributed 400,000 copies of their work and close to half a million in 1864. Francis Lieber was a key force behind the Loyal Publication League, serving as its secretary for a time. His 1861 lectures on the laws of war, reprinted by many Northern newspapers, served as a kind of guide for how to educate the public on legal and military issues. Lieber and other immigrant authors wrote several pamphlets designed to speak to the interests, attitudes, and backgrounds of new Americans, at least five of which were written in German.[110]

LPL pamphlets discussed particular battles and campaigns, commanders, and methods of waging war, including the use of martial law and the suspension of habeas corpus. Many writers addressed the causes of the war, identifying slavery as the fundamental cause but also critiquing the South as an aristocracy opposed to democracy. The pamphlets aimed to boost Northern morale and bolster citizens' commitment to the war. Authors made frequent reference to past wars, studied the historical process of emancipation in the ancient world, and reminded readers of the Founders' antipathy toward slavery. The 1863 pamphlets canvassed the ideas and justifications for starting, sustaining, and changing the nature of the Union war effort. Taken together, they offered a remarkably full airing of the most complex aspects of the war. Nothing comparable existed in the South, outside of newspaper editorials, which did not sustain arguments as complex or as deep as those in the LPL pamphlet series. Because of the political sensibilities of its founders, the LPL was resolutely Republican in its advocacy. During the 1864 presidential campaign, it condemned McClellan and the Democrats, eventually publishing a 150-page treatise enumerating McClellan's failings.[111]

The pamphlet literature drew strength from the increase in literacy in antebellum America, which had also fueled the rise of a new domestic literature. The participants in this movement—later termed the American Renaissance—turned their attention to the war's violence in music, poetry, and literature. Even prewar Democrats like Herman Melville became wartime boosters. The North's most famous anthem—the "Battle Hymn of the Republic"—came about because Julia Ward Howe sought to cleanse the lyrics of the popular favorite "John Brown's Body."[112] "John Brown's Body," probably written by a sergeant in the 20th Massachusetts Infantry in the war's opening months, celebrated "hanging Jeff Davis from a sour apple tree." Ward's version, though couched in more oblique metaphors, hardly eschewed violence. To the contrary, the song endorses military violence as a cleansing tool for a nation corrupted by the presence of slavery. The US Army is made God's "terrible swift sword," ready to cast judgment on the South. Death in a war for abolition is equated to the death of Jesus: "as He died to make men holy, let us die to make men free." Ward's song replaced the original's celebration of lynching with a call for broader and more anonymous violence.

The confidence that Northern boosters sought to instill swelled on a wave of battlefield victories in 1863. For them, the Union victories at Gettysburg and Vicksburg, both providentially announced on July 4, heralded God's favor in their cause. The actual military situation remained quite fraught—Lee's army won perhaps its greatest victory at Chancellorsville in May 1863—but news of success bred a righteousness that obscured doubts and engendered a deeper commitment to the North's hard war. The father of a young soldier, in cataloging the resources marshaled for the army, was "impressed with a feeling of intense and boundless admiration for a people who can thus pour out their bloody treasure to defend their possessions." Rather than intuiting a just cause and celebrating the material with which the Union sought to advance it, he reversed the formula, feeling a "profound conviction that the cause which such a people advocates and defends is just." Lincoln's attorney general, Edward Bates, a conservative from Missouri, detected this sentiment in the North and it worried him. "The right side, beginning, it may be, with patriotic indignation against treacherous crime, soon suffers that virtuous sentiment to be over-wrought, & transformed into a blind passion of revenge." The battles of 1863 only exacerbated this condition: "as successes increase & multiply, those who fancy themselves the chief agents of success, are apt to become puffed up with their own importance, & are easily persuaded, that, as all wisdom is with them, as all power ought to be lodged in their hands." The intoxicating effects of military success that worried Bates shaped Northerners' outlook. Even before the twin victories of 1863, some people had concluded that "Civil war, while it destroys weak nations, strengthens strong ones."[113]

Confederate confidence did not wane inversely as Union confidence rose. The war's conclusion seemed much further away in 1863 to contemporary eyes than it does to ours today. Diehard Confederates explained away even the defeat at Gettysburg. Lee's army retreated to Virginia, where it remained mostly untouched for the rest of the year. But in the western and trans-Mississippi theaters, Confederates could not ignore the increasingly large Southern space controlled by the US Army. If victory engendered confidence, what did defeat bring? For some Confederates, defeat generated anger, which they directed back at the Union forces in their midst. As new towns came under Union occupation, citizens reacted with barely concealed loathing. "Better, far better ... that Charleston should be laid in ashes, either by its barbarian foe or the hands of its own brave defenders," proclaimed the *Richmond Daily Dispatch*, "the burning of the town, is mercy compared with its occupation by Yankees, with the living death of New Orleans."[114]

Religious Rhetoric

Aside from the flood of reportage and propaganda generated by the popular press, people also received information and argument about the war from their religious leaders. In the overwhelmingly Protestant religious establishment of 1860s America, most ministers endorsed their section's war aims and methods and described the other side as an irreligious enemy. The competitive religious atmosphere fostered by the disestablishment clause of the Constitution compelled American ministers to attract parishioners. Though most took their charge to direct peoples' spiritual lives seriously, they also recognized the need to engage with issues of public concern. A minister without a pulpit could save no souls. The war fever in each region ensured that few ministers dissented loudly even if they opposed the war, which few did. Instead, ministers added a religious luster to the national cause of each section. They marshaled an old and powerful language to elevate their own cause and condemn that of their enemy.

Southern ministers maligned the North with special vigor. They had good experience with this practice. Southern ministers had been cultivating a separate Southern identity in sermons for decades. In wartime lectures and homilies, they venerated the Confederate side and used enemy casualty figures as evidence that their opponent was working against God's will. Already in 1861, the Reverend Henry Tucker lamented that *"thousands of our young men have been murdered."* The civilian language of "murder" created a position of Southern victimhood in which soldiers' deaths were not the cost of war but the evil deeds of a malicious and vindictive North. Tucker urged the strongest response: "to arms! To arms! Let us kill! Let us destroy! Let us exterminate the miscreants from the earth! Up with the black flag! They deserve no quarter! They alone are to blame for this horror of horrors." Tucker, like many ministers, made explicit the spiritual dimensions of the conflict—"we are God's children," he proclaimed. As suffering in the South mounted, Southern ministers redirected people's fatigue and anger toward the North. One of the most well-known Southern divines, Presbyterian minister Benjamin Morgan Palmer, referred to the war as a "holy cause"; the "wicked infidelity" of the North earned the scorn of God while the South's "fearful baptism of blood" was testament to God's love and support. A Tennessee Confederate went even further: "I really believe he who kills the greatest number of abolition thieves and their abettors is the best Christian."[115]

Ironically, defeat on the battlefield could also inspire confidence. Led by their ministers, white Southerners interpreted defeats as God's way of testing them. "I know we have sinned and richly deserve chastisement . . . and the Yankees may be used as the rod in God's hand," the Presbyterian Basil Manly Jr. wrote. "But, for all that, I cannot believe we should be either subjugated or exterminated by them."[116] Just as the God of the Old Testament had punished his favored people with trials, so he seemed to be testing those who now claimed they had earned his favor.

Northern ministers kept pace with their Southern peers when it came to war rhetoric. "War is not Christian work," Unitarian W. G. Eliot admitted, but "I hold it to be a Christian duty to defend our country from invasion and rebellion, peaceably if we can, forcibly if we must." Eliot demanded a Christian warfare: "there is also a difference in the conduct of warfare, and we may make it a war of barbarism, or of comparative humanity and civilization. . . . Let us do our part to keep Christian principles alive."[117] Northern politicians, led by Abraham Lincoln, kept reunion in view and so tried not to personalize the war or demean Southerners. Ministers felt less compunction about hewing this line. Though many echoed the party line that blamed the war on Southern elites, they also developed a fuller critique of white Southern life and political behavior that ennobled the Union cause. "We are upon Biblical ground, therefore, when we invoke God in doing battle for a just cause. . . . And, surely, we can appeal to God with pure hearts for the justness of our cause as a nation," preached a New York minister.[118] Many Northern preachers turned naturally to the story of Cain and Abel. Presented as the original parable of fratricidal violence, Northerners read in Cain's treachery a biblical parallel to the crime of the South. "In the whole history of human warfare," wrote one man, "from that first civil war in which Cain slew his brother and received the ineffaceable mark of God's displeasure, nothing—nothing exceeds in fiendish malignity the acts of those Southern men who in this war, are fighting on the side of treason and rebellion."[119]

The necessity of bloodshed to purge sin drew on a long trajectory of Christian thinking. As two modern theologians have argued, "at the center of western Christianity is the story of the cross, which claims God the father required the death of his Son to save the world." This interpretation, as dominant among Protestant Christians in the nineteenth century as it is today, produces a "theological claim that sanctions violence." The religious sanction offered by ministers bonded with the secular language of just war to produce a dangerous hybrid: just participants in a war further ennobled with divine favor felt few restraints on their conduct. Critics of this view could be found in the antebellum era. Hosea Ballou, an early proponent of Unitarian Universalism, argued strongly against the Christian sanction for violence. He believed that the idea that Christ's death was necessary to appease God's anger "has done more injury to the Christian religion than the writing of all its oppressors . . . the error has been fatal to the life and spirit of the religion of Christ in our world." But Ballou remained in the minority in the wartime North. More typical was a comment from one of his Unitarian brethren: "our atonement by blood has come."[120]

The rhetoric of the Civil War, both secular and religious, encompassed participants like a fog. Wherever they were and whatever position they occupied, it enveloped them. In conscious and unconscious ways, the rhetorical war shaped how people perceived and understood the physical war, even as changes in peoples' attitudes reshaped the conflict itself. Rhetoric influenced how participants on each side viewed themselves and their enemy, and it governed how they interacted during those pivotal moments when combatants met, whether they were in uniform or not. These meetings contained the potential for great violence. When Union officers approached civilian leaders to demand the surrender of a town, when Confederate officers accused Northern troops of abusing or murdering the prisoners they took, or when civilians stood before invading or occupying forces to demand exemption from the war's destruction—these moments were governed by the rhetorical positions people held.

Sometimes those attitudes exacerbated animosity and hastened a break-down in communication or worse, and sometimes they facilitated an exchange that deescalated the war. Civil War rhetoric could inspire or diminish the war's unnecessary violence.

Although most Civil War rhetoric inspired contempt and hatred for the enemy, the common language each side used—the emphasis on manly virtue, honor, respect for the laws of war, and victimhood—enabled discussion even as it raised the stakes of those conversations. Among soldiers, the "laws of war" become a buffer, a talisman that commanders on both sides invoked in discussions with the enemy. The *Official Records* chronicles thousands of discussions between Union and Confederate officers over the terms of the war. Because the armies operated with a premodern communications infrastructure, field commanders often established their own policies in spite of each side's official policy. Officers kept careful watch on the actions of their enemies and protested immediately and with vigor anything they regarded as violating the laws of war. The responses to these protests ranged from apologies to debate to outright rejection. Sometimes commanders ignored missives from their enemies, but because these letters were almost always released to local newspapers, the public nature of the discussions demanded responses. Neither side could appear to concede a point to the other, so some exchanges continued long past the point of usefulness.

The execution of William Mumford in New Orleans, the executions ordered by General John McNeill in Missouri, and the banishment of citizens all revealed the difficulties of communicating with the enemy. The conversations surrounding these events were shrouded in confusion because participants could not agree on what terms to use or the meaning of the few words they had in common. Were civilians in a combat zone legitimate targets? By taking actions that interfered with a military operation (like removing a flag that signaled an end to the fighting), could they transform themselves into irregular fighters and thus legally be killed? "Local defense" evoked a hallowed past in American history, but "guerrilla" put men outside the pale of law. Both sides agreed that "non-combatants" remained exempt from the war's violence, but national loyalty could alter who deserved that label. Any soldier out of a uniform or in the wrong place could be accused of being a "spy," a designation that nearly always carried the death penalty. The question of who could be identified as a "soldier" (and thus protected by the laws of war when captured) created the most fraught territory in the period after emancipation. Language mattered because the laws of war were predicated on real moral differences between the categories it considered.

Despite all the difficulties that exacerbated ill will and encouraged violence, neither side lost touch with those values that helped diminish the war's horrors. The most important of these for mitigating violence among white combatants was mercy, which rests on and reinforces a common humanity as one person extends sympathy to another. Lincoln spoke of mercy as one of the attributes of God—it appears in most of the proclamations of thanksgiving that he issued during the war—and he used it to characterize the pleas that reached his desk asking him to commute execution orders, whether of Union deserters or Confederate subjects of retaliation. To the frustration of his judge advocate general, Lincoln often suspended or modified execution orders for soldiers accused of deserting. Lincoln, like Davis, was the magistrate of last resort, and requests for mercy came only at the climactic moment of the long administrative processes that sentenced people to death. As a close reader of Shakespeare, Lincoln must have known the passage in the *Merchant of Venice*, when Portia, disguised as a lawyer, pleads with Shylock:

> But mercy is above this sceptered sway;
> It is enthronèd in the hearts of kings;
> It is an attribute to God Himself;
> And earthly power doth then show likest God's
> When mercy seasons justice.[121]

Lieber's code explained the necessity of executing guerrillas and threatening noncombatants as elements of justice because they made a shorter and more ordered war. Just as often, however, Union officers pursued nonviolent solutions. They followed the laws of war. They imprisoned guerrillas and denied Confederates the resources to fight rather than killing them outright. Sometimes they seasoned justice with mercy.

[6]

Discipline, Order, and Justice

Just rather than unjust actions increased the mortality rate in the first half of 1864. In those places where the US Army extended its occupation of Southern space, lethal violence subsided. In those parts of the South still controlled by Confederates, civilians suffered serious food shortages. Early in the year, Ulysses Grant assumed control of all the Union armies and deployed a strategy of logistical devastation across the whole Confederacy. Because the "rebellion has assumed that shape now that it can only terminate by the complete subjugation of the South or the overthrow of the government," Grant concluded that "it is our duty therefore to use every means to weaken the enemy by destroying their means of subsistence, withdrawing their means of cultivating their fields, and in every other way possible."[1] Both sides experimented with new technologies of warfare, which threatened to destabilize the precarious agreement about how to fight. Some of these changes introduced anonymous methods of killing that challenged the culture of honor at the root of both Northern and Southern manhood. Although these new weapons threatened to escalate the war's death toll, they were not deployed on a broad scale. The greater threat to life came from the battlefield clashes of regular forces. Both armies perfected their control over their soldiers, which brought some aspects of the conflict within the laws of war. Stronger discipline also ensured that when ordered to attack even entrenched enemy positions, soldiers obeyed. The year 1864 witnessed the same contradictory mix of forces and impulses that had characterized the war's first three years.

The Costs of Regular War

Historians typically portray 1864 as the year when the Union fully implemented its strategy of hard war and turned their military power on

Southern civilians, marking the apex of an increasingly deadly conflict.[2] Commanders' respect for the purposes and limits of military power focused the destruction and death meted out by both sides. The boundaries of permissible behavior had been worked out gradually over the previous three years, in newspaper exchanges between rival generals, in correspondence among and between Union and Confederate officials, and in the more subtle negotiation between the Northern and Southern publics and their respective political leaders over how their armies should fight. But boundaries only protect those within them, and the legal boundaries established by the laws of war only prohibited certain categories of behavior. Lethal violence, for instance, was not directed by soldiers at civilians except in a siege, when noncombatants' location rendered them vulnerable. Nonetheless, civilians suffered from the logistical devastation directed against the South in 1864. Some Southerners came to the brink of starvation. Because the laws of war were designed primarily to protect noncombatants, soldiers stood fully outside the boundary. The organized and efficient war of 1864 ensured many more military deaths. It also produced additional suffering for soldiers as their own armies subjected them to rigid control. They faced more lethal and more unpredictable weapons as inventors designed new killing technologies. Although participants may not have recognized it at the time, the rational, ordered war of 1864 made it a deadlier conflict.

The increased scale of soldier deaths could be seen in campaigns across northern Virginia. Ulysses S. Grant and Robert E. Lee commanded the largest armies in their respective nations and committed themselves to a vigorous and bloody war. Grant's campaign against Lee in early 1864 generated enormous casualties for the Union. Over the course of six weeks, his army incurred 54,000 casualties. Critical Northern newspapers labeled Grant a "butcher," though his men cheered the decisiveness with which he pursued Lee and refused to back down in the face of the tactical stalemates that had incapacitated his predecessors. Southern newspapers did not devise a similar coinage for Lee, even though he lost more men as a proportion of his total force than Grant—at least 30,000 over the same period.[3] The regularity of battlefield combat enabled Grant and Lee to turn a blind eye to the rapidly mounting casualty totals in their armies. Because those casualties came among just combatants lawfully engaged, they imposed no moral cost on either commander.

Both men accepted a level of death that would have been unimaginable two years earlier. The fact that most of these deaths came through regular combat and campaigning made them easier to absorb. Even when death arrived off the battlefield, both sides acknowledged its necessity. In a letter to Grant responding to a report of the murder of several black soldiers, Lee explained that "it was probably one of those acts of unauthorized violence proceeding from individual passions, which it is difficult to prevent, but which are not the less to be lamented."[4] Lee's explanation reflected his position as an elite commander: he saw this act as a breach of good conduct by a dishonorable man. Lee refused to recognize that the Confederacy's policies on black soldiers or slavery itself might have contributed to the incident. Grant accepted his explanation. He too was a man who believed in "authorized" violence but who understood that in a war, some participants would act irresponsibly. Certainly, in 1864, neither commander apologized for nor regretted the killing that ensued. Confederates accused Grant of waging a war of attrition, but nothing in the records suggests he fought vindictively or punitively. On the contrary, he targeted Lee's army because it embodied the nationalist enthusiasm of the people and because geographical conquests had failed to diminish Confederate war-making capacity or popular support.[5] Both Grant's decision to pursue Lee, "even if it takes all summer," and Lee's decision to resist derived from the cold military logic in which they had been trained. The Civil War did not operate by its own momentum; more tragically, it followed the rational and intentional plan of its human creators.

Policing the Armies

The regularity of conflict in the eastern theater proceeded from and enabled an expansion of the armies as institutions. In many respects, the armies' growth produced a more ordered and more just conflict.[6] The need for the Lieber Code arose because the war extended in time and complexity. The same could be said for each army's internal rules that regulated the conduct of men within their camps, on the march, and in battle. Both armies began the war relying on the prewar army's court-martial system, in which officers were appointed to serve as juries on military trials considering charges brought against soldiers.[7] Over time, this became routine duty. Each army held tens of thousands of such hearings during the course of the war.[8]

A more pressing question for the Union was how to handle civilians who engaged in the war as irregular combatants. Because they were not regular soldiers, they did not fall under the army's rules and regulations and so could not be tried by court-martial, though in many instances commanders held "drum-head" courts-martial that entailed abbreviated hearings and immediate punishment (often execution). US Lieutenant General Winfield Scott created the precedent for an alternative when he devised a system of military commissions in the Mexican-American War. Henry Halleck elaborated this system in response to the guerrilla war he faced when he was commander in Missouri. One student of this process concludes that "Halleck creatively combated guerrillas with a legal solution, expanding the jurisdiction of military commissions to include all those offenses constituting violations of the laws of war." Despite his frustration with the continuing irregular war in Missouri, Halleck adopted a solution that worked within existing institutions and the laws of war. This scholar concludes that "the use of legal processes allowed guerrillas to be quickly tried and detained, often for the duration of the war, without the collateral damage that would have been caused by more traditional violent reprisals and counter-raids." Francis Lieber extended Halleck's work by incorporating military commissions into General Orders No. 100. Article 13 specified that courts-martial would continue to be used for offenses that violated the army's rules and articles of war but that "military offenses which do not come within the statute must be tried and punished under the common law of war" by military commissions. For Halleck and Lieber, formalizing the rules for prosecutions possessed the virtue of bringing regular combatants and irregular combatants under the same legal system—one subject to oversight.[9]

Part of that oversight came when the US Congress created the system of judge advocate generals who monitored the prosecutions undertaken by the army. Lincoln appointed Joseph Holt of Kentucky judge advocate general of the US Army. Holt was a one-time slaveowner turned bitter enemy of the institution, a former Democrat now committed to advancing Lincoln's Republican agenda, and a white Southerner who strongly supported the Union. As Holt's biographer notes, Holt and his deputies functioned for military law "in much the same way that the attorney general was the premier arbiter of law in the civil realm." From September 1862 to November 1865, Holt's office reviewed nearly 68,000 courts-martial and military commission proceedings. This represented probably two-thirds of all the hearings by the US Army and a substantial investment of time and energy by the Union to confirm the fairness of the decisions that the army's criminal justice system reached. Holt's foremost interest was to serve the administration and protect the Union, but his many years of legal work trained him to also pursue fairness and equity for both defendants and victims of crimes.[10]

The Confederacy never developed a military commission system or a judge advocate general office equivalent to what the Union created, but by 1864, both sides had perfected their strategies for disciplining their soldiers. This meant that soldiers were subjected to tighter rules and harsher punishments for infractions than they had been in the war's first year.[11] The most fearsome display of the military's lethal power came in February 1864, when Confederate Major General George Pickett's army captured most of Company F of the 2nd North Carolina Union Volunteers during an attack on New Bern. Many of these men had belonged to a Confederate local defense force earlier in the war, though when North Carolina attempted to organize them into official state service, most refused. At some point after this, the men had volunteered or been forced into US military service. Pickett regarded them as deserters and executed twenty-two men between February 5 and 22 in nearby Kinston, North Carolina, the largest mass execution of soldiers in the Civil War. Pickett's most serious obstacle appears to have been finding the necessary wood, but he overcame this and constructed a gallows that allowed thirteen men to be executed simultaneously. Union officials protested, and the case lingered after the war, with Pickett narrowly escaping a murder charge. Notwithstanding even the legality of the executions, Pickett's zeal for capital punishment as a deterrent against desertion reflects an institutional outlook that devalued the human lives at stake. Over several months, Pickett's soldiers "were called out to witness a total of approximately seventy executions in Kinston by either hanging or firing squad."[12]

The Union offered a contradictory response to Pickett's actions. The local commander protested to Pickett, but Ulysses S. Grant acknowledged that the Confederacy could exercise lethal discretion over its soldiers. He went so far as to "claim no right to retaliate for the punishment of deserters, who had actually been mustered into the Confederate Army and afterward deserted and joined ours."[13] The deeper questions governing the fate of these twenty-two men was how their states established the loyalty of men at war and what steps they would take to punish violations of its order or to protect men unjustly accused of doing so. Historians seeking to understand the event have tried to identify the nature of the soldiers' initial Confederate commitment, though this effort has been frustrated by ambiguous or absent records.[14] Benjamin Butler, as always involved in these thorny questions of wartime justice, regarded the North Carolinians as US citizens who owed their allegiance to their natal state. They were conscripted by the Confederacy, and then escaped to reclaim their original lawful relation to the Union. "I do not recognize any right in the rebels to execute a United States soldier," Butler said, "because, either by force or fraud, or by voluntary enlistment even, he has been once brought into their ranks, and has escaped therefrom." Like Grant, Butler recognized the Confederacy's right to execute a soldier "who holds simply the character of a deserter," but once a man has reasserted his loyalty to the United States "by no law of nations, and by no belligerent rights, have the rebels any power over him, other than to treat him as a prisoner of war, if captured."[15] Company F's predicament reveals the unique nature of civil conflicts—each side claims a "natural" loyalty based on residence and geographic sovereignty that creates preconditions for conflict. Pickett refused to recognize the men's Union service as giving them any protection because he regarded their loyalty to the Confederacy as inalienable.

John Paris, the chaplain for the 54th North Carolina, gave a sermon after the executions that clarified the vision of national loyalty as a sacrament. He prefaced his sermon with the passage from Matthew (27: 3–5) describing Judas's renunciation of his betrayal of Jesus after he learns Jesus has been condemned. Northerners would have read this sermon ironically. For them, the story of Judas's betrayal captured the crime of the South writ large. "As sure as there is a God in heaven, justice and judgment will overtake the wicked," he preached. Northerners would have agreed. Paris's vision of national loyalty and obligation comported remarkably closely with how Northerners understood it. "With all the responsibilities of this solemn oath upon their souls and all the ties that bind men to the land that gave them birth," he said, the condemned had ignored "every principle that pertains to the patriot, disowning the natural, as well as lawful allegiance that every man owes to the government of the State which throws around him the aegis of its protection." In this case, the North Carolinians received no state's protection.[16]

Kinston was not the only mass execution and Pickett not the only Confederate general who regarded such actions as essential to maintaining the order that would see the army through its current troubled times. Two months later, Confederates executed fifteen more North Carolinians in Dalton, Georgia, though these men soldiered in the Army of Tennessee.[17] The same brutal efficiency applied in Dalton as in Kinston, except when it came to the actual execution, which required several minutes, repeated volleys, and point-blank firings to conclude. Both the US Army and the Confederate army executed soldiers for desertion throughout the war (and both commanders-in-chief often pardoned condemned men), but the escalation in scale appears to have drawn no comment from the high commands on either side. Brigadier General Alexander Welch Reynolds, the senior officer at Dalton, assumed that his soldiers would either support or be scared into compliance by the example he made of the North Carolinians.

The Union did not engage in a similar spate of large-scale executions, though they did continue to punish deserters, often with capital punishment. Francis C. Barlow, one of the Union's younger generals, was only twenty-nine in 1864. He commanded a division in the army's Second Corps. He expressed anger at Lincoln's pardon for deserters in his command, believing it to be "mistaken humanity to do so." Theodore Lyman, a staff officer for Major General George Gordon Meade, who traveled with Barlow and the Army of the Potomac in spring 1864, shared the same concern for Lincoln's "false merciful policy" for deserters. The core problem came from a lack of good men left to recruit into the armies.

The new recruits of 1863–64 were what he called "*poor material.*" Compounding the problem, Lyman complained, "they won't let us shoot the rascals, and few regiments have the discipline to mould them into decent troops." In fact, quite a few rascals were shot, though the Union's additional layer of administrative review (in the form of the judge advocate generals) reduced the number of executions from those ordered by officers in the field. The army's tactical commander, George Meade, like Barlow and Lyman, supported the strongest possible prosecution of deserters and stragglers, feeling it was the only way to keep the army together during this crucial campaign.[18]

Lyman was equally concerned that they could not make an example of stragglers in the army who stole food from civilians. He proposed that they "hang the perpetrators by the road where the troops pass, and put a placard on their breasts." Marsena Patrick, the provost general of the Army of the Potomac, held the same attitude but commanded the power to enforce it. Two men convicted of raping a local woman were executed together in front of a large crowd of soldiers, part of Patrick's efforts to impose discipline on his army and protect the civilians under his charge. Patrick had long been harder on his own troops than on Southern civilians. When he turned over command of a town in occupied Virginia to another US officer, he confessed that he felt sad, Patrick wrote, "at the thought that these helpless families are to be left to the tender mercies of an Abolitionist." The executions conducted by the Confederate and Union armies in spring 1864 were lawful under the rules of war and a symbol of the brutal efficiency that prevailed in both armies at the time.[19]

Desertion generated the most eager executioners in both armies, but that was hardly the only crime to draw the ire of commanders. In order to keep their militaries intact and responsive, both armies deputized their officers to regulate the conduct of their soldiers This was no easy feat during campaigns or the long stretches of camp life. The problems of drunkenness, robbery, and interpersonal violence consumed guards, provost marshals, and court-martial boards throughout the war. The Union provost marshal and court-martial records offer voluminous testimony about the violence committed by soldiers against each other, most of it inspired by alcohol. Wherever units remained in place for an extended period, the incidence of robberies, fights, attacks, and murders rose.

Military authorities regulated camps (at least the long-term winter camps), so personal violence committed among soldiers rarely went unpunished. But punishments rarely deterred such conduct. In fact, military discipline seems to have generated resistance among soldiers, who directed their anger against officers and their fellow enlisted men. Disciplinarians returned the favor. "After 1862," one historian writes, "the number of officers willing to shoot subordinates to back up their authority increased." This increase came partly from the perception among officers that the draft had brought more "roughs," uncivilized and poorly disciplined men, into the ranks. "Roughs were a separate class of men," this historian writes, "different from the early volunteers, and officers believed they had to back up their authority over this class with violence." Barlow and Lyman would have agreed.[20]

The military's criminal justice system, a well-tooled machine by spring 1864, reinforced army efficiency but provided little justice to civilians.[21] Although the army achieved a high conviction rate (85 percent) for those charges they brought, the numbers suggest that not every incident was brought to prosecution. The most comprehensive study reports 80,000 courts-martial general records for the US Army, although this may be an undercount because regimental courts-martial were not included in the tally.[22] Of these, 1,374 were murder cases and 350 trials were for rape, together accounting for just 2 percent of the crimes prosecuted.[23] Of the victims in the murder charges, 674 concerned civilians killed by soldiers, but in those 674 cases only thirty-five perpetrators were ultimately found guilty and executed, a conviction rate (5 percent) far below what the army usually achieved. The study concludes that fewer than a thousand men were convicted of murder during the war (out of a 2.1 million man army), and most of these were probably for events that took place in camp, for which more witnesses could be produced.[24] Although incidences of lethal violence committed by Northern soldiers against civilians were certainly rare, it seems equally true that not every soldier who killed a Southern citizen was held responsible in a court-martial.

The cases of men executed for rape or murder of civilians follow a similar pattern. The perpetrators preyed on people weaker than they were. In a majority of cases, the men lashed out with little cause or purpose beyond immediate gratification. For instance, Charles Sperry, a printer in New York state enlisted just before the draft in 1863. He was arrested once for being absent without leave, but by early 1864 had been promoted to sergeant. Serving in Fairfax County, Virginia, a stable region with few Confederates, he abandoned his post, got drunk, then assaulted and attempted to rape Annie Nelson, a fifteen-year-old girl. Sperry and a squad of soldiers arrived at the house after midnight and claimed to be searching for guerrillas. He attacked both Annie and her mother, and stopped only when other soldiers announced that a different group of Union soldiers were coming to search the house.[25] Sperry's actions, like many of those cataloged in the army's courts-martial prosecution records, reflect crimes of opportunity and power. The violence they committed was disconnected from the purpose of the war but enabled by the chaos of it. These were not political crimes against enemies of the state; they were interpersonal crimes performed under the cover of the authority that perpetrators claimed as soldiers.

The more mundane charges levied against soldiers in the US Army reflect the intent of army regulations as well.[26] The most common charges included desertion, conduct prejudicial to good behavior, absent without leave, sleeping on post, conduct unbecoming an officer, leaving a sentry post, and cowardice. The most serious cases, in which the army executed a soldier, usually concerned a crime against the institution rather than the public. Over the course of the war, the US Army executed 263 men, 181 of those (or almost 70 percent) for desertion. Of the capital cases, only 87 concerned men convicted of committing violent crimes (mostly murder and rape), and almost half of the murders concerned other service members.[27]

In short, soldiers suffered violence at the hands of the army, but that violence was more likely to protect the army than shield civilians. One of the leading scholars of Union military discipline finds the same conclusion: "more often than not, changes in the army's disciplinary system [were] to the benefit of the soldier / offender, leaving Confederate civilians more vulnerable to offenses because Union soldiers felt less deterred from committing certain crimes." But lethal violence remained unacceptable. "To prevent soldiers from engaging in retaliatory killings," this historian argues, "the army took special pains to prosecute and punish soldiers convicted of maliciously killing civilians, with the death penalty a common instrument of punishment."[28]

Black soldiers may have been treated differently from white soldiers, who were prosecuted primarily for intra-army crimes. Evidence reveals racial bias in the US Army's criminal justice system, from prosecutions to conviction rates to punishment. Unlike the pattern for soldiers more generally, most charges against black soldiers concerned crimes directed at civilians. Of the successful death penalty prosecutions brought by the army, thirty-five of the eighty-seven men (40 percent) executed for crimes other than desertion were black soldiers, though they made up only 20 percent of the Union's enlistees. More white than black soldiers were executed for desertion. In 1865, twenty-four out of thirty-five capital cases involved men from the USCT. The most infamous case of discriminatory conduct came just after the war's conclusion, when members of the 3rd US Colored Troops "mutinied" in Jacksonville, Florida. Protesting a long string of harsh punishments imposed by an inexperienced white commander, soldiers cut down a man strung up by his thumbs for stealing a jar of molasses and returned fire when officers shot at them. Six soldiers were executed for mutiny two weeks later and their bodies buried in unmarked graves at the water's edge.[29]

The Confederacy appears to have used its criminal justice system for self-regulation as well. They relied on the antebellum army's court-martial system to adjudicate violations of the army's *Articles of War* or laws of war more generally. And they focused overwhelmingly on disciplining their soldiers rather than on adjudicating soldier misconduct around civilians. The Confederate army prosecuted soldiers for the same set of crimes as the Union. The evidence on this topic is murky because when the Confederate government abandoned Richmond in April 1865, it burned most of the records relating to courts-martial in its armies. At least one collection survived this purge, a register of nearly 17,000 prosecutions over the years 1861–1865.[30] Given the size of the Confederate military—roughly 900,000 men—this set clearly only represents a small part of the total history of Confederate courts-martial. Nonetheless, it sheds light on a number of subjects. Nearly all of the charges under which the Confederacy prosecuted its soldiers related to issues of control—sleeping on post, drunkenness, straggling, desertion, and so on. In some rare cases, soldiers were charged with "conduct prejudicial to good order," which, in the US Army, covered problems with civilians. In the event, the Confederacy mounted "conduct prejudicial" prosecutions in only a small proportion of cases (11 percent).[31] The conclusion here is clear: the CSA used its military discipline system to create a more efficient army, not to police the conduct of the army in public.

If the policing of soldiers tended to benefit the armies more than the people they moved among, how did those people fare when they were subject to military justice? Beginning in mid-1862 (and especially after the release of the Lieber Code in 1863), the war department expanded the use of military commissions to all departments, and they came into wide use as a tool of the Union war effort.[32] The army held more commission hearings each year, peaking at 1,410 in 1864. Nearly 80 percent of the principals examined under commission rules were civilians, with about 8 percent classified as "guerrillas" and the remaining a mix of Union and Confederate soldiers.[33] As in Missouri under Halleck, commissions tried civilians for crimes under the laws of war: bridge-burning, sabotage of property, outright guerrilla conduct, and robbery. Some of the crimes prosecuted by the commissions overlapped with the authority of civil courts in some respects. Theft and property destruction, for instance, were regular crimes that could be prosecuted in civil courts, but in places like Missouri, martial law and commissions prevailed because the local courts were not reliably loyal.

At least 416 citizens were sentenced to death by military commissions, but of these, only 198 had their sentences upheld and presumably carried out. The remainder had their verdicts overturned, sometimes for irregularities in procedure during the hearings and sometimes by superior officers without explanation. Many of those originally sentenced to death had their verdicts upheld but the sentence modified to a term of imprisonment at hard labor, usually five or ten years. John H. Smith of Kentucky, for instance, was found guilty by a military commission in Louisville on December 1, 1863, on the charge of being a guerrilla. He was judged guilty of "taking up arms" as a "guerrilla, outlaw, and public robber" and consenting in and helping with the operations of the band. Despite his guilty verdict and death sentence, his punishment was adjusted to hard labor for the duration of the war. This suggests a degree of scrupulousness in legal procedure at odds with the image of a blood-thirsty US Army using whatever tools it needed to suppress irregular war.[34] If field officers (and many home front families with soldier-relatives fighting in irregular theaters) had their way, commission hearings would have given way to summary execution.

The hearing process included a lengthy review phase that in over half the cases reduced the sentence. Many of those men who had their capital sentences reduced were convicted of serious crimes—murder, bush-whacking, or spying—but were nonetheless jailed rather than killed. No doubt, many accused bushwhackers never made it before a commission, but those that did seem to have received fair treatment. In fact, of the 168 men charged with "being a guerrilla," dozens were found not guilty and released without punishment. Many of the men charged with the more general crime of violating the "laws of war" had come within Union lines either without a pass or with a Confederate uniform. Some had il-legally crossed a blockade line. In the field, a man in such a position could be accused and executed for being a spy.

The number of military commission hearings and courts-martial shows a linear increase throughout the war. More people—both soldiers and civilians—were brought before military courts and tried for crimes against army regulations or the laws of war. Does this evidence prove that the war grew more uncontrolled or more restrained over time? To an-swer this we need to know whether the pattern derives from a broadening of what constituted illegal behavior, more vigorous prosecution by the armies, or an actual increase in crimes committed over time. The creation of military commissions enabled the army to prosecute more people for a wider variety of crimes, but this change was made in 1862, and prosecu-tions continued to increase until the end of the war. Once the Lieber Code was passed, in early 1863, the crimes themselves were clearly fixed and the categories did not change again during the war. The behavior and comments of officers like Meade, Barlow, and Lyman regarding sol-diers who were recruited after 1862 offer a clue. The cultural perception among Union officers that these recruits were socially inferior and re-quired a harder hand to control suggests a more visible cause for the up-tick in prosecutions.[35] We cannot rule out the possibility that soldiers committed more violations in the latter half of the war, both against each other and against Southern civilians, but the bulk of the evidence suggests that enhanced enforcement not increased criminality is to blame. The linear pattern of an increasingly deadly Civil War is evident in the casualty totals from the battlefields, but this is not evidence that the war grew more random or more unjust. Rather than seeing the rising death toll on the battlefields as driving a more desperate and violent war, we must also recognize that this occurred even as participants committed themselves, in new and earnest ways, to a lawful and just war.

Starving the South?

Partly because of the US Army's apparatus of control, garrison towns remained mostly peaceful places in 1864. The appeal of stability and security drew many otherwise reluctant Southerners into the region's occupied cities. Residents of occupied towns had access to markets where they could purchase food, an increasingly rare commodity as the Union blockade tightened and the Confederacy directed Southern resources toward its army. For instance, Benjamin Butler initiated a relief commission in 1862 that provided vital aid for many of New Orleans's poorest citizens. Rations were not universally distributed. The order of distribution went: "1st Families of Federal Recruits 2nd Widows and friendless destitute 3rd Families of Confederate soldiers." By the end of 1863, the provost marshal general reported 6,000 families receiving food and clothing and another 10–12,000 requiring it. The benefits—ten ounces of food per person per day—were hardly extravagant, but they kept destitute families from collapse. Union commanders in other occupied cities established similar systems of relief. Once Grant captured Vicksburg, the occupiers distributed rations to people in the city and beyond its boundaries. During the winter of 1863–64, federal officers sold firewood and provisions to impoverished people in the surrounding region. As refugees poured into the city early in the new year, the federal distribution increased from 6,000 rations to 13,000, then to 32,000, feeding 558 families.[36]

People in those places outside Union control, and thus without relief systems of the sort created by the Union, suffered more. Confederate states established charitable aid systems—principally food relief—but these were more common in urban areas. In rural areas, poor people relied on local courts and the largesse of planters who might or might not choose to share surplus goods. Conditions deteriorated in these places in 1864. The Union provost marshals administering rural areas kept reports from loyal and disloyal citizens about living conditions. In late 1863, for instance, the provost marshal upriver from New Orleans recorded that "very many of them [inhabitants] are suffering to my certain knowledge for the bare necessities of life with starvation." He demonstrated little outright concern for the civilians themselves, instead worrying that "starving a neighborhood in the face, it opens a fertile field for smuggling." Much as the Union commanders who managed the army's soldiers, this officer fixated on administrative efficiency and compliance rather than the human toll of army policies.[37]

Field commanders had little incentive to challenge the Union war machine. They risked censure for mis-prioritizing the purpose of their command. More importantly, the decision by Lincoln and Grant to pursue logistical devastation presupposed that they accepted a certain level of civilian suffering. Neither man expressed any desire to deliberately harm noncombatants, and both kept the political goal of reunion persistently in view. Seeking to avoid a bloody war of attrition, the North denied Confederates the resources to fight. Confederates recognized their vulnerability in this regard. "In our country, land & labor constitute the back-bone of the Gov. break down the farming interest, & you conquer us at once," one man noted.[38] Surely a war that weakened Confederate soldiers rather than killing them was both politically more expedient and morally superior?

It was William T. Sherman who expressed the sentiment that Lincoln and Grant must have shared. "You might as well appeal against the thunder-storm as against these terrible hardships of war," he told Georgians. "They are inevitable, and the only way the people of Atlanta can hope once more to live in peace and quiet at home is to stop the war, which can alone be done by admitting that it began in error and is perpetuated in pride." What we "will have," Sherman asserted, was "a just obedience to the laws of the United States . . . and if it involves the destruction of your improvements we cannot help it." When the Confederate high command issued its official critique of the Lieber Code, they singled out the passage justifying logistical destruction. "War is not carried on by arms alone," Lieber wrote in Article 17, "it is lawful to starve the hostile belligerents, armed or unarmed, so that it leads to the speedier subjection of the enemy." This practice was, as Confederate leaders knew, legal and customary under the laws of war. Confederates also knew that their own army could cause equally severe harm to their own people. Robert E. Lee had complained about this in 1862, when he denounced the damage done by his army as it moved north through Virginia. "A great deal of damage to citizens is done by stragglers," he reported to Jefferson Davis, "who consume all they can get from the charitable and all they can take from the defenceless, in many cases wantonly destroying stock and other property." Lee knew this would diminish support for the Confederacy, but his solution—to have Richmond appoint an inspector general to review conduct and enforce good behavior—presumed extra manpower the Confederacy did not possess.[39]

Southern citizens suffered when Confederates destroyed canals, locks, bridges, and railroads on their own territory, which they did whenever necessary. For those who lived in the area, the damage imposed the same logistical challenges whether it was created by the Confederate or Union armies. In Virginia, one historian notes, "over a twelve-day span Imboden's men disrupted Federal communication with the West by driving off Federal defenders, dropping a half dozen B&O bridges . . . and destroying rolling stock, depots, water tanks, and several blockhouses." He also cut the C&O Canal in two places. Lee warned Imboden against "marauding" but was gratified with the results of the campaign, especially the horses and cattle he gained. Lee himself authorized thorough confiscation of foodstuffs, which may have allowed subjected parties to recover the following year but bore little difference from the Union's confiscation policies. When it came to impressment, Lee believed that what the army could take should "depend upon the wants of the Government. . . . If it requires all the meat in the country to support the army, it should be had." In Tennessee, Confederate soldiers followed a similar approach, committing such "wanton destruction" in the middle of the state that even Confederates declared it an "unpardonable outrage."[40]

Once the North committed to a hard war policy of resource destruction, commanders noted its effects on Southern civilians, but they neither modified those policies nor apologized for them. The faster that the South was driven to the point of collapse, the sooner the war would end. For many civilians, that point seemed to be approaching in 1864. Production of the South's main staple crops—corn and wheat—was down 60 percent. In Virginia, the continuous presence of armies in the state reduced the supply of foodstuffs irrespective of the Union's hard war policy. In July of 1864, William Gilmer wrote an article for the *Charlottesville Chronicle* in which he encouraged people to plant turnips, good food for refugees. More advice urging root crops appeared throughout the South. Turnips, onions, and other below-ground vegetables presented an advantage because roaming soldiers were unlikely to uncover them. As always in the Civil War, black Southerners experienced a worse conflict than white Southerners. Enslaved people subsisted on steadily reduced rations throughout the war. According to one scholar, "by the last months of the war, starving conditions were a major cause of slave flight from plantations."[41]

Some historians suggest that starvation may have caused civilian deaths during the war. Confederate officers asserted it continually during the war, and even Union officers referred to people in "a starving condition," but in almost every case the language is suggestive of hardship rather than literally true.[42] For instance, one soldier reported from Port Hudson in 1863 that "this place had also to succumb like Vicksburg to that grim monster Starvation but it was not until the last mule had been devoured that its brave commander would consent to a surrender."[43] Mule may have been the meat of last resort, but it still offered protein. Even at Vicksburg, food remained available, as it would throughout Sherman's siege of Atlanta. A scholar of the siege observes that the "strange reality is that Pemberton [managing Vicksburg's defenses] clearly had not run out of food." Grant discovered four days' rations of bacon and flour and 250 pounds of sugar.[44] The most comprehensive analysis of agriculture in the Confederacy reveals that the war reduced Southern food production significantly, which contributed to Union victory. Rather than chronicling starvation, however, this account identifies "hunger" as the most serious problem.[45] China's Taiping Civil War offers much more concrete evidence of mass death from starvation. After only a two-month siege of Hangzhou, Imperial forces entered the city's gates and found "thousands dead of starvation in the streets."[46] Nothing comparable ever occurred in America.

In private correspondence, Confederate officials were more circumspect with their language. Secretary of State Judah Benjamin called news reports that the Yankees would win by starving the South "too absurd for belief" in a letter to the Confederate diplomat John Slidell. "This starvation," Benjamin explained, "means simply short rations of meat for a very limited period, caused principally by the difficulties of transportation over our railroads." The Union policy of logistical destruction unquestionably generated great hardship, but there is little evidence of actual starvation. The American South was agriculturally self-sufficient before the war, and the war lasted only four years. Starvation is a slow process, as the soldiers who waged siege warfare against Southern cities discovered. Despite the awful conditions within Vicksburg—no one envied them "mule soup"—Grant knew that "waiting for starvation was not an option." Union and Confederate armies subsisted in central Virginia for nearly the whole of the war and by all reports consumed resources voraciously, yet the community studies of this region offer no evidence to substantiate the claim of significant civilian mortality from lack of food.[47]

Although intuition would suggest that diminished food supplies, from which all Southerners certainly suffered, would produce worse health and possibly fatalities, evidence from other conflicts suggests this is not always the case. During World War I, the Allied blockade of the North Sea prevented the importation of grain into Denmark, which forced the country to slaughter the hogs previously fed with grain and use domestic grain for bread. The result was a "remarkable fall in the death rate." In Britain during World War II, the German bombing and blockade strategy reduced the amount of meat, butter, and other fats, resulting in a decline in mortality from disease among children. In both cases, caloric restriction actually improved health rather than degraded it.[48]

In 1863 and 1864, malnutrition undoubtedly contributed to poor health and greater mortality among Southerners. Malaria and yellow fever plagued the Union armies as they moved south, with over 1.3 million soldiers suffering from the former disease during the war. Although

Southerners were more familiar with these maladies, they were hardly immune. Thousands of civilians suffered from these conditions, exacerbated by the Union's blockade, which prevented the importation of medicine. Black Southerners suffered worst of all. They surely suffered more from malnutrition than white Southerners, and rates of disease, especially for freedpeople making the perilous escape from slavery, were high. Thousands of freedpeople contracted smallpox between 1862 and 1868.[49]

What the Civil War did not generate were massive epidemics affecting the whole civilian population as happened in other wars.[50] The Revolutionary War provides an important point of contrast. During the course of that conflict, North America was ravaged by a smallpox epidemic. Despite a much less well developed communications infrastructure and record-keeping, ample evidence survived to document the effects of the disease on the civilian population.[51] Nothing similar exists for the American Civil War. We know that soldiers suffered from very high rates of traditional diseases, particularly measles and mumps, that produced high mortality in 1861 when men from different communities mingled in training camps. Once on the march, soldiers contracted and died from typhoid, yellow fever, and amoebic dysentery. Over the course of the war, twice as many soldiers died from disease as in battle. Despite these several hundred thousand deaths, there seem to be no significant cases of these diseases being transferred to civilian populations.[52] During Sherman's March in Georgia, his troops killed tens of thousands of animals (largely cattle and hogs), but in all the ample reportage on this event (much of it from angry Confederates with an incentive to record every ill effect of Sherman's passage through the state), there are no reports of disease from contamination.[53] The urban parts of the South that were occupied by the North generally experienced improvements in sanitation and hygiene because idle soldiers were detailed to clean.[54] The battles that did occur around cities—Richmond, Atlanta, Knoxville, and Mobile, for instance—might have been expected to produce cholera, which is transmitted by contaminated water, but this seems not to have been the case.[55] By comparison, in the Crimean War, over two-thirds of the 155,000 soldiers aligned against Russia died of cholera.[56] In the Taiping Civil War, cholera killed soldiers and civilians by the tens of thousands in cities along the Yangtze River in 1862.[57]

Technologies of War

The use of logistical pressure to bring a warring people to submission was hardly a new technique. Whatever people felt about its moral legitimacy, writers on both sides drew on the long history of warfare when they evaluated both the legitimacy and the effectiveness of the Union's strategy. This line of thinking suggests that if we want to understand the human damage done by war, we should look to the grand political decisions made about how each side fought. As a Northern observer remarked, "siege guns, shells, solid shot, telescopic rifles, and Minie bullets are as nothing compared with a proclamation."[58] But in other cases, new technologies of warfare challenged participants to think anew about how they wanted to make war. In particular, the introduction of weapons and tactics that allowed anonymous, sometimes mass, killing challenged the selectivity that marked regular conflict. Both Northern and Southern military engineers pursued these inventions, believing their devices would bring victory. Like most people in wars throughout history, Northerners and Southerners embraced new weapons.

Sometimes, participants stopped to consider the moral ramifications of weapons that heralded an unprecedented mode of killing, but more often they plunged ahead, seeking advantages wherever they lay. These ranged from increased use of snipers and mines to the deliberate explosion of the Union's City Point Harbor. At the same time, many individuals on both sides regarded anonymous killing as unproductive of military ends and more like murder than war. Had the war continued well past 1865, soldiers and their publics might have assimilated themselves to the new moral landscape, but there is substantial evidence that they resisted changes despite their desire to win the war. Nonetheless, political leaders, particularly in the Confederacy, supported new killing methods that diminished the traditional protections accorded to noncombatants and captured soldiers.

Battlefield Killing

Despite popular conceptions today of the Civil War as a uniquely deadly fighting experience, new technologies of war did not make battlefield combat a more deadly experience than it had been for previous generations of American soldiers. The technological conditions prevailing in mid-nineteenth-century America also kept the casualty total below that of many twentieth-century conflicts. The absence of air power, for instance, differentiated the Civil War, in terms of human casualties and damage to infrastructure, from World War II and later conflicts. Union destruction of the Southern industrial, transportation, and communication infrastructure proceeded by hand—during Sherman's march through Georgia, soldiers levered up cross-ties with crowbars and twisted rails by wrapping them around trees. New artillery devices ensured high casualties against opponents who charged breastworks, but even the innovative rifled musket proved less deadly than many contemporaries expected.[59]

Careful studies have undermined the idea that the rifled musket produced a deadlier conflict for infantrymen. After a detailed evaluation of the evidence on the effectiveness of the rifled musket, one historian concludes that "Civil War loss ratios were on the same level as those seen in major smoothbore battles of the eighteenth century."[60] The volley from a regiment of 500 men typically produced on average between three and seven casualties.[61] Sharpshooters, used first by the Union in 1862 and by the Confederacy in 1863, were more accurate and consequently more lethal, but they played a relatively small role in the conflict as a whole. Soldiers on both sides appreciated it when their own sharpshooters killed the enemy but were unnerved by being the targets.[62] The scale of Civil War armies, so much larger than anything seen during previous conflicts, ensured greater absolute numbers of casualties. In tactical terms, Union and Confederate soldiers learned from the same books and so planned the same sort of offensive and defense maneuvers.[63] This fair pairing of technology and tactics between North and South was unfortunate for regular soldiers, resulting in indecisive battles. Armies bled slowly, regrouped, and fought again.[64]

For uniformed soldiers, this required a commitment to killing that was sharply at odds with their prewar behavior. They did not relish killing other people.[65] Even for men reared in the physical violence of the nineteenth century's culture of honor, interpersonal violence was intimate and intentional, directed at a social purpose. Rebel soldiers may have grown to hate Yankees and vice versa, but this did not make killing any easier.

"The Army of the Potomac: A Sharp-shooter on Picket Duty." Winslow Homer's solitary figure wields a weapon of lethal menace far from the battlefield. The clinical detachment of sharpshooters unnerved observers at the time, who debated whether this form of fighting violated the laws of war.

Throughout the war, soldiers on both sides expressed fatigue and disgust at being required to kill and revulsion at their own actions. In a study of wartime killing in the twentieth century, one historian found that soldiers psychologically reconciled themselves to the task. She chronicles a range of reactions, from pleasure and pride to fear and guilt.[66] Nonetheless, soldiers had to be trained and ordered to kill. In World War I and after, "it was not possible to rely upon the instinctive flaring-up of martial aggression: military training regimes needed to reflect the 'civilian' codes of the new recruits." Even after World War I, the armies found that "no matter how thorough the training, it still failed to enable more combatants to fight."[67] A central component of the Civil War equivalent to this training was the rhetoric of righteousness nurtured by each side.

Even such deliberate propaganda may have failed to inspire. One of the war's popular songs, "Tenting Tonight on the Old Campground," captured the fatigue that soldiers felt. Both sides had patriotic and inspirational songs that rallied men against the enemy, but the success of "Tenting Tonight" after 1863 suggests a universal longing for the quiet of civilian life rather than more killing:

Many are the hearts that are weary tonight,
Wishing for the war to cease;
Many are the hearts looking for the right
To see the dawn of peace.[68]

Anonymous Killing

Peace seemed further away than ever in 1864 as military scientists devised more fearsome weapons. The most ubiquitous of the new weapons technologies were torpedoes, modified artillery shells set to explode with a pressure- or battery-activated trigger. Their initial design and use came in naval warfare, but Confederate engineers soon modified them to resemble modern land mines, which exploded when stepped on. The Confederacy invested heavily in their development and deployment throughout the war. Union officers feared them but generally respected their use as a means of defense on land and sea. Confederate and Union military leaders parted ways over the use of mines as offensive weapons that inflicted anonymous and random, though rarely purposeful, killing.

Matthew Fontaine Maury, a renowned oceanographer, led the Confederate navy's program of mine construction and deployment. Under his direction, Confederates barricaded Southern harbors with torpedoes and floated them into rivers. In strictly military terms, the torpedoes proved a cost-effective investment against the Union navy. Confederates never built a navy to rival the American one, but torpedoes sank between thirty-five and fifty Union ships and inspired fear and caution among many commanders.[69] The devices were so simple to construct that Confederate units around the South adopted the practice. Between 1862 and 1863, soldiers and guerrillas slowed down the Union's riverine invasion by firing on ships from shore. This drew fire back at them and at the towns that harbored them. The torpedoes offered a less risky approach. Confederates could build torpedoes, row into Southern rivers, and release them into the current. When a Union ship happened upon one, the perpetrators were long gone from the scene. Torpedoes proved effective; they created great anxiety and great anger among Union sailors, who regarded "their use as sneaky, treacherous, and unmanly." Union naval officers learned to push objects ahead of them in the water to detonate torpedoes before boats reached them. Their experiments with a variety of fenders, nets, and hooks lessened the damage they suffered but hardly provided full protection against the threat.[70]

American weapons designers had experimented with marine torpedoes before the Civil War, thus these were regarded as an unusual but not unprecedented part of naval warfare. The more serious problem, from the perspective of military ethics, came when Confederates invented "subterrra" torpedoes and placed these in what they hoped would be the path of Union armies. Confederate Brigadier General Gabriel J. Rains pioneered their use during the defense of Yorktown against George McClellan's Peninsula Campaign. McClellan, who adhered to the laws of war and promoted a limited conflict, objected strenuously when he received reports of Union soldiers injured by mines left by Rains. "The rebels have been guilty of the most murderous and barbarous conduct in placing torpedoes within the abandoned works," he informed the secretary of war, shortly after the battle. The devices killed several soldiers and injured another dozen. "I shall make the prisoners remove them at their own peril." McClellan put Confederate prisoners in jeopardy as a way to discourage the use of mines in the future. Confederate General James Longstreet likewise objected to their use simply to kill without materially impacting the enemy's advance. He commanded Rains to cease placing land mines because he did not "recognize it as a proper or efficient method of war." Rains appealed to the War Department with an argument used by commanders before and long after him. Sentries and pickets could be relieved of duty and replaced with mines that would detonate, warning Confederates of a breach of their line and at the same time "demoralize" the enemy. The response, from Secretary of War George W. Randolph, authorized the use of mines in defensive situations, such as in a parapet under assault, but prohibited them when the purpose was "merely to destroy life."[71]

Rains remained undeterred and looked for ways to expand Confederate use of mines. When Lee assumed command of the army outside

Richmond after the Battle of Seven Pines in June 1862, he detailed Rains to help develop naval defenses in Virginia. In late 1862, Rains was appointed head of the Army Torpedo Bureau, from which he managed research and production facilities in Richmond, Charleston, Wilmington, Savannah, and Mobile.[72] Confederates bragged about the success of these devices, whether they reported the sinking of Northern ships or advertised the harbors filled with torpedoes to ward off Northern attacks. Henry Hotze, the Confederate propagandist and publisher of the *Index* in London, celebrated their use in his articles.[73] In mid-1864, Rains was given a new position "superintending all duties of torpedoes" and a new budget of $350,000, an eighteen-fold increase over the previous year's allocation.[74] Much of those resources was directed toward planting mines in the path of Sherman's advance through Georgia, particularly around Augusta and Savannah. The Confederates invested heavily in this new way of war, and they received the enthusiastic backing of President Davis himself. By mid-1863, Davis abandoned the initially circumscribed uses that Randolph had authorized, writing to General Joseph Johnston to let Rains "fully apply his invention," something Johnston had resisted earlier in the war.[75] Secretary of War James Seddon clarified the administration's position at the time: "such means of offense against the enemy are approved and recognized by the Department as legitimate weapons of warfare."[76] Thousands of mines were deployed near and in cities in the South, including 2,363 around Richmond itself.[77]

Torpedoes generated Northern indignation the way the hard war angered Southerners. Union officers complained bitterly about them, and speakers made frequent reference to the practice when cataloging the atrocities and misbehavior of rebels in wartime. Private David F. Ritchie of New York had a typical reaction: "one of these devilish machines did its work before our battery reached the spot. A Pennsylvania regiment was passing the place of its concealment. One struck the torpedo fuse . . . and in an instant his body was flying in the air, a mangled mess. Never since the war began have I felt so ugly as when the remains of the poor soldier borne past and laid beneath a tree, the victim of an act of cowardice and barbarism." Marsena Patrick, provost marshal, reported from Virginia that "people say they [Confederates] are secretly placing Torpedoes etc. within the works, expecting them to be taken by the Yankees, who will then get blown up." Strangely, Patrick offered no comment on the practice, despite his persistent efforts to curtail unjust behavior by Union troops. Just before the war's end, he did report, again without comment, that a Confederate ship "ran into one of its own Torpedoes & blew up, yesterday—none of *our* people on board." His use of italics speaks louder and suggests he saw this unintended outcome as just desserts.[78]

Approaching Savannah late in 1864, William T. Sherman happened upon one of his junior officers whose horse had stepped on a hidden mine. The horse was killed and the man was preparing to have his leg amputated when Sherman rode by. "This was not war, but murder," Sherman explained later, "and it made me very angry." Eschewing his usual overstatement, Sherman's curt response indicated a deadly seriousness. Sherman immediately called up a detachment of Confederate prisoners and required them to march along the road with picks and spades to uncover and remove or detonate the devices. "They begged hard, but I reiterated the order, and could hardly help laughing at their stepping so gingerly along the road, where it was supposed sunken torpedoes might explode at each step."[79] They found no more, which may explain Sherman's cavalier recollection of an order that could have condemned prisoners to death.

One of Sherman's adjutants, Major Henry Hitchcock, came upon the scene at the same time and recorded his own impressions. Hitchcock was born in Alabama, trained as a lawyer, and served the US Army as a judge advocate, following in the footsteps of his father, Chief Justice of the Alabama Supreme Court. He knew the law and was aware of McClellan's precedent for using enemy prisoners to clear torpedoes. Hitchcock supported Sherman's order, angry that "these cowardly villains call us 'barbarous Yankees'—and then adopt instruments of murder in cold blood where they dare not stand and fight like men." Hitchcock believed that placing torpedoes at the entrance to a fort would be justifiable as a form of defense against invasion but not on a common roadway where they might kill a few soldiers but "could not possibly delay or interfere with such an army." "Quos Deus vult perdere prius dementat," Hitchcock pronounced, quoting (in Latin) the ancient Greek proverb, "those whom the gods would destroy, they first make mad." Even though land mines angered Union officers, once the war concluded, US officials never prosecuted Confederate torpedo designers or operators.[80]

The Union was said to have its own anonymous killing weapon, Greek fire. A chimerical substance that could be carried in incendiary shells thrown onto Southern cities, it would supposedly start fires that could not be extinguished. Lincoln authorized tests, and the confident inventor, Levi Short, managed to have his devices used in the bombing campaign against Charleston, South Carolina, in July 1863. The shells failed to achieve their intended effect—Charleston did not fall to the Union until February 1865—but they offered Confederates the opportunity to proclaim their victimization at the hands of murderous Yankees. P. G. T. Beauregard, the Confederate commander at Charleston, denounced the incendiary shells as "a villainous compound, unworthy of civilized nations." Confederates imagined their own apocalyptic weapons, often involving fire as well. One enterprising Southern citizen suggested to Jefferson Davis that they could stop Burnside's fleet from capturing Wilmington, North Carolina, by seizing all the area's turpentine, filling 1,000 barrels, "then breaking them open and setting fire to the water" near the Union fleet. The rabid secessionist Edmund Ruffin likewise recommended the use of fire rafts against Union vessels, "noting historical precedents." Ruffin was encouraged by reports about the use of torpedoes and hoped to expand the strategy in order to wreak havoc on Northern ships tied together along the James River. Ruffin, like other Southern architects of disunion, was called a "fire-eater" in antebellum parlance. His hatred of the Union now compelled him to hope Southerners could breathe rather than consume the deadly substance.[81]

Just conduct in war is predicated on selectively identifying legitimate targets—uniformed soldiers—rather than directing lethal violence without regard to the status of victims. The anonymous, mass-killing weapons with which both sides experimented disregarded this distinction. The most indiscriminate strategy of the Civil War—an early experiment in biological warfare—never came to fruition. The Kentucky physician Luke Pryor Blackburn, a widely recognized authority on yellow fever who had helped quell several epidemics in Southern cities before the war, served as a Confederate secret agent in Canada. We know today that

Blackburn's plan—to spread yellow fever by the distribution of clothing from infected patients—would not have accomplished what he intended. Yellow fever is transmitted via mosquitoes, but Blackburn was using his medical knowledge to create what he hoped would be a random and deadly epidemic in Northern cities. Blackburn also planned to send infected clothing to ports occupied by Northern soldiers in Virginia and North Carolina.[82]

In April 1864, Blackburn left Canada for Bermuda (an important base for Confederate blockade-runners) to assist in suppressing a yellow fever epidemic. While helping, Blackburn packed eleven large trunks filled with clothing from yellow fever victims for transportation to Northern cities. He hired a man to smuggle the trunks into the United States, though the contents were never distributed. The man later revealed the plot to the US Consul in Toronto. Blackburn even hoped to deliver a valise filled with infected clothes to the White House in order to infect Lincoln. Blackburn and his co-conspirators worked with secret agents that Jefferson Davis had sent to Canada early in the year in an attempt to destabilize the North through irregular actions launched across the Canadian border. Blackburn's attack, had it succeeded, would have had no parallel in the Civil War. In terms of its potential impact, it resembled air bombardments of civilians in World War II. During a 1793 outbreak in Philadelphia, 10 percent of the city's population died from the disease. A similar death toll in a Northern city in the 1860s could have claimed the lives of tens or even hundreds of thousands of people.[83]

The one actual case of a truly indiscriminate mass-casualty weapon came at the Union's City Point Harbor on the James River. On August 9, 1864, Confederate secret agents John Maxwell and R. K. Dillard detonated a clockwork torpedo that initiated a catastrophic explosion of artillery shells and ammunition stockpiled at the wharf. The improvised explosive device killed fifty-eight people outright, injured another 126, and caused $4 million in property damage.[84] The victims included a mix of soldiers, teamsters, stevedores, and civilians, all working in a zone far from the battlefield. The blast rocked Grant's headquarters, located at City Point, killing an orderly just outside his tent and injuring Orville Babcock, Grant's close friend and aide. Grant telegraphed news of the event to the War Department within minutes, though he and the rest of

"Explosion at City Point." Alfred Waud's sketch revealed the scale of the explosion unleashed by the Confederates' clockwork torpedo. If Union officers had recognized the event as a deliberate effort to kill remotely and anonymously, they would have surely retaliated.

his command believed for the remainder of the war that the incident was an accident, probably caused by mishandling explosive materials on the dock.[85] Grant appointed a committee to investigate the incident, though they too failed to unearth the real perpetrators.[86] This was due at least as much to a lack of imagination as to the well-concealed nature of the attack itself. Union officers had no frame of reference to imagine a deliberate attempt to kill and destroy on that scale with no evident military purpose.

The City Point bombing represents one of the largest atrocities of the Civil War. But Maxwell's superior officer endorsed him and his actions (as "a bold operator and well calculated for such exploits") in a report to General Rains, who sent it on to the secretary of war. The Confederate high command did not repeat the event but neither did it disavow it. Maxwell himself recognized the results of such an arbitrary form of war-making. "A party of ladies, it seems, were killed by this explosion," he confessed in his report. "It is saddening to me to realize the fact that the terrible effects of war induce such consequence." "Induce" was a particularly passive verb in this context; no one in the Union's or Confederacy's war to that date had regarded the killing of female civilians as a necessary consequence. Maxwell further consoled himself by asserting that his actions constituted "just retaliation" for "the ordeal to which our own women have been subjected, and the barbarities of the enemy's crusade against us and them." As Maxwell's War Department superiors certainly knew, his actions did not qualify as retaliation, which had to be public in order to compel the enemy to abandon the unjust behavior originally committed, and proportional, which the City Point bombing certainly was not. The nature of Maxwell's device ensured that he would not know who its victims were. The lack of selectivity in its potential victims, to say nothing of its scale, represented a willingness to abandon many of the conventions of warfare at the time, most importantly the idea of noncombatant immunity. Because the Union never knew the source of the explosion, the City Point bombing did not shape the war in any demonstrable way. Other new military technologies did influence the course of the war, though these generated new tactics (primarily ship design and movement) rather than inaugurating the wholesale abandonment of the principle of noncombatant immunity. This disregard for noncombatants would have to wait for twentieth-century wars.[87]

The preponderance of mass-casualty weapons were imagined by Confederates frustrated at translating battlefield successes into victory in the war. At various points, Confederate military officers and high-ranking politicians considered or pursued projects that adopted a less selective mode of war-making. Some of these, such as mines, worked, while others, like the idea of spread yellow fever, failed. The old Regular Army soldiers—Joseph Johnston, James Longstreet, Robert E. Lee—refused to follow this path. Instead, they hewed to the laws of war absorbed in the classrooms of West Point and in their socialization in the army after graduation.

The Perils of Prisoners

Throughout 1864, soldiers experienced increasing vulnerability when they became prisoners of war. The moment of capture emerged as a particularly fraught interval. In the war's early years, soldiers on both sides recognized flags of surrender and truce and allowed enemies to surrender individually. Once soldiers gave up their weapons, they effectively became noncombatants. The Lieber Code espoused the just war ideal: "A prisoner of war is subject to no punishment for being a public enemy, nor is any revenge wreaked upon him by the intentional infliction of any suffering, or disgrace, by cruel imprisonment, want of food, by mutilation, death, or any other barbarity."[88] In harmony with the code's legalistic approach, both sides devoted bureaucratic energy and resources to correctly identify, organize, and track the prisoners that each took during battle. An entire series of the *Official Records of the War of the Rebellion*— eight large volumes—pertains just to prisoner issues, and this hardly scratches the surface of the detailed lists kept by field commanders and provost marshals throughout the war.[89] The volume of attention that commanders gave to fairly treating captured soldiers stands out in sharp relief with the treatment accorded to prisoners in other nineteenth-century national and civil conflicts. In Mexico's Caste War of the Yucatán, both the Mayan Rebels and the Mexican government routinely killed enemies they captured in battle.[90] In the Taiping Civil War, tens of thousands of captured soldiers were put to death.[91]

Who Is a Soldier?

Prisoners encountered uncertainty and threats at various points. When Confederates faced black soldiers in 1864, they sometimes allowed them to surrender and sometimes fought them to the death. Soldiers on both sides also confronted more dangers inside prison camps, as logistical pressures reduced the rations that could be provided to prisoners. In addition, anxieties over escape attempts led camp commandants to increase surveillance and violence. The death rates from disease in prisoner-of-war camps were high in both Northern and Southern prisons, though this resulted largely from overcrowding and the same lack of understanding regarding communicable diseases that killed so many men in the ranks. Neither Union nor Confederate prison commandants designed their institutions to kill their prisoners, though on both sides callous neglect was more the rule than the exception.[92] The failure to find common ground on the exchange cartel was symptomatic of both the communication problems that plagued the war and the increasing animosity between participants.

In 1862, the two sides established an agreement that facilitated the parole and exchange of prisoners. This system was not perfect, but it usually ensured prison stays of only a few months as opposed to the indefinite imprisonment of 1864. In 1863, the North suspended the cartel because of the Confederacy's refusal to respect black soldiers as legitimate prisoners. After this, the commissioners for prisoner exchange met periodically, and sick or injured men were sometimes exchanged in small numbers after a battle, but starting in late 1863, prisoners began accumulating in greater numbers in camps on both sides. When some of the Confederate parolees captured at the fall of Vicksburg were recaptured at Chattanooga before being exchanged, it increased animosity late in the year. In April 1864, Benjamin Butler (who had been appointed the Union's lead negotiator on prisoner issues) met with his Confederate counterpart on prisoner exchange. The Union's decision to appoint Butler, a figure who was reviled more than any other in the Confederacy, signaled their willingness to politicize the exchange process. Confederates' willingness to meet with Butler repudiated their earlier declaration that Butler was liable for immediate arrest and execution and suggested the necessary flexibility with which Confederates approached such moments. In short, they failed to fulfill their worst threats when such actions would have compromised the lives of their soldiers. But holding a meeting did not guarantee agreement on the issues that divided them.

Butler wrung a concession from Robert Ould (the Confederate commissioner for prisoner exchanges) that the Confederates would treat as regular prisoners captured officers of USCT units and soldiers who had been free men of color. Butler refused to accept Ould's distinction between free men and slaves in the US Army. "We have no slaves in our Army," he asserted. The Emancipation Proclamation had freed those men, who then enlisted. The question for the Union was whether they would "permit the belligerents opposed to us to make slaves of the freed men that they capture in our uniform, simply because of their color." Ould's hope that Butler would concede to the exchange of white soldiers in order to satisfy the demands of soldiers' families revealed his careful reading of northern politics. Democratic newspapers and soldiers' relatives put considerable pressure on Butler. One Illinois man begged him to support exchange with no conditions if only to relieve the suffering at Andersonville: "35,000 it is said, are there *without* shelter, clothing or food sufficient to keep soul & body together, nearly two hundred are dying daily, while four hundred are raving maniacs already."[93]

The negotiations reveal Butler's twin goals of securing the release of Northern prisoners and maintaining the respect and support of the black community. Any agreement like the one Ould proposed, which subjected black soldiers to unjust imprisonment and suffering, would have jeopardized the latter goal. Grant intervened, bringing clarity and vigor to the Union's policy on prisoner exchange: "no distinction whatever will be made in the exchange between white and colored prisoners," he informed Butler. "The only question being, were they, at the time of their capture, in the military service of the United States. If they were, the same terms as to treatment while prisoners, and conditions of release and exchange must be exacted and had, in the case of colored soldiers as in the case of white soldiers." If Confederates did not observe this distinction, the cartel was dead. Another motive for Grant to refuse exchange was military necessity. As general-in-chief, Grant knew that he could refuse to exchange prisoners because the Confederacy had greater manpower demands. By 1864, they had fewer men to call up from the civilian population to replace soldiers lost to capture. Southerners accused Grant of callously sacrificing his men to Southern prisons in order to diminish Confederate armies. Little evidence supports this charge, but the "awful arithmetic" of the war was plain for everyone to see.[94]

Butler pressed the issue again later in 1864, responding to Ould's continued call for exchange with the following question: "will you please say whether you mean by 'prisoners held in captivity,' colored men, duly enrolled, and mustered into service of the United States." Butler drew on history and law, reminding Ould that the American navy refused to concede the right of Barbary pirates in the Mediterranean to enslave captured sailors. "Their children will hardly yield [the same principle] upon their own soil," he noted.[95] The influence of competing conceptions of race, manhood, and soldiering, the persistent irritation and diplomatic conflict over actual exchanges, and the blunt necessity of denying the

Confederates men for their armies combined to eliminate the possibility of exchange.

Conditions in Camps

With exchanges suspended, more prisoners accumulated in Northern and Southern camps, and they faced worse conditions. Throughout 1864, conditions in prison camps in both sections deteriorated. Inmates received smaller rations of less nutritious food, health care continued to be inadequate, few enjoyed enough protection from the elements (whether Southern summer heat or Northern winter cold), and guards in both places treated prisoners with increasingly cavalier violence. Although the breakdown of the Southern transportation network exacerbated the paucity of supplies that reached camps, Confederate Commissary General Lucius Northrop intentionally reduced the content and size of rations issued to prisoners before this problem manifested.[96] Reductions in the North were likewise deliberate rather than accidental or inevitable. US Secretary of War Edward Stanton seized opportunities to reduce the rations of Confederate prisoners in 1864 after receiving reports of the poor condition of Union men.[97]

The most infamous prison camp, at Andersonville, Georgia, witnessed appalling sanitary conditions and extraordinarily high death rates. The commandant of the camp, Henry Wirz, was executed after the war for his role in the deaths of 13,000 inmates, but most historians regard the violence committed against prisoners to have been more the result of neglect than any concerted effort. Much of the routine violence at Andersonville occurred among the prisoners themselves, a condition that reached its climax in 1864 when, with the commandant's permission, a self-appointed group of Union "regulators" executed six men who had perpetrated attacks, killings, and other crimes on prisoners in the camp. Nothing comparable occurred in Northern prisons, partly because none were as overcrowded as Andersonville. What constitutes responsibility here? Few people outside of central Georgia had any knowledge of the terrible conditions inside the prison, but the Confederate leadership did. Jefferson Davis received and read a letter from a Georgia soldier chronicling the abuses he witnessed. James Anderson, a private in the First

Georgia Reserves, had no love for the Union—his family had been driven from their home in New Orleans, yet he appealed to Davis under the auspices of the Golden Rule. "We should," Anderson believed, "'do as we would be done by.'" Instead, Confederate guards wantonly shot prisoners who neared the "dead line," usually two to three per day. "We have many thoughtless boys here who think the killing of a Yankee will make them great men," but Anderson believed that Davis would never sanction such practice. "I make this statement to you knowing you to be a soldier, statesman, and Christian, that if possible you may correct such things, together with many others that exist here." Davis forwarded the letter to his secretary of war but issued no orders for a change of policy.[98]

Northern sympathy for Confederate prisoners held in their camps diminished sharply after newspapers reported the condition of a group of sick men released in May 1864. Members of the Joint Committee on the Conduct of the War sent members to interview 500 men released by Richmond authorities. They were horrified to find the worst rumors true. "Dirty, emaciated, listless, suffering from frostbite and other ailments induced by exposure, many of the prisoners were little more than living skeletons." The report, widely distributed across the North, included pictures of abused men. Northern papers reprinted these images, complemented by narrative accounts. This material incensed Northerners over what they regarded as the deliberate starvation of Union prisoners. George Templeton Strong, who served on a committee to investigate the treatment of those soldiers, reached a damning conclusion shared by many Northerners: "Jefferson Davis's policy is to starve and freeze and kill off by inches the prisoners he dares not butcher outright." Strong misapprehended the conditions inside Union prison camps, where he assumed Confederate prisoners grew fat on the lavish rations. This perceived inequity only compounded his anger about the lack of Union retaliation for what he regarded as unjust abuse of prisoners. His conclusion reflected the ways that prisoner mistreatment could catalyze an increasingly harsh conflict. "God grant that this war may last till these fiends are exterminated from the surface of God's earth," he pledged, "no matter what insolvency it may bring on *me* for one! The *noyades* and fusillades and the Republican baptisms of the French Revolution were acts of mercy and charity compared with the lingering death Secessia is

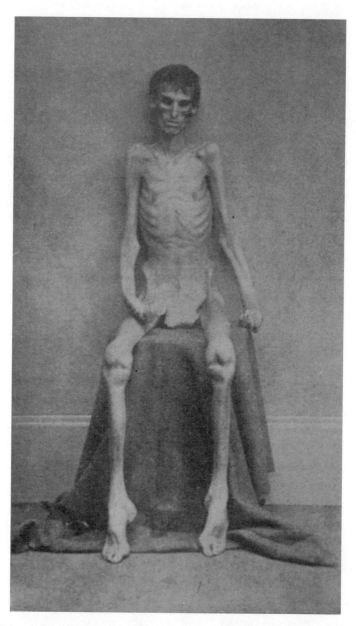

This Union prisoner of war, suffering from severe malnutrition and starvation at Belle Isle, Richmond, embodied for Northerners the unprincipled treatment of prisoners in Confederate hands. Woodcut reproductions of the image appeared in newspapers around the North, spurring calls for revenge.

inflicting deliberately and with murderous malice and forethought on thousands of prisoners of war."[99]

Over the course of the Civil War, 409,608 soldiers were captured by one side or the other. Of these, 30,218 Union soldiers died in Confederate prisons and 25,976 Confederate soldiers died in Union prisons. Comparing the mortality rates—15.5 percent for Union prisoners and 12.1 percent for Confederates—fails to do justice to the unnecessary deaths of these men. Much of the suffering and death among prisoners occurred in late 1864 and early 1865 as the number of men held in both Northern and Southern prisons skyrocketed. Many of these men died of diseases that killed their comrades in their own camps—dysentery, pneumonia, and smallpox—and these deaths may well have occurred regardless of location, but there is little question that incompetence, malign treatment, and administrative inefficiency created a perfect storm of conditions that increased the war's mortality total significantly.[100]

Children of God

The Confederate refusal to recognize black volunteers as legitimate soldiers, which culminated in a series of racial massacres in 1864, produced a deadlier Civil War for everyone. The Union pushed back, eventually forcing the Confederacy, at least at the highest levels of command, to respect black men as regular combatants. This concession provided little relief for the huge new prisoner-of-war populations that suffered under increasingly poor conditions in Northern and Southern camps. Many of the most dangerous issues in the Civil War, including the role of race, the mistreatment of prisoners, and new technologies of war came together in Georgia as William T. Sherman's army marched through the state. Although Sherman is remembered in myth as a monster who laid waste to the state without regard to the lives of its inhabitants, his siege of Atlanta and its occupation produced surprisingly few noncombatant fatalities. He banished citizens and destroyed property, which increased civilian suffering, but these actions followed the laws of war and may have forestalled worse outcomes.

Although Sherman's March was not as devastating as popular memories of the event would have us believe, it nonetheless drew soldiers and civilians into intimate and often destructive contact. This was particularly true for Southern women, both black and white, subject to the random violence of deserter bands and other criminals who followed in the US Army's wake. Because these men operated irregularly, military justice rarely reached them or curtailed their actions. Whatever threat Sherman posed, Georgia's citizens realized Union soldiers were preferable adversaries to the men who abandoned either army and preyed on the vulnerable.

Race and Violence in the Civil War

Jefferson Davis and Confederate military leaders retreated from the draconian positions they first articulated when confronted by black soldiers, but that did little to improve the experiences black Americans received at the hands of Confederates throughout the South. The most fraught decision came at the moment of capture. Would Confederates take black soldiers prisoner or simply kill them? Nearly all of the events that Civil War historians now regard as atrocities occurred when Confederates encountered USCT units and refused to allow them to surrender during military engagements. Rumors of these incidents spread among black troops, compelling some to fight to the death and escalating the war's death toll. Black Southerners also experienced unjust violence at the hands of Northerners as well, though nothing on the scale or severity of what they faced from Confederate soldiers. Conditions in Union contraband camps rivaled those in prison camps with the predictable result that rates of death for freedpeople living in them were high. In both prisons and contraband camps, a lack of concern for the victims of mistreatment—whether enemy soldiers or black Southerners—created unnecessary suffering and death.

A military historian's critique of how Europeans have selectively deployed the concept of just war sheds light on the dilemmas faced by black soldiers in the Civil War: "At the root of the Christian-humanist attempts to constrain war has been the recognition of the adversary as a human being possessing certain fundamental rights," he writes. "It was justifiable to kill him so long as he bore arms and so had accepted the risks inherent in that activity. But once he was disarmed he regained all the rights due to him as a child of God or a member of civil society." This perspective captures the moral framework that prevailed between white combatants in the US Civil War. The historian continues: "if he was seen not as a human being, however, but as a member of an inferior but still menacing race, it made no difference whether he was wearing a uniform and bearing arms or not—whether indeed he was man, woman, or child. He had no more rights than a wild animal or an insect."[1] This characterization reflected, all too often, how Confederates regarded black combatants in the conflict.

Racial Atrocities in the Civil War

Black men had served in the US Armed Forces since before the nation's founding, but Confederates regarded free black service and emancipation in general as unjust. They believed themselves authorized to respond in kind. Southern soldiers understood that refusing surrender allowed killing to continue beyond its military purpose. That refusal began with the first large-scale participation of black soldiers in battle at Milliken's Bend in Louisiana in 1863. In his official report, Confederate Major General Richard Taylor noted that "unfortunately" some of the soldiers had been captured. As USCT forces deployed in 1864, the scale of atrocities escalated. Reports emerged from all over the South of black soldiers suffering unjust violence at the hands of Confederates: Olustee, Florida, in February; Plymouth, North Carolina, Fort Pillow, Tennessee, and Poison Spring, Arkansas, in April; the Battle of the Crater in July; Saltville, Virginia, in October, and more.[2] The result of this pattern was that black soldiers experienced much higher casualty and mortality rates than white troops. Black troops played a key role in three out of five of the deadliest battles for the Union—Port Hudson, Fort Wagner, and Olustee.[3] All three battles were small by Civil War standards; they were violent because of the presence of black soldiers.

As hard as it may be for modern readers to appreciate, many Confederates believed that they fought the war in a just manner. Congressman Jabez L. M. Curry, like many of his Richmond colleagues, regarded the Union's emancipation policy as a major break in civilized warfare.[4] From this perspective, the Union's unjust actions required retaliation to restore balance to the war. The late 1863 and early 1864 debate in the Confederate Congress over retaliation took as its foundation the illegality of the Union's campaign against slavery. Beyond the legal problem of how to compel obedience to their view of the laws of war, Confederates believed that because emancipation was unjust, the presence of black soldiers fell outside the laws of war, and so the response had to be mediated by civil law. They refused to treat black men as regular prisoners because they did not regard them as regular soldiers.

The argument that Confederates targeted black soldiers for lethal violence with forethought and confidence in their own innocence may overstate the extent to which rationality governed Southern soldiers' actions. On the battlefield, Confederate soldiers responded emotionally to the presence of black opponents. They perceived black soldiers through the framework of slave rebellion, which tapped an ancestral fear among white Southerners. On the front lines, soldiers seem not to have rationalized or thought at all. After-battle accounts, usually from Confederates, share a common pattern—when Confederates killed injured soldiers, they did so in a frenzy but with a methodical precision.[5] The few Confederates who protested the mistreatment of black soldiers—and most of the racial massacres included at least one white Southern chronicler—were motivated by a sense of pity, not justice. More strategically, some Confederates regretted that reports of the killing of black soldiers created an unfavorable image of the country, but even these men regarded the problem as a matter of perception, not moral failure.

Given the incoherence of Confederate policy on the question of black soldiers and the visceral animosity of Southern soldiers, the possibilities for unjust violence were high wherever black and white men met on the battlefield. The massacre of black Union troops at Fort Pillow, Tennessee, stands out as the most well-known such event in the Civil War.[6] Initially a Confederate preserve along the Mississippi River north of Memphis, Fort Pillow was captured by the Union navy in 1862 and manned by a mixed force of white Tennessee Unionists and black Union soldiers. Confederates under the command of Major General Nathan Bedford Forrest attacked the fort in April 1864. Coming up from the river, they captured the facility and in the process shot, stabbed, or clubbed to death hundreds of black soldiers in the act of surrendering.[7] Several witnesses recounted a frenzy of violence inside the fort as Forrest's men used their revolvers, bayonets, and rifle butts to kill wounded or surrendering men. Achilles Clark, a Confederate sergeant in the attacking force, provided one of the most vivid descriptions of what happened there: "The slaughter was awful. Words cannot describe the scene. The poor deluded negroes would run up to our men[,] fall upon their knees and with uplifted hands scream for mercy but they were ordered to their feet and then shot down. . . . Their fort turned out to be a great slaughter pen. Blood, human blood stood about in pools and brains could have been gathered up in any quantity."[8] As one writer has proven, the dramatically unbalanced

"The War in Tennessee: Confederate Massacre of Federal Troops after the Surrender at Fort Pillow, April 12, 1864." The murder of surrendering black soldiers made immediate news in both the North and South and revealed the refusal of Confederate soldiers to respect black men as regular soldiers who merited the protection of the laws of war.

death rates between black and white Union soldiers in the garrison can only be explained by deliberate targeting by the Confederates.[9]

Fort Pillow offered a perfect storm of conditions that led to the massacre. The facility was closed after capture by the Union and only reopened two years later in February 1864, when it became "a safe haven once again for entrepreneurs, contrabands, and unionists."[10] That is to say, it held all those people—traders who collaborated with the US Army, runaway slaves, and white Unionists—that Confederate soldiers most despised. Inside the fort huddled an indeterminate number of civilians as well. The battle itself unfolded over a complex space, with Confederates coming up from the riverbank even as Union reinforcements tried to make their way by river to the fort. The Union chain of command collapsed during the battle, and on the Confederate side Forrest remained absent from the field during much of the fighting. Forrest also issued a flag of truce and demand for surrender in the middle of the attack, during which Confederate troops probably moved into better positions for attack. Forrest's troops, though officially commissioned, had long operated in a semi-irregular mode. Allowing them to enter a fort filled with black soldiers and white Unionists without oversight was grossly negligent.

Despite the official Confederate position that free black men serving in the US Army merited different treatment from ex-slaves (a distinction that required capturing and identifying enemy troops before determining their proper disposition), Forrest and his lieutenants regarded all black soldiers as slaves having escaped their masters. Once they adopted this perspective, Forrest and his men believed they were justified in killing or capturing with an intent to re-enslave the soldiers they faced. A slave trader before the war (and the first grand wizard of the Ku Klux Klan after it), Forrest expressed his racial hostility in covert ways. He had to perform an intellectual sleight of hand to conceal the murderous intent of his men. One biographer notes that although no evidence clearly demonstrates that Forrest ordered a massacre, "there was enough rancor between his men and the armed former slaves, as well as the Tennessee Unionists, that about all he had to do to produce a massacre was issue no order against one." Declining Confederate fortunes in the western theater, including the loss of all of eastern Tennessee in late 1863, compounded the frustration and disappointment among Confederates.[11]

Jefferson Davis never expressed any concern about the Fort Pillow Massacre. On the contrary, he accepted Forrest's report that the black soldiers killed inside the fort died because they refused to surrender. "Instead of cruelty," Davis wrote, "General Forrest, it appears, exhibited forbearance and clemency far exceeding the usage of war under like circumstances." This was after a report in which Forrest bragged that "the river was dyed with the blood of the slaughtered" which he hoped would "demonstrate to the Northern people that negro soldiers cannot cope with Southerners." The *Richmond Examiner* applauded the outcome of Fort Pillow and refused to apologize if Lincoln threatened retaliation. "We have shown that we, as a people, are heartily tired of a policy, dictated partly by sentimentality, partly by foolish deference to the good opinion of the world, partly by an official awe of Washington—a policy to which we have sacrificed too long the lives of our brave soldiers and our solemn sense of duty." In short order, the *Examiner's* editors disavowed all the normal restraints on barbarous action that had previously served as celebrated hallmarks of Confederate war-making. "Sentiment" could be read as the simple human reactions of pity, sympathy, and shame. Connecting this concept back to the revolution in emotional expression that gripped early nineteenth-century America, the denunciation could also be read as a disavowal of evangelical belief. One of the chief critiques of the evangelicalism of the Second Great Awakening had been its New Testament emphasis on Jesus's message of compassion and charity, a position at odds with both the necessary violence of slavery and of a cold-blooded war against the Yankees. The "foolish deference to the good opinion of the world" was a clumsy euphemism for diplomacy, something which held little hope in 1864, but it also reflected a willingness to cut off the Confederacy from the prevailing opinion of the civilized war that its leaders aspired to join. "Awe of Washington" perhaps denoted a respectful legacy of Southerners' long historic associations with the federal government or what the editors felt was an exaggerated fear of Northern retaliation. In any case, the *Examiner's* bold statement reflected Confederate frustration with precisely those structural aspects of the war that contained its violence.[12]

Although the scale of the Fort Pillow Massacre was unusual, the same impulse and outcome prevailed during engagements all over the Confederacy in 1864. Despite Robert E. Lee's reputation as a Christian gentleman who fought according to the laws of war, troops under his command committed atrocities against black soldiers throughout the Overland Campaign. During the second day of fighting at the Battle of the Wilderness, Confederates pursued wounded men separated from their commands, especially black soldiers, with special vigor, in some cases executing them and hanging their bodies along the roadside as trophies of war.[13] This practice of vindictive violence culminated in a massacre under very similar conditions to Fort Pillow during the Battle of the Crater outside Petersburg in July, though perhaps with an even higher casualty total.[14] On July 30, 1864, Union engineers detonated a massive mine placed in a carefully constructed tunnel dug under the Confederate line. Owing to confusion and poor command on the Union side, the black soldiers who had trained to lead the assault were held back and entered the crater created by the mine after Confederates had regrouped. Energized by the disorganized Federals and perhaps because they had heard black soldiers shout "Remember Fort Pillow!" and "No Quarter!," Confederates counterattacked with a vengeance. Like at Fort Pillow, Confederates refused to allow black soldiers to surrender. Lee's soldiers left ample testimony about their mistreatment of these men. One Georgian described how "the bayonet was plunged through their hearts & the muzzle of our guns was put on their temple & their brains blown out others were knocked in the head with the butts of our guns. Few would succeed in getting to the rear safe."[15] Lieutenant Colonel William Pegram told his wife that "black soldiers 'threw down their arms to surrender, but were not allowed to do so.'"[16] General Lee, always aware of what happened on his battlefields, surely knew about the behavior of his men, but took no action against it.[17] The *Richmond Examiner's* report supported the actions and encouraged the massacre, just as it had after Fort Pillow: "butcher every negro that Grant sends against your brave troops."[18]

During the Battle of Saltville in southwestern Virginia in late 1864, Confederates repulsed an attack by Union forces. Once again, Confederates murdered captured black soldiers. According to a historian of the event, "when the fighting ended, Confederate troops, disregarding their commanders' orders, began killing many of the wounded black troops that had fallen into their hands. The murders would continue for almost a week."[19] What marked this as distinct even from Fort Pillow is that many of the men killed had already been taken prisoner. The USCT soldiers at Saltville operated under command of Union Brigadier General Stephen Burbridge, who had wielded a heavy hand in neighboring Kentucky, alienating many locals. The soldiers had received little training and were pressed into regular units just before the raid commenced. The battle at Saltville, over control of an important salt works, was close quarter and Confederates were surprised to find black soldiers in the attacking force. Confederate George Dallas Mosgrove, a junior officer in the Fourth Kentucky Cavalry, recorded a sickening scene the morning after the battle. He "found the Tennesseans were killing negroes. . . . Hearing more firing at the front, I cautiously rode forward and came upon a squad of Tennesseans, mad and excited to the highest degree. They were shooting every wounded negro they could find. Hearing firing on other parts of the field, I knew the same awful work was going on all about me."[20] Champ Ferguson, the notorious Cumberland guerrilla, executed many men himself, including several taken out of a hospital or shot dead in their hospital beds.[21] As with other racial massacres, the Richmond press celebrated the victory.[22]

Northern newspapers chronicled these events in close detail. A Cincinnati paper called Fort Pillow "one of the most horrible that has disgraced the history of modern warfare." Responses split along partisan lines in the North. Conservative and Democratic papers disputed the facts, blamed incompetent Northern commanders, or regarded the black soldiers themselves as somehow liable. Republican and abolitionist papers blamed the savagery on the moral blindness induced by slavery. "The whole civilized world will be shocked by the great atrocity at Fort Pillow," the *Chicago Tribune* asserted, "but in no respect does the act misrepresent the nature and precedents of Slavery." Several called for retaliation in the strongest possible terms. The Joint Committee on the Conduct of the War, which had spent much of the war's first years criticizing Northern generals, turned its attention to the massacre. It deputized two members—one congressman and one senator—to visit the region to interview witnesses and gather evidence for a report. That report, filled with both accurate testimony and exaggerated material gathered hastily, left no doubt about the villainy of the Southern army. It pronounced the massacre the result "'of a policy deliberately decided upon and unhesitatingly announced'" and concluded that "'no cruelty which the most fiendish malignity could devise was omitted by these murderers.'" 60,000 copies were printed and distributed in the North.[23]

But just as with federal guerrilla policy, Confederate and state officials did not sustain draconian practices against all black soldiers. A long series of orders, opinions, and counteropinions circulated among the high command.[24] Despite the rhetoric and threats, the move to sell black soldiers into slavery or to kill every one captured (plus their officers) risked too great a threat to the deteriorating Confederate manpower base. Abraham Lincoln had pledged to retaliate by executing Confederate prisoners for every Union man killed. Even in lawless Missouri, Confederate regulars sometimes captured black soldiers and exchanged them with nearby Union officers for their own prisoners.[25] Because of the inconsistency of Confederate national policy on black soldiers, one historian notes, "the fate of individual black prisoners depended much more upon the attitudes of Confederate officers and men on particular battlefields."[26] This meant that many hundreds, perhaps thousands, of black soldiers died unjustly. The Davis administration's slow change on this issue was not merely a matter of saving face or protecting itself from criticism. Even a diehard such as Mississippian Henry Foote reconsidered his call for raising the black flag in response to black enlistment. Foote promoted a policy that distinguished between USCT soldiers who enlisted as free men in the North and those drawn from runaway slaves from the South. The former could be treated like regular public enemies while the latter could not. Foote assured his colleagues that "though it was a 'barbarous thing for the North to enlist negroes in its armies, he believed we were bound to recognize them as prisoners of war.'"[27] And some black soldiers were captured and sent to prison. Andersonville held perhaps one hundred such men, most captured at Olustee.[28]

Jefferson Davis embodied the frustration felt by many white Confederates at being unable to contend with the organized power of black soldiers. In mid-1864, he received a petition from the citizens of Northumberland County, Virginia. A detachment of black soldiers had entered the county and captured animals. Worse still, "the negroes were suffered to wander about from house to house without control, and wherever they went ladies were insulted, cursed, and reviled." The petitioners reported that four women "became unfortunate victims of brutal lust" before white citizens drove them from the area. Davis rejected the plea to exempt local men from the draft but penned an unusually long letter to his secretary of war. Davis recommended that those men who remained at home should be prepared to act and offered them the authority to "execute a summary punishment on such criminals as are described in this memorial." The men should then return to their homes so that the US Army would have no recourse. Whether Davis believed the report or not, he expressed "deep sympathy" and "sorrow . . . at my inability to give them ample protection." Recognizing that he lacked the power to defend his people from their most feared threat, Davis sanctioned abandoning the bounds of regular war by encouraging irregular violence against regular troops, knowing that the Union did have recourse in their antiguerrilla policies.[29]

Davis's recommendation that Confederate civilians respond outside the laws of war reflected the ad hoc nature of the white Southern response. This same inconsistency prevailed among regular troops. If black soldiers survived being captured, they might be killed later before they had a chance to be placed in a prisoner-of-war camp. After an 1863 skirmish in Louisiana, reports of murdered black prisoners reached Confederate Colonel John L. Logan, who to his credit investigated the incident. Subordinate officers reported that while escorting segregated groups of black captives, the men had tried to escape and had been shot. Throughout the Civil War, many captured soldiers escaped, but this explanation surfaces in almost every record of racial murders, including when the white officers of USCT units were killed after action but before imprisonment.[30] Logan was unpersuaded: "my own opinion is that the negroes were summarily disposed of . . . contrary to my wishes and against my own consent."[31]

Confederate behavior in this regard differed from how the British treated their enemies during the 1857 Indian Rebellion. British troops killed Sepoy soldiers in battle and refused surrender, as Confederates did, but they also organized public executions of rebels and trumpeted their policy for the world to hear. The British showed none of the reluctance to admit killing prisoners that surfaced in Confederate correspondence. The result was what a historian of the conflict calls a "war of extermination. All the rebels, because they took up arms against the British, were considered traitors. The massacres they perpetuated led the British to think of them, collectively, as murderers."[32] The Confederates may have never reached this high bar only because they feared the diplomatic consequences. They did not want to be seen as sanctioning murder. This may seem like a meaningless distinction, but for those black soldiers captured and not killed by the Confederates, it made a great deal of difference. Recognizing this difference does not excuse the murders that were committed under their flag, but it does remind us of the important role that Confederate aspirations toward statehood played in moderating the violence its armies committed.

In the absence of any real leadership from either commander-in-chief, soldiers along the Mississippi River experienced a more lethal war following the Fort Pillow Massacre. Two months later, Forrest himself wrote to Major General C. C. Washburn, the Union commander at Memphis, reporting, "the recent battle of Tishomingo Creek was far more bloody than it would otherwise have been but for the fact that your men evidently expected to be slaughtered when captured, and both sides acted as though neither felt safe in surrendering, even when further resistance was useless." Forrest attributed this to the fact "that all the negro troops stationed in Memphis took an oath on their knees, in the presence of Major-General Hurlburt and other officers of your army, to avenge Fort Pillow, and that they would show my troops no quarter." Washburn responded with a surprisingly candid assessment: yes, he believed that black soldiers had taken such an oath (though not in Hurlburt's presence) and "I have no doubt that they went into the field as you allege, in the full belief that they would be murdered in case they fell into your hands. The affair of Fort Pillow fully justified that belief." Washburn expressed satisfaction with Forrest's report of the soldiers' brave fighting and believed that "upon those who have aroused this spirit by their atrocities . . . be the consequences." Washburn may well have appreciated the vigor displayed by black soldiers incensed over Fort Pillow, but by allowing them to prepare to fight to the death he consigned many of them to that fate. Forrest, furious over the tone and implications in Washburn's letter, offered only a short statement of his position on black soldiers: "I regard captured negroes as I do other captured property and not as captured soldiers." Forrest's and Washburn's competing perspectives on the status of black men in arms reveals how an ethical problem expressed through legal and military terminology could escalate the war's killing.[33]

Black civilian supporters faced arbitrary violence from white Southerners as well. Sometimes the perpetrators belonged to the army and sometimes they were guerrillas. Regular noncombatants also acted according to antebellum legal and social practices that granted them authority over black bodies. A historian of this process notes that "in many sections of the no-man's-land [white Southerners] launched a campaign of terror against the newly freed blacks." In 1863, General Robert E. Lee's army brought the terror with them in their invasion of Pennsylvania.

Confederate cavalry and infantry units captured fleeing black refugees, chained them together, and sent these state-sanctioned slave coffles back into Virginia. In some cases, they appear to have caught runaway slaves, but in others, they kidnapped free people of color and sold them into slavery. As a recent history of Gettysburg concludes, "of the various ugly incidents stemming from Lee's Pennsylvania invasion, this was surely the ugliest." Hard numbers are elusive, but reports suggest hundreds of people were enslaved this way.[34]

In the Lower Mississippi River Valley, the Confederate army turned on black civilians in 1863 and 1864. No less an authority than Jefferson Davis's brother Joseph reported such events. In late 1863, after traveling to the Davis's plantations near Jackson, Mississippi, Joseph disputed the story spun by lieutenant Addison Harvey, the commander of a company of the First Mississippi Cavalry. Harvey reported that his unit had taken fire from armed black men and shot back in something like an equal fight. Joseph was unconvinced: "my opinion is they went expecting to find a large number of armed negroes and commenced shooting without waiting to see." Harvey's patrol had killed several of the Davis family slaves and others, most of whom Joseph regarded as "harmless." Joseph wrote his brother directly rather than contradicting Harvey in the newspaper because he was "unwilling to say or do any thing to prejudice the source for bad as they are still better than the Yankees but such atrocities should not go unpunished." Joseph's failure to publicly confront Confederate atrocities meant that they continued. Several weeks later, he reported that a Texas brigade was plundering, burning houses, and killing black noncombatants. "To kill a negro is tolerated extensively," he told his brother. By implicitly sanctioning wanton violence against innocent black civilians, white Southerners fostered a climate of lethal violence that could affect everyone.[35]

The Confederacy's response to the enlistment of former slaves as soldiers was not inevitable. Even a cursory historical assessment of the use of slaves in war reveals that in many conflicts, participants enlisted slaves as soldiers. The decision shifted on how people weighed "the doctrine of necessity," in which combatants privilege self-preservation over the consequences of arming enslaved people. What stands out, historically, is not the Union's enlistment of previously enslaved men into its armies but the

Confederacy's refusal to do so, until the war's closing weeks. All over the world, regimes both large and small have availed themselves of the labor of slaves in wartime, often as soldiers. In the midst of war, rulers have weighed the value of using bonded labor in the military against the possibilities of enslaved soldiers growing too strong to control or the threat of revolt or flight. In the colonial Americas, all the European colonizing powers recruited slaves who escaped from their rivals and incorporated them into colonial armies. The British who settled around Charleston lived in fear that the Spanish would entice their slaves away with promises of freedom in Florida, even though the English, French, and Dutch had all made similar arrangements with slaves who escaped from Spanish holdings.[36]

Confederates might have drawn on the model of the Spanish, who, in their colonial enterprises in the Caribbean, relied on slaves as soldiers. Spain's chief incentive was numbers—they did not possess the manpower to repulse the combined efforts of English, French, and Dutch efforts to seize their land claims. If the Spanish and Confederates shared a situation of necessity, they did not share a similar outlook on slavery. In particular, the Spanish system of slavery was less racialized than that in the Confederate South. This ideological factor is a crucial part of understanding why Confederates never seriously considered using slaves as soldiers. They valued preserving slavery and the white supremacy behind it more than independence. The Georgia politician Howell Cobb expressed the dilemma most clearly: "The day you make soldiers of them is the beginning of the end of the revolution. If slaves will make good soldiers our whole theory of slavery is wrong." Was this a misguided fear? A prominent historian of slavery suggests so, noting that "the increasing use of armed blacks from the early sixteenth to the early nineteenth century did not prevent or appreciably slow down the development of an enormous plantation system from Brazil to the Chesapeake and Mississippi Valley."[37]

The practice of indiscriminate violence against noncombatants continued into late 1864 and early 1865 even as the Confederates' regular military actions produced little result. South Carolina, the scene of few regular battles, produced some of the war's worst irregular atrocities. As Sherman's army moved into the state, enslaved people who escaped their masters but did not keep pace with the army were seized by Confederate irregulars. An enslaved man remembered that "'bush whackers . . . decapitated and their heads placed upon posts that lined the fields' as warnings 'of what would befall [other slaves] if they attempted to escape.'" Along the South Carolina coast, guerrilla bands attacked black people living on abandoned plantations near Beaufort, in March 1865. There, the guerrillas raided the settlement, shooting men in and around their homes, where their bodies lay until eaten by animals. In an upcountry district, a South Carolina county court executed eleven slaves for threatening rebellion.[38]

White Southerners' willingness to subject black Southerners to unnecessary and unjust violence demands an explanation distinct from what happened between soldiers on a battlefield. The episodes in Mississippi and South Carolina were intentional and premeditated. Irregular violence of this sort occurred within communities, so perpetrators and victims probably knew one another. From one perspective, it was simply a continuation of the practices long established within American slavery—whites could control and destroy black bodies at will. Rather than interpreting Confederate actions as "collective rage," one historian advises that they "should be viewed as a measured response" of the sort that white slaveholders committed against enslaved rebels all over the Americas. Faced, during the war, with black resistance to the Confederacy and support for the Union, perhaps it was inevitable that some white Southerners continued old habits. Americans had long worried about the degrading effect of slaveholding on masters themselves, in particular how it weakened the natural sympathy that should exist between human beings and replaced it with a sense of entitled dominance. Thomas Jefferson lamented, "the whole commerce between master and slave is a perpetual exercise of the most boisterous passions, the most unremitting despotism on the one part, and degrading submissions on the other." The result was that Southern men were "thus nursed, educated, and daily exercised in tyranny." How could the results be other than deplorable? Francis Lieber resorted to this explanation when he tried to account for Fort Pillow: "slavery chars a man's mind and nullifies his intellect."[39]

Modern scholars have embraced the term *atrocity* to describe these actions. The institutions that regulate and prosecute unjust military conduct in the modern world share a common definition of atrocity as one of three or four categories of offense—genocide, war crimes, crimes against humanity, or ethnic cleansing. Although the nature of these crimes differs, what unites them is that their victims are "the persons that should be most protected by States, both in times of peace and in times of war."[40] Despite this official standard, historians of different conflicts continue to use the concept in different ways.[41] Civil War historians use the term mostly to distinguish events like the refusal of Confederates to allow black soldiers to surrender or the deliberate targeting of black civilians from typical battlefield violence.[42] Because race was central to the worst moments of unjust fatalities in the Civil War, historians are properly reading modern definitions backward. Modern commentators regard genocide as signaling a desire to exterminate a whole people. Although such a posture was sharply at odds with whites' desire to control black labor in the South, the attitudes and actions of Confederates during the war sometimes came to resemble the modern definition. At the time, however, genocide lay in the future. Without the legal categories that would have given him intellectual refuge, Francis Lieber resorted to a more tragic mode when confronted by Fort Pillow. "Are you not also overwhelmed with grief that such savagery as that at Fort Pillow can be perpetrated by those who are after all our kin?," he wrote to the attorney general. "How slow is Progress and how quick is relapse!"[43]

Defending Black Soldiers

Lincoln's 1863 proclamation asserting the Union's willingness to retaliate for the unjust treatment of black soldiers created an important measure of protection. Because he never actually sanctioned retaliation in any specific cases, the threat may have lost some force, but it prevented the Davis administration from enacting the worst policies that it had initially adopted. Henry Halleck believed this was the case, writing privately that "the southern officers & soldiers are already beckoning Jeff Davis to not execute his threats, knowing that they must suffer the consequences."

Halleck hoped to deter unjust behavior by the Confederates "without too much bloodshed," but as general-in-chief of Union armies, he was committed to using retaliation if necessary. The United States followed the practice of other western powers who used emancipation and the enlistment of black soldiers as war policies. In Haiti, even the French, despite the excesses they blamed on slave insurgents in 1791, resorted to emancipation when the British and Spanish attacked the island. As the leading modern historian of that conflict explains, "in the place of stories of insurgent atrocities, the defenders of emancipation celebrated the heroism and idealism of their new, formerly enslaved, recruits."[44]

Lincoln knew that the scale and the media reaction to Fort Pillow demanded a more thorough response than he had given previous incidents. He took the unusual step of requesting formal opinions from his cabinet secretaries. This elicited a predictably contradictory set of recommendations. All agreed that the Union should respond, and several called for quick retaliation, but they disagreed about who could be targeted, when such action should commence, and whether they should engage diplomatically with Confederates first. The whole cabinet (except Francis Blair) envisioned some sort of retaliation. Most wanted this punishment directed at Confederate officers, and those in command at Fort Pillow if possible. On this point, Francis Lieber concurred, writing to Henry Halleck that "retaliation . . . must be restricted to the men under command of the general who allowed the perpetrators." As Lieber and Lincoln's secretaries knew, such a condition virtually ensured that no retaliation would occur, unless the US Army was lucky enough to capture Forrest and his senior aides. Denouncing them as beyond the laws of war if captured, as the Confederacy had done against Benjamin Butler in 1862, accomplished nothing until they possessed the men. Part of the reluctance to act came from a continuing belief that the Confederate rank and file were held in the army against their will, and retaliatory punishment would only alienate them from the Union. The political consideration at the heart of the war constrained how Lincoln responded to what everyone agreed was an unjust act in the war. The contrary force—the necessity of retaining the political support of black men for the Union—operated but not with enough power to compel action. Both Secretary of the Interior John Usher and Attorney General Edward Bates believed that the United

States was obligated to act on behalf of black soldiers. Once the Union enlisted black men into its ranks, "It [was] a simple duty [to protect them]," Bates explained, "the failure to perform which would be a crime and a national dishonor."[45]

Of the many dangers posed by Fort Pillow and the Confederate mistreatment of black soldiers in general was the problem of a response in kind from USCT soldiers. The Union general in charge of black recruiting for the region noted the reaction of his troops: "there is a great deal of excitement in town in consequence of this affair, especially among our colored troops." Rather than calling for an investigation and protesting the event through channels, he seemed to accept the inevitability of revenge. "If this is to be the game of the enemy they will soon learn that it is one at which two can play." Even Gideon Welles, Lincoln's staid secretary of the navy, anticipated such an event. He expected that Confederates' apparent commitment to a "vindictive" war "will unavoidably provoke retaliation by the race proscribed." A "war of extermination will be the consequence. No human effort will be wholly able to restrain the barbarous slaughter of the blacks on the one hand the rebels on the other after it shall have once been inaugurated." This was the race war that Confederates had predicted was the true purpose of the Emancipation Proclamation, but one they were creating. Lincoln's continuing concern to avoid such an outcome and to avoid any apparent responsibility for such an outcome undoubtedly shaped his cautious response to Fort Pillow. Despite a damning report from the Joint Congressional Committee on the Conduct of the War, which had already investigated the incident, Lincoln took no concrete action.[46]

Soldiers sometimes did. In South Carolina, the Fourth Massachusetts Cavalry destroyed several public buildings in Gillesonville after learning that a Union soldier who had previously been enslaved in the area had been captured by Confederates, beaten, and hanged. This regiment had been created by consolidating two veteran battalions of Massachusetts cavalrymen, one of which had fought in the Battle of Olustee, the site of a racial massacre in February 1864. Though not a massacre on the scale of Fort Pillow, the murder of black soldiers at Olustee had incensed those Union soldiers involved in the battle and may have toughened their resolve to resist such mistreatment again. But beyond a few isolated instances where the call of "Remember Fort Pillow" rang in the air, USCT regiments behaved with restraint. Sherman, never one to conceal evidence of vigorous conduct against Confederates, observed to Secretary of War Stanton that "thus far the negroes have been comparatively well behaved and have not committed the horrid excesses and barbarities which the Southern people so much dreaded."[47]

Regardless of what happened on the ground, Lincoln did not shift the Union's policy on retaliation. And he was not alone in resisting calls to use retaliation as a way to address the unjust killing of black men. Even leading black Americans, like Henry McNeal Turner, a minister in the African Methodist Episcopal church, opposed retaliating on Confederate prisoners in response to the racial massacres their armies committed. "I am sternly opposed to . . . the killing of all the rebel prisoners taken by our soldiers," Turner wrote in mid-1864, "true, the rebels have set the example, particularly in killing the colored soldiers; but it is a cruel one, and two cruel acts never make one humane one. Such a course of warfare is an outrage upon civilization and nominal Christianity." Turner knew too the diplomatic advantages of taking the restrained path. "Let us disappoint our malicious anticipators by showing the world that the higher sentiments not only prevail, but actually predominate."[48]

In the Rough Hands of the Union

In some cases, Union officers did more than stay neutral when they should have protected black lives. Because Lincoln established emancipation as a formal goal of the US Army and because the US Congress eventually passed the Thirteenth Amendment abolishing slavery, we tend to assume that the army supported black Americans in practice, but this was not always the case. The decentralized nature of the nineteenth-century military allowed departmental commanders and brigade-level officers to shape policy within their spheres of influence. For some of the conservative white Northerners serving in the army this meant a practice of malign neglect that produced additional suffering and death for black Southerners. We need to understand the source and nature of that violence, though its presence should not suggest a false equivalence between the Union's treatment of black people and that of the Confederacy.

As the Union army consolidated control of the Mississippi River Valley and expanded along the other tributaries of the Deep South, it exerted control over the labor of freedpeople. The provost marshals and other officials who managed affairs in occupied cities established clear guidelines for labor practices and made themselves available for complaints from both workers and planters. In rural areas of the South, the army often hired local white Unionists to supervise black laborers. By empowering these men, the US Army enabled abuses of the kind that the freedpeople had just fled, only now sanctioned by the US government. In late 1863, a sympathetic observer in Louisiana reported a "reign of terror" against black workers by the new provost marshal, "who is a citizen & been lately appointed to that office." The complainant asserted that even for the "the most simple offence," the provost marshal tied the hands of men and women behind them and hung them from the wall until an overseer came to release them. "I think this is rather cruel & is the commencement of again putting too much power in the hands of the Planters." The complaint was forwarded to the assistant adjutant general for the region who investigated and found the reports accurate. The case was sent on to General Banks, in command of Louisiana at the time, but no evidence indicates any redress of the underlying problems.[49]

A similar case, also from Louisiana, surfaced two months later, when a Union surgeon reported that a man (a white Unionist from New Orleans) supervising labor above the city had "shot dead a poor colored man who attempted to run from him on the Levee."[50] The provost marshal defended the overseer's actions, explaining that "a boy named Claiborn has worked on the levee but has been a lot of trouble, taking horses and running off nights and in various manners demoralising the rest of the Negroes." The marshal's conclusion would not have surprised skeptical black Southerners: "I think Mr. Wilder is humane to the Negroes generally. I know he is the only one I have yet been able to obtain that can successfully manage them in any work on the Levee. They don't complain and they aren't even being paid."[51] The casual violence practiced against black people, meted out by local whites empowered by the US Army, resembled the violence within the ranks. The paramount objective in both cases was the more efficient functioning of the army, in its capacity as a military institution and as the chief organizer of wartime labor.

In addition to the routine labor violence with which enslaved people were intimately familiar from before the war, the Union also failed to protect freedpeople who took up leases on abandoned plantations along the river in Mississippi and Louisiana. Working under the direction of white managers, the freedpeople on these free labor plantations were exposed to guerrilla raids that sought to re-enslave, terrorize, or kill them. The worst year was 1864, and though the death toll is hard to clearly identify, at least dozens of freedpeople were killed and hundreds recaptured.[52] An early historian of the process reports that "an agent . . . who visited ninety-five of the safest plantations found that from them the guerrillas had carried off 966 negroes and 2,314 horses and mules."[53] The same situation was observed by a would-be planter from Michigan writing to Republican Zachariah Chandler in mid-1864: "lessees and negroes had been left totally unprotected and Quantrell's guerrillas had a night or two before butchered some, stolen some & expelled the others, white and black, from the plantations which they had begun to work."[54] The problems continued as more plantations were struck. In all the cases, the planters blamed the federal government for failing to protect its charges. Military officials already knew from experiences in Missouri and Arkansas in previous years that half-hearted or temporary occupation only enabled violence, but they adopted the same practices that left Unionists in those western states vulnerable to similar raids and violence.

A more chilling example of Union mistreatment came in the midst of Sherman's March. In addition to destroying public works and seizing whatever food they could eat or carry, Sherman's troops liberated tens of thousands of enslaved people, many of whom followed the army hoping it would protect them from angry masters and marauding bands of Confederate deserters. Just outside Savannah, Union Major General Jefferson C. Davis's troops moved across Ebenezer Creek while being pursued by Confederate Major General Joseph Wheeler's cavalry. Hundreds of freedpeople marched with Davis's army corps. Davis's engineers had built pontoon bridges to enable the river crossing, but as soon as his soldiers crossed over, Davis had the bridge cut and pulled up onto the shore. Many of the freedpeople, trapped on the far bank and knowing that Wheeler's approaching cavalry would return them to slavery or worse, plunged into the swift, icy waters and drowned as they attempted to cross on their own. Hundreds of men, women, and children died in the panic. Although this episode was one of the largest civilian disasters of the war, it appears only briefly in most histories of Sherman's March, even ones sympathetic to emancipation.[55]

Observers at the time recognized the event for what it was—a deliberate act that produced needless civilian death. Colonel Charles D. Kerr of the 126th Illinois Cavalry, for instance, "witnessed the event, and wrote of the horror that ensued as, 'with cries of anguish and despair, men, women and children rushed by the hundreds into the turbid stream, and many were drowned before our eyes. From what we learned afterwards of those who remained upon the land, their fate at the hands of Wheeler's troopers was scarcely to be preferred.'" It reminded Davis's soldiers of the mistreatment of slaves by their masters. "A Minnesota private wondered: 'Where can you find in all the annals of plantation cruelty anything more completely indifferent and fiendish than this?'"[56]

Similar mistreatment came at the hands of officers who could not claim the justification of combat or campaign. At almost the same time that Davis abandoned the Georgians, another Northern officer expelled hundreds of freedpeople from a contraband camp located just outside Lexington, Kentucky. Camp Nelson served as one of the main recruiting centers for the USCT in the state. Slaveholding Unionists complained that their slaves were being enticed away and, in response, families were barred from the camp. But they continued living there until late November, when Union Brigadier General Speed S. Fry expelled the residents and destroyed their tents just as winter descended on the region. Four hundred people trudged through snow in search of shelter and food. About 250 returned after public condemnation of the action compelled the army to react, but over 100 of the returnees subsequently died from the exposure they suffered and the fate of the other 150 remains unknown.[57]

One of the black soldiers, Joseph Miller, testified that when he enlisted he was "told by the Lieut. in command to take my family into a tent within the limits of the Camp." This occurred in mid-October, despite the pre-existing order to stop accommodating families. Miller's wife, three sons, and daughter stayed with him in the camp until the evening of November 22, when an officer ordered them out by morning despite a sick child and nowhere to go. The guard charged with expelling people "told my wife and family that if they did not get up into the wagon which he had he would shoot the last one of them." His family made it six miles to an old meeting house, but by that time, Miller's son was dead. "I Know he was Killed by exposure to the inclement weather," Miller testified. The Millers returned to the camp when it was reestablished as a refugee center in January 1865, but by then they were all sick. Miller's remaining two sons, wife, and finally Miller himself all died at Camp Nelson. *The Liberator* and other radical papers in the North chronicled the catastrophe in detail, assigning blame to the Northern soldiers who were supposed to be protecting the people. Instead, "armed soldiers attack humble huts inhabited by poor negroes—helpless women and sick children—order the inmates on the pain of instant death, and complete their valorous achievements by demolishing dilapidated dwellings. The men who did all this were United States soldiers, and not Sepoys, and they acted under instructions from a Union General, and not Nena Sahib." The issue, like many concerning black Americans in the Civil War, was one of justice. "Let the potent, irresistible voice of a just and humane public demand of the authorities at Washington, that immediate steps be taken to arrest these barbarities, and to bring the responsible agents to stern account." No military official ever lost their position or was even seriously reprimanded for what occurred at Camp Nelson, but Miller's affidavit and supporting testimony from a white abolitionist who served in the quartermaster's department at the camp circulated through Northern newspapers, the halls of Congress, and into the Lincoln White House. As a result, the Union reopened the camp for escaping slaves, "a significant blow to slavery in Kentucky," but a measure of sympathy that came too late to help the Millers.[58]

The tragedy at Camp Nelson was even more preventable than the disaster at Ebenezer Creek, but the same impulse shaped both events. White Northerners, much like white Southerners, regarded black people as less sensitive (to cold, heat, pain, and other physical conditions) and more expendable. Even sympathetic officers of USCT units regarded these ideas as established scientific fact. Rough treatment began when black men were enlisted into the US forces. Particularly in the Mississippi River Valley (but also elsewhere), army recruiters forcibly enlisted black men into the USCT. Officers had quotas to meet and appear not to have considered the effect of men's absence on the fates of their families in these hostile and precarious places. This was not lethal violence, but it placed black men in the armies where they died at much higher rates than white men did. Grant, among others, received letters of complaint from former masters throughout 1864, not only about the seizure of their slaves, but also chronicling the abuse that ex-slaves reported they suffered at the hands of the military. Once regularly enrolled, black men suffered the worst assignments and consequently the highest death toll. Black soldiers assigned to fatigue duty in Louisiana died in droves, but this outcome did little to correct their commanders' erroneous view of racial difference. Sometimes, personal contact between white soldiers and black civilians diminished soldiers' racial hostilities, as occurred in Sherman's army. But in other cases, it seems to have inured white Northerners to the suffering that black civilians faced, even when in Union custody.[59]

Some of the worst treatment came in places and ways that remain hard to see from our historical distance. Contraband camps, the way stations to freedom through which hundreds of thousands of people passed, are only now receiving the attention they deserve.[60] Because they were controlled by the army but often staffed by missionaries and other volunteers, their records have not been preserved as well as other parts of the military story. But even with the limited information we have, we know that the camps were dangerous places to live. Unlike army camps, where soldiers were required to follow strict regulations in terms of sanitation and health practices, the residents of contraband camps received insufficient and often unhealthy rations. Lacking adequate supplies, they cobbled together housing as best they could. Over time, the results were often catastrophic.

The mortality rates in some contraband camps ran higher than in many Civil War prisons. "When we arrived," one missionary teacher reported about her stay in a camp, "the colored people had been there only about six weeks and 1800 were crowded into a few houses and tents and the mortality was very great. They were dying as they died at Hampton by hundreds and thousands. Every woman will say she lost three or more children."[61] Death from disease, exacerbated by the problems of exposure and malnutrition, killed thousands of people, perhaps more.[62] None of these deaths were deliberate violations of the laws of the war, but the people dying were noncombatants, and their protection merited greater attention from military authorities and officers on the ground.

When Northern soldiers or missionaries expressed sympathy for the suffering of black Southerners—whether at Ebenezer Creek or Camp Nelson—they did so because they felt moved by pity.[63] Unlike the mercy that white enemies sometimes showed for each other in the war, pity was generated by the superior position whites believed they occupied. In a different context, one historian has critiqued the willingness of white liberals in America to capitulate "to the historic tendency of posing blacks as objects of pity."[64] This analysis concerns the twentieth century and the rise of therapeutic diagnoses, but similar conditions prevailed in the mid-nineteenth century as abolitionists and others sought to alleviate the suffering they witnessed in the Civil War. The relief they provided (whether through charity or the army or federal government more generally) was much needed, but too often it reinforced rather than lessened the problems that emancipation was supposed to address.

Sherman's War

William T. Sherman's campaigns in Georgia have inspired passionate debate. In large measure, anti-Sherman writers dominate this literature. They condemn his war because it brought suffering to civilians and because he seemed indifferent to or pleased by that fact. Much of this critical judgment is built on hindsight and a lack of context. It is further bolstered by selectively quoting Sherman himself, something hard to avoid because his prolixity blended proposals, threats, and accurate descriptions of practice. Atlanta held strategic importance because of its location and east-west railway connections, but its current size and significance imply a scale absent in the mid-nineteenth century.[65] The tactics that draw so much fire from critics—the bombardment and deliberate destruction of a city and the expulsion of civilians—had been in long use by Union commanders in other theaters of the war. Throughout his campaign to pacify Georgia, Sherman executed a strategy of logistical, not human, devastation. This applied to both civilians and enemy soldiers. Sherman bombarded Atlanta and Savannah in order to force their surrender.[66] His strategy in the battles around Atlanta were not part of a campaign of attrition; he expected to outmaneuver and outfight John-ston and then Hood, which he did. The siege of Atlanta produced less hardship than that of Vicksburg the year before, and the siege of Savannah three months later took even less time and enacted fewer civilian casual-ties still.

But if Sherman's campaigns produced fewer noncombatant deaths than we might expect, they did increase noncombatant suffering. Sherman deferred the blame for civilian casualties to his opponents because they chose to fight in the city. "God will judge us in due time," he wrote, "and He will pronounce whether it be more humane to fight with a town full of women, and the families of 'a brave people' at our back, or to remove them in time to places of safety among their own friends and people." Beyond this legalistic response, Sherman appreciated that civilian suf-fering would hasten the end of the war. Like Robert E. Lee, Sherman recognized the importance of civilian morale and popular support. In this first fully popular war, the will of the enemy public became a necessary target. As a World War II historian observes about twentieth-century con-flict, "the more governments depended on the support of the governed, the more the morale and resources of the civilian population became a legitimate object of attack."[67]

Sherman's 1864 campaigns in Georgia consisted of three phases: the midyear campaign to capture Atlanta; the late summer decision to abandon and burn the city; and the fall campaign to capture Savannah. Throughout the phases, Sherman exercised a consistent approach to the strategic and logistical challenges he confronted. Sherman did not abandon the laws of war, as Confederates alleged, nor did his campaigns inspire a bloodthirsty cycle of revenge late in the war. For Georgians, es-pecially female residents of the state, his campaigns created fear, uncer-tainty, and sometimes violence. In particular, a small number of women on Georgia's home front experienced sexual violence at the hands of Union deserters or Confederate irregulars trailing in the wake of Sher-man's army. When Union soldiers violated the laws of war, especially with regard to sexual assaults on white women, the army prosecuted and pun-ished them, but Sherman refused to take responsibility for the actions of "bummers"—deserters from the Union army—and other irregular com-batants who took advantage of the chaos produced as Sherman's men marched through the state. The victims of these attacks properly ascribed the atmosphere that enabled such violence to the destabilizing effect of the Union's campaign.

Maneuver and Banishment

Sherman's army began its march south through Georgia in early May 1864. He hoped to capture or destroy Joseph Johnston's Army of Tennessee and to eliminate the industrial and transportation capacity of Atlanta, the most important Confederate city in the west. Fearing Sherman's numbers—his troops outnumbered Confederates two to one— Johnston retreated south toward Atlanta. His swift movement ensured that if Sherman wanted to keep pace with him, he could not invest time in garrisoning the towns through which they passed, though he did destroy resources as he went. Grant's order on this point was clear: "you I propose to move against Johnston's army, to break it up, and to get into the interior of the enemy's country as far as you can, inflicting all the damage you can against their resources."[68] This ensured that north Georgia communities were not subjected to bombardments or even much occupation.

The notable exception came in Roswell, Georgia, which occupied a narrow spot along the Chattahoochee River thirty miles north of Atlanta.[69] In addition to possessing strategic value as a place for Sherman's army to cross the river, the town contained three textile mills that supplied the Confederate army. The Union's division commander who entered the town, Brigadier General Kenner Garrard, ordered the destruction of the mills. In this action, Garrard implemented Sherman's strategy of logistical devastation, albeit one deployed with precision and deliberation. Garrard personally inspected the mills and ascertained ownership before ordering their destruction. Sherman approved Garrard's decision and further ordered him to "arrest all people, male and female, connected with those factories, no matter what the clamor, and let them foot it, under guard, to Marietta, whence I will send them by cars to the North."[70] The employees included 400 women and their children.

Sherman's order seems motivated partly by the initial response of a mill owner, Theophile Roché, who asserted that his position as a foreign national enabled him to claim neutrality, and thus immunity from destruction. When Sherman discovered that Roché supplied the Confederates with textiles, he adopted a much harsher line against the workers. Sherman's expulsion order explained that "being exempt from conscription, they [the mill workers] are as much governed by the rules of war as if in the ranks. The women can find employment in Indiana. This whole region was devoted to manufactories, but I will destroy every one of them." Within days, Union soldiers had detailed 100 wagons to carry nearly 1,000 women, children, and old men to Marietta, from which point they would be transported by railroads to Nashville. Sherman wanted the women sent north of the Ohio River, preferably into southern Indiana, but informed the Union commander in Nashville that "if any of the principals seem to you dangerous, you may order them imprisoned for a time." The jailing of "dangerous women" followed precedent as well, as provost marshals around the South had already been in the habit of arresting women who supplied guerrilla bands with resources. Confederates denounced the action as "atrocious villainy."[71]

Sherman never justified the Roswell banishment directly, but the precedent established by Ewing in western Missouri must have been on Sherman's mind when he made the decision to exile the workers. On the one hand, the Roswell banishment avoided the dangers that awaited Atlanta civilians after their source of livelihood had been destroyed, but it condemned them to the uncertainty and danger of refugee life that Missourians experienced under General Orders No. 11. Even conservative Northerners who opposed the destruction of private property—the mills—did not question the legitimacy of the removal of the women.[72] By July 20, the mill workers of New Manchester, Georgia, suffered a similar fate. About 200 female factory workers there were arrested and deported.[73]

Atlanta at Last

By mid-July, Sherman's troops pushed Johnston back into Atlanta itself. After initial infantry attacks failed, Sherman initiated a siege of the town. Over thirty-seven days in late July and early August, the US Army shelled

Atlanta. Confederates regarded this action as a wanton disavowal of just conduct in war. In a representative statement, an Atlanta Confederate argued that "this barbarous violation of the usages of civilized warfare only enabled [them] to murder a few noncombatants."[74] The Union's high command, on the other hand, spent no time discussing the propriety of the siege. As Vicksburg and other bombardments had demonstrated, Union officers respected sieges as a legitimate method of warfare. Interpreting the campaign against Atlanta requires filtering out the noise generated by two opposing but equally powerful forces. On the one hand, we have *Gone With the Wind*, the most influential American movie on the Civil War and one that enshrined the postwar mythology of Atlanta's destruction by portraying the campaign as Armageddon. On the other hand, we have William Tecumseh Sherman, who if he appeared in fiction would be regarded as an "unreliable narrator." He issued brutal bon mots throughout the war, and most detonated around Atlanta. For a historian, the temptation is great to let Sherman speak for himself.

But what Sherman said was not always what he did. The reports and communications of Sherman and his corps commanders reveal that his goal was capturing the Confederate army opposing him. Sherman's army left Chattanooga in May 1864 with clear instructions from Grant: "Neither Atlanta, nor Augusta, nor Savannah, was the objective, but the 'army of Jos. Johnston,' go where it might." Johnston's army may have been retreating, but that did little to diminish the costs of fighting. Between May and July, Sherman incurred significant casualties, over 20,000 from an army of 100,000. Once John Bell Hood was elevated to full command of the Confederate forces, Sherman knew the fighting would be severe, and by late July, Grant warned Sherman that the Confederacy, worried about Atlanta, might try to reinforce Hood. These demands on Sherman met the test of military necessity—Sherman attacked Atlanta because that is where Johnston went and where Hood stayed to fight.[75]

Sherman considered himself acting within the bounds of the laws of war. First, all the conditions that prevailed at Fredericksburg also prevailed at Atlanta. In both places, Confederate soldiers used the city as cover to fire on Union troops, and the city harbored both war industries and a crucial junction point in the Southern transportation network. These conditions alone offered sufficient grounds for a bombardment.

Second, Sherman's troops had been slowly approaching the city for two months, so no resident was surprised and trapped inside. By mid-July, only 4,000 of the city's wartime population of 20,000 still resided in Atlanta.[76] Sherman knew this, explaining to his wife that "most of the People are gone & it is now simply a big Fort."[77] Third, food supplies remained adequate. In fact, as one historian notes, "Confederate authorities were distributing 1,500 rations per day to the poor in the city."[78] Fourth, at no point did Sherman's army encircle the city in a way that would have denied exit. Sherman did not offer advance notice of shelling and did not help remove noncombatants, but there was ample opportunity for civilians to do so themselves. Last and most important, Confederate Joseph Johnston maneuvered his forces into the trenches that surrounded Atlanta and made the city a military target. City engineers had anticipated this moment and had spent more than a year building a ring of forts and trenches around the city.[79] A direct assault against these defenses would have been fruitless suicide for Union soldiers. Thus, Sherman could fairly reason, a siege of the city as a whole was the only way to dislodge Hood's army.

Sherman intended his bombardment to force Hood out of the city by reducing it "to ruins" if necessary.[80] The day before the bombardment began, Sherman ordered his corps commanders to advance to within cannon-range of the city. "If fired on from the forts or buildings of Atlanta no consideration must be paid to the fact that they are occupied by families, but the place must be cannonaded without the formality of a demand," he commanded.[81] When Hood refused to relent to the initial bombardment, Sherman increased the scale and scope of artillery he was using. Major General Oliver Otis Howard, one of Sherman's deputies in the campaign, remembered the bombardment this way: "For a month Hood kept to a defensive attitude, and, like a long storm, the siege operations set in. Sherman worked his right, with block after block, eastward and southward."[82] The location of the "blocks" was determined by Hood's placement of his forces. Even Hood himself, in his postwar reminiscences, explained Sherman's efforts in the same language: "Sherman had now been over one month continuously moving toward our left and thoroughly fortifying, step by step, as he advanced in the direction of the Atlanta railroad." Sherman's approach of simultaneous advances using all the methods available to him (he also sent a large cavalry detachment south around the city) reflected his belief in the necessity of maintaining unrelenting pressure on the Confederacy. Three weeks into the siege, he reminded his soldiers about the duration of the siege of ancient Troy (ten years) "and Atlanta is a more valuable town than Troy. We must manifest the character of dogged courage & perseverance of our race."[83]

Sherman pushed his infantry forces around the city, seeking to break the Confederate battle and rail lines, and maintained a heavy artillery fire. On August 1, he ordered the battalions of each wing to fire ten to fifteen shots per gun into the city from 4:00 PM until dark. "We keep hammering away all the time," he reported to Henry Halleck, "and there is no peace, inside or outside of Atlanta. I do not deem it prudent to extend any more to the right, but will push forward by parallels, and make the inside of Atlanta too hot to be endured." Three days later, Sherman increased the bombardment, calling on his artillery to fire continuously into the city. "I think those guns will make Atlanta of less value to them as a large machine-shop and depot of supplies," Sherman noted. Though he could hardly be sure of the effect his artillery was having on either soldiers or civilians, Sherman deduced its effect by Hood's efforts to find a way out. And deserters brought welcome news—that the Rebels had suffered "heavy" losses from the artillery.[84]

By late August, Sherman re-evaluated the effectiveness of his method and shifted course. He reached the conclusion that "our enemy would hold fast, even though every house in the town should be battered down by our artillery. It was evident that we must decoy him out to fight us on something like equal terms, or else, with the whole army, raise the siege and attack his communications." Accordingly, Sherman pulled his forces out of their entrenchments on the night of August 24 and moved directly against Hood. Sherman's most vigorous modern critic contends that Sherman's failure to compel the city's surrender by mid-August indicates that the bombardment was unnecessary, but Sherman had no way of knowing this when he initiated the artillery barrage. Whether or not it proved effective does not help us answer the question of whether he was justified in initiating it. Sherman felt he was. This critique would be persuasive if Sherman continued the bombing despite its failure, but he called an end when it became clear that the bombardment had failed to accomplish his strategic goal. Throughout the campaign, Sherman communicated regularly with Henry Halleck, the army chief of staff, and Ulysses S. Grant, by this time the Union general-in-chief. In all their telegrams and letters, they never discussed the question of civilian casualties as a result of a siege of the city. That silence, among correspondents who challenged each other on questions of both tactics and strategy in other contexts, suggests that Halleck and Grant, like Sherman, believed the nature of the attack justified. They supported the campaign and celebrated his accomplishments.[85]

Only after the city had fallen did Sherman comment on the legitimacy of the siege. Like most attacking commanders, Sherman blamed the Confederate decision to retreat into the city itself. Confederates "defended Atlanta on a line so close to town that every cannon-shot and many musket shot from our line of investment, that overshot their mark, went into the habitations of women and children," he wrote.[86] John Bell Hood, the Confederate commander, presented two faces to the conflict. During the bombardment, he never petitioned Sherman to stop shelling the town.[87] This silence is surprising. He had time and the skill—Hood wielded his pen effectively in the postwar period. But his failure to comment on the question of the legality of bombardment while it happened suggests he knew he held responsibility for civilian deaths because of his position around the city. In fact, once he abandoned Atlanta, Hood admitted to Sherman, "I made no complaint of your firing into Atlanta in any way you thought proper."[88] Only once his army had been forced to retreat did he condemn Sherman's failure to notify residents that he would be shelling the town and argued that Union misfiring was not accidental. "I have too good an opinion, founded upon both observation and experience, of the skill of your artillerists, to credit the insinuation that they for several weeks unintentionally fired too high for my modest field-works, and slaughtered women and children by accident and want of skill."[89] Hood was correct; Sherman directed shells over the Confederate lines into the city itself. Nonetheless, Hood was guilty of misrepresenting reality here as well. During weeks of shelling only twenty or so civilians died.[90] Not quite a slaughter.

After the fall of Atlanta, Hood and Sherman debated the campaign's sequence in the newspapers. In response to Hood's criticism that Sherman had failed to notify residents that the town would be shelled, Sherman bristled. "I was not bound by the laws of war to give notice of the shelling of Atlanta," Sherman lectured, "a 'fortified town, with magazines, arsenals, foundries, and public stores;' you were bound to take notice. See the books."[91] Sherman no doubt knew that General Edwin Sumner had notified Fredericksburg residents in 1862 prior to his bombardment, but he also knew that the Lieber Code condoned the element of surprise, though it seems unlikely that any Atlanta residents could have been surprised, with Hood's forces entrenching around the city's suburbs. Whether or not Sherman should have bombarded Atlanta when he knew some civilians remained inside, he defended his decision from the perspective of prior practice and the European laws of war.[92]

Regardless of its legal sanction, the bombardment caused enormous hardship among noncombatants and went much of the way toward destroying this important industrial city. For those civilians who remained, it was, as one resident noted, "'shells all night, shells all day, shells for breakfast, dinner, and tea, shells for all hours and sorts of weather."[93] Sherman did not seek out exclusively military targets in his bombardment. At times, Sherman directed artillery to pound the entrenched lines of the Confederates, and at other times, he instructed missiles be directed into the city. Sherman observed that "Hood is anxious to draw our fire from the town to their fort at White Hall, which is of no value to us. Let us destroy Atlanta and make it a desolation."[94] At times, the veil lifts, as when Sherman confessed to an old Southern friend that he was at that minute "pouring into Atlanta the dread missiles of war, seeking the lives of its people."[95] Sherman knew civilians remained in the city, though he apparently received no reports or intelligence on casualties.[96]

The experience of Sherman's siege of Atlanta should temper our belief that the Civil War became a war without limits, a thesis now widely popular among historians. Sherman conducted the siege of Atlanta in rough accordance with the laws of war, though he could have insulated himself still more by offering notice prior to the shelling. At the same time, the law had limits. Simply adhering to the letter of just war doctrine did not necessarily reduce violence. Civilians suffered enormously as a result of Sherman's bombardment. Several thousand people remained in the city, suffering the uncertainty, anxiety, injuries, and death that accrued from the thousands of shells launched around the clock. In addition, over 15,000 civilians fled their homes to an uncertain future as refugees. For these people, the laws of war provided no protection. If anything, the legitimacy of the Union's recourse to a siege reduced sympathy in the North for the suffering of Atlanta's inhabitants and steeled Sherman throughout over a month of shelling.

Sherman believed that in a people's war, the people suffer. "War is cruelty," he told the city's mayor, "and you cannot refine it, and those who brought war into our country deserve all the curses and maledictions a people can pour out."[97] The Civil War was initiated and sustained by (admittedly imperfect) democracies. And despite serious domestic opposition in each section, broad popular majorities of the North and South supported the war. It was truly a popular conflict. But like the apparatus of democratic politics, the apparatus of democratic war-making moves slowly. Atlanta's mayor could not surrender his town—its fate was protected by a national army commanded by a president in faraway Richmond who had the morale and future of the whole Confederacy to weigh against the suffering of a few thousand Georgians. The Confederate military commander on the scene could not risk his army being trapped or captured in a siege, so he abandoned the town and moved north to fight again another day. The residents of Atlanta, who generally supported the Confederacy, were doubly abandoned and left unprotected. Their suffering as a result of Sherman's siege of Atlanta was justified and awful. Atlanta in 1864 reveals the ways in which the US Civil War was at times a restrained conflict and at times a bloody, savage struggle. In some places, both of these statements were true at the same time.

Once Sherman captured Atlanta, the issue he faced was how or whether to occupy or garrison it. As the Union advanced into the Confederacy, it left detachments of soldiers in cities and small towns. These regiments were tasked with maintaining Union control, deterring or rooting out guerrilla forces, and administering an often hostile civilian population. In Memphis, Nashville, Corinth, Little Rock, Helena, Vicksburg, Baton Rouge, and New Orleans, tens of thousands of Union soldiers served as garrison troops. This amounted to several army corps taken out of active campaigning and combat. In order to avoid sacrificing more of his men, Sherman decided to expel Atlanta's remaining citizens and destroy the industrial and transportation infrastructure of the city. On September 7, 1864, he informed Hood that he intended to remove Atlanta's citizens. He proposed shepherding Unionist civilians north and allowing pro-Confederates passage south. He even offered to allow slaveholders to take their servants, "with the proviso that no force shall be used toward the blacks one way or the other" (and this almost two years after the Emancipation Proclamation took effect). According to Sherman, "Atlanta is no place for families or non-combatants." Hood agreed and submitted to the truce that Sherman proposed for the removal of citizens.[98]

Critics of Sherman have expended more of their ammunition on his expulsion order than on the bombardment. Sherman's strongest modern critic argues that his "ruthless depopulation of a surrendered city shocked the people of the South." According to this view, "the enormity of Sherman's crime against the citizens of Atlanta cannot be fully appreciated unless the results of his order are considered in terms of the human suffering and unhappiness which it caused." Happiness and comfort were not factors on the scale by which Sherman or any other Civil War commander assessed the military effectiveness or necessity of their actions. Other historians have persuasively argued that Sherman's decision was framed in terms of military necessity and concern about manpower. "He did not regard the measure as barbaric or cruel," one scholar writes, "and its execution was carried out with as much regard for the civilians as circumstances allowed." It is also worth imagining the fate of Atlanta's last residents if Sherman had left them in a partially destroyed city, in a region stripped of its resources, with few Confederate soldiers or even Georgia militia to provided protection against the violent deserter bands that patrolled the country. Such a fate could well have produced hardship far beyond that experienced by those families who were banished to regions of the South better equipped to support life.[99]

In the end, only 1,644 people evacuated, 8 percent of the number of Missourians expelled by General Orders No. 11.[100] Over half of those people who remained in the city through the bombardment appear to have stayed after its destruction. Before they left, the Confederates detonated an ammunition train that destroyed the huge Atlanta Machine Works, a major rolling mill that they wanted to prevent falling into Union hands. Before his troops left the city, Sherman continued their work by ordering "the destruction in Atlanta of all depots, car-houses, shops, factories, foundries." Best estimates suggest that 40 percent of the city was destroyed. As with the bombardment, Sherman saw civilian suffering as a natural consequence of their decision to support the Confederacy. "You might as well reason with a thunder-storm," he told a Southern friend who complained about the burdens of Union occupation. "War is the remedy our enemies have chosen. Other simple remedies were within their choice. You know it and they know it, but they wanted a war, and I say let us give them all they want; not a word of argument, not a sign of let up, no cave in till we are whipped or they are."[101]

At the time, Hood denounced Sherman's actions in terms quite similar to those used by his later critics—that it would impose too much suffering on civilians. Sherman responded by comparing his order to Johnston's conduct as he retreated through north Georgia. "It [the expulsion] is not unprecedented; for General Johnston himself very wisely and properly removed families all the way from Dalton down, and I see no reason why Atlanta should be excepted. Nor is it necessary to appeal to the dark history of war, when recent and modern examples are so handy. You yourself have burned dwelling-houses along your parapet, and I have seen to-day fifty houses that you have rendered uninhabitable because they stood in the way of your forts and men."[102] Hood's sarcastic rejoinder—that he had merely "offered and extended friendly aid to his unfortunate fellow-citizens who desired to flee from your fraternal embraces"—did not resonate with Sherman, who perhaps was aware that Hood had finished dead last in his class on ethics at West Point.[103] When the mayor and city council appealed to him to revoke his order, Sherman refused. Relying on Lieber's definition of military necessity, he would "not revoke my orders, because they were not designed to meet the humanities of the case, but to prepare for the future struggles in which millions of good people outside of Atlanta have a deep interest."[104] Henry Halleck defended Sherman's actions: "we are certainly not required to treat the so-called non-combatant rebels better than they themselves treat each other. Even here in Virginia, within fifty miles of Washington, they strip their own families of provisions, leaving them, as our army advances, to be fed by us, or to starve within our lines."[105]

Sexual Violence

After destroying Atlanta, Sherman's army moved across the state to Savannah. Sherman's march generated a mythology of military devastation that continues to shape public memory 150 years later. There is no question that his army destroyed a great deal—Sherman himself estimated about $100 million in property destroyed, of which 80 percent was "simple waste and destruction." Numerous studies of the campaign detail that the resources they destroyed, especially food, animals, storehouses, and mills, exacerbated civilian suffering in late 1864. These studies are equally clear that Sherman's men did not use lethal violence against civilians. Soldiers deployed military power selectively, but in the process, they caused a great deal of hardship. Georgia women, both black and white, experienced the full brunt of this power. As a historian of the campaign has argued, Sherman's men waged "domestic war" on women, as they entered homes and bedrooms, destroyed or stole clothes and personal items, insulted and sometimes threatened the inhabitants. This behavior reflected neither "cruelty nor vindictiveness," but rather an honest recognition that elite white women helped sustain the Confederate war effort. They were the enemy.[106]

Beyond the cultural and psychological war conducted by Sherman, how much harm came to women? Women's vulnerability to sexual violence varied considerably depending on their race, class, and location. Despite the tenacity of the myth of the black rapist, constructed by white Southerners in the last decades of the nineteenth century, white women in the Civil War appear to have been less at risk of rape than their black peers. According to one of the few studies of rape in the South during the nineteenth century, "most southerners of the slaveholding class did not believe that slaves posed such a threat during wartime. The war, despite the anxiety and uncertainty that it engendered, appears not to have spawned or fanned white fears of black rape." The state of Virginia brought only nine cases of wartime rape accusations against black men. In a state with an 1860 population of 1.5 million, this number must have undercounted actual rapes, though white Southerners had good reason to exaggerate rather than minimize the number of cases. In North Carolina, prosecutions of rape among civilians declined significantly during the war. A study of three Piedmont counties reveals only two rape cases (both for attempted rape) brought against black men during the war. This does not mean that rape stopped—rather it suggests how difficult it was for the county or state to track offenders during the war and a longstanding bias against "dissolute" women.[107]

Evidentiary problems complicate the study of Civil War rape.[108] Southern women were often reluctant to come forward because of the social opprobrium directed at female victims.[109] Nonetheless, many diehard Confederate women would probably have shared such stories if only to confirm the truth of Yankee barbarity. Women all over the South armed themselves as they anticipated attacks by Union soldiers and their sympathizers.[110] What emerges is a picture of Union soldiers perpetrating serious harassment and occasional violence against Southern women but mostly stopping short of rape. In South Carolina, Emma LeConte, who hated Yankees with a passion, observed the behavior of Union soldiers during the sack of Columbia: "terrified women and children . . . were offered every insult and indignity short of personal outrage."[111] In Mississippi a planter and Confederate colonel offered a similar assessment after a raid by black soldiers that killed several men around Deer Creek, Mississippi: "these unrestrained demons did not, even though nerved to indiscriminate plunder and murder of white men, in a single case offer to injure or insult women and children."[112]

Neither the Union nor the Confederacy used rape as an official strategy. Nonetheless, evidence exists that soldiers in the armies did perpetrate sexual assaults. In particular, Northern soldiers seem to have had fewer inhibitions about attacking black women. Anecdotal evidence from Sherman's March through Georgia suggests that black women were at much higher risk than white ones, even though black women supported rather than opposed the Union presence.[113] There was little opportunity for Southern soldiers to rape Northern women because they spent so little time in the region. It is unclear whether guerrillas used rape in any systematic way, though in regions without the main armies, reports of brutal attacks on women seem more common.[114]

Historians have performed almost no research on the violence Confederate soldiers may have committed against black or white women. The Confederate War Department burned most of the general order ledger books during the evacuation of Richmond in April 1865, and consequently historians have made little headway investigating the Confederate army the way they have the Union's. Because antebellum law held people who committed violence against enslaved people liable for damages, poor whites usually exercised caution when dealing with slaves. The ubiquitous white-on-black violence that characterized the New South lay in the future. Most of the violence that pervaded slavery occurred between masters and their own slaves. Some of this custom may have continued through the war, preventing Confederate soldiers from harming or killing enslaved people if their masters were present. But as black Southerners exercised more autonomy by running away or refusing to comply with plantation demands, white Southerners probably had fewer qualms.

One of Sherman's fiercest historical critics famously labeled him a "merchant of terror." The modern connotations of terroristic violence may mislead readers into seeing Sherman's work as the forbearer of America's brutal anti-insurgency campaigns in the Philippines and Vietnam. Sherman trafficked in the more ordinary, nineteenth-century meaning of terror. He allowed rumors of his army's brutality to furrow a path that terrified civilians. This was especially true for women, who heard wild stories about Sherman's men as they moved through the South.[115] Sherman let these rumors propagate because they served his larger goal of destabilizing the Confederate home front.[116] In this practice, he followed the lead of Union General John McNeil (of the Palmyra Massacre), who relished the terror he conveyed as his troops moved through northern Arkansas in early 1863. Citizens reportedly fled. McNeil blamed this on the "covers being on our guidons, for it rained most of the time, [and] they were taken for black flags, and the story that we were marching under that peculiarly Southern emblem widely circulated. Rape and murder were charged on us, causing the men to flee to the swamps."[117] No doubt, his reputation from Missouri advanced before the troops as well.

Sherman's success at instigating terror drew on years of Confederate newspaper stories that characterized Northern soldiers as little better than rapists in uniform. By 1864, the cumulative effect of this message created a framework within which Southern women anticipated the worst from their interactions with Union soldiers. "The yankeys says that if they conquer the south they will banish or hang all the men an made the fair daughters of the south hewers of wood & drawers of water," one woman wrote to Jefferson Davis. "In fact," she feared, they "will make or put us in a worse condition than the negroes . . . will build some yankee seraglio an put us in it to be used as prostitutes." She supported her dire prediction by relaying reports of Mississippi women being raped by black troops under the supervision of white officers. This charge—of the deliberate use of rape as a weapon of war, especially the rape of white women by black men—was almost certainly false. To the contrary, the US Army prosecuted black soldiers for sexual assault at much higher rates than they did for white soldiers.[118]

Nonetheless, the rumors created a viral climate of fear. Women in Sherman's path understood themselves as the targets of Sherman's campaign, even if they were not killed.[119] "Knowing little about when or where raids would commence," one historian notes, "women regarded themselves as victims of psychological torture." Women were afraid to undress for several days if the army was near for fear of being caught and vulnerable to rape.[120] This fear was not unwarranted. During the Roswell banishment in June, reports surfaced that drunk Union soldiers had assaulted refugee women while they awaited transportation in Marietta.[121] The stories about Marietta, like many of the interactions that occurred during Sherman's campaign, remain frustratingly hard to verify or dismiss, but some clear-cut cases do exist. Kate Nichols, the wife of James H. Nichols, a member of the Georgia Horse Guards, was "bedridden at their home in Midway, a bit south of Milledgeville, when she was raped by two Union soldiers."[122]

Recent scholarly work suggests that Sherman's campaign to break Southerners' psychological resistance failed because it did not diminish their nationalist support for the Confederacy. But from the perspective of social historians, who are more concerned with understanding how people experienced the war, the psychological dimensions of Sherman's campaign clearly debilitated people. Women, both white and black, Confederate and loyal, feared the advance of Sherman's troops. In comparison, fewer reports of assaults have surfaced (anecdotally) from the Army of the Potomac, perhaps because of the zealous prosecutions brought by its inspector general, Marsena Patrick. A conservative who disdained the immoral conduct of the men under his command, Patrick policed their conduct closely. When a Mrs. Stiles came to his office and reported being raped by Union soldiers, Patrick investigated the incident and discovered that the perpetrators had bragged about it. He mentioned it in four separate diary entries before reporting "they were identified by the woman & her cousin & both have been tried." They were executed in front of a large group of soldiers.[123]

Patrick was not the only officer who took a hard line against rape. When regular soldiers were accused of assaulting Southern women, especially white ones, the US Army prosecuted them vigorously. Military courts handled charges of rape, though how many assaults were reported to the authorities remains unknown. One historian reports that 200 Union soldiers faced charges of rape or sexual assault during the war, though how many men were accused but never charged also remains unknown. An officer in the First Kansas Colored Regiment reported that his soldiers committed "one of the most damnable crimes known to civilization." Three men (including a sergeant) from Company D went to the house of Mrs. Lee, whose husband was a Confederate prisoner at Fort Lincoln. Once there, they raped Lee and her sixteen-year-old daughter. The women identified the men before the local Union provost marshal and the men confessed. A court martial convened at ten o'clock in the morning found the men guilty by 1:00 PM, sentenced them at 3:00 PM, and executed them at 6:30 PM the same day. This sort of summary justice was more common for black soldiers, especially those convicted of assaulting a white woman, but it also reflected the US Army's vigorous prosecution of rapists.[124]

One of the many factors inhibiting successful prosecution of rapists during the Civil War was the legal regime surrounding rape in the nineteenth century. Most male prosecutors and judges expected victims to pass a nearly insurmountable bar in order to bring charges. This attitude carried over into the war years. In 1864, Mrs. A. E. Taylor chronicled an attack on her at her home in New Orleans that culminated in "the crime of raveshment on me." The men who raped her had worn Union hats and cloaks, though Taylor admitted that "a great many of the people at new orleans has got in their pocession united states dress." Taylor identified the source of her vulnerability: "the house i live in is far from all others, no guard here at night my husband has been seven months sick, they had evry apertunity to perpetrate their crime." Taylor's caution about mistakenly accusing an innocent man—"i could not bear the thought of exposing the soldgers for a crime they perhaps never done"—proved her undoing. The Union officer who received the complaint investigated but found only "an old forage cap" as evidence. "I see no reasonable grounds for supposing the outrage was committed by United States Soldiers," the officer wrote and concluded that "I see no way of detecting the offenders at present."[125]

The greatest legal obstacle was establishing that women relented only under the threat of death. As a scholar of this topic explains, "the legal definition of rape throughout antebellum America turned on the use of force and the lack of consent. . . . The best way to prove use of force and lack of consent was to produce evidence of a victim's resistance." This hurdle became an even more serious obstacle during the Civil War because soldiers often confronted women with weapons. They could threaten women with lethal force without creating any physical evidence to show a court. This problem manifested itself in one of the most brazen such attacks in the war. A large group of men from the 38th USCT broke into a house near their camp in southeastern Virginia. Most of the men then fled, but three remained—Dandridge Brooks, William Jackson, and John Sheppard. Brooks raped thirteen-year-old Eliza Woodson while her younger brother cowered in the corner of the room. Jackson and Sheppard chased Eliza's mother, Fanny, upstairs and raped her. The men stole goods from the house and returned to camp. They were captured quickly—the provost marshal tracked their boot prints back to camp, and neighbors offered corroborating testimony. Another member of the unit testified that Brooks "told me about his ravishings of the women at the house. He said they went to the Old woman and the Young one too. He said he fucked the young woman and the old one too."[126]

Although the defendants were all found guilty and executed, the court martial convened to assess the evidence revealed the lingering burden of proof on victims who brought rape charges. The judge's first concern was trying to determine the location and movement of women and soldiers within the house in order to determine whether the act that occurred was consensual. It required detailed questioning of Eliza Woodson to make clear that a rape had occurred and that the soldiers' access to weapons both facilitated the crime and the guilty verdict. The judge asked what happened when the soldier "entered" her.

> "When I hollered, he told me if I didn't hush, he would kill me."
> "What reason have you to think he would kill you?" asked the judge.
> "Because he had a pistol in his hand."

Even if Brooks had been free before the war (the record is unclear on this point), he would not have had access to a sidearm. The ubiquity of weapons during (and after) the war emboldened would-be perpetrators. It did so even in cases that involved simple assault rather than rape. When Charles Clark, of the First Pennsylvania Light Artillery, forced his way into a house in Virginia, he was asked on whose authority he came. Clark "drew his pistol saying 'This is my authority.'" Despite judges' demands for physical evidence of resistance to the attack, the presence of guns may have helped convict some wartime criminals. The episode in Virginia appears disconnected from the war itself and more a crime of opportunity committed in the midst of the conflict's closing moments. But in other cases, it is possible to imagine soldiers who used sexual violence to terrorize people because of their regional or national loyalties.[127]

Part of what facilitated sexual assault in the war was the routine nature of Union soldiers requesting entry into citizens' homes. In nearly all of the rape cases in which soldiers were executed, the men obtained access to private homes because of their authority as occupiers. They claimed to want to buy food, to search for stolen goods, to investigate reports of men who had committed violence, or any of the manifold excuses the war created to invade homes. Once inside, they had a private place in which to commit violence. Soldiers preyed on women living alone, often poor or elderly, and hoped to escape justice, though they rarely troubled to hide their actions. For Georgian women, this threat was heightened by the number of bummers who followed Sherman's army through the state taking advantage of the mayhem to rob and injure people. Sometimes dressed in uniforms, either real or stolen, these men were largely responsible for the apparent escalation of attacks on Southern women in the wake of Sherman's march. But because most of these acts happened outside the purview of the armies themselves, Sherman refused to recognize that his campaign created the conditions within which such horror could occur. His reliance on foraging parties to feed his army played a key role in this process.

The vulnerability of Southern women to violence committed by men outside the legal chain of command exposes the boundaries of the laws of war. In some cases, laws failed the noncombatant population they were designed to protect because they could be enforced only against regular soldiers. The law also failed to protect black soldiers murdered by Confederates. The men who perpetrated such deeds did not regard black men as legitimate combatants and so felt no compunction to treat them as they would regular enemy soldiers. Skeptics of the theory of just war argue that "in times of war, the law falls silent," meaning that normal legal rules are suspended during wartime.[128] Just war proponents seek to implement rules in order to keep war's violence within certain bounds. The Civil War reveals the importance of those laws and also their limits. As Sherman's campaign dramatized, the law was never fully silent, but it was hard to hear in certain spheres, especially those dominated by irregular fighters.

[8]

The Importance of States

By late 1864 and certainly by early 1865, the likelihood of Union victory in the war grew hard to ignore. In some places—Tennessee, most of the Confederate coast (both oceanic and riverine), northern Virginia, and garrison cities across the South—the Union had been in control for years. In other places—Arkansas, Georgia, Mississippi, Alabama—the absence of Confederate troops left the population defenseless. And in still others—central Virginia, South and North Carolina, Louisiana—Union troops pressed aggressively to exploit their manpower advantage. Without hindsight, participants could not see the war's end. As a result, many Confederate citizens and most soldiers fought on, hoping for the elusive victory that would turn the tide of the war. In March 1865, Lincoln announced a magnanimous posture toward Confederates that he hoped would facilitate reunion, but the prospect of the war's end only created new anxieties for white Southerners, unsure about what fate would await them with Union victory. Would they be dispossessed of citizenship? Have their property seized? Be tried for treason? These uncertainties could have fostered more violence in the war's closing months. In some places they did, but in most cases the war came to a peaceful conclusion.

Part of the reason the Civil War ended as it did was that it was fought by two well-organized modern states. Despite Lincoln's protests, it was clear that the Confederates had built a state, though not a permanent one. As Lincoln also knew, aspirational statehood created an incentive for Confederates to conduct the war according to traditional guidelines. One of the hallmarks of Western nations in the mid-nineteenth century was an ostensible commitment to the laws of war. Although Westerners violated these norms when they fought non-Western peoples, they nonetheless regarded fair conduct in war as a prerequisite for membership in the family of nations. The diplomatic campaigns waged by Federals and Confederates in Europe demonstrated that they understood the parameters of this system. This was a new condition, historically speaking, but present in the Western world from the mid-eighteenth century, when Jean-Jacques Rousseau wrote about "war 'not [as] a relationship between one man and another, but a relationship between the state and another.'" The importance of statelike behavior also influenced how people in North America perceived themselves and their enemy. Historians have spent a great deal of energy explaining how citizenship developed in the nineteenth century, focusing mostly on the transformation of imperial subjects into autonomous and empowered members of democracies. Becoming a citizen ensured rights and created obligations. The new states derived their power from the consent of the governed but also encouraged behaviors that sustained the new polities. Citizens had expectations about the state, especially during times of public crisis. In particular, both Confederates and Federals expected to fight a just war with armies that observed the laws of war.[1]

Knowing how the war ended makes it easy to see how states could function as institutions facilitating restraint. For instance, both the Union's decision to withhold punishment of Confederate prisoners and the Confederate decision to surrender depended on participants protecting their global reputation. Likewise, Lee's decision to deter a resort to guerrilla war by his men reflected a recognition that his state had lost the war. It was crucially important that if many other aspects of the Confederacy had collapsed, the army did not. It remained intact, and Lee's surrender originated from a Rousseauian conception of the purpose of warfare. In thinking about surrender, scholars have emphasized that Lee's decision may have been motivated by economic concerns—how to retain control of black labor in an unstable postwar South—or honor—virtuous men did not fight as guerrillas. Regardless of motives, the result had immediate consequences. Regular military conflict ended quickly in April 1865. Before that happened, both states demonstrated that nations could also spur violence. In practice, this meant each side sanctioned irregular actions that imperiled or took the lives of noncombatants. The war ended with the same paradoxes that had defined it all along.

Releasing the Dogs of War

Citizens of republican nation-states expected their governments to do what was necessary to preserve their existence. This encouraged national leaders to sanction unnecessary and often unjust violence. In some cases, unlawful violence occurred at the margins of a state. The decentralized nature of both nineteenth-century American polities ensured that these episodes would occur and that the central governments would repudiate them without actually taking any responsibility. Both states also encouraged a sense of righteousness, victimization, and other volatile emotions among their constituents. Jefferson Davis's public addresses, in particular, never failed to call out Union behavior in language intended to lay bare the moral gulf between the two sides. These efforts created animosities against the enemy that, despite the racial solidarity that prevailed in most contexts of the Civil War, could encourage unjust violence. Lincoln resorted to Davis's self-aggrandizing posture less often, but the North developed its own bloody rhetoric. Over the course of the war, the abolitionist posture that regarded slavery as not just a moral affront but a lethal influence on American life came to be more widely shared. Particularly after emancipation was adopted as a Northern war aim, many Northerners perceived their war as a civilizing mission, one that would remake the South, by force when necessary, into a modern, humane society. These forces, both Northern- and Southern-made, culminated in several late-war atrocities.

Sanctioned Irregular Actions

By mid-1864 both sides resorted to unjust violence in ways that they had consciously rejected earlier in the war. The incidents that stand out at this late point in the war were not ordered or approved by presidents or commanding generals. To the contrary, they occurred despite the repeated assertions by both Lincoln and Davis that they fought a civilized war against a savage foe. Nonetheless, all of the events discussed in this chapter received the implicit sanction of their respective governments. This marked a turning point, though one not universally observed by the war's participants. For both Northerners and Southerners, a primary motive seems to have been frustration. Union soldiers were angry about their inability to control the guerrilla war and to suppress the Confederacy despite military victories in all theaters. Confederates found their still-capable armies insufficient against the North, and their civilians subject to increasingly harsh conditions as Union armies devastated Southern resources. Even if Confederates received no support from the British or French, they took solace in European history. The *Amite City Daily Wanderer*, a rare Confederate Louisiana newspaper still publishing in 1864, "reminded readers that Spain had survived the burning of its cities and the destruction of its armies to prevail over the French by employing guerrilla tactics."[2]

The mildest of these late-war episodes involved the burning of Chambersburg, Pennsylvania, by Confederate forces under the command of Lieutenant General Jubal Early. The county seat of prosperous Franklin County, Chambersburg held 5,200 people in 1860, making it larger than Fredericksburg, Virginia, the partial destruction of which in 1862 had propelled Confederates into frenzied denunciations of uncivilized warfare. Confederate forces burned the town after holding it ransom for $100,000 in gold, a sum they knew residents could not satisfy. Early justified his actions as retaliation for the burning of the Virginia Military Institute and Governor John Letcher's house, both in Lexington, Virginia, by Union Major General David Hunter earlier in the year. After the war, Early explained that "a number of towns in the South, as well as private country houses, had been burned by the Federal troops. I came to the conclusion it was time to open the eyes of the people of the North to this enormity, by an example in the way of retaliation." A conservative who came to secession quite late, Early saw his actions within the limits of civilized war. In considering the episode from the vantage point of the 1890s, Early baldly stated, "I see no reason to regret my conduct on this occasion."[3]

Other Confederates were not so sanguine. Charles Morris, a lawyer and plantation owner, worked in the Quartermaster's Office in Richmond during the war. He wrote to his wife on August 4, 1864, about Early's burning of Chambersburg: "There is scarcely any [news] except the burning of Chambersburg by Early which seems to be authentic. I am sorry it has occurred because I am not a believer in the law of retaliation

& we must suffer more than we can make them. The war is becoming perfectly savage." Morris's experience as a law professor perhaps predisposed him to respect the laws of war, though his main motive seems to have been a strategic assessment that the Confederacy stood to lose more than the Union if both sides adopted indiscriminate destruction as the rule. One of Early's soldiers sheepishly addressed the topic in a letter to his wife, reversing himself several times in a few lines: "I am opposed to burning," Isaac White began, "but I supposed they deserved it + if they desire to retaliate we can play that game with them + play it well." Reversing course one last time he closed by noting "I do hope such warfare may cease." As Morris knew, and White seems to have suspected, the town's destruction did not qualify as legitimate retaliation because it was not proportional. Most of the Union destruction happened during campaigns and was directed at the resources of war. Private homes were sometimes burned though never, except in isolated instances along the Mississippi River, the whole of any town. Further, Early's initial request for ransom reflected something akin to a communal hijacking rather than an honest effort to right a specific violation committed by the Union. Early did not kill any civilians, and Chambersburg residents rebuilt their town, but it stands as one of the wanton acts of destruction in the war.[4]

Northerners expressed the same confidence in the justice of their cause. By early in 1864, according to one historian, "pride and self-righteousness (never in short supply) had replaced repentance and humility."[5] Terrible episodes occurred in Missouri, where the guerrilla war flared up again in 1864. After the terrific violence of the Lawrence Massacre and Schofield's General Orders No. 11, Union commanders hoped the state would remain quiet. Quantrill's bushwhackers moved south during the winter but returned in 1864. One Union officer, Captain Harry Truman, adopted the tactics of the guerrillas in his efforts to root out their civilian supporters.[6] For two weeks in June 1864, Truman "systematically terrorized Chariton County, Missouri in the name of the Union military effort." In total, he killed six civilian supporters of the guerrillas, beat and robbed many others, gathered intelligence from Unionist supporters, and generally created the kind of mayhem that guerrillas themselves usually caused.[7] Although Truman had been given wide latitude to conduct a "scouting expedition" charged with rooting out guerrillas and their supporters, his cavalier use of civilian informants and ad hoc posses that helped track down and murder men throughout the county eventually demanded a response from the Union command. Recalled to headquarters, Truman was sentenced to death by a military commission. The decision was overturned, however, and he was released after four months in prison. In this way, Truman received the public blame for the excessive acts of his raid but never really received much punishment. The Union could have its cake and eat it too.

The civilians of Missouri, especially Unionists, were left at the mercy of their neighbors. "Harry Truman awoke a sleeping giant of anti-Union sentiment that was eager to avenge the crimes committed by Truman and his men," writes one historian. Within days of his exit from Chariton, reports of retaliatory murders of Unionists started arriving at Union headquarters. Truman's behavior was not widely replicated, but it was a logical conclusion to the US Army's frustrating years of indecisive struggle against Missouri guerrillas. In other places, antiguerrilla groups left a wide wake of violence and destruction that alienated the people they were hoping to placate. In West Tennessee, Fielding Hurst, a staunch southern Unionist conducted a wide-ranging counterinsurgency campaign that drew the ire of both Confederates and the Union high command. In January 1864, Hurst's superior authorized him to "subsist upon the country" but cautioned that "peaceable and loyal citizens will be kindly treated and protected, and your whole energy will be given to the destruction of guerrilla bands which now infest the country. You are particularly warned against allowing your men to straggle from camp or go to their homes." By March, Confederate authorities were issuing requests for restitution of money that Hurst had confiscated and filing complaints about violence done to civilians. Shortly thereafter, the Confederacy publicly announced that Hurst and his officers, if captured, would not be treated as public enemies. The Union's subsequent instructions to Hurst, again requiring him to ensure his men did not straggle or pillage, were all but an admission that they knew he was doing so. Ominously, they noted that "any deviation from this rule may prove fatal to yourself and command." Nevertheless, Confederate reports of Hurst's misconduct kept coming.[8]

Kentucky was nearly as fractious and violent as Tennessee and Missouri. On August 14, 1864, the new Union commander for the state, Stephen

Burbridge, issued General Orders No. 59, which specified retaliatory measures for guerrilla attacks. Sympathizers living within five miles of an incident could be banished from Union lines. For every Unionist murdered, Burbridge pledged to shoot four guerrillas held as prisoners. A Kentucky historian records the executions of fifty men in nine Kentucky towns.[9] This stands as one of the most punitive anti-guerrilla policies undertaken by Union officials. Southern Appalachia, from western Virginia to northern Georgia, witnessed a huge amount of irregular war and violence in 1864–65. In East Tennessee, the Union provost marshal general, Samuel P. Carter, created the "National Guard of Tennessee," local self-defense units charged with suppressing Confederate activity in the area. Carter, believing that "'self-defense is a law of nature,' authorized any citizen to shoot on sight guerrillas and horse thieves."[10] Although Carter curtailed the worst abuses of these groups, the license he granted them was hardly better than Truman's approach.

In Missouri, whether in Chariton or elsewhere in the state, guerrillas maintained their campaigns of violence and robbery, rarely bothering to distinguish between pro-Confederate and pro-Union civilians. Bloody Bill Anderson, one of most murderous of Quantrill's gang, led an attack on Centralia, Missouri, in September 1864. He and his gang robbed residents and travelers on a train that came through town. Among the passengers were two dozen unarmed Union soldiers returning home on leave. Anderson's men stripped the soldiers and killed all but one. They left town, reconnoitered with more guerrillas—now numbering around 400—and set a trap for a pursuing force of Union regulars. The soldiers—about 115—rode into an ambush. A historian of irregular warfare explains the outcome: "Any Federals not killed in the ensuing slaughter were shot down when they tried to surrender. The rebels mutilated most of the bodies and scalped about a dozen of them." Anderson's guerrillas returned to the town and killed the remaining soldiers, bringing the day's death toll to "146 Union soldiers and 3 civilians." Anderson was hunted down by Union soldiers the following month and killed in a shoot-out. Other guerrillas suffered a similar fate in the waning months of the war, as Union officers dispatched targeted missions to capture or kill them. Union Brigadier General J. D. Stevenson summarized his efforts against a West Virginia bushwhacker with great cogency: "I sent out on Monday a small party to wipe out the notorious guerrillas, Mobberly and his band. They returned to-day with the body of Mobberly, and in the fight mortally wounded his right-hand man, Riley."[11]

Two last stories illustrate the desperation that gripped both sides in their efforts to break the war's stalemate as Lee and Grant bogged down outside Petersburg in the Virginia theater. In February 1864, Brigadier General Judson Kilpatrick met with Lincoln himself to discuss the idea of a Union cavalry raid on the Confederate capital that would liberate prisoners dying at a fast rate in Richmond's notorious camps, break up rebel communication lines, spread news of the Emancipation Proclamation, and also capture Jefferson Davis, an act within the laws of war but just barely.[12] Military approval came later, mostly because Lincoln had sanctioned the raid, though General Major George Gordon Meade confided to his wife that it seemed a "desperate" plan. Kilpatrick's raid bogged down quickly. Worse still, the commander of one wing of the attacking force, Ulric Dahlgren, was killed. Confederates discovered papers on Dahlgren's body that laid out a plan to burn the city and assassinate Jefferson Davis and his cabinet. Reports were published in the Richmond papers, prompting quick denials from the Union high command, all of which failed to persuade the Confederates, who took the papers to be true orders sanctioned from the highest level.[13] "Truly there is no depth of dishonor and villainy to which Lincoln and his agents are not capable of descending," the Richmond press thundered.[14] The notes themselves were written in Dahlgren's hand; a scholar of this episode speculates that "these murderous directions . . . could only have been based on instructions from his immediate superior, Judson Kilpatrick."[15]

Despite its infamy and inflammatory potential, the Dahlgren affair ended as these episodes often did in the Civil War. Lee pressed Meade for a clear repudiation for the intent of the orders, and Meade delivered: "neither the United States Government, myself, nor General Kilpatrick authorized, sanctioned, or approved the burning of Richmond and the killing of Mr. Davis and cabinet."[16] Whether Meade knew of or explained to Lee the full story remains unclear. He did not issue the Dahlgren orders, but Secretary of War Stanton could have suggested something like this to Kilpatrick. All of Lincoln's conversations with Kilpatrick revolved around the capture of Davis, not his or others' assassination. Although he stands free of blame for murder, his sanction for such a loose affair created the real possibility of precisely this sort of unjust action.

Jefferson Davis seems to have experienced the same fantasy of a far-off raid that would suddenly tilt the war in the Confederacy's favor at just the time that Lincoln was meeting with Kilpatrick.[17] Perhaps by this point in the war, Davis had begun to believe his own hysterical descriptions of the conflict. Despite the administration's ambivalent approach toward black soldiers, he continued to inflame the public with elaborate scenarios of the real purpose of emancipation: "with fiendish malignity the passions of a servile race have been excited by our foes into the commission of atrocities from which death is a welcome escape."[18] Davis advocated a range of approaches throughout 1864, some of which are detailed above. Both the bombing at City Point and Blackburn's plot to spread yellow fever in the North qualify as desperate but futile attempts to turn the course of the war. The Confederate Secret Service, responsible for the Blackburn plot, also initiated campaigns out of Canada into Vermont, and in New York City. During the latter raid, the chief perpetrator, Robert Cobb Kennedy, set fire to several buildings. Although foiled in his attempt to create a general conflagration in the city, several women and children died in the ensuing fire, and Kennedy was caught by city authorities.[19] In his approval of such raids, Davis had no intention of inflicting injury on noncombatants, but his reckless behavior, like Lincoln's, produced a situation where a violation of the laws of war was likely.

Outside the scope of officially sanctioned violence were episodes where the weakness and decentralization of the Confederate state enabled unjust violence to occur. One Confederate institution that operated without restraint or oversight were Confederate anti-deserter units, most sanctioned by county or state governments. These groups often perpetrated terrible violence on other Southerners. North Carolina's Quaker Belt, home to many of the state's anti-Confederates, witnessed the persistent raids of the Home Guard. This and other loosely organized militias tortured and killed civilians accused of protecting deserters. North Carolina's vigilantes drew on Confederate precedent. In the Shelton Laurel Massacre in 1863, pro-Confederate civilians in western North Carolina executed fourteen Unionist civilians. Texas, existing almost completely outside the regular fighting and campaigns of the war, witnessed some of the worst guerrilla actions. As a Texas historian has noted, "the ferocious efforts of Texans to eliminate dissent created for the state an image as the 'dark corner of the Confederacy' . . . Texas partisans and vigilantes hanged dissenters on the Trinity River, slaughtered German Unionists along the Nueces River, and lynched Federal recruits by the Rio Grande."[20]

Civilization and Violence

In addition to those times when state actors directly approved unjust practices, like the Truman raid in Missouri or the Confederate attack in New York City, the regimes of both places developed ideological justifications that encouraged unnecessary violence. Northerners crafted a wartime language that classified people along a binary axis: civilized or savage. This was not an exclusively racialized distinction—some white Americans came to appreciate the sacrifices that African American soldiers made on behalf of the Union—but it drew heavily on racial stereotypes and the idea of a hierarchy of moral intelligence. The Northern view of their purpose and conduct in the conflict resonated with prevailing imperial philosophies. In the Confederacy, what stands out is a growing reliance on scientific racism and a casual acceptance of brutal violence against people of color that resonated with events in other parts of the globe. Jefferson Davis justified this brutality by positioning white Southerners as the war's chief victims. Both of these ideologies of violence developed during the war. They grew out of the experience of conflict and helped sustain it. They also outlasted the war and shaped the postwar world in important ways.

The Union's belief that the savage could be civilized was best embodied by Secretary of State William Henry Seward. In the 1850s, Seward moved seamlessly from being a reform-oriented Whig to a Republican. He believed American nationalism represented the best of Western civilization.[21] Though famously bellicose toward the British during the war, he viewed the British Empire as a model for how the United States should engage the world. "British power" one historian notes, "helped shape [Seward's] view that imperial power could play a constructive and benign role in fostering the spread of 'civilization.'" Seward's Republican colleague Charles Sumner held the same view. Secession, for him, "was a challenge flung down by slavery to the civilization of the nineteenth century." Even as he criticized British behavior, Seward recognized a longer trajectory of global influence in which America and England would organize and improve the world. American borders, he believed, would extend "so that [they] greet the sun when he touches the tropic; and when he sends his glancing rays toward the polar circle." In order to achieve that goal, the North had to win the Civil War.[22]

By defeating the Confederacy, the North could bring the South out of its primitive reliance on racial bondage. "Seward understood nationalism to be a progressive historical force," one historian writes. But progress often requires sacrifice and sometimes (usually for opponents) conflict and death. The British had steeled themselves to this reality during their imposition of imperial control over India, especially after the Indian Rebellion. At the time, an American newspaper had asked "who in England talks of the moral rights of the Sepoys?" Learning from this example, Northerners like Seward knew that too much attention on the suffering of white Southerners would only delay a historical inevitability—the triumph of the free-labor North.[23]

The Northern cause was based on the "principle of order which is heaven's first law," asserted the *Continental Monthly* in 1864, and "also the cause of freedom." This explanation, which drew on Lincoln's arguments about the Union as the sole guarantor of self-government, called for the approbation of other enlightened peoples. With these twin foundations, the Civil War was, for the North, "preëminently, a just war, because waged in the combined interest of liberty and order."[24] This respect for order would have drawn the support of Seward, who believed in the paternalistic ethos of uplift that characterized so many imperial ventures of the nineteenth century. The necessity of suppressing secession demanded the highest sanction. Another Northern commentator observed that the military response to secession "marked it with an anathema as such as the Christian Church has put upon on an open denial of God." Like atheism, it "subverts the first principles of our political worship as free, order-loving, and covenant-keeping people."[25] Pamphlets like this one circulated in Union camps, and even illiterate soldiers absorbed the message as it was broadcast to them through the chaplain's sermons and regimental addresses by commanding officers. "Civilization," as a virtue to defend, appears ubiquitously in the addresses circulated in pamphlet form by the tens of thousands by the Loyal National League.[26]

Lincoln avoided the bellicose language favored by Davis, but his recourse to biblical phrasings and cadences could ennoble the Union cause in equally dangerous ways. His claim that the Union represented "the last best hope of earth" was widely absorbed and recast. Union Admiral Hiram Paulding, in a public comment in 1863, revised Lincoln's words to reflect an even more apocalyptic forecast: the Union represented "the last hope of freedom for the civilized world." The danger represented by such language was when it became not a retrospective explanation of Union virtue but a justification for military actions during the war. In 1961, the writer Robert Penn Warren wrote a famously caustic commentary on the Civil War centennial. He described the dual legacy of the war for Southerners and Northerners. The former earned the "Great Alibi," which offered the war as an explanation for all the South's human failings over the next century. The North earned the "Treasury of Virtue," which confirmed their moral superiority and created a reservoir of beneficence to cover whatever future sins the society produced. The North began writing checks from this account before it was fully funded. Northerners availed themselves of the moral sanction that compensated for other misdeeds during the war itself. Francis Lieber, who believed like Seward and Sumner that the Union cause embodied the future of civilization, also argued that the North's conduct improved that civilization. When he received his copy of General Orders No. 100, Lieber seemed almost wistful when he wrote to Halleck. "I think the No. 100 will do honor to our country," he said. "It will be adopted by the English, French, and Germans. It is a contribution by the U.S. to the stock of common civilization." This logic insulated the military from criticism. If the US Army was ennobling mankind's method of making war, the actions it took against guerrillas or their civilian supporters must themselves be just and proper.[27]

Confederates believed themselves civilized, of course, but they recognized that the society they hoped to preserve departed from the western trajectory toward freedom and liberalism. Before the war, the most extreme proslavery voices, people like George Fitzhugh and James Henry

Hammond, explicitly rejected the Northern emphasis on free labor, open markets, and an increasingly democratic political order. White Southerners flattered themselves that their society—with its emphasis on communal needs and genuine empathy between people—represented a morally superior social form. But this essential aspect of Southern self-image changed during the war. The willingness of Confederate soldiers to execute black troops and to murder enslaved people who sought their freedom contradicted the much-touted paternalism upon which slaveholders prided themselves. They leaned more heavily on the scientific racism, much of it crafted in the North before the war, that prevailed throughout the western world. In this scheme, violence against inferiors seemed appropriate, even "civilized," particularly in light of the repression of people of color elsewhere in the world.

Confederates also abandoned the language of pride and mastery that typified antebellum discourse, replacing it with a rhetoric of victimization and suffering. In Jefferson Davis's speeches to the Confederate Congress and his public addresses, he made frequent reference to "suffering." Sometimes he offered this term as a simple descriptor for the fate of his people. Depending on the audience, suffering was something maliciously enacted by the hated Yankees or something closer to a natural force that Confederates would bear as long as needed. Women and children suffered the worst; they were the most likely to be identified as "victims" by Davis. When Yankees suffered in Davis's speeches, it was only under the matchless military power of Confederate armies. Their suffering was just and expected, whereas Davis regarded the suffering of Southern civilians as always unjust. In his view, the mere presence of Union troops on Confederate soil violated their sovereignty and so represented an unjust act. Parsing the consistency of Davis's language is less useful than investigating the way his rhetoric transformed Southerners' self-image and contributed to the war's violence. Before the war, even during the secession crisis, Southerners represented themselves from a position of strength.[28] Lincoln's election insulted their sense of honor, an emotional register available only to those with confidence in their society. During the war, in contrast, Davis emphasized endurance. Absorbing the Yankees' punishment required strength and resiliency but positioned them as passive rather than active. Davis had few good options. Southern civilians experienced significant hardships during the war, and he labored to emphasize the unifying experience of the war's traumas within a society with a grossly unequal distribution of resources.

Nonetheless, the cumulative effect of Davis's rhetoric emphasized Confederate victimhood. Davis operated in a more forgiving political atmosphere when it came to evaluating the actions of the enemy. Where Lincoln worked continuously to enable reunion, Davis envisioned no such peace. With no countervailing influence, he had no reason to moderate his characterizations of the enemy. Lincoln condemned the perfidy of Confederate leaders but continued to believe in the goodness and even Unionism of nonelite Southerners long after their commitment to the Confederacy should have been obvious. Even then, Lincoln always considered the political implications of how he characterized his enemy. Because the Confederates wanted independence, the more Davis demonized the Union, the less likely reunion became. Davis's shrill denunciations of Yankees encouraged a relentless war against an invader that he characterized as bent on the worst sort of physical domination of white Southerners. Recent studies of South Carolina and Georgia suggest that Davis succeeded in convincing white Southerners that Lincoln deserved the blame for their suffering, rather than the decision to secede. Women in both states responded to Sherman's 1864 invasion not by calling for a truce but by urging their husbands, sons, and fathers to kill more Yankees.[29] Soldiers also absorbed Davis's characterization of the beleaguered South; their letters show a diminishing recognition of the Union soldiers as regular enemies and a growing view of them as feral beasts that deserved only death.

Leashing the Dogs of War

After a nineteenth century in which nations seemed a permanent solution to centuries of religious and ethnic conflict, the twentieth century set back the reputation of nationalism and nation-states. The genocidal campaigns conducted by regimes as varied as Ottoman Turkey, Nazi Germany, and Cambodia's Khmer Rouge operated through the infrastructure of modern states and defended their actions with the claims of territorial sovereignty and exclusive authority over violence that are central to how modern nation-states operate. Even with those terrible crimes on its ledger, the modern world of nations introduced a previously unknown degree of security. As one scholar has noted, "neighbours respect neighbours; in Europe all the signatories of the 1974 Helsinki agreement make no claims on others' territories—a previously unheard of situation for Europe. But this situation operated in practice across the world. . . . Nobody is carving up Somalia or Liberia in the way, say, Poland has been partitioned in the past."[30] Because the Civil War was a fight between nations, most of it occurred within legal and moral boundaries. The contours of those boundaries asserted themselves in the war's closing months.

Retaliation and Violence

In northern Virginia, where the war had raged incessantly for nearly four years, the worst aspects of Georgia and Missouri came together. In the face of the continued resistance of both irregular fighters and unruly civilians, Grant authorized a hard war approach similar to what Sherman practiced against the Confederate interior. His lieutenant, Philip Sheridan, directed a campaign of widespread burning and devastation in a once-fertile region of the state. Grant also sanctioned a hard hand against the partisan rangers and guerrillas in the region, one that nearly spiraled out of control. Once again, retaliation helped keep the war within bounds. But if those boundaries ensured a more just war for uniformed soldiers, they did little to diminish the suffering that civilians experienced.

In 1864, with Union troops focused on the main line of conflict between Fredericksburg and Richmond, irregular conflict raged in north-central Virginia, especially the region that came to be called "Mosby's Confederacy."[31] In 1863, John Singleton Mosby transformed the 43rd Virginia Cavalry Battalion into a partisan ranger unit that operated independently of Lee's army in the state. His battalion became perhaps the most militarily effective such unit in the Confederacy, but their operations—which usually involved small bands of Mosby's men attacking and harassing Union troops—generated a predictably punitive reaction from the Union, which saw little difference between Mosby's men and Missouri's guerrillas. Mosby described his operations as hewing to the lawful use of mobile forces: "the military value of the species of warfare I have waged is not measured by the number of prisoners and material of war captured from the enemy, but by the heavy detail it has already compelled him to make . . . in order to guard his communications and to that extent diminished his aggressive strength."[32] Mosby's unit was regularly commissioned, unlike Quantrill's guerrillas in Missouri, and it rarely targeted Unionist civilians in the region.[33] His selective approach to lethal violence and the unit's established command structure satisfied some of the aspects of regular public enemies that Lieber marked out in his treatise on guerrillas and in General Orders No. 100. On the other hand, his men operated in a decentralized fashion, rarely wore uniforms, and often retreated back into civilian life, all distinguishing characteristics of guerrillas. As a result of these practices and their effectiveness, they generated intense fear and apprehension among Union soldiers, which, in turn, compelled increasingly harsh efforts to curtail their operation.

Mosby, for his part, rejected the term "guerrilla" when applied to his men on the grounds of tactics, arguing that his "men fought in cavalry charges, with pistols."[34] The method of attack was a necessary though not sufficient part of what defined guerrillas in the Civil War, as Mosby knew. Sometimes, his men used the "long range gun" [rifle] to snipe at Union wagon trains and pickets. At other times, they seized Federals and killed them by execution. By focusing on tactics, Mosby deliberately ignored the irregular nature of how his men operated. They were rarely in uniform, for example. Mosby later claimed that his officers always "wore insignia," but these would never have been visible on an ordinary coat— often itself covered—during a surprise engagement. After periods of military action, his men could melt back into civilian life unnoticed.

After the war, Mosby recognized the importance of regularizing his command, so he asserted that he "reported directly to [Lee] and received instructions directly from him."[35] This exaggerated Lee's control over Mosby's unit and their actions. Mosby truthfully claimed that he reported to Lee, but Mosby himself retained full operational control over what his men did. This was a slightly more controlled version of Hindman's "Band of Ten" order from 1862 in Arkansas. There, the organization of local men into a self-defense force intent on slowing down the federal advance into the state devolved into chaos as the guerrillas quickly came to operate as criminals. In Virginia, Mosby's men did not target civilians, but their reliance on civilian support for food, fodder, shelter, and intelligence exposed all civilians to the rough handling that they received from Sheridan's men. By perpetuating an irregular war alongside the regular one, Lee and Mosby created an environment that left noncombatants vulnerable to military force.

Grant, for his part, was a West Point–trained officer and committed to the laws of war. By mid-1864 he had grown frustrated with the Union's inability to conquer the Confederacy and incensed by the field executions of Union soldiers by irregular Confederates. He clearly viewed Mosby as operating outside the laws of war whatever original sanction he could claim as the result of a commission from Lee. As a result, Grant, like Lee, behaved inconsistently. Two orders that Grant issued to Sheridan reveal how frustration could drive an otherwise thoughtful commander to extreme positions. In mid-August, he told Sheridan that "the families of most of Mosby's men are known, and can be collected. I think they should be taken and kept at Fort McHenry, or some secure place, as hostages for the good conduct of Mosby and his men." This escalated the standard practice in Missouri, where guerrilla families would have been expelled but not necessarily taken hostage. More ominously, he closed by noting that "where any of Mosby's men are caught hang them without trial."[36]

Grant would have known that Mosby's command was regularly enlisted, but was choosing to deny them protection as public enemies. He treated them solely in terms of their irregular operation. Another tactic involved eradicating the civilian support on which Mosby depended. "If you can possibly spare a division of cavalry," he wrote Sheridan, "send them through Loudoun County, to destroy and carry off the crops, animals, negroes, and all men under fifty years of age capable of bearing arms. In this way you will get many of Mosby's men. All male citizens under fifty can fairly be held as prisoners of war, and not as citizen prisoners. If not already soldiers, they will be made so the moment the rebel army gets hold of them." Grant was correct that these men would soon be in the army, for the Confederacy was implementing its last draft call, but they were noncombatants at that moment. Arrest meant survival rather than the field execution he sanctioned, but this was a much harder war than Sherman implemented in Georgia. Despite Grant's orders, the region did not descend into chaos. One historian explains, "Sheridan evidently did not direct his subordinates to comply [with Grant's order that Mosby's men should be hanged wherever they were found]. At least he did not publish an order to that effect."[37]

As Sheridan's troops implemented the logistical destruction that characterized much of the Union's war in 1864, Mosby's men targeted anyone they caught in the act of burning. In late August, a small unit of his command captured thirty members of the 5th Michigan Cavalry in the act of destroying several private homes near Berryville and executed summary justice. They "herded their captives into a ditch and shot them to death point blank."[38] The Confederates initially claimed that the Union soldiers died in the attack, but were forced to admit what happened when one of the Northerners—shot in the face but still alive—testified later. His evidence undergirded a newspaper article that revealed the truth. Mosby himself admitted the incident in his official report. One of his companies came upon the Northern soldiers burning houses and "such was the indignation of our men . . . that no quarter was shown, and about 25 of them were shot to death for their villainy."[39] Mosby's admission represented a remarkably frank assessment of one of the largest violations of the laws of war against uniformed soldiers in the conflict. After the war, he went further still, admitting "I had given orders to my men to bring me no prisoners caught in the act of house-burning. The order was superfluous; I could not have restrained them if I had wanted to."[40] Despite his claim to being a Partisan Ranger (that is, a lawfully recognized part of the Confederate Army), Mosby's actions in this regard reveal the impossibility of the Confederates' dual strategy—regular and irregular— against the Union. By enlisting men from the area—those most likely to be enraged by local destruction—by exercising loose oversight, and by giving them free rein to execute Union soldiers on the spot, Mosby's command compromised Davis's claim to fight a civilized war.

The Berryville Massacre and Mosby's irregular campaigns more generally raised the now old question of the right way for the Union to respond. Whom could they hold responsible? And what punishment would come for such behavior? The *New York Times*, echoing Grant's sentiments, declared about the Berryville incident that "Mosby has practically raised the black flag, but . . . the residents of this valley will regret the day he commenced operations here. The [Union] soldiers, naturally, are indignant at the bloody outrages perpetrated upon their companions, and whenever opportunity occurs, will no doubt retaliate." One more atrocity committed by Mosby's rangers pushed one of Sheridan's lieutenants, Major General George Armstrong Custer, to action. In an engagement with Mosby's men outside Front Royal, Union Lieutenant Charles McMaster was wounded and incapacitated. The evidence—including testimony from civilian witnesses—revealed that Mosby's rangers had murdered the officer. Even a sympathetic historian of Mosby concluded "the case presented by Mosby and Scott remains 'unconvincing' . . . McMaster . . . had surrendered and, when his captors could not lead him out with them, shot him where he stood."[41]

Custer commanded McMaster and the brigade that contained the Fifth Michigan. He was from Michigan and the murdered men had served with him since they gained fame as the "Wolverines" at Gettysburg. His response came swiftly but did not embrace the lawful retaliation for which the newspaper called.[42] Custer authorized the execution of six captured members of Mosby's cavalry regiment caught in Front Royal. Three were shot execution-style and left where they fell. Two more were mounted on horses and hung from a walnut tree. The youngest, a seventeen-year-old boy who had jumped on a horse to join the cavalry as they rode through town, was shot down in front of his mother while she begged for his life. One of his schoolmates watched the execution from her bedroom window; "his poor mother is almost crazy," she reported. None of the victims, and certainly not the young civilian, had committed a crime that merited death under the laws of war. They suffered execution to avenge the unlawful death of a Union officer. Lawful retaliation, which may have been an appropriate response to McMaster's killing or to the Berryville Massacre, would have been proportional.

This unjust episode nearly touched off a broader cycle of violence. One of Mosby's men remembered that news of the Front Royal executions circulated in camp. "There was at once a rumor set afloat that we were to fight thereafter under the black flag," and the men began eagerly preparing.[43] Instead, Mosby pursued a more lawful course. He believed that as members of a regularly commissioned Confederate cavalry unit, his captured men should have received the protection of prisoners of war, and in response he executed six of Custer's men. "I had every right of war that he had."[44] In an open letter to Sheridan, Mosby defined *his* action as a policy of retaliation and noted that "hereafter, any prisoners falling into my hands will be treated with the kindness due to their condition, unless some new act of barbarity shall compel me, reluctantly, to adopt a line of policy repugnant to humanity."[45] Mosby's proportional response and one that affected equivalent actors (all captured soldiers rather than Custer's inclusion of a civilian) hewed more closely to the practice of just retaliation. It seems to have worked. No executions followed on either side.[46]

In this case, as in others throughout the war, retaliation functioned to end breaches of the customary law of war. The manner of its execution reveals several important aspects of how this process happened during the Civil War. The breaches of the laws of war—whether by Mosby's men at Berryville or Custer's at Front Royal—were not ordered by Grant or Sheridan but decided independently by a brigade commander. The decentralized nature of the armies enabled this sort of violence to happen almost spontaneously or at least without oversight. That same structure also created a level of plausible deniability. Grant commented on neither Custer's nor Mosby's executions. His silence suggests that he understood Custer's actions were excessive and that Mosby's had effectively restored balance. Grant also knew what Mosby later asserted, that he "could hang 500 of his men where he could hang one of mine."[47]

But if retaliatory violence created the boundaries for lethal violence in the regular war, it provided little protection for civilians. The worst civilian suffering in Virginia came after Early's Army of the Valley was destroyed by Sheridan in three battles in September and October. Now in undisputed control of the Shenandoah Valley, Sheridan's men executed hard war with a vengeance. This was partly to deter support for Mosby and other guerrillas, partly to spur the hardship that Grant, Sherman, and Sheridan hoped would diminish civilian support for Davis and the Confederacy, and partly as simple vengeance against enemy civilians, who Union soldiers assumed supported local guerrillas. The physical violence that did occur was, like what happened on Sherman's March, random rather than planned or sanctioned. Unionists were typically spared, though Confederates sometimes had their homes and not just barns burned. The logistical destruction was supposed to target public infra-structure such as bridges and mills, but Sheridan's soldiers clearly held civilians responsible for the violence they suffered. "This, every living soldier who was in this campaign knows to be true," one reported, "the people were meek-faced citizens by day, and in the presence of any con-siderable body of Union troops; but as soon as the troops were out of sight, when darkness came on, they became desperate and bloodthirsty guerrillas; and in this character they stole upon our men like savages, and shot them down and dragged them away to the woods where some of them were found hung up by their heels with their throats cut." Ominously, this was not just an ordinary Union volunteer, but an army chaplain, who concluded by asking, "Could anything justify their course? Could any punishment be too severe?"[48]

To the Brink of Atrocity

The closest the United States came to using retaliation as a weapon of vengeance was during the early 1865 debate over the treatment of Union prisoners.[49] In mid-1864, the Northern public learned about the condi-tion of their men confined in Confederate prisons. Woodcuts published in Northern papers appeared to show more skeletons than men; strap-ping farm boys of the Midwest reduced to ninety pounds of listless bones. Editorials across the country called for vengeance.[50] Photographs of the men were left on the desks of senators and congressmen.[51] Even these underrepresented the true horror, according to a committee of distin-guished Northerners who investigated the condition of Union prisoners. "The best picture cannot convey the reality," they concluded, "nor create that startling and sickening sensation which is felt at the sight of a human skeleton, with the skin drawn tightly over its skull, and ribs, and limbs, weakly turning and moving itself, as if still a living man!"[52] In early 1865, the US Senate considered the issue.[53] Morton Wilkinson, a Republican senator from Minnesota, proposed that Confederate prisoners held by the United States receive the same "rations, clothing, and supplies" as "those furnished by the rebel authorities to Union troops held by them as prisoners of war." Wilkinson objected to what he regarded as the Con-federates' uncivilized method of waging war and also its result—that

Union soldiers returned from the South so weak that they could never fight again. His proposal for retaliation thus drew on the argument from military necessity. Although Wilkinson retained doubts about whether this was a truly Christian measure, he concluded that "I think the laws of war would justify a course of retaliation on the part of our Government."[54] Most of those who invoked Christianity in the debate disagreed. Just as Vattel and European history more broadly sanctioned particular forms of fighting, Christianity set clear limits on how nations could fight.[55]

Benjamin Wade, a radical Republican from Ohio, had fewer qualms. He introduced another resolution that required the rations and treatment of captured Confederates correspond to what Union prisoners received.[56] The brutality implicit in these resolutions created a divisive debate among Republicans and between Republicans and Democrats in the Senate.[57] It also produced an open debate over the meaning and intent of retaliation. Wade's Republican colleague Edgar Cowan summarized the proposal in plain language: "if the Confederates States of America starve our soldiers, we are therefore justified, or indeed bound, if we undertake to enforce the law of nations, to starve their soldiers." This Cowan refused to do. Although he supported retaliation, by which he meant an action that compensated for the barbarous treatment of Union soldiers, he would not support a perfect equivalency in treatment because this would unjustly kill innocent men. There had been "a time in the history of the world when an eye for an eye and a tooth for a tooth was the *lex talionis* of the universe; but ... that law, by a higher authority than ours, has been abrogated."[58]

Confederate mistreatment of Union prisoners raised serious concerns among Union policymakers, much more so than in the case of black soldiers unjustly killed. Francis Lieber, long an apostle for lawful warfare, could not understand how Christian Southerners (among whom he had lived for two decades) might sanction slavery, but Confederate conduct toward prisoners left him baffled. "It yet remains, as a simple psychological fact, inexplicable, how men, apparently under the influence of our common religion and civilization, can have become such fiends as the rebels have shown themselves by the treatment of our soldiers when captured by them," he wrote in the *New York Times*. Lieber referred here to "the bloodhounds, the calculated starvation, the loathsome cruelty, systematically and tauntingly practiced on our men." For Joseph Holt, Lincoln's judge advocate general, "criminal history presents no parallel to this monstrous conspiracy, and from the whole catalogue of infamous devices within reach of human hands, a system for the murder of men more revolting in its details could not have been planned." Holt regarded the system as beyond criminal law because it was undertaken by a military officer of a renegade state on behalf of furthering rebellion. Nonetheless, even Lieber rejected the idea that retaliation could remedy the conditions. "If what we read of the southern camps of prisoners of war be true," he told Charles Sumner, "and I fear much of it is true, our hearts must bleed that men, Americans, can become such fiends, but let us not retaliate fiendishness." Long an influential thinker among Northern politicians, he shaped the course of the retaliation debate through his correspondence.[59]

Where Cowan and Senate Democrats saw simple vengeance, Wade argued that his real purpose was to suppress Confederate atrocities. "Retaliation has in all the ages of the world been a means of bringing inhuman and savage foes to a sense of their duty, and has frequently had the effect to promote the objects of justice," Wade asserted.[60] But other senators believed that Wade's proposal would have entailed deliberately starving Confederate prisoners to death, something that would have cast them out of the company of nations. This they would not do. Influenced by Lieber, Wade's chief critic, Charles Sumner of Massachusetts, asserted that "any attempted imitation of rebel barbarism in the treatment of prisoners would be plainly impracticable, on account of its inconsistency with the prevailing sentiments of humanity among us; that it would be injurious at home, for it would barbarize the whole community; that it would be utterly useless, for it could not affect the cruel authors of the revolting conduct which we seek to overcome; that it would be immoral, inasmuch as it proceeded from vengeance alone."[61] The dispute between these two—a surprise to many because they represented the leading edge of radical Republicans in the Northern government—hinged on the importance of proportionality and the limits of retaliation imposed by common consent.

During the debate, Francis Lieber took his own turn to express the same sentiment in an editorial in Washington's *Daily Globe:* "These cruelties, therefore, would be simply revenge, not retaliation, for retaliation as an element of war, and of nations in general, implied the idea of stopping a certain evil." Sumner and Lieber won and Wade lost, and Northerners seemed quite glad of it. Although some papers had endorsed the call for vengeance, most celebrated the defeat of the resolution. The *Boston Daily Advertiser* was typical in this respect: "the people were as little willing as the Senate to enter upon retaliation in kind,—and to subject men to the tortures of starvation and cold, because rebels do the same." The much-advertised magnanimity displayed by Sumner, Lieber, and others could also have derived from the Union's position in the war in early 1865. Most Northerners expected to win within the coming months. Many of the most seriously ill Union prisoners had already been returned via exchange or liberated by Sherman's army. The US Army did not need these men back in uniform—their current forces were sufficient to defeat the Confederacy's remaining armies. The Union would gain nothing from punishing Confederate prisoners who had no army to which they could return.[62]

Surrender

Two key processes curtailed the potential violence of the Civil War more than all of the individual acts of sympathy or charity. The first was the decision of enslaved people not to perpetuate violence against white Southerners in their pursuit of freedom. The other was the ability of armies to surrender. At various points throughout the war, Union armies received the surrender of whole Confederate armies—at Fort Donelson, Vicksburg, Appomattox, and Durham Station, most famously. Lee's surrender in Virginia marked the effective end of military resistance and signaled the collapse of the Confederate state. Joseph Johnston's surrender two weeks later ended the career of the other major Confederate field army. Surrenders were a long-established procedure of states for concluding military hostilities. They were only possible where states could issue orders to stop combat and then to demobilize armed forces. The sharp break between the violence and destruction of 1864 and the cessation of combat in April 1865 revealed how seriously the United States and the Confederate States took the idea of surrender. Even though the Union policy of hard war gained focus and consistency throughout the war, Northerners engaged in no paroxysm of violence at war's end. This nineteenth-century behavior diverged sharply from many twentieth-century conflicts. In the US Civil War, one scholar observed, "unlike others now under way in the world, Federals carried out no genocide—no Kosovos, no Rwandas occurred on American soil." A more contemporary parallel was the 1871 Paris Commune, a quasi-secessionist effort by working-class Parisians to establish the national independence of the city. When the French National Army defeated the Communards, they refused to recognize their enemies as legitimate soldiers and spent a week in an orgy of executions. A recent study estimates that between 20,000 and 30,000 Parisian fighters were lined up in the streets and shot.[63]

The use of military surrender, as opposed to diplomatic agreement, to end the war became an option only in early spring 1865. The long and destructive siege of Petersburg yielded to a new phase of the war, one that brought a swift and peaceful conclusion to the terrible conflict. The defeat of Lee's army began to look like a possibility in March, as Grant's forces encircled the railroads leading into Petersburg (and then to Richmond). Beginning April 2, when Grant's forces finally broke through Lee's Petersburg lines, Confederates abandoned their trenches and then both cities altogether. Lee hoped to march his men west to obtain much-needed rations and supplies, then move south to combine with Joseph Johnston's army in North Carolina. Grant followed. He ordered Sheridan, his trusted cavalry commander, to pursue Lee. "The position and movement of the enemy will dictate your movements," Grant instructed. "All we want is to capture or beat the enemy."[64]

Union forces outnumbered the Confederates, and with Sheridan's cavalry moving west, parallel to Lee, the Union possessed a significant strategic advantage. If Grant had wanted to destroy Lee's army, he could have accomplished that. Grant believed no peace could come until "the military power of the rebellion was entirely broken," but like Lincoln, Grant regarded the purpose of the war as reunion and knew that needless killing and suffering would only postpone that objective. Historians' accounts of Grant's operational approach in the days after the fall of Richmond all agree that he sought to prevent Lee from reaching Johnston's army in North Carolina. On April 5, Sheridan, who seemed to relish a harder end than Grant, reported that "we are shelling their trains and preparing to attack their infantry immediately." This approach produced the desired results. One of Lee's chief aides—William B. Taylor—admitted the effect to his mother: "our army is ruined, I fear." Grant could have prolonged this approach, lobbing artillery into the vulnerable segments of Lee's army while attacking the flanks. The battles that occurred during the campaign—at Sailor's Creek and Farmville—were deadly encounters, but the Union captured many more than they killed. Grant quickly brought the active fighting to a close. He captured Lee's army through maneuver and pressure. On April 7, Grant appealed to Lee to surrender in order to prevent "any further effusion of blood."[65]

Both Union and Confederate soldiers benefited from the presence of Ulysses S. Grant in command of the army. A political moderate and a general who understood that politics were the purview of politicians, Grant never pursued a vindictive peace. Instead, he managed the surrender process in such a way as to peacefully transition the country away from war. Although Lee met with Grant at Wilmer McLean's house still not knowing how they would be treated, Grant offered generous terms. Lee's soldiers were issued paroles and allowed to depart for their homes after turning over weapons. Officers were allowed to keep their sidearms and cavalrymen kept their horses. Union quartermasters distributed thousands of rations to starving Confederates. Grant believed that these forgiving conditions represented "an extension of Lincoln's policy for amnesty and reconstruction."[66]

Despite his conciliatory posture at Appomattox, Grant understood that the war consisted of more than military affairs. Lee initially proposed a peace settlement, which would have ended the whole war with slavery's fate still uncertain. Grant rejected this approach because Lincoln had given him only the power to accept the surrender of Lee's army. Lincoln alone could negotiate or identify the war's absolute end. As a democratically elected representative he was best positioned to appreciate the war's deeper causes and the transformations of American life it had affected. In short, he wanted the war ended the right way.

One more condition had to be met for peace to reign—Lee's soldiers needed to understand that their war was over. Again, the command

THE SURRENDER OF GENERAL LEE.

"The Surrender of General Lee and His [Ent]ire Army to Lieut. General Grant, April 9th 1865." The ability of Lee and Grant to come to acceptable surrender terms enabled the US Civil War to come to a more peaceful conclusion than those that marked the end of other civil conflicts in the mid-nineteenth century.

structure of the Confederate army and Lee's own substantial personal authority over the men in his army played a key role in diminishing confusion at this pivotal moment. After surrendering, Lee drafted one last general order for his army—No. 9—that dismissed his soldiers "to return to their homes and remain until exchanged." Lee's men recognized the generosity of the terms Grant had issued. Even E. P. Alexander, Lee's artillery chief, who had advocated dispersing the army to fight as guerrillas rather than surrender, realized that the agreement "practically gave an amnesty to every surrendered soldier for all political offences."[67]

Events followed a similar pattern in North Carolina, where Confederate Joseph Johnston hoped to evade William Sherman's juggernaut and connect with Lee's army. Sherman proved as tenacious as Grant. His troops, having marched across Georgia and South Carolina, moved after Johnston with deliberation and intent. But they fought few battles in the state. The vast majority of Johnston's army ended their tenure as Confederate soldiers not face down during a battle but as prisoners, paroled at Durham Station in late April. In the event, Sherman went further than Grant, offering something more like full peace and a restoration of Southern state governments within the Union. Johnston happily agreed to the lenient conditions, but Grant, Secretary of War Stanton, and the new president Andrew Johnson all recognized the error. Stanton sent Grant to North Carolina to arrange new terms of surrender for Johnston's army. As one historian has observed, "Sherman's offer illustrates an alternative in 1865 that would have eliminated Reconstruction and constrained emancipation in ways that far exceeded the effects of Jim Crow." The administration's refusal to accept that offer signaled a shift from the early war posture that regarded reunion as the North's only goal.[68]

Still, the possibility for violence remained omnipresent through April. Some of Lee's men initially hoped to avoid the guards and slip out rather than surrender for a parole. They would then "take to the bushes," a euphemism for conducting guerrilla war. In order for surrenders to work, both sides had to respect them. As with the delicate negotiations that occurred when Southern towns surrendered to Union occupation, the success of surrender depended on trust and evident good will. When Philip Stephenson, an artillery private in the Army of Tennessee, surrendered at Meridian, Mississippi, his unit was treated with businesslike courtesy. "No excitement, no disorder," he remembered. "The Federal troops were kept well in hand, were not allowed to insult us, and they showed no disposition to do so. There was no marching out, lining us up opposite the Federal forces, and our general surrendering his sword to the victor, no pomp of parade and triumph." This was not the case everywhere, particularly after news of Lincoln's death circulated among US troops on April 15, 1865.[69]

In North Carolina, where William Sherman and Joseph Johnston were negotiating terms for Confederate surrender, one officer reported that "the terrible news of the assassination of our beloved President created a feeling of hatred and revenge in the heart of every soldier."[70] Union Major General Jacob Cox made a similar observation, noting on

April 17 that "the effect of the news of the assassination is very great in the army, and if active operations were to commence again it would be impossible to restrain the troops from great outrages."[71] Common soldiers echoed the sentiment. A young Illinoisan in Sherman's army recorded his thoughts after he heard the news of Lincoln's death: "the army is crazy for vengeance. If we make another campaign it will be an awful one. . . . We hope Johnston will not surrender. God pity this country if he retreats or fights us."[72] In Vicksburg, an Ohio soldier reported that news of Lincoln's death "brings sorrow to our harts but awaiks a spirit of revenge in every soldiers heart. last night General Dana, who commands at Vicksburg sent the cars down with the news and also notified the reble colonel who commands our camp that he had better get on the other side of the river for he would not be responsible for what was done after the boys herd the news. so Mr. Johny lit out last night and it very good thing for him that he did for I do not think his bacon would of been safe here 24 hours after herd the news."[73]

Sherman responded to the assassination by issuing Special Field Order No. 56, which framed the act as a feature of guerrilla war: "Thus it seems that our enemy, despairing of meeting us in open, manly warfare, begins to resort to the assassin's tools." Sherman understood that most Confederate soldiers did not sanction such actions, but he explained the killing as the "legitimate sequence of rebellion against rightful authority. We have met every phase which this war has assumed, and must now be prepared for it in its last and worst shape, that of assassins and guerrillas; but woe unto the people who seek to expend their wild passions in such a manner, for there is but one dread result." A Wisconsin captain poured out his rage in a letter to his wife in even more dramatic terms. Reeling from the news of the "treacherous murder," he hoped the government would authorize the army to drive out treason from the root. "If our leaders will but give us the word, we'll sweep over their states like a besom of destruction—fire & sword will desolate all they have." The injustice of Lincoln's death after he had steered the Union to safety gave cause for a renewed war on the same terms as those then followed by Confederates. "The wind of rebellion they have sown—let them reap the whirlwind of destruction & shame, desolation & sorrow." As so often throughout the war, rhetoric outpaced reality by several orders of magnitude. No more assassinations followed the attacks on Lincoln and Secretary of State Seward. As a result, the truce between Sherman and Johnston held while Grant and the War Department worked out a full end to hostilities.[74]

The states—Union and Confederate—structured surrender, but soldiers had to be willing to implement and respect it. Given their fatigue, most were happy to comply. For the vast majority of Civil War soldiers, the end of service arrived with a speed that would bewilder today's soldiers. Once the major Confederate armies surrendered, hundreds of thousands of men were mustered out and returned home. Several hundred thousand Union men remained in uniform to march in the Grand Review in Washington in late May, but many had already gone home, and others proceeded straight from the capital. Although survivors cherished the opportunity to reunite with families, the swiftness of the shift left many confused. "To tell the truth," one Union solider admitted in late April, "we none of us realize even yet that he [Lee] has actually surrendered. I had a sort of impression that we should fight him all our lives. He was like a ghost to children, something that haunted us so long that we could not realize that he and his army were really out of existence to us. It will take me some months to be conscious of this fact."[75]

A key question was how black soldiers and civilians would treat Lee's army at its surrender. Seven USCT regiments participated in the Appomattox Campaign. They displayed the same restraint toward their foe that freedpeople had demonstrated toward former slaveholders. This aspect of the surrender was a pivotal moment when black Americans could leverage their military service into a claim for full citizenship.[76] According to a historian of this experience, black Americans rejected vengeance because "it did not serve their political efforts for equality."[77] Whatever the motives, their actions helped reduce the potential chaos of the war's end. "Black magnanimity at Appomattox," another scholar notes, "was the exercise of moral authority—a conscious effort . . . to break the cycle of violence that slaveholders had so long perpetuated."[78]

And the states too drew back from imposing violence on surrendered soldiers. Simply because Confederate soldiers had received paroles did not necessarily make them exempt from a treason prosecution. Judges at different court levels all over the country issued indictments to try men for treason in the months after the war. The passage of the Fourteenth

Amendment in 1868 secured the legal fate of ex-Confederates, when "it became clear that the government would prosecute no former Confederate for treason." Ultimately, politics determined this decision. "Reunion was the primary goal of the war," one historian notes, "and it did not pay to create martyrs who might inflame the people expected to embrace renewed dominion by the federal government."[79] But still, the restraint appears quite exceptional in retrospect. "Never had any country been so generous in restoring the rights and lands of those who, with rifle and sword, tried to undo it," writes a historian of Reconstruction. "There would be no conquered provinces, no wholesale hangings, no abandonment of constitutional safeguards for the sake of the country's security."[80] The English Civil War, which provided a historical framework that Americans knew well, especially when Confederates proudly identified themselves as descended from the Cavaliers of old, ended with a similar lack of bloodshed but a more vigorous financial punishment for the defeated side. King Charles I was famously executed, but few participants faced lethal violence for the roles they played in the war. Instead, the victorious regime confiscated and redistributed the lands of nobles who had supported the king.[81]

The surrender of Confederate armies embodied the conclusion to war sanctioned by just war theory. In this sense, Appomattox and Durham Station succeeded by ending the massive bloodletting between regular soldiers that characterized the war's last year. Freedpeople, and the three and a half million enslaved people who remained in bondage behind Confederate lines, may well have regarded the settlement as premature. It is unlikely but possible to imagine that the United States would have imposed stricter terms on white Southerners before the war ended. As of April 1, 1865, the Thirteenth Amendment had been passed by Congress but ratified by only nineteen states. Slavery was not yet abolished in the United States. Radical Republicans believed that in addition to a permanent end to slavery, avoiding future conflict would require breaking the power of the South's planter class, but very little land had been redistributed. In World War II, the Allies required unconditional surrenders from Germany and Japan, which gave them the authority to impose structural changes on each country. Given the strength of conservative opinion in the wartime North, such an outcome was unlikely. Nonetheless, it is important to see the costs of surrender as well as its gains. For black Americans, justice, broadly conceived, may have been sacrificed for a just resolution of the military conflict.

Ending War

The surrenders at Appomattox and Durham Station and the capture of Jefferson Davis (who fled south and was arrested in Georgia) brought the regular war to a close. Ending the irregular war took more time. Both Federals and Confederates sought to rein in the guerrillas still active in many parts of the South. They also needed to muster out the hundreds of thousands of soldiers still under arms. These processes transpired unevenly over the ensuing months. In the midst of this dramatic interval, Abraham Lincoln was assassinated, casting a pall over the gospel of mercy that Lincoln had preached from the presidential pulpit.

Repudiating Guerrilla War

The peace treaties signed by Grant, Lee, Sherman, and Johnston ended the regular war with remarkable speed. But the conclusion to the irregular war arrived more haltingly and with less finality. Because guerrillas operated independently of the Confederate chain of command and fought local wars that rarely corresponded with the binary national framework, they did not respond to Lee's or Johnston's surrender by laying down their own arms. With Confederate regulars no longer a threat, the US Army turned its power to pursuing guerrillas still at large. In these places—Missouri, Arkansas, Mississippi, Georgia, the Carolinas, and Virginia—those that were not caught went quiet. Although Jefferson Davis confused the issue, Robert E. Lee refused to endorse an irregular campaign (as some of his lieutenants urged), and his final order directed them to lay down arms and return home. Neither of these decisions—by the US Army and Lee—were unexpected. Both conformed to the policies that each had pursued throughout the war. They both helped diminish the guerrilla conflict, though they did not mark a final conclusion. Some particularly bitter white Southerners refused to accept the war's end and carried their fight into the postwar period.

Jefferson Davis, in a typically awkward combination of arcane intellectual language and populist enthusiasm, complicated the guerrilla war's end. As the Confederate government fled the fires consuming Richmond (fires set by the Confederates themselves), Jefferson Davis issued his final address to the nation. In an act of willful delusion, Davis explained that now that the Confederate army was out of the Petersburg trenches, it was "free to move from point to point and strike in detail the detachments and garrisons of the enemy, operating on the interior of our own country." The language suggested the image of a giant guerrilla unit, though Davis actually saw no future in such a path. He had even taken the step of submitting the question to his cabinet, which unanimously opposed any extension of the fighting. James Seddon, the secretary of war and never a fan of irregular fighters, believed that a general turn toward guerrilla war "would 'lose entirely the dignity of regular warfare.'"[82]

Lee's longstanding opposition to irregular war put him in harmony with the Confederate cabinet. Because Sheridan's army moved south along Lee's line of march after leaving Petersburg, Davis's proclamation never reached Lee's army. Even without seeing it, however, Lee deterred his men from continuing the fight, both in his public message to his troops issued at Appomattox and in private correspondence to Davis, whom he warned that resorting to guerrilla warfare would impose "an enormous cost in 'individual suffering and the devastation of the country.'" Lee had reason to be specific about the consequences that he foresaw. During the retreat to Appomattox, Edward Porter Alexander, his artillery chief and one of Lee's inner circle, suggested that Lee allow his men "to scatter in the woods & bushes & either to rally upon Gen. Johnston in North Carolina, or to make their way, each man to his own state, with his arms, & to report to his governor." Alexander did not use the word "guerrilla," but permitting small groups of armed soldiers to move independently across the country while still in a state of war against the Union would have expanded the irregular conflict. Contemporaries interpreted Lee's actions in a similar way. Even Charles Francis Adams, the stalwart Yankee, "asserted a 'debt of gratitude this reunited country of ours—Union and Confederate, North and South—owes to Robert E. Lee, of Virginia' because Lee had considered, then forcefully rejected, what would have become a fruitless 'warfare without quarter' in an 'awful catastrophe.'"[83]

Some historians consider the debate about Lee academic. He never controlled the guerrilla bands that operated on behalf of the Confederacy, and they responded to local conditions rather than national ones. Where guerrillas operated as bandits, the difficulty of ending the war increased. As the most important history of the guerrilla war concludes: "By the summer of 1865, much of the Confederacy's guerrilla struggle had been divorced from the goals and purposes of the government for some time. Neither surrender nor decree could turn off the spigot of guerrilla violence."[84] Instead, small groups, maybe a dozen men or fewer, some long established and some newly constituted, took to plundering and to targeting both citizens and soldiers.

Although many people in the North and South believed guerrillas merited death, the Union's eagerness for vengeance faded. In May, Grant issued an amnesty proclamation to allow them to lay down arms. Some took advantage of this offer and accepted paroles. Those who refused found themselves facing more robust Union missions to eradicate them. Many of these men met the fate of Bloody Bill Anderson, the Missouri guerrilla captain, who was hunted down and killed by Union soldiers in October 1864. William Quantrill, Anderson's one-time commander, refused to lay down arms after Johnston's surrender and was killed by Union troops in May 1865. Guerrilla leaders in Arkansas, Virginia, and elsewhere met the same fate in the months after Appomattox.[85]

In Tennessee, Union soldiers arrested Champ Ferguson, perhaps the most violent of all the self-proclaimed guerrillas of the war. During the conflict, Ferguson killed at least fifty-three people, all the while disavowing any recognition of the laws of war to which other Southerners bound themselves. Ferguson shot unarmed men in hospital beds, underage and unarmed Union militia, and others. His band of men, mostly Kentuckians operating in Tennessee, harassed and attacked both regular Union forces and irregular pro-Union militia, but their private war had little impact on the course of the conflict. Instead, Ferguson's style of combat, to "take time by the forelock" as he said, took advantage of a power vacuum to abandon the conventions governing combat, captives, and the laws of war. Ferguson's trial took place in Nashville before a military commission, which charged him with "being a guerrilla and on twenty-three specifications of murder totaling fifty-three men." Ferguson's lawyers argued that the Union's orders of amnesty for irregular fighters should cover him. They also hoped that because he had a commission from the Confederate army, it could excuse his wartime actions. Although the trial was thorough—dozens of witnesses were called and it lasted several months—there was little suspense regarding the outcome. Ferguson operated far enough outside the laws of war to guarantee a guilty verdict. On October 20, 1865, Ferguson was executed. Some historians count Ferguson and Henry Wirz (the commandant of Andersonville Prison, who was executed shortly after Ferguson) as the only two men convicted of war crimes in the Civil War. This was not the actual charge for which either man was killed, but Ferguson's actions can be construed as criminal in the context of war because they did not correspond with military necessity or established rules for who could be killed.[86]

By October, those guerrillas who desired to withdraw had done so, but not all did. Some found the profits from banditry too appealing in the uncertain postwar environment, and others gravitated into political opposition to Reconstruction.[87] The latter subject has drawn the attention of both Civil War and Reconstruction scholars in recent years, some of whom see more continuity between the wartime and postwar years than earlier generations of scholars, who regarded Appomattox as a hard line ending the war.[88] The postwar resistance to meaningful freedom for black Southerners, for instance, began as resistance to emancipation during the war. Other lines of continuity can be drawn through these years, especially for participants who experienced them without the analytical categories of "Civil War" and "Reconstruction" that we use today. During the war, the North's political objectives shaped its military goals. Secession required that the Union reassert control over Southern states so that they could resume their normal relationship within the country, something that already occurred in Virginia and Louisiana by war's end. In the wake of Appomattox, those objectives became much more diffuse: protecting the rights and lives of freedpeople, reintegrating Southern states into the political order and Southern businesses into the economic order, and articulating a national culture that could encompass both North and South. The military policy to achieve these goals was hard for white Northerners to envisage. For regular uniformed soldiers, Appomattox marked real closure, but for participants whose lives and livelihoods hinged on the social and economic changes unleashed by war, less changed.

The Last Injustice

For Northerners, the Civil War started in treachery and ended in infamy. After the jubilation that gripped the country following Lee's surrender, the death of Abraham Lincoln less than a week later came as an inconceivable shock. The North was consumed by grief and horror. Lincoln was killed on Good Friday, and Northern ministers used their Easter sermons to proclaim his martyrdom for the cause of Union. For most Northerners, these moments in church were the first communal reckoning with this last act of the war's injustice.[89] The preaching and philosophizing they heard articulated a common reaction across the region, even among conservatives who had not lavished praise on Lincoln during the war. Northerners regarded Grant's magnanimity at Appomattox as an expression of the Union's humane and responsible reaction to the war's end. John Wilkes Booth, and the white South with him, rejected that generosity at Ford's Theater. Religious rhetoric portrayed the assassination as consistent with the Southern style of fighting during the war, one without regard for scruples. That lack of a common morality between North and South was, ministers explained, a product of slavery. Just as slavery had produced violence-prone masters in the antebellum era and bloodthirsty guerrillas during the war, Booth was the logical conclusion. Conversely, ministers glorified Lincoln, celebrating his virtues as the natural expression of a free republic. Although most ministers rejected calls for vengeance, Lincoln's murder nullified whatever charity Northerners may have felt after Lincoln's call in his second inaugural address. It was an inauspicious way to begin Reconstruction.

Having long fulminated against the Confederate way of war, Lieber and other Northerners regarded the assassination as typical of the South. "The applause to [Preston] Brooks, the secret societies, the filibusters, the murder in our war, the raiders, the Fort Pillow men, our riots here, the drunken lawlessness all over the South, the burning of their cities, the massacre now in Washington—it is all, all one fiendish barbarism," proclaimed Lieber.[90] Lieber was not the only one to identify a thread that carried through all the unjust actions of the antebellum decades and the war. Presbyterian Charles Robinson likewise believed "this is no isolated act. The history of this slaveholders' rebellion is full of such."[91] Other ministers had seen nothing but barbarism all along: "take as evidence the Southern conduct of the war," one wrote. "Let their cruelties—which would disgrace the wild tribes of Africa—speak; let the graves of the sixty thousand soldiers whom they murdered by starvation bear their testimony."[92] Whatever the guilt of individuals in the Confederate government, the crime was of a piece with "that state of society which was willing to unchain the fiends of war, to incarnadine sea and land, to immolate a Republic . . . to bore into Pandemonium itself and surge this consecrated earth with its sulphurous seas of flame, that it might continue to batten forever on slavery, and perpetuate eternally 'such abominations as are buried under the waters of the Dead Sea.'"[93]

Just as Northerners regarded the assassination as consistent with Southern war-making habits, so they ascribed all these actions to the same root cause. Booth "was but the dagger's point; Lee is its polished handle; slavery the force that drove it home," explained one eulogist.[94] Francis Lieber shared this view, along with many people in the North: "the assassination of the kindest magistrate any state ever had in a civil war, is another pro-slavery barbarism.—a fit illustration and logical sequel of a doctrine which defies all truth and law and honor."[95] Black Americans did not have to be told that slavery inspired violence. S. W. Rogers, a former slave and the editor of the New Orleans *Black Republican*, condemned the attacks on Lincoln and Seward as "a fitting finale of this brutal and bloody rebellion. They are the natural results of it. . . . They are the fell spirit of slavery breaking from the knife of the assassin—slavery, that for two hundred years has educated whole generations in cruelty and the spirit of murder; that, in the end, drove half a nation to a rebellion to destroy liberty, now whets the knife of the assassin to murder, in cold blood, the most illustrious exemplar of freedom."[96] Ascribing the murder to slavery provided in Northern minds the possibility of redemption—if white Southerners abandoned the peculiar institution, perhaps they would civilize over time.

When eulogists spoke about Lincoln, they characterized him as an embodiment of the natural goodness of the Union, what one speaker called "the incarnate spirit of true republicanism."[97] Minister after minister highlighted Lincoln's humble origins, his earnest efforts at self-improvement, and his humility in the face of the awesome task he confronted as president.[98] Contrasting the Union's cause, embodied by Lincoln, with the South, Charles Robinson declared Lincoln, "a good man, and just."[99] Robinson quoted the Gospel of Luke, comparing Lincoln not to the martyred Jesus (as many did after Lincoln's death on Good Friday) but to Joseph, the councilor who petitioned Pontius Pilate for Jesus's body, then wrapped and buried it in the tomb. This comparison drew attention to the care and protection that Lincoln had given to the nation itself. Other ministers echoed the message, particularly the emphasis on justice: "He was merciful," preached Henry Badger of Boston, "he was prompt to forgive; his delight was to pardon, to remit penalty, to modify extreme measures: but he was *just*, and he was *wise*."[100] Lincoln's goodness and innocence helped Northerners characterize the whole of the Union war effort as innocent.

Despite the contrast ministers drew between the blameless Lincoln and the vile South, they generally refrained from advocating vengeance. "Let the grave of ABRAHAM LINCOLN be unpolluted by the blood of Americans slaughtered for revenge," went one typical prayer.[101] But Lincoln's death and Northerners' interpretation of it in the context of the war alienated the two sides at the moment when empathy was important. "Talk to me no more of 'our misguided brethren,'" Charles Robinson declared. "Satan was of the same race as Gabriel, and educated at the same celestial school of love and grace; but one became a rebel, and between them ever thereafter was 'a great gulf fixed.' He cannot be brother of mine."[102] As Northerners began to consider the nature of reunion, they lamented that Southerners had delivered to Lincoln only malice, not charity.[103]

CONCLUSION
The Double-Edged Sword

Lincoln's murder shattered Northerners' euphoria about the Union's victory in the Civil War. Some blamed Jefferson Davis, others blamed slavery, but all recognized the real culprit: war was unfair. Even this moment of national triumph and unity was marred by unjust killing. In this sense, the war's end embodied the contradictions that had defined the whole experience. Looking back on the war 150 years later, we are left with a similar tangle of lessons.

Adhering to the laws of war, regular soldiers directed the majority of lethal violence at their enemies in battle. These events, no matter their scale, did not provide the decisive end that many people expected, but they did confine most of the war's killing to the armies. Irregular combatants perpetrated and met with irregular violence. Because they operated outside the laws of war, guerrillas did not receive the benefit of surrender, capture, and medical care when necessary. When Northerners faced irregulars, they exercised only as much restraint as commanders felt necessary at the moment. Similarly, the contradictory policies regarding black soldiers promulgated by the Davis administration offered broad license to the Confederacy's soldiers to kill black opponents without regard to the conventions of surrender that prevailed between white soldiers. According to the laws of war to which both sides publicly committed themselves, noncombatants should have been exempt from lethal violence. But the gender and race of citizens made them more vulnerable. Women, especially Southern women, absorbed the costs of hard war, suffering as the Union's policy of logistical devastation reduced food supplies. As Union armies moved through civilian spaces, women could be subjected to military violence if they supported guerrillas or resisted Union authority. Black people experienced even more vulnerability, with both Confederate and Union soldiers inflicting violence (though much more from the former than the latter). Beyond these supposedly fixed identities that shaped war experiences, the most important variable determining a person's likelihood of being a victim of the war was loyalty. Although both armies incidentally imposed hardship on their supporters (as when they impressed or confiscated supplies or animals), they directed their ire toward enemy citizens.

Civil War participants experienced unnecessary violence. The armies of both North and South killed people that they could or should have captured. The laws of war offered a general prohibition against directing violence toward noncombatants, and respect for those laws ensured less violence in the US Civil War than in other conflicts of the mid-nineteenth century. On the other hand, laws did not always help. Instead, sometimes they drove the death toll higher.[1] Union soldiers who captured guerrillas knew that they had legal cover to execute such men. The legal reasoning contained its own rationality. In Gideon Welles's melancholy framing: "violent and forcible measures are resorted to in order to resist and destroy the government, which have begotten violent and forcible measures to vindicate and restore its peaceful operation."[2] In many cases, however, Union commanders arrested and imprisoned suspected bushwhackers rather than killing them outright.

The war's participants made deliberate decisions when they directed violence against lawful enemies, irregular combatants, or noncombatants. They could never anticipate the unintended consequences of their actions, but they behaved according to ethical principles sanctioned by their societies. The decision about whether to execute guerrillas was often made spontaneously and at the whim of the men on the ground, a consequence of the Civil War's decentralized nature. This aspect of the war enabled rogue commanders to enact violence that was unauthorized (and often outside the laws of war), but such a system also facilitated a cooling-off period that helped avoid cycles of retributive violence. In such settings, the aggrieved party threatened retaliation if the accusations were true, which gave the accused party time to stall. The aggrieved party usually accepted this and waited for a response, at which point attention waned. This diplomatic system, structured around the public exchange of letters in newspapers, did not ensure perfect justice. Unjust violence sometimes went unpunished, but importantly, it only rarely resulted in over-punishment. As a result, the Civil War witnessed few of the cycles of retributive killing that have marked other conflicts. The decentralized war also ensured an inconsistent experience for Southern civilians living in occupied cities. In some places, departmental commanders and provost marshals supervised and controlled Union soldiers in their interactions with citizens. In others, soldiers had a freer hand to punish the enemy.

Whenever commanders on either side were challenged about the behavior of their soldiers, they defended themselves with the shield of military necessity. The Union's definition of military necessity was elastic enough to allow unnecessary and unjust violence against irregular combatants and occasionally noncombatants. The Confederacy used the same concept of lawful military necessity to explain the unjust killing of black soldiers. In order to preserve their social order, they could not accept black men as legitimate combatants. Although both sides marshaled strategic arguments for military necessity, Northern behavior was often tinged with malice against guerrillas and Confederate civilians, and Southern behavior against black people. People on either side disagreed about the justice of their respective claims. Confederates condemned the banishment of 20,000 citizens of western Missouri. Union commanders in the region believed it was necessary, and Lincoln accepted their reasoning. Lincoln declared emancipation "as a fit and necessary war measure" and enlisted black men into Union armies. Confederates believed that such an act necessitated a response that targeted such men with lethal violence.

Much of the war's unjust violence stemmed from the problem of guerrillas.[3] Not only did their irregular operation confuse the ability of Union soldiers to selectively identify legitimate targets of lethal violence, but the fear and paranoia they introduced into the conflict generated more insecurity for Southern noncombatants. The Confederacy's failure to aggressively condemn and police this process—to bring these men within the control of its regular armies—was a major failing of the regime, one that had terrible consequences for both Unionists and Confederates in the South. The Davis administration's acceptance of Union executions of guerrillas offers silent but eloquent testimony that they recognized the unjustness of this component of their war.

We can learn both from the decisions that Northerners and South-erners made and from the explanations they offered for those decisions. In World War II, both the Americans and the Japanese claimed that racial superiority justified their military behavior.[4] In the Civil War, both sides claimed moral authority, partly because of how they fought. The North adopted its superiority from a sense that it alone represented democracy. Southerners viewed their superiority from a cultural perspective—that slavery enabled a more generous and humane society to develop. Both of these were functions of the choices that Northerners and Southerners made, though sometimes their most rhapsodic propa-gandists spoke as though these characteristics were inherent in each people. Once mobilized, moral authority encouraged and justified a wide range of brutal actions in the war. Those brutalities, which overshadowed whatever misdeeds one's own side had committed, encouraged a sense of victimization. As a result, both sides finished the war thinking they had been victimized by a ruthless opponent. This legacy structured Recon-struction in the South in particular. White Southerners nursed what William Faulkner called the "canker suppuration of defeat" while Northerners entered an era of imperial expansion with a new moral cer-tainty underwritten by the Treasury of Virtue.

The wartime calculus created by the Civil War's participants sanc-tioned episodes of grim destruction and instances where the inertia of violence weakened. As a prominent military historian reminds us, "war is defined by *both* violence *and* restraint, consciously and unconsciously, ma-terially and mentally."[5] Moments of charity occurred wherever Union commanders and Confederate commanders or Southern politicians ne-gotiated surrenders—of forts, armies, and towns—without violence. They happened when soldiers surrendered on battlefields and became prisoners of war. They even happened when officers used threats of retaliation to demand an end to unjust practices. In most cases, a retaliatory order de-escalated the situation. The most pivotal moment of de-escalation was the decision by enslaved people to pursue freedom rather than revenge. Of the half a million people who fled to freedom during the war, only a tiny minority stopped to perpetrate violence against their masters or other white Southerners. Some of those enslaved people who remained behind Confederate lines pressed claims for autonomy with more vigor, but the bloody nightmare that Confederates predicted never transpired. Freed-people acted from a variety of motives—some practical, some strategic, and others ethical. Whatever the calculations, the result was a substantially more peaceful civil war.

A common expression is that we always fight the last war—because our training and organization come from what we know. We also fight previous wars all over again because those conflicts give us a vocabulary and a set of rules for how to understand the purpose, process, and limits of warfare. Like all human action, warfare is entangled with the past. Alongside this temporal dimension lies a spatial one. We determine when war is just and what actions in war are acceptable in relation to what other people around the globe have done and are doing. The global context within which the Civil War occurred helped moderate the most extreme behavior. As much as historians talk about the Civil War as an exclusively American conflict—a "brothers' war"—evidence suggests Northerners and Southerners made sense of the war and, in particular, the violence of war, with reference to global examples. They associated their enemy's behavior with the most infamous examples at hand—Sepoy, British, or Native American. As one of Lincoln's cabinet secretaries explained, "every consideration due to our position in the family of nations—to humanity, to civilization should prompt us, in the existing condition of the country, to maintain an habitual and scrupulous observance of the usages of modern warfare."[6] In the nineteenth century, even civil wars were world wars.

Federals and Confederates interacted with Europeans and others around the world as members of nation-states. The national identity of each place structured foreign affairs, shaped internal politics and, in important ways, the nature of the war that each state waged. Citizens both North and South identified with their nation. Historians have spent a great deal of time assessing the nature, meaning, and significance of nationalism in the Civil War era. Both places included substantial dissenting communities, but for white citizens, national affiliation played a sustaining role in their commitment to the war. Nationalism both enabled the war's destructiveness and moderated its excesses. In the North and South, martial nationalism emboldened a jingoistic posture that sanctioned the mistreatment of outsiders (especially those, like guerrillas and black soldiers, who were regarded as outside of the national framework altogether). Conversely, the nature of nationalism in mid-nineteenth-century America required believers to pledge adherence to standards of conduct that at times limited the war's violence. Both Northerners and Southerners disclaimed responsibility for their own excesses even as they cataloged the injustices they suffered. If the terrible violence of the twentieth century has taught us anything it is that we cannot "arbitrarily select from a national heritage what we like and proclaim it as patrimony to the exclusion of everything else." "Just the opposite," writes a historian of modern Poland, "if people are indeed bonded together by authentic spiritual affinity—I have in mind a kind of national pride rooted in common historical experiences of many generations—are they not somehow responsible also for horrible deeds perpetrated by members of such an 'imagined community?'"[7]

Like so much else about the Civil War, nationalism proved a double-edged sword, equally capable of taking life as of defending it. Even those wars that we envision as "good" are rarely consistently so. Observant states often violate the principles of just war and use those rules to excuse unnecessary harm and injustice. Nonetheless, the experience of the Civil War demonstrates the importance of rules—of the ways that popular democracies encourage good conduct and of the centrality of states watching and policing each other. Rules of war occasionally observed are better than no rules at all. The moral disasters of the twentieth century enabled scholars to see how nation-states and the patriotism they required generated previously unimaginable violence. But the Civil War demonstrates that nation-states can also encourage people to articulate and enforce rules of war. Nineteenth-century Americans, both North and South, promoted moral behavior in and by their armies because they believed in their nation-states. International observers supplied additional pressure, calibrating their diplomatic responses to the war based partly on their moral reckoning of each side's method of war-making. These institutions, forces, and choices compelled the Confederacy to participate in the war as a state rather than as a guerrilla republic. They required Lincoln to treat the Confederacy's soldiers as citizens of a sovereign nation rather than as a band of lawless rebels who should suffer the fate marked out for traitors in the Constitution. The horrible toll of the Civil War should not blind us to the still more terrible possibilities that participants' respect for customary rules of warfare prevented. The contradictions of the Civil War remind us of a dreadful calculation: the occasional necessity of conflict and the costs it necessarily imposes.

Notes

Acknowledgments

Illustration Credits

Index

NOTES

AFIC   *American Freedmen's Inquiry Commission*, National Archive and Record Administration, Record Group 94, M619, Rolls 199–200.

BAP   *The Black Abolitionist Papers*, vol. 5: *The United States, 1859–1865*, C. Peter Ripley, Roy E. Finkenbine, Michael F. Hembree, and Donald Yacovone, eds. Chapel Hill: University of North Carolina Press, 1992.

CG   *Congressional Globe*

CWAL   *Collected Works of Abraham Lincoln*, ed. Roy P. Basler, 8 vols. New Brunswick, NJ: Rutgers University Press, 1953.

CWH   *Civil War History*

CS   Confederate States of America

FSSP   *Freedom: A Documentary History of Emancipation, 1861–1867*, ed. Ira Berlin, et al., 6 vols. Cambridge: Cambridge University Press, 1982–.

HH   Henry E. Huntington Library, San Marino, CA

JAH   *Journal of American History*

JCWE   *Journal of the Civil War Era*

LiebC   *Instructions for the Government of Armies of the United States in the Field, prepared by Francis Lieber, LL.D.*, Originally Issued as General Orders No. 100, Adjutant General's Office, 1863. Washington, DC: Government Printing Office, 1898.

LOC   Library of Congress

LP   *Abraham Lincoln Papers*, Library of Congress, Series I (unless otherwise noted)

LSU   Special Collections, Hill Memorial Library, Louisiana State University, Baton Rouge, Louisiana

MPC   *A Compilation of the Messages and Papers of the Confederacy*, ed. James D. Richardson. Nashville: United States Publishing, 1905.

NARA   National Archives and Records Administration, Washington, DC

NL   Newberry Library, Chicago, IL

NYPL   New York Public Library, New York

OR   United States War Department. *The War of the Rebellion: A Compilation of the Armies*, 128 vols. Washington, DC: Government Printing Office, 1880–1901.

ORN   United States Naval Records Office. *Official Records of the Union and Confederate Navies.* 30 vols. Washington, DC: Government Printing Office, 1894–1922.

PJD   *The Papers of Jefferson Davis,* 11 vols. Baton Rouge: Louisiana State University Press, 1970–2016.

PMR   U.S. Provost Marshal Records, National Archives and Records Administration, Record Group 393, Part 1

POCBB *Private and Official Correspondence of Gen. Benjamin F. Butler,* ed. Jessie Ames Marshall, 5 vols. Norwood, MA: Plimpton Press, 1917.

PUSG *Papers of Ulysses S. Grant,* ed. John Y. Simon, 31 vols. Carbondale: Southern Illinois University Press, 1969–2009.

TAS   George A. Rawick, ed. *The American Slave: A Composite Autobiography.* Westport, CT: Greenwood Press, 1977–1979.

RG   Record Group (NARA)

SHSP *Southern Historical Society Papers* (proceedings of the Confederate Congress), vols. 44–52 (1923–1959).

UVA   Albert and Shirley Small Special Collections Library, University of Virginia, Charlottesville, VA

INTRODUCTION. THE PUZZLE OF THE CIVIL WAR

1. For accounts that emphasize violence, see Daniel E. Sutherland, *A Savage Conflict: The Decisive Role of Guerrillas in the American Civil War* (Chapel Hill: University of North Carolina Press, 2009); Clay Mountcastle, *Punitive War: Confederate Guerrillas and Union Reprisals* (Lawrence: University Press of Kansas, 2009); Barton A. Myers, *Executing Daniel Bright: Race, Loyalty, and Guerrilla Violence in a Coastal Carolina Community, 1861–1865* (Baton Rouge: Louisiana University Press, 2009). For studies that emphasize restraint, see Mark Grimsley, *The Hard Hand of War: Union Military Policy toward Southern Civilians, 1861–1865* (Cambridge: Cambridge University Press, 1995); Mark E. Neely, Jr., *The Civil War and the Limits of Destruction* (Cambridge, MA: Harvard University Press, 2007). Wayne Hsieh and others have begun advocating a middle ground. Hsieh, "Total War and the American Civil War Reconsidered: The End of an Outdated 'Master Narrative,'" *JCWE* 1 (Fall 2011): 394–408; William Blair, *With Malice toward Some: Treason and Loyalty in the Civil War Era* (Chapel Hill: University of North Carolina Press, 2014); D. H. Dilbeck, *A More Civil War: How the North Waged a Just War* (Chapel Hill: University of North Carolina Press, 2016).

2. Wayne Lee has suggested a similar framing of the Anglo-American experience of war in the seventeenth, eighteenth, and nineteenth centuries. The Civil War occurred at a moment that "marked such a dramatic shift

in the demographic and industrial capacity to destroy, at the same time that Europeans and Americans increasingly sought to draw boundaries around acceptable forms of violence." Wayne Lee, *Barbarians and Brothers: Anglo-American Warfare, 1500–1865* (New York: Oxford University Press, 2011), 243.

3. Stephen Platt, *Autumn in the Heavenly Kingdom: China, the West, and the Epic Story of the Taiping Civil War* (New York: Vintage, 2012); Nelson A. Reed, *The Caste War of the Yucatán*, rev. ed. (Stanford, CA: Stanford University Press, 2001); Terry Rugeley, *Yucatán's Maya Peasantry and the Origins of the Caste War* (Austin: University of Texas Press, 1996); Michael Geyer and Charles Bright, "Global Violence and Nationalizing Wars in Eurasia and America: The Geopolitics of War in the Mid-Nineteenth Century," *Comparative Studies in Society and History* 38 (October 1996): 619–657.

4. John Merryman, *Massacre: The Life and Death of the Paris Commune* (New York: Basic Books, 2014).

5. Grimsley, *The Hard Hand of War*, 43–46; Stephen Ash, *When the Yankees Came: Conflict and Chaos in the Occupied South* (Chapel Hill: University of North Carolina Press, 1999), 52–53; Chandra Manning, *What This Cruel War Was Over: Soldiers, Slavery, and the Meaning of the Civil War* (New York: Knopf, 2007), 68.

6. It is important to note that in the South, "enemies" could designate fellow Southerners. After the passage of the Conscription Act in early 1862, some soldiers returned home and joined reluctant Unionists who fought as guerrillas against the Confederate government. Sutherland, *A Savage Conflict*, 181, 186.

7. Jonathan D. Spence, *God's Chinese Son: The Taiping Heavenly Kingdom of Hong Xiuquang* (New York: Norton, 1996), xxi; Jürgen Osterhammel, *The Transformation of the World: A Global History of the Nineteenth Century* (Princeton, NJ: Princeton University Press, 2014), 120–121; Douglas M. Richmond, *Conflict and Carnage in the Yucatán: Liberals, the Second Empire, and Maya Revolutionaries, 1855–1875* (Tuscaloosa: University of Alabama Press, 2015), 27; Geyer and Bright, "Global Violence."

8. "Law of Nations," *Advocate of Peace* (November / December 1863): 357–360 and "International Law: Grotius on War and Peace," *The Knickerbocker Monthly: A National Magazine* 62 (August 1863): 150–157. Several recent books have articulated the ways in which participants in the Civil War relied upon or influenced international laws of war. See Stephen C. Neff, *Justice in Blue and Gray: A Legal History of the Civil War* (Cambridge, MA: Harvard University Press, 2010), 56; and Denis K. Boman, *Lincoln and Citizens' Rights in Civil War Missouri* (Baton Rouge: Louisiana State University Press, 2011), 7–8.

9. Despite a century and a half of writing, historians have no reliable number of civilian casualties in the Civil War. A precise count is probably beyond the reach of even the most dedicated statistician. Most historians rely upon James McPherson's figure of 50,000 "war-related civilian deaths" in the South. *Battle Cry of Freedom: The Civil War Era* (New York: Oxford, 1988), 619, n53. But this was, as he wrote, only a "fair estimate" based on his assumptions about the conflict.

10. David Armitage's global history of the Declaration of Independence persuasively shows that establishing sovereignty in the United States required that other countries accept the declaration, which generally they did. This same dynamic was at work during the Civil War as well. Armitage, *Global History of the Declaration of Independence* (Cambridge, MA: Harvard University Press, 2008).

11. Daniel Sutherland's *A Savage Conflict* offers the most comprehensive account. His work builds on local or regional studies that have broadened and deepened our sense of the nature of irregular conflict in the Civil War.

12. For a useful, contextualized interrogation of this question see D. H. Dilbeck, *A More Civil War: How the North Fought a Just War* (Chapel Hill: University of North Carolina Press, 2016), Chapter 6.

13. Harry S. Stout, *Upon the Altar of the Nation: A Moral History of the Civil War* (New York: Vintage, 2006); Charles Royster, *The Destructive War: William Tecumseh Sherman, Stonewall Jackson, and the Americans* (New York: Vintage, 1991).

14. Mary Dudziak, *War Time: An Idea, Its History, Its Consequences* (New York: Oxford University Press, 2013), 23. Charles Royster's *The Destructive War,* one of the most influential books in shaping modern ideas about violence in the conflict, presents the Civil War as an autonomous force that drove violence to greater and greater heights. Modern war in the twentieth century attained an institutional shape and power that made it an independent factor, something that operated beyond the control of any individual or even any nation-state. I am not convinced that this characterization applies to nineteenth-century warfare. The Civil War encouraged great mobilization and organization of military and civilian resources, in both the Union and the Confederacy, but it was not the colossus that haunted the modern world. Regardless, history as a discipline demands that we recognize change as a result of human action. We build machines and governments and markets and institutions that operate independently, but as historians we recognize those abstractions as products of individual decision-making. The Civil War did not *become* violent because of some natural force or inevitable pattern in the making of war. Where violence prevailed, it was because people made the decision to commit or sanction it; this was also the case where restraint prevailed. We can identify those moments when the war's participants chose vio-

lence or restraint. These help us recognize the tipping points of historical change in the Civil War.

15. Lincoln to Thomas C. Fletcher, February 20, 1865, *CWAL*, VIII: 308; Lincoln to Clinton B. Fisk, October 13, 1863, *CWAL*, VI: 511; "Fragment on Proslavery Theology," October 1, 1858, *CWAL*, III: 204. Walt Whitman used the concept similarly, as when he called "Charity and Love! sister throbbings in the heart of great Humanity!" Walt Whitman, "One Wicked Impulse! A Tale of a Murderer Escaped," *The Brooklyn Daily Eagle and Kings County Democrat*, September 9, 1846.

16. Kurt Vonnegut, *Slaughterhouse Five, or The Children's Crusade* (1969. New York: Random House, 1997), 24.

17. George Caleb Bingham, *"But I Forget That I Am a Painter and Not a Politician"*: *The Letters of George Caleb Bingham*, ed. Lynn Wolf Gentzler (Columbia: State Historical Society of Missouri, 2011), 315.

1. WHO CAN MAKE WAR?

1. *The Iliad*, trans. Robert Fagles (New York: Penguin, 1990).

2. And long after. Robert Wiebe, *The Search for Order, 1877–1920* (New York: Hill and Wang, 1966), xiii.

3. John Majewski, *A House Dividing: Economic Development in Pennsylvania and Virginia before the Civil War* (Cambridge: Cambridge University Press, 2000); Jim Huston, *Calculating the Value of the Union: Slavery, Property Rights, and the Economic Origins of the Civil War* (Chapel Hill: University of North Carolina Press, 2003); and Marc Egnal, *Clash of Extremes: The Economic Origins of the Civil War* (New York: Hill and Wang, 2009).

4. Daniel Walker Howe, *What Hath God Wrought: The Transformation of America, 1815–1848* (New York: Oxford University Press, 2007).

5. Leonard Richards, *The Slave Power: The Free North and Southern Domination, 1780–1860* (Baton Rouge: Louisiana State University Press, 2000); Eric Foner, *Free Soil, Free Labor, Free Men: The Ideology of the Republican Party before the Civil War*, 2nd ed. (1970. New York: Oxford University Press, 1995).

6. Henry W. Halleck, *International Law; or, Rules Regulating the Intercourse of States* (San Francisco: H. H. Bancroft, 1861). Travers Twiss, a British jurist, wrote on the rules of international law in the 1850s and was regarded as a useful guide as well. Travers Twiss, *The Law of Nations Considered as Independent Political Communities* (London: Longman, Green, Longman, and Roberts, 1861).

7. John Fabian Witt, *Lincoln's Code: The Laws of War in American History* (New York: Free Press, 2013), 181–183; D. H. Dilbeck, *A More Civil War: How the North Fought a Just War* (Chapel Hill: University of North Carolina Press, 2016), 23–24, 182–185.

8. Laura Edwards, *The People and Their Peace: Legal Culture and the Transformation of Inequality in the Post-Revolutionary South* (Chapel Hill: University of North Carolina Press, 2009).

9. John S. Carlile, Senate, July 30, 1861, *CG*, 37th Congress, First Session, 340.

10. James Turner Johnson, *Just War Tradition and the Restraint of War: A Moral and Historical Inquiry* (Princeton, NJ: Princeton University Press, 1981), x.

11. This anxiety also surfaced in Americans' reactions to the revolutions and counterrevolutions of 1848. Timothy Mason Roberts, *Distant Revolutions: 1848 and the Challenge to American Exceptionalism* (Charlottesville: University Press of Virginia, 2009).

12. Sherman to James M. Calhoun et al., September 12, 1864, in *Sherman's Civil War: Selected Correspondence of William T. Sherman, 1860–1865*, ed. Jean V. Berlin and Brooks D. Simpson (Chapel Hill: University of North Carolina Press, 1999), 707–709; Gregory P. Downs, "The Mexicanization of American Politics: The United States' Transnational Path from Civil War to Stabilization," *American Historical Review* 117 (April 2012): 387–409.

13. Garry Wills, *Lincoln at Gettysburg: The Words that Remade America* (New York: Simon and Schuster, 1992), 41–43; Thucydides, *History of the Peloponnesian War* (New York: Penguin, 1972), Book 2, 43, p. 150, Book 2, 41, p. 148. I am grateful to Nate Andrade, Christine Kooi, and Sue Marchand for conversations that clarified my understanding of this text.

14. Peter Carmichael, "'Truth is mighty & will eventually prevail': Political Correctness, Neo-Confederates, and Robert E. Lee," *Southern Cultures* 17 (Fall 2011): 6–27; Henry Ward Beecher, *Freedom and War. Discourses on Topics Suggested by the Times* (Boston: Ticknor and Fields, 1863), 183; Fitzhugh quoted in John Hope Franklin, *The Militant South 1860–1861* (1956. Urbana: University of Illinois Press, 2002), 248; Charles Royster, *The Destructive War: William Tecumseh Sherman, Stonewall Jackson, and the Americans* (New York: Vintage, 1991), 256–257, 294–295.

15. Randolph Roth, *American Homicide* (Cambridge, MA: Harvard University Press, 2009), 3–8.

16. Ted Robert Gurr, "Political Protest and Rebellion in the 1960s: The United States in World Perspective," and Charles Tilly, "Collective Violence in European Perspective," both in *Violence in America: Historical and Comparative Perspectives*, 2nd ed., ed. Hugh Davis Graham and Ted Robert Gurr (Beverly Hills, CA: Sage, 1979), 49–76, 83–118; Richard Hofstadter, "Reflections on Violence in the United States," in *American Violence: A Documentary Reader* (New York: Knopf, 1970), 6. The United States has typically maintained a higher murder rate than Western Europe but has a lower rate of the communal violence that characterized both rural and urban European life. More

recently, Steven Pinker distinguishes a higher homicide rate in the United States compared to other Western democracies, although it is "close to the median rate for the entire world." Pinker, *The Better Angels of Our Nature: Why Violence Has Declined* (New York: Viking, 2011), 91–92; Roth, *American Homicide*, 14, 15. A useful discussion of scholarly explanations for the high US murder rate can be found in Jill Lepore, "Rap Sheet: Why is American History So Murderous?," *New Yorker*, November 9, 2009, 79–83.

17. Ned Blackhawk, *Violence Over the Land: Indians and Empires in the Early American West* (Cambridge, MA: Harvard University Press, 2006); Brian DeLay, *War of a Thousand Deserts: Indian Raids and the U.S.-Mexican War* (New Haven, CT: Yale University Press, 2009); Brian Sandberg, "Beyond Encounters: Religion, Ethnicity, and Violence in the Early Modern Atlantic World, 1492–1700," *Journal of World History* 17 (January 2006): 1–25.

18. Carroll Smith-Rosenberg, *This Violent Empire: The Birth of an American National Identity* (Chapel Hill: University of North Carolina Press, 2010), 216.

19. Roth, *American Homicide*, 297–298, 384, and chapter 7.

20. Edward L. Ayers, *Vengeance and Justice: Crime and Punishment in the Nineteenth-Century South* (New York: Oxford University Press, 1985)

21. Charles W. Wills, *Army Life of an Illinois Soldier: Letters and Diary of Charles W. Wills*, ed. Mary E. Kellog (Carbondale: Southern Illinois University Press, 1996), May 11, 1862, p. 13. Wills reported similarly abused men coming from other parts of Alabama and Tennessee as well. See entries for May 12 and 17, 1861.

22. Thavolia Glymph, *Out of the House of Bondage: The Transformation of the Plantation Household* (Cambridge: Cambridge University Press, 2008); and Elizabeth Fox-Genovese, *Within the Plantation Household: Black and White Women of the Old South* (Chapel Hill: University of North Carolina Press, 1988).

23. Thomas D. Morris, *Southern Slavery and the Law, 1619–1860* (Chapel Hill: University of North Carolina Press, 1999); Mark V. Tushnet, *The American Law of Slavery, 1810–1860: Considerations of Humanity and Interest* (Princeton, NJ: Princeton University Press, 1981).

24. Dickson D. Bruce, Jr., *Violence and Culture in the Antebellum South* (Austin: University of Texas Press, 1979), chapters 5 and 6; Franklin, *The Militant South*, chapter 5.

25. Richard Maxwell Brown, *Strain of Violence: Historical Studies of American Violence and Vigilantism* (New York: Oxford University Press, 1975), Appendix 4, 320–323.

26. Edward Baptist, *Creating an Old South: Middle Florida's Plantation Frontier before the Civil War* (Chapel Hill: University of North Carolina Press, 2002), 88.

27. Bertram Wyatt-Brown, *Southern Honor: Ethics and Behavior in the Old South* (New York: Oxford University Press, 1982). Some of the commonplace attitude that Southerners were more prone to violence may have come from sectional pressure rather than any more fundamental social difference. See R. Don Higginbotham, "The Martial Spirit in the Antebellum South: Some Further Speculations in a National Context," *Journal of Southern History* 58 (February 1992): 3–26.

28. Christopher J. Olsen, *Political Culture and Secession in Mississippi: Masculinity, Honor, and the Antiparty Tradition, 1830–1860* (New York: Oxford University Press, 2000), 5.

29. Edward L. Ayers, *Vengeance and Justice: Crime and Punishment in the 19th-Century American South* (New York: Oxford University Press, 1984), 16.

30. Bruce, *Violence and Culture in the Antebellum South*, 6; Franklin, *The Militant South*, 12–13.

31. Tyler Anbinder, *Five Points: The 19th Century New York City Neighborhood that Invented Tap Dance, Stole Elections, and Became the World's Most Notorious Slum* (New York: Free Press, 2010); Tyler Anbinder, *Nativism and Slavery: The Northern Know Nothings and the Politics of the 1850s* (New York: Oxford University Press, 1982); Andrew Mach, "Transatlantic Tales and Democratic Dreams: Archbishop Gaetano Bedini, Alessandro Gavazzi, and the Struggle to Define Republican Liberty in a Revolutionary Age, 1848–1854" (MA thesis, West Virginia University, 2014); Sean Wilentz, *Chants Democratic: New York City and the Rise of the American Working Class, 1788–1850* (New York: Oxford University Press, 1984); Gregg D. Kimball, *American City, Southern Place: A Cultural History of Antebellum Richmond* (Athens: University of Georgia Press, 2000); Werner H. Steger, "'United to Support, But Not Combined to Injure': Free Workers and Immigrants in Richmond, Virginia, during the Era of Sectionalism, 1847–1865" (PhD diss., George Washington University, 1999).

32. David Grimstead, *American Mobbing, 1828–1861: Toward Civil War* (New York: Oxford, 1998), viii; Brown, *Strain of Violence*, Appendix 3, 303–319; David Williams, *I Freed Myself: African American Self-Emancipation in the Civil War Era* (New York: Cambridge University Press, 2014), 32. The editors of a recent essay collection on antislavery violence argue that "by emphasizing the continuing role of violence within the antislavery movement, the collection takes a step toward reestablishing an appreciation of the movement as a major precursor of the much more violent Civil War." John R. McKivigan and Stanley Harrold, "Introduction," in *Antislavery Violence: Sectional, Racial, and Cultural Conflict in Antebellum America* (Knoxville: University of Tennessee Press, 1999), 2.

33. William A. Blair, *With Malice toward Some: Treason and Loyalty in the Civil War Era* (Chapel Hill: University of North Carolina Press, 2014), 19–20; Steven Hahn, *The Political Worlds of Slavery and Freedom* (Cambridge, MA: Harvard University Press, 2009), 38–39.

34. Stanley Harrold, *Border Wars: Fighting over Slavery before the Civil War* (Chapel Hill: University of North Carolina Press, 2010).

35. Hahn, *Political Worlds*, 37.

36. Historians divide over whether most of the violence in America is perpetrated by radicals or conservatives. Richard Hofstadter argued the latter in "Introduction," *American Violence*. McKivigan and Harrold suggest that both sides contribute. McKivigan and Harrold, "Introduction," *Antislavery Violence*, 1.

37. Edward Everett to Horace Maynard, October 3, 1857, quoted in William E. Gienapp, "The Crime against Sumner: The Caning of Charles Sumner and the Rise of the Republican Party," *CWH* 25 (Fall 1979): 223.

38. Jeremiah Wilbur to William H. Seward, June 20, 1856, in Gienapp, "The Crime against Sumner," 234.

39. Nicole Etcheson, *Bleeding Kansas: Contested Liberty in the Civil War Era* (Lawrence: University Press of Kansas, 2004), 104–105, 193–194.

40. Caroline E. Janney, "Written in Stone: Gender, Race, and the Heyward Shepherd Memorial," *CWH* 52 (June 2006): 117–141.

41. Garrison to Charles K. Whipple, July 19, 1846, *The Letters of William Lloyd Garrison*, vol. III: *No Union with Slaveholders, 1841–1849*, ed. Walter M. Merrill (Cambridge, MA: Harvard University Press, 1973), 352.

42. Halleck, *International Law*, 319.

43. Drew McCoy, *The Elusive Republic: Political Economy in Jeffersonian America* (Chapel Hill: University of North Carolina Press, 1980); and Max Edling, *A Revolution in Favor of Government: Origins of the U.S. Constitution and the Making of the American State* (Cambridge: Cambridge University Press, 2003); Matthew Karp, *This Vast Southern Empire: Slaveholders at the Helm of American Foreign Policy* (Cambridge, MA: Harvard University Press, 2016).

44. Henry Wheaton, *Elements of International Law*, 6th ed. (Boston: Little Brown, 1855), 27.

45. Linda Colley, *Forging the Nation 1707–1837*, 3rd ed. (New Haven, CT: Yale University Press, 2009); David Bell, *The Cult of the Nation in France: Inventing Nationalism, 1680–1800* (Cambridge, MA: Harvard University Press, 2003); H. Ernest Gellner, *Nations and Nationalism*, 2nd ed. (Ithaca, NY: Cornell University Press, 2009); E. J. Hobsbawm, *Nations and Nationalism since 1780*, 2nd ed. (Cambridge: Cambridge University Press, 1992).

46. Buchanan's December 3, 1860, "Annual Message to Congress."

47. Halleck, *International Law*, 64. Italics in the original. Unless otherwise noted, all quotations include original spelling, punctuation, and emphasis.

48. Wheaton, *Elements of International Law*, 30.

49. Davis, "Inaugural Address," February 18, 1861, in Richardson, *MPC*, I, 32, 36.

50. Davis, "Address to Congress," April 29, 1861, in Richardson, *MPC*, I, 63–65.

51. Thomas Bender, *A Nation among Nations: America's Place in World History* (New York: Hill and Wang, 2006), 144–146, 178.

52. Daniel W. Crofts, "Late Antebellum Virginia Reconsidered," *Virginia Magazine of History and Biography* 107 (Summer 1999): 253–286; Joel Parker, "The Character of the Rebellion, and the Conduct of the War," *North American Review* (October 1862): 510; Don Doyle, *The Cause of All Nations: An International History of the Civil War* (New York: Basic Books, 2014); Twiss, *The Law of Nations Considered*, 144.

53. Wheaton, *Elements of International Law*, 29. Lincoln's Attorney General cited this passage, among others, in his defense of the president's power to suspend habeas corpus that he provided Lincoln in mid-1861. Edward Bates to Lincoln, July 5, 1861, *LP*; Wheaton, *Elements of International Law*, 73–75; "The Right of Secession," *North American Review* (July 1861): 212–244; Halleck, *International Law*, 332.

54. Robert Toombs to William L. Yancey, Pierre A. Rost, A. Dudley Mann, March 16, 1861, *MPC*, II, 4.

55. *SHSP* 44 (1923): 53–54; George Rable, *God's Almost Chosen People: A Religious History of the Civil War* (Chapel Hill: University of North Carolina Press, 2010), 39.

56. Lincoln, Second Inaugural, March 4, 1865; Alexander W. Randall, "Governor's Message," *Wisconsin Daily Patriot*, May 15, 1861.

57. Lincoln, First Inaugural, March 4, 1861; Henry Everett Russell, "The War a Contest for Ideas: I. The Idea of Political Equality. II. The Idea of Nationality," *The Continental Monthly: Devoted to Literature and National Policy (1862–1864)* May, 1864 (5): 578–579.

58. David Armitage, *Civil Wars: A History in Ideas* (New Haven, CT: Yale University Press, 2017), 167, 177–178.

59. Elisha R. Potter, *Upon the Present National Difficulties* (Providence: Cooke, Jackson, 1863), 27, in *Civil War Politics: Pamphlets*, vol. 2, NL; Wayne Lee, *Barbarians and Brothers: Anglo-American Warfare, 1500–1865* (New York: Oxford University Press, 2011), 233; *New York Times*, July 13, 1861.

60. Michael Howard, "Constraints on Warfare," in *The Laws of War: Constraints on Warfare in the Western World*, ed. Michael Howard, George J. Andreopoulos, and Mark R. Shulman (New Haven, CT: Yale University Press, 1994), 1–11;

Stephen C. Neff, *War and the Law of Nations: A General History* (Cambridge: Cambridge University Press, 2005); William V. O'Brien, *Conduct of Just and Unjust Wars* (New York: Praeger, 1982); Johnson, *Just War Tradition*. Many of the most recent treatments of just war in US history have addressed it largely as rhetoric. Jill Lepore's study of King Philip's War in the seventeenth-century Massachusetts colony and Peter Silver's examination of eighteenth-century Indian-European conflict in the Pennsylvania colony both show the power of language to catalyze real violence. They also demonstrated the persistence of a surprisingly robust conversation among European immigrants about who they could attack and in what ways. Jill Lepore, *The Name of War: King Philip's War and the Origins of American Identity* (New York: Vintage, 1999); and Peter J. Silver, *Our Savage Neighbors: How Indian War Transformed Early America* (New York: Norton, 2007).

61. Francis Lieber to Edward Bates, May 15, 1862, Box 23, Lieber Papers, HH.

62. Blair, *With Malice toward Some*, 3, 69–70, 78.

63. *SHSP* 49 (1930): 153.

64. Hobsbawm, *Nations and Nationalism*, 73–77; and also the work of Anthony D. Smith, especially *The Ethnic Origins of Nations* (Oxford: Basil Blackwell, 1986); and *The Antiquity of Nations* (Cambridge: Polity, 2004).

65. David Armitage's history of the uses of the Declaration by other nations implicitly shows this process at work when Americans feel sympathy for other people emulating our model of national independence. David Armitage, *The Declaration of Independence: A Global History* (Cambridge, MA: Harvard University Press, 2008).

66. Stephen Cushman, *Belligerent Muse: Five Northern Writers and How They Shaped Our Understanding of the Civil War* (Chapel Hill: University of North Carolina Press, 2014), 86; David M. Crowe, *War Crimes, Genocide, and Justice: A Global History* (New York: Palgrave Macmillan, 2014), 40–41. For examples of this process, see "The Laws of War," *Richmond Daily Dispatch*, March 15, 1862; "Art. IV.—Enmities and Barbarities of the Rebellion," *Danville Quarterly Review* (December 1864): 606–609; "Art. X Speeches at the Annual Banquet of the Lord Mayor of London," *North American Review* (January 1862): 212–214; James A. Hamilton, "State Sovereignty: Rebellion against the United States by the People of a State Is Its Political Suicide" (New York: Baker & Godwin, 1862).

67. L. Lynn Hogue, "Lieber's Military Code and Its Legacy," in *Francis Lieber and the Culture of the Mind*, ed. Charles R. Mack and Henry H. Lesesne (Columbia: University of South Carolina Press, 2005), 56.

68. Michael Walzer, *Just and Unjust Wars: A Moral Argument with Historical Illustrations*, 4th ed. (New York: Basic Books, 2006), 137–138.

69. Blair, *With Malice toward Some*, 3.

70. Hugo Grotius, *The Rights of War and Peace*, ed. Knud Haakonssen (Indianapolis, IN: Liberty Fund, 2005), Bk. 2, Ch. XXI, Bk. 3, 1420–12; Emer de Vattel, *The Law of Nations*, ed. Béla Kapossy and Richard Whatmore (1758. Indianapolis: Liberty Fund, 2008), Book II, Chapter XVIII, Sec. 339, p. 459.

71. *LiebC*, Arts. 27–28. See also Union General-in-Chief Henry Halleck's comment: "The law of retaliation in war has its limits . . . the object . . . being, not revenge, but prevention." Henry W. Halleck, "Retaliation in War," *American Journal of International Law* 6 (January 1912), 110. Halleck practiced what he preached, rescinding a retaliatory order issued by Gen. E. A. Paine because "such a policy was 'contrary to the rules of civilized war, and if its spirit should be adopted the whole country would be covered with blood. Retaliation has its limits, and the innocent should not be made to suffer for the acts of others over whom they have no control.'" Halleck quoted in Dennis K. Boman, *Lincoln and Citizen's Rights in Civil War Missouri* (Baton Rouge: Louisiana State University Press, 2011), 94.

72. *SHSP* 44 (1923): 244.

73. *CG*, 38th Congress, Second Session, Part 1: 408.

74. *CG*, 38th Congress, Second Session, Part 1: 469.

75. Lee to Davis, June 25, 1863, in *The Wartime Papers of R. E. Lee*, ed. Clifford Dowdey (Boston: Little Brown, 1961), 530–531.

76. Walzer, *Just and Unjust Wars*, 207, 208–216.

2. THE RISING OF THE PEOPLE

1. William Whiting, *The War Powers of the President and the Legislative Powers of Congress in Relation to Rebellion, Treason, and Slavery*, 2nd ed. (Boston: N. L. Shorey, 1862), 46, 51, 58.

2. "The Southern Rebellion," April 20, 1861, *The Press* (Philadelphia); *New-York Daily Tribune*, April 23, 1861; *New York Times*, April 21, 1861; Daniel E. Sutherland, *A Savage Conflict: The Decisive Role of Guerrillas in the American Civil War* (Chapel Hill: University of North Carolina Press, 2009), 6; John Lockwood and Charles Lockwood, *The Siege of Washington: The Untold Story of the Twelve Days That Shook the Union* (New York: Oxford University Press, 2011), 88–92. The following paragraphs draw heavily on the Lockwoods' excellent account of this dramatic period.

3. Jones quoted in Lockwood and Lockwood, *Siege of Washington*, 114.

4. "The Work of the Mob—Destruction of Bridges," *New-York Daily Tribune*, April 23, 1861.

5. Lockwood and Lockwood, *Siege of Washington*, 114–122.

6. Thomas Hicks and George Brown to Abraham Lincoln, April 18, 1861, *LP*.

7. *Philadelphia Press*, April 20 and 22, 1861; *New-York Daily Tribune*, April 22 and 28, 1861; *New York Times*, April 21 and 25, 1861; *Chicago Tribune*, April 24 and May 9, 1861; Gideon Welles to MJW, April 28, 1861, Welles Papers, LOC.

8. H. D. J. Pratt to Abraham Lincoln, Saturday, April 20, 1861; H. Pollock to Abraham Lincoln, Monday, April 22, 1861, *LP*; Andrew H. Reeder to Simon Cameron, Wednesday, April 24, 1861, *LP*; *Philadelphia Press*, April 22 and 24, 1861; *Chicago Tribune*, April 25, 1861; Lockwood and Lockwood, *Siege of Washington*, 234–235.

9. Louis Gerteis, *Civil War St. Louis* (Lawrence: University Press of Kansas, 2001), 97–115, 113; *Chicago Tribune*, May 14, 1861; *New York Tribune*, May 12, 1861; "Missouri," *U.S. Service Magazine* 1 (March 1864), 227.

10. *Chicago Tribune*, May 11, 1861; *Philadelphia Press*, May 15, 1861.

11. "War Movements," *New York Sun*, April 23, 1861.

12. Dickson D. Bruce, Jr., *Violence and Culture in the Antebellum South* (Austin: University of Texas Press, 1979), 166; Wayne Wei-Siang Hsieh, *West Pointers and the Civil War* (Chapel Hill: University of North Carolina Press, 2009), 13–14.

13. *Regulations for the Army of the Confederate States* (New Orleans: Henry P. Lathrop, 1861), 134.

14. Lee, G. O. No. 73, June 27, 1863, in *The Wartime Papers of R. E. Lee*, ed. Clifford Dowdey (Boston: Little Brown, 1961).

15. Hsieh, *West Pointers and the Civil War*, 94.

16. J. David Hacker, "A Census-Based Count of the Civil War Dead," *CWH* 57 (December 2011): 307–348; James Q. Whitman, *The Verdict of Battle: The Law of Victory and the Making of Modern War* (Cambridge, MA: Harvard University Press, 2012), 5, 209–210.

17. Jaime Martinez, *Confederate Slave Impressment in the Upper South* (Chapel Hill: University of North Carolina Press, 2013); Glenn Brasher, *The Peninsula Campaign and the Necessity of Emancipation: African Americans and the Fight for Freedom* (Chapel Hill: University of North Carolina Press, 2014); *POCBB, I*, 107 .

18. Kate Masur, "'A Species of Philological Vegetation': The Word 'Contraband' and the Meanings of Emancipation in the United States," *JAH* 93 (March 2007): 1050–1084; David Williams, *I Freed Myself: African American Self-Emancipation in the Civil War Era* (New York: Cambridge University Press, 2014), 73–81.

19. The historian Kate Masur argues that Butler's language deliberately blurred the distinction in the laws of war between what could be done to neutrals as opposed to enemy combatants. Masur, "'A Species of Philological Vegetation,'"

1054. Her interpretation is persuasive, but few people at the time had enough familiarity with the details of the laws of war to notice this difference. Burrus M. Carnahan offers a contrary reading that emphasizes the legality of the order under domestic law. Carnahan, *Act of Justice: Lincoln's Emancipation Proclamation and the Law of War* (Lexington: University Press of Kentucky, 2007), 84–85.

20. Butler to Stanton, May 25, 1862, *OR*, I, 15: 439–441.

21. Butler to Stanton, May 25, 1862, *OR*, I, 15: 439–440; James G. Hollandsworth, Jr., *The Louisiana Native Guards: The Black Military Experience during the Civil War* (Baton Rouge: Louisiana State University Press, 1998), 12–16; Joseph T. Glatthaar, *Forged in Battle: The Civil War Alliance of Black Soldiers and White Officers* (New York: Meridian, 1990), 7–9; Hollandsworth, *The Louisiana Native Guards*, 16–17, 1–9; George S. Denison to Salmon P. Chase, September 9, 1862, in Butler, *POCBB*, II, 270.

22. Miles to Davis, June 11, 1862, *OR*, II, 3: 898.

23. Winthrop Jordan, *Tumult and Silence at Second Creek: An Inquiry into a Civil War Slave Conspiracy*, rev. ed. (Baton Rouge: Louisiana State University Press, 1995); Williams, *I Freed Myself*, 56–59, 64–68; Herbert Aptheker, *American Negro Slave Revolts* (1943. New York: International, 2013), 359–367; Ruggles to Butler, in Butler, *POCBB*, II, 67–69; Butler to Sarah H. Butler, July 25, 1862, in Butler, *POCBB*, II, 109–110; *AIFC*, Roll 199: James McKaye, "The Emancipated Slave Face to Face with His Old Master," 27.

24. Butler to Weitzel, November 2, 1862, *OR*, I, 15: 162; Weitzel to Strong, November 5, 1862, *OR*, I, 15: 171–172.

25. Butler to Weitzel, November 6, 1862, *OR*, I, 15: 165.

26. Carnahan, *Act of Justice*, 61–62.

27. William A. Blair, *With Malice toward Some: Treason and Loyalty in the Civil War Era* (Chapel Hill: University of North Carolina Press, 2014), 67.

28. *London Globe*, February 4, 1861; "Humiliating," *New York Times*, May 18, 1861; Sinclair Tousey to the *New York Times*, August 7, 1861.

29. Lee to John Winder, July 5, 1861, *The Wartime Papers of R. E. Lee*, 57.

30. Davis to Lincoln, July 6, 1861 (221–222), *PJD 1861*. Robert Toombs had already established the Confederacy's willingness to retaliate if the United States did not respect letters of marque. Toombs to Yancey, Rost, and Mann, May 18, 1861, *MPC*, II, 27.

31. Jefferson Davis "to the Congress of the Confederate States," Richmond, November 18, 1861, *PJD 1861*, 417–418. Excerpts of this speech, often including the section on prisoners at sea, were reprinted in many Southern newspapers.

32. Mark Weitz, *The Confederacy on Trial: The Piracy and Sequestration Cases of 1861* (Lawrence: University Press of Kansas, 2005), 161, 189; Blair, *With Malice toward Some*, 75.

33. Judah P. Benjamin to John Winder, in "The Retaliatory Measures," *Cincinnati Catholic Telegraph and Advocate*, November 30, 1861; Weitz, *The Confederacy on Trial*, 198; *Pittsfield (MA) Sun*, May 9, 1861; "Privateers of the South—What the North may do, in Retaliation," *San Francisco Bulletin*, May 8, 1861.

34. London *Morning Post*, March 17, 1862; Henry Hotze, *Henry Hotze, Confederate Propagandist: Selected Writings on Revolution Recognition, and Race* (Tuscaloosa: University of Alabama Press, 2008).

35. D. H. Dilbeck, "'The Genesis of This Little Tablet with My Name': Francis Lieber and the Wartime Origins of General Orders No. 100," *JCWE* 5 (June 2015), 237; *The Prize Cases*. 67 U.S. 625 (1863); Cowan, Senate, July 30, 1861, *CG*, 37th Congress, First Session, 341; Andrew Kent, "The Laws of War during the Civil War," *Notre Dame Law Review* 85 (2010), 1841.

36. Edward Everett, *An Address Delivered at the Inauguration of the Union Club* (Boston: Little Brown, 1863), 48, in *Civil War Politics: Pamphlets*, vol. 1, NL.

37. Blair, *With Malice toward Some*, 88.

38. Francis Lieber to Edward Bates, November 9, 1862, Box 23, Lieber Papers, HH; James A. Hamilton, "State Sovereignty: Rebellion Against the United States by the People of a State Is Its Political Suicide" (New York: Baker and Godwin, 1862), 27.

39. Anne Rubin, *A Shattered Nation: The Rise and Fall of the Confederacy, 1861–1868* (Chapel Hill: University of North Carolina Press, 2005), 14–25; Davis, Inaugural Address, February 22, 1862, *MPC*, I, 188; William J. Cooper, *Jefferson Davis, American* (New York: Vintage, 2000), 401. Even much later in the war, Davis recited and reasserted the Confederate claim to just cause in the war. See Davis, "Message to Congress," January 12, 1863, *MPC*, I, 286–289, and Davis, "Message to Congress," December 7, 1863, *MPC*, I, 379.

40. Thomas M. Key to Stanton, June 16, 1862, LoC, Edwin M. Stanton Papers, Reel 3; Davis, Message to Congress, July 20, 1861, in *MPC*, I, 119–120. Similar language appears in most of Davis's public addresses. See, for instance, Davis, "Message to Congress," November 18, 1861, *MPC*, I, 141; Davis "Fasting Proclamation," May 3, 1862, *MPC*, I, 227; Davis, "Message to Congress," August 18, 1862, *MPC*, I, 233; and many others.

41. George Rable, *Damn Yankees! Demonization and Defiance in the Confederate South* (Baton Rouge: Louisiana State University Press, 2015), 55–56; John T. Wightman, *The Glory of God, The Defense of the South. A Discourse delivered in*

the Methodist Episcopal Church, South (Portland, ME: B. Thurston, 1871), in *Civil War Pamphlets, 1861–71*, NL; Russell, August 30, 1862, *SHSP* 44 (1925): 281.

42. For a brilliant analysis of the often unintended role of metaphors and figurative language in the context of a military conflict, see Louis Perez's analysis of the American role in the Spanish American War. Perez, *Cuba in the American Imagination: Metaphor and the Imperial Ethos* (Chapel Hill: University of North Carolina Press, 2011).

43. *CG*, 37th Congress, First Session; "The Pickens-and-Stealing's Rebellion," *The Atlantic Monthly* (June 1861); *Speech of Hon. E. C. Benedict, in the Assembly of the State of New York, April 6, 1864* (Albany: Weed, Parsons, 1864), 3, in *Civil War Politics: Pamphlets*, vol. 3, NL; Everett, *An Address Delivered at the Inauguration of the Union Club*; Speech of Admiral Paulding, "Opinions of Prominent Men concerning The Great Questions of the Times Expressed in their letter to the Loyal National League, on Occasion of The Great Mass Meeting of the League" (New York: C. S. Wescott & Co., 1863), 31; Speech of Oliver Morton in "The Sumter Anniversary, 1863. Opinions of Many Loyalists concerning The Great Question of the Times," Mass Meeting at Union Square, New York (New York: C. S. Westcott, 1863), 42.

44. *Speech of Hon. W. J. Heacock, of Fulton and Hamilton, In Favor of a Vigorous Prosecution of the War.* No. 18, Documents from the N.Y. State Union Central Committee (Albany: Weed, Parsons & Co, 1863), 4, in *Civil War Politics: Pamphlets*, vol. 1, NL; Speech of Judge Daly, Loyal Reprints No. 3: "The Great Mass Meeting of Loyal Citizens, at Cooper Institute, March 6, 1863," NYPL, 9–10.

45. *Proceedings of the Convention of Loyal Leagues held at Mechanics Hall, Utica* (New York: Wm. C. Bryant & Co., 1863), 50.

46. Francis Lieber to Edward Bates, July 23, 1861, Box 23, Lieber Papers, HH; Alexander W. Randall, "Governor's Message," *Wisconsin Daily Patriot*, May 15, 1861.

47. J. Matthew Gallman, *Defining Duty in the Civil War: Personal Choice, Popular Culture, and the Union Home Front* (Chapel Hill: University of North Carolina Press, 2015), 130; "Loyalty," *North American Review* (January 1862): 153–174; Henry Ward Beecher, *Freedom and War. Discourses on Topics Suggested by the Times* (Boston: Ticknor and Fields, 1863), 90.

48. Charles Stillé, *How a Free People Conduct a Long War: A Chapter from English History* (New York: Anson D. F. Randolph, 1863), 25.

49. Gallman, *Defining Duty in the Civil War*, 132; Goodwin, *Christianity versus Treason and Slavery: Religion Rebuking Sedition*, Resolutions endorsed by the Protestant Episcopal Church of Pennsylvania, 4, 10.

50. Gallman, *Defining Duty in the Civil War*, 133; D. R. Brewer, *The Wrath of Man Compelled to Praise God. A Sermon* (New York: Anson D. F. Randolph, 1862), 5–6, in *Civil War Politics: Pamphlets*, vol. 1, NL.

51. Henry W. Bellows, *The State and the Nation—Sacred to Christian Citizens. A Sermon Preached in All Souls' Church, New York* (New York: James Miller, 1861), in *Civil War Pamphlets, 1861–71*, NL; B. H. Nadal, *A Christian Nation's Ordeal. A Fast-Day Sermon.* (Washington, DC: M'Gill & Witherow, 1864), 5, 14; James A. Thome, "What Are We Fighting For?," Occasional No. 2, American Reform Tract and Book Society (Cincinnati, OH: nd).

52. Peter J. Parish, "The War for the Union as a Just War," in *Aspects of War in American History*, ed. David K. Adams and Cornelis A. van Minnen (Keele, UK: Keele University Press, 1997), 95.

53. Henry Alden, "Pericles and President Lincoln," *Atlantic Monthly* 65 (March 1863), 389; Charles D. Drake, *The Rebellion: Its Character, Motive, and Aim*, delivered in Washington, MO, July 4, 1862, np, 7, in *Civil War Politics*, vol. 1, NL.

54. D. A. Washbrook, "India, 1800–1860: The Two Faces of Colonialism," in *The Oxford History of the British Empire: The Nineteenth Century*, ed. Andrew Porter (Oxford: Oxford University Press, 1990), 395–421. A useful recent survey of the event written for a popular audience is Pramod K. Nayar, *Indian 1857: The Great Uprising* (New Delhi: Penguin, 2007).

55. "Important from Charleston," *New York Times*, April 17, 1861; "Our New Orleans Correspondence," *New York Times*, January 3, 1863; "A Peep at Diplomacy," *New York Times*, September 8, 1863; "Affairs in England," *New York Times*, November 7, 1863.

56. "From Rebeldom," *New York Times*, January 3, 1862. See also "Our Enemy.—The reports of atrocities committed by the Southern,"*Christian Recorder*, August 10, 1861; "American Topics Abroad," *New York Times*, June 28, 1861; "What General Banks Thinks of the Rebellion," *New York Times*, August 5, 1861; "Our Lookout Valley Correspondent," *New York Times*, May 5, 1864; "What Can be Done for Our Prisoners?," *New York Times*, December 27, 1864. Confederates used the word in the same way. See "What Brave Men Can Do," *Richmond Daily Dispatch*, August 20, 1863.

57. J. W. Thayer to Edwin M. Stanton, February 27, 1864, *OR*, I, 34(2): 443. See also S. R. Curtis to "Citizens of Kansas City," March 4, 1864, *OR*, I, 34(2): 500; and Henry C. Daniel to Jefferson Davis, October 3, 1862, *OR*, II, 4: 923.

58. "News from Washington," *New York Times*, May 1, 1862; and "Foreign Censors Again," *New York Times*, July 20, 1862.

59. "Rebel Ferocity," *New York Times*, September 4, 1862.

60. "Notes of the War—The Situation of Affairs in the West," *Charleston Mercury*, August 25, 1863.

61. "Great War Meeting," *New York Times*, December 4, 1863; "What Shall We Do With Them?," *Atlantic Monthly*, April 1, 1862.

62. "Crushing Slavery in Rebellion," *Liberator*, May 27, 1864.

63. Arthur Jaffray, June 11, 1862 to *London Daily News*, reprinted as "European View of our Great Struggle: A Candid and Generous Englishman" in *New York Times*, July 10, 1862.

64. Ned Blackhawk, *Violence Over the Land: Indians and Empires in the Early American West* (Cambridge, MA: Harvard University Press, 2006); Peter J. Silver, *Our Savage Neighbors: How Indian War Transformed Early America* (New York: Norton, 2007); John K. McMahon, *History of the Second Seminole War, 1835–1842*, rev. ed. (Gainesville: University Press of Florida, 1985); Wayne E. Lee, *Barbarians and Brothers: Anglo-American Warfare, 1500–1850* (New York: Oxford University Press, 2011).

65. These references are ubiquitous, and a simple keyword search of Civil War–era newspapers turns up many hits. For examples of the casual tone, see "Civilized Warfare," *Charleston Mercury*, October 3, 1862; "Address of the Legislature," *Wisconsin Daily Patriot*, October 7, 1861.

66. "Spirit of the Rebellion," *Christian Recorder*, September 28, 1861.

67. Beecher quoted in George Rable, *God's Almost Chosen People: A Religious History of the Civil War* (Chapel Hill: University of North Carolina Press, 2010), 70, 158.

68. Charles Royster, *The Destructive War: William Tecumseh Sherman, Stonewall Jackson, and the Americans* (New York: Vintage, 1991), 241.

69. Sutherland, *A Savage Conflict*, chapter 3.

70. Robert R. Mackey, *The Uncivil War: Irregular Warfare in the Upper South, 1861–1865* (Norman: University of Oklahoma Press, 2004), 6; Paul Anderson, *Blood Image: Turner Ashby in the Civil War and the Southern Mind* (Baton Rouge: Louisiana State University Press, 2002), 129–132; Sutherland, *A Savage Conflict*, 127; Sherman to Grant, October 9, 1862, *OR*, I, 17(2): 273.

71. Clay Mountcastle, *Punitive War: Confederate Guerrillas and Union Reprisals* (Lawrence: University Press of Kansas, 2009), 79.

72. Lowndes Davis quoted in Sutherland, *A Savage Conflict*, 15.

73. Sutherland, *A Savage Conflict*, 14–15; Mark Geiger, *Financial Fraud and Guerrilla Violence in Missouri's Civil War, 1861–1865* (New Haven, CT: Yale University Press, 2010), 100–102.

74. Sutherland, *A Savage Conflict*, 20–25; Mackey, *Punitive War*, 24–30.

75. Brian D. McKnight and Barton A. Myers, "Introduction," in *The Guerrilla Hunters: Irregular Conflicts during the Civil War* (Baton Rouge: Louisiana State

University Press, 2017), 4–6; Martin Crawford, *Ashe County's Civil War: Community and Society in the Appalachian South* (Charlottesville: University Press of Virginia, 2001), 112; Judkin Browning, *Shifting Loyalties: The Union Occupation of Eastern North Carolina* (Chapel Hill: University of North Carolina Press, 2011), 138; Jonathan Dean Sarris, *A Separate Civil War: Communities in Conflict in the Mountain South* (Charlottesville: University of Virginia Press, 2006), 101.

76. John D. Fowler, "'We Can Never Live in a Southern Confederacy': The Civil War in East Tennessee," in *Sister States, Enemy States*, ed. Kent T. Dollar, Larry H. Whiteaker, and W. Calvin Dickinson (Lexington: University Press of Kentucky, 2009), 97–119, offers a good survey of this period. For more detailed treatments that elucidate the shifting contest among civilians, irregular combatants, and soldiers of both armies see Noel C. Fisher, *War at Every Door: Partisan Politics and Guerrilla Violence in East Tennessee, 1860–1869* (Chapel Hill: University of North Carolina Press, 1997); and W. Todd Groce, *Mountain Rebels: East Tennessee Confederates and the Civil War, 1860–1870* (Knoxville: University of Tennessee Press, 1999).

77. Fisher, *War at Every Door*, 62.

78. Fowler, "We Can Never Live in a Southern Confederacy," 109.

79. David Donald, "The Confederate Man as Fighting Man," *Journal of Southern History* 25 (May 1959), 178–193; "To Arms! To Arms!," Michael G. Harman, June 6, 1861, HH.

80. Dennis K. Boman, *Lincoln and Citizens' Rights in Civil War Missouri* (Baton Rouge: Louisiana State University Press, 2011), 129; James Turner Johnson, *Just War Tradition and the Restraint of War: A Moral and Historical Inquiry* (Princeton, NJ: Princeton University Press, 1981), 67.

81. Michael Walzer, *Just and Unjust Wars: A Moral Argument with Historical Illustrations*, 4th ed. (New York: Basic Books, 2006), 185.

82. Jordan Lewis Reed, "American Jacobins: Revolutionary Radicalism in the Civil War Era," Ph.D. diss, University of Massachusetts-Amherst, 2009; Lee, *Barbarians and Brothers*, 236; Williamson Murray and Wayne Wei-Siang Hsieh, *A Savage War: A Military History of the Civil War* (Princeton, NJ: Princeton University Press, 2016), 5, 515.

83. *SHSP* 44 (1923): 122, 129.

84. "An Act to authorize the formation of volunteer companies for local defence," October 13, 1862, *The Statutes at Large of the Confederate States of America, Passed at the Second Session of the First Congress; 1862* (Richmond: B. M. Smith, 1862), 90; *SHSP* 49 (1930): 98.

85. *SHSP* 40 (1930): 110.

86. Henry Foote of Mississippi introduced a bill to retaliate in August 1862. It was referred to committee and never passed. *SHSP* 44 (1925): 176–177.

Confederates could not even agree that Partisan Rangers should be protected like other troops when the Union regarded them as irregular forces. An effort to retaliate when Partisans were treated like "lawless bands of robbers and murderers" failed in the House. *SHSP* 44 (1923): 9. At a few points, Confederate leaders called on the United States to treat captured guerrillas as regular prisoners, but given their own summary execution of men caught out of uniform (usually regarded as "spies"), this was a half-hearted effort at best and never convinced the Union to even consider changing its policies.

87. Judah Benjamin to R. G. Barkham [and same to Samuel P. Gresham], March 19, 1862, *OR*, IV, 1: 1008.

88. General Order No. 54, August 1, 1862, *OR*, II, 4: 836–837.

89. James M. McPherson, *Embattled Rebel: Jefferson Davis as Commander in Chief* (New York: Penguin, 2014), 250.

90. Francis Lieber, "Guerilla Parties Considered with Reference to the Laws and Usages of War," *OR*, III, 2: 306; Charles Esdaile, *Fighting Napoleon: Guerrillas, Bandits and Adventurers in Spain, 1808–1814* (New Haven, CT: Yale University Press, 2004). Though this was the origin of the term *guerrilla*, Max Boot notes that "the practice is as ancient as mankind." Boot, *Invisible Armies: An Epic History of Guerrilla Warfare from Ancient Times to the Present* (New York: Liveright, 2013), xxii.

91. Curtis to Bartholow, March 30, 1863, *OR*, I, 22(2): 184; Mackey, *Punitive War*, 23–29; Lieber, "Guerilla Parties," 307; Banks to Richard Taylor, September 3, 1863, *PMR*, Department of the Gulf, #1738: Letters Sent, Box 5.

92. Lieber, "Guerilla Parties," 303, 305; Andrew Lang, "Challenging the Union Citizen-Soldier Ideal," in *The Guerrilla Hunters: Irregular Conflicts during the Civil War*, ed. Brian D. McKnight and Barton A. Myers (Baton Rouge: Louisiana State University Press, 2017), 313.

3. SOLDIERS AND CITIZENS

1. *LiebC*, Art. 23.

2. Gregory P. Downs, *After Appomattox: Military Occupation and the Ends of War* (Cambridge, MA: Harvard University Press, 2015), 6. William Whiting offered a detailed explanation at the time: "the President has the authority to establish military governments over enemy territory in time of war,—1st. Because such governments are necessary to the successful prosecution of hostilities, and to secure the objects for which war has been waged. 2d. Because the Constitution, by making him Commander-in-Chief of the army, confers on him the right to use all proper means of warfare, including war-governments and war-courts; and 3d. Because the Supreme Court have recognized this authority, and have

given to it the sanction of law by their decisions." Whiting, *Military Government of Hostile Territory in Time of War* (Boston: John L. Shorey, 1864), 66.

3. Gerald Capers, *Occupied City: New Orleans under the Federals, 1862–1865* (Lexington: University of Kentucky Press, 2014), 12; Chester G. Hearn, *The Capture of New Orleans, 1826* (Baton Rouge: Louisiana State University Press, 1995), 8, 16; Richard Nelson Current, *Lincoln's Loyalists: Union Soldiers from the Confederacy* (New York: Oxford University Press, 1992), 89–93, 213–216.

4. Chester G. Hearn, *When the Devil Came Down to Dixie: Ben Butler in New Orleans* (Baton Rouge: Louisiana State University Press, 1997), 64; Capers, *Occupied City*, 48.

5. Capers, *Occupied City*, 49; Hearn, *When the Devil Came Down to Dixie*, 70, 73–74; Bradley Clampitt, *Occupied Vicksburg* (Baton Rouge: Louisiana State University Press, 2016), 27.

6. Hearn, *When the Devil Came Down to Dixie*, 134.

7. Special Order No. 70, June 5, 1862, *OR*, II, 3: 645.

8. Butler to Stanton, June 10, 1862, *OR*, II, 3: 673–674. Butler's subordinate John Phelps explained it with greater brevity: Mumford "swung . . . for trampling on the national flag." J. W. Phelps to R. S. Davis, June 16, 1862, *FSSP*, I, Book 1: 212.

9. Butler to Stanton, April 29, 1862, *POCBB*, I: 425–428.

10. Hearn, *When the Devil Came Down to Dixie*, 138.

11. *New Orleans Delta*, undated, *OR*, II, 4: 134; *Richmond Dispatch*, "The Murderer Butler," July 5, 1862; *Hannibal (Missouri) Herald*, June 10, 1861; *POCBB*, I: 577.

12. George Randolph to Robert E. Lee, June 29, 1862, *OR*, II, 4: 792–793; and Lee to McLellan, July 6, 1862, *OR*, II, 4: 134; McClellan to Stanton, July 11, 1862, *OR*, II, 4: 170; Davis to Lee, August 1, 1862, *OR*, II, 4: 835. The Mumford affair also drew the repeated attention of the Confederate Congress. *SHSP* 44 (1925): 176; Halleck to Lee, August 7, 1862, *OR*, II, 4: 350.

13. Even critical historians find that New Orleans citizens received gentle treatment compared to other Southern places later in the war. Historian Gerald Capers, no fan of Butler, writes, "certainly in comparison with other areas of the South and with subsequent wars, the consequences in New Orleans were not nearly so bad as its residents thought at the time." Capers, *Occupied City*, 72; Hearn, *When the Devil Came Down to Dixie*, 81–94.

14. Hearn, *When the Devil Came Down to Dixie*, 133, 141.

15. Butler to Stanton, June 8, *PMR*, Department of the Gulf, #1738: Letters Sent.

16. Davis, speech at Richmond, January 5, 1863, *PJD*, 9, 10–16; Annual Address to Congress January 12, 1863, Printed in the *Journal of the CSA Congress*, January 14, 1863, 11–20; Davis, speech in Macon, September 23, 1864, *PJD*, 11, 61–63; *POCBB*, II: 557–562.

17. Stephen Ash, *When the Yankees Came: Conflict and Chaos in the Occupied South* (Chapel Hill: University of North Carolina Press, 1999), 77.

18. Welles Orders, August 18, 1862, sent to Farragut, Porter, etc., LOC, Gideon Welles Papers, Reel 5: Letterbooks.

19. Lee to Lazarus Lindsay, May 21, 1862, quoted in Michael Ballard, *Vicksburg: The Campaign that Opened the Mississippi* (Chapel Hill: University of North Carolina Press, 2004), 34; *OR*, I, 15: 475; *OR*, I, 15: 474.

20. Katherine Bentley Jeffrey, ed., *Two Civil Wars: The Curious Shared Journal of a Baton Rouge Schoolgirl and a Union Soldier on the USS Essex* (Baton Rouge: Louisiana State University Press, 2016), 100; Michael Bennett, *Union Jacks: Yankee Sailors in the Civil War* (Chapel Hill: University of North Carolina Press, 2004), 89, 90; Clay Mountcastle, *Punitive War: Confederate Guerrillas and Union Reprisals* (Lawrence: University Press of Kansas, 2009), 69–79.

21. Farragut to Lovell, June 17, 1862, *OR*, I, 15: 484–485.

22. *OR*, I, 15: 150. Residents of cities surrounded or besieged by Union armies experienced the same degree of uncertainty as those who faced the Northern navy. The example of Chattanooga, besieged briefly by Union General James Negley on June 7–8, 1862, manifested many of the same dynamics as the river towns discussed above. The Union shelled the city and did little damage, though Confederates denounced it as uncivilized conduct. J. Henry Haynie, *The Nineteenth Illinois: A Memoir of a Regiment of Volunteer Infantry* (Chicago: M. A. Donohue & Co., 1912), 173; H. A. Hambright to Negley, June 8, 1862, *OR*, I, 10(1): 919+; "News by Telegraph. The Bombardment of Chattanooga," *Charleston Mercury*, June 9, 1862; *Richmond Examiner*, June 10, 1862; Entry of June 9, 1862, in William R. Snell, *Myra Inman: A Diary of the Civil War in East Tennessee* (Macon, GA: Mercer University Press, 2000), 155; "From Chattanooga," *Macon Telegraph*, June 10, 1862.

23. William Blair, *With Malice toward Some: Treason and Loyalty in the Civil War Era* (Chapel Hill: University of North Carolina Press, 2014), 5, 103–105.

24. *PMR*, Dept. of the Cumberland, #1091.

25. *PMR*, Department of the Gulf, Entry #1844, Book 1: Provost Marshal, Letters Received, #1845, Box 1: Letters Received, 1863, #1845, Box 3: Letters Received, 1864.

26. John Carroll Elder Diary (Mss#4353), LSU; "Private diary of Commander H. H. Bell," *ORN*, I, 18: 706.

27. Charles East, ed., *Sarah Morgan: The Civil War Diary of a Southern Woman* (New York: Touchstone, 1992), 95.

28. Farragut to Lovell June 17, 1862, *OR*, I, 15: 484–485.

29. For a contrary view of the Union's occupation of southern Louisiana, and especially the bombardment of Baton Rouge, see Samuel Hyde, Jr., *Pistols and*

Politics: The Dilemma of Democracy in Louisiana's Florida Parishes, 1810–1899 (Baton Rouge: Louisiana State University Press, 1996), 111–115.

30. East, *Sarah Morgan*, 87.

31. *OR*, I, 15: 508–509.

32. James Taylor Graves to unknown, January 4, 1863, James Taylor Graves Papers, NL; Norman E. Clarke, Sr. *Warfare along the Mississippi: The Letters of Lieutenant Colonel George E. Currie* (Mt. Pleasant: Central Michigan University Press, 1961), 122; William T. Shepherd to "Dear Mother and Father," October 20, 1862, in Kurt Hackemer, ed., *To Rescue My Native Land: The Civil War Letters of William T. Shepherd, First Illinois Light Artillery* (Knoxville: University of Tennessee Press, 2005), 239–240.

33. Lee to Lovell, *OR*, I, 6: 652–653.

34. Mountcastle, *Punitive War*, 25–29; W. Wayne Smith, "An Experiment in Counterinsurgency: The Assessment of Confederate Sympathizers in Missouri," *Journal of Southern History* 35 (August 1969): 361–380; Thomas Worthington to commanding officer of the 42nd Missouri Vols., January 3, 1865, NARA, RG109, #465 (M416), Union Provost Marshal's File of Two or more Name Papers Relating to Citizens, Roll 1, Entry #13981.

35. Charles Wills, diary entries of January 17 and March 20, 1862, in Mary E. Kellogg, ed., *Army Life of an Illinois Soldier: Letters and Diary of Charles W. Wills* (Carbondale: Southern Illinois University Press, 1996); Daniel Sutherland, *A Savage Conflict: The Decisive Role of Guerrilla in the American Civil War* (Chapel Hill: University of North Carolina Press, 2009), 124–125; Butler to Williams, June 1, 1862, *OR*, I, 15: 25; Dudley to Hoffman, June 9, 1862, *OR*, I, 15: 20.

36. Butler to Sister Maria Clara, September 2, 1862, *OR*, I, 15: 563.

37. Meeting on the Right Bank, August 11, 1862, *OR*, I, 15: 795–796; Davis to Pond, *PJD*, 10: 452–453; *OR*, I, 26(1): 704–705. Pond remained committed to a regular war against the Union, admitting that he was "willing to see the war carried forward by legitimate means, and in accordance with the rules of civilized and decent warfare."

38. Butler to Stanton, in *POCBB*, II: 13.

39. Joseph Allen Frank and George A. Reaves, *"Seeing the Elephant": Raw Recruits at the Battle of Shiloh* (New York: Greenwood Press, 1989).

40. Ulysses S. Grant, *Personal Memoirs of U.S. Grant* (New York: Charles L. Webster, 1885), I, 356.

41. Robert R. Mackey, *The Uncivil War: Irregular Warfare in the Upper South, 1861–1865* (Norman: University of Oklahoma Press, 2004), 30.

42. Ash, *When the Yankees Came*, 47; Andrew William Fialka, "Controlled Chaos: Spatiotemporal Patterns within Missouri's Irregular Civil War," in *The Civil War Guerrilla: Unfolding the Black Flag in History, Memory, and Myth*, ed.

Joseph M. Beilein and Matthew C. Hurlbert (Lexington: University Press of Kentucky, 2015), 43–70.

43. Christopher Phillips, *The Rivers Ran Backward: The Civil War and the Remaking of the American Middle Border* (New York: Oxford University Press, 2016), 175–181.

44. Castel, "Estimate of the Number of Guerrillas who Operated in Southern and Border States during the Civil War," *Civil War Times Illustrated* (October 1974), 50.

45. Mark E. Neely, *The Civil War and the Limits of Destruction* (Cambridge, MA: Harvard University Press, 2007), 71. Daniel Sutherland has provided the fullest response to this argument. Daniel E. Sutherland, "Sideshow No Longer: A Historiographical Review of the Guerrilla War," *CWH* 46 (1): 5–23; and Sutherland, *Savage Conflict*, ix.

46. Ash, *When the Yankees Came*, chapter 3; Richard S. Ewell to Lizinka Bown, March 5, 1862, Folder E-332, Museum of the Confederacy, Richmond, Virginia. My thanks to Peter Carmichael for alerting me to this passage. For a similar sentiment before the fall of Mobile, Alabama, see Thomas H. Higginbotham to Sallie Higginbotham, August 5, 1864, Dore Schary Collection, NYPL.

47. This paragraph draws on Richard B. McCaslin, "The Price of Liberty: The Great Hanging at Gainesville," in *The Fate of Texas: The Civil War and the Lone Star State*, ed. Charles D. Grear (Fayetteville: University of Arkansas Press, 2008), 53–67. Northeast Florida, which the Union invaded four separate times, was similarly unsettled. By 1864, a motley mix of civilians and former soldiers began a debilitating campaign of mining the St. John's River, which derailed Union control of the region for months. The Union response exacerbated the social uncertainty by forcing guerrilla units and activities deeper underground. See Daniel L. Schafer, *Thunder on the River: The Civil War in Northeast Florida* (Gainesville: University Press of Florida, 2010), chapter 10.

48. NARA, Record Group #109, #182: Papers Relating to Confederate Sympathizers, Deserters, Guerrillas, and Prisoners, 1861–1865, Box 1; *PMR*, Arkansas, Letters Received, Book 360; Stathis Kalyvas, *The Logic of Violence in Civil Wars* (Cambridge: Cambridge University Press, 2006), 104–145.

49. My description of this process draws generally on the records of Union provost marshals across the South. One collection that illustrates the difficulties and demands of identifying disloyal Southerners is NARA, RG 109, #182: Papers Relating to Confederate Sympathizers, Deserters, Guerrillas, and Prisoners, 1861–1865, Box 1.

50. Affidavit of A. P. Appleby, February 15, 1865, NARA, Record Group #109, #182: Papers Relating to Confederate Sympathizers, Deserters, Guerrillas, and Prisoners, 1861–1865, Box 1.

51. George Pottiser to PM of Carrollton, MO, March 26, 1865, NARA, RG #109, #182: Papers Relating to Confederate Sympathizers, Deserters, Guerrillas, and Prisoners, 1861–1865, Box 2.

52. Sutherland, *A Savage Conflict*, 134–135, 147–150, 177–179.

53. Sherman to Rawlins, September 26, 1862, *PUSG*, 6, 429.

54. For similar events, see J. H. Hammond, Special Orders No. 283, *OR*, I, 17(2): 280–281; Stephen Hurlburt to John Rawlins, February 20, 1863, *OR*, I, 22(1): 230; and the burning of Donaldsonville, Louisiana, discussed above.

55. Sherman to Grant, October 9, 1862, *OR*, I, 17 (2): 272–274; *PUSG*, 6.

56. Williams Report, June 10, 1862, *PMR*, Department of the Gulf, Entry #1756; Department of the Gulf, Letters Received 1862, Box #1; Grant to Thomas A. Davies, October 30, 1862, *PUSG*, 6, 225; Entry of August 31, 1862, *The Civil War Diary of Gideon Welles, Lincoln's Secretary of the Navy, The Original Manuscript Edition*, ed. William E. Gienapp and Erica L. Gienapp, vol. 1: 1861– March 30, 1864 (Urbana: University of Illinois Press, 2014).

57. Quoted in Judkin Browning, *Shifting Loyalties: The Union Occupation of Eastern North Carolina* (Chapel Hill: University of North Carolina Press, 2011), 157; Mackey, *Uncivil War*, 36. A similarly hyperbolic call was made by the South Carolina governor in response to Sherman's invasion in December 1864. "Arm yourselves, fellow citizens, and shoot down every one of these thieves on any provocation—it is our only mode of redress." Lorien Foote, *The Yankee Plague: Escaped Union Prisoners and the Collapse of the Confederacy* (Chapel Hill: University of North Carolina Press, 2016), 63.

58. Mark Neely singles out this episode as one of the events that historians have used to identify the turn toward a total war. Neely, *Civil War and the Limits of Destruction*, 41–49. Neely opens his chapter by focusing on Michael Fellman's work on Missouri, which did initiate more careful research into the contours of violence in the Civil War, but Fellman made only one brief mention of the Palmyra executions. The event did not serve as the linchpin of his argument, as Neely suggests. Michael Fellman, *Inside War: The Guerrilla Conflict in Missouri during the American Civil War* (New York: Oxford University Press, 1989), 113–114.

59. Neely, *Civil War and the Limits of Destruction*, 43.

60. Dennis K. Boman, *Lincoln and Citizen's Rights in Civil War Missouri: Balancing Freedom and Security* (Baton Rouge: Louisiana State University Press, 2011), 134–135; Neely, *Civil War and the Limits of Destruction*, 46–49.

61. Samuel R. Curtis to T. H. Holmes, December 27, 1862, *OR*, I, 22(1): 879–880; Samuel R. Curtis to T. H. Holmes, December 24, 1862, *OR*, I, 22(1): 860–861.

62. Boman, *Lincoln and Citizens' Rights in Missouri*, 136; Lincoln to Charles Drake, *CWAL*, VI: 500.

63. Lance Janda, "Shutting the Gates of Mercy: The American Origins of Total War, 1860–1880," *Journal of Military History* 59 (January 1995), 16. Many officers went through this same process of gradually endorsing a harder war. On William T. Sherman, see Charles Royster, *The Destructive War: William Tecumseh Sherman, Stonewall Jackson, and the Americans* (New York: Vintage, 1991), 106–107. Christopher Phillips argues that "the western way of war had become the nation's." Phillips, *The Rivers Ran Backward*, 241.

64. Sherman to Rawlins, October 18, 1862, *OR*, I, 17(2): 280; Sherman to P. A. Fraser, October 22, 1862, *OR*, I, 17(2): 287–288; Sherman to Valeria Hurlburt, November 8, 1862.

65. Kristin Streater, "She-Rebels on the Border: Gender and Politics in Civil War Kentucky" (PhD diss., University of Kentucky, 2001); Streater, "'She-Rebels' on the Supply Line: Gender Conventions in Civil War Kentucky," in *Occupied Women: Gender, Military Occupation, and the American Civil War*, ed. LeeAnn Whites and Alecia P. Long (Baton Rouge: Louisiana State University Press, 2009), 88–102.

66. John Q. Anderson, ed., *Brokenburn: The Journal of Kate Stone, 1861–1868*, reprint (Baton Rouge: Louisiana State University Press, 1995), 188–203.

67. Ash, *When the Yankees Came*, 55, 61.

68. Hearn, *When the Devil Came Down to Dixie*; Alecia P. Long, "(Mis)remembering General Order No. 28: Benjamin Butler, the Woman Order, and Historical Memory," in Whites and Long, *Occupied Women*, 21, 25–30; Jacqueline G. Campbell, "'The Unmeaning Twaddle about General Order 28': Benjamin F. Butler and Confederate Women in Occupied New Orleans," *JCWE* 2 (March 2012): 24.

69. Browning, *Shifting Loyalties*, 4, 75–76.

70. J. L. Chandler to Lt. Col. Anderson, September 28, 1863, Book #353: Letters received, *PMR*, Department of Arkansas. Because Chandler was the provost marshal for the Department of Little Rock, he figures prominently in the correspondence that fills the many boxes of records filed in *PMR*, Department of Arkansas. The image of daily life in Little Rock and environs obtained through these reports contrasts with what Mackey and Sutherland portray, especially for late 1864–1865. One explanation is that as a garrison town, it was unusually stable.

71. Quoted in Thavolia Glymph, *Out of the House of Bondage: The Transformation of the Plantation Household* (Cambridge: Cambridge University Press, 2008), 115.

72. LeeAnn Whites, "Forty Shirts and a Wagonload of Wheat: Women, the Domestic Supply Line, and the Civil War on Western Border," *JCWE* 1 (January 2011): 56–78; and Joseph M. Beilein, Jr., *Bushwhackers: Guerrilla*

Warfare, Manhood, and the Household in Civil War Missouri (Kent, OH: Kent State University Press, 2015).

73. Stephanie McCurry, *Confederate Reckoning: Power and Politics in the Civil War South* (Cambridge, MA: Harvard University Press, 2010).

74. Helen Kinsella, *The Image before the Weapon: A Critical History of Distinction between Combatant and Civilian* (Ithaca, NY: Cornell University Press, 2011).

75. Leonard Richards, *Who Freed the Slaves: The Fight Over the Thirteenth Amendment* (Chicago: University of Chicago Press, 2015), 69.

76. Garrison quoted in Henry Mayer, *All on Fire: William Lloyd Garrison and the Abolition of Slavery* (New York: St. Martin's Press, 1998), 121, 237–238.

77. Garrison to Charles K. Whipple, July 19, 1862, *The Letters of William Lloyd Garrison*, vol. 3: *No Union with Slaveholders, 1841–1849*, ed. Walter M. Merrill (Cambridge, MA: Harvard University Press, 1973), 353; Frederick Douglass, "My Opposition to War: An Address Delivered in London, England, on May 19, 1846," *Liberator*, July 3, 1846. John Blassingame, et al, eds., *The Frederick Douglass Papers*. Series 1: *Speeches, Debates, and Interviews*, 5 vols. (New Haven, CT: Yale University Press, 1979), 1: 261; Henry Mayer, *All on Fire: William Lloyd Garrison and the Abolition of Slavery* (New York: St. Martin's Press, 1998), 479.

78. Douglas quoted in Patrick Rael, *Eighty-Eight Years: The Long Death of Slavery in the United States, 1777–1865* (Athens: University of Georgia Press, 2015), 203.

79. Rael, *Eighty-Eight Years*, 203–206; Manisha Sinha, *The Slave's Cause: A History of Abolition* (New Haven, CT: Yale University Press, 2016), 256–265.

80. Child quoted in Julie Roy Jeffrey, *The Great Silent Army of Abolitionism: Ordinary Women in the Antislavery Movement* (Chapel Hill: University of North Carolina Press, 1998), 177.

81. Garrison quoted in Sinha, *The Slave's Cause*, 556.

82. Lewis Perry, *Radical Abolitionism: Anarchy and the Government of God in Antislavery Thought* (Ithaca: Cornell University Press, 1973), 269.

83. "Proclaim Liberty throughout All the Land, to All the Inhabitants Thereof," *Liberator*, December 13, 1861. Adams's comments were quoted widely in other newspapers. "The Question of Slavery and the Present Rebellion," *New York Times*, May 16, 1861; "The Beginning of the End," *Harper's Weekly*, September 14, 1861; James Oakes, *Freedom National: The Destruction of Slavery in the United States, 1861–1865* (New York: Norton, 2013), 36–39.

84. Oakes, *Freedom National*, 345–352; Burrus M. Carnahan, *Act of Justice: Lincoln's Emancipation Proclamation and the Law of War* (Lexington: University Press of Kentucky, 2007), 8–10, 14–23.

85. Perry, *Radical Abolitionism*, details the changes in abolitionist-pacifists' views; see chapter 8 in particular. Minister quoted in George Rable, *God's Almost Chosen People: A Religious History of the Civil War* (Chapel Hill: University of North Carolina Press, 2010), 156; W. Caleb McDaniel, *The Problem of Democracy in the Age of Slavery: Garrisonian Abolitionists and Transatlantic Reform* (Baton Rouge: Louisiana State University Press, 2013), 113–115, 215; Mayer, *All on Fire*, 520–521, 554.

86. Stephen Ash, *Firebrand of Liberty: The Story of Two Black Regiments that Changed the Course of the Civil War* (New York: Norton, 2008), 5–11, Higginson quoted on p. 5; Frank Cirillo, "'The Power of Civilized Warriors to Unmake Slaves': White Abolitionists and the Emancipation Process, 1861–1862," paper presented at the Society for Civil War Historians Annual Meeting, June 2016, 7; "George Julian's Journal—The Passage of the 13th Amendment," *Indiana Magazine of History* 11, no. 4 (December 1915): 327.

87. Blair, *With Malice toward Some*, 84.

88. *American Destiny: What Shall It Be, Republican or Cossack? An Argument Addressed to the People of the Late Union, North and South* (New York: Columbian Association, 1864), 26, in *Civil War Politics: Pamphlets*, vol. 1, NL.

89. Blair, *With Malice toward Some*, 85–86.

90. Elisha R. Potter, *Upon the Present National Difficulties* (Providence: Cooke, Jackson, 1863), 8, in *Civil War Politics: Pamphlets*, vol. 2, NL.

91. Stephen D. Engle, *Gathering to Save a Nation: Lincoln and Union's War Governors* (Chapel Hill: University of North Carolina Press, 2016).

92. *FSSP*, II, Book 1: 75.

93. Perry, *Radical Abolitionism*, 271.

94. Andrew to Stanton, December 7, 1861, *FSSP*, I, Book 1: 353–354.

95. *FSSP*, I, Book 1: 356–357.

96. William B. Hesseltine, *Lincoln and the War Governors* (New York: Knopf, 1955), 219.

97. John Andrew to Benjamin Butler, April 25, 1861, Albert G. Browne, Jr., *Sketch of the Official Life of John A. Andrew, as Governor of Massachusetts* (New York: Hurd and Houghton, 1868), 96–97.

98. Benjamin Butler to John Andrew, May 9, 1861, Browne, *Sketch*, 98–99, 100.

99. Andrew to Edwin Stanton, May 19, 1862: Browne, *Sketch*, 71fn. The full letter is at *OR*, III, 2: 45; Engle, *Gathering to Save a Nation*, 207–209. John H. Matsui argues that a similar shift of attitude occurred among the soldiers (and officers) of the North's first majority Republican-led army, the brief-lived Army of Virginia. Soldiers accommodated themselves quickly to commander John Pope's harder war against disloyal citizens of the state in 1862. Matsui, *The

First Republican Army: The Army of Virginia and the Radicalization of the Civil War (Charlottesville: University Press of Virginia, 2016), especially Chapter 6.

100. Bruce Tap, *Over Lincoln's Shoulder: The Committee on the Conduct of the War* (Lawrence: University Press of Kansas, 1998), 26; T. Harry Williams, "The Committee on the Conduct of the War: An Experiment in Civilian Control," in *The Selected Essays of T. Harry Williams* (Baton Rouge: Louisiana State University Press, 1983), 15–30; Chandler quoted in Tap, *Over Lincoln's Shoulder*, 101–102; Speech of George Julian, "The Sumter Anniversary, 1863. Opinions of Many Loyalists concerning The Great Question of the Times" (New York: C. S. Westcott, 1863), 100; Linus H. Shaw, *The War, and Its Cause* (Waltham: Josiah Hastings, 1861), 5, in *Civil War Politics: Pamphlets*, vol. 2, NL.

101. Daniel W. Crofts, *Lincoln and the Politics of Slavery: The Other Thirteenth Amendment and the Struggle to Save the Union* (Chapel Hill: University of North Carolina Press, 2016), 9.

102. Samuel Kirkwood, speech at Des Moines, September 4, 1861, in H. W. Lathrop, *The Life and Times of Samuel J. Kirkwood: Iowa's War Governor* (Iowa City, 1893), 149; Kirkwood, Inaugural Address, January 14, 1862, in Lathrop, *Life and Times*, 197; Engle, *Gathering to Save a Nation*, 274; Kirkwood, Speech in Fayette County, September 8, 1863, in Lathrop, *Life and Times*, 257.

103. William Bender Wilson wrote "Curtin's First Military Telegraph," in *Andrew Gregg Curtin: His Life and Services*, ed. William H. Egle (Philadelphia: Avil, 1895), 347–348.

104. Silvana Siddali, *From Property to Person: Slavery and the Confiscation Acts, 1861–1862* (Baton Rouge: Louisiana State University Press, 2005), 2–3.

105. *American Destiny: What Shall It Be, Republican or Cossack? An Argument Addressed to the People of the Late Union, North and South* (New York: Columbian Association, 1864), 12, in *Civil War Politics: Pamphlets*, vol. 1, NL; *American Society for Promoting National Unity*, "God is Our Refuge and Strength" (New York: John F. Trow, 1861), 4, in *Civil War Politics*, vol. 1, NL.

106. *The Diary of Edward Bates, 1859–1866*, ed. Howard H. Beale (Washington, DC: Government Printing Office, 1933), 331; Henry Ward Beecher, *Freedom and War: Discourses on Topics Suggested by the Times* (Boston: Ticknor and Fields, 1863), 188.

107. E. V. Sumner to Mayor and Common Council, November 21, 1862, *OR*, I, 21: 783.

108. Robert E. Lee to Samuel Cooper, November 22, 1862, *OR*, I, 21: 1026–1027.

109. George Rable, *Fredericksburg! Fredericksburg!* (Chapel Hill: University of North Carolina Press, 2002), 161.

110. Rable, *Fredericksburg*, 162; Richard F. Miller, *Harvard's Civil War: A History of the Twentieth Massachusetts Volunteer Infantry* (Hanover, NH: University Press of New England, 2005), 195.

111. Rable, *Fredericksburg*, 163.

112. Summerhayes quoted in Miller, *Harvard's Civil War*, 197.

113. Virgil W. Matoon, quoted in Rable, *Fredericksburg*, 164.

114. Francis Augustín O'Reilly, *The Fredericksburg Campaign: Winter War on the Rappahannock* (Baton Rouge: Louisiana State University Press, 2003), chapter 4; Miller, *Harvard's Civil War*, 199–206; Rable, *Fredericksburg*, 168–171.

115. Rable, *Fredericksburg*, 177–182; Mason quoted in Miller, *Harvard's Civil War*, 207.

116. Rable, *Fredericksburg*, 84–86, 427–430.

117. Abbott to "My Dear Carry," December 21, 1862, in *Fallen Leaves: The Civil War Letters of Major Henry Livermore Abbott*, ed. Robert Garth Scott (Kent, OH: Kent State University Press, 1991), 150, 155; Aide quoted and discussed in Gary W. Gallagher, "Introduction," *The Fredericksburg Campaign: Decision on the Rappahannock* (Chapel Hill: University of North Carolina Press, 1995), vii, xiifn1.

118. Rable, *Fredericksburg*, 166, 183.

119. Lee to Seddon, December 12, 1862, and Lee to Cooper, April 10, 1863, both in *The Wartime Papers of R. E. Lee*, ed. Clifford Dowdey (Boston: Little Brown, 1961), 359, 367; Rable, *Fredericksburg*, 181.

120. William Osborn Stoddard, *Inside the White House in War Times* (New York: Charles Webster, 1890), 178–179.

4. KINDLING THE FIRES OF LIBERTY

1. Mark Grimsley, *The Hard Hand of War: Union Military Policy toward Southern Civilians* (Cambridge: Cambridge University Press, 1995), 210–211; Keith Wilson, "In the Shadow of John Brown: The Military Service of Colonels Thomas Higginson, James Montgomery, and Robert Shaw in the Department of the South," in *Black Soldiers in Blue: African American Troops in the Civil War Era*, ed. John David Smith, (Chapel Hill: University of North Carolina Press, 2002).

2. George C. Rable, *Damn Yankees! Demonization and Defiance in the Confederate South* (Baton Rouge: Louisiana State University Press, 2015); Jason Phillips, "A Brother's War? Exploring Confederate Perceptions of the Enemy," in *The View from the Ground: Experiences of Civil War Soldiers*, ed. Aaron Sheehan-Dean (Lexington: University Press of Kentucky, 2007), 67–90; Mark E. Neely, Jr. *The Civil War and the Limits of Destruction* (Cambridge, MA: Harvard University Press, 2007), 153.

3. Barbara Fields, *Slavery and Freedom on the Middle Ground: Maryland during the Nineteenth Century* (New Haven, CT: Yale University Press, 1984); Clarence L. Mohr, *On the Threshold of Freedom: Masters and Slaves in Civil War Georgia* (Athens: University of Georgia Press, 1986); Lynda J. Morgan, *Emancipation in Virginia's Tobacco Belt, 1850–1870* (Athens: University of Georgia Press, 1992); Susan O'Donovan, *Becoming Free in the Cotton South* (Cambridge, MA: Harvard University Press, 2007); Kate Masur, *An Example for All the Land: Emancipation and the Struggle over Equality in Washington, D.C.* (Chapel Hill: University of North Carolina Press, 2010); Ira Berlin, *The Long Emancipation: The Demise of Slavery in the United States* (Cambridge, MA: Harvard University Press, 2015).

4. Gary W. Gallagher, *The Union War* (Cambridge, MA: Harvard University Press, 2011); Chandra Manning, *What This Cruel War Was Over: Soldiers, Slavery and the Civil War* (New York: Knopf, 2007).

5. John Sifton, *Violence All Around* (Cambridge, MA: Harvard University Press, 2015), 136.

6. Adam I. P. Smith, *The Stormy Present: Conservatism and the Problem of Slavery in Northern Politics, 1846–1865* (Chapel Hill: University of North Carolina Press, 2017); Andrew Mach, "'The Name of Freeman Is Better Than Jesuit': Anti-Catholicism, Republican Ideology, and Cincinnati Political Culture, 1853–1854," *Ohio Valley History* 15 (Winter 2015): 3–21; Tyler Anbinder, *Nativism and Slavery: The Northern Know Nothings and the Politics of the 1850s* (New York: Oxford University Press, 1992).

7. David Grimsted, *American Mobbing, 1828–1861: Toward Civil War* (New York: Oxford University Press, 1998), 101. Grimsted estimates that 80 percent of the fatalities in "insurrections" were enslaved people.

8. Lincoln, "First Inaugural," *CWAL*, IV: 265.

9. John P. Wederstrandt to Shepley, September 19, 1862, *FSSP*, I, Book 1: 220; Winthrop D. Jordan, *Tumult and Silence at Second Creek: An Inquiry into a Civil War Slave Conspiracy*, rev. ed. (Baton Rouge: Louisiana State University Press, 1996); Joshua D. Rothman, *Flush Times and Fever Dreams: A Story of Capitalism and Slavery in the Age of Jackson* (Athens: University of Georgia Press, 2012).

10. William Lambert, "public address," December 2, 1859, *BAP*, 51–52; Edward L. Ayers and Scott Nesbitt, "Seeing Emancipation: Scale and Freedom in the American South," *JCWE* 1 (April 2011): 3–22.

11. Colin Woodward, *Marching Masters: Slavery, Race, and the Confederate Army during the Civil War* (Charlottesville: University Press of Virginia, 2014), 121–122; David G. Smith, "The Capture of African Americans during the Confederate Invasions of Pennsylvania: Part of a Virginia Way of War?," paper presented to the Douglas Southall Freeman Southern Intellectual History Conference, Richmond, VA, February 2002.

12. Earl Hess, *Civil War in the West: Victory and Defeat from the Appalachians to the Mississippi* (Chapel Hill: University of North Carolina Press, 2008), 235; Amy Taylor, *Embattled Freedom: Journeys through the Civil War's Slave Refugee Camps* (Chapel Hill: University of North Carolina Press, forthcoming), 56–57.

13. William C. Davis, *Battle at Bull Run: A History of the First Major Campaign of the Civil War* (Baton Rouge: Louisiana State University Press, 1977); G.O. No. 16, September 23, 1861, *FSSP,* I, Book 1: 348–349; Stephen W. Sears, *George B. McClellan: The Young Napoleon* (New York: Ticknor and Fields, 1988), 227–228.

14. Jaime Martinez, *Confederate Slave Impressment in the Upper South* (Chapel Hill: University of North Carolina Press, 2013); de Joinville quoted in Glenn David Brasher, *The Peninsula Campaign and the Necessity of Emancipation: African Americans and the Fight for Freedom* (Chapel Hill: University of North Carolina Press, 2014), 135–148; James Marten, "A Feeling of Restless Anxiety: Loyalty and Race in the Peninsula Campaign and Beyond," in *The Richmond Campaign,* ed. Gary W. Gallagher (Chapel Hill: University of North Carolina Press, 2000), 121–152; Louis S. Gerteis, *From Contraband to Freedman: Federal Policy toward Southern Blacks, 1861–1865* (Westport, CT: Greenwood Press, 1973).

15. Willie Lee Rose, *Rehearsal for Reconstruction: The Port Royal Experiment* (Indianapolis: Bobbs-Merrill, 1964); Patricia Click, *Time Full of Trial: The Roanoke Island Freedmen's Colony, 1862–1867* (Chapel Hill: University of North Carolina Press, 2001); O'Donovan, *Becoming Free*; Silvana Siddali, *From Property to Person: Slavery and the Confiscation Acts, 1861–1862* (Baton Rouge: Louisiana State University Press, 2005), 94, 225, 249–255.

16. Christopher Phillips, *The Rivers Ran Backward: The Civil War and the Remaking of the American Middle Border* (New York: Oxford University Press, 2016), 261. Brian D. McKnight describes a similar degree of chaos in the Cumberland region of Tennessee and Kentucky, east of Nashville. McKnight, *Confederate Outlaw: Champ Ferguson and the Civil War in Appalachia* (Baton Rouge: Louisiana State University Press, 2011), 123; Daniel E. Sutherland, *A Savage Conflict: The Decisive Role of Guerrilla in the American Civil War* (Chapel Hill: University of North Carolina Press, 2009), chapter 10.

17. Judkin Browning, *Shifting Loyalties: The Occupation of Eastern North Carolina* (Chapel Hill: University of North Carolina Press, 2014), 6, 88; Stephen Ash, *When the Yankees Came: Conflict and Chaos in the Occupied South, 1861–1865* (Chapel Hill: University of North Carolina Press, 1999), 158; James Oakes, *Freedom National: The Destruction of Slavery in the United States, 1861–1865* (New York: Norton, 2012).

18. Manisha Sinha, *The Slave's Cause: A History of Abolition* (New Haven, CT: Yale University Press, 2016); Lincoln, "Address at Sanitary Fair," *CWAL*, VII: 302.

19. James McPherson, *For Cause and Comrades: Why Soldiers Fought the Civil War* (New York: Oxford University Press, 1993); William J. Cooper, Jr., *Jefferson Davis, American* (New York: Vintage, 2000), 8; Alexander Stephens, "Corner Stone Speech," Savannah, Georgia, March 21, 1861, available at http://teaching americanhistory.org/library/document/cornerstone-speech/.

20. Oakes offers a slightly different reading, arguing that "slavery's opponents argued that military emancipation was fully constitutional because it was the accepted practice under the laws of war, laws which were themselves embedded within the constitution." Oakes, *Freedom National*, 40.

21. Lincoln to James C. Conklin, August 26, 1863, *LP*.

22. "How to End the War," *Douglass' Monthly*, May 1861; H. Ford Douglas to Ralph Roberts, January 11, 1863, in *BAP*, 169–170.

23. Daniel W. Crofts's recent book, *Lincoln and the Politics of Slavery: The Other Thirteenth Amendment and the Struggle to Save the Union* (Chapel Hill: University of North Carolina Press, 2016), offers the most persuasive and comprehensive account of the attitudes of this community toward slavery on the eve of war. William Barrows, *The War and Slavery; and their Relations to each other. A discourse delivered in the Old South Church, Reading, Mass* (Boston: John M. Whittemore, 1863), 10, in *Civil War Pamphlets, 1861–71*, NL; Chase quoted in Eric Foner, *The Fiery Trial: Abraham Lincoln and American Slavery* (New York: Norton, 2010), 219.

24. *Blackwood's Edinburgh Magazine* 92 (Nov. 1862): 636; "The Emancipation Proclamation in England," *Richmond Daily Dispatch*, October 25, 1862; "The London Press on Mr. Gladstone's Speech," *Richmond Daily Dispatch*, November 1, 1862; "An English Opinion of the American Constitution, *Richmond Daily Dispatch*, December 13, 1862.

25. "A Word for the Negro," February 12, 1863, in *Henry Hotze, Confederate Propagandist: Selected Writings on Revolution Recognition, and Race* (Tuscaloosa: University of Alabama Press, 2008), 194.

26. Lieber to Edward Bates, June 8, 1862, Box 23, Lieber Papers, HH. Other legal experts concurred. See William Whiting: "it is in accordance with the law of nations and with the practice of civilized belligerents in modern times, to liberate enemy's slaves in time of war by military power." Whiting, *War Powers of the President, and the Legislative Powers of Congress, in Relation to Rebellion, Treason, and Slavery*, 2nd ed. (Boston: J. L. Shorey, 1862), 69; Daniel Gardner, *A Treatise on the Law of the American Rebellion and our True Policy, Domestic and Foreign* (New York: John W. Amerman, 1862); *AFIC*, "Final Report," May 15,

1864, *OR*, III, 4: 347; Matthew J. Mancini, "Francis Lieber, Slavery, and the 'Genesis' of the Laws of War," *Journal of Southern History* 77 (May 2011), 337.

27. *LiebC*, Articles 42–43.

28. Philip D. Morgan and Andrew Jackson O'Shaughnessy, "Arming Slaves in the American Revolution," in *Arming Slaves: From Classical Times to the Modern Age*, ed. Christopher Leslie Brown and Philip D. Morgan (New Haven, CT: Yale University Press, 2006), 187, 182.

29. Diary entry of July 23, 1863, in *The Civil War Diary of Gideon Welles, Lincoln's Secretary of the Navy, The Original Manuscript Edition*, ed. William E. Gienapp and Erica L. Gienapp (Urbana: University of Illinois Press, 2014), 257; William A. Blair, *With Malice toward Some: Treason and Loyalty in the Civil War Era* (Chapel Hill: University of North Carolina Press, 2014), 97–98; Foner, *The Fiery Trial*, 242; Whiting, *War Powers of the President*, 46, 51, 58; *Speech of Gen. A. J. Hamilton, of Texas at the War Meeting at Faneuil Hall* (Boston: T. R. Marvin & Son, 1863), 46, in *Civil War Politics*, vol. 1, NL.

30. Lincoln, *CWAL* VI: 29; Philip Paludan, "The Civil War Considered as a Crisis in Law and Order," *American Historical Review* 77 (October 1972): 1013–1034; Burrus M. Carnahan, *Act of Justice: Lincoln's Emancipation Proclamation and the Law of War* (Lexington: University Press of Kentucky, 2007), 141.

31. *Henry Hotze, Confederate Propagandist: Selected Writings on Revolution Recognition, and Race* (Tuscaloosa: University of Alabama Press, 2008), 192; George Rable, *Damn Yankees! Demonization and Defiance in the Confederate South* (Baton Rouge: Louisiana State University Press, 2015), 124–125; William J. Cooper, *Jefferson Davis, American* (New York: Vintage, 2000), 439.

32. *SHSP* 44 (1925): 7; James A. Seddon to Robert Ould, *OR*, II, 6: 44; James A. Seddon to Robert Ould, June 24, 1863, *OR*, II, 6: 45; John R. Eakin, as quoted in Gregory J. W. Urwin, "'We Cannot Treat Negroes . . . as Prisoners of War': Racial Atrocities and Reprisals in Civil War Arkansas," in *Black Flag over Dixie: Racial Atrocities and Reprisals in the Civil War*, ed. Gregory J. Urwin (Carbondale: Southern Illinois University Press, 2004), 139; Jefferson Davis, "President's Annual Address to Congress," January 12, 1863, *Journal of the CSA Congress*, January 14, 1863, 17–18.

33. *SHSP* 49 (1930): 29–30; Clark and Henry, September 29, 1862, Senate and Hill, October 1, 1861, Senate; Howard C. Westwood, "Captive Black Union Soldiers in Charleston: What to Do?," in Urwin, *Black Flag over Dixie*, 34–35; Lee to Davis, June 10, 1863, in *The Wartime Papers of R. E. Lee*, ed. Clifford Dowdey (Boston: Little Brown, 1961), 508.

34. Seddon to Beauregard, November 20, 1862, quoted in James McPherson, *Embattled Rebel: Jefferson Davis as Commander in Chief* (New York: Penguin, 2014), 121.

35. Westwood, "Captive Black Union Soldiers," 35. Under Davis's order, white officers were to be treated in the same fashion.

36. Confederate Congressional debates, First Congress, Second Session and beginning of Third Session.

37. Retaliatory Act, May 1, 1863, Statutes at Large, CSA, First Congress, Third Session, ed. James M. Matthews (Richmond: R. M. Smith, 1863).

38. Westwood, "Captive Black Union Soldiers," 34–51, 47; *SHSP*, 52 (1930): 25; Lee to Davis, June 25, 1863, *The Wartime Papers of R. E. Lee*, 530–531.

39. Longstreet, quoted in Colin Woodward, *Marching Masters*, 23; Urwin, "Introduction," in Urwin, *Black Flag over Dixie*, 7.

40. Ash, *When the Yankees Came*, 163; Judkin Browning, *Shifting Loyalties: The Occupation of Eastern North Carolina* (Chapel Hill: University of North Carolina Press, 2014), 90, 81–82; Katharine Bentley Jeffrey, ed. *Two Civil Wars: The Curious Shared Journal of a Baton Rouge Schoolgirl and a Union Sailor on the USS Essex* (Baton Rouge: Louisiana State University Press, 2016), 123.

41. Chandra Manning, *Troubled Refuge: Struggling for Freedom in the Civil War* (New York: Knopf, 2016), 107; September 12, 1865, *FSSP*, I, Book 1: 387; O. A. A. Gardner to Curtis, February 16, 1863, *FSSP*, I, Book 1: 445–446; Oakes, *Freedom National*, 403–404.

42. Stephanie M. H. Camp, *Closer to Freedom: Enslaved Woman and Everyday Resistance in the Plantation South* (Chapel Hill: University of North Carolina Press, 2004), 129.

43. Fisk to Jas. E. Yeatman, March 25, 1865, *FSSP*, I, Book 1: 489; *FSSP*, I, Book 1: 615–616; Charles W. Joyner, *Down By the Riverside: A South Carolina Slave Community*, 2nd ed. (Urbana: University of Illinois Press, 1984), 55.

44. G.O. No. 4, July 4, 1862, *FSSP*, I, Book 1: 795–797.

45. Rothman, *Flush Times and Fever Dreams*; Jordan, *Tumult and Silence at Second Creek*.

46. REL to Seddon, January 10, 1863, *The Wartime Papers of R. E. Lee*.

47. W. E. B. Du Bois, *Black Reconstruction in America, 1860–1880* (1935. Cleveland: Meridian Books, 1962), chapter 4; Steven Hahn, *The Political Worlds of Slavery and Freedom* (Cambridge, MA: Harvard University Press, 2009), 58; Stephanie McCurry, *Confederate Reckoning: Power and Politics in the Civil War South* (Cambridge, MA: Harvard University Press, 2010), 261. Hahn is largely concerned with how we interpret the political meaning and shape of slave resistance, 72–73. He argues for the similarities between the US Civil War and Haitian Revolution by emphasizing the central roles of enslaved people and the outcomes. See chapter 2, esp. 87–97. My emphasis here is on how the process of fighting between black and white people during the Civil War shaped the broader pattern of violence in the war.

48. Ashli White, *Encountering Revolution: Haiti and the Making of the Early Republic* (Baltimore: Johns Hopkins University Press, 2010).

49. Augustus S. Montgomery to Maj-Genl Foster, May 12, 1863, *OR*, I, 18: 1067–1077; Seddon to Moore, July 18, 1863, *OR*, I, 18: 1067–1077. The War Department officer John B. Jones interpreted it as evidence that "a plan to incite servile insurrection has been adopted," but merely recorded the bureaucratic forwarding through channels in the department. John B. Jones, *A Rebel War Clerk's Diary* (New York: Sagamore Press, 1958), 217.

50. Semmes, October 1, 1862, Senate, *SHSP* 44 (1925), 26; *Speech of Hon. W. J. Heacock, of Fulton and Hamilton, In Favor of a Vigorous Prosecution of the War*, No. 18 Documents from the N.Y. State Union Central Committee (Albany: Weed, Parsons & Co, 1863), 5, in *Civil War Politics*, vol. 1, NL; Charles S. May, *Sustain the Government* (Lansing: John A. Kerr, 1863), 13, in *Civil War Politics*, vol. 2, NL.

51. Lincoln, "Emancipation Proclamation," *CWAL*, VI: 30.

52. Lincoln to Johnson, *OR*, III, 3: 103.

53. Testimony of B. K. Lee, Jr., AIFC, Roll 200; Testimony of Solomon Bradley, AFIC, Roll 200. Robert Smalls uses similar language in his deposition. Testimony of Robert Smalls, AFIC, Roll 200.

54. John David Smith, "Let Us All Be Grateful," in Smith, *Black Soldiers in Blue*, 1–79; Kathryn Shively Meier, "Lorenzo Thomas," in Smith, *Black Soldiers in Blue*, 268; Thomas to Senate Military Affairs Committee, May 30, 1864, *FSSP*, II, Book 2: 530–531; *American Freedmen's Inquiry Commission*, Preliminary Report, June 30, 1863, *OR*, III, 3: 435; Testimony of Col. Higginson, AFIC, Roll 200.

55. *New York Times* quoted in Stephen Ash, *Firebrand of Liberty: The Story of Two Black Regiments That Changed the Course of the Civil War* (New York: Norton, 2008), 196–197, 193; Meier, "Lorenzo Thomas," 268, 257.

56. Richard M. Reid, *Freedom for Themselves: North Carolina's Black Soldiers in the Civil War Era* (Chapel Hill: University of North Carolina Press, 2014), xii, 1–8; *FSSP*, II, Books 1–2; Ash, *Firebrand of Liberty*, xi–xii; soldier quoted in Richard Lowe, "Battle on the Levee: The Fight at Milliken's Bend," in Smith, *Black Soldiers in Blue*, 127–128.

57. *FSSP*, I, Book 1: 80–81; Reid, *Freedom for Themselves*, 113–114; Barton Myers, *Executing Daniel Blight: Race, Loyalty, and Guerrilla Violence in a Coastal Carolina Community, 1861–1865* (Baton Rouge: Louisiana State University Press, 2011), 85, 96, 88–89.

58. Myers, *Executing Daniel Blight*, 114; Reid, *Freedom for Themselves*, 134–135.

59. Lowe, "Battle on the Levee," 125. Lowe does offer solid evidence that some group of Confederates murdered two Union officers commanding these

troops the next day (both Louisianans). Lowe, "Battle on the Levee," 126, 134n40, 125.

60. Joseph T. Glatthaar, *General Lee's Army: From Victory to Collapse* (New York: Free Press, 2008), 19–20.

61. Kirby Smith, as quoted in Westwood, "Captive Black Union Soldiers," 41; *FSSP*, II, Book 2: 578. Smith was not the only one to arrive at this solution. Before the Battle of Olustee, Florida, in 1864, Col. Abner McCormick instructed his troops to "teach them [black troops] a lesson. I shall not take any negro prisoners in this fight." McCormick quoted in David J. Coles, "'Shooting Niggers Sir': Confederate Mistreatment of Union Black Soldiers at the Battle of Olustee," in Urwin, *Black Flag over Dixie*, 73.

62. James G. Hollandsworth, Jr., *The Louisiana Native Guard: The Black Military Experience during the Civil War* (Baton Rouge: Louisiana State University Press, 1998), 71; quotation from commanding officer of the 17th Arkansas Mounted Infantry in *OR*, II, 4: 258–259, 244, 289, 960–961; George L. Andrews to J. A. Logan, August 5, 1863, and Logan to Andrews, August 8, 1863, *PMR*, Department of the Gulf, Entry #1756, Letters Received 1863 (Box #2).

63. Cooper, *Jefferson Davis, American*, 439; James McPherson, *Embattled Rebel*, 171–172.

64. Hannah Johnson to Abraham Lincoln, July 31, 1863, in Ira Berlin and Leslie S. Rowland, eds. *Families and Freedom: A Documentary History of African-American Kinship in the Civil War Era* (New York: New Press, 1997), 81–82.

65. General Orders No. 252, July 31, 1863, *OR*, II, 6: 163. Roy P. Basler, the editor of Lincoln's papers, notes that the order was drafted by the War Department and signed by Lincoln. *Collected Works of Abraham Lincoln* (New Brunswick, NJ: Rutgers University Press, 1953), VII: 357n1.

66. James G. Hollandsworth, Jr., "The Execution of White Officers from Black Units by Confederate Forces during the Civil War," in Urwin, *Black Flag over Dixie*, 60; Theodore Hodgkins to Abraham Lincoln, April 18, 1864, in Ira Berlin, Joseph P. Reidy, and Leslie S. Rowland, eds., *Freedom's Soldiers: The Black Military Experience in the Civil War* (Cambridge: Cambridge University Press, 1998), 118–120; Burrus M. Carnahan, *Lincoln on Trial: Southern Civilians and the Law of War* (Louisville: University Press of Kentucky, 2010), 73.

67. Westwood, "Captive Black Union Soldiers," 34–51.

68. Foner *The Fiery Trial*, 254–255.

69. Douglass to George L. Stearns, August 1, 1863, quoted in Smith, "Let Us All Be Grateful," 47; James Oakes, *The Radical and the Republican: Frederick Douglass, Abraham Lincoln, and the Triumph of Antislavery Politics* (New York: Norton, 2007), 213–214; *Speech of Hon. Charles D. Drake, delivered before the National*

Union Association, at Cincinnati, October 1, 1864, np, 15, in *Civil War Politics,* vol. 1, NL.

70. *SHSP* 49 (1930): 167.

71. *FSSP,* II, Book 1: 232–263; *FSSP,* II, Book 1: 244; *FSSP,* II, Book 1: 262.

72. Grant to Taylor, June 22, 1863, NARA, Department of the Tennessee, PM Papers, #4709, Letters Sent, Book 1 of 4.

73. Lincoln, "Annual Message to Congress," December 8, 1863, quoted in Smith, "Let Us All Be Grateful," 63.

74. Ira Berlin's recent study of the end of slavery emphasizes violence as "ubiquitous" in the process of emancipation, though he considers the full range of antislavery activism over a century. When he writes that "the mobilization of warring armies that transformed the war for the union into a war for freedom ratcheted up the level of violence," he is correct, though most of that violence fell on the soldiers (both black and white) of the regular armies. Berlin, *The Long Emancipation,* 159, 31, 45.

75. Grant to Jesse Root Grant, May 6, 1861, *PUSG,* 2, 20.

76. *AFIC,* "Preliminary Report," June 30, 1863, *OR,* III, 3: 451; *AFIC,* "Final Report," May 15, 1864, *OR,* III, 4: 333.

77. Ash, *When the Yankees Came,* 160–162; Michael Fitzgerald, *Urban Emancipation: Popular Politics in Reconstruction Mobile, 1860–1890* (Baton Rouge: Louisiana State University Press, 2002), 21; Yael A. Sternhell, *Routes of War: The World of Movement in the Confederate South* (Cambridge, MA: Harvard University Press, 2012); David Silkenat, *Driven from Home: North Carolina's Civil War Refugee Crisis* (Athens: University of Georgia Press, 2016).

78. Diane Sommerville, *Rape and Race in the Nineteenth Century South* (Chapel Hill: University of North Carolina Press, 2004); 1920s history text quoted in Anne Sarah Rubin, *Through the Heart of Dixie: Sherman's March and American Memory* (Chapel Hill: University of North Carolina Press, 2014), 85; George Rable, *Civil Wars: Women and the Crisis of Southern Nationalism* (Urbana: University of Illinois Press, 1991), 116–120; Nancy Bercaw, *Gendered Freedoms: Race, Rights, and the Politics of Household in the Delta, 1861–1875* (Gainesville: University Press of Florida, 2003), 64.

79. *FSSP,* II, Book 1: 374; Sinha, *The Slave's Cause.*

80. *Appeal of the Western Freedmen's Aid Commission in behalf of the National Freedmen* (Cincinnati: NP, 1864), 5.

81. Testimony of George Cato, *TAS,* S.1, vol. 11, 99.

82. Laurent Dubois, "Avenging America: The Politics of Violence in the Haitian Revolution," in *The World of the Haitian Revolution* (Bloomington: Indiana University Press, 2009), 111–124; White, *Encountering Revolution,* 177–180.

NOTES TO PAGES 170–172

83. Laurent Dubois, *Avengers of the New World: The History of the Haitian Revolution* (Cambridge, MA: Harvard University Press, 2004), 110–111.

84. Dubois, "Avenging American," 120–122; C. L. R. James, *The Black Jacobins: Toussaint L'Ouverture and the San Domingo Revolution*, 2nd ed. (New York: Vintage, 1963), 370–374; John Barrow, 1806, quoted in *The Haitian Revolution: A Documentary History*, ed. David Geggus (Indianapolis: Hackett, 2014), 199; Ronald Angelo Johnson, *Diplomacy in Black and White: John Adams, Toussaint Louverture, and Their Atlantic Alliance* (Athens: University of Georgia Press, 2014), 120–130.

85. Matthew J. Clavin, "American Toussaints: Symbol, Subversion, and the Black Atlantic Tradition in the American Civil War," in *African Americans and the Haitian Revolution: Selected Essays and Historical Documents*, ed. Maurice Jackson and Jacqueline Bacon (New York: Routledge, 2010), 108; Patrick Rael, *Eighty-Eight Years: The Long Death of Slavery in the United States, 1777–1865* (Athens: University of Georgia Press, 2015), 157; Sinha, *The Slave's Cause*, 563–564. Cuban historian Ada Ferrer sees a similar process at work in Cuba, where enslaved people "talked, interpreted, and imagined what Haiti might portend." Ferrer, *Freedom's Mirror: Cuba and Haiti in the Age of Revolution* (New York: Cambridge University Press, 2014), 11.

86. A recent scholar has argued that white Americans changed their attitudes as well: "Many overcame their racialized views of the diaspora to see revolutionary images from Saint-Domingue as not dissimilar to those that played out on mainland soil in the 1770s." Johnson, *Diplomacy in Black and White*, 10.

87. White, *Encountering Revolution*, 2; Brandon R. Byrd, "An Experiment in Self-Government: Haiti in the African American Political Imagination, 1863–1915" (PhD diss., University of North Carolina, 2014), 15.

88. Abraham Bishop, 1791, quoted in Geggus, *The Haitian Revolution*, 194.

89. *FSSP*, II, Book 1: 80.

90. Matthew J. Clavin, *Toussaint Louverture and the American Civil War: The Promise and Peril of a Second Haitian Revolution* (Philadelphia: University of Pennsylvania Press, 2010), 1–3.

91. Julius Scott, "The Common Winds: Currents of Afro-American Communication in the Era of the Haitian Revolution" (PhD diss., Duke University, 1986); Greg Grandin, *The Empire of Necessity: Slavery, Freedom, and Deception in the New World* (New York: Metropolitan, 2014), 177.

92. Clavin, "American Toussaints," 115.

93. Mitch Kachun, *Festivals of Freedom: Memory and Meaning in African American Emancipation Celebrations, 1808–1915* (Boston: University of Massachusetts Press, 2006).

94. William Wells Brown, "From St. Domingo," 1854, in Jackson and Bacon, *African Americans and the Haitian Revolution*, 188.

95. Byrd, "An Experiment in Self-Government," 22–24; Grandin, *Empire of Necessity*, 197–198.

96. Mitch Kachun, "Antebellum African Americans, Public Commemoration, and the Haitian Revolution: A Problem of Historical Mythmaking," in Jackson and Bacon, *African Americans and the Haitian Revolution*, 93–107.

97. Brandon R. Byrd, "Black Republicans, Black Republic: African Americans, Haiti, and the Promise of Reconstruction," *Slavery and Abolition* 36 (2015), 546.

98. Quoted in Byrd, "An Experiment in Self-Government," 33; Clavin, *Toussaint Louverture*, chapter 4.

99. Clavin, *Toussaint Louverture*, chapter 1; Scott, "The Common Winds," 307–308.

100. Thomas Wentworth Higginson, "Gabriel's Defeat," *Atlantic Monthly* 10 (September 1862), 337.

101. Albert Raboteau, *Slave Religion: The "Invisible Institution" in the Antebellum South* (New York: Oxford University Press, 1978), 174–176; Charles F. Irons, *The Origins of Proslavery Christianity: White and Black Evangelicals in Colonial and Antebellum Virginia* (Chapel Hill: University of North Carolina Press, 2008), 4–6; Jon Butler, *Awash in a Sea of Faith: Christianizing the American People* (Cambridge, MA: Harvard University Press, 1990), 283; Whitemarsh B. Seabrook, quoted in Raboteau, *Slave Religion*, 169.

102. Raboteau, *Slave Religion*, 250; Eugene Genovese, *Roll Jordan Roll: The World the Slaves Made* (New York: Vintage, 1972), 252–255.

103. Raboteau, *Slave Religion*, 309–314. According to David Chappell, this same prophetic faith continued into the twentieth century, when it played a crucial role in shaping the modern Civil Rights movement. See David L. Chappell, *A Stone of Hope: Prophetic Religion and the Death of Jim Crow* (Chapel Hill: University of North Carolina Press, 2004). Donald G. Mathews's emphasis on slaves' premillennial quietism conveys a similar outlook. Mathews, *Religion in the Old South* (Chicago: University of Chicago Press, 1977), 223–224.

104. Maria quoted in Raboteau, *Slave Religion*, 309.

105. Mathews, *Religion in the Old South*, 225, 229.

106. David Williams, *I Freed Myself: African American Self-Emancipation in the Civil War Era* (Cambridge: Cambridge University Press, 2014), 88, 163–167; Herbert Aptheker, *American Negro Slave Revolts*, 6th ed. (New York: International, 2013), 363; Interview of John Ogee, *TAS*, S2, 8.7: 2974; Mary Chesnut quoted in Thavolia Glymph, *Out of the House of Bondage: The Transformation of the Plantation Household* (Cambridge: Cambridge University Press, 2008), 97; Crystal Feimster, *Southern Horrors: Women and the Politics of Rape and Lynching* (Cambridge, MA: Harvard University Press, 2011), 15–17.

107. John Rock, October 6, 1864, in *BAP*, 304–307.

108. Camp, *Closer to Freedom*, 119. Camp's astute cultural history emphasizes control of space as the essential attribute of American slavery. She demonstrates that the Civil War allowed enslaved people to accelerate the practice of truancy and escape that characterized much of the preceding decades. In a careful study, she never observes violence practiced against whites by escaping slaves. See especially chapter 5.

109. Charles Dewey to James Bowen, Feb. 19, 1864, *PMR*, Department of the Gulf, #1845, Box 1: Letters Received.

110. John M. Brooks et al. to Banks, nd (probably early 1864), *PMR*, Department of the Gulf, #1845, Box 1: Letters Received, 1863.

111. Unknown to J. A. Judson, May 1, 1865, *PMR*, Department of North Carolina and Virginia, #3230: Letters Sent; Testimony of William Moore, *TAS*, 7.6, 2769.

112. Glymph, *Out of the House of Bondage*, 108, 114; Hahn, *Political Worlds of Slavery and Freedom*, 71.

113. George L. Davis to James Bowen, August 21, 1863, *PMR*, Department of the Gulf, #1845, Box 1: Letters Received, 1863.

114. S. W. Sawyer to H. Kallenstroth, August 21, 1863, *PMR*, Department of the Gulf, #1845, Box 1: Letters Received, 1863; Ash, *When the Yankees Came*, 154–155, 167.

115. Interview of Thomas Cole, *TAS*, 4.1: 225–235.

116. Ash, *When the Yankees Came*, 155; Rubin, *Through the Heart of Dixie*, 82; Glymph, *Out of the House of Bondage*, 100, 108; Hahn, *Political Worlds of Slavery and Freedom*, 71; Woodward, *Marching Masters*, 113. The interviews with exslaves contain 456 entries for "runaway slaves." Only eighteen entries describe violence in conjunction with escape. This is an admittedly crude index that could undercount violence for many reasons, but as recent histories of slavery have shown, former bondspeople expressed no reluctance to describe the violence committed against them under slavery.

5. UNNECESSARY VIOLENCE

1. For texts that emphasize the code's positive influence, see John Fabian Witt, *Lincoln's Code: The Laws of War in American History* (New York: Free Press, 2012); and D. H. Dilbeck, *A More Civil War: How the Union Waged a More Just War* (Chapel Hill: University of North Carolina Press, 2016). For more critical evaluations, see Mark Grimsley, *The Hard Hand of War: Union Military Policy toward Southern Civilians, 1861–1865* (Cambridge: Cambridge University Press, 1995); and Michael Fellman, *Inside War: The Guerrilla Conflict in Missouri during the American Civil War* (New York: Oxford University Press, 1989). On

the difficulty of assessing the code's influence, L. Lynn Hogue notes, "it is easier to discover when a policy like the Code fails to work because it does not prevent a violation than it is to know how many times the existence of a norm fostered compliance with the Code." Hogue, "Lieber's Military Code and Its Legacy," in *Francis Lieber and the Culture of the Mind*, ed. Charles R. Mack and Henry H. Lesesne (Columbia: University of South Carolina Press, 2005), 57.

2. *LiebC*, Art. 14. Lincoln articulated a similar conception of military necessity, arguing "armies, the world over destroy enemie's property when they can not use it; and even destroy their own to keep it from the enemy." In short, "civilized belligerents do all in their power to help themselves, or hurt the enemy, except a few things regarded as barbarous or cruel—Among the exceptions are the massacres of vanquished foes, and non-combatants, male and female." Lincoln to James C. Conklin, August 26, 1863, *LP.* Harry Stout similarly criticizes the Lieber Code for using the concept of "military necessity" to sanction actions that the code itself had outlawed in principle. Harry Stout, *Upon the Altar of the Nation: A Moral History of the Civil War* (New York: Viking, 2006), 192–193; Daniel Sutherland raises a similar point in *A Savage Conflict: The Decisive Role of Guerrillas in the American Civil War* (Chapel Hill: University of North Carolina Press, 2009), 128.

3. Burrus M. Carnahan, "Lincoln, Lieber, and Laws of War: The Origins and Limits of the Principle of Military Necessity," *American Journal of International Law* 92 (April 1998), 216–217.

4. Norman E. Clarke, Sr., ed. *Warfare along the Mississippi: The Letters of Lieutenant Colonel George E. Currie* (Mt. Pleasant: Central Michigan University Press, 1961), 84.

5. Grant to Pemberton, December 15, 1862, Department of the Tennessee, #4709, Letters Sent, Book 1 of 4, NARA, PM Records.

6. Grant to Pemberton, March 2, 1863, NARA, Department of the Tennessee, PM Papers, #4709, Letters Sent, Book 1 of 4.

7. *LiebC*, Art. 44; *LiebC*, Art. 82.

8. Capt Godwin to P. H. Sheridan, August 5, 1863, *PMR*, Dept. of the Cumberland, #1091.

9. *PMR*, Department of the Gulf, Entry #1756, Letters Received 1863 (Box #3).

10. Lieber's biographer Frank Freidel asserts that "more than one Union officer who had been administering occupied territory informed Lieber how helpful the order had been." Frank Freidel, *Francis Lieber: Nineteenth-Century Liberal* (Baton Rouge: Louisiana State University Press, 1948), 338.

11. Halleck to Schofield, May 22, 1863, NARA, Headquarters of the Army, RG 108 Entry 8: Reports and Important Letters Sent, Volume 1.

NOTES TO PAGES 185–188

12. Mark Grimsley, "The Erosion of Noncombatant Immunity during the American Civil War," unpublished paper, Kings College, London, 1985, 20.

13. Mountcastle also emphasizes the fundamental vagueness in the code that allowed advocates of both conciliation and harsh treatment to cite it as an authority. Clay Mountcastle, *Punitive War: Confederate Guerrillas and Union Reprisals* (Lawrence: University of Kansas Press, 2009), 43–45. Gideon M. Hart argues "as a legal code, the Lieber Code was incredibly effective because it granted enormous power to military courts by setting forth a broad and flexible foundation for military jurisdiction." Hart, "Military Commissions and the Lieber Code: Toward a New Understanding of the Jurisdictional Foundations of Military Commissions," *Military Law Review* (Spring 2010), 48.

14. James A. Seddon to Robert Ould, June 24, 1863, in *OR*, II, 6: 41–47.

15. *LiebC*, Art. 82; Dennis K. Boman, *Lincoln and Citizens' Rights in Civil War Missouri: Balancing Freedom and Security* (Baton Rouge: Louisiana State University Press, 2011), 44–46; Lincoln to Frémont, September 2, 1861, *LP*.

16. Stephen Ash, *When the Yankees Came: Conflict and Chaos in the Occupied South* (Chapel Hill: University of North Carolina Press, 1999), 63–64.

17. "List of Property Seized and Disposed of," *PMR*, Department of Arkansas, #365.

18. The same is true for Missouri, where thousands of men accused of "bushwhacking," "rank bushwhacking," or "spying" were tried and released rather than being imprisoned or worse. See, for instance, NARA, RG 109, #182: Papers Relating to Confederate Sympathizers, Deserters, Guerrillas, and Prisoners, 1861–1865, Box 1.

19. "List of Property Seized and Disposed of," *PMR*, Department of Arkansas, #365.

20. *PMR*, Department of the Gulf, #1845, Box 4: Letters Received, 1864.

21. Roger Pickenpaugh, *Captives in Gray: The Civil War Prisons of the Union* (Tuscaloosa: University of Alabama Press, 2009), 22–24.

22. NARA, M598, Department Relating to Confederate Prisoners of War, 1861–1865, vol. 29–30: Relating to Individual Prisons or Stations: Alton, IL, Register of Prisoners, 1862–1865. This was true in 1862 as well, when the prison held suspected disloyal citizens from Missouri. "List of Prisoners," *OR*, II, 2: 250–252. Some undetermined number of the 14,000 "political prisoners" arrested by the Lincoln administration included Southern guerrillas. Mark E. Neely, Jr., *The Fate of Liberty: Abraham Lincoln and Civil Liberties* (New York: Oxford University Press, 1991), 233–234.

23. Robert R. Mackey, *The Uncivil War: Irregular Warfare in the Upper South, 1861–1865* (Norman: University of Oklahoma Press, 2004), 59–62; Mountcastle, *Punitive War*, 40.

24. Grant to Henry Halleck, October 23, 1862, *Papers of Ulysses S. Grant*, vol. 6.

25. Grant to Col. J. Hilderbrandt, November 20, 1862, *PMR*, Department of the Tennessee, #4709, Letters Sent, Book 1 of 4. Another example appears with regard to Capt. Faulker's cavalry. See Grant to Pemberton, December 15, 1862, and Grant to Commanding officer at Alton, December 15, 1862, *PMR*, Department of the Tennessee, #4709, Letters Sent, Book 1 of 4.

26. Grant to T. A. Davies, October 29, 1863, *PMR*, Department of the Tennessee, #4709, Letters Sent, Book 1 of 4.

27. Robert Leslie Wiles Papers, NL; Anna M. Farrar to Jefferson Davis, June 20, 1863, *PJD*, 9, 231; Helena PM, May 9, 1863, *PMR*, Department of Arkansas, Part 2, Entry 4702, Letters Sent, Orders Issued, and other Records of the Provost Marshal, vol. 123. She was not the only woman thus threatened. William M. Wiley, the provost marshal at Murfreesboro, Tennessee, issued the same warning to two other woman in his department in early 1863. Wiley to Mrs. M. Murray and Mrs. Martha Sands, February 22, 1863, *PMR*, Dept. of the Cumberland, #1091.

28. William Blair, *With Malice toward Some: Treason and Loyalty in the Civil War Era* (Chapel Hill: University of North Carolina Press, 2014), 145.

29. Sherman to Pemberton, November 18, 1862, *OR*, II, 4: 723–725; Robert Leslie Wiles Papers, Diary entry November 12, 1863, NL.

30. Burrus M. Carnahan, *Lincoln on Trial: Southern Civilians and the Law of War* (Lexington: University Press of Kentucky, 2010), 107.

31. Michael Walzer, *Just and Unjust Wars: A Moral Argument with Historical Illustrations*, 4th ed. (New York: Basic Books, 2006), 160–162; Hugo Grotius, *The Rights of War and Peace*, ed. Richard Tuck (Indianapolis: Liberty Fund, 2005), Book III, Chapter IV, 1281; Henry W. Halleck, *International Law; or, Rules Regulating the Intercourse of States* (San Francisco: H. H. Bancroft, 1861), 538.

32. *Regulations for the Army of the Confederate States* (New Orleans: Henry P. Lathrop, 1861), 135; Wayne Wei-Siang Hsieh, *West Pointers and the Civil War* (Chapel Hill: University of North Carolina Press, 2009), 66.

33. *Regulations for the Army of the Confederate States*, 134.

34. *LiebC*, Art. 18. Working from the World War II examples of places such as Leningrad, Walzer reaches the opposite conclusion, arguing that attacking soldiers have a moral obligation to facilitate the exit of noncombatants from the city. Only once this has been accomplished is the battle "morally permissible"; Walzer, *Just and Unjust Wars*, 169.

35. J. G. Foster to Samuel Jones, June 16, 1864, *OR*, I, 35(2): 134–135.

36. Lee to Cooper, August 19, 1863, *Wartime Papers of R. E. Lee*, ed. Clifford Dowdey (Boston: Little Brown, 1961), 318; Jackson quoted in Dennis E. Frye,

Harpers Ferry under Fire: A Border Town in the American Civil War (Virginia Beach: Donning Co., 2012), 86–89.

37. Lee to Imboden, June 7, 1863, *OR*, I, 27(3): 865; James Broomall, "'This Debatable Land': The Chesapeake and Ohio Canal's Civil War," Historic Resource Study, Chesapeake and Ohio Canal National Historical Park, chapter 3, p. 19 (manuscript draft in author's possession).

38. J. G. Foster to Samuel Jones, June 16, 1864, *OR*, I, 35(2): 134–135.

39. Grant to Banks May 25, 1863, NARA, Department of the Tennessee, PM Papers, #4709, Letters Sent, Book 1 of 4; Banks to Farragut, 28, 1863, *PMR*, Department of the Gulf, #1738: Letters Sent, Box 5.

40. Edward Wood to Jane Wood, July 2, 1863, in *A Fierce, Wild Joy: The Civil War Letters of Colonel Edward Wood, 48th Indiana Volunteer Infantry Regiment*, ed. Stephen E. Towne (Knoxville: University of Tennessee Press, 2007); *PUSG, 8*, 376–377; David Dudley Field, Loyal Reprints No. 3: "The Great Mass Meeting of Loyal Citizens, at Cooper Institute, March 6, 1863," 8, NYPL.

41. Mark M. Smith, *The Taste of Battle, The Smell of the Siege: A Sensory History of the Civil War* (New York: Oxford University Press, 2015), 90, 92; "The Siege and Fall of Vicksburg," *Richmond Daily Dispatch*, July 25, 1863; Bradley Clampitt, *Occupied Vicksburg* (Baton Rouge: Louisiana State University Press, 2016), 7; "Confederate Bill of Fare," July 4, 1863, Hotel de Vicksburg. The full bill of fare is printed in Andrew F. Smith, *Starving the South: How the North Won the Civil War* (New York: St. Martins, 2011), 103–104.

42. Christopher Phillips, *The Rivers Ran Backward: The Civil War and the Remaking of the American Middle Border* (New York: Oxford University Press, 2016), chapter 6; Christopher Phillips, "The Hard-Line War: The Ideological Basis of Irregular Warfare in the Western Border States," in *The Civil War Guerrilla: Unfolding the Black Flag in History, Memory, and Myth*, ed. Joseph M. Beilein, Jr., and Matthew C. Hulbert (Lexington: University Press of Kentucky, 2015), 24–25.

43. Edward Bates to Simon Cameron, September 30, 1861, NARA, RG 153—Records of the Judge Advocate General, Entry 12—Opinions of the Attorney General, Volume 4 (1855–1868); Grant to Butler, August 18, 1864 NARA, Headquarters of the Army, RG 108, Entry 100, Volume 1.

44. Charles Laforest Dunham to Mrs. Simeon H. Dunham, April 16, 1863, Dunham to Hercey Dunham, June 21, 1863, Dunham to Mrs. Simeon H. Dunham, August 5–6, 1863, in Arthur H. DeRosier, Jr., ed., *Through the South with a Union Soldier* (Johnson City: East Tennessee State University Research Advisory Council, 1969), 66, 79.

45. General references to the practice of hostage taking can be found in Samuel Hyde, Jr., *Pistols and Politics: The Dilemma of Democracy in Louisiana's Florida Parishes* (Baton Rouge: Louisiana State University Press, 1996), 115; Ash, *When the Yankees Came*, 66.

46. Grant to John A. McClernand, *PUSG*, 2, 316.

47. Halleck, *International Law*, 652–674.

48. *LiebC*, Art. 54, 55.

49. As usual, General David Hunter serves as an exception to this generalization. He urged Lincoln to establish a widespread system of hostages to counteract the Confederacy's mistreatment of black soldiers. Hunter to Lincoln, May 27, 1863, *OR*, II, 5: 711–721. Gideon Welles raised the same issue though he was much more circumspect about the practice. Diary entry for May 5, 1864, *The Civil War Diary of Gideon Welles, Lincoln's Secretary of the Navy, The Original Manuscript Edition*, ed. William E. Gienapp and Erica L. Gienapp (Urbana: University of Illinois Press, 2014), 402.

50. B. S. Curd and William M. Price to Capt. Price, August 15, 1861, in Reynolds to Fremont, August 15, 1861, in C. C. Marsh to Fremont, August 18, 1861, *OR*, I, 3: 448–450.

51. E. B. Tyler to F. H. Pierpont, November 2, 1861, NARA, RG109, #465 (M416), Union Provost Marshal's File of Two or more Name Papers Relating to Citizens, Roll 1; Hurst to Grierson, May 29, 1864, *OR*, I, 39(2): 56.

52. George W. Randolph to Jefferson Davis, August 9, 1862, *PJD*, *8*; Bragg to H. G. Wright, December 1, 1862, *OR*, II, 5: 2–3.

53. Grant to Sheridan, August 16, 1864, *PUSG*, *12*, 13. Nathaniel Banks made a similarly inflated threat in response to the murder of a Union officer in Louisiana. See Banks to Halleck, May 5, 1863, *OR*, I, 15: 311–312.

54. Simon B. Buckner to Isaac C. Dyer, January 31, 1863, and Dyer to Buckner, February 4, 1863, *PMR*, Department of the Gulf, Entry #1756, Letters Received 1863 (Box #3); Edwin H. Webster to E. M. Stanton, January 26, 1864, NARA, RG109, #465 (M416), Union Provost Marshal's File of Two or more Name Papers Relating to Citizens, Roll 1; David F. Riggs, "Robert Young Conrad and the Ordeal of Secession," *Virginia Magazine of History and Biography* 86 (July 1978), 259–274.

55. General George Thomas, frustrated by his inability to pacify Kentucky, wrote to superiors in Washington that "we shall be compelled to send disloyal people of all ages and sexes to the south, or beyond our lines." J. J. Reynolds to George E. Flynt, February 11, 1863, *OR*, I, 23(2): 54–57; *LiebC*, Art. 44; William Whiting, *The War Powers of the President and the Legislative Powers of Congress in Relation to Rebellion, Treason, and Slavery*, 2nd ed. (Boston: N. L. Shorey, 1862), 97.

56. J. J. Reynolds to George E. Flynt, February 10, 1863; Thomas, February 11, 1863, both in *OR*, I, 23(2): 54–57; Halleck to Rosecrans, March 5, 1863, *OR*, I, 23(2): 107–109; Earl Hess, *The Civil War in the West: Victory and Defeat from the Appalachians to the Mississippi* (Chapel Hill: University of North Carolina Press, 2008), 181–183; Phillips, *Rivers Ran Backward*, 189–192.

57. Diary entry of August 14, 1862, in Mary E. Kellogg, ed., *Army Life of an Illinois Soldier: Letters and Diary of Charles W. Wills* (Carbondale: Southern Illinois University Press, 1996), 125.

58. Special Order No. 73, R. M. Gordon, October 26, 1863, *PMR*, Department of Arkansas, Part 2, Entry 4702, Letters Sent, Orders Issued, and other Records of the Provost Marshal, Vol. 123. Mary Stearns, also banished and threatened with arrest as a spy, received a designation as "a camp follower and Common Woman." Helena Provost Marshal, May 9, 1863, *PMR*, Department of Arkansas, Part 2, Entry 4702, Letters Sent, Orders Issued, and other Records of the Provost Marshal, Vol. 123.

59. Grant to Halleck, July 10, 1862, and Alvin P. Hovey to Thompson, July 16, 1862, *PUSG*, 5, 192–193.

60. Grant to Hurlburt, January 3, 1863, *PMR*, Department of the Tennessee, #4709, Letters Sent, Book 1 of 4; for other Tennessee banishments, Andrew Johnson to Edwin Stanton, April 4, 1862, in LoC, Edwin M. Stanton Papers, Reel 2.

61. General Orders No. 12, March 2, 1863, *PMR*, Department of Arkansas, Part 2, Entry 4702, Letters Sent, Orders Issued, and other Records of the Provost Marshal, Vol. 123.

62. Although Confederates did not occupy enough Unionist territory to make this problem as acute as it was for federal troops, in those places where they could not trust noncombatants, some officers used banishment to impose order. Late in 1863, in southwestern Mississippi and eastern Louisiana, regions that had seen frequent Union occupation, the Confederate commander proposed to expel disloyal residents. "All citizens living in this district who have taken the oath of allegiance to the Federal government are hereby ordered with their families outside the Confederates lines in 24 days after the publication of this order or be treated as alien enemies." Copy of an order from Col. Francis Porvens, December 12, 1863, *PMR*, Department of the Gulf, Entry #1756, Letters Received 1863 (Box #3).

63. Jno. F. Phillips to J. W. Barnes, February 7, 1865, NARA, RG109, #182: Papers Relating to Confederate Sympathizers, Deserters, Guerrillas, and Prisoners, 1861, 1865, Box 1.

64. Bradley Clampitt, *Occupied Vicksburg* (Baton Rouge: Louisiana State University Press, 2010), 190–196; Phillips, *Rivers Ran Backward*, 195–196.

65. E. P. Sanderson to Rosecrans, July 9, 1864, NARA, RG109, #182: Papers Relating to Confederate Sympathizers, Deserters, Guerrillas, and Prisoners, 1861–1865, Box 1.

66. Jefferson Davis, "Message to Congress," August 18, 1862, *MPC*; Jefferson Davis, "Message to Congress," May 2, 1864, *PJD, 10:* 378; *SHSP* 49 (1930): 25.

67. *FSSP*, I, Book 1: 407; Sutherland, *A Savage Conflict*, 194; Anne E. Marshall, *Creating a Confederate Kentucky: The Lost Cause and Civil War Memory in a Border State* (Chapel Hill: University of North Carolina Press, 2010), 23–31; Phillips, "The Hard-Line War."

68. See Lincoln's correspondence with various Missourians, all at odds with one another. *LP*, August–October, 1863.

69. Christopher Phillips, "'A Question of Power Not One of Law': Federal Occupation and the Politics of Loyalty in the Western Border Slave States during the American Civil War," in *Bleeding Kansas, Bleeding Missouri: The Long Civil War on the Border*, ed. Jonathan Earle and Diane Mutti Burke (Lawrence: University Press of Kansas, 2013), 139.

70. Stanley Harrold, *Border Wars: Fighting over Slavery before the Civil War* (Chapel Hill: University of North Carolina Press, 2010); and Kristin Oertel, *Bleeding Borders: Race, Gender, and Violence in Pre–Civil War Kansas* (Baton Rouge: Louisiana State University Press, 2009).

71. Boman, *Lincoln and Citizen's Rights*, chapter 8; Charles F. Harris, "Catalyst for Terror: The Collapse of the Women's Prison in Kansas City," *Missouri Historical Review* 89 (April 1995), 292.

72. Matthew M. Stith, *Extreme Civil War: Guerrilla Warfare, Environment, and Race on the Trans-Mississippi Frontier* (Baton Rouge: Louisiana State University Press, 2016), 93.

73. Fialka, "Reassessing Guerrillas: A Spatial and Temporal Analysis of Missouri's Civil War," (MA thesis, West Virginia University, 2013). This pattern was not unique to Missouri. A report from Tullahoma, Tennessee, was typical: "during the temporary evacuation of this place lately by the U.S. forces . . . the guerrillas came into town and robbed peaceable citizens of loyal character and behaved in a most shameful and cowardly manner." Thomas Worthington to Unknown, January 3, 1865, NARA, RG109, #465 (M416) Union Provost Marshal's File of Two or more Name Papers Relating to Citizens, Roll 1, Entry #13981.

74. Boman, *Lincoln and Citizen's Rights*, 172; Fellman, *Inside War*; Thomas Hindman, *OR*, I, 22(1): 83.

75. Harris, "Catalyst for Terror," 293–294; Ann Davis Niepman, "General Orders No. 11 and Border Warfare during the Civil War," in *Kansas City, America's*

Crossroads: Essays from the Missouri Historical Review 1906–2006, ed. Diane Mutti Burke and John Herron (Columbia: State Historical Society of Missouri, 2007), 101.

76. Albert Castel offered one of the few censuses of guerrillas, estimating 2,000 to 2,500 for Missouri over the course of the war, though more recent authors suggest that his estimates may be 50 percent too low. Albert Castel, "Estimate of the Number of Guerrillas Who Operated in Southern and Border States during the Civil War," *Civil War Times Illustrated* (October 1974), 50. In October, James Rollins estimated "a few hundred lawless men." Rollins to Lincoln, October 8, 1863, *LP.* Schofield, who had cause to overstate the numbers, guessed 500 men for midsummer in western Missouri. Schofield's report, December 10, 1863, *OR,* I, 22(1): 15.

77. Harris, "Catalyst for Terror," 295.

78. W. R. Penick to Curtis, March 23, 1863, *OR,* I, 22(1): 244; see also James McFerran to Ewing, August 10, 1863, *OR,* I, 22(1): 546–547, in which he does enact it, sending seven families of guerrilla supporters outside the lines.

79. General Orders No. 10, August 18, 1863, *OR,* I, 22(2): 460–461; Schofield's report, December 10, 1863, *OR,* I, 22(1): 16; Harris, "Catalyst for Terror," 299. After the war, one of Quantrill's lieutenants, William Gregg, offered a different explanation. Asked whether he killed citizens in Lawrence, he responded "that's not so. There wasn't a citizen in the whole state of Kansas. They were soldiers . . . every man big enough to carry a gun was a soldier—and we killed them in retaliation for the killings by Redlegs, who came over into Missouri and raided homes. It was war, that's all." *Kansas City Times,* August 20, 1910. My thanks to Joe Beilein for drawing my attention to this passage.

80. *OR,* I, 22(1): 583.

81. "Quantrell," *Richmond Daily Dispatch,* December 3, 1863; "Quantrell's invasion of Kansas," *Augusta Chronicle,* September 4, 1863; "The Destruction of Lawrence, Kansas," *Charleston Mercury,* August 30, 1865.

82. "The Rebels Applaud and Indorse the Lawrence Massacre," *Freedom's Champion* (Atchison, Kansas), October 15, 1863; "A Night of Horror," *Chicago Tribune,* August 24, 1863; "Massacre in Kansas," *Philadelphia Press,* August 25, 1863.

83. *OR,* I, 22(2): 473.

84. John Grenier, *The First Way of War: American War Making on the Frontier, 1607–1814* (New York: Cambridge University Press, 2005), 22, 24, 102–104.

85. Niepman, "General Orders No. 11 and Border Warfare during the Civil War," 106; Officer quoted in Phillips, *Rivers Ran Backward,* 240; Boman, *Lincoln and Citizen's Rights,* 215; Albert Castel, "Order No. 11 and the Civil War on the Border," *Missouri Historical Review* 62 (July 1963), 364–365; soldier

quoted in Thomas Goodrich, *Black Flag: Guerrilla Warfare on the Western Border, 1861–1865* (Bloomington: Indiana University Press, 1995), 100.

86. Schofield to Townsend, September 14, 1863, *LP*; *Chicago Tribune*, August 27, 1863; *Philadelphia Press*, August 28, 1863; *New York Times*, September 4, 1863; Castel, "Order No. 11 and the Civil War on the Border," 363.

87. Lincoln to Schofield, October 14, 1863, *CWAL*, VI: 492–93; Burrus M. Carnahan, *Lincoln on Trial: Southern Civilians and the Law of War* (Lexington: University Press of Kentucky, 2010), 65; Halleck's report, November 25, 1863, *OR*, I, 22(1): 11; Andrew Fialka, "A Spatial Approach to Missouri's Domestic Supply Line," in *The Guerrilla Hunters: Irregular Conflicts during the Civil War*, ed. Brian D. McKnight and Barton A. Myers (Baton Rouge; Louisiana State University Press, 2017), 288–291.

88. Schofield to Townsend, September 14, 1863, *LP*.

89. "The destruction of Lawrence, (Kansas) Escape of the Guerillas Leavenworth," *Daily National Intelligencer*, August 24, 26, September 9, 1863.

90. Boman, *Lincoln and Citizen's Rights*, 212; John M. Schofield, *Forty-Six Years in the Army* (New York: Century Co., 1897), 81.

91. Lane, quoted in *Daily National Intelligencer*, September 5, 1863.

92. Schofield to Edward D. Townsend, September 14, 1863, *LP*, Schofield to Townsend, September 14, 1863, *LP*; James Moss to Willard Hall, September 27, 1863, *LP*; Chicago *Tribune*, August 24, 26, 27, 1863; *New York Times*, September 4, 1863.

93. Carney to Schofield; *OR*, I, 22(1): 576; Schofield to Carney, *OR*, I, 22(1): 578; Lincoln, *CWAL*, VI: 423; Lincoln to Charles Drake and others, *CWAL*, VI: 502–503.

94. Castel, "Order No. 11 and the Civil War on the Border."

95. Bingham to *St. Louis Missouri Republican*, March 12, 1869, in *"But I Forget That I Am a Painter and Not a Politician": The Letters of George Caleb Bingham*, ed. Lynn Wolf Gentzler (Columbia: State Historical Society of Missouri, 2011), 296.

96. Diane Mutti Burke argues that General Orders No. 11 should be viewed in the long history of displacement and violence in the region (against Native Americans, Mormons, and then in the Civil War). "Given border residents' long history of using violence and forced eviction as a political and security tool, General Thomas Ewing's decision to depopulate western Missouri in the summer of 1863 should not be particularly surprising." Diane Mutti Burke, "Scattered People: The Long History of Forced Eviction in the Kansas-Missouri Borderlands," in *Civil War Wests: Testing the Limits of the United States*, ed. Adam Arenson and Andrew R. Graybill (Oakland: University of California Press, 2015), 82.

97. Lincoln, *CWAL*, VI: 500–504.

98. Simone Weil, "The Iliad, or the Poem of Force," in *War and the Iliad* (New York: New York Review Books, 2005), 23.

99. Michael Fellman similarly tries to recenter American warmaking practices in the global mainstream, even when those practices include the deliberate use of terror. Fellman, "Introduction," *In the Name of God and Country: Reconsidering Terrorism in American History* (New Haven, CT: Yale University Press, 2010), 1–13.

100. Andrew Mack, "Why Big Nations Lose Small Wars: The Politics of Asymmetric Conflict," *World Politics* 27 (2): 175–200.

101. "The Probable Influence of the New Military Element on our Soil and National Character," *United States Service Magazine* (June 1864), 598; "The Great Civil Wars," *The Monthly Religious Magazine* 33 (February 1865), 8; Charles Royster, *The Destructive War: William Tecumseh Sherman, Stonewall Jackson, and the Americans* (New York: Vintage, 1991), 241; see also Harry Stout, *Upon the Altar of the Nation: A Moral History of the Civil War* (New York: Vintage, 2006), 132.

102. Davis "to the Congress of the Confederate States," November 18, 1861, *PJD, 1861*, 413; Davis "to the Congress of the Confederate States," November 18, 1861, *PJD, 1861*, 417; George C. Rable, *Damn Yankees! Demonization and Defiance in the Civil War* (Baton Rouge, Louisiana University Press, 2015); "Northern Outrages," *Richmond Dispatch*, August 6, 1862; "Why the Difference?," *Richmond Dispatch*, November 5, 1863.

103. On the importance of proper burials for soldiers, see Drew Gilpin Faust, *This Republic of Suffering: Death and the American Civil War* (New York: Knopf, 2008), and Mark S. Schantz, *Awaiting the Heavenly Country: The Civil War and America's Culture of Death* (Ithaca, NY: Cornell University Press, 2008).

104. Corinth *War Eagle*, July 31, 1862. See also Joseph T. Glatthaar, *General Lee's Army: From Victory to Collapse* (New York: Free Press, 2008), 61–62.

105. Joan Cashin, "Trophies of War: Material Culture in the Civil War Era" *JCWE* 1 (September 2011): 339–367; Michael C. C. Adams, *Living Hell: The Dark Side of the Civil War* (Baltimore: Johns Hopkins University Press, 2014), 166; *Harper's Weekly*, June 7, 1862, and February 7, 1863; Mobile *Register and Advertiser*, April 22, 1864; "The Rebel Barbarities," *Liberator*, March 28, 1862; "Whence Flow the Rebel Barbarities," *Liberator*, June 13, 1862; *Report of Lewis H. Steiner, M.D. Inspector of the Sanitary Commission, Containing a Diary kept during the Rebel Occupation of Frederick, Maryland* (New York: Anson D. F. Randolph, 1862), 11.

106. Paul Anderson, *Blood Image: Turner Ashby in the Civil War and the Southern Mind* (Baton Rouge: Louisiana State University Press, 2002), 72.

107. Royster, *The Destructive War*, 356–366; Harry Stout argues that historians who emphasize Sherman's words over his actions are seeking to "absolve Sherman of moral culpability," but even Stout admits that Sherman had clear limits, which prevented the "deliberate 'slaughter' of women and children" of which his enemies accused him. Stout, *Upon the Altar of the Nation*, 371–372.

108. "Late from the Enemy's Lines," *Macon Daily Telegraph*, April 26, 1864.

109. Levi Bishop, "Mission of the Democracy," *An Address delivered before the Democratic Literary Association of Cincinnati*. February 4, 1864, 4, in *Civil War Politics*, vol. 1, NL.

110. "Report of the Executive Committee," No. 44: Proceedings of the First Anniversary Meeting of the Loyal Publication League, 1864, and No. 78: Proceedings of the Second Anniversary Meeting, February 11, 1865 (NY: LPL, 1865), NYPL; Nos. 19, 53, 55, 59, 71, NYPL.

111. No. 81, NYPL.

112. Sarah Vowell, "'John Brown's Body' and the 'Battle Hymn of the Republic,'" in *The Rose and the Briar: Death, Love and Liberty in the American Ballad*, ed. Sean Wilentz and Greil Marcus (New York: Norton, 2005), 81–89.

113. *Speech on the War by Maj. L. Chandler Ball, Paymaster U.S.A. Delivered at Hoosick Falls, December 9th, 1863* (Washington, DC: Chronicle Print, 1863), in *Civil War Politics: Pamphlets*, vol. 1, NL; Bates to Lieber, October 8, 1863, Box 2, Lieber Papers, HL; Judge Daly, Loyal Reprints No. 3: "The Great Mass Meeting of Loyal Citizens, at Cooper Institute, March 6, 1863," NYPL.

114. Gary W. Gallagher, "Lee's Army Has Not Lost Any of Its Prestige: The Impact of Gettysburg on the Army of Northern Virginia and the Confederate Home Front," in *Lee and His Army in Confederate History* (Chapel Hill: University of North Carolina Press, 2001), 83–114; *Richmond Daily Dispatch*, August 31, 1863.

115. Mitchell Snay, *Gospel of Disunion: Religion and Separatism in the Antebellum South* (Chapel Hill: University of North Carolina Press, 1997); Henry Holcombe Tucker, "God in War: A Sermon Delivered Before the Legislature of Georgia, in the Capitol at Milledgeville," Milledgeville, GA: Boughton, Nisbet, & Barnes, 1861), 5, 7, 16, available at http://docsouth.unc.edu/imls/tuckerh/tuckerh.html; James W. Silver, *Confederate Morale and Church Propaganda* (New York: Norton, 1957), chapter 5; Daniel W. Stowell, *Rebuilding Zion: The Religious Reconstruction of the South, 1865–1877* (New York: Oxford University Press, 1998), chapter 2; and Stout, *Upon the Altar of the Nation*, though he makes clear that Northern ministers were as active in this endeavor as Southern ones. Gardiner H. Shattuck, Jr., *A Shield and a Hiding Place: The Religious Life of Civil War Armies* (Macon, GA: Mercer University Press, 1987), 35; quoted in George Rable, *God's Almost Chosen People: A Reli-*

gious History of the American Civil War (Chapel Hill: University of North Carolina Press, 2011), 164.

116. Basil Manly Jr. quoted in Stowell, *Rebuilding Zion*, 37.

117. W. G. Eliot, *Loyalty and Religion. A Discourse for the Times, delivered in The Church of the Messiah, St. Louis* (St. Louis: George Knapp & Co., 1861), 11, in *Civil War Politics: Pamphlets*, vol. 1, NL; Edward Everett, *An Address Delivered at the Inauguration of the Union Club* (Boston: Little Brown, 1863), in *Civil War Politics: Pamphlets*, vol. 1, NL, 46.

118. Joseph Parrish Thompson, "Peace through Victory," no. 60 (New York: LPL, 1864): 7, NYPL.

119. *Speech on the War by Maj. L. Chandler Ball, Paymaster U.S.A. Delivered at Hoosick Falls, December 9th, 1863* (Washington, DC: Chronicle Print, 1863), 6; No. 7: "Character and Results of the War. How to Prosecute and How to End it. A Thrilling and Eloquent Speech by Major-General B. F. Butler" (March 26, 1863), NYPL; *Philadelphia Inquirer*, October 18, 1862.

120. Rita Nakashima Brock and Rebecca Ann Parker, *Proverbs of Ashes: Violence, Redemptive Suffering, and the Search for What Saves Us* (Boston: Beacon, 2001), 8; Ballou quoted in Brock and Parker, *Proverbs*, 30; quoted in Rable, *God's Almost Chosen People*, 164.

121. William Shakespeare, *Merchant of Venice*, Act 4, Scene 1.

6. DISCIPLINE, ORDER, AND JUSTICE

1. Grant to Steele, April 11, 1863, NARA, Department of the Tennessee, PM Papers, #4709, Letters Sent, Book 1 of 4.

2. Mark Grimsley, *The Hard Hand of War: Union Military Policy toward Southern Civilians 1861–1865* (Cambridge: Cambridge University Press, 1995); Buck T. Foster, *Sherman's Mississippi Campaign* (Tuscaloosa: University of Alabama Press, 2006); Joseph T. Glatthaar, *Partners in Command: The Relationships between Leaders in the Civil War* (New York: Free Press, 1994), 208.

3. Edward H. Bonekemper III, *A Victor, Not a Butcher: Ulysses S. Grant's Overlooked Military Genius* (Washington, DC: Regnery, 2004).

4. Grant to Lee, March 23, 1865, *OR*, II, 8: 393.

5. Gary Gallagher, "Our Hearts Are Full of Hope: The Army of Northern Virginia and the Confederacy in the Spring of 1864," in *Lee and His Army in Confederate History* (Chapel Hill: University of North Carolina Press, 2001), 115–147; Gary Gallagher, *The Confederate War* (Cambridge, MA: Harvard University Press, 1997), 61–112. Wayne Hsieh notes "throughout the entire campaign [Grant] constantly attempted to turn Lee's army, rather than simply throw troops against entrenched Confederates in frontal assaults.

Furthermore, Grant's own reference to attrition in his summary report on operations from 1865, 'to hammer continuously against the armed force of the enemy and his resources, until by mere attrition, if in no other way,' saw attrition as a method of last resort, as opposed to Grant's preferred technique." Wayne Wei-Siang Hsieh, *West Pointers and the Civil War* (Chapel Hill: University of North Carolina Press, 2009), 178.

6. Mark E. Neely, Jr., *The Civil War and the Limits of Destruction* (Cambridge, MA: Harvard University Press, 2007), 30–34.

7. Steven J. Ramold explains that "the Articles [of War] were regulations that defined the soldier's place within the army structure and delineated the powers the government and the army had over the average soldier's existence." Ramold, *Baring the Iron Hand: Discipline in the Union Army* (Dekalb: Northern Illinois University Press, 2010), 312.

8. Lorien Foote provides the clearest explanation of the Union's system of military justice. Foote, *The Gentlemen and the Roughs: Violence, Honor, and Manhood in the Union Army* (New York: New York University Press, 2010), 11–16. The Confederacy's system operated in a similar fashion, though with an insufficient manpower supply, it no doubt had a harder time fielding officers to hear charges.

9. Gideon M. Hart, "Military Commissions and the Lieber Code: Toward a New Understanding of the Jurisdictional Foundations of Military Commissions," *Military Law Review* 203 (Spring 2010), 3, 12–14, 21. In his study of Missouri, the historian Dennis Boman likewise defends Halleck's use of commissions as within rules of war and as fairly conducted. Dennis K. Boman, *Lincoln and Citizen's Rights in Civil War Missouri: Balancing Freedom and Security* (Baton Rouge: Louisiana State University Press, 2011), 81, 84; *LiebC*, Art. 13.

10. Elizabeth Leonard, *Lincoln's Forgotten Ally: Judge Advocate General Joseph Holt of Kentucky* (Chapel Hill: University of North Carolina Press, 2011), 159, chapter 5; Hart, "Military Commissions," 64n401. William Marvel offers a substantially less charitable reading of Holt, describing him as "duplicitous," ideologically malleable, and unconcerned with civil liberties. Marvel, *Lincoln's Autocrat: The Life of Edwin Stanton* (Chapel Hill: University of North Carolina Press, 2015), 250–253.

11. This is certainly true for desertion, which only emerged as a well-defined offense after the enactment of draft acts. Aaron Sheehan-Dean, *Why Confederates Fought: Family and Nation in Civil War Virginia* (Chapel Hill: University of North Carolina Press, 2007), chapter 2.

12. Donald E. Collins, "War Crime or Justice? General George Pickett and the Mass Execution of Deserters in Civil War Kinston, North Carolina," in *The Art of Command in the Civil War*, ed. Steven E. Woodworth (Lincoln: Univer-

sity of Nebraska Press, 1998), 54–56, 63; Judkin Browning, *Shifting Loyalties: The Union Occupation of Eastern North Carolina* (Chapel Hill: University of North Carolina Press, 2011), 164.

13. Grant to Johnston, March 26, 1864, *OR*, II, 6: 991.
14. The exact status of the men in their initial Confederate service remains frustratingly vague. Donald Collins notes that half of them "began their military careers serving the Confederacy in one capacity or another" (Collins, "War Crime or Justice?," 54), and Lesley Gordon writes that "these men had once donned the colors of the state's home guard but, when threatened with Confederate conscription, opted for the Union blue." Lesley J. Gordon, *General George Pickett in Life and Legend* (Chapel Hill: University of North Carolina Press, 1998), 130.
15. Butler to Grant, April 14, 1864 in US Congress, House, "Murder of Union Soldiers in North Carolina," 34th Congress, 2d. sess., 1866, Ex. Doc. No. 98, Serial 1263, 2–3. Full investigation (including witness interviews), most of the correspondence, and newspapers accounts can be found in this report.
16. John Paris, *A Sermon Preached before Brig-Gen. Hoke's Brigade, at Kinston, N.C. on the 28th of February, 1864* (Greensborough, NC: A. W. Ingold, 1864), 6, 7.
17. Peter Carmichael, "The War for the Common Soldier" (unpublished manuscript, 2018, copy in the author's possession), chapter 5.
18. Barlow to "My Dear Mother," April 9, 1864 in *"Fear Was Not in Him": The Civil War Letters of Major General Francis C. Barlow, U.S.A.*, ed. Christian G. Samito (New York: Fordham University Press, 2004), 174; Lyman Diary entries of May 23 and August 8, 1864, in *Meade's Headquarters 1863–1865: Letters of Colonel Theodore Lyman*, ed. George R. Agassiz (Boston: Atlantic Monthly Press, 1922), 117; Lyman Diary entry of August 8, 1864 in *Meade's Headquarters*, 209; Carmichael, "War for the Common Soldier," 312.
19. Lyman Diary entry of May 23, 1864, in *Meade's Headquarters*, 117; Carmichael, "War for the Common Soldier," 302; Patrick quoted in John H. Matsui, *The First Republican Army: The Army of Virginia and the Radicalization of the Civil War* (Charlottesville: University Press of Virginia, 2016), 68.
20. Foote, *Gentlemen and the Roughs*, 136, 139.
21. Ramold, *Baring the Iron Hand*, 343, 384.
22. Thomas Lowry, "Research Note: New Access to a Civil War Resource," *CWH* 49 (March 2003): 53. Lorien Foote's estimate is approximately 75,000–100,000 over the course of the war. Foote, *Gentlemen and the Roughs*, 10.
23. Lowry, "Research Note," 59, 58.
24. Lowry, "Research Note," 56. Stephen Ramold found a similar rate (83 percent conviction) in his study of Union army discipline, which relied on a 5,000-man sample of courts-martial. Ramold, *Baring the Iron Hand*, 328.

NOTES TO PAGES 242–244

25. Sperry, Charles: 13th NY Cav, NARA, RG 153, Microfilm 1523.

26. Table from Lowry, "Research Note," 56.

27. During the Vietnam War, JAG officers prosecuted tens of thousands of soldiers in courts-martial and nonjudicial punishments, but the number convicted of serious crimes was tiny. In Vietnam between 1965 and 1972, the army tried 103 soldiers for murdering Vietnamese civilians. Forty were convicted, twenty-five were convicted of lesser charges, and thirty-eight acquitted. Charges for other serious crimes against civilians numbered ninety, of whom half were convicted. According to one study of the system, "If the military justice system is indeed supposed to be a deterrent, then it did indeed fail." William Allison, *Military Justice in Vietnam: The Rule of Law in an American War* (Lawrence: University Press of Kansas, 2006), 68. Allison focuses on violence internal to the army (such as fragging), but if the US Army could not protect its own officers what chance did Vietnamese civilians stand? His study offers little support for the belief that the military justice system protected Vietnamese civilians or sought justice in any reliable way for violations of war by US soldiers. See Allison, *Military Justice in Vietnam*, 88–89.

28. Ramold, *Baring the Iron Hand*, 7, 295.

29. NARA, RG 153, Microfilm 1523: Proceedings of the U.S. Army Courts Martial and Military Commissions of Union Soldiers Executed by U.S. Authorities, 1861–1866; John F. Fannin, "The Jacksonville Mutiny of 1865," *Florida Historical Quarterly* 88 (Winter 2010): 368–396.

30. NARA, RG109, Adjutant and Inspector General, Judge Advocate General's Office. Records of Confederate Courts-Martial, chapter 1, vols. 194–199.

31. To evaluate the records at a more granular level, I recorded all the charges from one month included in volume 198 (March–April 1864). I selected this month at random. Based on my survey of the remainder of the volumes, it seemed to capture the same crimes in the same numbers. It yielded a total of 209 total cases, below the monthly average for the whole collection.

32. Courts-martial continued to be used to try soldiers accused of crimes.

33. The conclusions reached in this paragraph and the subsequent two were derived from my own statistical analysis of the data gathered and generously shared with me by Gideon M. Hart. The data set does not include general orders for the Department of the Tennessee, which means it may undercount the total number of military commission hearings during the war. Nonetheless, the 3,300 cases included represent a significant majority of those conducted by the Union. Email correspondence with Gideon Hart, May 15, 16, 18, 2015, in the possession of the author. John Witt, working with Hart, estimates about 4,000 commission hearings. John Fabian Witt, *Lincoln's Code: The Laws of War in American History* (New York: Free Press, 2013), 267.

Thomas Lowry asserts that a total 5,460 military commission hearings were held by the North, substantially more than in the Hart data set, though Lowry does not indicate where he found this figure. Lowry, "Research Note," 54.

34. This was certainly true at the highest levels, where Holt met personally with Lincoln and his secretary John G. Nicolay, discussing dozens of cases in detail over the course of hours. Leonard, *Lincoln's Forgotten Ally*, 159.

35. Foote, *Gentlemen and the Roughs*, 129.

36. Stephen Ash, *When the Yankees Came: Conflict and Chaos in the Occupied South* (Chapel Hill: University of North Carolina Press, 1995), 92; Butler, August 7, 1862, Special Order No. 246; Banks to Bowen, Dec. 23, 1863, *PMR*, Department of the Gulf, Entry #1844, Book 1: Letters Received; E. S. Whittmore to Banks January 3, 1863, *PMR*, Department of the Gulf, Entry #1756, Letters Received 1863 (Box #5); Bradley R. Clampitt, *Occupied Vicksburg* (Baton Rouge: Louisiana State University Press, 2016), 98–99.

37. William A. Blair, *Virginia's Private War: Feeding Body and Soul in the Confederacy* (New York: Oxford University Press, 1998), 75–76, 99–101; A. Groom, PM, to W. O. Fiske, December 17, 1863, *PMR*, Department of the Gulf, Entry #1756, Letters Received 1863 (Box #3).

38. William Wirt Gilmer, August 9, 1864, Gilmer Family Papers, UVA.

39. Sherman to Calhoun, et al., September 12, 1864, in *Sherman's Civil War: Selected Correspondence of William T. Sherman, 1860–1865*, ed. Jean V. Berlin and Brooks D. Simpson (Chapel Hill: University of North Carolina Press, 1999), 707–709; *LiebC*, Art. 17; James A. Seddon to Robert Ould, June 24, 1863, *OR*, II, 6: 42; Burrus M. Carnahan, *Lincoln on Trial: Southern Civilians and the Law of War* (Lexington: University Press of Kentucky, 2010), 78; Lee to Davis, September 22, 1862, *OR*, I, 19(2): 617–619.

40. Spencer Tucker, *Brigadier General John D. Imboden: Confederate Commander in the Shenandoah* (Lexington: University Press of Kentucky, 2003), 144; Lee to James L. Kemper, January 29, 1864, in *The Wartime Papers of R. E. Lee*, ed. Clifford Dowdey (Boston: Little Brown, 1961), 663; quoted in Earl Hess, *The Civil War in the West: Victory and Defeat from the Appalachians to the Mississippi* (Chapel Hill: University of North Carolina Press, 2008), 180.

41. D. H. Dilbeck, *A More Civil War: How the North Waged a Just War* (Chapel Hill: University of North Carolina Press, 2016); Andrew F. Smith, *Starving the South: How the North Won the Civil War* (New York: St. Martins, 2011), 184; Gilmer, July 28, 1864, Gilmer Papers, UVA.; Edward T. Warren to his Jenny Warren, March 12, 1864, Warren Letters, UVA; Thavolia Glymph, *Out of the House of Bondage: The Transformation of the Plantation Household* (Cambridge: Cambridge University Press, 2008), 113, quote from 113n53.

42. Jefferson Davis's habit of forecasting starvation appears throughout his wartime speeches. "Proclamation," December 23, 1862, in *MPC*, I, 273; Davis's Message to Congress, December 7, *MPC*, I, 379. Despite his suggestive title, Andrew Smith's book *Starving the South* shows that hunger, not literal starvation, weakened Confederate armies and civilians.

43. Howard Tully to Thomas Higginbotham, July 15, 1863, Dore Schary Collection, NYPL.

44. Clampitt, *Occupied Vicksburg*, 34–35; Justin S. Solonick, *Engineering Victory: The Union Siege of Vicksburg* (Carbondale: Southern Illinois University Press, 2015), 213.

45. R. Douglas Hurt, *Agriculture and the Confederacy: Policy, Productivity, and Power in the South* (Chapel Hill: University of North Carolina Press, 2015), 161–162, 192.

46. Stephen R. Platt, *Autumn in the Heavenly Kingdom: China, the West, and the Epic Story of the Taiping Civil War* (New York: Vintage, 2012), 238.

47. Benjamin to Slidell, March 24, 1863, *MPC*, II, 462; Benjamin to James Mason, May 20, 1863, *MPC*, II, 488; Solonick, *Engineering Victory*, 115; Daniel Sutherland, *Seasons of War: The Ordeal of a Confederate Community, 1861–1865* (New York: Free Press, 1995); Richard R. Duncan, *Winchester Divided: A Virginia Community at War, 1861–1865* (Baton Rouge: Louisiana State University Press, 2007); Crandall A. Shifflett, *Patronage and Poverty in the Tobacco South: Louisa County, Virginia, 1860–1900* (Knoxville: University of Tennessee Press, 1982).

48. Leonard A. Sagan, *The Health of Nations: True Causes of Sickness and Well-Being* (New York: Basic Books, 1987), 51–52. It is important to note that both these societies maintained more modern food supply networks before the respective conflicts, and thus citizens went from eating refined grains to more whole grains. The British blockade of Germany during World War I likewise did not produce starvation. Rather, it generated "mass malnutrition [that] greatly heightened the normal effects of ... diseases such as influenza and typhus." Michael Walzer, *Just and Unjust Wars: A Moral Argument with Historical Illustrations*, 4th ed. (New York: Basic Books, 2006), 173.

49. Andrew Bell, *Mosquito Soldiers: Malaria, Yellow Fever, and the Course of the American Civil War* (Baton Rouge: Louisiana State University Press, 2010), 7, 129. Jim Downs, *Sick from Freedom: African American Illness and Suffering during the Civil War and Reconstruction* (New York: Oxford University Press, 2012), chapter 4. Precise numbers are hard to pinpoint. Downs demonstrates the pervasive neglect by Union commanders and appalling suffering experienced by escaping slaves as a result. The worst clusters and highest number of fatalities from the disease appear to have occurred after 1865.

NOTES TO PAGES 251–252

50. Margaret Humphreys identifies "several small yellow fever epidemics" at port cities along the Atlantic coast, though "the most interesting story, for sanitarians, was the epidemic that did not happen." That is, Benjamin Butler's troops in New Orleans kept the city clean and free of yellow fever through the war. According to Humphreys, "cholera was less of a threat than yellow fever during the war." Margaret Humphreys, *Marrow of Tragedy: The Health Crisis of the American Civil War* (Baltimore, MD: Johns Hopkins University Press, 2013), 95–96, 275.

51. Elizabeth Fenn counts at least 130,658 deaths from smallpox between 1775 and 1782 as compared to 25,000 soldiers who died fighting in the Continental Army. Elizabeth A. Fenn, *Pox Americana: The Great Smallpox Epidemic of 1775–82* (New York: Hill and Wang, 2001), 275. Humphreys counts 19,000 US troops who contracted smallpox during the war, with about 7,000 dying from the disease. In US POW camps 10,000 Confederate soldiers contracted the disease and at least 2,500 died as a result. Humphreys, *Marrow of Tragedy*, 285.

52. A review of the *Richmond Daily Dispatch* reveals numerous references throughout the war to the major killers of the antebellum period—yellow fever, typhus, cholera—but none signaled any fear about epidemics among the civilian population. Health histories of the conflict chronicle a great deal of death from infection and disease, but nothing that suggests an epidemic. Bell, *Mosquito Soldiers*.

53. Lisa Brady, *War Upon the Land: Military Strategy and the Transformation of Southern Landscapes during the American Civil War* (Athens: University of Georgia Press, 2012);

54. This was especially true in New Orleans, where Benjamin Butler's soldiers scoured the city's network of canals that remove wastewater from the below-ground city. See Jo Ann Carrigan, "Yankees versus Yellow Jack in New Orleans, 1862–1866," *CWH* (1963): 248–260; Joy J. Jackson, "Keeping Law and Order in New Orleans under General Butler," *Louisiana History* (1993): 51–67.

55. Shauna Devine shows how much military doctors learned about cholera after the war. Devine, *Learning from the Wounded: The Civil War and the Rise of American Medical Science* (Chapel Hill: University of North Carolina Press, 2014), chapter 6.

56. Jürgen Osterhammel, *The Transformation of the World: A Global History of the Nineteenth Century* (Princeton, NJ: Princeton University Press, 2015), 191.

57. Platt, *Autumn in the Heavenly Country*, 305–307.

58. Joel Parker, "The Character of the Rebellion, and the Conduct of the War," *North American Review* 95 (October 1862): 524.

59. Mark E. Neely, Jr., "Was the Civil War a Total War?," *CWH* 37 (March 1991): 5–28; Earl Hess, *Civil War Infantry Tactics: Training, Combat, and Small-Unit Effectiveness* (Baton Rouge: Louisiana State University Press, 2015), xii–xiii.

60. Hess, *Civil War Infantry Tactics*, xiii.

61. The average casualty figure is 3.4–7.5, cited in Brent Nosworthy, *The Bloody Crucible of Courage: Fighting Methods and Combat Experience of the Civil War* (New York: Carroll and Graf, 2003), especially chapter 30, 584.

62. Timothy Orr, "'The Greatest Terror to the Enemy': The Combat Debut of Berdan's Sharpshooters during the 1862 Peninsula Campaign," *Vulcan: The International Journal of the Social History of Military Technology* (2014): 1–40.

63. Hess, *Civil War Infantry Tactics*, 60.

64. The historian Earl Hess notes that "the idea that one army can 'destroy' the other . . . is a chimera more common in dreams than reality." Hess, *Civil War Infantry Tactics*, 235.

65. Dave Grossman, *On Killing: The Psychological Cost of Learning to Kill in War and Society*, rev. ed. (1995. New York: Back Bay, 2009), 1–30.

66. Joanna Bourke, *An Intimate History of Killing: Face to Face Killing in 20th Century Warfare* (New York: Basic, 1999), xix, 358–361.

67. Quotations in Bourke, *Intimate History*, 59, 61. A handful of Civil War soldiers, primarily guerrillas, thrived on killing in a way sharply at odds with how most men experienced it. See, for instance, Brian D. McKnight, *Confederate Outlaw: Champ Ferguson and the Civil War in Appalachia* (Baton Rouge: Louisiana State University Press, 2011).

68. Walter Kittredge, "Tenting Tonight on the Old Campground," 1863.

69. Milton F. Perry, *Infernal Machines: The Story of Confederate Submarine and Mine Warfare* (Baton Rouge: Louisiana State University Press, 1965), 4.

70. Daniel Schafer, *Thunder on the River: The Civil War in Northeast Florida* (Gainesville: University Press of Florida, 2010), 206–216; quotation in Michael Bennett, *Union Jacks: Yankee Sailors in the Civil War* (Chapel Hill: University of North Carolina Press, 1994), 194.

71. Herbert M. Schiller, *Confederate Torpedoes: Two Illustrated 19th Century Works with New Appendices and Photographs* (Jefferson, NC: McFarland, 2011), 4; Perry, *Infernal Machines*, 23–24; McClellan to Stanton, May 4, 1862, *OR*, I, 11(3): 134–135. Lincoln's attorney general endorsed his decision, writing in his diary that he hoped McClellan would "put the prisoners of the highest rank foremost in this dangerous duty." Bates quoted in Perry, *Infernal Machines*, 23; Sorrel to Rains, May 11, 1862, *OR*, I, 11(3): 509; George W. Randolph, *OR*, I, 11(3): 509–511.

72. Schiller, *Confederate Torpedoes*, 5.

73. *The Index,* "Notes on the Events of the Week," January 1, 1863; "The Naval Defeats of the Federals," February 19, 1863, "The Defenses of Charleston," April 9, 1863; "Letter from Richmond," April 16, 1863.

74. Quoted in Perry, *Infernal Machines,* 165. Jefferson Davis confessed that "large numbers of army and navy officers have been employed in torpedo service." *CSA Journal of the Senate,* June 11, 1864, 223.

75. Davis to Johnston, July 9, 1863, *OR,* I, 24(1): 199–200.

76. Seddon to Johnston, May 27, 1863, *OR,* I, 18: 1083.

77. Schiller, *Confederate Torpedoes,* 7.

78. Speech of George Julian, in "The Sumter Anniversary, 1863. Opinions of Many Loyalists concerning The Great Question of the Times" (New York: C. S. Westcott, 1863), 100; Norman Youngblood, *The Development of Mine Warfare: A Most Murderous and Barbarous Conduct* (Westport, CT: Praeger, 2006), 43; David F. Ritchie, *Four Years in the First New York Light Artillery: The Papers of David F. Ritchie* (Hamilton, NY: Edmonston, 1997), 44; Patrick, *Inside Lincoln's Army,* November 16, 1863, and March 18, 1865, 307–308, quotation on 471.

79. Sherman quoted in Charles Royster, ed., *Memoirs of General W.T. Sherman* (New York: Library of America, 1990), 670. Sherman used Confederate POWs to clear mines around Fort McAllister in Savannah: see Perry, *Infernal Machines,* 166; and he had issued similar orders at the start of the campaign: see Sherman to J. B. Steedman, June 23, 1864, *OR,* I, 38(4): 579.

80. Hitchcock, *Marching with Sherman,* 161, 162. In a preview of the US Army's recruitment of Nazi rocket designers, "some [Confederate torpedo inventors] joined their former enemies and demonstrated the secrets." Perry, *Infernal Machines,* 195. The Union also vacillated on whether to charge Confederate weapons designers with violating the laws of war during the conflict. When they captured Lt. William T. Glassell after he deployed a spar torpedo against two ships in Charleston Harbor, the Union abandoned its plans to prosecute him for "conducting an illegal form of warfare" and instead exchanged him for another naval officer. Craig Symonds, *The Civil War at Sea* (New York: Oxford University Press, 2012), 173.

81. Neely, *Civil War and the Limits of Destruction,* 1–2, 143–145; "Greek Fire and Other Inflammables," *United State Service Magazine* 1 (January 1864): 50–55; Beauregard quoted in G. R. Hasegawa and B. Guelry, *Villainous Compounds: Chemical Weapons and the American Civil War* (Carbondale: Southern Illinois University Press, 2015), 21; David S. Parker to Jefferson Davis, January 16, *PJD, 8:* 20; Edmund Ruffin to Jefferson Davis, August 25, 1864, *PJD, 10:* 623.

82. Jane Singer, *The Confederate Dirty War: Arson, Bombings, Assassination and Plots for Chemical and Germ Attacks on the Union* (Jefferson, NC: McFarland, 2005), 76–85; Bell, *Mosquito Soldiers,* 103–106.

83. Edward Steers, *Blood on the Moon: The Assassination of Abraham Lincoln* (Lexington: University Press of Kentucky, 2001), 47–51, 54; J. D. Haines, "Did a Confederate Doctor Engage in a Primitive Form of Biological Warfare? The Northern Press Thought So" *America's Civil War* 12 (September 1999): 12–13.

84. Perry, *Infernal Machines*, 133. Laura June Davis describes a similar, though more personal, campaign conducted by Confederate guerrillas operating as boat burners on the Lower Mississippi River after the fall of Vicksburg. They "engaged in a 'hidden war,' operating within the sinister intersections of irregular warfare, sabotage, and espionage." She concludes that they destroyed at least forty US ships, resulting in dozens of casualties and deaths and millions of dollars in property damage. Davis, "Irregular Naval Warfare along the Lower Mississippi," in *The Guerrilla Hunters: Irregular Conflicts during the Civil War*, ed. Brian D. McKnight and Barton A. Myers (Baton Rouge: Louisiana State University Press, 2017), 213–235.

85. Grant to Halleck, August 9, 1864, *PUSG*, *11*, 384; Meade to his wife, August 9, 1864, *The Life and Letters of George Gordon Meade*, vol. 2, ed. George Meade (New York: Charles Scribner's Sons, 1913).

86. After the war ended, a copy of Maxwell's report was found and sent to Washington. Joseph Holt issued a warrant for Maxwell's arrest, but he was never taken into custody.

87. Report of John Maxwell, December 16, 1864, *OR*, I, 17(1): 954–956.

88. *LiebC*, Art. 56.

89. The records of the local provost marshal offices in National Archives Record Group 393 are filled with lists, reports, and orders pertaining to prisoners, many of which are not included in the *Official Records*.

90. Nelson A. Reed, *The Caste War of the Yucatán*, rev. ed. (Stanford, CA: Stanford University Press, 2001), 203–204, 209–210, 238; Douglas M. Richmond, *Conflict and Carnage in the Yucatán: Liberals, the Second Empire, and Maya Revolutionaries, 1855–1875* (Tuscaloosa: University of Alabama Press, 2015), 40.

91. Platt, *Autumn in the Heavenly Kingdom*, 210–211, 232, 267.

92. Much of the postwar writing, most of it based on nonexistent or exaggerated evidence and designed explicitly to slander one side or the other, has obscured this topic for decades but recent studies have established a clearer picture. James M. Gillispie, *Andersonvilles of the North: The Myths and Realities of Northern Treatment of Civil War Confederate Prisoners* (Denton: University of North Texas Press, 2008); and William Marvel, *Andersonville: The Last Depot* (Chapel Hill: University of North Carolina Press, 1994). Charles Sanders's recent work departs from the consensus that the high death tolls were accidental; he argues that deliberate mistreatment killed many thousands of men.

Charles W. Sanders, Jr., *While in the Hands of the Enemy: Military Prisons of the Civil War* (Baton Rouge: Louisiana State University Press, 2005), 2–5. For a historiography of the issue, see James Gillispie, "Prisons," in *A Companion to the U.S. Civil War*, ed. Aaron Sheehan-Dean, 2 vols. (Malden, MA: Wiley, 2014), 1: 456–475.

93. Butler to Stanton, April 9, 1864, *POCBB*, IV, 50; Johnson Harvey to Butler, August 28, 1864, *POCBB, V*, 115.

94. Grant to Butler, April 17, 1864, *PUSG, 10*, 301–302; Sanders, *While in the Hands of the Enemy*, 4, 257.

95. Butler to Ould, August 23, 1864, *POCBB, V*: 97–103.

96. Sanders, *While in the Hands of the Enemy*, 187–188, 226.

97. Sanders, *While in the Hands of the Enemy*, 179–180, 271; Roger Pickenpaugh, *Captives in Gray: The Civil War Prisons of the Union* (Tuscaloosa: University of Alabama Press, 2009), 189–191.

98. James E. Anderson to Jefferson Davis, June 23, 1864, *PJD, 10:* 481; and *OR*, II, 7: 403. Anderson may have been overestimating the number of killings. William Marvel's meticulous history of Andersonville reveals that eleven Union prisoners died from being shot by sentries and at least thirty-one Confederates were killed in similar conditions in Union prisons. Marvel, *Andersonville*, 173.

99. Report quoted in Bruce Tap, *Over Lincoln's Shoulder: The Committee on the Conduct of the War* (Lawrence: University Press of Kansas, 1998), 202. The first images of suffering Union prisoners appeared in *Harper's Weekly* in December 1863, by which time prison memoirs were already on the market. Benjamin G. Cloyd, *Haunted by Atrocity: Civil War Prisons in American Memory* (Baton Rouge: Louisiana State University Press, 2010), 24. Diary entry September 27, 1864, George Templeton Strong, *Diary of the Civil War, 1860–1865* (New York: Macmillan, 1962), 494.

100. Sanders, *While in the Hands of the Enemy*, 1; Gillispie, "Prisons," 470. Pickenpaugh notes that "the end of prisoner exchanges opened a new and much harsher chapter in the story of Civil War prisons." Roger Pickenpaugh, *Camp Chase and the Evolution of Union Prison Policy* (Tuscaloosa: University of Alabama Press, 2007), 3.

7. CHILDREN OF GOD

1. Michael Howard, "Constraints on Warfare," in *The Laws of War: Constraints on Warfare in the Western World*, ed. Michael Howard, George J. Andreopoulos, and Mark R. Shulman (New Haven, CT: Yale University Press, 1994), 8.

2. Gregory Urwin's pathbreaking *Black Flag over Dixie: Racial Atrocities and Reprisals in the Civil War*, ed. Gregory J. W. Urwin (Carbondale: Southern

Illinois University Press, 2004); and George S. Burkhardt's *Confederate Rage, Yankee Wrath: No Quarter in the Civil War* (Carbondale: Southern Illinois University Press, 2007) offered a full portrait of these events, but new research continues to identify more such incidents. See, for instance, Peter Luebke, "What Does the Northern Neck Have to Do with the Crater?," blog post, quoted in Brendan Wolfe blog post, "Explaining a Massacre," July 27, 2009, in blog of Encyclopedia of Virginia, Virginia Center for the Humanities, available at http://blog.encyclopediavirginia.org/2009/07/explaining-a-massacre/#more -821, and Christopher Phillips, "The Hard-Line War: The Ideological Basis of Irregular Warfare in the Western Border States," in *The Civil War Guerrilla: Unfolding the Black Flag in History, Memory, and Myth*, ed. Joseph M. Beilein, Jr., and Matthew C. Hulbert (Lexington: University Press of Kentucky, 2015), 30–31.

3. The casualty figures are 267 per 1,000 men for Port Hudson, 265 per 1,000 for Olustee, and 214 per 1,000 for Fort Wagner. By comparison, casualty figures for Union troops were 212 per 1,000 at Gettysburg, 162 per 1,000 at Shiloh, and 155 per 1,000 at Antietam. Thomas L. Livermore, *Numbers and Losses in the Civil War in America: 1861–1865*, reprint (Bloomington: Indiana University Press, 1957), 75–76. Only Cedar Mountain and Stones River (among the deadliest battles for the Union) did not feature high numbers of black casualties. This rate reflected the entry of black men into the war after the point at which both sides had perfected their strategies for exacting maximum casualties, the willingness of white Union commanders to expend black lives in ill-conceived attacks, and the refusal of Confederate forces to accept the surrender of black troops.

4. Jabez L. M. Curry, *Proceedings of the First Confederate Congress, Fourth Session*, February 3, 1864, House, 365.

5. David J. Coles, "'Shooting Niggers Sir': Confederate Mistreatment of Union Black Soldiers at the Battle of Olustee," in Urwin, *Black Flag over Dixie*, 65–88; Weymouth T. Jordan, Jr., and Gerald W. Thomas, "Massacre at Plymouth, April 20, 1864," in Urwin, *Black Flag over Dixie*, 153–202; Brian D. McKnight, *Confederate Outlaw: Champ Ferguson and the Civil War in Appalachia* (Baton Rouge: Louisiana State University Press, 2011), 147–151.

6. Unlike other racial atrocities, there is a lengthy written record on Fort Pillow, including a Congressional investigation. John Cimprich, *Fort Pillow, a Civil War Massacre, and Public Memory* (Baton Rouge: Louisiana State University Press, 2005). At almost the same time as Fort Pillow, Confederates massacred black soldiers after besieging a Union outpost in Plymouth, North Carolina. See Jordan and Thomas, "Massacre at Plymouth."

NOTES TO PAGES 273–278

7. Cimprich, *Fort Pillow*, 80–83; Jack Hurst, *Nathan Bedford Forrest: A Biography* (New York: Vintage, 1993), 171–175; Brian Steel Wills, *The River Was Dyed with Blood: Nathan Bedford Forrest & Fort Pillow* (Norman: University of Oklahoma Press, 2014), 107–115.

8. John Cimprich, *Fort Pillow*, 81.

9. John Cimprich and Robert C. Mainfort, Jr., "The Fort Pillow Massacre: A Statistical Note," *Journal of American History* 76 (December 1989): 830–837; Cimprich, *Fort Pillow*, 85; Wills, *The River Was Dyed with Blood*, 115–116.

10. Cimprich, *Fort Pillow*, 71

11. Wills, *The River Was Dyed with Blood*, 123; Hurst, *Nathan Bedford Forrest*, 177. Cimprich concludes that "no evidence provides unquestionable proof of Forrest's guilt or innocence regarding the massacre." Cimprich, *Fort Pillow*, 83. Although Forrest may not have ordered the massacre, troops under his command committed one, and he merited responsibility, as all commanders did, for the actions of his troops.

12. *OR*, I, 32(1): 617; Cimprich, *Fort Pillow*, 94; *Richmond Examiner*, April 29, 1864, 2.

13. Robert K. Krick, *9th Virginia Cavalry* (Lynchburg, VA: H. E. Howard, 1982), 34.

14. Bruce Suderow, "The Battle of the Crater: The Civil War's Worst Massacre," in Urwin, *Black Flag over Dixie*, 207–209.

15. Georgian quoted in Kevin Levin, *Remembering the Battle of the Crater: War as Murder* (Lexington: University Press of Kentucky, 2012), 15–29; Suderow, "Battle of the Crater," 203–207.

16. Lieutenant Colonel William Pegram quoted in Levin, *Remembering the Battle of the Crater*, 28; Colin Edward Woodward, *Marching Masters: Slavery, Race, and the Confederate Army during the Civil War* (Charlottesville: University of Virginia Press, 2014), 146–152.

17. Joseph T. Glatthaar, *General Lee's Army: From Victory to Collapse* (New York: Free Press, 2008), 425.

18. Levin, *Remembering the Battle of the Crater*, 31.

19. Thomas D. Mays, "The Battle of Saltville," in *Black Soldiers in Blue: African American Troops in the Civil War Era*, ed. John David Smith (Chapel Hill: University of North Carolina Press, 2002), 200–226.

20. George Dallas Mosgrove quoted in Mays, "Battle of Saltville," 212.

21. Brian D. McKnight, *Confederate Outlaw: Champ Ferguson and the Civil War in Appalachia* (Baton Rouge: Louisiana State University Press, 2011), 147–151.

22. Mays, "Battle of Saltville," 214, 216–217.

23. Cincinnati paper quoted in Cimprich, *Fort Pillow*, 90–99; Wills, *The River Was Dyed with Blood*, 125–127; Theodore Hodgkins to Stanton, April 18, 1864,

FSSP, II, Book 2: 587–588; *Chicago Tribune* quoted in Bruce Tap, *Over Lincoln's Shoulder: The Committee on the Conduct of the War* (Lawrence: University Press of Kansas, 1998), 195, 196–200, 203.

24. Howard C. Westwood, "Captive Black Union Soldiers in Charleston: What to Do?," in Urwin, *Black Flag over Dixie*, 34–51; Brainerd Dyer, "The Treatment of Colored Troops by the Confederates, 1861–1865," *Journal of Negro History* 20 (July 1935), 285.

25. Report T. R. Livingston, May 28, 1863, *OR*, I, 22(1): 322.

26. Roger Pickenpaugh, *Captives in Blue: The Civil War Prisons of the Confederacy* (Tuscaloosa: University of Alabama Press, 2013), 186.

27. Foote, *SHSP* 12 (1930), 33 and Curry, *SHSP* 12 (1930), 365.

28. Pickenpaugh, *Captives in Blue*, 189–195; William Marvel, *Andersonville: The Last Depot* (Chapel Hill: University of North Carolina Press, 1994), 155; Douglas R. Egerton, *Thunder at the Gates: The Black Civil War Regiments That Redeemed America* (New York: Basic Books, 2016), 230–231.

29. *OR*, I, 40(2): 704–705; and Jefferson Davis to James Seddon, July 26, 1864, *PJD*, 10, 705–706.

30. Union Major Bradford, for example, was killed after surrendering Fort Pillow to Forrest. See the correspondence of Washburn and Forrest, June 19 and 23, 1864, *OR*, I, 32(1): 589–590.

31. Logan quoted in Pickenpaugh, *Captives in Blue*, 188.

32. Bruce Watson, *The Great Indian Mutiny: Colin Campbell and the Campaign at Lucknow* (Westport, CT: Praeger, 1991), 105; Edward J. Thompson, "British Atrocities," in *India in 1857: The Revolt Against Foreign Rule*, ed. Ainslie T. Embree (Delhi: Chanakaya, 1987), 105–111.

33. Forrest to Washburn, June 14, 1864, *OR*, I, 32(1): 586; Washburn to Forrest, June 19, 1864, *OR*, I, 32(1): 589; Forrest to Washburn, June 23, 1864, *OR*, I, 32(1): 590.

34. Quotations in Stephen V. Ash, *When the Yankees Came: Conflict and Chaos in the Occupied South, 1861–1865* (Chapel Hill: University of North Carolina Press, 1995), 168–169, and Stephen Sears, *Gettysburg* (Boston: Houghton Mifflin, 2003), 112, 82; see also David G. Smith, "Race and Retaliation: The Capture of African Americans during the Gettysburg Campaign," in *Virginia's Civil War*, ed. Peter Wallenstein and Bertram Wyatt-Brown (Charlottesville: University Press of Virginia, 2005), 137–151. Black soldiers were also reenslaved in Lee's invasion of Maryland in 1862; Aaron Sheehan-Dean, *Why Confederates Fought: Family and Nation in Civil War Virginia* (Chapel Hill: University of North Carolina Press, 2007), 76.

35. Joseph to Jefferson Davis, November 11, 1863, *PJD 10*, 61–62; Joseph to Jefferson Davis, December 1, *PJD 10*, 96–97.

36. Christopher Leslie Brown and Philip D. Morgan, eds., *Arming Slaves: From Classical Times to the Modern Age* (New Haven, CT: Yale University Press, 2006); David Brion Davis, "Introduction," in Brown and Morgan, *Arming Slaves*, 6; Jane Landers, "Transforming Bondsmen into Vassals: Arming Slaves in Colonial Spanish America," in Brown and Morgan, *Arming Slaves*, 137.

37. Landers, "Transforming Bondsmen into Vassals," 136–137; Howell Cobb to James A. Seddon, January 8, 1865, in Robert F. Durden, *The Gray and the Black: The Confederate Debate on Emancipation* (Baton Rouge: Louisiana State University Press, 1972), 184; David Brion Davis, "Introduction," in Brown and Morgan, *Arming Slaves*, 8.

38. Chandra Manning, *Troubled Refuge: Struggling for Freedom in the Civil War* (New York: Knopf, 2016), 77; Ash, *When the Yankees Came*, 169; Lorien Foote, *The Yankee Plague: Escaped Union Prisoners and the Collapse of the Confederacy* (Chapel Hill: University of North Carolina Press, 2016), 35.

39. Levin, *Remembering the Battle of the Crater*, 29; Mays, "Battle of Saltville," 222; Thomas Jefferson, *Notes on the State of Virginia*, Query 18; Lieber to Halleck, April 19, 1864, Box 28, Lieber Papers, HH.

40. United Nations, "Framework of Analysis for Atrocity Crimes: A Tool for Prevention," 2014, available at http://www.un.org/en/genocideprevention /documents/publications-and-resources/Framework%20of%20Anal- ysis%20for%20Atrocity%20Crimes_EN.pdf. The 1998 "Rome Statute of the International Criminal Court" includes "the crime of aggression." "Rome Statute of the International Criminal Court" (1998) and the US Army in- clude "ethnic cleansing." Sarah Sewall, Dwight Raymond, and Sally Chin, *Mass Atrocity Response Operations: A Military Planning Handbook* (Cambridge, MA: Carr Center for Human Rights Policy, Harvard Kennedy School, and the U.S. Army Peacekeeping and Stability Operations Institute, 2010); quo- tation from United Nations, "Framework of Analysis," 1.

41. A recent report on Northern Ireland notes that "the disappearance of Jean McConville was eventually recognized as one of the worst atrocities that oc- curred during the long conflict in Northern Ireland known as the Troubles." McConville was a widowed mother of ten, murdered by the IRA, who accused her of collaborating with the British. Her disappearance resulted in the children being separated and cycled into foster care and institutional homes. In this context, the criteria for atrocity is its social impact, not necessarily the manner of her death (many others in Northern Ireland suffered worse fates) or the scale (larger groups of people were killed). Patrick Radden Keefe, "Where the Bodies are Buried," *New Yorker*, March 16, 2015, 42.

42. The historian Philip Paludan represents an exception when he uses the term *atrocity* to describe the murder of a group of white Unionists in western North

Carolina. Phillip Shaw Paludan, *Victims: A True Story of the Civil War* (Knoxville: University of Tennessee Press, 1981).

43. Francis Lieber to Edward Bates, April 19, 1864, Box 23, Lieber Papers, HH.

44. Halleck to Lieber, August 4, 1863, Box 9, Lieber Papers, HH; Laurent Dubois, "Avenging America: The Politics of Violence in the Haitian Revolution," in *The World of the Haitian Revolution*, ed. David Patrick Geggus and Norman Fiering (Bloomington: Indiana University Press, 2009), 118.

45. Lincoln to Cabinet members, April 3, 1864, *CWAL*, VII: 328; Lieber to Halleck, April 19, 1864, Box 28, Lieber Papers, HH; Stanton to Lincoln, and Montgomery Blair to Lincoln, May 6, 1864, *LP*; Bates to Lincoln, May 4, 1864, *LP*.

46. Chetlain to E. B. Washburne, April 14, 1865, *OR*, I, 32(3): 364; Welles to Lincoln, May 5, 1864, *LP*; Charles Carleton Coffin, "The May Campaign in Virginia," *Atlantic Monthly* (July 1864): 124–133.

47. *Liberator*, March 17, 1865; *Daily Ohio Statesman*, February 17, 1865; Coles, "'Shooting Niggers Sir'"; Sherman to Stanton, April 23, 1864, LOC, Edwin M. Stanton Papers, Reel 7. In many cases, violence may have been only narrowly averted. During a skirmish in Virginia late in 1864, a white officer reported that "one Sergt. made three of them surrender, and they [went] down on their knees and begged for mercy, which they would not have gotten had it not been for the officers." Charles Griswold to Mary Griswold, October 30, 1864, Griswold Family letters MSS6158, NYPL.

48. George Rable, *God's Almost Chosen People: A Religious History of the Civil War* (Chapel Hill: University of North Carolina Press, 2010), 365; Turner, July 9, 1864, *Christian Recorder*, in Jean Lee Cole, *Freedom's Witness: The Civil War Correspondence of Henry McNeal Turner* (Morgantown: West Virginia University Press, 2013), 132.

49. Robert Bennie to G. H. Hanks, Sep. 7, 1863, PMR, Department of the Gulf, #1845, Box 1: Letters Received, 1863.

50. John E. Fallon (surgeon) to the AAAG, November 17, 1863, PMR, Department of the Gulf, Entry #1756, Letters Received 1863 (Box #2).

51. A. Grover to H. L. Berson, November 26, 1863, PMR, Department of the Gulf, Entry #1756, Letters Received 1863 (Box #2). More reports of violence done to black workers in outlying parishes surface in the provost marshal's papers for southern Louisiana, including a soldier's wife who saw a fellow worker whipped until she miscarried and died. PMR, Department of the Gulf, #1845, Box 1: Letters Received, 1863.

52. Nicholas Guyatt, drawing on Eric Foner's work, asserts that "Confederate raiders killed hundreds of freedpeople who'd been put to work under the new system without adequate protection from the military." Guyatt, "'An Im-

possible Idea?' The Curious Career of Internal Colonization," *JCWE* 4 (June 2014): 242; Eric Foner, *Reconstruction: America's Unfinished Revolution* (New York: Harper and Row, 1988), 58. Foner's sources do not offer statements as categorical as those that Foner and Guyatt make. Foner's sources include David H. Overy, *Wisconsin Carpetbaggers in Dixie* (Madison: State Historical Society of Wisconsin, 1961); Vernon Lane Wharton, *The Negro in Mississippi, 1865–1890* (New York: Harper and Row, 1965).

53. Wharton, *The Negro in Mississippi*, 38; Louis S. Gerteis, *From Contraband to Freeman: Federal Policy toward Southern Blacks, 1861–1865* (Westport, CT: Greenwood, 1973), 158.

54. Martha Bigelow, "Plantation Lessee Problems in 1864," *Journal of Southern History* 27 (August 1961), 359; John Eaton, *Grant, Lincoln, and the Freedmen: Reminiscences of the Civil War* (New York: Longman Green, 1907), 157–158.

55. Jacqueline Jones, *Saving Savannah: The City and the Civil War* (New York: Vintage, 2009), 202; Anne Bailey, *War and Ruin: William T. Sherman and the Savannah Campaign* (Wilmington, DE: Scholarly Resources, 2003), 93–94; John Marszalek, *Sherman: A Soldier's Passion for Order* (New York: Free Press, 1993), 312–313.

56. Kerr quoted in Anne Sarah Rubin, *Through the Heart of Dixie: Sherman's March in American Memory* (Chapel Hill: University of North Carolina Press, 2014), 23, 89; Minnesota private quoted in Joseph T. Glatthaar, *The March to the Sea and Beyond: Sherman's Troops in the Savannah and Carolinas Campaign* (Baton Rouge: Louisiana State University Press, 1995), 64.

57. Amy Murrell Taylor, "How a Cold Snap in Kentucky Led to Freedom for Thousands: An Environmental Story of Emancipation," in *Weirding the War: Stories from the Civil War's Ragged Edges*, ed. Stephen Berry (Athens: University of Georgia Press, 2011), 191–214; Jim Downs, *Sick from Freedom: African American Illness and Suffering during the Civil War and Reconstruction* (New York: Oxford University Press, 2012), 18–21.

58. Statement of Joseph Miller, *FSSP*, I: 269–270; Taylor, "How a Cold Snap," 192, 196; "Cruel Treatment of the Wives and Children of U.S. Colored Soldiers," *Liberator*, December 9, 1864.

59. Downs, *Sick from Freedom*, 11, 35–36; Michael T. Meier, "Lorenzo Thomas and the Recruitment of Blacks in the Mississippi River Valley, 1863–1865," in Smith, *Black Soldiers in Blue*, 249–275; Willie Lee Rose, *Rehearsal for Reconstruction: The Port Royal Experiment* (New York: Vintage, 1964), describes the eastern version of this process; *PUSG, 10*; James G. Hollandsworth, Jr., *The Louisiana Native Guards: The Black Military Experience during the Civil War* (Baton Rouge: Louisiana State University Press, 1998), 97–98; Glatthaar, *The March to the Sea and Beyond*, 96–97, 107–108.

60. Manning, *Troubled Refuge;* and Amy Murrell Taylor, *Embattled Freedom: Journeys through the U.S. Civil War's Slave Refugee Camps* (Chapel Hill: University of North Carolina Press, forthcoming).

61. Testimony of Lucy Chase, AIFC, Roll 200.

62. Manning, *Troubled Refuge,* 116–117, 136–137, 193; Gerteis, *From Contraband to Freeman,* 121. The historical demographer David Hacker is currently conducting research that could rewrite our understanding of black mortality in the Civil War. His preliminary research suggests that tens of thousands of black civilians, perhaps as many 50,000, died during the war from all causes in both sections. David Hacker, "The Impact of War and Emancipation on the Black Population of the United States," paper presented at the annual meeting of the Southern History Association, St. Petersburg, Florida, November 5, 2016.

63. Gerteis, *From Contraband to Freeman,* 28–29, 34–35, 99–100.

64. Daryl Michael Scott, *Contempt and Pity: Social Policy and the Image of the Damaged Black Psyche, 1880–1996* (Chapel Hill: University of North Carolina Press, 1997), xiii, 184.

65. William Link's book shows how much Atlanta's present shape and economic power was built on its recovery from the war and how much that process was underwritten by a narrative of suffering that other cities (even those that experienced longer or more destructive occupation) did not match. Link, *Atlanta, Cradle of the New South: Race and Remembering in the Civil War's Aftermath* (Chapel Hill: University of North Carolina Press, 2013).

66. Ash, *When the Yankees Came,* 52; William T. Sherman, "The Grand Strategy of the Last Year of the War," in *Battles and Leaders of the Civil War,* ed. Robert Underwood Johnson and Clarence Clough Buell, 4 vols. (New York: Thomas Yoseloff, 1956), 4: 247–259 and *Memoirs of General W. T. Sherman,* ed. Charles Royster (New York: Library of America, 1990). The historian Stephen Davis argues that "the Union commander evidenced no pangs of regret for the systematic shelling; in fact, he seemed to take a personal interest in the destruction of the city." Davis, "'A Very Barbarous Mode of Carrying on War': Sherman's Artillery Bombardment of Atlanta," *Georgia Historical Quarterly* 79 (Spring 1995), 67. In his history of the federal assault on Savannah, Charles Colcock Jones, Jr., makes no mention of civilian casualties or even the bombardment itself. Jones, "The Siege and Evacuation of Savannah, Georgia, in December 1864" (Augusta, GA: Chronicle Publishing, 1890).

67. Sherman to Hood, September 10, 1864, *OR,* I, 39(2): 416; R. J. Overy, *The Bombers and the Bombed: Allied War over Europe, 1940–1945* (New York: Viking, 2014), 30. This was the motive for Allied commanders who planned the bombing of Bulgaria in 1944 as its government toggled between its early-war

alliance with Germany and the emerging power of the Soviets. Overy, *The Bombers and the Bombed*, 2–12.

68. Grant to Sherman, *OR*, I, 32(3): 245–246.

69. The next two paragraphs draw upon Mary Deborah Petite, *"The Women Will Howl": The Union Army Capture of Roswell and New Manchester, Georgia, and the Forced Relocation of Mill Workers* (Jefferson, NC: McFarland and Company, 2008); Ruth Beaumont Cook, *North across the River: A Civil War Trail of Tears* (Birmingham, AL: Crane Hill Publishers, 1999); and Hartwell T. Bynum, "Sherman's Expulsion of Roswell Women in 1864," *Georgia Historical Quarterly* 54 (Summer 1970): 169–182.

70. Sherman to Kenner Garrard, July 7, 1864, *OR*, I, 38(5): 76–77.

71. Sherman to Halleck, quoted in Petite, *"The Women Will Howl,"* 85; Sherman to Joseph Webster, July 9, 1864, *OR*, I, 38(5): 92–93; *Richmond Enquirer,* August 11, 1864.

72. "Wanton Destruction of Property," *Hartford Courant,* July 23, 1864; *Columbus Daily Enquirer,* August 4, 1864, page 2.

73. Petite, *"The Women Will Howl,"* 110–111.

74. Quoted in Stephen Davis, *What the Yankees Did to Us: Sherman's Bombardment and Wrecking of Atlanta* (Macon, GA: Mercer University Press, 2012), 227–228.

75. *Memoirs of Sherman,* 489; Grant to Sherman, *Memoirs of Sherman,* 489; *Memoirs of Sherman,* 516, 533, 558.

76. Davis, *What the Yankees Did to Us,* 96.

77. Sherman to Ellen Sherman, August 2, 1864, in *Sherman's Civil War: Selected Correspondence of William T. Sherman, 1860–1865,* ed. Brooks D. Simpson and Jean V. Berlin (Chapel Hill: University of North Carolina Press, 1999), 681.

78. Stephen Davis, *Atlanta Will Fall: Sherman, Joe Johnston, and the Yankee Heavy Battalions* (Wilmington, DE: Scholarly Resources, 2011), 158.

79. Davis, "A Very Barbarous Mode," 60.

80. Sherman to Halleck, July 21, 1864, and Sherman to Howard, August 8, 1864, *OR*, I, 39(5): 211, 429.

81. Special Field Order No. 39, July 19, 1864, *OR*, I, 38(5): 193.

82. O. O. Howard, "The Struggle for Atlanta," in Johnson and Buell, *Battles and Leaders of the Civil War,* 4: 320.

83. Sherman to Grant, August 7, 1864, *PUSG, 11,* 381n.

84. Sherman to Schofield, August 1, 1864, *OR*, I, 38(5): 324; Sherman to Halleck, August 7, 1864, in *Sherman's Civil War,* 574–575; R. W. Johnson to W. D. Whipple, August 11, 1864, *OR*, I, 38(5): 459.

85. *Memoirs of Sherman,* 576; Davis, *What the Yankees Did to Us,* 240–241, 249; Lee Kennett, *Marching through Georgia: The Story of Soldiers and Civilians during*

Sherman's Campaign (New York: HarperCollins, 1995) 128; Grant to Sherman, August 7, *PUSG, 11,* 381.

86. Sherman to Hood, September 10, 1864, *OR,* I, 39(5): 514. Common soldiers with Sherman maintained the same silence on the morality of the bombardment. See Charles T. Kruse to "Dear Parrents," July 28, 1864, in Charles T. Kruse Papers, NL; Charles Wills, July and August entries, 1864, in Charles Wright Wills, *Army Life of an Illinois Soldier: Including a Day-by-Day Record of Sherman's March to the Sea: Letters and Diary of Charles W. Wills,* compiled by Mary E. Kellogg (Carbondale: Southern Illinois University Press, 1996); Charles Laforest Dunham to "Mother," August 10, 1864, in Arthur H. DeRosier, Jr., *Through the South with a Union Soldier* (Johnson City: East Tennessee State University Research Advisory Council, 1969), 137.

87. Davis, *Atlanta Will Fall,* 158.

88. Hood to Sherman, September 11, 1864, in *Sherman's Civil War,* 596.

89. Hood to Sherman, September 12, 1864, in Sherman, *Memoirs,* 2: 122.

90. Stephen Davis, "How Many Civilians Died in Sherman's Bombardment of Atlanta?," *Atlanta History* 45, no. 4 (2003): 4–23; Davis, *What the Yankees Did to Us,* 243–249.

91. Sherman to Hood, September 14, in *Sherman's Civil War,* 602. The historian John Walters criticized him on this score as well: "although the bombardment of a besieged city without notice was considered by most military men of the day as a violation of the accepted rules of war, no considerations on this score had deterred Sherman." John B. Walters, *Merchant of Terror: General Sherman and Total War* (Indianapolis, IN: Bobbs-Merrill, 1973), 128.

92. With two exceptions, previous scholars of the topic have described the siege without analyzing it in the context of the existing laws of war. Aside from John Walters (who labeled Sherman a "merchant of terror") and Stephen Davis, historians do not pass negative judgment against Sherman for his decision to turn his guns on the city. Richard McMurry, who has written the most cogent and clearest assessment of the campaign, concludes: "although the bombardment damaged some buildings and on occasion killed or injured soldiers and civilians, it soon became obvious that the artillery could neither cut off rail traffic into and out of Atlanta nor force Hood and the Rebels to evacuate the city." Richard M. McMurry, *Atlanta 1864: Last Chance for the Confederacy* (Lincoln: University of Nebraska Press, 2000), 164. For similar conclusions, see Kennett, *Marching through Georgia,* 117–127; Lee Kennett, *Sherman: A Soldier's Life* (New York: HarperCollins, 2001), 251; B. H. Liddell Hart, *Sherman: Soldier, Realist, American* (New York: Praeger, 1958); Earl Hess, *The Civil War in the West: Victory and Defeat from the Appalachians to the Mississippi* (Chapel Hill: University of North Carolina Press, 2012), 227. McMurry's main

concern is tactical effectiveness, not justice. Albert Castel provides the fullest chronicle of the campaign, and he too implicitly sanctions Sherman's decision. "Under the rules and practices of war," Castel notes, "Atlanta (since it was the headquarters of an army, was a railroad and supply center, and was fortified and garrisoned) was a legitimate target of bombardment." Castel concludes by noting that "although Sherman deserves to be criticized for not having offered to allow the city's civilians an opportunity to leave once he knew, as he assuredly did, that many of them remained, Hood is equally at fault for not having requested such permission." Albert Castel, *Decision in the West: The Atlanta Campaign of 1864* (Lawrence: University Press of Kansas, 1992), 489.

93. Castel, *Decision in the West*, 488.

94. Sherman to Howard, August 10, 1864, *OR*, I, 38(5): 452.

95. Sherman to Daniel Martin, August 10, 1864, in *Sherman's Civil War*, 686–688.

96. Sherman to Thomas, August 10, 1864, *OR*, I, 38(5): 448.

97. Sherman to Calhoun, September 12, 1864, *OR*, I, 39(5): 418–419. The historian Charles Royster saw this dynamic in more mystical terms: "Sherman believed that killing and wounding so many soldiers on both sides, as well as violently intimidating and punishing so many southern civilians, were parts of the process by which Americans attached themselves to their nation." Charles Royster, *The Destructive War: William Tecumseh Sherman, Stonewall Jackson, and the Americans* (New York: Vintage, 1991), 322.

98. Sherman to Hood, September 7, 1864, *OR*, I, 38(5): 822; Hood to Bragg, September 9, 1864, *OR*, I, 39(2): 825.

99. Walters, *Merchant of Terror*, 129; Mark Grimsley, *The Hard Hand of War: Union Military Policy toward Southern Civilians, 1861–1865* (New York: Cambridge University Press, 1995), 188.

100. Marszalek, *Sherman: A Soldier's Passion*, 285; Davis, *What the Yankees Did to Us*, 315–324.

101. Sherman to James Guthrie, August 14, 1864, in *Sherman's Civil War*, 694; Sherman to Daniel Martin, in *Sherman's Civil War*, 686–688.

102. Sherman to Hood, September 10, 1864, in *Sherman's Civil War*, 594.

103. Hood to Sherman, September 11, 1864, in *Sherman's Civil War*, 595; Stephen Cushman, *Belligerent Muse: Five Northern Writers and How They Shaped Our Understanding of the Civil War* (Chapel Hill: University of North Carolina Press, 2014), 77.

104. Sherman to Calhoun, in *Sherman's Civil War*, 600.

105. Halleck to Sherman, September 28, in *Sherman's Civil War*, 603.

106. Sherman to Halleck, December 22, 1864, *OR*, I, 44: 13; Lisa Tendrich Frank, *The Civilian War: Confederate Women and Union Soldiers during Sherman's March* (Baton Rouge: Louisiana State University Press, 2015), 4–5.

107. Diane Sommerville, *Rape and Race in the Nineteenth Century South* (Chapel Hill: University of North Carolina Press, 2004), 122; Victoria Bynum, *Unruly Women: The Politics of Social and Sexual Control in the Old South* (Chapel Hill: University of North Carolina Press, 1992), 117.

108. In no case does the absence of evidence prove evidence of absence and this is especially true for a topic like sexual assault, which creates numerous hurdles to evidentiary recording and retention over a century and a half. Emancipation used to be regarded as a scholarly black hole because it was assumed enslaved people and freedpeople did not leave written records. After decades of diligent research, we now have robust histories of emancipation written from the perspective of black Southerners. Scholars researching sexual violence in the war may make similar advances in coming years.

109. Jane E. Schultz, "Mute Fury: Southern Women's Diaries of Sherman's March to the Sea, 1864–1865," in *Arms and the Woman: War, Gender, and Literary Representation*, ed. Helen M. Cooper, Adrienne Auslander Munich, and Susan Merrill Squier (Chapel Hill: University of North Carolina Press, 1989), 59–79; Rubin, *Through the Heart of Dixie*, 48.

110. Crystal Feimster, *Southern Horrors: Women and the Politics of Rape and Lynching* (Cambridge, MA: Harvard University Press, 2011), 19; Sarah Morgan Dawson, *Sarah Morgan: The Civil War Diary of a Southern Woman*, ed. Charles East (New York: Touchstone, 1992), 65.

111. Emma LeConte, *When the World Ended: The Diary of Emma LeConte*, ed. Earl Schenck Miers (1957; Lincoln: University of Nebraska Press, 1987), 58. Michael Fellman came to a similar conclusion in his study of Missouri, where he argued that "all the evidence indicates that Union soldiers and guerrillas did not shoot, violate, or beat women who aided the enemy": Michael Fellman, *Inside War: The Guerrilla Conflict in Missouri during the American Civil War* (New York: Oxford University Press, 1989), 201; and in his study of Sherman: Michael Fellman, *Citizen Sherman: A Life of William Tecumseh Sherman* (New York: Random House, 1995), 226. See also Daniel Sutherland, *A Savage Conflict: The Decisive Role of Guerrillas in the American Civil War* (Chapel Hill: University of North Carolina Press, 2009), 177.

112. Quoted in J. S. McNeily, "War and Reconstruction in Mississippi, 1863–1890," *Publication of the Mississippi Historical Society*, II (Jackson, MS, 1918), 199.

113. Royster, *The Destructive War*, 342; Grimsley, *Hard Hand of War*, 199; Reid Mitchell, *The Vacant Chair: The Northern Soldier Leaves Home* (New York: Oxford University Press, 1993), 104–110; Rubin, *Through the Heart of Dixie*, 49; Steven J. Ramold, *Baring the Iron Hand: Discipline in the Union Army* (Dekalb: Northern Illinois University Press, 2010), 300; Feimster, *Southern Horrors*, 21–22; Frank, *The Civilian War*, 110–111. The threat against black

women appears to have been higher elsewhere also. Harry Stout chronicles a record of the "ravishing of negro women" on the South Carolina Sea Islands from 1862. Harry S. Stout, *Upon the Altar of the Nation: A Moral History of the American Civil War* (New York: Viking, 2006), 142. The experience during Turchin's looting of Athens, Alabama, in May 1862 supports the pattern. It including one attempted rape and one rape of two enslaved women. William A. Blair, *With Malice toward Some: Treason and Loyalty in the Civil War Era* (Chapel Hill: University of North Carolina Press, 2014), 135.

114. Sutherland, *Savage Conflict*, 216, 274.

115. "In theory, Sherman advertised himself as a terrorist—an advertisement calculated to instill profound, disabling fear in the hearts of Confederate civilians even more than their military. . . . In practice—and this must be emphasized—Sherman and his army were selective destroyers. Unlike terrorist actions employed in other wars against civilian populations . . . Sherman's soldiers generally refrained from raping white women or killing masses of civilians." Michael Fellman, "Terrorism and Civil War," in *In the Name of God and Country: Reconsidering Terrorism in American History* (New Haven, CT: Yale University Press, 2010), 60.

116. With no planes from which to drop pamphlets and no internet over which to broadcast messages, Sherman relied on the Confederate grapevine telegraph, which served his purpose better in many respects because the source and conduits were Southerners themselves. Jason Phillips, "The Grape Vine Telegraph: Rumors and Confederate Persistence," *Journal of Southern History* 72 (November 2006): 753–788; Lisa Tendrich Frank, "Bedrooms as Battlefields: The Role of Gender Politics in Sherman's March," in *Occupied Women: Gender, Military Occupation, and the American Civil War*, ed. LeeAnn Whites and Alicia P. Long (Baton Rouge: Louisiana State University Press, 2009), 37–38; Frank, *The Civilian War*, 158–159; Ash, *When the Yankees Came*, 200.

117. McNeil's report, March 16, 1863, *OR*, I, 22(1): 241.

118. Mary Westmoreland to Jefferson Davis, October 22, 1863, *Papers of Jefferson Davis*, 10: 31; E. Susan Barber and Charles F. Ritter, "'Physical Abuse . . . and Rough Handling:' Race, Gender, and Sexual Justice in the Occupied South," in Whites and Long, *Occupied Women*, 63.

119. Frank, "Bedrooms as Battlefields," 33–34, 36.

120. Schultz, "Mute Fury," 63–64, quotation on p. 60.

121. Petite, *"The Women Will Howl,"* 65–66.

122. Rubin, *Through the Heart of Dixie*, 49, quotation on p. 48; see also Frank, *The Civilian War*, 111.

123. Frank, *The Civilian War*; and Jacqueline Glass Campbell, *When Sherman Marched North from the Sea: Resistance on the Confederate Home Front* (Chapel

Hill: University of North Carolina Press, 2005); Diary entries of June 25, 26, 27, and 28, 1864, in *Inside Lincoln's Army: The Diary of Marsena Rudolph Patrick, Provost Marshal General, Army of the Potomac*, ed. David S. Sparks (New York: Thomas Yoseloff, 1964), 389.

124. Ash, *When the Yankees Came*, 201; Mitchell, *The Vacant Chair*, 104; Grimsley, *Hard Hand of War*, 220; Frank, *The Civilian War*, 112. "Although not perfect," two authors recently wrote, "the system functioned to bring to justice soldiers who committed sexual crimes." Barber and Ritter, "'Physical Abuse . . . and Rough Handling,'" 49. Ramold, *Baring the Iron Hand*, 297–298; Thomas Goodrich, *Black Flag: Guerrilla Warfare on the Western Border, 1861–1865* (Bloomington: Indiana University Press, 1995), 118–119.

125. Mrs. A. E. Taylor to New Orleans PM, January 20, 1864, PMR, Department of the Gulf, #1845, Box 3: Letters Received, 1864; George Webster to R. R. Brown, January 23, 1864, PMR, Department of the Gulf, #1845, Box 3: Letters Received, 1864.

126. Sommerville, *Rape and Race*, 43; Feimster, *Southern Horrors*, 20–21; Trial of Dandridge Brooks, et al., NARA, RG94, Microfilm 1523.

127. Transcript of case of Charles Clark and William Dormandy, Special Order No. 131, October 14, 1862, NARA, RG94, Microfilm 1523. This same scenario (with soldier using gun to demand compliance from a woman he raped) played out in other cases, including John Bell, John Wesley Cook, Spencer Lloyd, and John M. Smith, NARA, RG94, Microfilm 1523.

128. The Latin phrase is *inter arma enim silent legēs* and goes at least as far back as Cicero.

8. THE IMPORTANCE OF STATES

1. David Bell, *The First Total War: Napoleon's Europe and the Birth of Warfare as We Know It* (New York: Mariner, 2008) notes that this was a unique interval in world history. Rousseau, quoted in David M. Crowe, *War Crimes, Genocide, and Justice: A Global History* (New York: Palgrave Macmillan, 2014), 36; Rogers Smith, *Civic Ideals: Conflicting Visions of Citizenship in U.S. History* (New Haven, CT: Yale University Press, 1999); Judith Sklar, *American Citizenship: The Quest for Inclusion* (Cambridge, MA: Harvard University Press, 1998).

2. Samuel Hyde, *Pistols and Politics: The Dilemma of Democracy in Louisiana's Florida Parishes, 1810–1899* (Baton Rouge: Louisiana State University Press, 1996), 135.

3. Everard H. Smith, "Chambersburg: Anatomy of a Confederate Reprisal," *American Historical Review* 96 (April 1991): 432–455; Jubal Early, *War Memoirs: Autobiographical Sketch and Narrative of the War Between the States*, reprint (1912. Bloomington: Indiana University Press, 1960), 401, 404.

4. Charles Morris to Mary Minor Morris, August 4, 1864, Section 1, Charles Morris Papers, Mss1 M8315a, Virginia Historical Society, Richmond, Virginia. My thanks to Brian Luskey for drawing this episode to my attention. Isaac White Letters, Special Collections Department, University Libraries, Virginia Tech, Ms97–013, available at http://spec.lib.vt.edu/mss/white/white.htm.

5. George Rable, *God's Almost Chosen People: A Religious History of the Civil War* (Chapel Hill: University of North Carolina Press, 2010), 353, 358.

6. Andrew Fialka, "Captain Harry Truman: A Case Study of the Union Military's Use of Guerrilla Tactics against the Civilian Population in Civil War Missouri" (B.A. honors thesis, University of Missouri, 2010), 16–17; Truman may not have been the only Yankee who operated outside the laws of war. A Confederate captain reported that Union soldiers in the northwestern part of the state had "murdered every Southern man that could be found." Peevy to Holmes, April 17, 1863, *OR*, I, 22(2): 823–826.

7. Fialka, "Captain Harry Truman," 19. Another Missourian who operated in the same mode for the Union was John R. Kelso. A native of the state, he hunted pro-Confederate guerrillas, often using disguises and subterfuge and killing many. John R. Kelso, *Bloody Engagements: John R. Kelso's Civil War*, ed. Christopher Grasso (New Haven, CT: Yale University Press, 2017).

8. Fialka, "Captain Harry Truman," 76–77; S. L. Woodward to Hurst, January 11, 1864 *OR*, I, 32(2): 66; Forrest to Buckland, March 22, 1864, *OR*, I, 32(3): 117; B. H. Grierson to Hurst, March 24, 1864, *OR*, I, 32(3): 145–146.

9. Execution data from Marshall Myers, "Union General Stephen Gano Burbridge: The Most Hated Man in Kentucky," in *Kentucky's Civil War, 1861–1865*, ed. Jerlene Rose (Clay City, KY: Back Home in Kentucky, 2005), 144; Anne E. Marshall, *Creating a Confederate Kentucky: The Lost Cause and Civil War Memory in a Border State* (Chapel Hill: University of North Carolina Press, 2010), 23; William A. Blair, *With Malice toward Some: Treason and Loyalty in the Civil War Era* (Chapel Hill: University of North Carolina Press, 2014), 208.

10. Carter quoted in Lorien Foote, *Yankee Plague: Escaped Union Prisoners and the Collapse of the Confederacy* (Chapel Hill: University of North Carolina Press, 2016), 101.

11. Daniel Sutherland, *A Savage Conflict: The Decisive Role of Guerrillas in the American Civil War* (Chapel Hill: University of North Carolina Press, 2009), 203; Stevenson to Stanton, April 5, 1865, *OR*, I, 46(3): 590.

12. Stephen W. Sears, "Raid on Richmond," in *Controversies and Commanders: Dispatches from the Army of the Potomac* (Boston: Houghton Mifflin, 1999), 228–229, 232–233.

13. Peter Luebke, "Kilpatrick-Dahlgren Raid," April 5, 2011, Encyclopedia Virginia online, Virginia Foundation for the Humanities, available at

http://www.encyclopediavirginia.org/Kilpatrick-Dahlgren_Raid#start _entry.

14. Quoted in Sears, "Raid on Richmond," 241.

15. Sears, "Raid on Richmond," 245–246, quotation on 237.

16. Sears, "Raid on Richmond," 243.

17. Sears believes the Dahlgren affair directly influenced the Confederate turn toward secret actions against Lincoln and other Union targets. "It was easy to rationalize such efforts ... when everyone involved could point to the fact that the Federals under Kilpatrick and Dahlgren had shown no compunction about pillaging and burning Richmond and killing President Davis and his advisors." Sears, "Raid on Richmond," 248. Although the Dahlgren raid accelerated this attitude, ample evidence exists of Confederate experiments in sabotage and mass casualty weapons from before this time.

18. Davis, "Fast Day Proclamation," October 26, 1864, *MPC*, I, 564.

19. "Confession of Kennedy, the Rebel Incendiary," *Baltimore Sun*, March 28, 1865, LVI, 1.

20. Victoria Bynum, *Unruly Women: The Politics of Social and Sexual Control in the Old South* (Chapel Hill: University of North Carolina Press, 1992), 143; Barton Myers, *Rebels Against the Confederacy: North Carolina's Unionists* (Cambridge: Cambridge University Press, 2014), 137–149, 167; Phillip Shaw Paludan, *Victims: A True Story of the Civil War* (Knoxville: University of Tennessee Press, 1981); Quotation by Richard B. McCaslin, "Foreword," in David Pickering and Judy Falls, *Brush Men and Vigilantes: Civil War Dissent in Texas* (College Station: Texas A&M University Press, 2000), xiv.

21. This attitude was ubiquitous in Republican newspapers as well. "'The war is drawing to an end,' the *Continental Monthly* predicted in summer 1862, 'but a greater and nobler task lies before the soldiers and free men of America—the extending of *civilization* into the South.'" Quoted in Bruce Tap, *Over Lincoln's Shoulder: The Committee on the Conduct of the War* (Lawrence: University Press of Kansas, 1998), 198.

22. Jay Sexton, "William H. Seward in the World," *JCWE* 4 (September 2014): 399; Charles Sumner, "Letter of the Hon. Charles Sumner, U.S. Senator from Massachusetts, April 9, 1863," in Loyal National League of the State of New York, *Opinions of Prominent Men Concerning the Great Questions of the Times* (New York: C. S. Westcott, 1863), 13; Lieber to Sumner, June 20, 1864, Box 44, Lieber Papers, HH; Seward quoted in Walter Stahr, *Seward: Lincoln's Indispensable Man* (New York: Simon and Schuster, 2012), 139.

23. Sexton, "William H. Seward," 414; *Tuskegee Republican*, January 7, 1858.

24. Henry Everett Russell, "The War a Contest for Ideas," *The Continental Monthly: Devoted to Literature and National Policy (1862–1864)* 5 (May 1864): 578–584.

25. George L. Prentiss, "The National Crisis: Being and Address, Delivered before the Phi Beta Kappa Society in Dartmouth College, July 30, 1862" (New York: W. H. Bidwell, 1862), 11, in *Civil War Pamphlets, 1861–71*, vol. 1, NL; Joel Parker, *The Character of the Rebellion, and the Conduct of the War* (Cambridge: Welch, Bigelow, 1862), 40, in *Civil War Politics*, vol. 2, NL.

26. Loyal National League, *The Sumter Anniversary, 1863: Opinions of Loyalists Concerning the Great Questions of the Times* (New York: C. S. Westcott, 1863). Modern scholars have grown more skeptical of the universal claims of international law, which depended too much in their origins on racialized visions of the world's people. See Jennifer Pitts, "Empire and Legal Universalisms in the Eighteenth Century," *American Historical Review* 117 (2012): 92–121; and Andrew Fitzmaurice, "Liberalism and Empire in Nineteenth-Century International Law" *American Historical Review* 117 (2012): 122–140.

27. Lincoln, "Annual Message to Congress," December 1, 1862, *CWAL*, V, 537; H. Paulding, "Letter of Admiral Paulding," in Loyal National League, *Opinions of Prominent Men*, 31; Robert Penn Warren, *The Legacy of the Civil War* (Cambridge, MA: Harvard University Press, 1961); Lieber to Halleck, May 20, 1863, Box 27, Lieber Papers, HH.

28. Charles B. Dew, *Apostles of Disunion: Southern Secession Commissioners and the Causes of the Civil War* (Charlottesville: University Press of Virginia, 2001); Matthew Karp, *This Vast Southern Empire: Slaveholders at the Helm of American Foreign Policy* (Cambridge, MA: Harvard University Press, 2016).

29. Jacqueline Glass Campbell, *When Sherman Marched North from the Sea: Resistance on the Confederate Home Front* (Chapel Hill: University of North Carolina Press, 2005); and Lisa Tendrich Frank, *The Civilian War: Confederate Women and Union Soldiers during Sherman's March* (Baton Rouge: Louisiana State University Press, 2015).

30. Quotation from Peter J. Taylor, "The State as Container: Territoriality in the Modern World-System," *Progress in Human Geography* 18 (1994): 158; and Steven Pinker, *The Better Angels of Our Nature: Why Violence Has Declined* (New York: Viking, 2011).

31. Principally Fauquier, Rappahannock, and Warren counties. John Heatwole's study of this campaign, *The Burning: Sheridan's Devastation of the Shenandoah Valley* (Charlottesville, VA: Rockbridge Publishing, 1998), chronicles many scenes of devastation.

32. Mosby to Stuart, September 30, 1863, quoted in *The Memoirs of Colonel John S. Mosby*, ed. Charles Wells Russell (Boston: Little, Brown, 1917), 262.

33. Robert R. Mackey, *The Uncivil War: Irregular Warfare in the Upper South, 1861–1865* (Norman: University of Oklahoma Press, 2004), chapter 3.

34. John Singleton Mosby, "Monument to Mosby's Men," *SHSP* 27 (1899), 271. Mosby's final defense of his men used the evidence of Grant's willingness to parole his men alongside Lee's to prove their legitimacy. *SHSP*, 273. But this retroactive decision, taken at a time when Lincoln was asking for charity, does not satisfy the case for how Mosby's men behaved during the war itself.

35. Mosby, "The Monument to Mosby's Men," *SHSP*, 269.

36. Grant to Sheridan, August 16, 1864, *OR*, I, 43(1): 811.

37. Grant to Sheridan, August 16, 1864, *OR*, I, 43(1): 811; Jeffry D. Wert, *Mosby's Rangers: The True Adventures of the Most Famous Command of the Civil War* (New York: Simon and Schuster, 1991), 197.

38. Michael J. Bennett, "The Black Flag and Confederate Soldiers," in *This Distracted and Anarchical People: New Answers for Old Questions about the Civil War–Era North*, ed. Andrew L. Slap and Michael Thomas Smith (New York: Fordham University Press, 2013), 157. Jeffry D. Wert recounts the episode in similar terms, though he notes that two men had their throats cut. See Wert, *Mosby's Rangers*, 195–196.

39. Report of John S. Mosby, *OR*, I, 43(1): 634.

40. John S. Mosby, "The Monument to Mosby's Men," *SHSP*, 1899, 275.

41. "The Middle Division," *New York Times*, August 25, 1864; Wert, *Mosby's Rangers*, 214.

42. Wert attributes Custer's decision to "memories of the burned wagons at Berryville, the dead Michigan troops in the ditch at Benjamin Morgan's, the disappearance of pickets and forage details [all of which] kindled the flames ignited by McMaster's fatal wounding." Wert, *Mosby's Rangers*, 215.

43. John W. Munson, *Reminiscences of a Mosby Guerrilla* (New York: Moffat, Yard, and Co., 1906), 149.

44. Mosby, "Retaliation," *SHSP* 27 (1899), 268.

45. Mosby to Sheridan, *OR*, I, 43(2): 920; Wert, *Mosby's Rangers*, 246–252. Lee endorsed the action on the same principle—that retaliation might be the only method of preventing "the cruel conduct of the enemy toward our citizens." Lee, quoted in John S. Mosby, "Retaliation," 317.

46. A similar retaliatory event—in which the Union executed six Confederate prisoners following the execution of six Union prisoners—is chronicled in Oliver R. Barrett, "Lincoln and Retaliation," *Lincoln Herald* (December 1947): 2–7, 23. In another similar event, occurring after Lee had surrendered, Sherman's commanders did not retaliate at all. Mark Bradley, *This Astounding Close: The Road to Bennett Place* (Chapel Hill: University of North Carolina Press, 2000), 105.

47. Mosby, "Monument," *SHSP,* 274.

48. Heatwole, *The Burning,* 69–70; Edwin M. Haynes, quoted in Heatwole, *The Burning,* 93.

49. Before the debate over prisoner treatment and even before the confirmations of atrocities in rebel prisons, the US commissary general proposed, and the secretary of war approved, a 20 percent reduction in the food allotment to Confederate prisoners. W. Hoffman to E. Stanton, May 19, 1864, *OR,* II, 7: 150–151; and "Circular," W. Hoffman, June 1, 1864, *OR,* II, 7: 183–184. Scholars of Civil War prisons argue that this policy shift stemmed from anger among officials (principally the Commissary General W. Hoffman, the Quartermaster General Montgomery Meigs, and Edwin Stanton, the secretary of war). James M. Gillispie, *Andersonvilles of the North: The Myths and Realities of Northern Treatment of Civil War Confederate Prisoners* (Denton: University of North Texas Press, 2008), 58–64. Gillispie's own evidence from the camps at Alton, Rock Island, and elsewhere indicate that the "retaliation" rations did not significantly affect the mortality rates in Union camps. Gillispie, *Andersonvilles of the North,* 117, 145, 162, 202, 246.

50. Reporting on Andersonville and Belle Isle, in Richmond, filled the papers beginning in spring 1864. See, for example, *Columbus Daily Enquirer,* July 27, 1864; *New York Herald,* September 19, 1864; *Philadelphia Inquirer,* November 16, 1864.

51. Mark E. Neely, *Retaliation: The Problem of Atrocity in the Civil War* (Gettysburg, PA: Gettysburg College, 2002), 11.

52. United States Sanitary Commission, *Narrative of Privations and Sufferings of United States Officers and Soldiers while Prisoners of War in the hand of the Rebel Authorities . . .* (Philadelphia: King & Baird, 1864), 25.

53. Mark Neely, *Civil War and the Limits of Destruction* (Cambridge, MA: Harvard University Press, 2007), 187–188.

54. *CG,* 38th Congress, Second Session, December 20, 1864, 73–74.

55. *CG,* 38th Congress, Second Session, Part 1, 413, 388, 390, 454.

56. *CG,* 38th Congress, Second Session, January 16, 1864, 267.

57. Confederates denied all the charges leveled against them in the course of the debate. Their rebuttal appeared in their own *Report of the Joint Select Committee appointed to investigate the condition and treatment of prisoners of war,* Confederate States Congress, March 3, 1865.

58. *CG,* 38th Congress, Second Session, January 24, 1865, 383.

59. Lieber, "Stonewall Jackson and Our Prisoners," included in Lieber to Halleck, January 9, 1865, Lieber Papers, HH; Holt quoted in "Trial of Henry Wirz," 40th Congress, 2nd Session, House of Representatives, Ex.Doc. No. 23, 809; Lieber to Sumner, December 24, 1864, Lieber Papers, HH.

60. Benjamin Wade, *CG*, 38th Congress, Second Session, Part 1, January 23, 1865, 364. Wade's resolution did include a provision for improving conditions in Northern prisoner-of-war camps once the Confederates demonstrated they had done the same.

61. Charles Sumner, *CG*, 38th Congress, Second Session, Part 1, January 24, 1865, 381. Sumner adopted Lieber's formulation of this critique almost word for word: "It seems then that retaliation in this case is—impracticable, because God by thanked, our people would not carry it out (the Northern man is eminently a hardhearted being); injurious, if it would be carried out, for it would barbarize our own people; useless, because it would not affect the hard hearts could indulge in the heaven-crying cruelties—a very shame to humanity itself; and therefore, immoral or criminal in turn because useless inflictions of suffering, no matter on whom is cruelty." Lieber to Sumner, January 22, 1865, Lieber Papers, HH.

62. Francis Lieber, quoted in Henry W. Halleck, "Retaliation in War," *American Journal of International Law* 6 (January 1912), 113; *Boston Daily Advertiser*, February 4, 1865, 2; "Retaliation," *Albany Evening Journal*, April 12, 1865, 2; *National Daily Intelligencer*, February 2, 1865; *New Orleans Times*, March 9, 1865.

63. Bertram Wyatt-Brown, "Death of a Nation," in *The Shaping of Southern Culture: Honor, Grace, and War, 1760s-1880s* (Chapel Hill: University of North Carolina Press, 2001), 230–231; John Merryman, *Massacre: The Life and Death of the Paris Commune* (New York: Basic Books, 2014), 253–254.

64. Grant to Sheridan, April 2, 1865, *OR*, I, 46(3): 488.

65. Grant, "Final Report," *OR*, I, 46(1): 11; Sheridan to Grant, April 5, 1865, *OR*, I, 46(3): 582; Taylor to "Dear Mamma," April 5, 1865, *OR*, I, 46(3): 582; Grant to Bowers, April 3, 1865, *OR*, I, 46(3): 509; Grant to Stanton, April 4, 1865, *OR*, I, 46(3): 545. Elizabeth Varon, *Appomattox: Victory, Defeat, and Freedom at the End of the Civil War* (New York: Oxford University Press, 2014), 7; William Marvel emphasizes "Grant's determination to beat Lee's army into submission," though his narrative chronicles the importance of strategy. Marvel, *Lee's Last Retreat: The Flight to Appomattox* (Chapel Hill: University of North Carolina Press), 37; Grant to Lee, April 7, 1865, *OR*, I, 46(3): 619.

66. Varon, *Appomattox*, 62.

67. Lee, "General Orders No. 9," *OR*, I, 46(1): 1267; Alexander, quoted in Varon, *Appomattox*, 72; J. Tracy Powers, *Lee's Miserables: Life in the Army of Northern Virginia from the Wilderness to Appomattox* (Chapel Hill: University of North Carolina Press, 1998), 283.

68. Bradley, *This Astounding Close*, 171–180, 206–213, 226–232; Gregory P. Downs, *After Appomattox: Military Occupation and the Ends of War* (Cambridge, MA: Harvard University Press, 2015), 17.

69. Powers, *Lee's Miserables*, 282; Wyatt-Brown, "Death of a Nation," 232.

70. Report of Edward S. Salomon, May 29, 1865, *OR*, I, 47(1): 673; Diary entry of April 18, 1865, *Fighting for Liberty and Right: The Civil War Diary of William Bluffton Miller*, ed. Jeffrey L. Patrick and Robert J. Willey (Knoxville: University of Tennessee Press, 2005), 335; Caroline E. Janney, *Remembering the Civil War: Reunion and the Limits of Reconciliation* (Chapel Hill: University of North Carolina Press, 2013), 57.

71. Abstract of the Journal of Maj. Gen. Jacob D. Cox, U.S. Army, Doc. No. 237: April 17, *OR*, I, 47(1): 937.

72. Charles Wright Wills, *Army Life of an Illinois Soldier: Including a Day-by-Day Record of Sherman's March to the Sea: Letters and Diary of Charles W. Wills*, compiled by Mary E. Kellogg (Carbondale: Southern Illinois University Press, 1996), 371.

73. Charles T. Kruse to "Dear Parrents," April 18, 1865, in Charles T. Kruse Papers, NL; Sanford McCall to "Dear Niece," May 2, 1865, Sanford McCall Letters, UVA.

74. *OR*, I, 47(2): 239; Thomas Stevens to his wife, April 23, 1865, in George M. Blackburn, ed., *"Dear Carrie . . .": The Civil War Letters of Thomas N. Stevens* (Mt. Pleasant, MI: Clarke Historical Library, 1984). Bradley, *This Astounding Close*, 163–165.

75. Aaron Sheehan-Dean, ed., *The Civil War as Told by Those Who Lived It: The Final Year* (New York: Library of America, 2014), 709.

76. Varon, *Appomattox*, 94–100, 139. Varon notes that black soldiers manifested this same control after news of Lincoln's assassination.

77. Blair, *With Malice toward Some*, 8.

78. Varon, *Appomattox*, 101; Blair, *With Malice toward Some*, 261.

79. Blair, *With Malice toward Some*, 240–243, 307, 8.

80. Mark W. Summers, *The Ordeal of the Reunion: A New History of Reconstruction* (Chapel Hill: University of North Carolina Press, 2014), 6.

81. Michael Braddick, *God's Fury, England's Fire: A New History of the English Civil Wars* (London: Allen Lane, 2008), 556–558; Barbara Donagan, *War in England, 1642–1649* (Oxford: Oxford University Press, 2008), 369–398; Wayne Lee, *Barbarians and Brothers: Anglo-American Warfare, 1500–1865* (New York: Oxford University Press, 2011), 116–118.

82. Davis, "Address," April 4, 1865, in *MPC*, I, 569; Daniel E. Sutherland, *A Savage Conflict: The Decisive Role of Guerrillas in the American Civil War* (Chapel Hill:

University of North Carolina Press, 2009), 267–269; the best review of the literature around Davis's intent can be found in William B. Feis, "Jefferson Davis and the 'Guerrilla Option': A Reexamination," in *The Collapse of the Confederacy*, ed. Mark Grimsley and Brooks D. Simpson (Lincoln: University of Nebraska Press, 2001), 104–128. Like Sutherland, Feis argues that Davis did not support turning to a guerrilla strategy. Seddon quoted in Sutherland, *A Savage Conflict*, 268.

83. Marvel, *Lee's Last Retreat*, 59; Lee to Davis, April 19, 1865, quoted in Marvel, *Lee's Last Retreat*, 189; Edward Porter Alexander, *Fighting for the Confederacy: The Personal Recollections of General Edward Porter Alexander*, ed. Gary Gallagher (Chapel Hill: University of North Carolina Press, 1989), 531. Brooks D. Simpson offers a contrary reading in a blogpost: Simpson, "Lee's Choice at Appomattox Revisited," Crossroads, Brook D. Simpson's blog, December 14, 2010, available at https://cwcrossroads.wordpress.com/2010/12/14/lees-choice-at-appomattox-revisited/. Charles Francis Adams, "Lee at Appomattox," in *Lee at Appomattox and Other Papers* (Boston: Houghton, Mifflin, 1903), 2.

84. Sutherland, *A Savage War*, 270.

85. Sutherland, *A Savage War*, 273–274.

86. Brian D. McKnight, *Confederate Outlaw: Champ Ferguson and the Civil War in Appalachia* (Baton Rouge: Louisiana State University Press, 2011), 166, 151, 160–173.

87. Sutherland, *A Savage War*, 276–277; Mark L. Bradley, *Bluecoats and Tarheels: Soldiers and Civilians in Reconstruction North Carolina* (Lexington: University Press of Kentucky, 2009), 100–104.

88. Gregory P. Downs has offered the most challenging and comprehensive version of this argument. He argues that a "post-surrender wartime" prevailed that gave the president and Congress wide latitude to use the military to enforce the terms of Reconstruction. Downs, *After Appomattox*. Downs's work is part of a group of books that critically reexamine the idea of "wartime" itself. See Mary Dudziak, *Wartime: An Idea, Its History, Its Consequences* (New York: Oxford University Press, 2013); and Rosa Brooks, *How Everything Became War and the Military Became Everything: Tales from the Pentagon* (New York: Simon and Schuster, 2016).

89. Martha Hodes, *Mourning Lincoln* (New Haven, CT: Yale University Press, 2015), 98–99; Richard Wrightman Fox, *Lincoln's Body: A Cultural History* (New York: Norton, 2015), 67.

90. Lieber to Halleck, April 15, 1865, Box 28, Lieber Papers, HH.

91. Charles S. Robinson, *The Martyred President: A Sermon Preached in the First Presbyterian Church, Brooklyn, N.Y.* (New York: John Trow, 1865), 15, 25; Henry C. Badger, *The Humble Conqueror: A Discourse Commemorative of the Life*

and Services of Abraham Lincoln (Boston: William V. Spencer, 1865), 13; Herrick Johnson, *"God's Ways Unsearchable": A Discourse on the Death of President Lincoln* (Pittsburgh: W. G. Johnston, 1865), 10.

92. Quotation from John Falkner, *A Sermon on the Services and Death of Abraham Lincoln* (New York: John Trow, 1865), 12; Morgan Dix, *The Death of President Lincoln* (Cambridge, MA: Riverside Press, 1865), 4.

93. Allyn Hall, *Eulogy of Abraham Lincoln* (Hartford, CT: A. N. Clark, 1865), 53.

94. Gilbert Haven, *The Uniter and Liberator of America* (Boston: James P. Magee, 1865), 24; Hodes, *Mourning Lincoln*, 128–130.

95. Lieber to Halleck, April 16, 1865, Box 28, Lieber Papers, HH; Lieber to Sumner, April 15, April 23, 1865, Box 46, Lieber Papers, HH; Badger, "The Humble Conqueror," 13.

96. Rogers, April 22, 1865, in C. Peter Ripley, Roy E. Finkenbine, Michael F. Hembree, and Donald Yacovone, eds., *BAP*, 315–316.

97. Emma Hardinge, *The Great Funeral Oration on Abraham Lincoln* (New York: American News Co., 1865), 20; Fox, *Lincoln's Body*, 179.

98. Hodes, *Mourning Lincoln*, 115–116. A representative sample of the apotheosizing of Lincoln can be found in Richard H. Steele, *Victory and Mourning* (New Brunswick, NJ: Terhune and Van Anglen's Press, 1865), 11–12.

99. Robinson, *The Martyred President*, 7; Alex H. Bullock, *Abraham Lincoln: The Just Magistrate, the Representative Statesman, the Practical Philanthropist* (Worcester, MA: Charles Hamilton, 1865), 45, 47.

100. Badger, *The Humble Conqueror*, 14; N. H. Chamberlain, *The Assassination of President Lincoln* (New York: G. W. Carleton, 1865), 5–6; Frank L. Robbins, *A Discourse on the Death of Abraham Lincoln* (Philadelphia: Henry B. Ashmead, 1865), 12; Thomas Tousey, *Discourse on the Death of Abraham Lincoln* (Rochester, NY: C. D. Tracy, 1865), 21.

101. Johnson, *"God's Ways Unsearchable,"* 11; Haven, *The Uniter and Liberator of America*, 24. Hodes sees a more complex ministerial message that often blended vengeance and mercy: Hodes, *Mourning Lincoln*, 136–138.

102. Robinson, *The Martyred President*, 16–17.

103. "Our beloved President becomes a victim to the very magnanimity he was inculcating." Robinson, *The Martyred President*, 18.

CONCLUSION. THE DOUBLE-EDGED SWORD

1. Laws sometimes drove the death toll higher in earlier wars as well. In her study of the English Civil War, Barbara Donagan writes that "what is legal is not, of course, necessarily just or equitable." Donagan, *War in England, 1642–1649* (Oxford: Oxford University Press, 2011), 394.

2. Diary entry of June 3, 1863, *The Civil War Diary of Gideon Welles, Lincoln's Secretary of the Navy, The Original Manuscript Edition*, ed. William E. Gienapp and Erica L. Gienapp (Urbana: University of Illinois Press, 2014), 205.

3. "The guerrilla conflict in all its guises—Unionist and rebel guerrillas, partisan rangers, lone bushwhackers, guerrilla hunters, deserter bands, and outlaw gangs—made the war a far bloodier affair than the armies alone could have done." Daniel E. Sutherland, *A Savage Conflict: The Decisive Role of Guerrillas in the American Civil War* (Chapel Hill: University of North Carolina Press, 2011), 277.

4. Thomas Dower, *War without Mercy: Race and Power in the Pacific War* (New York: Pantheon, 1987); Michael Bess, *Choices Under Fire: Moral Dimensions of World War II* (New York: Vintage, 2006), 7, chapter 1.

5. Wayne Lee, *Barbarians and Brothers: Anglo-American Warfare, 1500–1865* (New York: Oxford University Press, 2011), 2; Donagan, *War in England*, 9, 397.

6. John P. Usher to Lincoln, May 6, 1864, *LP*.

7. Jan Gross, *Neighbors: The Destruction of the Jewish Community in Jedwabne, Poland*, reprint (2001. New York: Penguin, 2002), 89.

ACKNOWLEDGMENTS

Writing a book is supposedly a solitary pursuit, but this project has allowed me to engage with so many people I've come to appreciate the social dimension of writing as much as the quiet moments. The conversations—in person, over email, and through print—that I have had with friends and colleagues have enriched my life and enabled me to write this book. For that, I am grateful.

The archivists at the various archives I visited have been unfailingly courteous and helpful. The staff at the National Archives deserves special thanks for their patience with helping me sort through army records. Trevor Plante, in particular, extended great courtesy throughout my many visits there. In the same camp, the interlibrary loan staff at West Virginia University and Louisiana State University played a crucial role in helping me obtain the materials on which this study is based. Germain Bienvenu, at LSU's Hill Library, offered valuable help on both manuscript materials and images. At both WVU and LSU, I have been fortunate to have had supportive chairs and deans who enabled me to conduct research trips. A Manship Fellowship from the LSU College of Humanities and Social Sciences in the summer of 2014 allowed me to spend a week at the Henry Huntington Library reading Francis Lieber's papers. The resources available through the Fred C. Frey Chair at LSU have enabled additional trips and writing time. I am grateful to the Frey-Eaton families for their generosity in supporting this position.

The community of Civil War scholars has been a wonderful place to make an intellectual home. The generosity and intelligence of my colleagues have been both helpful and inspiring. Keith Bohannon has proved himself the master of anything related to Georgia and much beyond. He responded quickly and helpfully to a series of queries on my part. Jim Ogden was likewise helpful in my studies of Tennessee and Georgia and connected me with other people who shared written material and ideas, most importantly Larry Stephens and Bob Davis. I met Andrew Fialka

ACKNOWLEDGMENTS

when he was a student, but he quickly evolved into a peer from whom I learned. He generously read and commented on a draft chapter despite being a new dad and writing his own dissertation. Sarah Gardner read much of the manuscript and offered encouraging words and valuable suggestions, for which I am grateful. Susannah Ural and I have talked about the ideas in this project for a long time. She hosted an event at the University of Southern Mississippi with Anne Marshall and Lesley Gordon that was both great fun and intellectually stimulating. Similar thanks go to Anne Marshall (again) and Andy Lang for organizing a great conference at Mississippi State University. The group they assembled, including Drew Bledsoe, D. H. Dilbeck, Lorien Foote, Lesley Gordon, and Susan O'Donovan, all participated in robust conversation that helped me conceptualize the whole project. Lorien, in particular, has answered questions and encouraged me for a long time. I have benefited from her broad knowledge and her example of inquisitive scholarship. Gary Gallagher encouraged and prodded, when the latter was called for. As always, he proved a great counselor and even lent an office for a particularly productive week of writing in Charlottesville.

I owe serious thanks to all the friends who read pieces of the work in progress or listened to ideas. Wayne Hsieh did both, offering his typically penetrating comments. Johann Neem and Carl Bon Tempo both ventured out of their fields to offer their usual mix of encouraging and challenging ideas. Jim Broomall shared his knowledge of Maryland and West Virginia, including work in progress that was quite helpful. I disappointed Mark Simpson-Vos, which still pinches, and makes me all the more grateful for the encouragement, support, and motivation he provided and the friend he has become. A host of people allowed themselves to be buttonholed at a conference or over email to answer queries or test ideas. I am grateful to all them, including Joe Beilein, Bill Blair, Don Doyle, Matt Gallman, Luke Harlow, Carrie Janney, Watson Jennison, Susanna Lee, Bill Link, Peter Luebke, Chandra Manning, Jim Marten, Barton Myers, Megan Kate Nelson, George Rable, Brian Schoen, Jay Sexton, Yael Sternhell, Amy Taylor, LeeAnn Whites, and Michael Woods. Ed Ayers did not read any of the book, but his influence hovers over it. As I discovered a more complex and tangled story than the one I initially envisioned, I kept hearing his admonition not to ignore or try to resolve the points of

448

tension and contradiction but to embrace them as the core of the story. I have tried to do justice to the admirable model of scholarship he set for those of us lucky enough to work with him.

Stathis Kalyvas commissioned an essay on the Civil War and violence that I expected to be a short detour. That piece mushroomed into the current book, and I owe him thanks for initiating it and for a great weekend in New Haven talking about civil wars. Joe Glatthaar read the whole manuscript and offered trenchant and valuable criticism throughout. He is a model of honest scholarly engagement and generosity. I owe a special thanks to Gideon Hart, who generously shared his research files on the US Army's military commission hearings. I drew insights from his own research into this topic and greatly appreciate his willingness to share and explain the spreadsheets that he constructed.

I have been graced with funny, friendly, and helpful faculty colleagues, most of them friends as well, who have supported this project over a long time. At the University of North Florida, Dale Clifford, my first and beau ideal department chair, drew on her own broad military history knowledge to pose insightful questions and encourage me in the early phases of the project. Greg Domber provided comic relief with his wry observations about the world and discussed a wide range of the issues in this book. He also earns special thanks for helping me puzzle through a particularly difficult Sherman letter one day at the Library of Congress. At WVU, Brian Luskey proved a great colleague, became a good friend, and offered sage advice on a range of issues. I was fortunate to find another great and supportive group of colleagues at LSU. Andy Burstein and Nancy Isenberg helped me settle into Baton Rouge and have encouraged and supported me since I arrived. Christine Kooi and Sue Marchand both discussed early modern and European history on the many occasions when I reached the limits of my knowledge. Cat Jacquet responded to a lot of queries. Despite the grim nature of what we usually discussed, she always made me laugh. I am grateful for her advice and her friendship. Steve Andes and Brendan Karch both listened with great generosity to questions that only tangentially intersected with their own work and offered valuable ideas. Victor Stater gracefully fielded too many questions about the English Civil War and British history and has proven a terrifically supportive department chair. Gaines Foster, in particular, merits praise and thanks for his willingness to be interrupted on a daily basis as I tried out ideas. He also read the whole manuscript and offered his always insightful comments and then patiently waited while I figured out how he was right.

I have been lucky to hold positions where I could hire students to help with research and luckier still to find students who have been so generous and intellectually creative. At WVU, Adam Zucconi, Andrew Fialka, and Zac Cowsert all helped out. At LSU, Garrett McKinnon, Adam Lawrence, Macy Allen, and Luke Hargroder all performed valuable labor. I am grateful for their assistance and their friendship.

The outside readers for Harvard University Press were enormously helpful. One remains anonymous, so I can only express my deep appreciation of the insights and encouragement that person provided during a crucial phase of the project. Greg Downs performed herculean labors with his report—pages of insightful, generous, and challenging critique of the manuscript. I had already benefited from previous conversations with Greg, and his comments helped make this a much stronger book. At Harvard University Press, Andrew Kinney has been a supportive and encouraging editor, and Olivia Woods has provided efficient and friendly support for all manner of production questions. Editors extraordinaire Kate Brick and Anne McGuire shepherded the book through the copyediting process with speed and grace. I am grateful for the careful attention with which they read the manuscript and the wise counsel about language they offered.

Pete Carmichael occupies a special spot in the pantheon of thank-yous. He provided so many research leads, talked through so many ideas, and encouraged and pushed me for so long that a simple acknowledgment hardly satisfies. He has been an essential part of how I have learned to be a historian. For that alone, I would be grateful. His steadfast friendship, and that of Beth Carmichael, has made our relationship all the more valuable to me. A group of friends and family have gamely listened to my discussions of banishment and murder and other awful topics. Neil Connelly shares my love of books and writing and never failed to ask how my own writing was going. I have taken cheer from his model of perseverance and relished his success. The whole Schrobilgen clan suffered through conversations about military mayhem during what should have been peaceful summers. Kathleen Schrobilgen even read parts of the book, which merits a special sister-in-law award. Steve Galpern and Patti Simon provided access to the storied "Scholar's Retreat" in Arlington, Virginia, which offered a wonderful resting spot during trips to the National Archives and Records Administration. Their friendship and support has been crucial. Anand Mishra and Kimberley Marchant, and Lorelai and Kieran, allowed their vacations to be invaded by often unpleasant topics, but they always responded with love and interest. Anand read several early parts of the manuscript and offered very helpful advice. Although I've been supplanted by better house guests, I will always think of the spare bedroom as my room. My mother, Lois Dean, and brother, Jonathan Dean, have heard far more than they ever wanted to about Civil War violence, but both remained enthusiastic nonetheless. Jon spent valuable Mackinaw time reading and commenting on the manuscript. Having long admired both his writing and his thoughtfulness, I am grateful to have his insights on this project.

My immediate family has likewise lived with this project longer than they should have. My daughter Annie asked once whether I read any books that did not have "murder" or "death" in the title. For a long time, the answer to that question was unfortunately no. That is partly because even longer ago, my son Liam asked why I taught about war if war was bad. His honest and important question compelled me to think more deeply about why I study the Civil War and what value that has for us today. I hope he finds this book a compelling answer to his query. Megan steadies me and brings joy to my life. She listened to innumerable ramblings, patiently waited out aimless venting sessions, and read the whole manuscript with her keen and critical eye. More important than any of that is her love, which inspires me every day.

ILLUSTRATION CREDITS

p. 18.   Francis Lieber. Brady-Handy Collection, Library of Congress Prints and Photographs Division, Washington, DC, LC-DIG -cwpbh-01402.

p. 47.   "The Sixth Regiment of the Massachusetts Volunteers Firing into the People in Pratt Street, While Attempting to Pass through Baltimore *en route* to Washington, April 10, 1861." *Frank Leslie's Illustrated Newspaper* 11, no. 284 (April 30, 1861): 376–377. Library of Congress Prints and Photographs Division, Washington, DC, LC-USZ62-132929.

p. 76.   "Southern Chivalry: Dedicated to Jeff Davis." Illustration by Thomas Nast, *Harper's Weekly* 7, no. 319 (February 7, 1863): 88–89. ©HarpWeek, LLC.

p. 90.   "Bluebeard of New Orleans." The Historic New Orleans Collection, 1993.76.115.

p. 98.   "Ruins at Donaldsonville." Photograph by McPherson & Oliver, Marshall Dunham Photograph Album (Mss. 3241), Louisiana and Lower Mississippi Valley Collections, Louisiana State University Libraries, Baton Rouge.

p. 100. "A Harvest of Death, Gettysburg, Pennsylvania." Photograph by Timothy H. O'Sullivan, July 4, 1863. Print by Alexander Gardner. Digital image courtesy of Getty's Open Content Program, The J. Paul Getty Museum, Getty Research Institute, Los Angeles.

p. 156. "1st US Colored Infantry." Photograph by Matthew B. Brady, Civil War Photographs Collection, Library of Congress Prints and Photographs Division, Washington, DC, LC-USZC2-6431.

p. 178. *A Ride for Liberty—The Fugitive Slaves* (recto), ca. 1862 by Eastman Johnson. Gift of Gwendolyn O. L. Conkling, American Art Collection, Brooklyn Museum, New York, 40.59a-b.

p. 188. "A Rebel Guerrilla Raid in a Western Town." Illustration by Thomas Nast, *Harper's Weekly* 6, no. 300 (September 27, 1862):

453

616–617. Library of Congress Prints and Photographs Division, Washington, DC, LC-DIG-ppmsca-35363.

p. 218.   *Order No. 11, 1865–70.* George Caleb Bingham, Cincinnati Art Museum, 1958.515. The Edwin and Virginia Irwin Memorial / Bridgeman Images.

p. 254.   "The Army of the Potomac: A Sharp-shooter on Picket Duty. [From a painting by W. Homer, Esq.]," *Harper's Weekly* 6, no. 307 (November 15, 1862): 724. Harris Brisbane Dick Fund, 1929, The Metropolitan Museum of Art, New York, 29.88.3(5).

p. 261.   "Explosion at City Point." Illustration by Alfred R. Waud, *Harper's Weekly* 8, no. 400 (August 27, 1864): 545. Gift, J. P. Morgan, 1919, Morgan Collection of Civil War Drawings, Library of Congress Prints and Photographs Division, Washington, DC, LC-DIG-ppmsca-21253.

p. 268.   "Unidentified Emaciated Prisoner of War, from Belle Isle, Richmond, at the U.S. General Hospital, Div. 1, Annapolis." Photograph by A. Hill Messinger, U.S. General Hospital, Div. 1, Annapolis. Civil War Photographs Collection, Gift; Col. Godwin Ordway, 1948, Library of Congress Prints and Photographs Division, Washington, DC, LC-DIG-ppmsca-33758.

p. 274.   "The War in Tennessee: Confederate Massacre of Federal Troops after the Surrender at Fort Pillow, April 12, 1864." *Frank Leslie's Illustrated Newspaper* 18, no. 449 (May 7, 1864): 97. Art and Picture Collection, The New York Public Library, Astor, Lenox, and Tilden Foundations.

p. 340.   "The Surrender of General Lee and His [Ent]ire Army to Lieut. General Grant, April 9th 1865." Published by John Smith, Philadelphia, ca. 1865. Marian S. Carson Collection, Library of Congress Prints and Photographs Division, Washington, DC, LC-DIG-pga-08989.

INDEX